PEACE AND CONFLICT SERIES
Ron Milam, General Editor

Also in this series:

The Air War in Vietnam
by Michael E. Weaver

Crooked Bamboo: A Memoir from Inside the Diem Regime
by Nguyen Thai; edited by Justin Simundson

Girls Don't! A Woman's War in Vietnam
by Inette Miller

Rain in Our Hearts: Alpha Company in the Vietnam War
by James Allen Logue and Gary D. Ford

ADMIRALS UNDER FIRE

THE US NAVY AND THE VIETNAM WAR

EDWARD J. MAROLDA
FOREWORD BY JOHN LEHMAN

TEXAS TECH UNIVERSITY PRESS

Copyright © 2021 by Texas Tech University Press
All rights reserved. No portion of this book may be reproduced in any form or by any means, including electronic storage and retrieval systems, except by explicit prior written permission of the publisher. Brief passages excerpted for review and critical purposes are excepted.

This book is typeset in EB Garamond. The paper used in this book meets the minimum requirements of ANSI/NISO Z39.48-1992 (R1997). ∞
Designed by Hannah Gaskamp

Library of Congress Cataloging-in-Publication Data

Names: Marolda, Edward J., 1945– author.
Title: Admirals Under Fire: The US Navy and the Vietnam War / Edward J. Marolda.
Other titles: US Navy and the Vietnam War
Description: [Lubbock, Texas]: [Texas Tech University Press], 2021. | Series: Peace and Conflict | Includes bibliographical references and index. | Summary: "An examination of how America's top naval leaders—Admirals Zumwalt, Moorer, Sharp, Holloway, and Felt—dealt with the challenges of the Vietnam War and its aftermath, with a discussion of their relationships with Presidents Kennedy, Johnson, Nixon, Ford, and Carter and Secretaries of Defense McNamara, Laird, and Schlesinger."—Provided by publisher.
Identifiers: LCCN 2020053118 (print) | LCCN 2020053119 (ebook) |
ISBN 978-1-68283-089-5 (cloth) | ISBN 978-1-68283-090-1 (ebook)
ISBN 978-1-68283-248-6 (paper)
Subjects: LCSH: Vietnam War, 1961–1975—Naval operations, American. | United States. Navy—History—Vietnam War, 1961–1975. | United States. Navy—Officers—Biography. | Admirals—United States—Biography.
Classification: LCC DS558.7 .M34 2021 (print) | LCC DS558.7 (ebook) |
DDC 959.704/348092273—dc23
LC record available at https://lccn.loc.gov/2020053118
LC ebook record available at https://lccn.loc.gov/2020053119

First paperback edition 2025

Texas Tech University Press
Box 41037
Lubbock, Texas 79409-1037 USA
800.832.4042
ttup@ttu.edu
www.ttupress.org

This book is dedicated to the men and women of the US Navy who served their country with honor during the Vietnam War era.

CONTENTS

IX   ILLUSTRATIONS
XIII   FOREWORD
XVII ACKNOWLEDGMENTS
XIX   INTRODUCTION

CHAPTER 1
3   **STEAMING INTO THE ABYSS**

CHAPTER 2
44 **AT THE BRINK**

CHAPTER 3
72 **UPPING THE ANTE**

CHAPTER 4
90 **COMMAND IN CRISIS**

CHAPTER 5
132 **NAVY TROUBLES**

CHAPTER 6
151 **WHITE KNIGHT OF THE DELTA**

CHAPTER 7
196 **FIGHTING TO RETREAT**

CHAPTER 8
222 **TEST OF FIRE**

CHAPTER 9
253 **A NEW BROOM**

CHAPTER 10
275 **REVOLUTION IN THE NAVY**

CHAPTER 11
305 **FIGHTING WASHINGTON**

CHAPTER 12
326 **THE END GAME**

CHAPTER 13
361 **CONCLUSION**

379 NOTES
455 BIBLIOGRAPHY
475 INDEX

ILLUSTRATIONS

4	Admiral Harry D. Felt, in charge of the US Pacific Command from 1958 to 1964
18	Map of the Republic of Vietnam
24	US Ambassador Frederick Nolting welcomes Admiral Felt to Saigon
46	Admiral Ulysses S. G. Sharp confers with Vice Admiral Thomas Moorer, 1964
53	Admiral Sharp at his Camp Smith headquarters in Hawaii
75	Admiral Sharp directed the Rolling Thunder bombing campaign against North Vietnam
78	Route packages map
94	Admiral Sharp and General William C. Westmoreland, 1965
107	Admiral Sharp, deep in thought, Hawaii headquarters
108	Admiral Sharp and a Marine colonel, South Vietnam
115	Captain James L. Holloway III, commanding officer of USS *Enterprise*
118	Admiral Moorer presenting Rear Admiral Holloway with his second Legion of Merit award
121	Admiral Sharp conferring with President Lyndon B. Johnson
128	Admiral Sharp's book *Strategy for Defeat*

133	Admiral Thomas H. Moorer, CNO, September 1967
148	Admiral Moorer and Rear Admiral Tran Van Chon inspect a unit of the Vietnam Navy
158	General Creighton W. Abrams and Vice Admiral Elmo R. Zumwalt Jr.
160	Map of Mekong Delta
163	Admiral Zumwalt speaks to sailors involved in Operation Sea Float
183	Secretary of Defense Melvin Laird and Admiral Zumwalt
190	Admiral Zumwalt and Rear Admiral Robert S. Salzer confer, May 1971
200	President Richard M. Nixon and Admiral Moorer on USS *Saratoga,* May 1969
208	The Joint Chiefs of Staff, January 1971
225	Map of North Vietnam's main offensive thrusts during Easter Offensive, 1972
239	Vice Admiral Holloway and South Vietnamese President Nguyen Van Thieu
251	Map of Haiphong safe port approaches
255	JCS chairman Moorer, Secretary of the Navy John Chafee, and Admiral Zumwalt
261	Admiral Zumwalt's book *On Watch*
269	Admiral Hyman G. Rickover delivers speech
286	Admiral Zumwalt discusses racial discrimination with a group of sailors
316	CNO Zumwalt swears in Admiral Holloway as next Vice Chief of Naval Operations, 1973

324   Admirals Holloway, Zumwalt, and Moorer, Secretary of Defense James R. Schlesinger, Vice Admiral William P. Mack, Annapolis, 29 June 1974

328   President Nixon and Admiral Holloway, with Secretary of the Navy John Warner

337   Admiral Holloway and Chief Machinist's Mate Lilton Davis confer

342   Admiral Holloway testifies before congressional committee

FOREWORD

Vietnam has continued to be a source of deep emotional conflict for all those who served there and very many of those who did not. The nature and sources of this turmoil are unique to each individual, but a major chasm is the patriotism and love of country cohabiting with the dishonest and deeply wrong policy and decisions of American leaders. It was widely known that targets were picked not to do maximum damage but to send signals. Hundreds of aviators died or became POWs while attacking "suspected truck parks" and bridges that were rebuilt overnight, while power stations, dams, and MiG bases were off limits.

Revelations in recent years have reopened these deep wounds: Secretary of Defense Robert S. McNamara admitting that he believed from the beginning that the war could not be won; John F. Kennedy in tapes played in Ken Burns's series *The Vietnam War* stating that he believed the same but that he would not change policy until after his reelection fourteen months hence (this while knowing that Americans in combat would be dying every single day of those long months); revelations from the archives that some were secretly providing North Vietnam with the next day's targets nominally so they could warn endangered civilians, but in fact enabling them to focus and reinforce their air defenses, resulting in hundreds of unnecessarily lost airplanes and pilots.

Veterans of the war thought that they had been subjected to intolerable limitations and rules of engagement (ROE) because of stupid policies, but to learn of the actual betrayals of trust in such detail was to rip the scabs from these veterans' wounds.

Dr. Edward J. Marolda was one of those Vietnam veterans. But above all he is one of the nation's leading scholars of both the US Navy's history and of the Vietnam War and is arguably *the* preeminent scholar of naval policy, strategy, and operations in that savage contest.

The author of numerous previous books and articles, in this volume he takes on a daunting task: challenging the reader to see the naval war for Vietnam primarily—although not exclusively—through the eyes of five leading naval commanders: four-star admirals Harry Felt, "Oley" Sharp, Tom Moorer, Bud Zumwalt, and Jim Holloway.

Four-star admirals are typically an experienced, sagacious, and energetic lot, with a great deal of wisdom to offer and the savvy and clout to translate that wisdom into action. I knew well three of the five whose experience Dr. Marolda highlights: Admirals Moorer, Holloway, and Zumwalt.

But this is not just their story. While Dr. Marolda focuses heavily on their capabilities, beliefs, accomplishments, and setbacks, he does not neglect those of their contemporaries. In many ways, this book serves as a "who's who" of the naval direction of the war. There is significant discussion of the roles played by the Secretaries of the Navy, especially Paul Nitze but also Paul Ignatius, John Chafee, and John Warner. And much attention is also paid to the views and actions of Admirals Arleigh Burke, George Anderson, David McDonald, and Jack McCain (father of the recently deceased war hero, US senator, and presidential candidate). Future four-star admiral and Chairman of the Joint Chiefs of Staff Bill Crowe appears periodically, mostly as a captain and riverine warfighter in the Mekong Delta, as does the brilliant but irascible father of our nuclear navy, Hyman Rickover—often a nemesis of almost everybody mentioned above.

Army 1st Lieutenant Marolda served in the war zone. As it did for so many of his generation, the war had a profound effect on his future. It became the prime motivator for his decision to become a professional historian, searching for the truth of the war's policies and combat operations. For me, the war deepened an understanding of the efficacy of seapower—properly funded and applied—as the key tool in America's national security arsenal. It also taught me the searing tragedy of the duplicitous and deeply flawed political misuse of that power.

America's command of the world's seas during the Vietnam War enabled us to accomplish truly herculean tasks: We supplied and maintained whole armies, air forces, and naval fleets continuously in-country and on-station and engaged with the enemy over 7,000 miles from our continental shores—without significantly compromising our overt forward presence in the Mediterranean or our more covert forward presence in the North Atlantic and the Pacific. With sea supremacy assured, we were also able to create and deploy an innovative fleet of 1,000 or so riverine and coastal craft, block and sever enemy waterborne supply lines, and use our navy's carrier aircraft and naval gunfire—at a cost—to punish that enemy at will.

At will. There was the rub. What we needed was the will, from our political leadership and the American people, to wage the war properly and to see it through. Marolda, with discipline and objectivity, takes the reader through the constant policy changes, misperceptions, and failures to solidify the will that over time foredoomed the enterprise. Key, time-proven naval operations like blockades, mining, air strikes, and amphibious assaults were implemented partially, inconsistently, or not at all—not because of lack of US Navy tactical acumen or technical skill but due to faulty premises and prohibitions at the high elected and appointed civilian echelons of our government.

Serving with deep frustration and seeking to persuade President Lyndon B. Johnson and his civilian advisors were the five admirals whose thinking and actions are the threads that tie this book together. At the same time as they were advising and arguing, testifying and lobbying Congress, they were also directing and leading the tens of thousands of naval officers and sailors under their command, exercising their military skills and judgment to try to implement the deeply flawed orders they received from on high to defeat a muscular and tenacious foe fully supported by China and the Soviet Union.

But the lessons from that tragic lost war were not forgotten. They were deeply ingrained in those who fought that war in actual combat and home in the political arena. It was later my good fortune—and that of the four-star admirals of my time—to serve under a president and in an administration that was deeply imbued with those lessons and determined to apply them in the proper application of military, and especially naval, force in the face of a powerful and hostile antagonist, one emboldened years before by the often feckless American policies and operations observed in Vietnam. We defeated that antagonist, and much of the credit must go to flag officers like Bud Zumwalt and Jim Holloway, who—having learned from their experiences in the Vietnam War—infused a spirit and a strategy in our navy that enabled the naval rebuilding and deployment by new political leadership that went on to win the Cold War at sea.

Admirals Zumwalt, Holloway, Felt, Sharp, and Moorer were fine leaders and heroes of World War II, the Korean War, and Cold War operations. That they could not win the Vietnam War, despite deep commitment and prodigious efforts, was a tragedy. But there is much to be learned from their example—and that of their fellow flag officers and civilian masters. Their intertwined stories needed to be told, and we should all be grateful to Dr. Marolda for giving their Vietnam War experiences their proper due.

The Honorable John Lehman
Secretary of the Navy, 1981–1987

ACKNOWLEDGMENTS

This author owes a huge debt of gratitude to the many individuals and institutions that helped bring this history to completion. Former Secretary of the Navy John Lehman graciously penned the foreword and provided significant insights on naval and other leaders with whom he worked during his eventful years of public service. I especially want to thank the highly respected and widely published historians, political scientists, retired naval officers, and other colleagues who patiently waded through all or portions of the original manuscript. Vice Admiral Robert F. Dunn, USN (Ret.), former President of the Naval Historical Foundation; John B. Hattendorf, Ernest J. King Professor Emeritus of Maritime History at the US Naval War College; Thomas C. Cutler; Thomas C. Hone; Norman Polmar; John Darrell Sherwood; Paul Stillwell; David A. Rosenberg; and Captain Peter M. Swartz, USN (Ret.) employed their considerable expertise on the modern history of the US Navy in support of the work. Enhancing my understanding of the roles played in the war by the Department of Defense, the Joint Chiefs of Staff, the other armed services, and the governments of North and South Vietnam were the following scholars: Jeffrey J. Clarke; Mark Clodfelter; Graham A. Cosmas; Christopher J. Lamb; Lien-Hang T. Nguyen; and James H. Willbanks. The work benefited on so many levels from the considerable insight and information they graciously provided.

Especially helpful to my research endeavors were Dale Gordon, John Hodges, Laura Waayers, John Gustav Keilers, and Greg Martin of the Naval History and Heritage Command's archives. Critical to exploitation of the US Naval Institute's oral history collection were Paul Stillwell, Eric Mills, and Rick Russell. Steve Maxner, Director of the Vietnam Center and Archives at Texas Tech University, and archivist Sheon Montgomery helped me navigate and extract valuable information from their first-rate collection of Vietnam War documents and images. Stacey Parillo and Elizabeth Delmage of the Naval War College's Naval Historical Collection were especially helpful to my photo research. David Winkler of the Naval Historical Foundation facilitated my access to that organization's oral history collection and other relevant materials. Peter Swartz proved indispensable to an understanding of the studies produced by the Center for Naval Analyses.

This work benefitted immeasurably from the professional and dedicated editorial and prepublication work of Christie Perlmutter and her colleagues Travis Snyder, Joanna Conrad, Hannah Gaskamp, and John Brock of Texas Tech University Press.

My special thanks to Jim Hornfischer, a renowned naval historian of the modern US Navy and a gifted writer who provided invaluable advice on the style, readability, and presentation of this work.

Finally, I want to thank Beverly, my devoted wife of fifty-two years, my sons Jeffrey, Brian, and Michael, and my grandson Nicholas for their patience and understanding as I toiled away cloistered in my office instead of fully enjoying the fruits of retirement.

Grateful as I am for the collaboration of my colleagues and family, and the support of relevant archives, libraries, and other institutions of research and learning, this author accepts full responsibility for the conclusions drawn in this work and for any errors in fact.

INTRODUCTION

In 1997, H. R. McMaster, a graduate of the US Military Academy at West Point and the University of North Carolina doctoral program in history, published a seminal study on US military leadership during the Vietnam War entitled *Dereliction of Duty*. He later won laurels for combat leadership during the Gulf War, ascended to the highest ranks of the US Army, and served as the National Security Advisor to President Donald Trump. Focusing in his book on the Joint Chiefs of Staff (JCS) during the early years of the war, McMaster "discovered that the military's role in Vietnam decision making was little understood and largely overlooked." He attempted to fill that gap by asserting that the JCS, and by extension the military in general, "became accomplices in the president's [Lyndon Baines Johnson's] deception and focused on a tactical task, killing the enemy." McMaster added that "General [William C.] Westmoreland's 'strategy' of attrition in South Vietnam was, in essence, the absence of strategy. The result was military activity (bombing North Vietnam and killing the enemy in South Vietnam) that did not aim to achieve a clearly defined objective."[1]

In short, US generals and admirals at the highest levels failed in their duty to arm their civilian superiors with sound and balanced military advice and became complicit in the execution of a flawed national strategy. Jeffrey Record, in his work, "Why We Lost in Vietnam," asserted that "the military certainly shared with civilian authority that combination of unwarranted self-confidence in America's ability to prevail in Indochina." He added that "the Joint Chiefs of Staff, Pacific Command, and MACV [Military Assistance Command, Vietnam] were not well-served by their civilian superiors, but neither did they serve their country well." He concluded that "the military's performance left much to be desired [and] spent much of its time . . . shooting itself—and the American cause in Vietnam—in the foot."[2]

The primary object of this book is to address the accuracy of those assertions and assess the success or failure of the leadership exercised by four-star admirals Harry D. Felt, Ulysses S. Grant Sharp, Thomas H. Moorer, Elmo R. Zumwalt Jr., and James L. Holloway III. From 1958 to 1968, Felt (1958–1964) and Sharp (1964–1968) oversaw all US military forces in a vast theater, which encompassed Vietnam, as Commander in Chief, Pacific (CINCPAC). Moorer, Zumwalt, and Holloway were members of the Joint Chiefs of Staff, and during the last years of the war, Moorer served as chairman. These three flag officers also led the US Navy as Chief of Naval Operations (CNO) from 1967 to 1978.

Library shelves are filled with thousands of books detailing how such legendary admirals as Ernest J. King, Chester W. Nimitz, Raymond A. Spruance, and William F. Halsey led US and allied naval forces to victory against the Axis nations in the latter years of World War II. They achieved success because they were especially gifted statesmen and military leaders at the strategic and operational levels. But they also succeeded because they were blessed with focused civilian leadership, a coherent global strategy, the industrial might of the United States, the strong support of the American people, and the fighting prowess of the Allied soldiers, sailors, airmen, and Marines who by 1944 and 1945 were clearly overpowering their Axis adversaries.

An even greater challenge for any military leader is to cope with distrustful or ill-prepared civilian superiors, a flawed strategy, a discontented populace, and above all a failing war. The key naval leaders of the Vietnam War had to contend with an approach to the conflict that was nothing like their experiences in World War II and the Korean War. The Vietnam War, a so-called "limited war," quickly became a no-win situation that divided the American people, resulted in an enormous outlay of lives and resources, and seriously undercut US national security and foreign policy. These men also had to deal with the negative consequences to the US Navy from the war and destabilizing changes in American society. Racial discord, drug abuse, anti-war and anti-establishment sentiment, and a host of other personnel and material ills beset the service during and after the fighting. These naval leaders were also faced with the rise of Soviet nuclear-missile and naval power and an increasingly serious global threat to US interests. In short, the Vietnam War and its aftermath thoroughly tested the mettle of America's top naval leaders during one of the most trying times in US history.

From the early 1960s to the late 1970s, the five officers under study, all Naval Academy graduates, rose in rank and took on increasingly demanding duties. Tours as mid-level and senior-level officers found them commanding major deployed forces, arming them with considerable insight into the planning and execution of combat operations. Each of these men reached the highest ranks in the US military establishment with roles in the design and implementation of US national strategy and security policies relating to the war in Southeast Asia.

Admiral "Don" Felt helped craft President John F. Kennedy's counterinsurgency strategy and championed the employment in South Vietnam of Army Green Berets, Navy SEALs, and other special operations forces. He witnessed the rise of the southern communist guerrillas, the Viet Cong, and worked to stem the collapse of internal order after the assassination of South Vietnam's President Ngo Dinh Diem. Admirals "Oley" Sharp and Tom Moorer helped design a pressure campaign against Hanoi that included the super-secret Operation 34 Alpha coastal raids and the pivotal August 1964 Desoto Patrol mission of US destroyer *Maddox* (DD-731). They executed the retaliatory air strikes in response to Hanoi's real and supposed attacks on US warships in the Tonkin Gulf incident. They also oversaw the deployment of major US ground forces to South Vietnam during 1965 and establishment of the Market Time patrol to interdict North Vietnam's infiltration of war materials by sea. Sharp, an early advocate but later harsh critic of the "graduated escalation" strategy, was the officer in charge of the three-year, trouble-plagued Rolling Thunder bombing campaign. The admiral became the most prominent military leader of the postwar period to speak out about the mismanagement of Rolling Thunder by President Johnson and Secretary of Defense Robert S. McNamara.

Tom Moorer became Richard M. Nixon's closest military advisor and oversaw execution of the "secret" bombing of Cambodia and subsequent ground incursion into that country, the Lam Son 719 invasion of Laos, the mining of Haiphong harbor, and the "Christmas bombing" of North Vietnam. He accommodated the penchant of Nixon and Henry Kissinger, the former's assistant for national security affairs, for secrecy and bureaucratic maneuvering in direction of the war effort. Moorer was crucial to the White House effort in ensuring that the Paris Peace Accords (Paris Agreement) of 1973 provided for the return of American prisoners of war.

"Bud" Zumwalt gained fame as the dynamic combat leader of US naval forces fighting in South Vietnam's Mekong Delta in the years after the Tet Offensive of 1968. He also earned the praise of General Creighton W. Abrams, the officer in charge of the Military Assistance Command, Vietnam, and Melvin Laird, the secretary of defense, for his efforts to strengthen the Vietnam Navy as part of the "Vietnamization" program. The exposure of his son, a naval officer, and other American sailors under his command to the toxic Agent Orange defoliant, however, troubled his conscience. Admirers credited his victories in Vietnam as the reason for the admiral's selection as the youngest ever Chief of Naval Operations, but his detractors ascribed that accomplishment to political pull by high-ranking civilians in the Nixon administration. As head of the Navy, he revolutionized and greatly improved the service's treatment of African American, female, and enlisted sailors. He took positive steps to help the Navy overcome post–Vietnam personnel and material shortfalls. But racial turmoil, drug abuse, disciplinary lapses, and anti-war activities that troubled aircraft carrier *Constellation* (CVA-64) and other ships and shore stations during his four years in command clouded that legacy. So too did his public and heated disputes with Admiral Hyman Rickover, "the Father of the Nuclear Navy," Kissinger, and most important the president. Indeed, Nixon came close to firing Zumwalt at various times during the admiral's days in command of the Navy.

Jim Holloway experienced the war firsthand as the commanding officer of nuclear-powered aircraft carrier *Enterprise* (CVAN-65) during two combat tours off Vietnam and in command of the Seventh Fleet during the Linebacker bombing campaign of 1972. He led naval forces that achieved great tactical feats but also suffered from Washington's checkered execution of strategy and policy. As a member and on occasion acting chairman of the Joint Chiefs, Holloway was involved in management of the seaborne evacuations from Cambodia and South Vietnam and the recovery from Cambodia's Khmer Rouge government of merchant ship SS *Mayaguez* and her crew in 1975. As CNO in a time of resource scarcity, Holloway furthered Zumwalt's efforts to improve the lot of Navy sailors and the material condition of the fleet. He also acted to bring stability to a service troubled by the aftereffects of a failed war, the public's disenchantment with the military, and his predecessor's missteps. In many ways, his positive actions from 1974 to 1978 putting the Navy on an even keel proved just as taxing as fighting the war.

These five officers significantly influenced the course of the war and its aftermath, but the evolution of the conflict also strongly influenced their views on the use of military force, America's responsibilities and role in the world, and the civil-military relationship. Like millions of other Americans, these men had to come to terms with America's first lost war and what it meant for the future of the nation and the armed forces. In retirement, Don Felt and Oley Sharp devoted considerable effort rationalizing their involvement in wartime decision-making. Tom Moorer, Bud Zumwalt, and Jim Holloway, as the uniformed heads of the Navy and as members of the Joint Chiefs of Staff, could not focus solely in the postwar period on Vietnam, since they had to deal with troubles in the Middle East, internal problems of the services, and myriad other serious issues. But for good or ill, the Vietnam experience clearly colored their decision-making and advice to the president and Congress on the issues of the day. The Vietnam War was the defining event in the lives of these flag officers, and their involvement in that long-ago conflict offers insight to today's leaders on the uses and limitations of military power and the functioning of the civil-military relationship.

ADMIRALS UNDER FIRE

CHAPTER 1

STEAMING INTO THE ABYSS

Admiral Harry D. Felt became the most powerful American military leader west of San Francisco when he took charge of the Pacific Command (PACOM) in July 1958. The Navy flag officer oversaw all US military forces in the Asia-Pacific region for the next seven years. From his headquarters at Camp H. M. Smith overlooking the historic Pearl Harbor naval base in Hawaii, Felt commanded more than 900,000 soldiers, sailors, airmen, and Marines operating close to 7,000 aircraft and 500 warships and support vessels. CINCPAC's subordinate commands included the US Pacific Fleet as well as major Army, Air Force, and Marine formations. The operational area for which he was responsible stretched from the US West Coast across the vast Pacific and into the Indian Ocean, and from the Aleutian Islands as far south as the Antarctic—an expanse of 85 million square miles. In addition to his military duties, Felt served as one of America's most prominent diplomats in uniform. CINCPAC was the chief US military representative to the Southeast Asia Treaty Organization (SEATO) and to the allied governments of Japan, South Korea, Australia, New Zealand, and the Philippines.

Admiral Harry D. Felt, in charge of the US Pacific Command from 1958 to 1964, opposed the employment of American naval and ground combat forces in Vietnam. Naval History and Heritage Command (NHHC) 80-G-1017094.

Born in Topeka, Kansas, on 21 June 1902, Don Felt moved with his family to the nation's capital ten years later, settling near the Rock Creek Park neighborhood. He attended Central High School. His strong-willed mother worked to instill discipline and a love of education in the boy, but like many young men he showed more interest in playing games and hunting than academics. With the encouragement of his uncle, Senator William Thompson, and extra work at a prep school, however, in 1919 Felt entered the US Naval Academy. Other midshipmen remembered him for his positive attitude and "famous ear-splitting grin." His non-regulation, easygoing demeanor won him "a place among his classmates" but also earned him demerits for various infractions. Despite being nicknamed "shorty" and "shrimp," short-statured Felt played intramural baseball for three years. He graduated in the respectable middle rank of the brigade of midshipmen and was commissioned Ensign in the US Navy in June 1923.[1]

Bored with duty on board surface ships in the years after graduation, Don Felt "got the aviation bug." He applied for and was accepted to flight training at Naval Air Station Pensacola, Florida. Kathryn Cowley, whom Felt met and wed there, later related that he had found his niche in the Navy in aviation and wanted little more after that than to "fly, fly, fly."[2] Felt excelled in various naval aviation billets in the late 1930s, and the outbreak of war in 1941 found him in command of a dive-bombing squadron operating from aircraft carrier *Lexington* (CV-2). By August 1942, Felt, now a commander, had been fleeted up to lead the air group of *Saratoga* (CV-3) and earned a Navy Cross and a Distinguished Flying Cross for his skillful and courageous combat performance against Japanese forces off Guadalcanal. He led an attack that sank the enemy aircraft carrier *Ryujo*. Felt capped his World War II combat experience in command of escort carrier *Chenango* (CVE-28) during the bloody fight for Okinawa against Japanese Kamikaze air attacks. For success in battle, Felt's ship earned a Navy Unit Commendation, and he was awarded the Legion of Merit with Combat "V."[3]

Felt's assignment to a US military mission in Russia from March 1944 to February 1945 opened his eyes to the threat posed by communist ideology and Stalin's USSR. During that time, he learned that his rooms were routinely "bugged" and that he was under constant surveillance by his hosts. Despite the World War II Allies' endorsement of Soviet entry into the war against Japan at the Yalta Conference of February 1945, Felt intimated to his wife that he hoped "we don't let the Russians in."[4] His worldview also broadened with attendance at the National War College and assignment as commander of the Navy's small but diplomatically important Middle East Force. He met with numerous foreign dignitaries in the region and learned much about the local cultures. He joined the faculty at the Naval War College in Newport, Rhode Island, in the late 1940s and served into the early 1950s, and while there strengthened his understanding of political-military affairs.

Felt's responsibilities as deputy head of the Navy's Strategic Plans Section during the Korean War exposed him not only to the service's "big picture" but also to US foreign and national security policy.

Strengthening that education was his tutelage under the section's head, Arleigh Burke, already known in the Navy as a strategic thinker and likely future Chief of Naval Operations. Felt related that "that was the beginning . . . of Burke and Felt working together as a team."[5] Burke, a Naval Academy classmate of Felt's, also clearly valued their professional and personal connection. Soon after Burke took the reins of the Navy as Chief of Naval Operations in August 1955, he named Felt Commander Sixth Fleet, a three-star billet, but less than four months later decided he needed him back at the Pentagon as his second-in-command or Vice Chief of Naval Operations (VCNO) with the rank of four-star admiral. That accelerated promotion clearly reflected Burke's confidence in Felt's abilities.[6]

Burke remembered that even though he and Don Felt "used to have a lot of big arguments," his subordinate was "extremely loyal to the Navy [and] he had his nose to the grindstone." Burke added that "it wasn't pleasant [because] it isn't pleasant to fight continuously with a good friend [but] it operated extremely well."[7] Indeed, the VCNO handled the day-to-day administration of the Navy so the CNO could concentrate on high-level global and national security issues. Like the executive officer of every command in the Navy, the VCNO was expected to be a no-nonsense enforcer of the commander's will—and Felt did not disappoint.

Don Felt had a reputation throughout the Navy as a hard-ass, a demanding, irascible, and dictatorial perfectionist. Staff officers called to his Pentagon office would enter it trembling, expecting to be chewed out even for some minor infraction. Regarded by some as "mean as hell," he was rumored to eat "admirals for breakfast, lunch, and dinner." While acknowledging Felt's caustic persona, Burke and many other flag officers considered him a top-notch leader who could be counted on to accomplish whatever mission he undertook. Lawson Ramage, who had earned the Medal of Honor for his submarine exploits in World War II, served under Felt in the Pentagon. He remembered that his boss would "really do his homework" by thoroughly mining relevant materials and discussing the pros and cons of a subject with trusted advisors before calling in a subordinate to execute an action. Ramage considered Don Felt a "great man."[8]

Felt's first direct experience with the belligerence of the Asian communist countries had occurred during his tour as the commander of a Seventh Fleet aircraft carrier task force in 1954. On 22 July, fighter planes of the People's Republic of China (PRC) shot down a British Air Cathay airliner traveling between Bangkok and Hong Kong, killing eighteen civilian passengers and crew members. Rear Admiral Felt immediately ordered the launch of aircraft from carrier *Philippine Sea* (CV-47) to search for survivors. Suspecting that the Chinese might also attack his search planes, necessarily flying close to the water, Felt positioned the fighter cover high above the sea. On the 26th, when a pair of Chinese LA-7 fighters arrived as expected and dove on the American search planes, Felt's AD Skyraiders shot down the attackers.[9]

The young admiral participated in the Taiwan Strait Crisis of 1954–1955 when Mao Zedong's communist forces shelled the Chinese Nationalist island of Jinmen (Quemoy) and seized an island in the Dachen (Tachen) group. The Eisenhower administration supported the Chinese Nationalists and feared that the communists might also invade the large island of Taiwan, seat of Chiang Kai-shek's Nationalist and pro-American government. Felt believed that because Mao was concerned that the United States might employ nuclear weapons in defense of its ally, in April 1955 the communist leader stopped the shelling and recommended negotiations to end the crisis. This experience convinced Felt that in the face of a determined US military stand, the Asian communists would invariably back down. He did not consider the possibility that Mao had no intention of invading Taiwan but was merely drawing international attention to his geopolitical grievances and galvanizing the Chinese people to stand up to the Americans in Asia.[10]

By the late 1950s, Don Felt and other US leaders concluded that the Asian communist countries would be more likely to work to undermine the non-communist governments of the region through insurgencies and guerrilla warfare than to conduct outright invasions. They understood that conventional French forces had been unable during the First Indochina War to defeat the guerrilla and unconventional tactics of Ho Chi Minh's Vietnamese army. The communist leader had exploited control of the countryside to mount ceaseless surprise attacks on isolated outposts, eventually confining French forces to the lowlands around Hanoi and Haiphong.

US leaders searched for ways to oppose communist inroads in Asia without having to use nuclear weapons or even conventional forces.

The ground war in Korea, fought much like World War II, had proven especially costly in terms of American lives, resources, and domestic support. Advocates for a change in US policy from stressing nuclear retaliation to a more flexible approach, exploiting the full range of measures available to the United States, included naval leaders. Burke, writing to Lord Louis Mountbatten, British First Sea Lord and Chief of Staff of the Royal Navy, suggested that "if we go too far on the megaton [nuclear] road we will, I think, have found that the free world will have been lost by erosion, and *perhaps not even military erosion*" (italics added).[11]

Former Army Chief of Staff General Maxwell D. Taylor proved to be an especially influential advocate for a new flexible approach to US defense policy. He criticized the Eisenhower administration's overemphasis on readiness for nuclear war, which he argued limited America's options in international crises. In his 1960 book, *The Uncertain Trumpet*, the general contended that the United States should be able to fight communist aggression in Southeast Asia and elsewhere with military measures that did not risk global nuclear war. Taylor wanted the conventional forces of the military services strengthened so they could prevail in regional conflicts, "brushfire wars," counterguerrilla campaigns, and counterinsurgencies.[12]

TROUBLE IN LAOS

Arleigh Burke thought so highly of Don Felt's leadership skills that he considered recommending his friend and chief subordinate to succeed him as Chief of Naval Operations when Burke expected to step down in 1958. But the Defense Reorganization Act of 1958 removed the CNO from the operational chain of command and empowered the regional commanders in chief, or "cincs," so Burke wanted Felt in one of those newly empowered billets. Alarmed by what he considered the belligerence of the Asian communist nations, Burke wanted his man on the spot as the Pacific commander in chief. Burke considered Felt the "ideal man" for the CINCPAC billet.[13]

When Don Felt took the helm as Commander in Chief, Pacific, he took on major new responsibilities. Just the year before, the Joint Chiefs of Staff had disestablished the Army-led Far East Command, formerly headed by General Douglas MacArthur, and the Air Force-led Alaska Command, and transferred their area responsibilities to CINCPAC. Felt became responsible for military-to-military and diplomatic interaction with foreign officials from Japan in the north to Australia in the south and as far west as Pakistan. Furthermore, Felt had to oversee development of a new staff separate from that of the Commander in Chief, Pacific Fleet (CINCPACFLT). Previously, a Navy flag officer had been the "dual-hatted" head of both CINCPAC and CINCPACFLT. Burke had also recommended Felt for the job because he considered him tough enough and astute enough to handle challenges from the Army and the Air Force, which wanted one of their general officers to lead the joint-forces Pacific Command.[14]

Felt strongly endorsed Burke's new approach to conflict resolution and de-emphasis on "massive retaliation." After the Taiwan Strait crisis of 1958, however, he worried that US forces lacked sufficient readiness for conventional warfighting. Early in his term, Felt ordered subordinates to ensure that all of his command's contingency plans provided for operations where nuclear weapons might not be used.[15]

As US strategic concepts changed in the last years of Eisenhower's presidency, American leaders grew concerned that the Sino-Soviet bloc had inaugurated a more aggressive, worldwide effort to subvert non-communist governments.[16] In November 1959, Admiral Herbert G. Hopwood, the Pacific Fleet commander, expressed alarm about the assertive behavior of Mao's China. He observed that "we are entering a new era of intensified cold and limited war in South and South East Asia." He related that Chinese communists had previously "attempted to win friends and influence the many new and violently nationalistic governments in this area." He feared that "they have now decided to use force and/or threat of [force] as a major instrument of policy for the predictable future."[17] Felt believed that Southeast Asia was Communist China's prime target. He related in retirement that "we discovered a Red Chinese plan for the take-over of Southeast Asia."[18]

While one doubts that such a singular and one-dimensional plan existed, to meet this threat and to help indigenous peoples keep free of "the slavery of Communism," CINCPAC called for an increase in US forces in Southeast Asia.[19] The first test of how US forces would deal with a communist insurgency occurred in the remote, mountainous country of Laos—the "Land of a Million Elephants"—where communists, anti-communists, and "neutralists" vied for power. In keeping with his previous thinking on the matter, Felt had his Pacific Command develop Operation Plan 32(L)-59 that focused solely on US non-nuclear forces countering an indigenous communist insurgency. The concept of operations called for the rapid deployment of the Marine, Army, and Navy units of CINCPAC's Joint Task Force 116 to airfields in Laos along the Mekong River. The main purpose of the task force was to back up local non-communist troops engaged in counterinsurgency operations.[20]

Soon, however, Felt became convinced that stronger actions were needed to counter what he interpreted as intervention into the Laotian situation by North Vietnamese regular forces. In calling for the deployment to Laos of Joint Task Force 116, Felt apprised leaders in Washington that "the time for decision and action is now" and that "the leadership and inspiration of communist aggression in Laos is located outside that country."[21] At Don Felt's urging, Washington ordered deployment of the US Seventh Fleet into the South China Sea hoping it would help scare off external support for the Laotian communists. At the same time, Felt grew increasingly concerned that the deployment of the task force might trigger a Chinese or North Vietnamese invasion. He wanted to contain the insurgency, not start a war. He cabled the JCS that he was "trying to keep us from having the same kind of experience as the French during their catastrophic Indo China war when they won many a battle but lost the campaigns."[22]

The crisis abated at the end of 1959, but in fall 1960 a political confrontation developed in Laos between the head of the armed forces, Phoumi Nosavan, and Prime Minister Souvanna Phouma. Felt reported to the JCS that "Phoumi is no George Washington [but] he is anti-communist which is what counts most in the sad Laos situation."[23] CINCPAC considered Souvanna's government a puppet of the communist bloc. In December, when Souvanna requested and received a Soviet airlift of arms, ammunition, and supplies, Phoumi's forces, with US support, overthrew the government and seized the capital of Vientiane. Unsure of Soviet intentions in this episode, in a temporary bit of bravado Felt declared that "we should find out by knocking off the present [Soviet] airlift." He personally believed that "the Reds are bluffing as they were in the Taiwan Strait affair and will back down if we are firm." He concluded that the United States had to "draw the line in Laos."[24] Of course, shooting down Soviet transport planes could have significantly inflamed the situation, locally if not worldwide. Washington did not endorse his ill-thought-out scheme.

When strong communist forces ejected government troops from the Laotian Plain of Jars at the end of the year, CINCPAC concluded that all of Laos would soon fall. He called for unilateral US military intervention. Burke, however, in one of the earliest instances of what later in the Vietnam War would be labeled "graduated response," recommended a step-by-step reaction to the other side's actions. He advised Don Felt not to escalate the confrontation faster than necessary and to "leave the enemy all possible opportunity to disengage." He added that the goal is holding Laos, not conquering DRV [Democratic Republic of Vietnam] or Red China."[25]

At the time, the Soviet Union and China were supplying the Pathet Lao (indigenous Laotian communist forces) with military material, and North Vietnamese troops were feverishly developing in southern Laos what would later be called the Ho Chi Minh Trail. In 1959 and 1960, the North Vietnamese and their Pathet Lao allies established a trail system replete with rest areas, truck parks, supply caches, and guides. In the same period, more than 4,500 communist military personnel infiltrated into South Vietnam from North Vietnam via this logistical pipeline.[26]

Despite the presence in Southeast Asia of major US naval forces in spring 1961, the Kennedy administration decided against intervention in Laos. One factor was the recently concluded Bay of Pigs fiasco in Cuba that embarrassed President Kennedy. He related that "if it hadn't been for Cuba, we might be about to intervene in Laos."[27] Moreover, the president's civilian advisors and some of his top military leaders opposed a large-scale US intervention there. The conferees understood that success in Laos might ultimately require the use of nuclear weapons if China also entered the fray. Burke continued to press for intervention until Kennedy pointedly told him to drop the matter. Burke then gave Kennedy a short memo predicting that the failure to act in Laos would result in the eventual loss of all Southeast Asia.[28]

Kennedy and Secretary of Defense Robert S. McNamara were not happy with their military advisors. They concluded that the Joint Chiefs of Staff had not provided the president with accurate advice during the Bay of Pigs operation. Vice Admiral Ulysses S. G. Sharp, the chief planner on the Navy staff, related that he attended a meeting of the chiefs with the president in the Pentagon in May 1961. The president chided the military heads and said that he wanted them to provide him not only with military advice but also with their insights on relevant economic and psychological factors. Despite this schooling, Kennedy's "unhappiness with the Chiefs

[that] hung like a cloud over their relationship with the President" did not dissipate.²⁹

The president and his defense secretary increasingly relied on only one military leader, Maxwell Taylor. Kennedy assigned Taylor as his military advisor at the White House and soon afterward named him JCS chairman. Kennedy came to admire the general's erudition, political skills, and combat record in World War II. The Kennedy people liked Taylor because he was "articulate but presentable," unlike Air Force General Curtis LeMay and the other rough-edged military leaders.³⁰ McNamara later gushed that Taylor "was the wisest uniformed geopolitician and security adviser I ever met" and a "scholar who spoke six or seven languages."³¹ Taylor became the face of the US military at the White House—the only face.

In addition, Kennedy increasingly favored the advice of his civilian secretary of defense. McNamara had served in uniform as a statistician with the Army Air Forces during World War II and in 1946 joined the Ford Motor Company. In November 1960, recognizing the superlative managerial skills and strong leadership traits that McNamara had displayed over the previous fourteen years, Henry Ford named him president of the firm. Only several months later, the newly elected president decided that he wanted McNamara to be his secretary of defense. Kennedy believed that McNamara possessed the leadership qualities, organizational skills, and dynamism to run a government department that consumed half of the federal budget and whose Army, Navy-Marine Corps, and Air Force components operated all over the world. Kennedy was enthralled by McNamara's seeming mastery of things related to America's Cold War policies, nuclear warfare, and the Pentagon bureaucracy. McNamara dazzled presidents and journalists alike with his no-nonsense command presence, detailed knowledge of weapon systems, managerial techniques, and adept handling of congressional questioning. Vice President Lyndon Johnson was equally impressed with McNamara, considering the man one of the most intelligent and effective government officials he had ever known.³²

In contrast to his managerial experience, McNamara had had no significant exposure to national security policy, the US armed forces, or America's Cold War global posture. He remembered when he was an ROTC (reserve officer training corps) cadet in the 1930s that "nobody took the military seriously [and] my classmates and I saw [the regimentation] as a pointless ritual, irrelevant to our world."³³ While at Ford, he had had neither the time nor the inclination to become familiar with the nature of military strategy or the operational arts. Hence, he had little understanding of what the famous Prussian strategist Karl von Clausewitz referred to as the "fog of war": unforeseen problems like misinterpreted orders, garbled communications, faulty intelligence, equipment and supply failures, and violently changing weather that could foil the most precisely planned operation.[34]

While suggesting to Kennedy that he felt himself "unqualified" for the job and "with a limited grasp of military affairs," McNamara did not withdraw his name from nomination. Indeed, McNamara was supremely confident in his ability to face any challenge, analyze the problem based on statistical measures, and push through a solution. Roswell Gilpatrick, who served in the defense department from 1961 to 1964, contended that "no cabinet officer in my time has ever been closer to his Chief than McNamara was to John F. Kennedy and Lyndon B. Johnson, both of whom treated him as first among equals."[35] Maxwell Taylor, who served under McNamara as the Joint Chiefs chairman from 1962 to 1964, considered him "a man of decision who tackled fearlessly the tough problems of defense and refused to yield to the temptation to sweep them under the rug."[36] Paul Nitze, who worked for McNamara as the Navy secretary and later as the deputy secretary of defense, remembered that "McNamara was determined to understand and be sure that he understood all the various important things that went on in the Pentagon," including such things as base structures, pay scales, logistics, and similar aspects.[37]

Even when possessed of such great power as that of the secretary of defense, McNamara never clearly understood the nature of the conflict in Southeast Asia. He later admitted that he "was not even close to an East Asian expert" and that he "had never visited Indochina, nor did I understand or appreciate its history, language, culture, or values." McNamara recalled that the same applied to President Kennedy and the other civilian and military members of the national security establishment. He confessed that he and his advisors were "simpleminded about China."[38]

McNamara developed an antipathy toward US military leaders early in his term in office. The secretary of defense ultimately fired Chief of Naval Operations George W. Anderson because McNamara thought the admiral did not defer to his handling of the naval quarantine during the Cuban Missile Crisis. After the Department of Defense

Reorganization Act of 1958, the JCS chairman remained in the chain of command but the uniformed heads of the services no longer had the authority to direct armies in the field or fleets at sea. During the Vietnam War, strong-willed service chiefs did press their views on operational matters, but unofficially. In contrast, the secretary of defense was empowered to direct the execution of the president's policies and strategies.

Captain Elmo R. "Bud" Zumwalt Jr., who was one of Navy secretary Nitze's staff subordinates at the time, remembered an episode during the missile crisis. Admiral Anderson and his head planner, Vice Admiral "Oley" Sharp, wanted the junior officer in essence to tell McNamara that the Navy would handle the quarantine patrol off Cuba. Nitze reportedly told Zumwalt, "you get back to Admiral Sharp [and by implication Anderson] and tell him that I have personally directed that he is to carry out McNamara's orders." Zumwalt thought this was "a classic example of military versus civilian authority as Paul Nitze saw it." Zumwalt agreed with his boss, stating that "frankly, there was, in my judgement, absolutely no excuse for them [Anderson and Sharp]. If ever there was a clear-cut case of doing something in the way of using military power to send a signal [to the Soviets], this was it."[39]

That same evening, McNamara and Nitze entered the Navy's Flag Plot in the Pentagon, the command center for the quarantine of Cuba. Nitze remembered that Anderson suggested to McNamara that the Navy had known how to manage a blockade "since the days of John Paul Jones" and that McNamara should "go back to his office."[40] While Nitze and Zumwalt considered McNamara's actions the proper exercise of civilian control over the military, others considered them an example of civilian micromanagement of military operations. Anderson had a different and more accurate interpretation of the event, suggesting that it was a minor affair. The admiral thought "the so-called incident in Flag Plot" so insignificant that it was "not even of sufficient importance for me to write down in my diary."[41] Nonetheless, McNamara later fired Anderson over this episode and the admiral's resistance to the Navy's buying a plane that the defense secretary wanted.

The animus between McNamara and the military was reciprocated in spades. Tom Moorer later observed with his usual biting sarcasm that "you can't come from a soap factory [and] take over the Secretary of Defense's job."[42] McNamara, on his part, believed that the chiefs of staff of the armed forces came close to triggering a nuclear war during the Cuban Missile Crisis. At the same time, he ascribed the latter confrontation's successful outcome to his and Kennedy's skillful management and diplomacy. Moorer later opined that "this crowd over in the Pentagon under McNamara had gotten to be field marshals, every one of them by virtue of the Cuban Missile Crisis."[43]

Even before the missile crisis, Kennedy and McNamara had overseen management of another crisis in Laos, according to US intelligence under threat from 7,000 to 10,000 North Vietnamese troops. Both communist and US leaders used military force to gain advantage in Laos. The Pathet Lao, with Chinese and North Vietnamese troop support, routed Lao government forces at Nam Tha in May 1962. Under Kennedy's direction, Felt sent the Seventh Fleet to the South China Sea and deployed US Army and Marine combat forces up to the Thai border with Laos. Felt underestimated the enemy's staying power, glibly assuring McNamara that Seventh Fleet planes could "wipe Tchepone [a small communist-occupied town on the Ho Chi Minh Trail] off the face of the earth."[44] Washington, however, deliberately kept the approach to the confrontation "low-key" and kept the assigned forces in the region small enough to avoid provoking a strong Soviet or Chinese reaction. At one point, Kennedy even intimated to British Prime Minister Harold Macmillan that he did not consider Laos of great strategic importance.[45]

Kennedy banked on diplomacy to resolve the Laos crisis, hoping for the "neutralization" of the country. Having reached a rough equilibrium of force in the region, both sides pressured their subordinate allies to accept a coalition government in Laos headed by Souvanna Phouma. The contending nations then gathered in Geneva, Switzerland, and on 23 July 1962 signed the Geneva Declaration and Protocol on Neutrality of Laos. The Geneva Agreement ended legal justification for the presence of foreign military units in Laos, and after 1962 the United States did not deploy regular forces into that country.

North Vietnam, however, continued to operate there, at first clandestinely but later openly. As Moorer pithily noted, the North Vietnamese "paid no more attention to the Geneva Accords than one of those elephants up there did."[46] By the end of 1962, 10,000 to 20,000 North Vietnamese military personnel had infiltrated from North to South Vietnam through the Laotian "panhandle." McNamara later considered neutralization as having been the best solution for the Laos problem. Ultimately, however, this decision planted the seeds for the American debacle in Vietnam. Freed from the threat of overt

US military intervention, Laos became a communist sanctuary and a never-ending threat to South Vietnam's continued existence.[47] It was a diplomatic blunder of the highest order.

Don Felt did not credit diplomacy with stabilizing the military situation in Laos. He believed that, like the Lebanon and Taiwan Strait crises of the late 1950s, a forthright stand by the United States had limited communist gains there. He deemed that the presence of strong US military forces in the region, even if not ashore, and their potential for further action had been a primary factor in moderating North Vietnamese and Chinese behavior. CINCPAC also learned to be wary about alarmist and frequently exaggerated calls for massive US ground intervention by local leaders. Of equal importance, the admiral came to understand that in keeping with the "flexible response" approach, there were many options available to resolving conflicts in Indochina that did not entail boots on the ground.

AN ANTIDOTE TO COMMUNIST INSURGENCY

Admiral Felt was an early champion of readiness for low-level warfare and "counterinsurgency," the latter defined as "the entire scope of military, paramilitary, political, economic, psychological, and civic actions taken by or in conjunction with the government of a nation to defeat insurgency."[48] There was little in Don Felt's early experiences in the Navy, however, that revealed a strong interest in or affinity for anything other than the type of conventional warfare in which he had engaged in World War II. One might think that Don Felt was a typical old-school officer. Indeed, he had served a midshipman tour while at the US Naval Academy on board *Olympia*, Admiral of the Navy George Dewey's flagship during the 1898 Battle of Manila Bay! As a young ensign, Felt served on board battleship *Mississippi*, a coal-burning warship. But when Felt taught at the Naval War College in the 1950s, he introduced guerrilla and counterguerrilla warfare to the curriculum. His CINCPAC Operation Plan 32-59 for the defense of Southeast Asia stressed that the communist nations would "seek to gain their objectives by means other than war."[49]

In fact, the leadership in Hanoi did not decide in January 1959 at the 15th plenum of the Vietnamese Worker's Party to launch a ground invasion of South Vietnam. Instead, North Vietnamese leaders called for an unconventional, guerrilla campaign to unite all of Vietnam. Southern Vietnamese communists who had migrated to North

Vietnam in 1954 made their way down the Ho Chi Minh Trail and strengthened the insurgency in the South. Under North Vietnamese direction, the Viet Cong waged a campaign of assassination and intimidation to eliminate or cow South Vietnamese villagers. These guerrilla forces, with increasing effectiveness, attacked Army of the Republic of Vietnam (ARVN) troops and installations countrywide. Lieutenant General Samuel T. Williams, Chief of the Military Assistance Advisory Group, Vietnam, a command subordinate to Felt's CINCPAC, did not favor counterinsurgency warfare. He focused on beefing up the conventional capability of the South Vietnamese army to fight like-sized regular enemy forces that might one day storm across the demilitarized zone (DMZ) at the 17th parallel. Don Felt remembered that countering that mindset by "Singing Sam" [actually nicknamed "Hanging Sam"] Williams was "the beginning of my troubles" over how to combat the VC threat.[50]

Instead, the admiral wanted to provide resources to the South Vietnamese military for the development of specialized counterguerrilla units. He facilitated the deployment to South Vietnam of teams of US Army Special Forces—the Green Berets. In April 1960, at the behest of the JCS, CINCPAC produced a plan labeled "Counter-Insurgency Operations in South Vietnam and Laos" that drew upon successful efforts against insurgencies in the Philippines and Malaya. The document posited that the main purpose of counterinsurgency operations was to provide security to the local population on a continuing basis. Key to this control was a government's ability to retain the political allegiance of its people and ensure their economic and social welfare. Felt emphasized that maintaining internal security was not an exclusively military job. He later said that "the key to victory, the key to success, the key to winning in South Vietnam" was to understand that you had to have an integrated program "to break the connection between the rural population and the Viet Cong."[51]

The document specifically called for a carefully planned and well-coordinated campaign against the Viet Cong employing combat forces, paramilitary troops, police, and civilian agencies. It also stressed how important it was for the South Vietnamese government to improve its political and economic connection to the people. Felt told officials in Washington that a sizeable US outlay of material and financial resources was essential if the goal was a successful counterinsurgency campaign. He added that "if Communist expansion is to be prevented

The Republic of Vietnam. Naval History and Heritage Command (NHHC).

without resorting to overt warfare, there is no alternative to making the expenditures required."[52]

Despite Don Felt's impassioned advocacy, the plan languished in the Eisenhower bureaucracy until the end of 1960. The new Kennedy administration moved with greater speed, and in February 1961 approved a somewhat revised plan that provided support for a 20,000-man increase in the South Vietnamese armed forces and strengthening of the paramilitary forces. Ngo Dinh Diem, President of the Republic of Vietnam, accepted the US prospectus but resisted specific recommendations to improve his government's political and economic support of the South Vietnamese people—a basic pillar of the plan. Felt considered Diem a strong leader who was "doing a good job" running the government, but this incident should have suggested to the admiral that Diem did not have the determination or even the desire to satisfy his citizens' most pressing needs. It soon became evident that Diem's primary goal was to establish the primacy of his Catholic minority in the hierarchy of the predominantly Buddhist country and ensure his own political survival.[53]

To complement the political and social aspects of counterinsurgency, in 1960 Don Felt's mentor Arleigh Burke called for the development of naval special forces. That September, the CNO suggested that the Navy adopt relevant concepts and techniques in order to exploit America's maritime advantage. As a direct consequence of Burke's interest, that same month the Navy staff established an Unconventional Activities Working Group to study the subject. Hence, even before the advent of the Kennedy administration and its focus on Green Berets, the Navy and its leaders were looking at alternative methods of warfare for the conflict in Southeast Asia.[54]

The strongest push for the adoption of counterinsurgency measures, however, originated with the Kennedy administration. During the election campaign of 1960, the future president warned that the Soviet Union planned to advance its global interests through "limited brushfire wars, indirect non-overt aggression, intimidation and subversion, internal revolution ... and the vicious blackmail of our allies."[55] As if to confirm Kennedy's suspicions, on 6 January 1961 Soviet Premier Nikita Khrushchev publicly stated his intention to support "wars of liberation or popular uprisings," suggesting South Vietnam as a test case.[56] When the president met with the JCS on 23 February, Kennedy zeroed in on the need for the US military to improve its capability for guerrilla and counterguerrilla warfare. After the meeting, Burke intimated to Felt that "there is going to be an awful lot of guerrilla warfare training by US forces all over [the] world, I'll betcha!"[57]

The still unresolved crisis in Laos and the failure of the Bay of Pigs paramilitary operation in Cuba in spring 1961 had a profound effect on Kennedy. He told the economist John Kenneth Galbraith that he could not abide any more "defeats."[58] Those crises gave added impetus to Kennedy's desire to develop a robust US counterinsurgency capability. He established a group under General Taylor and including Admiral Burke to suggest ways to improve the US ability to combat insurgencies. The Navy head specifically proposed helping friendly governments threatened by communist subversion with US military and civic action groups. As an example, Burke suggested employing naval construction units (Seabees) in underdeveloped countries. McNamara echoed the president's concerns and told the Joint Chiefs that the United States needed to develop a national approach to the counterinsurgencies surfacing all around the world and especially in Vietnam.[59]

Understanding the president's top priority, the Navy's chief planner, Vice Admiral Sharp, rued then that the Navy "has done little, if anything, to increase the emphasis on counter-guerrilla warfare." He added, "Since this type of operation is held in such high regard in high places, we had better get going."[60] Despite his misgivings, the Navy staff had actually moved ahead with an innovative approach to the naval aspects of guerrilla warfare. Planners recommended creation of specialized teams in the Atlantic and Pacific fleets consisting of twenty to twenty-five officers and fifty to seventy-five enlisted men whose primary mission would be to develop a Navy capability in guerrilla and counter-guerrilla operations. These units, offshoots of the existing "frogman" underwater demolition teams, would be designated by the acronym SEAL, "a contraction of Sea, Air, Land . . . indicating an all-around, universal capability."[61]

That same spring, halfway around the world, the deterioration of internal security in South Vietnam prompted some in the administration to recommend the deployment there of strong US ground forces. Don Felt adamantly opposed the proposal, now and perhaps for the first time disagreeing with his mentor and confidant Burke on a major Vietnam-related issue. CINCPAC's primary argument was that such an action would usurp Vietnamese responsibilities for fighting the enemy. Henry L. Miller, who served on Felt's CINCPAC staff, later observed that "Admiral Felt's policy was to help the Vietnamese get organized, get trained, given the military equipment to fight their own war, but to keep US troops out of that country."[62] Don Felt was prophetic in May 1961 when he warned that the deployment of US troops would "commit the US to another Korea-type support and assistance situation" and that "if we go in, we can't pull out at will without damaging repercussions."[63] In the end, Diem informed Washington that short of an overt North Vietnamese invasion, he neither needed nor wanted major US combat units in his country.

With that proposition shelved, at least for a while, the administration reemphasized counterinsurgency warfare. On 11 May 1961, an interdepartmental task force issued what it labeled the "Presidential Program," the basic objective of which was to support Diem's government. To prevent a Viet Cong victory, the document called for military, political, economic, psychological, and covert actions and an increase of the South Vietnamese armed forces to 200,000 men.[64] One aspect of the Presidential Program was US support for the South Vietnamese Coastal Force, sometimes referred to as the "Junk Force." Diem had established the Coastal Force in April 1960 in response to Felt's Counterinsurgency Plan that promoted the use of South Vietnamese paramilitary units to intercept seaborne infiltration from North Vietnam. The Presidential Program provided American advisors and some weapons and communications equipment. Washington significantly strengthened the Coastal Force in early 1962 when McNamara met with Felt in Hawaii and agreed to a sizeable increase in funding for the organization. The United States paid for the construction of 644 motorized junks to operate from twenty-eight bases along the coast of South Vietnam. Felt insisted that the crew members be South Vietnamese fighting men, in this case lightly armed militiamen in black pajamas, rather than American sailors.[65]

In May 1961, even while understanding that major ground combat units would not be deployed to South Vietnam, the CNO alerted his staff to the future possibility of US naval forces operating on the country's myriad inland waterways. On 3 May, Burke observed, "I know this is going to be difficult, but we are going to have to take over such operations as river patrol in the Saigon Delta, in the Mekong River, and other areas."[66] Felt was relieved that the Navy took no action on this idea before Burke stepped down as CNO on 1 August.

Much more to Don Felt's liking was a proposal by the Navy's Washington staff to create Seabee naval construction units specifically dedicated to the counterinsurgency mission. Seabee technical assistance teams (STATS) would be tasked with helping countries like South Vietnam preempt subversion of its villagers by improving their physical environment. Although armed for defense, the Seabees would help the government win and maintain the allegiance of its rural population by digging water wells, bridging canals, building schools, and completing other construction projects throughout the country.[67]

Washington proponents of the deployment of regular US forces to the conflict arena, however, redoubled their efforts. In August 1961, the JCS suggested air and sea patrols of South Vietnam's 1,200-mile coastline by US Seventh Fleet units to interdict suspected North Vietnamese seaborne infiltration of arms and other munitions. CINCPAC strongly advised against the proposed measure. Felt argued that the primary objective was to help the Vietnamese forces develop their own capabilities. He suggested that "one of the keys to success in dealing with our Asian friends is to encourage and assist their own initiative."[68] He also believed that American sailors would not be as effective as their Vietnamese counterparts in identifying North Vietnamese boats trying to evade coastal patrols. Don Felt's well-reasoned opposition influenced the JCS and Secretary McNamara to shelve the idea—for a time.

At the end of August, soon after he became Chief of Naval Operations, Admiral George W. Anderson rhetorically queried his staff about the development of Seabee technical assistance teams and in a larger sense Navy preparation for counterinsurgency warfare: "How far do we go in this business?"[69] In a fashion answering his own question, Anderson then put off the SEAL development program citing lack of personnel sufficient for the job. By the end of October 1961, the Navy had sent only four officers for unconventional warfare instruction at the Army's Special Warfare Center at Fort Bragg, North Carolina. Anderson, a naval aviator, typified many US Navy officers who believed that the primary function of the naval service was to win a war at sea against the Soviet Navy that involved aircraft carriers, submarines, and powerful surface ships. They considered the development of a special warfare capability as an unnecessary and wasteful deviation from their "real" mission.

Meanwhile, South Vietnam's internal security showed signs of collapse. Battalion-size Viet Cong attacks fueled by troops and munitions infiltrated from North Vietnam took an increasing toll of South Vietnamese forces. So worried was Diem that at the end of September 1961 he informed Felt, US Ambassador Frederick Nolting, and Lieutenant General Lionel C. McGarr, the new chief of the Military Assistance Advisory Group, Vietnam, that US combat units might be needed to prevent a communist victory. The Joint Chiefs as well as other defense and state department officials thought that the time for major US intervention had arrived. Before authorizing that step, Kennedy dispatched General Taylor to South Vietnam on a fact-finding mission. Even during the visit, Taylor, McNamara, and the JCS continued to press for intervention with perhaps 8,000 troops. Don Felt helped torpedo the proposal. CINCPAC briefed Taylor, on the way to South Vietnam, about the dire situation in Indochina. Still, he only favored the introduction of engineer, helicopter, and logistic units for selective assistance to the Vietnamese. He recommended deferring the deployment of troops, at least for the time being.[70]

Diem once again changed his mind, insisting that only US support units were needed to help him cope with the insurgency. Secretary of State Dean Rusk also thought the proposed action would work against US diplomatic interests. Feisty Admiral Felt once again manned the barricades against intervention. CINCPAC averred that the deployment to Vietnam of American soldiers would reignite charges of "white colonialism throughout the world, prompt Communist countermeasures on a like scale, result in a long-term deployment, and ultimately engage US personnel in combat" with the Viet Cong.[71]

Concluding, however, that there was a groundswell in Washington and even in Saigon for stronger action in Southeast Asia, Felt suggested that the US could take alternative actions that would not trigger a war with China. Reflecting his comfort with the current theoretical approach to international security threats, the admiral suggested that the United States "use forces flexibly in a way of our own choosing."[72] That thinking was in line with the Taylor mission's final report that called for a new US–South Vietnam relationship, a "limited partnership" in which "Americans must, as friends and partners—not as arm's-length advisors—show them how the job might be done—not tell them or do it for them."[73] On 14 November, Kennedy informed Diem that the United States would dispatch some US support units to his country but only as a backup to the South Vietnamese armed forces.

Meeting at Felt's Hawaii headquarters in December 1961, McNamara apprised the room full of US civilian and military officials that money was no object in the preservation of the South Vietnamese state and that all assistance short of ground combat troops could be made available. Rear Admiral Arnold F. Schade, on the Navy's Washington staff, remarked that "if we get by short of introducing US

US Ambassador Frederick Nolting welcomes Felt to Saigon during one of the admiral's visits to South Vietnam. In the end, the naval leader lost touch with the reality of the conflict in the embattled country. NHHC VN Collection.

or SEATO troops, it will be a long hard pull" and added, in perhaps one of the first uses of the memorable phrase, "we can't see any light at the other end of the tunnel yet."[74]

Glimmers of hope with regard to the counterinsurgency campaign did arise early in February 1962 when McNamara once again flew to CINCPAC headquarters to meet with Don Felt and other relevant civilian and military leaders. The assembled group learned that the number of Viet Cong attacks had decreased from late 1961 and that government troops were registering some success. Felt and the others were optimistic: "South Vietnam had earlier been described as a country going down a steep slope to disaster. We can't say that the direction has been reversed—for the moment the slope has leveled out a bit." At the same time, he cautioned that long-term success would only come when the Vietnamese villagers felt safe from Viet Cong attack.[75] General McCarr was so confident that he assured McNamara that, with some additional resources for the South Vietnamese, the war would be over by the end of 1963.[76]

In March 1962, during his next meeting with SECDEF, Felt reported that based on favorable reports from General Paul D. Harkins, the first commander of the newly established Military Assistance Command, Vietnam (MACV), the "pendulum seems to be swinging our way."⁷⁷ Following a tour of naval installations throughout South Vietnam in late July, Admiral Anderson buttressed Felt's optimistic appraisal. The CNO thought President Diem "appeared knowledgeable and seemed to be coming around" to being less dictatorial. He added that "what we saw is a sound basis for cautious optimism."⁷⁸ There certainly was cause for optimism as US regular forces began stiffening South Vietnamese military operations in the new "limited partnership" program.

While only a short time before Don Felt had opposed a US Navy anti-infiltration patrol of South Vietnam's coast, he now complied with that tasking, if only to forestall the deployment ashore of American troops. He wanted the operation to augment training of the Vietnam Navy's Sea Force and to infuse it with a "can do" spirit.⁷⁹ That unit, with escorts, motor gunboats, LSTs and other amphibious ships, operated along South Vietnam's coastline and on the open ocean. Another important goal of the operation was to determine whether there was significant seaborne infiltration from North Vietnam. Hence, in December 1961, Seventh Fleet and Vietnam Navy units began conducting surface and air patrols from the 17th parallel eastward to the Paracel Islands. In an effort to ascertain if there were any communist infiltration of arms and supplies from Cambodia into the Mekong Delta, US and South Vietnamese naval forces launched a similar effort in the Gulf of Thailand. The allies did not discover significant infiltration either there or near the 17th parallel, so CINCPAC readily ended the entire anti-infiltration program off South Vietnam on 1 August 1962. Before and especially after the patrols, Felt and other US Navy leaders doubted the existence of seaborne infiltration. As related in a postwar interview, Captain Joseph B. Drachnik, the head naval advisor in South Vietnam, was convinced that "there was no effective infiltration by sea." He added, "Mr. McNamara told me later when I was on his staff in the Pentagon that he too was convinced."⁸⁰

No sooner had the US ended its coastal patrols, however, than the North Vietnamese mounted a major seaborne infiltration effort. Directed by Group 759 (after January 1964 Brigade 125), from late 1962 to late 1963 North Vietnamese ships carried out twenty-three missions delivering 1,318 tons of munitions to sites in the Mekong Delta and central South Vietnam. Sometimes flying the flag of the People's Republic of China to conceal their origin, the vessels steamed on moonless nights to points offshore beyond waters patrolled by South Vietnamese naval forces and then made quick dashes to the beach to deliver their war material to Viet Cong guerrillas. The maritime infiltration of war materials by a force of approximately twenty-five North Vietnamese steel-hulled and wooden-hulled trawlers increased dramatically. According to North Vietnamese sources, during 1964 and early 1965, Brigade 125 carried out eighty-eight missions to the South, delivering tons of guns and ammunition and North Vietnamese military and political cadres. The communist seaborne infiltration program, while largely unsuccessful after the intervention of US Navy units in 1965, lasted in some form until the end of the war.[81]

Despite Admiral Anderson's ambivalence about naval special forces, he authorized the establishment on 1 January 1962 of SEAL Team 1 in the Pacific Fleet and SEAL Team 2 in the Atlantic Fleet. If the CNO had any doubts about Kennedy's interest in naval involvement in counterinsurgency warfare, they must have been erased when the CNO learned later that month that the "President was quite emphatic ... that he wanted people from all Services trained in antiguerrilla warfare."[82] As a financial and professional incentive, the president let it be known that he saw knowledge of counterinsurgency warfare as a prerequisite to flag and general officer promotion. On 6 January, Anderson ordered that all Navy personnel in Vietnam or headed to Vietnam be trained in the use of small arms for defense against guerrillas and in July established the Navy's formal "Counterinsurgency Education and Training Program."[83]

But even while initiating these programs, Anderson complained to his Pacific Fleet commander that "we are constantly besieged with inquiries as to what the Navy is doing in this realm."[84] In November 1963, the same month of his assassination, Kennedy thus apprised Anderson and the new Secretary of the Navy, Paul Nitze: "When I was in Norfolk in 1962 I noted particularly the members of the SEAL Teams. I was impressed by them as individuals and with the capability they possess as a group." He emphasized that "the need for special forces in the Navy and Marine Corps will increase."[85]

Anderson concurred with Felt's opposition to the establishment of a US Navy "River Warfare Force" as proposed in August 1962 by Captain Drachnik. The CNO observed that creation of such a capability "does not appear to be justified." Instead, he suggested "improving the River Force capabilities of our friends, the Vietnamese."[86] Top naval leaders continued to stress that aside from advisors, SEALs, STATs, and a few other specialized units, regular US naval forces should not become directly involved in fighting the war in South Vietnam; that was the responsibility of the armed forces of the Republic of Vietnam.

Small detachments of SEALs first deployed to South Vietnam in spring 1962 to begin training South Vietnamese "Biet Hai" and other commandos in small boat, sabotage, and clandestine maritime operations. SEALs would be a permanent fixture of the naval war in Vietnam for the next ten years. Moreover, after some bureaucratic and logistical delays, the first Seabee technical assistance teams arrived in South Vietnam in January 1963 and were soon hard at work supporting the South Vietnamese internal security program. Teams of thirteen specially trained Seabees constructed fortifications for Army Green Berets and their Vietnamese and "Montagnard" tribal allies all along the borders with Laos and Cambodia. The units also drilled wells in the Mekong Delta to provide rural villagers with clean water, served their medical needs, and constructed airfields, roads, and bridges throughout South Vietnam. Felt was so pleased with the success of the STAT program that in summer 1963 he authorized deployment of additional teams to Vietnam.[87]

Felt did not favor a large American military presence in South Vietnam—especially a US Army presence. Early in 1962, McNamara proposed creating a joint command for South Vietnam separate from the Pacific Command that would logically be headed by an Army general. There was even consideration that the CINCPAC command itself should be led by a non-Navy flag officer. With justification, Felt argued, as did a majority of the JCS, that his security responsibilities in the Pacific—a vast maritime domain—demanded one overall regional commander, a four-star admiral. Of course, the Navy and its leaders as far back as World War II were as determined as admirals Ernest King and Chester Nimitz to keep the entire Pacific theater in their hands. Persuaded by the strong logic of Don Felt's argument and understanding the partisan ramifications, McNamara did an about-face. For the duration of the war in Vietnam, the US Military Assistance Command, Vietnam, would serve as a subordinate command under CINCPAC.[88]

TAKING THE FIGHT TO HANOI

In addition to backing the use of special forces and military support units in South Vietnam, Felt favored putting military pressure on

North Vietnam, the command center for the insurgency. In November 1960, even as he wrestled with crises in Laos, the admiral had suggested overturning "some Communist apple carts" through clandestine actions in their rear areas.[89] The following year, Felt provided the White House with a list of military actions that might be taken against North Vietnam, including air strikes, amphibious raids, and the mining of Haiphong harbor. The attacks could be made "singly but progressively" and could be "graduated dependent on the politico/military objectives." During the 1962 crisis over Laos, the JCS called for major air strikes against targets in North Vietnam to punish the leaders in Hanoi for supporting the Pathet Lao.[90]

In April 1962, CINCPAC observed that North Vietnam's power plants, railroads, bridges and the homes of communist leaders were vulnerable to air attack and that "we should exploit this vulnerability." Unsurprisingly, Don Felt advanced his thoughts in the context of the "flexible response" and "graduated escalation" strategic approaches then widely accepted not only by civilian but also by military strategists. He suggested that "we should strive for a direct cause-and-effect relationship." Hence, "a mining of Dong Ha–Saigon railroad ideally would be followed within a week by slightly larger destruction of the DRV Lao Kay–Hanoi line."[91] Anderson heartily endorsed a campaign to harass the North Vietnamese. The CNO suggested tailoring US actions in the North to enemy actions in the South: "step up the harassment campaign as Viet Cong activities increase and slow it down as the Viet Cong slow down."[92] Perhaps forgetting this operational advice, Anderson later lambasted the "concept of gradualism, or [the] gradual approach [since] nothing other than winning, once military forces are committed, is acceptable."[93]

Such a harassment campaign was already in motion. Under CIA direction, relatively slow and lightly armed motorized junks and other craft landed South Vietnamese saboteurs and intelligence agents in North Vietnam. Other men were infiltrated by land or air; these unlucky volunteers were ultimately, if not immediately compromised and either killed or "turned" to become counterspies. In August 1962, General Harkins proposed to Washington that SEALs and naval logistic personnel based in Danang support a clandestine maritime operation against North Vietnam. US fast craft crewed by non-Americans would sortie from that port for actions on the enemy coastline. In September, Felt readily endorsed the concept since he was dismayed by the slow progress and inadequacy of the CIA program.[94]

That same month, the Kennedy administration's Special Group (Counterinsurgency or 5412 for the room in which they met), composed of White House, State Department, Defense Department, JCS, CIA, and other representatives, concurred with Harkins's concept. But the real push came from McNamara, who ordered the secretary of the Navy to purchase Norwegian-built "Nasty"-class fast patrol boats (PTFs). Cost was no object. Felt later remembered McNamara saying with regard to spending, "Gee, I've got a 50-billion-dollar budget. If I can't spend two or three million dollars . . . something's wrong."[95]

Accordingly, a pair of Nasty craft, complemented by two US-built motor torpedo boats of early 1950s vintage, armed with 20mm guns and crewed by Navy personnel, were transported across the Pacific and deployed to Danang. Also operating at that port was a US naval group that trained Vietnamese personnel in boat operations and repaired the vessels, a SEAL detachment that worked with Vietnamese commandos, and a trio of formerly CIA fast patrol craft (PCF), or Swift boats.

While the Johnson administration continued to support political and military actions in South Vietnam, it began to focus on North Vietnam as well. Following a classic flexible response approach, McNamara aimed to discourage Hanoi's southern campaign through a program of increasingly painful military pressures. Based on Operation Plan 34, a document Felt directed his staff to develop in mid-1963, the CIA's Chief of Far Eastern Operations, William Colby, produced a three-phase blueprint for covert operations against North Vietnam. Johnson approved continued work on what was then labeled Operation Plan 34A. But, in a foretaste of his later direct involvement in military operations, the president insisted that the proposed actions limit any physical damage in North Vietnam, not generate retaliation, avoid an adverse international reaction, and enable the US government to deny involvement.

Despite Don Felt's view that the CIA should continue to take the lead in pressuring North Vietnam, he complied with the president's wishes. McNamara now became especially enthusiastic about annoying Hanoi. On 20 December, after reviewing 34A's proposed concept of operations, the defense secretary ordered the Navy to buy more Nastys from Norway. The following day, McNamara told the president that the plan presented a wide variety of operations "from which I believe we should aim to select those that provide maximum pressure with minimum risk." He was also keen on not jeopardizing Johnson's political ambitions with more overt actions.[96]

On 16 January 1964, Johnson gave the go-ahead; Operation Plan 34A would start on 1 February. But the president authorized only Phase I, which entailed the least-risk psychological, intelligence-gathering, and sabotage actions. Since the CIA had transferred control of most covert operations in North Vietnam to the Defense Department in late 1963, a new US office in Saigon, the Special Operations Group (MACSOG, or later Studies and Observation Group) would control 34A actions. MACSOG worked in close coordination with McNamara's Washington-based Special Assistant for Counterinsurgency and Special Activities (SACSA), Marine Brigadier General Victor H. "Brute" Krulak, a legendary World War II warrior.

The signal of US resolve that Washington wished to send communist leaders in Hanoi did not reach them via initial 34A operations. The first boat foray, an unsuccessful attempt to sabotage a ferry on Cape Ron, took place on 16 February 1964, but not until the end of May were all the boats finally armed and ready and the South Vietnamese sufficiently trained for their dangerous missions to the north. In April, US Ambassador to South Vietnam Henry Cabot Lodge complained that 34A operations were having no impact on Hanoi. Admiral Sharp, Commander in Chief, Pacific Fleet since September 1963, observed that "we have spent a lot of time, effort and money on the PTF program." He regretted that "some of our early reservations on the PTF concept are becoming reality." Felt and Sharp also considered employing US destroyers to help the 34A force carry out its combat missions, but Washington never acted on that suggestion.[97]

Only on 27 May 1964 did Operation 34A carry out its first successful mission, when the maritime force captured a North Vietnamese fishing junk and its six-man crew. The South Vietnamese brought the boat and crew to Lao Cham Island near Danang, questioned the men for intelligence, provided them with propaganda materials, and returned the vessel and sailors to waters above the Demilitarized Zone. During June and July, the maritime force registered somewhat more success, destroying a storage facility ashore and dropping a bridge near Hao Mon Dong and capturing more North Vietnamese junks and fishermen. On the night of 30 June–1 July near the mouth of the Kien River, a pair of PTFs landed a combat team that destroyed a reservoir pump house, while losing two men in a firefight with defending troops.[98]

COUNTERINSURGENCY ON THE ROPES

Meanwhile, the cautious optimism of 1962 had evaporated in the face of troubling developments in South Vietnam. On 2 January 1963, at the hamlet of Ap Bac in the Mekong Delta, Viet Cong forces ambushed and thoroughly drubbed a South Vietnamese unit strengthened with US-supplied armored personnel carriers, artillery, helicopters, and advisors. The enemy shot down five helicopters and killed 83 soldiers, including three Americans. With little understanding of guerrilla warfare, General Harkins characterized the battle—as if it had occurred in World War II—as a victory since the enemy had abandoned the battlefield. Felt blamed the press for biased reporting and accepted Harkins's rosy evaluation of the war effort in South Vietnam. Indeed, Don Felt naively believed Harkins's assertion that he had a plan that would defeat the insurgency by the end of 1965.[99]

Don Felt railed against journalists who reported that the counterinsurgency effort was failing and that the ineptitude of Diem's government was the cause. CINCPAC accused the newsmen, whom he considered "not quite dry behind the ears" and irresponsible, of trying to destroy Diem. He admonished them to "get on the team."[100] At the end of the month that featured the disastrous battle at Ap Bac, Felt issued a public statement emphasizing that the war was going well and that the government was "gradually reestablishing its control over the rural population." Felt itemized positive trends: the weekly average of Viet Cong attacks had dropped by half since early 1962, and attacks by battalion-size enemy forces were rare. He credited part of this result to a new aggressiveness on the part of ARVN and paramilitary forces that were killing the Viet Cong on a five-to-one ratio. Felt enhanced his optimistic prognosis with the statement that the US team was confident that the South Vietnamese "will defeat the communist guerrillas and establish decent civil control of the nation."[101]

On 31 January 1963, *The Washington Post* reported that Felt predicted that South Vietnam would win its war against the Viet Cong within three years. In May, Felt testified before the House Foreign Affairs Committee that the South Vietnamese government had made significant progress during the past six months in the military, political, social, and economic spheres. He suggested that the people were not supporting the Viet Cong because the government "meets their basic social needs such as medical care, education, sanitation and agricultural assistance."[102]

Don Felt, like the leaders in Washington, did not shy away from micromanaging Harkins's actions from afar. In January 1963, State Department officials Roger Hilsman, Michael Forrestal, and Army Major General Edward L. Rowney complained that Felt was "trying to run the war even in practical detail." They contended that the admiral "runs the South Vietnam operation like a ship [in that] he interferes in details of tactical planning" and prevented Harkins from communicating directly with the Joint Chiefs of Staff. The trio suggested that Washington "cut CINCPAC out as regards operations [and] policy decisions."[103] At one point, Kennedy wondered whether Felt kept Harkins on too tight a "leash." As a result, Ambassador Taylor personally instructed Felt to give Harkins "more latitude" in his areas of responsibility.[104] In short, Felt was being told to ease up on his efforts to micromanage the situation in Vietnam. General Westmoreland, Harkins's successor, who wanted a more robust US military effort, did not have a high regard for Felt. He mentioned the admiral, his boss in the chain of command, only twice in his 425-page memoir and spoke disparagingly of Felt as "a man of small physical stature who commanded autocratically."[105]

Eventually, even Felt began to question the optimistic reports coming out of Saigon. In January 1964, CINCPAC dispatched Navy Captain Phil Bucklew to South Vietnam to determine the extent of communist infiltration along the country's myriad waterways. The day before Bucklew departed on his mission, Don Felt called him to his quarters. With moccasined feet propped up on his desk, the admiral told the officer that he wanted to know "why all I get from Vietnam are glowing reports of our accomplishments and meanwhile we are getting the hell kicked out of us."[106] Felt later admitted that McNamara, Harkins, and he had relied too heavily on optimistic statistical reports of progress in the counterinsurgency struggle from Diem's government and from senior American advisors. CINCPAC admitted with regard to the counterinsurgency programs that "we got fooled [and] hoodwinked." He lamented that "the actual performance . . . was not nearly as good as presented to Diem and as presented to us." He blamed much of that failure on Diem, who had no serious plan to combat the insurgency and didn't provide the necessary leadership.[107]

Communist attacks and defeats of ARVN units increased throughout the year. Security in the countryside deteriorated considerably. Political and religious turmoil in South Vietnam caused Washington an even greater headache. Beginning in the spring, South Vietnamese Buddhists began noisy street demonstrations in Saigon to protest Diem regime policies and actions. The government's police forces reacted swiftly and violently. The crisis spread to other cities during the summer. The self-immolation of Buddhist monks in the capital, in full view of international media, revealed the depth of opposition to Diem and his government.

The Kennedy administration now began to accept the possibility that Diem would be ousted in a coup d'état that might not only end the US connection to the Republic of Vietnam but also endanger the lives of Americans in the country. During Felt's visit to Saigon at the end of October, Ambassador Lodge convinced the admiral that there would be no coup. He told Felt that "there isn't a Vietnamese general with hair enough on his chest to make it go." Don Felt later admitted that even though he visited Diem on the morning of 1 November, he "had no idea that there would be a coup."[108] Later that day, shortly after Felt departed Saigon on a military transport, a cabal of South Vietnamese military leaders overthrew the government and killed Diem. In following months, the political situation in South Vietnam worsened. As Vice Admiral Tom Moorer, then Commander Seventh Fleet, later observed, "they had a series of coups—a coup a day, just like a tropical shower."[109]

Hanoi took note of South Vietnam's changing fortunes with the death of Diem. At the 9th plenary session of the Vietnamese Communist Party in December 1963, General Secretary Le Duan led the charge to intensify the military campaign against Saigon before the United States could intervene in force to save its ally. Le Duan and other hardliners sidelined Ho Chi Minh and browbeat moderate Politburo members to embrace more aggressive policies.[110]

Ngo Dinh Diem's assassination seriously eroded but did not destroy Felt's belief that it was possible for the South Vietnamese, with limited US assistance, to overcome the communist threat. CINCPAC took a number of actions to bolster the armed forces of Vietnam and their ability to successfully prosecute the war. Not only did he continue to oppose the deployment of US regular forces to South Vietnam but also he resisted increasing efforts by McNamara and certain Army leaders to beef up the overall American military presence.

Concerned by reports that the enemy was transporting arms and ammunition via Cambodia and along the rivers and coastal waters of the Mekong Delta, in January 1964 McNamara suggested that Felt dispatch a team to South Vietnam to investigate. The nine-man Vietnam Delta Infiltration Study Group, headed by Captain Bucklew, interviewed key American and Vietnamese naval officers and put together what became known as the Bucklew Report. The document affirmed that the enemy was moving supplies into and throughout the Mekong Delta and called for action to improve the Vietnam Navy's response. Bucklew recommended greater coordination and cooperation between the South Vietnamese naval and ground forces; river pilots and customs agents to monitor waterway activity; an augmentation of resources for the Vietnam Navy; and establishment of the billet of chief of naval operations to increase the maritime arm's clout within the army-dominated Joint General Staff.[111]

Felt concurred with the report's conclusions, and with JCS approval it became the guiding document of 1964 for South Vietnam's Chien Thang, or Victory Plan, and for the US naval advisory effort. A significant factor in CINCPAC's endorsement of the Bucklew Report was its emphasis on South Vietnamese actions and the absence of any call for a US Navy river force. Navy leaders in Washington during early 1964 strongly opposed a significant Navy contribution of conventional forces to the conflict in South Vietnam. Marine Commandant General Wallace Greene was especially bothered that of the Joint Chiefs, only one—CNO Admiral David L. McDonald—had never visited South Vietnam. Greene recommended that as soon as possible the president should direct the admiral to go to South Vietnam and "acquaint himself with the situation, especially in regard to the Navy."[112] That action did not occur during 1964. Moreover, according to Bucklew, McDonald had concluded that "there will never be need for aircraft carriers out there," so the Navy would only provide limited support for the predominantly "army situation." Moreover, Admiral Horacio "Rivets" Rivero, who became the Vice Chief of Naval Operations in July, didn't want the Navy to "degenerate into a river force." Bucklew related that Rivero "put it in writing, that the Navy would not become involved in any shallow river, muddy warfare."[113]

TURNING UP THE HEAT

Following the catastrophic events of November 1963 and the subsequent collapse of security in South Vietnam, many US leaders called for direct military action against North Vietnam. Even before Kennedy's death, Felt had pushed for air strikes against communist forces in Laos and possibly North Vietnam. Washington rejected these proposals, McNamara informing CINCPAC that the president considered such actions untimely.[114]

In January 1964, Vice Admiral Alfred G. Ward, then the Navy's chief planner, proposed a series of increasingly strong measures against Hanoi culminating in the mining of Haiphong harbor and a naval blockade of the country. Felt cautioned that a blockade was considered an act of war and an action not to be taken lightly on the doorstep of China. He also said that a blockade would be difficult to execute. Partly influenced by Don Felt's reasoning, the JCS did not recommend implementation of a blockade. CINCPAC was convinced that lesser actions would suffice to moderate Hanoi's behavior. The following month, VCNO Admiral Claude V. Ricketts, representing the CNO on the JCS, called for air strikes on military and industrial targets throughout North Vietnam to break Hanoi's will to continue supporting the insurgency in South Vietnam. He alluded to the Lebanon and Taiwan Strait crises of 1958 and the Cuban Missile Crisis of 1962 as instances where the threat of overwhelming US military retaliation had compelled communist leaders to back down.[115]

On 2 March, the Joint Chiefs also called for overt military action against North Vietnam, in a "sudden blow for shock effect." But they would also accommodate measures in an ascending order of intensity that would begin with raids, sabotage, and the harassment of shipping and ending with a massive bombing and sea blockade. The military heads concluded that China would not intervene as a result of these actions. Not only did Johnson not approve of the JCS approach, but General Taylor suggested to Marine General Greene that Taylor's "neck and the SecDef's neck were on the chopping block" if they pushed the JCS proposal.[116] Felt's CINCPAC Operation Plan 38-64, "Military Operations to Terminate Aggression in Southeast Asia," a worst-case contingency plan, anticipated the massive use of air and naval power to defend the region and to strike "punitive and crippling" offensive operations against China. The use of nuclear weapons was not ruled out. The Joint Chiefs approved the CINCPAC plan on 29 July 1964.[117]

Nevertheless, newly installed President Johnson and his chief advisors doubted the confrontation would reach that point since they considered North Vietnam a military lightweight. In one instance, the president characterized North Vietnam as a "damn little piss-ant country" and on another occasion as a "raggedy-ass little fourth-rate country" that would fold under pressure.¹¹⁸ Secretary of the Navy Nitze, an early supporter of the flexible response approach, opined that US air and naval power "would favor the United States so greatly that regardless of what North Vietnam did we would prevail in a comparably short period of time."¹¹⁹ Ricketts felt much the same way, observing that if Chinese armies entered North Vietnam they could be destroyed by air and naval power and ground troops deployed along the coast.

Other Navy leaders discounted North Vietnam as the primary actor in the Indochina conflict. The CNO asked Vice Admiral Rufus L. Taylor, Director of Naval Intelligence, for an assessment of North Vietnamese intentions. The intelligence head saw China, rather than North Vietnam, as the main culprit behind the recent adverse developments in Indochina. Taylor pointed to the buildup of forces in southern China and substantial transfer of arms and munitions to the Vietnamese communists as proof of Mao's intention to dominate the region through his Vietnamese and Laotian allies. The admiral concluded that "we should be prepared at an early date to either commit US forces in sufficient strength to ensure victory for our side or get out before it is too late."¹²⁰ In short, the head of Navy intelligence was calling for war, even if it involved China. CNO McDonald remembered McNamara saying, "We can win this little war with both hands tied behind our backs."¹²¹ Nitze also remembered that before 1965 McNamara was supremely confident that the conflict would be won in a reasonable period of time. Tom Moorer suggested that when the war began, the North Vietnamese "didn't have anything but a few machine guns."¹²²

The Joint Chiefs doubted that strong military actions against North Vietnam would trigger the Johnson administration's biggest fear: Chinese or even Soviet intervention. General Krulak, an authority on counterinsurgency, believed that the Soviets would not go to war with the United States over Indochina. Moscow might protest a US mining of Haiphong, for instance, but do nothing more. General Earle Wheeler, the JCS chairman, assured the president that militarily the United States was a match for both North Vietnam and China. In spring 1965, General Taylor thought it would likely take months, not years, to compel Hanoi to reconsider its aggressive behavior. McNamara later admitted that "we never carefully debated what US force would ultimately be required, what our chances of success would be, or what the political, military, financial, and human costs would be if we provided it." He regretted that "we were at the beginning of a slide down a tragic and slippery slope."¹²³

Despite this optimistic appraisal of the balance of forces, Admiral Felt supported Johnson's efforts to avoid provoking Chinese or Soviet intervention through direct US military actions against North Vietnam. General Westmoreland and State Department officials also cautioned against strong measures against Hanoi because they feared that the South Vietnamese government and armed forces could not cope with a major escalation of the war. Maxwell Taylor, one of the intellectual fathers of flexible response, encouraged the graduated application of finely calibrated military pressure. Observers also understood that in an election year, the Johnson administration would not approve a potentially unpopular direct attack on North Vietnam.[124]

Don Felt continued to back the administration's graduated pressure program. Given the later course of the war, one can only conclude that the admiral was overly optimistic when he suggested that the clandestine actions embodied in Operation Plan 34A could influence Hanoi to end its support of the southern insurgency. He contended that the selective application of military, diplomatic, and psychological pressures would deter the North Vietnamese and not trigger Chinese intervention. Don Felt apparently forgot this advocacy when he claimed in his post–retirement oral history that the "gradualism concept was . . . imposed on us," and that in war "there's only one way, and that is to win the damned thing as quickly as you can, and that wasn't done."[125]

CINCPAC was in accord with Johnson's and Westmoreland's desire to reinvigorate the counterinsurgency campaign in South Vietnam before taking especially drastic actions against North Vietnam. So too were Generals Taylor and Harold K. Johnson and Admiral McDonald on the JCS. General Greene, however, "had the feeling that Admiral McDonald was [only] saying what he thought the President would like to hear."[126] Only Air Force general Curtis LeMay and Greene called for massive air strikes against North Vietnam. National Security Action Memo (NSAM) 288, approved by the president on 17 March and affirmed during McNamara's meeting with Felt in Hawaii on 1 and 2 June 1964, emphasized the primacy of actions in South Vietnam over those proposed for North Vietnam.[127]

That same spring, CINCPAC developed a blueprint, Operation Plan 37-64, for direct attack on North Vietnam, but it adhered closely to Washington's emphasis on limited retaliatory measures and graduated escalation. Don Felt's plan embodied "tit-for-tat" retaliatory air strikes in response to communist attacks in South Vietnam. Reflecting Felt's long-held belief that the struggle ashore was primarily between North and South Vietnam, the plan emphasized that the South Vietnamese air force would take the lead, with US land-based squadrons acting only in support.[128]

Hanoi's surge of combat-trained southern "returnees" down the Ho Chi Minh Trail after Diem's assassination in November 1963 drew US attention in spring 1964.[129] Laotian Prime Minister Phouma, who had switched his previous allegiances and now looked to the United States for support in response to communist actions in Laos, authorized the use of Laotian air space by American low-level reconnaissance aircraft. In line with the administration's objective of "sending Hanoi a message" without committing US forces to direct attacks on North Vietnam, McNamara directed the Navy and the Air Force to initiate aerial reconnaissance missions over central and southern Laos in Operation Yankee Team. On 19 May, Air Force aircraft based in South Vietnam executed the first "reconnaissance/show of force" flight, and two days later a pair of photo-reconnaissance planes from carrier *Kitty Hawk* (CVA-63) overflew the Plain of Jars.[130]

Aircraft carriers *Bon Homme Richard* (CVA-31) and *Constellation* (CVA-64) joined *Kitty Hawk* in the Gulf of Tonkin within striking distance of North Vietnam. The presence of the Seventh Fleet was designed not only to support the reconnaissance flights but also to awe communist leaders in Hanoi with the naval power of the United States. Between 21 May and 9 June, Navy and Air Force squadrons carried out more than 130 flights over central and southern Laos. Apparently, the communists were not discouraged by this display of American aerial might since on 6 June 1964 an enemy antiaircraft gun shot down the RF-8A Crusader photo-reconnaissance plane flown by Lieutenant Charles F. Klusmann from *Kitty Hawk*'s air wing.[131]

Washington's tight control of operations surfaced during Yankee Team operations. General Greene recorded at the time that "McNamara has pretty much field-marshaled the entire effort in Southeast Asia [but] his whiz-kid-Ford-Motor-company management techniques apparently aren't paying off."[132] Proposals for future missions had to be sent to Washington for McNamara's personal approval days in advance of the operation. On 2 June, the Seventh Fleet commander had confidentially voiced his concern to McDonald. Tom Moorer complained that with Washington determining how many aircraft would conduct a mission, the type of camera the photo planes would use, and other tactical factors, the missions had become unnecessarily complicated and unproductive.¹³³ The following spring, Westmoreland voiced similar complaints about war management from afar. He related to JCS chairman Wheeler that "the more remote the authority . . . the more we are vulnerable to mishaps resulting from such things as incomplete briefings and preparation, loss of tactical flexibility and lack of tactical coordination."¹³⁴ These verities fell on deaf ears in Washington. McNamara considered himself superior to military leaders with regard to managerial decision-making, cost-accounting, and even warfighting.

Right after Klusmann's shoot-down, McNamara gave specific instructions for the next Yankee Team missions. He ordered the start of operations on 7 June by two reconnaissance planes and eight escorting fighters. The escorts were to be armed with an "optimum mix of weapons for anti-aircraft suppression [and] authorized to employ retaliatory fire against any source of anti-aircraft fire." On the second mission of the day, communist gunners shot up Commander Doyle Lynn's F-8D Crusader, forcing the naval aviator to bail out. Air Force and Navy search and rescue units retrieved the pilot from the jungle the next day and whisked him to safety.

Reviewing the event, the secretary of defense expressed the view that naval commanders had improperly positioned and armed their aircraft for the mission and not followed his wish to destroy the enemy antiaircraft site. CINCPAC replied that in future actions the operators should have more latitude.¹³⁵ McNamara rejected Felt's recommendation because the defense secretary had become less concerned about signaling Hanoi than losing aircraft. He was already considering a new, minimum-risk approach in Laos. He ordered that most future reconnaissance missions avoid the heavily defended Plain of Jars and fly elsewhere in Laos above 10,000 feet, out of reach of North Vietnamese antiaircraft guns. This measure dramatically reduced losses—but negated the overall strategic objective. With US aircraft flying at high altitudes and far above the heavy cloud ceiling during the typical Laotian monsoon season, there was little for Hanoi to fear from American air power. As judged by the continued heavy troop and logistic flow down the Ho Chi Minh Trail, the North Vietnamese showed no inclination to stop supporting the southern insurgency.¹³⁶

Washington's micromanagement of the war and disregard of Felt's advice only increased in the waning days of his service. As one indication of that trend, Greene remembered that before a conference of defense department civilian and military leaders at CINCPAC headquarters in Hawaii on 3 June 1964, McNamara did not provide Don Felt with an agenda or brief him on the issues to be discussed.[137]

The admiral, however, won the fight to continue the Pacific Command's control of bombing operations external to South Vietnam. General Harkins in Saigon had asserted that he should have that authority since what transpired in Laos and North Vietnam impacted directly on the conflict in South Vietnam. Supported not only by his subordinate Air Force component commander but those Air Force leaders serving under MACV, Felt argued that the Pacific-wide responsibilities of his command demanded his control of out-country operations. Washington agreed.

FIGHTING TO HOLD BACK THE TIDE

Admiral Harry D. Felt's signal achievement during his first five years as Commander in Chief, Pacific, was delaying the deployment of major American ground combat forces to the mainland of Asia, anticipating the dangers of that weighty and potentially long-term commitment. He understood that the South Vietnamese government had to be at the forefront of the fight against its internal and external enemies. His direct role in the management of the crises in Laos exposed him to the complexities and difficulties of the political-military situation in Indochina. He came to understand that the nuclear-heavy, "massive retaliation" approach of the Eisenhower administration had little utility to the security challenges he faced. Under his leadership, the Pacific Command developed war plans that provided for various non-nuclear contingencies. Given greater operational authority by the Department of Defense Reorganization Act of 1958, Felt exercised significant influence over Washington's early handling of the crises in Laos. His stature as head of the vast Pacific theater and the logic of his arguments made it clear that a Navy flag officer should continue to fill the key CINCPAC billet. Appropriately, his command would oversee the war's major bombing campaigns. Don Felt's close professional and personal relationship with CNO Burke and thus his access to the JCS enhanced his clout in the decision-making process during the latter years of the Eisenhower administration and at least the early months of the Kennedy administration.

Felt's service during World War II and in Korea had schooled him in conventional operations, but he readily adapted his strategic thinking to the new realities of the Cold War. Felt was an early and enthusiastic champion of the conflict resolution theories of "flexible response" and "graduated escalation," which made perfect sense in the era when the Soviet Union and then China possessed nuclear weapons. He was in the forefront of those civilian and military leaders who pushed for the adoption of a counterinsurgency strategy in South Vietnam to combat indirect aggression, as reflected in his Counterinsurgency and Victory plans. He understood that for counterinsurgency to work in South Vietnam, it was vital for President Diem to focus on the social and economic betterment of his people and win the battle for their "hearts and minds." He supported development of the paramilitary Coastal Force and facilitated the deployment to Vietnam of Green Berets, SEALs, Seabee technical assistance teams, and other specialized counterinsurgency units, even while he resisted establishment of regular US Navy river and coastal patrols. He accurately identified North Vietnam as a key facilitator of the Viet Cong struggle in South Vietnam. The greatest challenges to Felt's leadership, however, would occur during his last two, tumultuous years as head of the Pacific Command.

Don Felt's tenure as CINCPAC, on balance, cannot be considered a model demonstration of leadership under stress. By 1964, the counterinsurgency campaign and the government in South Vietnam that he had championed were in deep trouble. People in major cities violently expressed their disdain for the government, and South Vietnamese military leaders then ousted and killed Diem. The Viet Cong began savaging one ARVN unit after the other, killing American advisors, overrunning population centers, and terrorizing the countryside. Felt did not understand the strong sympathy of many southerners for unification with their northern cousins and their desire to rid the country of foreigners. Like many Americans at the time, Felt saw the struggle in Vietnam in the context of the global fight against communism. The admiral ended up having to compromise his opposition to the employment of US regular forces by implementing the Kennedy administration's "limited partnership" approach. When even that measure failed to make a difference, he joined civilian and military leaders in calling for the 34A covert operations against North Vietnam and measures in Laos involving regular US air forces. Felt also developed plans that anticipated one-time, tit-for-tat strikes and ultimately a major air campaign against North Vietnam.

While Don Felt understood the theory of counterinsurgency, he had little contact with those American personnel in-country actually working to implement it. Indeed, despite complaining of micromanagement by Washington, the often-abrasive admiral also engaged in that counterproductive method of leadership. Until too late, the admiral readily accepted General Harkins's optimistic and misleading reports of progress. He doubted the accuracy of the less-than-positive accounts by American journalists and advisors in the field. He engaged in wishful thinking. Like other US civilian and military leaders, he discounted the existence of North Vietnam's major operation to deliver war munitions to South Vietnam by sea. As an indication of his isolation from the reality on the ground, the last time Felt visited Diem he had no inkling that within hours the coup's executors would arrest and kill the Vietnamese president. The admiral boarded his military transport plane and headed back to Pearl Harbor oblivious to the firestorm about to erupt behind him.

A significant cause of Don Felt's loss of power and influence over developments in Indochina resulted from changes in America's civil-military relationship. President Kennedy and later Johnson and their defense secretary, Robert McNamara, distrusted the military and relied much more heavily than Eisenhower on the advice of their civilian counselors. Moreover, these leaders, who had had little military experience, were determined to run the operational aspects of the war from Washington. In many instances, Felt and his Pacific Command headquarters became little more than facilitators of the administrations' operational orders and policy directives. Moreover, Kennedy and Johnson and their top civilian subordinates increasingly dealt directly with the MACV generals who sometimes disdained and often ignored their CINCPAC superior. Felt made so little impression on McNamara that the admiral is only referred to three times in his apologia, *In Retrospect*, and the former defense secretary identified Felt as commander of the Pacific Fleet rather than the military leader of all US forces in Asia.[138]

Don Felt also shared a major failing of the entire US national security establishment at the outset of the Vietnam War. He concluded that the power of the United States was so great and that of North Vietnam so weak that Hanoi would buckle under US military pressure without prompting Chinese or Soviet interference. Felt's models for action were America's deployment of the Navy during the Taiwan Strait and Cuban Missile crises, but those maritime operations did not apply to the continental struggle for Vietnam, or indeed the Indochinese peninsula.

Moreover, the admiral underestimated the determination of the North Vietnamese and their Viet Cong allies to prevail in a long struggle.

On 30 June 1964, Don Felt turned over the CINCPAC command to Oley Sharp. Washington was even then considering something that Felt had long resisted: the extended employment in Vietnam of regular US ground, air, and naval forces. The admiral departed his Hawaii headquarters before Washington made that decision, but in keeping with the "graduated escalation" theoretical approach he had long advocated, it was inevitable. His military and civilian successors would take that fateful step in 1965.[139]

CHAPTER 2
AT THE BRINK

When Admiral Sharp succeeded Felt as Commander in Chief, Pacific, he recognized that the course of the war in South Vietnam pointed toward the intervention there by major US Army and allied combat forces, a measure his predecessor had long opposed. Having served since September 1963 as Commander in Chief, Pacific Fleet, Sharp was well aware that the nature of the conflict was in flux. Sharp was much less enamored than Felt with counterinsurgency and covert operations. He increasingly emphasized the direct employment of US military power. But the new CINCPAC also understood and endorsed the administration's focus on the graduated application of force against Hanoi.[1]

Born on 2 April 1906 in Chinook, Montana, Ulysses S. Grant Sharp Jr. was named after his grandmother's sister's husband, the eighteenth president of the United States and the Civil War's most victorious U.S. Army general. Childhood friends nicknamed the blond, blue-eyed, husky boy "Oley," then a term often given to boys who seemed to look to them like Swedes. Following in the footsteps of numerous uncles who served in the Army or the Navy, he entered the US Naval Academy in 1923. With a cousin in the Naval Academy's First Class, as a plebe Sharp suffered when the "sins of his kin were transmitted to him threefold." Despite having to endure that challenge, the boy earned the respect and friendship of his classmates. They discovered "a streak of the philosopher in his attitude toward life." Moreover, they observed that "true optimism and many friends go hand in hand and [Oley's] undaunted cheerfulness has won himself a host of them."[2]

After graduation in 1927, Sharp served on board aircraft carrier *Saratoga* (CV-3) and battleship *New Mexico* (BB-40). In the early years of World War II, he fought German U-boats while on convoy escort duty in the Mediterranean, Western Atlantic, and Caribbean. He understood the terrible cost of war when he learned in March 1943 that his brother, Lieutenant Commander Thomas F. Sharp, and the submarine in which he served patrolling Japanese waters had disappeared. *Pickerel* (SS-177) and her entire crew were never seen again. In command of destroyer *Boyd* (DD-544) during 1943 and 1944, Commander Sharp took part in some of the war's fiercest actions in the Gilbert, Mariana, and Philippine islands and during the hard-fought Battle of the Philippine Sea. The Navy awarded him two Silver Star medals for his coolheaded leadership and bravery under fire. Sharp earned the respect of superiors and subordinates alike for his performance in command and staff billets during the Korean War. Oley Sharp married Patricia O'Connor and they raised two children, Patricia Ann and Grant, the latter of whom graduated from the US Naval Academy, attained flag rank, and served with distinction in the Persian Gulf War as General Norman Schwarzkopf's strategist. Following the death of his first wife, in 1987 Sharp married Nina Blake.[3]

Sharp's keen understanding of the nature of twentieth-century naval warfare soon drew the attention of the Navy's leaders, who tasked him in August 1954 with planning operations under the Pacific Fleet commander, Admiral Felix B. Stump. John Hyland, who later commanded the Pacific Fleet, characterized Sharp as tough, smart, and a Stump favorite. He continued to impress superiors with his grasp of international affairs in the Strategic Plans Division on the Navy staff in Washington. Tom Moorer, who worked under Sharp in several capacities, considered the naval leader "a very sound thinker [with] an excellent appreciation of global strategy as well as local strategy and tactics."[4] After a short stint in command of the West Coast-based First Fleet, Vice Admiral Sharp returned to the Pentagon in 1960 where he routinely worked twelve-hour days. When he did take some time off, he blazed through the Army and Navy Country Club's golf course, usually shooting in the low 80s. Sharp served as the Navy's chief planner and in that capacity helped develop the operational scheme for the naval quarantine of Cuba during the 1962 missile crisis. The Navy not only awarded him a Distinguished Service Medal for that stellar performance but in September 1963 made him Pacific Fleet commander, a four-star billet.[5]

Four-star Admiral Ulysses S. G. Sharp, then the Pacific Fleet commander, confers in early 1964 with his Seventh Fleet commander, Vice Admiral Thomas H. Moorer. NHHC VN Collection.

HOSTILITIES IN THE GULF OF TONKIN

In January 1964, Oley Sharp and Tom Moorer oversaw one aspect of Washington's pressure campaign against North Vietnam. They directed Seventh Fleet units to gather intelligence on North Vietnam's coastal defenses in support of MACV's Operation Plan 34A. To carry out that task, the Navy commanders exploited the Desoto Patrol, a program in existence since 1962. Destroyers collected electronic and other intelligence along the Soviet, Chinese, North Korean, and North Vietnamese coastlines.[6] In contrast to previous missions, however, in 1964 patrolling destroyers were permitted to steam as close as four miles from North Vietnamese islands and eight miles to the mainland. Sharp considered neither China nor North Vietnam a threat to the proposed operation since "CHICOM [Chinese communists'] air attack on Desoto ship highly unlikely and North Vietnam air capability for attack almost non-existent."[7] In fact, he did not approve US air support for the warship slated for the mission. Between 28 February and 9 March, destroyer *John R. Craig* (DD-885), with a MACV officer on board as an observer, navigated along the North Vietnamese coastline without incident.[8]

The honeymoon soon ended as the North Vietnamese beefed up their coastal defenses, deployed troops and naval vessels to threatened areas in the south of the country, and fought the 34A program. Still, leaders in Washington and Saigon continued to favor 34A and the Desoto Patrol as ways to turn up the heat on North Vietnam. Westmoreland wanted information from the destroyer patrols on the enemy's coastal ground forces and radar sites and naval vessels capable of intercepting the South Vietnamese-crewed boats operating out of Danang. On 10 July, Sharp, the newly made CINCPAC, directed Moorer, now CINCPACFLT, to launch a destroyer patrol in August to provide intelligence for Westmoreland's 34A force.[9]

CNO McDonald questioned the usefulness of the Desoto Patrol in the Gulf of Tonkin. He wanted to ensure that the Navy was not just "DeSoto patrolling once a quarter because it has been going on for some time."[10] Sharp countered that with the onset of air operations in Laos, an upsurge in 34A activity, and the increasing possibility of direct US attacks on North Vietnam, intelligence of the enemy coastline was never more essential.

Moorer concurred and said that the advantages of the destroyer patrols far outweighed the disadvantages. The operations captured valuable intelligence on communist military forces and provided the destroyer sailors with beneficial training. Perhaps the most important justification to Tom Moorer was the opportunity "to assert our traditional belief in the right of free use of international waters . . . the importance of [which] has been emphasized [time] and again [but] is particularly worthy of repetition at this time."[11] With back-to-back assignments in Asia, first as commander of the Seventh Fleet and then as commander in chief of the Pacific Fleet—in the period from October 1962 to March 1965—Tom Moorer became especially familiar with the Kennedy and Johnson administrations' approach to the Vietnam problem and played a significant role in the evolution of the conflict during those seminal years.

Moorer was born in 1912 in the rural community of Mount Willing, Alabama. His father, Richard R. Moorer, practiced dentistry there for many years and served for a time in the state legislature. His mother, Hulda Hull Hinson Moorer, taught at the local school before she focused on her son's upbringing. Tom Moorer excelled in school, graduating as the valedictorian of Cloverdale High School in Montgomery at the tender age of fifteen. His father persuaded Alabama Senator James T. "Cotton Tom" Heflin to appoint young Moorer to the US Naval Academy in 1929. Moorer excelled there in the technical sciences (a lifelong focus), played football, and impressed his classmates with his drive and intellect. They were most impressed with his "likeable nature, friendly disposition, and will to succeed." Indeed, his classmates predicted that he would "surely be a credit to his profession." Tom Moorer finished at Annapolis in the top half of his 1933 class.[12]

After graduation and commissioning, he served in heavy cruisers *Salt Lake City* (CA-25) and *New Orleans* (CA-32) but, intrigued by the prospect of soaring high above the earth, Moorer decided he would give naval aviation "a try." During flight training at Naval Station Pensacola, Florida, he met and wed Carrie Ellen Foy. They raised four children: Thomas, Ellen, Richard, and Robert.[13]

From the time he earned his gold wings in 1936 to the end of his career in 1974, Moorer was known as a champion of the Navy's aviation community. During the late 1930s and early 1940s he served on board three of the Navy's first aircraft carriers: *Langley* (CV-1), *Lexington* (CV-2), and *Enterprise* (CV-6). The 7 December 1941 Japanese attack on Pearl Harbor found him flying a PBY 5 flying boat in Patrol Squadron 22. Posted to the South Pacific, Moorer endured an attack by Japanese fighters that shot up his aircraft and wounded him in the leg. He managed to land his badly damaged plane in the water and got his entire crew into a life raft. Rescued by a Philippine merchant ship, Tom Moorer and his crew found themselves in the water again when enemy planes sank the vessel. The intrepid officer later said that "I was born again on the 19th of February 1942." He recalled that he "was in the water and those bombs were falling all around, and the ship was blowing up." He remembered telling the Lord "that anything that happened to me from then on was an anticlimax." He added, "I wasn't going to ever worry about anything again. And I haven't."[14]

Moorer and all but one of his men eventually made it to safety. For his quick thinking and bravery that day, the Navy awarded the officer Silver Star and Purple Heart medals. Later in the war, he earned a Distinguished Flying Cross. He was then assigned to the Royal Navy as a mine warfare observer, an experience that served him well during the Vietnam War when Washington considered mining the ports of North Vietnam. His time with the US Strategic Bombing Survey in Japan after the war exposed him to the pluses and minuses of air power.

During the 1950s, Tom Moorer served in various fleet, shore-based, and staff assignments that earned him plaudits. He was the senior naval officer at the Naval Ordnance Test Station at China Lake, California, the service's primary missile research center. It was a perfect fit for the technologically savvy Moorer. His attendance at the Naval War College in Newport, Rhode Island, honed his strategic sense and worldview. In 1957, the Navy promoted the forty-five-year-old Moorer to rear admiral, then the youngest officer to attain that rank. He burnished his reputation as a strategic thinker with service under Arleigh Burke in the Strategic Plans Division and as the director of the Long-Range Objectives Group. When Tom Moorer took command of the Seventh Fleet in the Western Pacific in October 1962, he was already known Navy-wide as a "comer." By 1965, *Time* magazine was characterizing him as "America's fastest-rising sailor." Oley Sharp considered Tom Moorer "an outstanding candidate [to be the] next Chief of Naval Operations."[15]

As North Vietnamese defenses against the 34A force hardened during July 1964, McNamara complained about the slow pace of the operation and its minimal impact on Hanoi. The secretary of defense suggested that the 34A maritime force end the landing of saboteurs and instead use the PTF's weapons to shell coastal targets. But Sharp knew that the boats' low-caliber deck guns, recoilless rifles, rockets, and mortars would hardly impress Hanoi with the might of allied military power. Surprisingly for a US naval officer, Oley Sharp argued that the best way to get Hanoi's attention was to let the South Vietnamese air force bomb targets in North Vietnam. CINCPAC lost that argument. Hence, on the night of 31 July, four of the 34A PTFs shelled military targets on the islands of Hon Me and Hon Nieu. Enemy naval vessels attempted but failed to intercept the South Vietnamese boats. Several other units carried out a similar shore bombardment on the night of 3 August.[16]

On 31 July, Desoto Patrol destroyer *Maddox* (DD-731), steaming on a northwesterly course along a pre-designated track, began her patrol of North Vietnam's coastal waters. On 1 August, the warship reached a point four-and-a-half miles southeast of the small islet of Hon Mat. In the early hours of 2 August, personnel in a Naval Security Group communications interception van installed earlier on the ship picked up intelligence that North Vietnamese fast attack vessels were heading their way. Soon afterward, Captain John J. Herrick, the officer in tactical command of the Desoto Patrol mission, sent out to higher authorities a "flash" (highest priority) message stating "contemplate serious reaction my movements [vicinity] Pt Charlie [a point on a pre-designated mission track] in near future. Received info indicating possible hostile action."[17] Herrick ordered the ship away from the coast and dispatched another message in which he warned that "if info received concerning hostile intent by DRV is accurate, and have no reason to believe it is not, consider continuance of patrol presents an unacceptable risk."[18]

Admiral Roy L. Johnson, Moorer's relief as the Seventh Fleet commander, took note of Herrick's concern but directed him to resume the patrol. About the same time, Johnson and Sharp learned from intelligence that the North Vietnamese were gearing up their defenses in the area and might attack *Maddox*. In the early afternoon, lookouts and radars in the destroyer picked up concentrations of naval vessels close to shore. Among the group was Section 3 of North Vietnamese PT Squadron 135, consisting of Soviet-made P-4 torpedo boats T-333, T-336, and T-339. In the early afternoon, North Vietnamese naval leaders ordered the unit to execute a torpedo attack on the "enemy."[19] As the National Security Agency (NSA) later observed, the signals intelligence community "could be proud of its efforts that day [because] everyone in the Pacific command [including Herrick] was aware of the approaching attack."[20]

Even as *Maddox* headed east and then southeast to move away from the threat, the North Vietnamese P-4s, capable of 52-knot speeds, closed the ship on an intersecting course. At 1540H (twelve hours ahead of Washington time), Herrick sent out a "flash" precedence message to higher headquarters and aircraft carrier *Ticonderoga* (CVA-14), the latter charged with providing the Desoto Patrol with air support, stating that the ship was "being approached by high speed craft with apparent intention of torpedo attack." The captain stated that he intended "to open fire if necessary self defense."[21] At 1608H, *Maddox* fired two shots from her 5-inch/38-caliber guns to deter the fast attack vessels, now only 9,800 yards off her starboard quarter and closing. The PT boats did not attempt with radio, signal flags, lights, pyrotechnics, or other means of communication to indicate the reason for their hostile approach.

Maddox then opened fire with her guns, and when the enemy boats got as close as they could, they launched torpedoes at the destroyer and fired on her with their onboard weapons. The torpedoes missed, but one round from a North Vietnamese gun put a hole in the destroyer's superstructure. Even as the surface action ended and *Maddox* retired to the Yankee Station carrier operating area in the southern waters of the Gulf of Tonkin, four *Ticonderoga* F-8 Crusader attack planes (one of them piloted by later Medal of Honor recipient and vice-presidential contender Commander James B. Stockdale) arrived overhead and immediately pounced on the PTs. Fire from the American aircraft left one of the attacking boats burning and dead in the water. Despite the damage, this boat and the other two eventually made it back to North Vietnam.

Understanding that one of Washington's highest priorities in summer 1964 was to increase military pressure on North Vietnam, Tom Moorer wasted little time debating the Navy's next moves. Shortly after the 2 August action, the admiral ordered Herrick back to the coast of North Vietnam, emphasizing that "in view [of] *Maddox* incident consider it in our best interest that we assert freedom of the seas and resume Gulf of Tonkin patrol earliest."[22] Moorer not only reinforced *Maddox* with Forrest Sherman-class destroyer *Turner Joy* (DD-951) but also directed the pair to resume their patrol where the North Vietnamese had concentrated their naval forces; the area was now a virtual hornet's nest. Tom Moorer, the combat-tested warrior, was not about to back down from a fight.

Indeed, he had a strong belief in military honor. When he took command of the Seventh Fleet in 1962, he returned to a retired Japanese admiral and World War II veteran a centuries-old Samurai sword that the officer had surrendered to Moorer at the end of the conflict. Moorer had the sword professionally reconditioned and then presented it to the man. Moorer understood that the sword, in his possession since the end of the war, had a substantial monetary value but felt it "worth a lot more to me to see the great joy it gave that fellow."[23]

Oley Sharp and Tom Moorer believed that the attack on *Maddox* provided the administration with a golden opportunity to convince

North Vietnam that it risked war with the military might of the United States. The flag officers were convinced that even if the North Vietnamese had sent several vessels from its minuscule navy against *Maddox*, the leaders in Hanoi were unlikely to start a major conflict. They believed that North Vietnamese leaders would back down in the face of American power rather than continue to test it.

The president and his secretary of defense were also surprised that rather than buckle under the increasing military pressure, Hanoi had come out fighting. Johnson thought a rogue shore command or boat commander might have precipitated the attack on *Maddox*. Since late 1963, the administration had bombed North Vietnamese forces in Laos and launched covert sabotage and naval bombardment operations against North Vietnam itself, but Johnson later contended that the Desoto Patrol was not meant to be "provocative."[24] He claimed that "we would give Hanoi the benefit of the doubt—this time—and assume the unprovoked attack had been a mistake." The North Vietnamese were warned of grave consequences if they attacked US forces again.[25] These were strong pronouncements, but the administration's actions were decidedly less forceful. Washington authorized Sharp and Moorer to resume the Desoto Patrol but with the understanding that the destroyers would approach no closer than eleven nautical miles to North Vietnam and stay well clear of the other US-initiated operation, 34A. Moreover, if North Vietnamese forces attacked the destroyers or the aircraft supporting them, the US units were not allowed to go after them in "hot pursuit" near North Vietnamese territory.[26]

The two destroyers executed their patrol on 3 August without incident, but at least two naval leaders expressed concern that the potential for conflict remained high. After the 2 August battle, Herrick had suggested ending the patrol since "it is apparent that DRV has cut [*sic*] down the gauntlet and now considers itself at war with U.S. It is felt that they will attack U.S. forces on sight with no regard for cost." He added, "consider resumption of patrol can only be safely undertaken by [destroyer/cruiser] team and with continuous air cover."[27] On 3 August, Admiral Johnson echoed these sentiments when he suggested ending the patrol on the 4th.

The determined Pacific Fleet commander wasted little time responding. Moorer told Commander Seventh Fleet that "termination of Desoto Patrol after two days of patrol OPS [subsequent] to *Maddox*

Admiral Sharp, the Commander in Chief, Pacific Command from 1964 to 1968. He oversaw a force of 500 warships, 7,000 aircraft, and almost one million soldiers, sailors, airmen, and Marines. NHHC NH 93802.

incident . . . does not in my view adequately demonstrate U.S. resolve to assert our legitimate rights in international waters."[28] Instead, he instructed Herrick to spend the next four days steaming back and forth along the hotly contested coastline near Hon Me. In essence, he was daring Hanoi to try another aggressive action.

Admiral Sharp weighed in on the Washington-driven directive that prevented the destroyers from chasing attacking enemy naval vessels into waters close to shore. CINCPAC emphasized that "a United States ship has been attacked on the high seas off North Vietnam." He suggested that "now, our friends and enemies alike will await what additional moves the United States will take." He expressed surprise, however, that the JCS directives "appear to be a retreat at a time when aggressive measures are necessary."[29] The logic of the argument did not persuade the secretary of defense. He advised the president against allowing the ships to steam closer to North Vietnam and carrying out "hot pursuit" if they were attacked. McNamara felt that "no military purpose would be served by it." Accordingly, the JCS reaffirmed the decision that the destroyers not enter North Vietnamese waters, even in hot pursuit.[30]

On 4 August, *Maddox* and *Turner Joy* continued their patrol, coming no closer than sixteen miles to the North Vietnamese littoral, and that night retired to a steaming area far out in the middle of the gulf. At

2040H, Herrick received information from naval intelligence "indicating attack by PGM [gunboat]/P-4 imminent."³¹ During the next hour, the two ships picked up radar contacts that they considered hostile and closing on them at a fast rate. At 2239H, *Turner Joy* opened up on one contact and for the next several hours both ships fired on reported contacts and dropped depth charges to ward off suspected trailing vessels. *Ticonderoga* aircraft arrived overhead to provide support, but only two pilots reported the possibility of an enemy presence on the sea below. Well before daylight, the two destroyers had left northern waters and joined the other ships of the Seventh Fleet to the south.

Even as *Maddox* and *Turner Joy* had taken the radar contacts under fire and begun their evasive maneuvers on that dark night, Pacific commanders prepared their forces for strong retaliatory measures against North Vietnam. CINCPAC directed his naval forces to pursue and destroy any attacking vessels up to three miles from offshore islands and eleven miles from the mainland. Seventh Fleet commander Roy Johnson, now comprehending Moorer's intent, instructed Herrick not to depart the northern gulf, since the patrol was to resume on 5 August.³²

Sharp requested "punitive U.S. air strikes . . . in increasing stages of severity" against North Vietnamese naval vessels along the coast; against three naval facilities; and against the fuel tank farm at Vinh. He also requested authority from the JCS to allow US warships as close as three miles to the mainland and to allow aircraft to enter North Vietnamese air space in hot pursuit.³³ Shortly afterward, the admiral asked Washington for authorization to consider hostile and to attack any aircraft, including Chinese Communist aircraft, "whose actions and behavior indicate within reasonable certainty that air attack on U.S. forces is intended."³⁴

As these events unfolded in the Gulf of Tonkin, President Johnson and Secretary of Defense McNamara met with top civilian and military officials just before and after noon (EDT) on 4 August to determine the course of action. McNamara concurred with many of Oley Sharp's recommendations and, perhaps for the only time in the war, suggested an aerial mining operation to close five North Vietnamese naval bases. The secretary of defense, never shy about giving detailed instructions to the military, ordered the airlift of 100 Mark 50 sea mines to carriers in the Gulf of Tonkin. Following lunch at the White House on 4 August, President Johnson agreed with the unanimous opinion of his advisors that the events on the night of 4 August in the gulf, following the torpedo attack against *Maddox* two days earlier, demanded retaliation against North Vietnam. The president gave the order to execute a one-time strike.[35]

As preparations went forward for Operation Pierce Arrow, doubts surfaced about what had actually happened out in the gulf on the night of 4 August. Herrick communicated to Moorer, "review of action makes many reported contacts and torpedoes fired appear [doubtful]." He suggested that "freak weather effects on radar and overeager sonarmen may have accounted for many reports [since there had been] no actual visual sightings by *Maddox*." He recommended an evaluation of the evidence before any further action was taken.[36] Less than half an hour later, the captain added that the "entire action leaves many doubts except for apparent ambush at beginning." At the same time, Herrick reported information he had received from *Turner Joy* indicating that the destroyer had been fired upon and illuminated by searchlight and had hit at least one of the attacking vessels with her gunfire.[37]

When queried by the Joint Staff about Herrick's doubts, Sharp responded that a new message from the task group commander reported that Herrick was "certain that original ambush was bonafide." Herrick also passed on information he had received from *Turner Joy* indicating that some of her crew had reported seeing enemy boats and a torpedo passing close aboard the destroyer.[38] Still, CINCPAC suggested to McNamara that Pierce Arrow be delayed until the reality of a North Vietnamese attack could be confirmed. Admiral Johnson later related that "McNamara wanted to get direct communications with Maddox; he wanted to talk to [the commanding officer] and I said it couldn't be done." Bridling at this interference from Washington with an ongoing military operation, the fleet commander admitted, "I lied but I told him that anyway."[39] Tom Moorer, with his characteristic sarcasm, later observed that "Washington wanted to know everything. They wanted to know how many waves hit the bow at seven o'clock last night and were the stars twinkling."[40] The secretary of defense decided that preparations for the planned strike would continue but told Sharp that "we obviously don't want to do it unless we are damned sure what happened."[41]

The National Security Agency provided Sharp with the supposed "smoking gun" that finally convinced not only Sharp but almost everyone else in the national security chain of command connected with the

Tonkin Gulf incident that North Vietnamese naval vessels had attacked *Maddox* and *Turner Joy* on the night of 4 August. It is now clear, however, that an attack never occurred. The NSA misinterpreted intercepted North Vietnamese radio transmissions suggesting an attack; eyewitness accounts by the men on the destroyers and in the planes overhead proved inconclusive; and the Navy's operational reports revealed much of the information gathered to be imprecise or contradictory. Moreover, since the Tonkin Gulf incident more than half a century ago, neither archival records nor personal accounts have surfaced in Vietnam or the United States to refute Hanoi's unchanged contention that its navy did not attack on 4 August.[42]

Nonetheless, at 1725 EDT CINCPAC informed McNamara that based on intelligence and reports from the ships he was convinced an attack had taken place. Apparently having been unwilling to wait to be "damned sure," McNamara had already given the execute order for Operation Pierce Arrow.[43] The administration's strategy throughout 1964 had been to apply increasingly heavy military pressure on Hanoi, but Johnson and McNamara vitiated their own approach; fearing Chinese intervention, they made sure that Pierce Arrow would be seen as a one-time affair. Johnson and McNamara instructed Sharp to ensure that no US aircraft in the operation flew near China's Hainan Island or got within fifty miles of the PRC. Following the operation, Johnson told a number of congressmen that he "did not want the leaders in Peking to misunderstand the reason our planes were over the Tonkin Gulf." He wanted them to know that "the retaliation was aimed only at North Vietnam, not Red China, and that the objective was limited."[44]

The first strike of Operation Pierce Arrow occurred at 1315H on 5 August when six F-8 Crusaders from *Ticonderoga* attacked enemy gunboats and P-4s at Quang Khe and Ben Thuy. At 1325H, sixteen other *Ticonderoga* aircraft bombed and strafed the petroleum tank farm near Vinh. Attack planes from *Constellation*'s Carrier Air Wing 14 then hit North Vietnamese naval craft near Hon Gai and in the Lach Truong/Hon Me area. The strikes achieved good tactical results. North Vietnam lost ninety percent of its fuel storage capacity when the facility at Vinh went up in flames. The sixty-four-plane operation also destroyed or damaged thirty-three enemy naval vessels. North Vietnamese antiaircraft fire accounted for two naval aviators, Lieutenant (junior grade) Richard C. Sather, who went down with his crippled aircraft, and Lieutenant (junior grade) Everett Alvarez Jr., who ended up in North

Vietnam's Hoa Lo prison, soon be known as the "Hanoi Hilton."[45]

Soon after these actions in the Gulf of Tonkin, the United States Congress took a step that would have a long-term impact on the role of the United States in Southeast Asia. On 7 August, the Gulf of Tonkin Resolution, as proposed by the Johnson administration, was passed unanimously in the House of Representatives and approved in the Senate by an eighty-eight to two vote. Based on the events in the Gulf of Tonkin, this measure authorized the president to use the US Armed Forces to assist in the defense of the non-communist nations of Southeast Asia. This resolution would serve as the legal basis for the armed support provided by the United States to South Vietnam for the rest of the war.[46]

THE PRESSURE CAMPAIGN LOSES STEAM

In the wake of Pierce Arrow, which President Johnson and his advisors considered an appropriately measured answer to Hanoi's aggressive behavior, naval leaders ordered *Maddox* and *Turner Joy* to resume their patrol off North Vietnam. Not everyone was game. John Herrick expressed concern that his ships were experiencing equipment failures and lacked sufficient ammunition. He put forth another reason why he pressed for postponing the mission. He communicated that *"Maddox* considered to be [prime] target after evasion of several attempts at destruction." He added that he believed the "DRV Navy will go to any lengths to achieve destruction of *Maddox* to save face."[47] His arguments got nowhere with his superiors, who considered Herrick's actions decidedly less than heroic. Emphatic orders came down from Sharp, Moorer, and Johnson, decorated warriors all, to continue the mission. The ships went back in on the 5th protected by a large gaggle of aircraft from *Ticonderoga* and *Constellation*. *Maddox* and *Turner Joy* spent the next four days patrolling no closer than eleven miles to North Vietnam. Despite Herrick's fears, this time the North Vietnamese navy did not contest the American presence offshore.

Sharp wanted to keep the pressure on Hanoi. He encouraged the Joint Chiefs to authorize another Desoto Patrol and the deployment of troops to South Vietnam to protect airfields used by US aircraft. CINCPAC emphasized that once pressure was applied to the other side, it should not be relaxed. He cautioned that a decrease of activity could be seen as a "sign of weakness and lack of resolve."[48] Oley Sharp's advice from the field went unheeded by Johnson and McNamara, who adopted a "low-risk" policy. Not until mid-September did the administration agree to another Desoto Patrol.⁴⁹

On 17 and 18 September, destroyers *Morton* (DD-948) and *Richard S. Edwards* (DD- 950) in the charge of Captain Ernest E. Hollyfield Jr. returned to the coast of North Vietnam for another mission. In contrast to the previous destroyer forays, however, this time the ships were instructed to approach no closer than twenty miles to the mainland and no closer than twelve miles to offshore islands. Late on the 18th, and forty-five miles out in the middle of the gulf, the ships' radars picked up fast-approaching contacts as close as 7,000 yards. As on the 4th of August, the ships went to General Quarters, sped up, maneuvered to avoid to any torpedoes, and began firing on the suspicious contacts. The captain reported several contacts disappearing from radar screens when they were hit by gunfire. A pilot providing overhead cover reported seeing two wakes near *Richard S. Edwards*. By midnight, the destroyers had exited the central gulf. Sharp and CNO McDonald, convinced an attack had occurred, pressed for retaliatory strikes against North Vietnam within nine hours. Having been unsatisfied with the proof of a North Vietnamese attack on 4 August, this time both civilian and military leaders demanded positive evidence before launching strikes. When naval search parties found no debris in the area of the supposed nighttime battle and US intelligence detected no unusual North Vietnamese naval activity on the 19th, Washington cancelled the proposed mission.⁵⁰

Still, Westmoreland, Sharp, and Moorer called for more Desoto Patrols. Westmoreland—Commander, US Military Assistance Command, Vietnam (COMUSMACV)—emphasized that the presence off North Vietnam of US warships and the 34A force diverted Hanoi's attention from the fighting in South Vietnam. The two admirals stressed that the most important factor was to assert America's traditional insistence on freedom of the seas. Oley Sharp asked rhetorically, "If they can keep us out of the Gulf of Tonkin what do we do when they try to stop us using the Straits of Malacca [between Singapore and Indonesia]?"⁵¹ One might say this was the maritime equivalent of President Eisenhower's Domino Effect. Moorer observed that "if the patrol were not to be resumed, the CHICOMS could claim that the United States stood down to their threat and is in fact a paper tiger."⁵²

Despite the admirals' advocacy, the president never authorized another Desoto Patrol in the Gulf of Tonkin and during the months after the August incident kept the 34A force on a tight leash. Johnson and McNamara were determined not to draw attention to the crisis in Southeast Asia before the November presidential election. Another factor in their reluctance to heighten involvement was their concern over the poor state of governance in South Vietnam. After the assassination of Diem, the administration continued to decry the lack of a new strong, trustworthy South Vietnamese leader. General Wheeler, the JCS chairman, bemoaned the fact that the South Vietnamese "don't have any George Washington." CNO McDonald wondered if "there are any good people in the government, any available around whom the South Vietnamese could rally?" None of the Joint Chiefs had an answer. No operations took place in September, and heavy weather compromised the few relative pinpricks launched in October and November. The bombardment of a radar station at Mach Nuoc on 8 December proved to be the last strike of the year.[53]

In the immediate aftermath of the Gulf of Tonkin incident, the JCS endorsed Sharp's Operation Plan 39-65 that anticipated the use of overwhelming air power to counter an attack by China on South Vietnam with or without US allies. The counterattack would concentrate on China's economic, military, and logistical infrastructure. In April, the president's Special Assistant for National Security Council (NSC) Affairs, McGeorge Bundy, publicly stated that if China mounted a major intervention into Southeast Asia, that nation would not be considered a "privileged sanctuary" as it was in the Korean War.[54] At JCS direction, Sharp concentrated four attack carriers, one antisubmarine carrier, an amphibious formation, and forty-one other warships in the Western Pacific. He established an antisubmarine barrier between China and waters to the south. The Navy and Air Force members of the Joint Chiefs expressed confidence that US air and naval power, rather than ground forces, would be strong enough to defeat a Chinese invasion of Southeast Asia. But by the end of September, the White House had ordered the JCS to return most of these forces to their ports in Japan, Okinawa, and the Philippines.[55]

Lyndon Johnson had no stomach for a major war on his watch. He regarded the conflict in Southeast Asia as an irritant and a distraction from his ambitious goals for social reform in the United States. The president, who rose to prominence as a leader of the US Senate during the 1950s, took great pride in his legislative skills. His advocacy was a prime factor in passage of the seminal Civil Rights Act of 1964 and the Voting Rights Act of 1965, no mean feats for a white Southerner in the heated civil rights era. Buoyed by his success in those endeavors, Johnson continued to pour his energies into his Great Society. As Vice Admiral Lloyd Mustin observed, "the president didn't want the country to get behind the war. He wanted peace as usual, and business as usual at home."[56] Johnson's approach to the Vietnam question was to put off hard decisions and avoid alienating his liberal supporters or right-wing opponents.

Lyndon Johnson did not have the credentials to be a wartime president. In World War II, the Navy awarded Naval Reserve Lieutenant Commander Lyndon Johnson a Silver Star medal, normally recognition of great courage in battle. Johnson's award, however, resulted from his presence as an observer on board an Army Air Forces B-26 bomber on a mission over New Guinea that may or may not have come under enemy fire. During the 1950s he chaired the Senate Armed Services Committee, but his exposure to the military was minimal. He generally kept generals and admirals at arm's length and indeed was suspicious of the military. He did not take part in the debates over the "massive retaliation" or "flexible response" strategic approaches. His experience with and understanding of US foreign policy during this era of the Cold War was similarly lacking. He retained the worldview of a rural politician whose only connection with other cultures was to the Mexican American community in central Texas. Finding himself suddenly president of the United States on Kennedy's death, and recognizing his shortcomings in defense and foreign policy, Johnson kept on board his predecessor's primary cabinet officers. The most prominent among them was Secretary of Defense McNamara, then at the height of his power and influence. Johnson pleaded with the Kennedy men to stay on with him; he apparently told them, "I need you more than he did."[57]

THE SINO-SOVIET ALLIANCE WITH NORTH VIETNAM

The Chinese saw the half-hearted US actions in fall 1964 as a clear indication of US irresolution. China dispatched seventeen MiG-15 and MiG-17 jet fighters to North Vietnam only one day after Pierce Arrow, agreed to train Vietnamese pilots, and began building airfields in southern China for Hanoi's use. Beijing sent another thirty-six MiGs to North Vietnam in succeeding months. In October, China entered the exclusive global nuclear club by detonating its first atomic bomb. Mao admitted to his inner circle after the nuclear test that China was a long way from nuclear parity with the United States. President Johnson, however, could not be confident that Mao would not use even one nuclear weapon against American troops deployed on China's southern border.[58]

The question of Chinese intervention in the conflict was undoubtedly the most significant factor in the graduated escalation and limited war strategies of the Johnson administration. As President Johnson and his top civilian and military advisors considered the potential consequences of their military actions in Southeast Asia during the mid-1960s, their worst fear was that legions of Chinese troops would pour across the border into Vietnam to defend Ho Chi Minh's regime. They remembered a massive Chinese army crossing the Yalu River in late 1950, laying an ambush in the cold, barren mountains of North Korea, and then springing an attack that forced a hasty and costly withdrawal by US and UN forces. It is worth remembering, however, that there had been no Chinese military presence in North Korea prior to the outbreak of the Korean War. Such was not the case with North Vietnam.

Indeed, Chinese involvement in the struggle for Vietnam had occurred long before Johnson and his top politico-military advisors gave that factor serious consideration. From 1950 to 1965, the People's Republic of China had invested an enormous amount of political, ideological, economic, and military resources in the defense and development of the Democratic Republic of Vietnam. In January 1950, the PRC became the first nation to recognize the DRV. That April, Beijing established the Chinese Military Advisory Group, with 281 military advisors posted to the headquarters of Ho Chi Minh's Viet Minh forces. The People's Liberation Army's General Chen Geng developed the plan by which Ho's troops destroyed French forces in the border region of northern Vietnam in 1950. In 1951 and 1952, the Chinese equipped six Viet Minh infantry divisions. Chinese strategic planning and logistic support to the Viet Minh forces during the pivotal battle for the French redoubt at Dien Bien Phu proved key to Ho's overwhelming victory there in May 1954.[59]

The PRC, for the first time on an international stage, championed North Vietnam's cause at the Geneva Conference in July 1954, helping oust France from Indochina. At another conference in Geneva, in 1962, the Chinese were pivotal to the establishment of an international agreement that declared Laos "neutral" in the fight for Indochina. That accomplishment enabled the DRV to develop the Ho Chi Minh Trail through southern Laos and renew the armed struggle to unite Vietnam. Mao also considered the DRV as a buffer against a US presence on China's southern border.

Mao was personally and ideologically invested in the future of the DRV. He and Ho were longtime communist revolutionaries and comrades in arms. During the 1950s and early 1960s, when the PRC and the Soviet Union were locked in ideological combat, Beijing could count on North Vietnam's support. The North Vietnamese had even less use than the Chinese for Nikita Khrushchev's "peaceful coexistence" with the West. Mao backed North Vietnam to prove his Marxist-Leninist bona fides and to strengthen his assertion that he was the leader of the communist movements in Asia. Moreover, frustrated by his inability to achieve his goals in the face of US air and naval power in Korea and in the Strait of Taiwan during the 1950s, in the 1960s he saw an opportunity for success in the mountainous jungles of Indochina.[60]

When the DRV launched its unification campaign in 1959, Mao did not hesitate to fuel the effort. In August, Ho traveled to China and met one of Mao's chief subordinates, Zhou Enlai, who assured the Vietnamese leader that China would supply North Vietnam with weaponry and financial assistance. China's substantial support of North Vietnam helped Ho generate guerrilla warfare in South Vietnam during the early 1960s. In December 1962, the PRC was the first government to recognize the National Liberation Front—the political arm of the Viet Cong. Between 1956 and 1963, the PRC provided Hanoi with 270,000 rifles, more than 10,000 artillery pieces, 28 naval vessels, and millions of rounds of ammunition. Before 1965, 70 percent of the supplies China provided to the Viet Cong were delivered by sea.[61]

In June 1964, Mao assured the North Vietnamese Army's chief of staff, General Van Tien Dung, on an official visit to Beijing, that if the US invaded the North, China would intervene with combat troops. Mao told the Vietnamese general that "our two parties and two countries must cooperate and fight the enemy together." When visiting Hanoi in July, Zhou Enlai reiterated Mao's pledge of support and that China would match US actions up to and including the deployment of combat troops to North Vietnam.[62]

That same year, the Chinese leader even urged Hanoi to bring on a major conflict with the United States. He told the North Vietnamese that their previous guerrilla attacks in South Vietnam were just "scratching the surface." He suggested Hanoi send more troops south and "turn it into a bigger war." He told the North Vietnamese not to be afraid of US intervention, since it would be no worse than having another Korean War. He assured the Vietnamese that if the US invaded, "the Chinese army will march in at once. Our troops want war now." Zhou Enlai intimated to Egypt's President Gamal Abdel Nasser that China's aim was to draw a huge US Army into Vietnam where it would serve as an "insurance policy" against a US attack on China's budding nuclear weapons program. The Chinese wanted the Americans there "because we will have a lot of their flesh close to our nails." In short, "they will be close to China [and] in our grasp [and they] will be our hostages."[63] In late 1964, high-level Chinese officials suggested in an issue of the official Soviet newspaper *Pravda* that a "war in Southeast Asia would not be such a bad thing."[64]

Strong evidence that these were not idle boasts and that the Chinese considered a major war with the United States likely in 1964 or 1965 was Mao's massive "Third Front" campaign to relocate more than 1,000 defense and industrial plants to China's hinterland and far from the striking power of the US Seventh Fleet and B-52 bombers based throughout the Western Pacific. The effort begun in 1964 ultimately cost China more than 200 billion yuan and, according to one account, consumed at least two-thirds of China's developmental resources. Moreover, the effort required the relocation to the far west of over four million people to build new factories, open mines, and create a supporting rail and road system.[65]

In the wake of the Gulf of Tonkin incident, China geared up for war. Beijing put its 500,000-man ground, air, and naval forces in southern China in a state of combat readiness and deployed five air force and antiaircraft divisions on the border with North Vietnam. The People's Liberation Army Navy, which operated 1,000 combat vessels, including thirty-two submarines, increasingly deployed units to southern China. The PRC agreed to train Ho's pilots and began building additional airfields in its southern Kwangsi and Yunnan provinces to bolster the air defenses of the two nations. In December, the PRC agreed to dispatch 300,000 troops to North Vietnam to free up North Vietnamese forces for the fight in the South.[66] Despite his competition with the USSR for leadership of the communist world, in March 1965 Mao signed an agreement that enabled the Soviet Union to ship munitions by rail to North Vietnam through China.[67]

On the other hand, Mao's assistance to Hanoi was not open-ended. Beijing made it clear that Chinese troops would only serve as a reserve force to the North Vietnamese Army if the United States invaded. In essence, Mao "was only willing to fight the Americans down to the last Vietnamese."⁶⁸ Moreover, in the wake of the Tonkin Gulf incident, Beijing prohibited its air force units from attacking US aircraft that flew into Chinese air space. In June 1965, Mao withdrew an earlier pledge to provide North Vietnam with Chinese air cover, similar to Stalin's backtracking on Soviet air support for Chinese ground operations in Korea. Chinese-manned fighter aircraft would not take part in the defense of North Vietnam. Zhou Enlai and other Chinese officials repeatedly warned Washington through diplomatic channels that US air or other attacks on China would spark all-out war with the PRC; they did not say the same for North Vietnam. Washington came to understand that the Chinese had, in the words of Assistant Secretary of State for Far Eastern affairs William P. Bundy, "drawn a line [in the sand] for the United States." He concluded that if the United States confined its attacks to the air over North Vietnam, stayed clear of the southern border, and did not directly attack China, Beijing would not come into the war.⁶⁹

On 11 January 1965, Beijing issued a directive that instructed its pilots not to fire on the Americans who strayed over the border unless they fired first. When two groups of US Navy F-4 Phantoms inadvertently entered China's air space over Hainan Island in April, the Americans reportedly fired first but lost an ensuing engagement. Shot down with their plane on that occasion were Lieutenant (junior grade) Terrence Murphy and his radar intercept officer, Ensign Ronald Fegan. For the remainder of the war, Chinese aircraft tangled with US planes on only a few occasions. Once, Admiral Sharp worked to avoid trouble with China when a carrier pilot went down on Hainan. Pacific Fleet commander Hyland phoned the admiral and pleaded with him to authorize an immediate rescue operation. Sharp told Hyland that he was saddened by the loss of the young American pilot, but he could not approve his subordinate's request. He explained to the Pacific Fleet commander that he would not risk triggering Chinese intervention and—one might add—Washington's wrath.⁷⁰

Despite Beijing's caution in the aerial arena, at 0830 on 9 June 1965, the first Chinese troops entered North Vietnam. Ultimately, 320,000 soldiers of the People's Liberation Army would serve there. They operated antiaircraft artillery and railroad repair, minesweeping, and logistical equipment. Between 1965 and 1968, the PRC deployed twenty-three antiaircraft divisions to the allied nation. By 1967, 170,000 Chinese troops served in the neighboring nation. Beijing's reports, while clearly exaggerated, concluded that during the war their antiaircraft units shot down 1,707 US aircraft, damaged another 1,608, and captured 42 American aircrewmen. The PRC reportedly suffered anywhere from 6,900 to 20,000 dead and wounded military personnel. Chinese engineers also built roads that served communist troops in Laos. In addition, Chinese intelligence agents and technical experts traveled down the Ho Chi Minh Trail and as far as Hue and Danang to gather information on US military technologies.[71]

By July 1970, Mao had pulled Chinese troops out of North Vietnam over political disagreements with Hanoi and fears about Soviet forces concentrated on his northern border. Nonetheless, the PRC's support for the war effort did not stop, if only to continue competing with the Soviet Union for favor with the Vietnamese in the worldwide struggle for communist hearts and minds. Between 1968 and 1975, the Chinese provided their Vietnamese allies with huge stocks of aircraft, tanks, naval vessels, rifles, and ammunition. In 1971, Beijing signed seven economic and military agreements with Hanoi, which amounted to almost half of the PRC's total foreign assistance for that year. Mao took these measures in support of Hanoi despite hosting President Richard Nixon's momentous February 1972 visit to China. Communist solidarity trumped the potential of a US-PRC rapprochement.[72]

Hence, President Johnson's fears that all-out military operations against North Vietnam might trigger a massive Chinese intervention were well founded. If not eager for war, Mao was not deterred by the prospect. He considered Chinese intervention in the Korean War as a success that could be replicated in Indochina. He believed that the conflict in Korea had showed that his army could stand up to US land, air, and sea power; displayed international solidarity with the other communist movements; strengthened China's role as the main communist power in Asia; unified the Chinese people in support of the Chinese Communist Party; and stimulated the Soviet Union to provide China with military hardware and economic assistance. Moreover, Vietnam, unlike the Korean peninsula, could not be isolated by US air and naval power. The heavily jungled and forested regions of Indochina clearly benefitted the communist side.

Lyndon Johnson also had to contend with Soviet support to Hanoi. Moscow's policy toward Vietnam had been especially tentative before

1964. A Soviet-Vietnamese meeting in Moscow in February, during which Khrushchev demanded that Hanoi side with Moscow against Beijing, was a low point in Soviet-DRV affairs. He cautioned China and North Vietnam to avoid stimulating a massive US intervention. The Soviets considered Southeast Asia of secondary importance to their global interests and feared fighting a conflict far from the USSR. At one point, when Mao suggested that the United States was a "paper tiger," the Soviet leader replied, "Yes, of course [but] the tiger does have missile claws and nuclear teeth."[73]

The outbreak of hostilities between North Vietnam and the United States during the Tonkin Gulf incident of August 1964 witnessed a dramatic change in Soviet policy. Soviet leaders, absent Khrushchev who was deposed in October, came to understand that North Vietnam was determined to wage war to achieve its political ends. The Soviets also understood that in their struggle with China for leadership of the global communist movement, they would be roundly condemned if they did not aid North Vietnam in its fight for survival against the Americans.[74]

By early 1965, Soviet military material began to flow into North Vietnam. By the end of May, US intelligence reported the presence in North Vietnam of one hundred military vehicles equipped with antiaircraft guns. Between 1965 and 1968, the Soviets provided Hanoi with almost $2 billion worth of surface-to-air missiles, fighter aircraft, antiaircraft artillery, and ordnance. The Soviet Union's major contribution to North Vietnam was the development of integrated air defenses. Between 1,000 and 3,000 military advisors helped to develop a sophisticated air defense system that tied in advanced communications, air alert stations, and radars. Lethal SA-2 Guideline surface-to-air missiles, MiG-17 and MiG-21 fighter interceptors, and an array of 8,000 antiaircraft guns stiffened the defenses.

The training provided by Soviet advisory personnel eventually enabled the North Vietnamese defenders to bring down 922 US fixed-wing aircraft between 1965 and 1968. While military equipment comprised the bulk of the USSR's largesse, the Soviets also provided industrial and telecommunications gear, trucks, medical supplies, machine tools, iron ore, and nonferrous metals. The Soviet Union, especially after 1970, became the principal supplier of military and economic assistance to North Vietnam. Moscow hosted North Vietnamese military personnel at training schools and bases in the Soviet Union. Many of those students went on to instruct Viet Cong and North Vietnamese troops fighting in South Vietnam in the use of Soviet-supplied ordnance.[75]

In short, Soviet and Chinese assistance to Hanoi proved to be a major factor in North Vietnam's defeat of the United States in the struggle for Vietnam, and indeed Indochina. It enabled North Vietnam to survive and outlast the US aerial onslaught free from the threat of invasion and to prosecute its wartime objectives in South Vietnam, Laos, and Cambodia.

MISREADING THE ENEMY

The 34A attacks, the Desoto Patrols, and the retaliatory strike of 5 August did not discourage Hanoi from pressing its war effort in South Vietnam. Indeed, the British Consul in Hanoi reported that these actions aroused the North Vietnamese to greater effort and buoyed their confidence, even to the point of arrogance. Communist sources also made clear that the US actions strengthened Le Duan's hand in pushing for a more aggressive campaign in the South and the decision to speed up the deployment of division-size units of the North Vietnamese Army. The lessening of US military activity in September further persuaded the leaders in Hanoi that the United States was not about to launch an all-out assault on North Vietnam. The Politburo decided that before the American military intervened in force, it was an opportune time to destroy the armed forces of South Vietnam. North Vietnam's 325th Division began moving south soon afterward. Meeting with North Vietnamese officials in Beijing, Mao speculated that because of its global commitments and small number of combat divisions, the United States would not be able to respond quickly. As would soon become clear, Hanoi and Beijing had badly underestimated the American ability to swiftly deploy major combat forces to South Vietnam.[76]

Oley Sharp and his superiors in Washington were equally deluded about the true situation in Indochina. They continued to believe that Hanoi could be discouraged by increasingly punitive measures. CINCPAC Operation Plan 37-65, issued the same day Congress passed the Tonkin Gulf Resolution, entailed counter-infiltration measures on the South Vietnam-Cambodia-Laos border areas and one-time reprisal strikes by air and naval forces. Naturally, gauging the effectiveness of these measures would be difficult and take months. Only if and when these actions had failed to change the situation on the ground did the plan consider a systematic bombing campaign against ninety-four of

North Vietnam's military installations, railroads, airfields, and industrial plants. In support of his plan, Oley Sharp suggested only the establishment of a US operating facility at Danang and an amphibious exercise. Washington did not approve either of these decidedly limited recommendations. Air Force General LeMay and Marine General Greene, chiefs of staff of their services, stood alone in their advocacy of major air attacks on North Vietnam.[77]

Tom Moorer went somewhat further than his boss. The Pacific Fleet commander argued that "we should stop treading water in midstream and take positive action against NVN [North Vietnam]," even if it meant direct confrontation with China. He considered it "a necessary risk" if Southeast Asia were not to fall to communist aggression. Moorer stressed that "time is running out on us."[78] Still, the admiral did not push for the intervention ashore of US combat divisions. Instead, Moorer called for the creation of robust air and naval facilities at Danang and three other locations on the coast and enhanced advisory and material support to the South Vietnamese government. Only when these measures had failed to change the situation on the ground did he consider it necessary to launch a major effort against North Vietnam, to include an all-out bombing campaign, aerial mining of ports, and a maritime blockade.[79]

In the aftermath of the Gulf of Tonkin incident, to be safe the Johnson administration prepared for an expanded conflict in Southeast Asia, but at the same time ruled out strong actions against North Vietnam. As laid out in a national security action memo signed by the president on 10 September 1964, the United States continued its focus on trying to stabilize the political and military situation in South Vietnam. Johnson disapproved reprisal strikes against North Vietnam for the Viet Cong attack on the air base at Bien Hoa in South Vietnam on 1 November that killed four Americans and destroyed twenty-four aircraft. Proximity to the presidential election was a significant factor influencing Johnson's decision.[80]

Ambassador Maxwell Taylor, Westmoreland, Sharp, and Moorer did not call for all-out war against North Vietnam but rather heavy reprisal strikes against select targets carried out over the short term. Taylor and Sharp were two of the foremost advocates of graduated escalation. Surprisingly, given his later heated condemnation of such limited action, Sharp concluded that heavy reprisal strikes had the potential to defeat North Vietnamese aggression and return peace and stability to the region. Only Tom Moorer had suggested that the "objective of the reprisal must be to eliminate NVN strength to support the insurgency in the South," rather than "tit-for-tat operations [which] are not sufficient."[81]

Hanging over all their deliberations was the specter of China's possible entry into the conflict. Greene recorded that during the 2 November JCS meeting with McNamara, General Taylor and the defense secretary suggested that a major military effort in Vietnam might get the Chinese involved. The president worried that China and even the Soviet Union had signed secret treaties with North Vietnam and that any misstep by the US air forces might prompt intervention. Johnson once mused that "in the dark at night" he "would lay awake" and ask himself "an endless series of questions [such as] what if one of the targets you picked today triggers off Russia or China?"[82] Later in the war, while speaking to sailors on board aircraft carrier *Constellation*, Johnson assured them that he didn't want a wider war because the North Vietnamese "have two big brothers that have more weight and people than I have."[83] McNamara too shared Johnson's fear of major Chinese or Soviet intervention and admitted that it significantly influenced the manner in which he and the president ran the air war against North Vietnam.[84]

The Joint Chiefs downplayed the likelihood of Chinese intervention and at one point considered a Navy-Marine amphibious landing and beachhead on the coast of North Vietnam. Vice Admiral Lloyd Mustin, the chief operations officer on the Joint Staff and member of the State Department's Joint Planning Group, argued in November that ending Hanoi's support of the insurgencies in the region did not necessitate the defeat of North Vietnam or China. Hence US objectives in South Vietnam could be achieved without risking a major conflict.[85]

Oley Sharp referred derisively in his memoir to "the apparent specter of the mythical 'hordes' of Chinese coming down from the north."[86] Nonetheless, in November 1964 the admiral reinforced the administration's desire to avoid taking any measures that might fire up the Chinese. CINCPAC cautioned the JCS that an air and mining campaign and a blockade had a "high probability of provoking [an unspecified] CHICOM reaction."[87] As an alternative, the admiral recommended a program of graduated pressures that entailed air strikes on select targets in Laos and North Vietnam that were far from the border with the PRC. Sharp anticipated "systematic and progressive attacks of ever-increasing intensity." Sufficient time would be allowed between the strikes to see how the Vietnamese and Chinese reacted. If they did not cave in to the pressure, the campaign was to resume "its inexorable and increasingly destructive march toward Hanoi." CINCPAC was confident such an approach would cause Hanoi to end its support to the Viet Cong and Pathet Lao.[88] Compare that recommendation with his later castigation of the "civilian side of the house [that] wanted to see a campaign of gradually increasing military pressures," which he labeled an approach of "carrot and stick."[89]

Sharp's basic concept was embodied in a presidential directive issued on 1 December 1964. The document emphasized that the military actions were designed to "give the impression of a steady, deliberate approach, and to give the U.S. the option at any time (subject to enemy reaction) to proceed or not, to escalate or not, and to quicken the pace or not."[90] This of course was the essence of the Johnson administration's "graduated escalation" approach to the conflict against North Vietnam from 1965 to 1968. In his influential post–retirement book, *Strategy for Defeat*, Oley Sharp lambasted both Johnson and McNamara for adopting just such a strategy against North Vietnam, but he was one of its founding fathers.[91]

Admirals Sharp and Moorer shared the Johnson administration's illusions about the nature of the conflict with Hanoi in 1964. They dismissed the military strength and staying power of North Vietnam, its close connection with the Sino-Soviet bloc, and the real threat of an even greater Chinese intervention to thwart US aims. In keeping with the graduated escalation approach, they routinely called for ever stronger measures to pressure the North Vietnamese into compliance with Washington's desires. The two flag officers, among the most professionally skilled, world-wise, and accomplished leaders in the Navy, sincerely believed that US air and naval power would prevail in any conflict with Hanoi. Unlike more bellicose members of the Joint Chiefs, they did not call for the invasion or the overthrow of North Vietnam's Communist government.

Sharp and Moorer were the two most central overseers of the 34A maritime program and the Desoto Patrol. The North Vietnamese foray against *Maddox* and supposed nighttime attack on *Maddox* and *Turner Joy* seriously challenged President Johnson's and their assumptions about the nature of the confrontation. Nonetheless, once battle had been joined, the two combat-hardened, honor-bound warriors called for a swift, strong response. As naval leaders, they understood the concept of freedom of the sea, a bedrock tenet of US foreign policy since the founding of the republic. The admirals correctly reasoned that not following the Pierce Arrow strikes with additional 34A and Desoto Patrols and other retaliatory measures conveyed weakness and irresolution. Indeed, Johnson's inaction prompted Le Duan to double down on North Vietnam's support for the Viet Cong war effort and to push for a military victory before the United States could prevent it.

Johnson and McNamara, however—unlike the admirals—began to understand that Hanoi's determination to resist American pressure, the communist-bloc's robust military, economic, and ideological support for Hanoi, and China's military might just across the border boded ill for US objectives in Indochina. In the new year, Johnson, McNamara, and their naval leaders in the Pacific would be compelled to steer a different course in their determination to win the struggle against North Vietnam.

CHAPTER 3
UPPING THE ANTE

The Johnson administration, concerned about its failure to deter North Vietnam's aggressive actions in the wake of the Tonkin Gulf incident, moved to stiffen its pressure campaign. Navy and Air Force aircraft launched Barrel Roll, an operation to interdict logistic traffic along the rudimentary roads in Laos between North and South Vietnam. The planes flew "armed route reconnaissance" in search of targets of opportunity or bombed preselected military sites. At the same time that entire North Vietnamese divisions were heading south, Washington adopted a minimalist approach to the operation. The first mission approved personally by the president entailed two strikes, each one carried out by four aircraft and conducted three days apart.

John T. McNaughton, McNamara's principal deputy and most trusted advisor, told the military that the purpose of the mission was to send a signal of deeper US involvement, "the signal to be more psychological . . . than of pure military effectiveness."[1] Tom Moorer believed that McNaughton, formerly a Harvard Law School professor, "lacked common sense."[2] The admiral disparaged McNaughton and other defense department civilians, "none of whom [had] ever heard a gun fired in anger." He added, "They tell everybody how to fight a war [and] they read Greek and *Macbeth* [but] they don't learn a damn thing about how to fight a war."[3] Bud Zumwalt, who served as a mid-level officer in the Pentagon with McNaughton, recalled that "he was, by nature, very distrustful of the military mind and used to be quite open in saying so." Zumwalt must have softened his opinion of McNaughton, however, since he later offered that had McNaughton not been killed in an airplane crash, he would have been an even stronger advocate than Secretary of the Navy John Chafee for Zumwalt becoming CNO.[4]

The Barrel Roll strikes in Laos did not have the desired effect, since the destruction on one occasion of a number of jungle huts and the failure to destroy a targeted bridge hardly sent Hanoi a signal of US military might. Sharp accepted an additional complication to Barrel Roll when he agreed to clear planned operations through the US Ambassador to Laos, William H. Sullivan. The diplomat demanded direct involvement in control of the operation. Strikes in December continued to return limited results. When the US ambassadors to Laos, South Vietnam, and Thailand and a CINCPAC representative gathered in Saigon early in 1965 to discuss Barrel Roll, the consensus was that the air operations were probably "unrecognized by Hanoi and Peiping [Peking] as increments of pressure designed to influence the (North Vietnamese) will to continue aggression."[5]

Sharp was especially disappointed that the US air forces had detected in Laos little evidence of enemy traffic and that the "effects achieved have been negligible compared to [the] effort expended."[6] A large part of the problem, he argued, stemmed from Washington's stifling control of operations from 8,000 miles away. He reported that his subordinate commands had profound uncertainty over their authority to launch particular missions.[7] To make Barrel Roll more effective, Sharp and Westmoreland proposed to the JCS concentrated, persistent air assaults on two vital transportation bottlenecks, or "chokepoints." Interdicting the Mu Gia and Nape passes, through which ran roads between North Vietnam and Laos, stood the chance of slowing if not stopping the enemy's logistic traffic. Sharp admitted that while this was a limited plan, it was a first step toward more meaningful operations.[8]

On 28 February 1965, the Navy carried out the first chokepoint strike when aircraft from *Coral Sea* (CVA-43) pounded Mu Gia with delayed-action bombs, rockets, and cannon fire that cratered the road in many places and buried a large section with landslides. Moorer was ecstatic, proclaiming the operation an outstanding success. The Pacific Fleet commander considered it fortuitous that one of McNamara's civilian staff members, Alain C. Enthoven, happened to be visiting *Coral Sea* at the time. The admiral related to the CNO that "this operation was worth a thousand words in explaining to him our Navy" and the utility of an aircraft carrier with its striking power all in one floating package.[9]

Moorer's elation was short-lived. Despite several successful strikes by Navy and Air Force units during early March, neither the US ambassador to Laos nor Sharp expressed happiness with Barrel Roll. Sullivan felt the signal to Hanoi was not getting through because execution of the program had been inconsistent. Sharp concurred with that assessment. CINCPAC knew that Barrel Roll was not impressing Hanoi. As with the other air operations then underway in Indochina, Sharp began suggesting that the United States should focus more on physically interdicting the Ho Chi Minh Trail. At least partly based on CINCPAC's recommendations, that same month the JCS approved a more comprehensive, systematic, and long-term program to cut the Ho Chi Minh Trail.[10]

The escalation of North Vietnam's war effort and assault on US facilities and personnel in South Vietnam intensified on 7 February 1965 when Viet Cong forces mortared the US advisors' barracks at Pleiku in South Vietnam's Central Highlands, killing or wounding 117 American servicemen. Despite some reluctance on the part of the State Department, the president's civilian and military advisors called for an immediate counterstrike, and intelligence sources minimized the threat of Chinese intervention. On the 11th, McDonald, then acting JCS chairman, met with the president and other members of the national security establishment at the White House. The CNO informed the president that it was the unanimous view of the JCS that the US should strike back immediately with *"adequate force"* (italics added) in retaliation for the recent attacks.[11]

Johnson reluctantly ordered Flaming Dart I, a multi-plane assault on North Vietnamese barracks far from the border with China and just north of the Demilitarized Zone. That same day, aircraft from carriers *Ranger* (CVA-61) and *Coral Sea* rolled in on the 275 widely spaced barracks and administrative buildings at Dong Hoi, destroying or damaging twenty-two of them. Similar operations by US Air Force and South Vietnamese air force planes ran afoul of heavy weather or command-and-control glitches. Sharp did not think Flaming Dart I "a very effective attack," and Moorer agreed that it was "at best a qualified and inadequate reprisal."[12]

Apparently not discouraged by the leaders in Hanoi, three days later Viet Cong saboteurs detonated an explosive device at the US

Sharp directed the Rolling Thunder bombing campaign against North Vietnam, believing that a graduated escalation of military force against Hanoi would bring success in the war. Naval War College (NWC) Sharp Collection MSC 247-03-01-46.

barracks in Qui Nhon, a port on the South Vietnamese coast, causing forty-four American casualties. As authorized by the president, the US and Vietnamese air forces struck North Vietnamese barracks at Chap Le while the Navy assaulted Chanh Hoa. Despite a cascade of bombs and rockets, the strike by the air wings of carriers *Hancock* (CVA-19), *Ranger*, and *Coral Sea* managed to destroy or damage only twenty-three of the seventy-six buildings at the target. The dispersion of the structures, miserable flying weather, and enemy antiaircraft defenses made the task of the aviators especially difficult. On 3 March, McNamara told the chief of staff of the Air Force that he was not pleased with the overall bombing effort.[13]

Moorer later expressed his deep frustration with civilian analysts in the defense department who micromanaged operations and who opined that "the number of bombs you dropped . . . should have knocked out X barracks and you're only reporting Y barracks." The admiral lamented that "they were trying to fine tune it down to that point."[14] Apparently, Johnson and his civilian advisors did not heed the advice given by former President Dwight D. Eisenhower on 17 February to enunciate an overall strategy and then allow the field commanders to determine its execution. Instead, Johnson took note only of the former president's endorsement of his pressure campaign against North Vietnam.[15]

LEADERSHIP SQUABBLES

Westmoreland, not for the last time, used the limited results from the Flaming Dart strikes to push for control of allied air power in Indochina. He complained that CINCPAC's planning measures had caused confusion at the Seventh Air Force's Tan Son Nhut headquarters near Saigon. COMUSMACV then and later felt that "it would have been better if there had been a single, operational commander for Southeast Asia."[16] Sharp responded that the Air Force and Navy commands had received the same information and directives. He added, "The Navy's carrier forces, operating under similar instructions and orders, were not confused and had carried out their preparations and strikes smoothly and with a minimum of fuss in accordance with the basic operations order."[17] Sharp bluntly informed Westmoreland that CINCPAC would control the air campaign outside of South Vietnam and that he "would appreciate it if you would accept that fact."[18]

Oley Sharp fiercely guarded his oversight of air operations in Southeast Asia because he considered it essential to his Pacific-wide responsibilities. After the war, he reaffirmed that his control of the air war worked for him and the JCS, and if he had to do it over again, he wouldn't have changed it.[19] He was determined to maintain direct control of the interdiction air campaigns against North Vietnam and Laos through his subordinate Pacific Fleet and Pacific Air Forces commands. Sharp's Air Force subordinate, General Hunter Harris Jr., agreed with that assessment, as did Air Force leaders in Washington. They believed that the existing Rolling Thunder command-and-control arrangements well served Air Force interests. A Joint Staff study concurred with that finding.[20]

Nonetheless, Sharp did accommodate Westmoreland's wish for MACV to control air power resources that directly influenced the fight in South Vietnam. As a result, in April 1966 the admiral approved MACV overseeing air operations in Route Package 1, the bombing zone just north of the DMZ. Westmoreland suggested that he and Sharp "got along very well." The general admitted that we "had some disagreements, but very few, and none was acrimonious."[21] Sharp also made a division of air operations permanent; the Air Force would operate in the northwest of North Vietnam, the area closest to its Thailand air bases, and the Navy would work the route packages closest to the Gulf of Tonkin and the carriers. Air Force leaders were unhappy with Sharp's route packages and suggested he had set up the system to favor the Navy in a sortie-rate competition with the Air Force. Some Air Force leaders considered CINCPAC "Navy oriented."[22] Sharp, however, worked to improve coordination and cooperation between his Air Force and Navy component commanders. At one point, CINCPAC chastised General Joseph H. Moore Jr., the Vice Commander Pacific Air Forces, and Admiral Roy L. Johnson, CINCPACFLT, for their squabbling over route package assignments. He told them to negotiate arrangements for the sharing of targets throughout North Vietnam.[23]

The leadership skills of Oley Sharp and Tom Moorer were sorely tested in dealing with their civilian superiors and advisors in the White House and the Pentagon. McNamara came to rely on the advice of Assistant Secretary of Defense for International Security Affairs McNaughton, National Security Advisor McGeorge Bundy, and other civilians rather than their four-star military counterparts, most of whom had been successful combat commanders and warriors in World War II and the Korean War. Indeed, McNamara considered the JCS "a miserable organization" focused on the parochial needs of the individual services rather than the national good.[24] John Blandford, counsel to the House Armed Services Committee, has suggested that McNamara

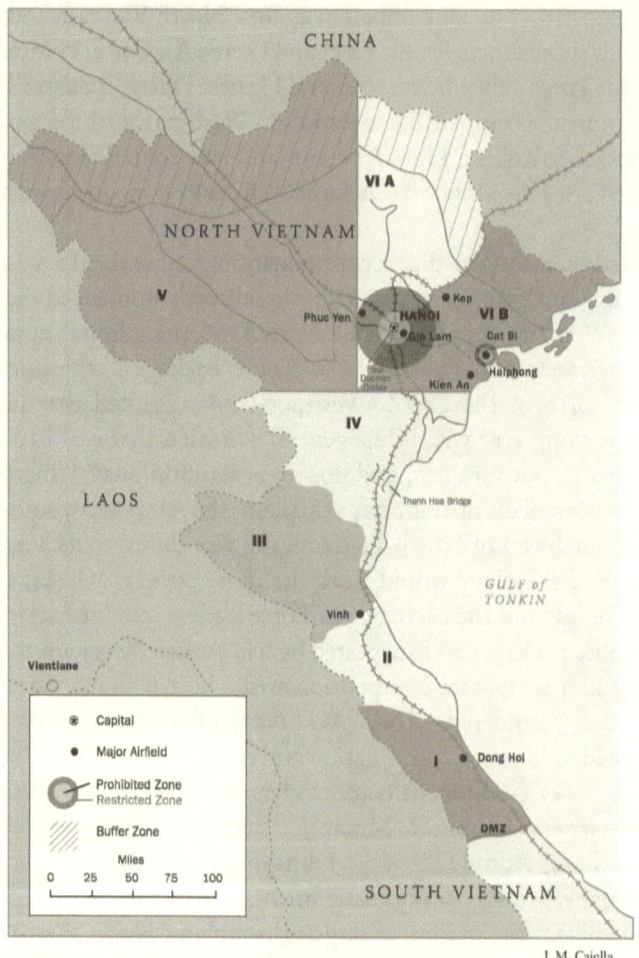

Route Packages map. Sharp mandated the use of separate operational areas, or "Route Packages," for Air Force and Navy air units engaged in Rolling Thunder strikes. NHHC.

"was the wrong man in the wrong job at the wrong time" because he frequently ignored professional military advice, which he badly needed. Maxwell Taylor thought that McNamara was the best secretary of defense ever but admitted that he was "probably the only man in uniform who ever said that."[25]

The secretary of defense blamed the military for failing to send Hanoi the powerful message he desired through the Flaming Dart strikes. With sharp sarcasm, he told the Joint Chiefs that "although the four missions left . . . operations at the targets relatively unimpaired, I am quite satisfied with the results." But he clearly knew that had not been the result. He expressed his true evaluation of Flaming Dart by complaining that the attacking forces had knocked out only sixty-nine of 491 buildings at the target sites. He observed that future communications of resolve would "carry a hollow ring unless we accomplish more military damage than we have to date." Not content to leave it at that, the secretary suggested that his military commanders try different tactical approaches: "Can we not better meet our military objectives by choosing different types of targets, directing different weights of effort against them, or changing the composition of the force?"[26]

The operational commanders, however, had not been and would not be empowered to make those choices. Moorer suggested that a cause for the loss of seven naval aircraft between June 1964 and the end of February 1965 was that air operations in Indochina had been oriented toward political aims, with operational objectives considered secondary. He elaborated: "Three of the aircraft were lost in attacks on targets under very poor weather conditions which forced the employment of low altitude delivery tactics." He concluded that "with greater tactical freedom, these strikes might have been postponed or alternate targets struck [but] adequate target flexibility was not available."[27]

In the wake of the less than satisfactory Flaming Dart strikes, Sharp mused that the North Vietnamese would not be discouraged by such "tit-for-tat" retaliatory actions.[28] Several weeks later, CINCPAC testified before Congress that he now recognized Hanoi's determination to bring about the US withdrawal from South Vietnam. He believed that the enemy had concluded that "if they can kill Americans, harass U.S. personnel, and destroy U.S. facilities the American public will, in time, become so tired of the war that we will abandon our efforts there."[29] While not the admiral's desired outcome, this statement proved to be an accurate prophecy.

Even when the exhaustion of previous efforts at deterrence necessitated the launch of continuous bombing operations against North Vietnam, the service chiefs, with the exception of Air Force Chief of Staff John P. McConnell, did not push for an all-out, no-holds-barred campaign. On 24 February, Marine General Greene proposed a number of actions to demonstrate US resolve to prevail in Vietnam, including the use of South Vietnamese, and if necessary US, forces to "commence systematic destruction—in a rising crescendo—of targets in North Vietnam by air attack, amphibious raids, covert operations, and naval gunfire."[30]

The majority of the Joint Chiefs now thought it probable that Chinese "volunteers" would enter North Vietnam and that the Soviets would supply Hanoi with air defense weapons, including possibly SA-2 surface-to-air missiles. A plan developed by the Joint Chiefs called for a *two-month* operation focused on selected targets below North Vietnam's 19th parallel. Attacks on these sites would not be tied to specific Viet Cong outrages in South Vietnam but would constitute part of a systematic anti-infiltration campaign. Sharp concurred with the approach. The JCS target list complied with the White House objective of restricting attacks to North Vietnamese military sites while avoiding political and economic targets, especially in populated areas.[31]

Sharp was frustrated with Washington's failed attempts to deter North Vietnam's aggressive behavior. Hence, he increasingly proposed military solutions that would improve the allied situation on the ground and convince Hanoi that it could not prevail in an extended conflict with the United States. The admiral suggested that the US air forces should focus on disrupting the enemy's supply line to the south, the Ho Chi Minh Trail. He expressed confidence that that approach would "slowly *strangle* [italics added] the VC." Ironically, a similar air effort to cut enemy supply lines to communist forces during the Korean War—that failed to achieve the goal—was labeled Operation Strangle.[32]

On 13 February 1965, Johnson gave final approval for Operation Rolling Thunder, a systematic bombing campaign against North Vietnam. In his memoir, Johnson implied that he merely followed the advice of his advisors in ordering a bombing campaign that adhered to a "slowly ascending tempo," but he had pressed repeatedly for just such a measured approach.[33] Dwight D. Eisenhower endorsed Johnson's decision at a White House meeting three days later. The former president observed that the bombing program would weaken North Vietnam's will to continue the war. He suggested that if China or the Soviet Union openly intervened in the conflict, Johnson should deploy up to eight Army divisions to Indochina and warn the communist powers of "dire results," implying the use of nuclear weapons.[34]

Complications that would vitiate Rolling Thunder's military effectiveness throughout the three-year campaign forced postponement of the first planned strike. Political turmoil in Saigon, heavy weather, and concerns about possible Soviet and Chinese reactions delayed succeeding missions. General Wheeler, the JCS chairman, gave voice to the Johnson-McNamara approach to the bombing campaign. The administration was endeavoring to "steer a careful course which would lead to the greatest possible effect on the enemy both in and out of RVN while keeping at a minimum the chances of bringing the Chinese Communist[s] into open battle." He admitted that Rolling Thunder brought with it "sizable and vexing domestic and international political problems."[35]

Rolling Thunder finally began on 2 March 1965 when US Air Force and South Vietnamese aircraft heavily damaged military facilities at Xom Bang and Quang Khe and sank two gunboats offshore. Having been granted a grace period by Washington after the Pierce Arrow retaliatory strike in August 1964, North Vietnam's air defense forces then were well-armed and ready. Antiaircraft fire shot down six American and South Vietnamese planes and killed two pilots. Almost two weeks passed before the allied air forces worked out command-and-control problems to launch the next preplanned strike.

The Navy joined the fight on 15 March when ninety-four aircraft of the Attack Carrier Striking Force (Task Force 77) destroyed an ammunition depot at Phu Qui as part of Rolling Thunder 6. Admiral Moorer, just before his departure for the United States to take command of the Atlantic Fleet, argued again that operational commanders should be allowed to choose from a list of preselected targets based on their knowledge of weather conditions, enemy air defenses, and other tactical considerations. He complained that essential flights by reconnaissance aircraft over the only preselected target available to the fleet alerted the North Vietnamese to the impending attack. At one point, McNaughton sympathized with some of Moorer's complaints but explained that restrictive rules of engagement were necessary because Washington was sensitive to the danger of Soviet involvement and heavy losses of American aircraft. Tom Moorer later related that when the military suggested destroying the Soviet-installed SAM sites in North Vietnam before they became operational, McNaughton denied the request. According to the admiral, McNamara's civilian advisor believed that "the North Vietnamese are not going to shoot at you, they're just putting those there as a deterrent [and that] they just want to scare you."[36]

That same day, the president convened a meeting in Washington of his national security team that, while not directly responding to

Moorer's complaints, addressed the overall issue of command and control of air operations over North Vietnam. Johnson relaxed some of the restrictions that had complicated early Rolling Thunder operations. He authorized the services to select from a list of primary and alternate targets and in a wider geographic area, without prior approval from Washington. At the same time, he prohibited even reconnaissance flights above the 20th parallel, and if the US aircraft encountered MiGs, they were to back off. Rolling Thunder was finally off and running—if fitfully.

NAVAL AND GROUND FORCES JOIN THE FRAY

By early 1965, Sharp and Moorer understood that the US armed forces would soon be executing major air operations in Laos and North Vietnam. An incident in February also made it clear that the conflict was about to take on a greater maritime dimension. On the 16th, a US Army helicopter pilot flying past Vung Ro, an isolated bay on South Vietnam's central coast, spotted a camouflaged, steel-hulled vessel offloading onto the beach what looked to be military supplies. South Vietnamese air and naval forces converged on the site. During the next three days and nights, the attacking forces fought Viet Cong guerrillas for possession of the ship and its cargo. Afterward, South Vietnamese soldiers and sailors and their US military advisors discovered on board the captured ship and in nearby areas ashore over 100 tons of war material, including small arms ammunition, mortar rounds, grenades, rifles, submachine guns, and explosives. Documents found on board verified that the ship with its mostly Chinese- and Soviet-made munitions had departed from North Vietnam.

The Seventh Fleet commander, Vice Admiral Paul P. "Brick" Blackburn Jr., informed the Pacific Fleet commander that he considered the event at Vung Ro Bay "positive proof that sea infiltration is occurring and raises the strong possibility that at least a portion of the unconfirmed reports of the past were, in fact, true."[37] His suspicions about the existence of significant North Vietnamese seaborne infiltration verified, Westmoreland pressed for establishment of a major US Navy-led maritime interdiction effort.

Tom Moorer heartily endorsed COMUSMACV's call for a coastal patrol. Much like Sharp, Moorer was increasingly dubious that North Vietnam could be deterred by erratically ordered pinprick air strikes in Laos and North Vietnam. Both officers, however, were confident that

US naval and air forces could cut the supply lines from North Vietnam. CINCPACFLT recognized that a change in the course of the war was at hand. He told Admiral McDonald, "It seems clear that our national policy towards SVN [South Vietnam] is shifting from one in which we attempted to maintain an 'advisory' image in SVN to one of active and overt U.S. participation."[38]

Throughout his long service in uniform, Moorer had expressed rock-solid confidence in the value of sea power and the Navy's ability to support operations ashore. He now made a pitch to the CNO for the major commitment of naval forces in Southeast Asia. He emphasized that his fleet had the power and "we are ready to go." Moorer suggested that in addition to coastal patrol, his naval forces could assist the South Vietnamese military with shore bombardment, aerial mining, commando raids, over-the-beach logistic support, submarine reconnaissance, amphibious lift of ARVN units, and carrier strikes against Viet Cong guerrillas. Moorer wanted to reinforce "the President's reported belief that the Navy offers the most effective and uncomplicated means to bring pressure to bear" in Southeast Asia. In a not uncommon Navy approach to taking action before getting permission to do so, Moorer informed the CNO that "unless you feel to the contrary, I will push in this direction."[39] With another officer this might have seemed presumptuous, but Moorer was already considered as the prime candidate for McDonald's job.

Reacting quickly to Westmoreland's request, on 11 March the Seventh Fleet established Market Time, an operation that would engage the US Navy and in short order the US Coast Guard for the duration of the long conflict.[40] US maritime patrol forces operated all along the 1,200-mile coastline from the DMZ in the north to the border with Cambodia in the south. The coastal patrol employed destroyers, minesweepers, shore-based SP-2H Neptune patrol planes, and even for a time P-5B Marlin seaplanes. Also engaged in the operation were destroyer escorts, Swift boats, patrol gunboats, LSTs, and Coast Guard cutters. The Vietnam Navy contributed coastal patrol ships and its sizeable junk fleet. P-3A Orion patrol planes flying from bases in South Vietnam, the Philippines, and Thailand eventually stiffened the air patrol of the coast.[41]

Not every naval flag officer wanted to connect the service to Army-dominated operations on the mainland. Admiral Rivero stressed that Market Time should be directed by the Pacific Fleet rather than "some other command, such as COMUSMACV."⁴² He got his wish until the end of July. By then, however, it had become clear that since the coastal patrol directly supported the allied war effort in South Vietnam, Westmoreland should oversee the operation, with his Navy subordinate on the MACV staff, Rear Admiral Norvell G. Ward, in direct command. The latter officer also served as Chief of the Naval Advisory Group. Consequently, Ward established the Coastal Surveillance Force (Task Force 115) under MACV to manage the maritime effort.

Even more momentous than President Johnson's employment of the US armed forces in air operations against Laos and North Vietnam and naval operations off the coast of South Vietnam was his decision to send US combat troops into battle in Indochina. Since the end of the Korean War, during which the US Army had suffered embarrassing defeats and heavy casualties at the hands of China's People's Liberation Army, many US leaders were determined to avoid a similar commitment ashore on the Asian mainland. The so-called "Never Again Club" of Army and Marine generals helped presidents Eisenhower and Kennedy decide against the deployment of US troops to Vietnam in 1954 and Laos in the early 1960s.⁴³

In the latter months of 1964, both Sharp and Moorer, strong advocates for the use of air and naval power, also opposed the movement ashore of major ground units. The issue surfaced in the wake of the Gulf of Tonkin incident when Westmoreland called for troops to defend the Danang, Bien Hoa, and Tan Son Nhut airfields from Viet Cong attacks. As an indication of the overly optimistic thinking among Johnson's civilian advisors, on 31 August 1964 McGeorge Bundy considered it "at least possible that a couple of brigade-size units . . . might be good medicine everywhere."⁴⁴ CINCPAC, with the concurrence of his Pacific Fleet commander, persuaded the JCS not to go that route with Army troops and suggested that in any emergency Marines positioned throughout the Western Pacific could be rushed to threatened airfields.⁴⁵

The admirals considered Danang, however, as different from the other sites. In contingency plans, Danang was considered key to the deterrence of China and to air operations in Laos and North Vietnam. From Danang, Air Force and Marine planes provided US forces with fighter, search and rescue, and other aerial support. In addition, the 34A maritime force operated from Danang against targets on North Vietnam's coast. Sharp regarded the base as a visible but vulnerable symbol of the

US commitment to the defense of all Southeast Asia. Late in the year, the admiral asked for and received approval to deploy a Marine air defense missile battalion and an infantry company to Danang.

Oley Sharp and Tom Moorer strongly opposed using US ground forces to help the South Vietnamese military fight the Viet Cong. In October 1964, when the JCS suggested the employment of the Seventh Fleet's Special Landing Force of Marines to counter a feared but never-launched Viet Cong offensive against Quang Ngai City, seventy-five miles southeast of Danang, Moorer urged caution. He argued that before the deployment of any US troops, "every effort should be made to undertake this operation with RVN resources." He clearly recognized the long-term consequences of putting major US combat units on South Vietnamese soil: "If landing of U.S. ground troops is ordered, it should be borne in mind that this will be the first such landing of U.S. forces in Southeast Asia in a potentially imminent combat situation." He advised that "prior to any such landing, determination should be made as to length of time U.S. forces will be maintained ashore and also the method of withdrawal."[46]

Events conspired to weaken Moorer's argument. The Viet Cong attacks on the Bien Hoa airbase in November and Saigon's Brinks Hotel in December convinced Johnson that only US ground troops could salvage the situation in South Vietnam. On 30 December, the president stated, "I have never felt that this war will be won from the air." Instead, he looked to the use of special forces, Army Rangers, and Marines to "stiffen" the Vietnamese military against the Viet Cong. In essence, Johnson had begun to focus on defeating communist forces in South Vietnam rather than bombing North Vietnam into submission.[47]

On 28 December 1964, at Binh Gia near Saigon, for the first time in the war a sizeable Viet Cong force cut off and threatened to destroy several first-line South Vietnamese units. The communist troops fought off an ARVN relief force strengthened with tanks, artillery, aircraft, and American advisors; stayed on the battlefield for four days; and inflicted more than 400 casualties on the South Vietnamese army. Binh Gia heralded the enemy's transition from guerrilla warfare to big-unit battle. US intelligence also detected major North Vietnamese formations moving down the Ho Chi Minh Trail. After Binh Gia, Westmoreland—but more importantly President Johnson—suggested that it might take a major deployment of US ground troops to stem the communist tide in South Vietnam.[48]

The immediate concern of the national security establishment, however, was for the safety of Danang. Fearing North Vietnamese or even Chinese retaliation for air strikes against North Vietnam, Westmoreland and the JCS called for the dispatch to Danang of a 5,000-man Marine expeditionary brigade with additional air support. Sharp and Moorer were in full accord with the measure because they considered Danang vulnerable and wanted to act before the enemy did. On 26 February, the president authorized the landing of Brigadier General Frederick J. Karch's 9th Marine Expeditionary Brigade (MEB). The unit's mission was to defend the airfield, port facilities, and other US installations against attack from any source. Operational orders emphasized that the Marines would not take part in day-to-day actions against the Viet Cong.[49]

At 0600 on 8 March 1965, the Seventh Fleet's amphibious task force commander, Rear Admiral Donald W. Wulzen, gave the traditional order to "land the landing force." While delayed for a few hours because of a heavy swell in the harbor, that morning naval amphibious units landed the first battalion-size American combat formation to set foot on South Vietnamese soil. By the end of April, the 9th MEB and its integral Marine fighter, attack, and helicopter squadrons totaling 8,878 officers and men were on the ground. Westmoreland had wanted the landing at Danang to be a low-key affair and blamed Sharp for dashing that hope. The general later related that when the Marines were told they were to land, "it was like pulling the plug from a bathtub [and] any semblance of a low profile quickly disappeared." Westmoreland sniffed that "under Admiral Sharp's direction *rather than mine*" (italics added), the Marines stormed ashore "in full battle regalia as if re-enacting Iwo Jima."[50]

Even as the Marines landed, national leaders had been considering an expanded role for US ground forces. In late February, the president dispatched Army Chief of Staff General Harold K. Johnson on a fact-finding mission to Saigon. The commander in chief wanted the general to return with recommendations on the future direction of US strategy. During Johnson's 5 to 12 March visit to South Vietnam, he met with Ambassador Taylor, Sharp, and Westmoreland. While Sharp attended these meetings, he was not the principal official present. When Taylor began his term as US ambassador in July 1964, President Johnson had given him an unusually broad grant of authority. In addition to the usual duties of an ambassador, Taylor understood that the president wanted him to take on "responsibility for the whole military effort in South Vietnam" and that he was "authorized the degree of command and control which I might consider appropriate." Westmoreland considered Taylor as his superior officer. Taylor recognized that the directive might trouble Sharp. While the admiral accommodated this arrangement and it supposedly "worked well," at least in Taylor's estimation, it reflected the president's view even then that the Pacific Command was not the prime mover with regard to in-country actions.[51]

Taylor continued to favor putting military pressure on North Vietnam, but Westmoreland called for a more direct US commitment to the southern conflict in light of ARVN's rapid disintegration and the surge south of North Vietnamese troops. In the end, General Johnson returned to Washington with the strong recommendation that US Army combat units be deployed in defense of South Vietnam. He warned prophetically, however, that it might take five years and 500,000 troops to accomplish US objectives there. This prognosis was a shock to McNamara, who had not "been thinking in anything approaching such terms," and the JCS, which "had not looked much beyond a 3- or 4-month campaign."[52]

Meeting with his principal advisors on 15 March 1965, the president finally decided that the defense of South Vietnam required US ground troops. The JCS and Westmoreland favored deploying large Army formations to Saigon and the Central Highlands, areas of enemy strength. Admiral Sharp and Ambassador Taylor, in line with their earlier concerns about a heavy commitment of US troops to the fight ashore, argued instead for the establishment of firm lodgments along the coast. On 29 March, the secretary of defense tentatively sided with the enclave proponents, observing that once a logistic foundation was well established, the troops could move into the interior. A critical factor was the consensus among the key leaders of the national security establishment that US ground troops would soon seek combat with Viet Cong and North Vietnamese forces. Hence, the primary role for US forces in South Vietnam had changed from supporting ARVN operations to going head-to-head with the enemy.[53]

Despite later downplaying his role, Oley Sharp finally supported the deployment of ground troops to South Vietnam and their new mission to fight the Viet Cong. Indeed, he alluded to the Marine Corps' "distinguished record in counter-guerrilla warfare."[54] Having ruled out an invasion of North Vietnam, US ground troops would have no alternative but to fight what would soon become a war of attrition, searching for and destroying enemy forces. McNamara later put the onus of that ultimately bankrupt strategy on Westmoreland, but COMUSMACV was only the operational commander; McNamara and his Washington cohort developed and ordered execution of the attrition strategy. On 1 April, after meeting with the National Security Council, President Johnson formally authorized reorientation of the mission of the Marines in Danang from air base defense to offensive combat operations. Johnson's decision became US policy with promulgation of National Security Action Memorandum 328 on 6 April 1965. That directive served as the foundation for a ground campaign in South Vietnam that soon overshadowed all other aspects of the conflict.[55]

On 30 March 1965, Tom Moorer had relinquished command of the Pacific Fleet before moving on to lead the Atlantic Fleet. In his parting remarks during the turnover ceremony on board aircraft carrier *Bennington* (CVS-20), he expressed the view he shared with Oley Sharp that a major war was on the horizon. The admiral observed that he felt "like a fire chief that leaves a roaring fire just when he gets the hoses hooked up and is ready to turn on the water."[56] Despite his new posting, Moorer would return as a fire chief and make an even greater impact than he already had on the course of the Vietnam War.

By early 1965, the Johnson administration no longer determined the course of action against North Vietnam but instead reacted to the enemy's moves. The Viet Cong's bloody attacks on American-occupied facilities in Saigon, Pleiku, and Qui Nhon and defeat of ARVN main force units at Binh Gia prompted the Flaming Dart strikes and eventually the Rolling Thunder bombing campaign. The early ineffectiveness of these operations then influenced Sharp and other US leaders to focus on cutting North Vietnam's supply lines to the southern battlefield through the Barrel Roll operations in Laos and the Market Time patrol of South Vietnam's coastline. During these months, admirals Sharp and Moorer complied uneasily with Washington's operational directives. At the same time, they began to shine light on what they considered flaws in the execution of US strategy and the micromanagement of air operations from Washington.[57] In theater, Sharp shot down Westmoreland's attempt to gain control of air operations. He did, however, enable COMUSMACV to direct air strikes in Route Package 1 north of the DMZ. Further, CINCPAC approved Westmoreland's headquarters overseeing the Navy-Coast Guard anti-infiltration operation. Like Admiral Felt before them, Sharp and Moorer opposed the deployment of US ground troops to South Vietnam to fight the Viet Cong. They did, however, see the need to protect Danang from enemy attack, so they advocated what they thought would be a short-term deployment there of Marine combat troops. Soon, however, President Johnson decided that only US Army infantry divisions could salvage the situation in South Vietnam. The admirals dutifully complied with their marching orders from the commander in chief and prepared for what they knew would be a long, hard slog.

CHAPTER 4

COMMAND IN CRISIS

As Rolling Thunder got underway, Admiral Sharp continued to press the administration's case for the gradual application of force against North Vietnam. While the JCS briefly considered a twelve-week bombing campaign that would culminate in strikes on military sites in the heart of North Vietnam, Sharp supported a more limited focus on transportation targets south of the 20th parallel. On 4 April 1965, he concluded that the destruction of bridges there would not only degrade the enemy's transportation system but "demonstrate our strength of purpose [and] at the same time make support of the VC as onerous as possible."[1]

That same month, however, Sharp came to recognize that Washington would not give him the authority to employ the military power he considered essential to bending the will of North Vietnam. On the 20th, he attended a meeting in Honolulu with McNamara, Wheeler, Westmoreland, Taylor, McNaughton, and William Bundy. To the admiral's chagrin, McNamara suggested that Rolling Thunder had not and probably would not break Hanoi's will to resist. This conclusion was a tacit admission that the strategy Johnson and McNamara had pushed since early 1964 of pressuring North Vietnam into submission was doomed. Only years later did the former secretary of defense admit that he and his military leaders had "greatly underestimated Hanoi's determination, endurance, and ability to reinforce and expand Vietcong strength in the South."[2]

Hence, the chief promoter and executor of graduated escalation began to weaken that approach even as it struggled to get off the ground. McNamara said that the new US goal would be to deny a North Vietnamese victory through the full application of American combat power—but in South Vietnam. In June he told the other cabinet secretaries that since a traditional victory against North Vietnam was not possible, the object of US policy should be to achieve a "stalemate" that would convince the leaders in Hanoi that they could not win.[3]

From that point on, the requirement for aircraft, weapons, and ordnance to fight the air war in the South took precedence over Rolling Thunder. Sharp later labeled Johnson's and McNamara's change of strategy in spring 1965 as the "fateful decision" that led "to our ultimate loss of South Vietnam." Sharp complained that by giving top priority to the campaign in the South and not the North, "we were denying ourselves the advantage of our immensely superior firepower and technology, fighting a war with one hand tied behind our backs."[4] As late as 1995, Sharp held to the view that "we had the forces we needed to win [but] we weren't allowed to use them."[5]

McNamara's report to Johnson on the meeting in Honolulu concluded that everyone there agreed that the current tempo of operations in Rolling Thunder was "about right." Then and throughout the war, McNamara controlled the information he put before the president, and in this instance it was limited. McNamara's summarization did not accurately reflect Sharp's views. Indeed, the admiral later wrote that it was "in fact, a distortion of the view that I took at that conference."[6] Thomas L. Hughes, a State Department official at the time, remembered that in dealing with Vietnam issues, "the real-life effect of McNamara on the bureaucracy was regularly one of intimidation [and] hobbling if not silencing those in government."[7]

Despite his later complaints, in 1965 Sharp did not call for the overwhelming employment of US air resources against North Vietnam. General William W. Momyer, the Seventh Air Force commander, understood that Sharp preferred a more measured application of power. Sharp continued to believe that systematic air attacks on North Vietnam would eventually create "a feeling of helplessness among the military and general frustration, anxiety, and fear among the people" that would continue until they finally decided to "leave their cousins" in South Vietnam in peace. He expressed guarded optimism that the bombing of North Vietnam was having the desired effect.[8] His statement reminds one of the common wisdom during World War II that city-leveling strategic bombing would bring the German people to their knees when in fact the civilian population endured the aerial hell and supported their troops to the end.

With justification, Johnson, McNamara, and their civilian advisors grew increasingly pessimistic about the prospects of the direct campaign against North Vietnam that had not only failed to deter Hanoi but also prompted robust support from the Sino-Soviet bloc. They doubted that they could achieve either a quick or a cheap victory against Hanoi. Johnson and McNamara began to place their hopes on diplomacy to resolve the conflict on terms favorable to the United States. In late July, McNamara advised the president that Rolling Thunder could be a useful and cost-effective tool for promoting negotiations with Hanoi and without risking war with China or the Soviet Union.[9]

Throughout the spring and summer, the JCS called for a major assault on North Vietnam to include mining of the nation's ports, interdiction of the rail and road connections to China, the destruction of POL (petroleum, oil, lubricants) storage sites, and the neutralization of military airfields.[10] Johnson rejected these recommendations, observing that interdiction of the Ho Chi Minh Trail and defeat of the enemy by US ground forces in South Vietnam stood the best chance of bringing success. Indeed, on 28 July the president announced the immediate deployment to South Vietnam of 50,000 US troops, an expeditionary force that would grow to more than 543,000 by May 1968.

During the same period, Sharp worked to accommodate the divergent views of Army General Wheeler and Air Force General McConnell. The JCS chairman wanted the focus of air operations to be on the interdiction of troops and supplies headed for South Vietnam. The Air Force chief pressed for more robust attacks on North Vietnam's industry and economy. Sharp supported both measures, believing that Rolling Thunder could hurt North Vietnam's domestic capacity for war and the nation's ability to support the Viet Cong. In August 1965, Sharp reported to Washington that even though the Rolling Thunder resources given to him had been limited, the campaign was succeeding and "we are on the threshold of realizing the full impact of a cumulative effect." Still, he warned his correspondents not to expect immediate or spectacular results, since "it is a campaign of pressure."[11] The admiral was beginning to enter the realm of wishful thinking.

Sharp continued energetically lobbying Washington for authority to increase military pressure. It was hardly surprising when the naval officer suggested using Seventh Fleet warships to bombard coastal targets and sink coastal vessels. McNamara repeatedly denied Sharp's requests to unleash the cruisers and destroyers of the fleet against targets on the enemy coast. In May 1966, CINCPAC correctly argued that the Navy's warships could hit targets ashore when bad weather and darkness limited the effectiveness of aircraft. He also reminded the Joint Chiefs that unlike aircraft, the ships would not have to contend with strong enemy defenses. The JCS endorsed Sharp's proposal, suggesting that naval bombardment could be a valuable adjunct to the bombing campaign. McNamara did not reply to the Joint Chiefs and CINCPAC even after Wheeler on several occasions personally raised the issue with the defense secretary.

In October, McNamara finally authorized naval gunfire attacks, in Operation Sea Dragon, against boats moving war supplies south along the coast of North Vietnam's panhandle. To Sharp's dismay, however, the defense secretary prohibited the bombardment of targets ashore, even against supply-laden boats that had grounded themselves on the beach to avoid interception at sea. On another occasion, Sharp learned from intelligence that North Vietnamese heavy artillery and antiaircraft guns emplaced in the northern portion of the DMZ and just to the north of it were bombarding allied troops and shooting down planes in South Vietnam. Sharp and Westmoreland urgently requested authority to launch artillery and naval gunfire attacks on those threatening sites. The JCS endorsed the request but had to report back to them that McNamara had not "favorably considered" the recommendation.[12]

In December, the JCS again asked McNamara for a ruling on the May request for the use of naval bombardment against military targets in southern North Vietnam. To buttress their case, the chiefs reported that between October and December just two destroyers had severely limited the enemy's use of the sea between the 17th and 18th parallels. The two warships had sunk 382 coastal craft and damaged 285 others, and in self-defense destroyed a number of enemy shore batteries. The naval operation also had the benefit of compelling the North Vietnamese to divert forces to coastal defense. In January 1967, General Krulak, the commander of Fleet Marine Force, Pacific, also pressed McNamara to authorize strikes against all enemy military targets on the coast in range of the Navy's guns. With the approval in February 1967 of Rolling Thunder 54, Johnson and McNamara finally allowed the Sea Dragon force to operate as far north as the 20th parallel and

Sharp and General William C. Westmoreland, Commander US Military Assistance Command, Vietnam (MACV), confer in September 1965. Sharp, Westmoreland's superior in the chain of command, complained when Washington bypassed the admiral to deal directly with the general. NWC Sharp Collection MSC 247.

to hit targets ashore as well as to continue interdicting coastal traffic. Nonetheless, for the remainder of Rolling Thunder, neither Sharp nor anyone else in the chain of command could persuade the administration to open up the entire North Vietnamese coastline to the powerful naval gunfire of the Seventh Fleet.[13]

McNamara's—and by extension Johnson's—reluctance to unleash the fleet against the enemy coast reflected their debilitating hesitance to take even reasonable measures against North Vietnam for fear of antagonizing the Sino-Soviet bloc. It also revealed their abysmal lack of understanding of the military capabilities of the forces under their command. And finally, it showed that they did not trust the professionalism and combat experience of their military subordinates.

Sharp increasingly recognized that Rolling Thunder was only moving forward "with the "rapidity of a tortoise," but he did not give up working to improve the bombing operation and indeed sang its praises when others saw only gradual failure. Having personally tied his professional star to the air campaign, he did not request reassignment or retirement even though, as he said, "One had the feeling of being in Lewis Carroll's Wonderland—totally unrealistic."[14] Moreover, Washington had charged Sharp with executing Rolling Thunder, and as a military leader he tried to accomplish the mission assigned him to the best of his ability.

A gulf began to develop between Johnson and McNamara and their top military commander in the Pacific, however. Once the president gave primacy to the ground war in South Vietnam, he frequently bypassed CINCPAC and communicated directly with Westmoreland. Johnson's main interest in Rolling Thunder was to keep it tightly controlled, lest the admirals and generals trigger Chinese or Soviet intervention, torpedo diplomatic initiatives underway, inflame international opinion, or worse yet stoke growing anti-war sentiment in the United States that would threaten his domestic programs and indeed his presidency.[15]

THE CIVIL-MILITARY DIVIDE

Johnson ran the air war from Washington, more than 8,000 miles from Vietnam. His biographer remembered that "in Johnson's view, limited bombing was seduction, not rape, and seduction was controllable, even reversible."[16] No previous commander in chief had so involved himself in operational approaches, target selection, and tactics. Johnson later observed, "I spent ten hours a day worrying about all this, picking targets one by one."[17] Every Tuesday, the president gathered around him for lunch at the White House his "brain trust" that included McNamara, Secretary of State Dean Rusk, and National Security Advisor McGeorge Bundy (until Walt Rostow replaced him). Oley Sharp criticized the Tuesday lunch meetings as a "fine example of carrying strategic direction of the armed forces to an extreme of informality."[18] Even McNamara admitted that Johnson's method of operations was "a major factor contributing to the deficiencies . . . of the administration's management of the war."[19]

Given the nature of the gathering, the discussion routinely focused on tactical rather than strategic matters, and these men had much more on their plates than Vietnam. During Rolling Thunder, Johnson and his national security team had to deal with the Dominican Republic intervention of 1965, a military coup that same year in Indonesia, the

Arab-Israeli Six-Day War of 1967, and North Korea's seizure of the US intelligence ship *Pueblo* (AGER-2) in January 1968. The ongoing Cold War with the Soviet Union, the nuclear arms buildup, and similar issues consumed much of Johnson's and McNamara's time and attention. Moreover, Johnson's frequent stays away from Washington, primarily at his ranch in Texas, lessened the effectiveness of the Tuesday lunch meetings. Astonishingly, only late in the game—in October 1967— did Johnson invite a military representative, the Chairman of the Joint Chiefs of Staff, to attend the Tuesday meeting, or other key gatherings related to Rolling Thunder. Sharp later observed that the omission was a "flagrant example of his persistent refusal to accept the civilian-military partnership in the conduct of our military operations."[20]

One reason for Johnson's distance from his military leaders was that he considered them one-dimensional. He complained that "all the military chiefs did was come in every morning and tell him, 'Bomb, bomb, bomb,' and then come back in the afternoon and tell him again, 'Bomb, bomb, bomb.'"[21] Johnson later suggested that "it's hard to be a military hero without a war." He surmised that "heroes need battles and bombs and bullets in order to be heroic." He revealed that that was "why I am suspicious of the military [because] they're always so narrow in their appraisal of everything." He added, "I made sure that I had more control over the generals than any other civilian President in history." Apparently, he "knew what the generals wanted [which was] to bomb the hell out of North Vietnam."[22]

McNamara held similar views of the military. Captain Elmo Zumwalt, then working for Navy secretary Nitze, had a personal reason for disliking the defense secretary. On one occasion, McNamara summoned the naval officer to his office to gather information for a message to the Atlantic Fleet commander and then rattled off a list of things he wanted in the communication. When McNamara realized Zumwalt had written nothing down he threw a tablet of paper and a pencil at the naval officer, who, "furious," let the writing materials remain on the floor but continued memorizing McNamara's verbal instructions. Nitze later remarked that McNamara told him that if Zumwalt "missed a single point, fire him." Zumwalt, however, recognized by some for his ability to retain complex data, related that he did not fail to remember the information precisely.[23]

Supremely confident in his mastery of national strategy and defense policy, McNamara was in essence the US military's representative at the

White House. In that capacity, however, he was subject to Johnson's notorious persona. Bud Zumwalt remembered that in Johnson you had "a powerful President, a vindictive President, a President who could break people and throw them away in the blink of an eye, and a President who intended to be reelected." McNamara was under great pressure to comply with the wishes of his boss.[24]

The year before, McNamara had persuaded Johnson to appoint Wheeler, a sharp but much less forceful or intellectually gifted leader than Maxwell Taylor, as chairman of the JCS. Wheeler typified the officers who filled that billet during the period. The men who served on the Joint Chiefs during the 1960s lacked the towering stature of their predecessors: George C. Marshall, Ernest J. King, Henry "Hap" Arnold, and the other iconic leaders of World War II. Wheeler had the statutory authority to present the views of the JCS directly to the president, but he surrendered that responsibility to McNamara. In contrast to the JCS, the Office of the Secretary of Defense (OSD) then held the power and largely determined the military budget. The service chiefs on the JCS had to fight with McNamara for their aircraft carriers, bombers, and armored fighting vehicles. Zumwalt related that by the time he achieved flag rank, the OSD rather than the Joint Staff established the policies.[25]

Wheeler had the onerous task of presenting the often divergent views of the JCS members about the Vietnam situation to a strong-willed secretary of defense and an equally strong-willed president, neither of whom easily accepted advice from the chiefs of the armed services. Tom Moorer, who liked the man, thought that Wheeler went along with the measures taken by Johnson and McNamara although the general "knew they were wrong . . . or not the correct ones to take, [but that] he was more or less carried along with the tide."[26] Moorer maintained that by the end of Wheeler's term as JCS chairman, the chiefs "were blue in the face" from proposing actions that were never taken. The admiral recalled that when he relieved Wheeler as chairman, "I went below [in the Pentagon] to see him, and I never will forget it. He was sitting at his desk . . . with his face in his hands. When I walked in, he looked up and saw me and said, 'you will never survive' [in the job]."[27]

During Senate hearings on the air war in North Vietnam in August 1967, the testimony of Admiral Sharp and his subordinate commanders made it clear that Johnson and his civilian advisors routinely disregarded their counsel. Wheeler, however, testified that all was well between the civilian and military leaders of the defense department. Despite Wheeler's support for his boss during the hearings, McNamara later implied that Wheeler was unable to handle the stress of his job as evidenced by a heart attack that killed him.[28]

McNamara was able to dominate an equally unremarkable Chief of Naval Operations. The defense secretary replaced Anderson with McDonald, whom McNamara thought would be much more pliable than his predecessor. McDonald later admitted, "I didn't want the job; never had wanted it, didn't want it then." He would have preferred a "sunset" assignment in London because "life was nice over there."[29] Nonetheless, McDonald accepted the appointment. Zumwalt recalled that McDonald enthusiastically embraced the concept of civilian authority over the military. James L. Holloway III, then a Pentagon staff officer, was much less charitable. Even though Jim Holloway was, like McDonald, a naval aviator, he related that he had "zero admiration" for the man. "He'd never done anything, in my book, that qualified him to lead troops in battle, whether the battle was in the Pentagon or not." Holloway remembered one Pentagon meeting with McDonald that related to unit deployments. McDonald suggested that "if that's what SECDEF wants, that's what SECDEF gets. I don't want to make it rough for him. I said when I took this job I didn't want to [do] something that would get me fired like [Admiral Anderson] was."[30]

Earlier, when a majority of the members of the JCS wanted a non-naval officer to replace Don Felt as CINCPAC, McDonald had pleaded with McNamara to continue filling the position with a Navy flag officer. McNamara sided with McDonald on this and other issues of importance to the Navy. McDonald later told Tom Moorer that one of his primary objectives as CNO was to make sure the Navy kept fifteen carriers in the fleet. To meet that goal, McDonald needed the support of not only McNamara but also Johnson. During a meeting with the president at his Texas ranch, Johnson, well known for his invasion of personal body space, put his arm around the admiral's shoulders and whispered to him, "Don't you worry too much about that [new] carrier, boy."[31] McDonald admitted that "these things made me sort of obligated to Mr. McNamara"—and, one might add, President Johnson.[32]

Later in the war, McNamara restored funding in the annual DOD budget for the construction of a nuclear aircraft carrier in order to secure the admiral's support for a Vietnam-related measure unpopular initially unimpressed with the POL option, but a CIA study persuaded him that such a campaign just might impede Hanoi's logistics effort. On April Fools' Day, President Johnson authorized CINCPAC to plan for strikes on seven POL storage areas, a cement plant, and four bridges in northeast North Vietnam.[50]

As happened throughout Rolling Thunder, however, external factors caused the president to draw back from strong measures. Political turmoil rocked South Vietnam throughout April. In May, international pressure for a bombing halt to stimulate peace negotiations again led Johnson to delay the POL strikes. Hopeful that the visit of an envoy of the Canadian government to Hanoi in June might bring about peace talks (it didn't), the president once again delayed authorization. Even when National Security Advisor Walt Rostow, CIA director William Raborn, and even McNamara pressed for the POL strikes, Johnson continued to delay a decision. Throughout the war, Johnson's management of the air war was characterized by ambivalence, tentativeness, and indecision. For once, however, the president decided to act. Mustin informed Sharp that he had not seen such an interest by the administration in aerial operations against North Vietnam since the Pierce Arrow retaliatory strike of August 1964.[51]

Johnson finally ordered the POL campaign to begin on 24 June. He made it clear that his object was not to destroy North Vietnam's war-making capacity but to compel the nation's leaders to negotiate peace. Afraid that the bombing in populated areas might kill civilians or trigger Soviet or Chinese complaint, Johnson demanded that the missions be mounted only by veteran air crews and on clear days to ensure bombing precision. Mustin sent a message to Sharp in which he explained that "we know [Johnson's instructions] are completely nauseous and tell you how to blow your nose, but they were prepared as a 'sacrifice' to obtain strike authority." Poor weather and a leak by *The Wall Street Journal* detailing the forthcoming operation caused another delay.[52]

On 29 June, after almost six months of Johnson administration vacillation and indecision, Sharp's Navy and Air Force squadrons struck their assigned targets. A force of twenty-eight planes from *Ranger* dropped their bombs on the Haiphong POL complex, which erupted in fire and smoke that rose to 20,000 feet. Simultaneously, *Constellation* planes sought out other POL facilities on the Don Son Peninsula southeast of the port. On 1 July, other carriers executed devastating strikes against fuel storage sites at Dong Nham and Bac Giang in the Red River Delta. As part of the POL campaign, American aircraft executed their heaviest raids against the enemy on 25 August, flying 146 sorties with no losses. In succeeding months, the US air forces completed as many as 173 bombing missions over North Vietnam in a single day. By September, North Vietnam's major above-ground POL storage facilities had been largely destroyed.[53]

It was too late. Recognizing that their POL storage areas were at risk, during the first half of 1966 the North Vietnamese began storing more and more of their POL in 55-gallon drums and spreading their stocks in small concentrations throughout the country. As usual, the president further vitiated the military operation when he disapproved strikes on the storage facilities near Kep and Phuc Yen airfields, home to some Soviet and Chinese military personnel. The POL storage there was thought to constitute two-thirds of North Vietnam's remaining capacity. Johnson and McNamara feared that strikes against these sites might induce China, even though in the throes of the Cultural Revolution, to take some irrational military action. Naturally, they might have considered that since Mao was focused on the domestic turmoil in China, he would not opt to start trouble on his southern border.[54]

Combat commanders soon recognized the futility of the POL campaign. Rear Admiral David C. Richardson, the Task Force 77 commander, remembered one occasion when an assigned target consisted of dispersed and buried oil drums heavily defended by SAMs and antiaircraft guns. He knew that "we would have consumed more fuel in half the strike group than we could possibly have destroyed if every drum had been full and we'd hit every drum, and there was also the danger [from the air defenses]. The risk-to-reward danger was cockeyed." Richardson protested to Sharp, who recognized the absurdity of the situation and scrubbed the mission. It had also become clear to Sharp that with dispersal of the POL stocks and continuing imports, the fuel shortage would not seriously impede Hanoi's war effort nor appreciably diminish supply traffic down the Ho Chi Minh Trail.[55]

McNamara was especially disappointed by the results of the POL campaign and took to heart the conclusion of a Defense Department-sponsored JASON Summer Study Group that Rolling Thunder would fail. Having already undermined the graduated escalation approach that he had championed since the Kennedy administration, McNamara turned completely against the campaign in North Vietnam. Instead, he called for the construction of a barrier of mines, wire, and sensors, backed up by troops, along the southern border of the DMZ from the South China Sea to Laos. The intent, in conjunction with air operations against the Ho Chi Minh Trail, was to physically block the infiltration of North Vietnamese troops and supplies into South Vietnam.

Sharp and other military leaders greeted the proposal with skepticism and even derision. They complained that the operation would consign highly trained combat troops to static positions, require a massive building effort, and consume huge amounts of technological and other resources. The Air Force and Navy considered the measure "Maginot Line thinking," and the Marines were even more scathing in their opposition to the scheme. The "McNamara Wall"—or as Sharp referred to it, the "Edsel Line" (after a failed auto line of McNamara's former employer, the Ford Motor Company)—was never completed and had little effect on North Vietnamese infiltration into South Vietnam.[56] Mustin observed that, "despite all sorts of special priorities and gimmicks the whole thing fell apart like the dinosaurs from its own monstrosity."[57]

Sharp, the JCS, and Westmoreland continued to argue that widespread attacks on North Vietnam's major power plants, port facilities, and key locks and dams would drive home the point to the population that resistance to US power was futile. They suggested that similar attacks on hydroelectric plants and irrigation dams during the Korean War had made Pyongyang more willing to compromise at the Panmunjom cease-fire negotiations. To pacify the military, Johnson approved a select number of missions. Sharp's forces then hit several power plants and a steel factory. Reacting to international opinion that the strikes had torpedoed a prospective US–North Vietnamese meeting in Warsaw, in December Johnson again pared the target list.

Oley Sharp also became increasingly pessimistic about the efficacy of the aerial interdiction campaign in Laos and indeed recognized that his forces could only hinder, not stop, enemy movement south on the trail. In December 1966, Sharp exhorted his JCS colleagues to mount a stronger effort in Southeast Asia: "Let's roll up our sleeves and get on with the war. We have the power. I would like to have the authority to use it." He understood that McNamara would receive the message but he "did not expect a reply... nor did I receive one."[58] Frustrated by McNamara's delays in approving actions he recommended, on occasion Sharp employed an approach long known by naval leaders as UNODIR (unless otherwise directed). In essence, he told Washington that he intended to carry out an operation until told not to. Nonetheless, by then he could do little to effect a major change in the administration's strategic approach to the war.[59]

SHARP AND THE IN-COUNTRY WAR

In contrast to his laser-like focus on the air operations against North Vietnam, Admiral Sharp devoted much less time to the naval campaign in South Vietnam. These operations on the country's inland waterways are only briefly covered in the formerly classified 1,000-page CINCPAC command histories for 1967 and 1968.[60] US Navy leaders had long resisted the deployment of small boat forces to patrol the country's thousands of miles of navigable rivers and canals. They were equally leery about deploying naval units in support of Army ground operations.[61]

Nonetheless, in 1965 and 1966, Westmoreland's MACV command established the River Patrol Force and the Army-Navy Mobile Riverine Force (MRF). One former leader of the naval component of the MRF related that Army Chief of Staff Johnson "told me that he finally had to shame Admiral McDonald" into supporting creation of the unit.[62] Once established, however, the MRF proved to be a formidable fighting force, decimating large Viet Cong troop units during 1967 and liberating major population centers during the enemy's Tet Offensive of 1968.[63] Army Major General George C. O'Connor, who commanded the 9th Infantry Division during this period, related that the MRF "carried the war to the enemy in the Delta [and] major losses were inflicted on the enemy."[64] Ultimately, however, both Army and Navy leaders soured on the MRF mission and in 1968 and 1969 sent its 9th Infantry Division troops home and dispersed its naval units to various operational sectors in South Vietnam.[65]

Despite their successes, the River Patrol Force and the MRF quickly faded from Sharp's memory. The *Report on the War in Vietnam*, issued jointly by the admiral and Westmoreland in 1969, covered in detail the fights for Khe Sanh and Hue but made no mention of the MRF battles in the Mekong Delta. There is nothing on the MRF in Sharp's two-volume oral history or in his take on the war, *Strategy for Defeat*. Arthur Price, one-time commander of the River Patrol Force, several times after the war asked the retired CINCPAC for information on the Navy's in-country river operations. According to Price, Sharp "spent an hour and a half screening his records . . . and

Sharp is captured deep in thought at his headquarters in Hawaii. He grew increasingly frustrated with his inability to convince President Johnson and Secretary of Defense Robert McNamara that heavier bombing would turn the tide in the war. NWC Sharp Collection MSC 247 07-01-26.

he said he 'couldn't find a damn thing' that had to do with the river forces in the delta."⁶⁶

Oley Sharp took somewhat more interest in the amphibious actions conducted all along the coast of South Vietnam by the Navy's Amphibious Ready Group and the Marine Corps' Special Landing Force. The purpose of the ARG/SLF, which consisted of four or five amphibious ships and a Marine infantry battalion, a helicopter squadron, and supporting arms, was to operate as a ready reserve for Western Pacific-wide contingencies. The ARG/SLF was under the operational control of Commander Seventh Fleet, who reported to Commander in Chief, Pacific Fleet, Sharp's naval component commander. Sharp welcomed the opportunity to employ these forces in support of combat operations in South Vietnam. When General Lewis Walt, the III Marine Amphibious Force (MAF) commander, asked for the ARG/SLF as an offshore reserve during Operation Starlite, CINCPAC immediately approved the request. This operation in August 1965 brought about the decimation of the 1st Viet Cong Regiment and is considered the most successful coordinated amphibious operation of the war.⁶⁷

Sharp, during a visit to Vietnam, discusses combat operations with a Marine colonel, whose boss, General Lewis W. Walt, Commander III Marine Amphibious Force, appears behind them. Sharp worked to satisfy the operational needs of Marine, Army, Navy, and Air Force commands in South Vietnam. USMC A184867.

When it became clear in 1965 that President Johnson wanted US ground troops to directly engage the Viet Cong, Sharp gave the go-ahead for the employment of US Marines. In July, he approved the initiation of a series of amphibious strikes ashore to enhance the Market Time anti-infiltration patrol. In Operation Dagger Thrust, the ARG/SLF targeted Viet Cong concentrations along the central coast of South Vietnam until 2 October 1965, when CINCPAC ordered its termination. He dispatched the formation, his only strategic reserve force in the Western Pacific, to Indonesia in connection with the politically inspired violence then wracking that country. While the diversion caused heartburn for Westmoreland and some Marine leaders focused on the fight for Vietnam, Sharp acted with his Pacific-wide responsibilities in mind.

General Victor Krulak, then commander of the Fleet Marine Force, Pacific, concurred with Sharp's view that the ARG/SLF was not an "in-country" resource. Westmoreland, however, loathed going through the Navy to use the SLF. Indeed, the general considered amphibious landings in Vietnam as a continuation of his ground campaign. He called for and got a conference with naval leaders to hash out the command arrangements. The upshot of that meeting was that Sharp gave Westmoreland greater access to the amphibious planning process. He did not, however, surrender operational control of these Navy and Marine forces to MACV. Westmoreland remembered that the arrangement "worked out, but not entirely to the full satisfaction of all parties," especially himself.[68]

Despite the new arrangements, later Dagger Thrust raids proved as unproductive as the first. The Seventh Fleet commander, Roy Johnson, concluded that "the excessive time involved in planning and coordinating with the MACV levels resulted in completely stale intelligence." By the time he could launch an operation, the enemy had gotten wind of it and "had flown the coop."[69] Westmoreland too found that the amphibious operations rarely caught the enemy by surprise and were too costly in Marine lives and resources.

During planning for the March–April 1966 amphibious Operation Jackstay, which involved US and South Vietnamese ground, air, and naval forces targeting guerrilla units in the Rung Sat swamp southeast of Saigon, Westmoreland once again made a pitch for operational control of the units involved. Hyland, the Seventh Fleet commander, with Sharp's support, told the general that the command-and-control arrangements were in accord with well-established Navy-Marine Corps amphibious doctrine. Hyland, however, promised Westmoreland that the Navy would be responsive to his and his staff's advice and would end the operation whenever the general wished. While a showcase of multinational and multiservice cooperation, Jackstay ultimately consumed a lot of military resources for little operational gain. The experiment was not repeated.

During the remainder of 1966, the ARG/SLF spent most of its time deployed in northern I Corps. To assuage Westmoreland's fears about a possible enemy thrust from North Vietnam, Sharp reinforced the Navy-Marine floating reserve and deployed it to waters close to the DMZ. The ARG/SLF carried out twenty-four amphibious operations during that period in support of Army, Marine, and ARVN operations. In 1967, Sharp ordered the creation of a second ARG/SLF and an extended commitment to inland combat operations. Sharp partially accommodated the view of MACV and Marine generals ashore who "did not want troops floating off the coast when they could be 'in-country' [and] in combat."[70]

In December 1967, the command-and-control issue surfaced once again. That month, the enemy ambushed a battalion landing team of the SLF engaged in Operation Badger Tooth, killing forty-eight Marines and wounding another eighty-six. The presumed mishandling of the operation prompted renewed calls from MACV and a few Marine leaders for the SLF battalions to operate under MACV direction. Generals Krulak and III MAF commander Robert Cushman, however, argued that it was still necessary to maintain the independence of the afloat force.[71]

Oley Sharp also informed Westmoreland that the ability of the ARG/SLF to respond to theater-wide contingencies still warranted CINCPAC control of the naval force. Indeed, even then US leaders were considering an amphibious invasion of North Vietnam. Sharp, however, sympathized with the needs of Westmoreland and the Marine division commanders for troops, and considered permanently assigning one of the SLFs to III MAF and basing it ashore. The issue became moot in the wake of the Tet and post–Tet emergency in I Corps when the Marine battalions of both SLFs operated continuously as part of III MAF. But just before Sharp's relief as CINCPAC, the admiral, with the support of General Creighton Abrams, Westmoreland's successor, ordered reconstitution of the force offshore. North Korea's seizure of the *Pueblo* in January 1968 had once again emphasized CINCPAC's need for a theater reserve force. Hence, throughout his tour as CINCPAC, Sharp kept his eye on his Pacific-wide commitments but also worked to provide the Army and Marine troops ashore with essential ground combat support from the sea.[72]

Sharp also opposed the efforts of Westmoreland and his Air Force subordinates to gain direct control of Navy aircraft carriers and shore-based Marine squadrons. COMUSMACV and General William W. 'Spike" Momyer, the strong-willed Seventh Air Force commander, were especially keen in late 1967 and early 1968 to take charge of the III Marine Amphibious Force's air operations. Marine leaders expressed outrage at what they considered a power grab by the Air Force in general and Momyer in particular. Discussions between Marine and Air Force leaders on occasion resulted in "verbal fists flying."[73]

Since the early twentieth century, the Marine Corps had considered its air component an essential part of the "air-ground team," which entailed Marine aircraft directly supporting the operations of Marine infantrymen. That system functioned with great success throughout

World War II and the Korean War, and many Marines considered the combination sacrosanct. With its independent fleet of aircraft carriers, the Navy naturally supported that position as well. Since establishment of the US Air Force in 1947, its leaders and theorists had enunciated an air power doctrine that suggested all the military's aircraft should be centrally controlled and directed by one of its officers. The Air Force eventually gained responsibility for close air support by fixed-wing aircraft of US Army troops in combat. But the air power control issue had especially dogged interservice relations during the war in Korea and in the early years of the Vietnam conflict.

Observers considered the message from Westmoreland to General Cushman, then the III MAF commander, regarding MACV's control of air power as a trial balloon. It immediately drew heated opposition from the Marines, and Sharp reportedly "blew it out of the sky."[74] CINCPAC reiterated that he, not Westmoreland, would decide who exercised operational control of the Marine air assets. At one point, Krulak told fellow Marine flag officers that "we have a CINCPAC to thank for putting his foot down and saying, 'No, the Marines fight as a team. I will not see them broken up.'"[75] Marine leaders feared that breaking up the air-ground team might endanger the service's identification with amphibious warfare and indeed "the future of the Corps itself."[76]

Oley Sharp, however, was a practical, undogmatic, and joint-minded leader. He was increasingly persuaded by Westmoreland's argument that the MACV command should be able to bring the full weight of US air power against the enemy in I Corps. The issue surfaced during discussions about the defense of Khe Sanh, a Marine-manned fortified base close to Laos and North Vietnam. President Johnson obsessed about the Marine deployment there, concerned that an enemy storming of the base would imperil the overall US effort in Southeast Asia. He feared a repeat of the Viet Minh seizure of the Dien Bien Phu redoubt in 1954 that doomed France's war effort in the First Indochina War. Sharp shared Johnson's anxiety, contending that the US loss of Khe Sanh would be a huge psychological victory for Hanoi. As a reflection of their concern for Khe Sanh, Sharp and Westmoreland directed their staffs to investigate the use of tactical nuclear weapons to defend the base, even though they understood that the president was then not prepared to take that step.[77]

The air control issue came to a head in March 1968, even though the military situation around Khe Sanh had by then improved somewhat.

At the same time, I Corps had become much less of a Marine preserve as additional Army divisions deployed there in the fight for Hue. Westmoreland was irritated with what he considered III MAF's parsimonious provision of Marine air support to Army units in combat. The general was so vexed that Marine leaders in I Corps were ignoring his directives to improve the situation that he "blew his top." He later observed that "that was the issue—the one issue—that arose during my service in Vietnam to prompt me to consider resigning."[78]

That same month, Westmoreland finally got CINCPAC's blessing with regard to "single management" of air power. Sharp decided that the general commanding forces in the combat theater should be listened to in a crisis situation. Sharp, however, insisted that both he and Westmoreland rule on Marine suggestions for improvements to the air support system that would ensue. In the short term, Westmoreland and his Air Force supporters had their way with single management of air power; Momyer would exercise "mission direction" (not quite full operational control) over US air assets. MACV and III MAF, however, worked out compromise solutions that accommodated both commands' requirements and enabled Marine leaders to continue directing Marine aviation in air support of Marine infantry units.[79]

Sharp, however, had to contend with top Marine and Navy leaders who did not support the single-manager decision. CNO Moorer agreed with the opposition of Marine commandant General Leonard F. Chapman to the idea. Hyland, the Pacific Fleet commander, worried that the decision would imperil continued Navy control not only of carrier operations but also those of the amphibious and naval gunfire support forces. Krulak, CINCPAC's subordinate, intimated to Sharp that "he could be in for trouble" with the Marines for supporting Westmoreland.[80]

Aware that the single-manager issue was far from settled, in May 1968 Sharp dispatched a team headed by his operations chief, Marine Brigadier General Homer G. Hutchinson Jr., on a fact-finding mission to Saigon. The resulting report concluded that the single-management system was not performing the way the Marines thought it should. Sharp's time in command was about to end, so he decided that the ever-contentious issue should be ruled on in Washington. Finally, on 15 May 1968, Deputy Secretary of Defense Nitze reaffirmed the earlier decision to centralize the direction of air support in South Vietnam under MACV. Sharp's successor at CINCPAC,

Admiral John S. McCain, blessed the single-management decision, as did Westmoreland's successor, Abrams. In a larger sense, the doctrinal principal of centralized control of air power, long espoused by the Air Force, had won the day and established a precedent for the future.[81] During Operation Desert Storm in 1991, for instance, Air Force General Charles A. Horner served as the "air boss," charged with directing the combat operations of Air Force, Navy, Marine, and allied aircraft.

Sharp's role in the single-management controversy demonstrated that he worked to carry out his CINCPAC duties in a nonpartisan, "purple-suit" manner, accommodating the differing viewpoints of his civilian and military superiors in Washington and his subordinates in theater. Westmoreland related that "although Navy oriented, 'Oley' Sharp eschewed parochialism and dealt fairly with all the services." The general added that "no commander could ever hope for greater support than I received from Admiral Sharp at CINCPAC."[82]

USS ENTERPRISE *JOINS THE BATTLE*

Captain James Lemuel Holloway III reinforced Rolling Thunder with the awesome combat power of his ship, *Enterprise* (CVAN-65), America's first nuclear-powered aircraft carrier, when he conned her into the waters off Vietnam in December 1965. It was no accident that the Navy chose Holloway, one of its most promising officers and a future Chief of Naval Operations, to lead its most modern and powerful warship into battle. Born in Charleston, South Carolina, on 23 February 1922, Jim Holloway soared academically at the Saint James School in Hagerstown, Maryland, and his four years there nourished in him a deep spiritual and moral ethos. He burnished his academic skills and won unmatched wrestling championships at the US Naval Academy, graduating in June 1942. He earned a bronze star for his combat exploits as a surface warfare officer at the pivotal Battle of Leyte Gulf in World War II and a Distinguished Flying Cross and three Air Medals as a naval aviator in the Korean War. Holloway turned in superior performances as the commanding officer of Attack Squadron 83 during the Lebanon and Quemoy-Matsu crises of 1958. He then served with distinction on the staff of the Deputy Chief of Naval Operations (Air Warfare) in the Pentagon.[83]

Holloway was the son of Jean Hagood Holloway and James L. Holloway Jr., the latter retiring as a four-star admiral in the postwar period after having served as the Navy's chief of personnel, superintendent of the US Naval Academy, and commander of US Naval Forces, Eastern Atlantic and Mediterranean. He also authored the Holloway Plan that led to the development of the post–World War II Naval Reserve Officers Training Corps (NROTC). While proud of his father's accomplishments, the future Chief of Naval Operations only briefly mentioned his father in his autobiographical *Aircraft Carriers at War* and in his oral history with the US Naval Institute. Indeed, the son elaborated on what was clearly a touchy issue, reminding readers that "there has often been a tacit presumption that my father was in a position to advance my career as I gained seniority in the Navy." The younger Holloway emphasized that, "on the contrary, as a retired officer he had little or no influence over his own future, much less mine."[84] Bud Zumwalt, Jim Holloway's classmate at the Naval Academy, later remarked that "a father's achievements can place an unfair burden on the boy." He suggested that Holloway, "although an outstanding naval officer who succeeded me as Chief of Naval Operations, always thought he was being compared to his dad."[85]

On 2 December 1965, soon after arriving off Vietnam, aircraft from *Enterprise*'s Carrier Air Wing 9 struck Viet Cong positions near Bien Hoa, South Vietnam. During 1965 and 1966, *Enterprise* and sixteen Navy carriers operated not only from Yankee Station in the Gulf of Tonkin but also temporarily from Dixie Station, located southeast of Cam Ranh Bay. One purpose of the latter carrier staging area was to enable air crews to get accustomed to the combat environment in the South before they operated in the more lethal skies over North Vietnam. Another purpose was to relieve operational pressure on the Air Force, then woefully short of airfields in South Vietnam. Air Force leaders griped that Sharp and Westmoreland gave higher priority to the construction of ports and supply depots than to their airfields.[86]

The 94,700-ton *Enterprise*, whose crew and air wing totaled more than 5,000 men, operated up to ninety aircraft grouped in two F-4B Phantom and four A-4C Skyhawk squadrons, as well as individual aerial tankers, photo reconnaissance and electronic countermeasures aircraft, and helicopters. During these early, heady days of the war, Jim Holloway expressed the supreme confidence common among America's warriors that their technologically advanced aircraft and weapons, veteran leaders, and thoroughly trained enlisted men would make short work of the

Captain James L. Holloway III served as the commanding officer of America's first nuclear-powered aircraft carrier, USS *Enterprise* (CVAN-75), during two tours off North Vietnam. NHHC NH 103853.

enemy. Holloway, who had commanded a fighter squadron in Korea, was especially gratified to learn how much more proficient the fleet had become since that war. He observed that "there was not the tremendous commitment in Korea that I saw in Vietnam . . . to get things done."[87]

While the Navy's combat leaders carried out their orders, the overly restrictive rules of engagement exacted a heavy toll. Sixty-seven Seventh Fleet squadron commanders, executive officers, and air wing commanders were killed in action or went missing during the war. Admiral Richardson, one-time commander of the fleet's Attack Carrier Striking Force, later observed bitterly that "their commander-in-chief's concern [was] far more for the civilians in the hostile country than for his own pilots."[88]

In addition to complicated rules of engagement, the air crews of *Enterprise* and the other carriers at Yankee Station had to contend with heavy weather over Indochina. Jim Holloway's ship arrived off North Vietnam during the annual winter monsoon that blanketed the country with thick clouds and blinding rain squalls. Holloway related that "the weather on that first cruise was terrible and . . . mission after mission was aborted."[89] Frequently, pilots had to switch their attack to an alternate site when the primary target was obscured by clouds. They were less well briefed on the enemy's air defenses there, however, so losses of crews and planes increased. Richardson related how poor weather helped negate a systematic bombing campaign. During late summer and early fall there would be seventeen to nineteen days when strike missions were possible, but during the winter monsoon from January to April, only two or three days free of heavy weather. He stressed that "the adverse impact of the weather . . . never registered in the thinking back in Washington."[90]

Even at this early stage of Rolling Thunder, Task Force 77 air crews complained about rules of engagement that limited their operational flexibility and increased their exposure to the enemy's air defenses. Holloway related that naval aviators were coming back to the ship and saying, "This is really screwy, Skipper. We went in and bombed a warehouse and I just bombed the thing last week."[91] The North Vietnamese knew that the American pilots had to approach targets along definite headings to avoid hospitals, churches, and other off-limits sites, so they set up their antiaircraft defenses accordingly. According to Holloway, to get to their targets the strike groups had to fly through "The Valley of Death."[92]

Holloway and his fellow combat leaders especially railed against McNamara's handling of air operations. The captain recalled one episode in which the secretary of defense was displeased with the results of a photo reconnaissance mission, so he said: "I'm taking charge here. I want this [mission] flown at 6,000 feet." When informed that the mountains in that area rose to 12,000 feet, the defense secretary suggested the plane fly at 6,000 feet above the mountains. Complying with orders, the plane returned with photos of nothing but clouds that apparently blanketed the target at 4,000 feet. When upbraided for the poor result, the carrier's mission planners explained to McNamara's staff that "you tell us what to do and we are carrying out your orders." They added, "We knew the clouds were there and we wondered, 'What the hell is going on?'"[93] Air crewmen returning home for Pentagon duty began referring to the bombing campaign as "Rolling Blunder."[94]

The way Jim Holloway handled his command responsibilities, despite sometimes inept direction from above, demonstrated his gifts as a leader. On 23 December 1966, he was ordered by Commander Task Force 77 to launch a major strike against targets around Hanoi even though heavy weather was expected to obscure many of the sites. Enemy surface-to-air missiles filled the sky over Hanoi and shot down two *Enterprise* aircraft, resulting in the death of three men and the capture of another. Holloway's boss informed him that he understood that the weather was a problem, but "everyone up the line—Seventh Fleet, CinCPac, and Washington—wants those targets hit hard to show Hanoi we mean business." He ordered a restrike on Christmas Eve day. In briefing his air wing and squadron commanders, dejected after the failure of the earlier mission and the loss of their shipmates, Holloway did not blame his superiors for ordering an operation in such heavy weather. He appealed instead to his commanders' professionalism and dedication. He told them, "You are career naval officers and combat-experienced pilots" and reminded them that "this is not mission impossible." The strike went off as planned and without loss, and the air crews got to enjoy a stand-down on Christmas Day.[95]

When *Enterprise* returned to San Francisco in June 1966 after her first Vietnam tour, on hand to greet the first nuclear-powered aircraft carrier and her nuclear-trained commanding officer at the pier was Admiral Hyman G. Rickover, often referred to as the "Father of the Nuclear Navy." No individual was more responsible than the admiral, who served in uniform for almost thirty years, for the development of nuclear power and the safe operation of US nuclear-powered surface ships and submarines. He was also known Navy-wide as an unforgiving task master who would chew out or fire officers on the spot for failing to ensure the operational safety of their ships. When Holloway's ship docked, however, Rickover was ecstatic. Holloway later observed that he thought Rickover "felt beholden to me for having such a successful cruise."[96] Holloway recognized the reason for Rickover's elation: *Enterprise*'s successful combat tour had given the admiral's dream of a fleet of nuclear-powered aircraft carriers a big boost.

Admiral Moorer (right), then CNO, has just presented Rear Admiral Holloway with a second Legion of Merit award for his wartime command of *Enterprise*. On hand to witness the event was Admiral Hyman G. Rickover, who strongly supported Holloway's Navy career. NHHC 2017.11.02.

Jim Holloway's wife Dabney (Rawlings) Holloway was also on hand to welcome home her husband and the father of their daughters Lucy and Jane and son James L. Holloway IV.[97] Rickover proposed that the two naval officers confer privately over a steak dinner to discuss nuclear reactors. Rickover's civilian assistant, however, diplomatically suggested that the newly returned warrior might want to see his wife first. The legendary admiral understood. Before Holloway's return to Vietnam, Rickover paid several visits to *Enterprise* to satisfy himself that her commanding officer had the engineering and reactor departments ready for any Atomic Energy Commission inspection. He was not disappointed. One upshot of the experience was that Holloway had gained a powerful ally in Washington.[98]

Unlike many of his contemporaries, Jim Holloway recognized the benefits to the Navy and to his career of a positive relationship with the informational media. During construction of *Enterprise* and his combat command experience off Vietnam, he welcomed interest in his ship's activities by newspapers and reporters. He remembered the attention showered on the ship and her crew when *Enterprise* returned from the first tour. He observed that the three major San Francisco Bay area newspapers devoted their front pages to the ship's visit. The article beneath the *Oakland Tribune*'s lead story declared, "This nation's most powerful lady returned from the war today, her nuclear power churning her through Golden Gate as thousands of welcomers cheered her on." Holloway later observed that "I had my hands full" with the publicity generated by the *Enterprise*. He was called on frequently to receive the keys to area cities and to deliver lunchtime speeches at local clubs. The media in Hawaii covered the visit of 20,000 people to the ship, then en route to Vietnam for her next combat deployment in fall 1966.[99]

On 10 December 1966, *Enterprise*, now with combat-tested naval aviators and experienced flight-deck crewmen, rejoined Task Force 77 at Yankee Station. All-weather, day-night A-6 Intruder attack planes had replaced many of the less-capable A-4 Skyhawks, and many of the air wing's aircraft now carried advanced Sidewinder and Sparrow air-to-air missiles, flak-suppression weapons, and bombs. On the negative side, Jim Holloway found that the ship's officers and men complained about the seeming ineffectiveness of Rolling Thunder. He found that after two years of combat, his aircraft were hitting the same targets as before. The White House-established rules of engagement that unnecessarily exposed air crews to the enemy's most lethal defenses also remained in force. Navy and Air Force aircraft had to operate against the most sophisticated air defense system then in existence. North Vietnam boasted heavy concentrations of Soviet-supplied surface-to-air missile batteries, radar-guided antiaircraft artillery, and fighter aircraft. As in the previous deployment, heavy weather severely complicated air operations. Holloway remembered that persistent bad weather that stymied the air campaign frustrated all the levels of command, "from the White House to the flag officers at sea."[100]

Holloway recounted one particularly costly mission mounted by aircraft from *Enterprise* against a truck park south of Hanoi in May 1967. As soon as a quartet of A-6 Intruders and eight escorting F-4 Phantom fighters crossed the "beach" into North Vietnam, their warning systems alerted them to multiple surface-to-air missile launches. Soon afterward, the formation had to deal with North Vietnamese MiG interceptors. As the Intruders dove on the target, a barrage of SAMs came up at them, destroying one plane and forcing the two crewmen to eject. They spent the next six years in North Vietnam's infamous prison system. Damaged by enemy fire and flying low to avoid trailing MiGs, a Phantom smashed into the ground, killing the executive officer of Fighter Squadron 94 and his bombardier/navigator. By the time *Enterprise* completed her second tour at Yankee Station in June 1967, her air wing had carried out 11,470 combat sorties and delivered more than 14,000 tons of ordnance, at a cost of eighteen air crewmen and twenty planes.[101]

ROLLING THUNDER AT ITS ZENITH

By spring 1967, all of Johnson's chief civilian advisors had rejected the notion that Rolling Thunder would be able to break Hanoi's will or destroy its war-making capability. In his mea culpa book, *In Retrospect*, McNamara admitted that by then "our policy was failing."[102] During that same period, the domestic and international anti-war movement had become so widespread and vocal that Johnson had to pay attention. Hundreds of thousands of Americans demonstrated in the nation's major cities. In July, Johnson weighed three options: increase the bombing of the North; restrict it to the region below the 20th parallel; or keep it at the same level. The consummate compromiser, not wishing to further antagonize either his civilian or his military advisors or the anti-war movement, Johnson chose the third option—it satisfied no one.

By mid-1967, Johnson considered Oley Sharp antagonistic to his policies. The admiral, despite being repeatedly shot down, kept aggressively pressing the White House for authority to expand the target list. His actions clearly did not endear him to Johnson. Washington increasingly ignored or bypassed the Commander in Chief, Pacific. He later admitted that his "first-hand knowledge of . . . major strategy [reviews] was minimal at the time, since relatively little information filtered through to Honolulu."[103]

At one point, Johnson selected Westmoreland to serve as the senior US military representative at a meeting with America's Asian allies in Manila; Sharp was not invited. Even earlier, when Johnson and McNamara launched a secret "peace feeler" through Moscow, they restricted the information to generals Wheeler and Westmoreland, who were, unlike Sharp, thought to "appreciate the subtleties of the administration's position." Hence, Oley Sharp was left in the dark about information about US policy that would be discussed with the Soviets and the North Vietnamese. Lieutenant Henry Mustin, Vice Admiral Lloyd Mustin's son and Sharp's personal aide, related a remembrance of Admiral Moorer's. According to the CNO, the president "contemptuously and routinely referr[ed] to Sharp as *That Man*." Johnson would

Sharp conferring with the president. By 1968, Johnson considered his Pacific commander persona non grata at the White House and spoke of him with derision as "that man." NWC Sharp Collection MSC 247 06-01-54.

ask rhetorically, "What is *That Man* saying now?'" (original italics)[104] Gerald Miller suggested that Oley Sharp was "a perfect example of loss of authority." He observed that "Sharp couldn't even pick the targets. He couldn't map the strategy of the campaign. He couldn't do anything without reference not just to the office of the Secretary of Defense but the White House itself."[105]

Nor did Sharp's pointed and persistent complaints about administration policies sit well with McNamara. At a Saigon conference in July 1967, Sharp once again called for mining Haiphong and lifting most restrictions on bombing. Straining credulity, Sharp asserted that "the trend in the air war in the north was changing in our favor." McNamara showed his reaction by thanking Westmoreland for his briefing while ignoring the Pacific commander. No surprise, Wheeler told Sharp that McNamara said nothing to him because "he was furious [about] your presentation."[106] McNamara later identified the military leaders with whom he had served and admired including Army generals Taylor, Wheeler, Westmoreland, and Andrew Goodpaster; Marine general David Shoup; and admirals Burke and McDonald. Sharp's name did not appear on his list. McNamara later denigrated the admiral, saying that Sharp had deliberately misled him over a US air strike that showered a Soviet freighter in Haiphong with shrapnel. With obvious bitterness, McNamara contended that "this was the only occasion during my seven years at the Defense Department that [he had been subject to] an outright lie by a military officer."[107] Whatever the merits of that case, it demonstrated McNamara's disdain for a combat-decorated military officer who had done his utmost to carry out his and Johnson's Vietnam policies.

Oley Sharp and other four-star military leaders appeared in August 1967 before the Senate Armed Services Committee, headed by Senator John C. Stennis (D) of Mississippi, to report on the air war in Vietnam. Johnson understood that the flag officers planned to vent their frustration about the heavy political controls on the bombing effort. He acted to lessen the thunder of his antagonists. On 9 August, the opening day of the hearings, the president authorized attacks on twenty-five formerly restricted targets (from a list of seventy recommended by CINCPAC and the JCS). McNamara instructed Sharp to inform the committee that targets proposed by CINCPAC had been approved.

In preparation for Sharp's testimony, his executive assistant, Captain Rembrandt C. Robinson (later killed in a helicopter accident in the Gulf of Tonkin) provided a sympathetic committee member, Democratic Senator Stuart Symington, with a follow-up question: "When were those strikes approved?" Sharp was pleased to respond under questioning that they had been under consideration for almost eighteen months. For the next two weeks, Sharp and other witnesses pilloried the administration's bombing policies, which became public record with release of the hearings' final report shortly afterward. Wheeler and the other Joint Chiefs did not reinforce Sharp's testimony and indeed avoided criticizing the administration.[108]

In his testimony, Sharp once again advocated the mining of North Vietnam's ports and the relaxation of restrictions on some targets. He observed, "We had begun to hurt the enemy in his home territory . . . and he was suffering painful military, economic, and psychological strains."[109] At the same time, neither CINCPAC nor the other senior military leaders who spoke recommended an all-out attack on North Vietnam, in contrast to their postwar assertions. For instance, Sharp and Air Force General McConnell nixed the idea of employing B-52 bombers in the North because they considered them too vulnerable to the enemy's surface-to-air missiles and MiGs. The Linebacker strikes of late 1972 did, however, demonstrate that the heavy bomber fleet, while suffering losses, could and did penetrate the defenses around Hanoi to complete their missions.

Neither did they push for bombing the irrigation dams, dikes, and hydropower plants of the Red River Delta to flood the country's primary rice fields, even though McConnell testified that in neither World War II nor the Korean War "was there any attempt to preserve the agricultural base" if it was required to end the war.[110] Sharp continued to argue for stronger actions against the enemy but within the parameters of the Johnson administration's policy.

McNamara later remembered his own appearance as "one of the most stressful episodes of my life." Nonetheless, in his testimony the former Ford Company executive stonewalled or danced around the negative particulars of the bombing. Despite what was evident to everyone connected with Rolling Thunder since 1965, McNamara baldly stated that "no gulf existed between military and civilian officials over target selection." McNamara later admitted to former Secretary of State Dean Acheson that his testimony, as in many other instances, "was the truth, but not the whole truth."[111] His testimony also revealed that McNamara considered himself a master of military decision-making and implied that previous witnesses were not so well endowed. After three years of war, however, McNamara's credibility had been severely damaged. The Stennis committee's final report stressed that there were indeed sharp differences of opinion between the civilian and military witnesses. It also expressed regret that McNamara had "discounted the professional judgement of our best military experts and substituted civilian judgement in the details of target selection and the timing of strikes."[112]

Johnson's grudging act of opening up critical targets in North Vietnam to attack did not last. With the end of the Stennis hearings, he no longer needed to appease the military. Instead, he saw a glimmer of hope that Dr. Henry Kissinger, his representative sent on a secret mission to Paris, might be able to draw North Vietnamese representatives into negotiations. But the North Vietnamese, recognizing that their forces had the upper hand on the battlefield and that Johnson was desperate for a cessation of hostilities, closed that door once more.[113]

THE UNHAPPY LEADER

The military's influence with the president, such as it was, reached a high point in late fall 1967. The Joint Chiefs chairman then attended the Tuesday lunches at the White House on a routine basis. At the same time, Johnson recognized that he and McNamara no longer saw eye to eye on the major issues of the war and it was time for the latter to move on. Johnson hoped that some additional bombing might persuade the North Vietnamese to come to an understanding. The president's goal was to keep the military pressure on North Vietnam, but within clearly defined limits. He wanted to keep "hawks" in the Congress and among the public appeased as he tried to negotiate a cease-fire with Hanoi. Hence, while the president did not approve all twenty-four targets recommended by CINCPAC and the JCS on 16 December 1967, he did agree to ten. Johnson dismissed the conclusion of the JASON Summer Study Group's second report of the year—commissioned by McNamara—that there was little Rolling Thunder could do to affect Hanoi's will or significantly reduce infiltration.[114]

Unrealistically, Oley Sharp continued to see value in the bombing campaign. He still thought it possible to achieve the "widespread disruption and deterioration of the North Vietnamese economy."[115] Sharp argued that the enemy was paying an enormous cost in men and materials to supply the war in the South and that the interdiction program had delayed and weakened enemy offensive operations. CINCPAC persisted in saying that the full application of Rolling Thunder, along with continued progress on the ground in South Vietnam, would bring ultimate success to allied arms. That same month, Sharp was buoyed by positive reports from Westmoreland, who concluded that the North Vietnamese realized that they were losing the war. On 26 December, CINCPAC considered an enemy offensive early in the next year "remote."[116] In Sharp's 1967 year-end report, he predicted that "the enemy is no longer capable of a military victory."[117] In a *Reader's Digest* article published in spring 1969, he averred that the United States could have won the war by the end of 1967.[118]

Hanoi dangled the prospect of negotiations on 29 December when the North Vietnamese foreign minister announced that if the United States stopped the bombing campaign, talks could begin with Washington. Johnson once again took the bait. He responded by prohibiting strikes close to Hanoi and alluded to the possibility of negotiations in his State of the Union address on 3 January 1968. Hanoi's true intentions became clear on the 30th and 31st of the month when 70,000 communist troops attacked thirty-six of South Vietnam's forty-four provincial capitals and the major cities of Saigon and Hue during the annual Tet holiday. US, South Vietnamese, and allied forces eventually retook every population center during succeeding months and inflicted terrible punishment on enemy forces, killing or capturing tens of thousands of combatants. Westmoreland, pressed by Wheeler, requested an additional 206,000 troops to secure what COMUSMACV considered a victory. Sharp too believed that the United States now had the upper hand and could win the war. Nonetheless, Sharp's endorsement of Westmoreland's request mattered little, since Washington once again bypassed CINCPAC in the debate over the troop increase. That request and the shock of Tet, which Johnson did not see as signs of success, convinced the president that his military advisors had misguided him on the true situation in Vietnam.[119]

The Tet Offensive broke the president's will. Exhausted by his daily exposure to "that bitch of a war," beset by the anti-war movement in the United States and abroad, and understanding that he would be unable to secure peace on favorable terms, Johnson was psychologically spent. One of the president's biographers has concluded that "Johnson came frighteningly close to clinical paranoia." Close observers reported Johnson being "irascible . . . suspicious [and] inconsistent." Despite Johnson's distaste for the war, Tom Moorer remembered that the president was obsessed with it.[120]

At a late March meeting of the "wise men" convened by Clark M. Clifford, who replaced McNamara as the secretary of defense on 1 March 1968, the conferees concluded that the war was unwinnable. Clifford and almost all the others at the meeting recommended an end to the bombing and US withdrawal from South Vietnam. Moorer later related that "Clifford just supported any kind of withdrawal, bombing cessation, or anything."[121] Bud Zumwalt suggested that Nitze "went to work on Clark Clifford and educated him" and converted him from the "hawkiest hawk in town" to an advocate for withdrawal.[122] Nitze, however, had a different take on Clifford, whom he believed had become "an absolute incontinent cut-and-runner" willing to compromise US interests with regard to the Soviet Union in order to end the bombing of North Vietnam.[123]

When anti-war candidate Eugene McCarthy almost beat Johnson in the Democratic primary in New Hampshire, and Robert Kennedy entered the race soon afterward, Johnson realized the bleakness of his political future. Secretary of State Rusk's suggestion to Johnson that he should declare a unilateral halt to Rolling Thunder promised a way out. On 31 March, in a televised address to the nation, Johnson announced not only an end to the Rolling Thunder campaign above the 19th parallel (Rolling Thunder continued in the constricted area south of that line until 31 October, when Johnson ended all bombing in North Vietnam) but also his withdrawal from the 1968 presidential race. The Joint Chiefs assented to Johnson's bombing cessation, concluding that it would not do serious harm to the US military situation in South Vietnam.[124] This pronouncement was a clear indication that even the military leaders in Washington had given up on Rolling Thunder. Moorer, the Navy's JCS member, later admitted that "I made a big mistake in agreeing to temporarily stopping the bombing." He suggested that even though the president had promised to resume the air attacks if Hanoi violated the bombing halt, he knew that Johnson would be gone from the White House by 20 January 1969, so he didn't have to back up his pledge.[125]

As he had been for some time, Sharp admitted that he was left in the dark about these discussions in March. He was caught "completely unaware of [the] major policy shift." He later vented his frustration: "The handwringers [now] had center stage; the anti-war elements were in full cry." He complained that "the most powerful country in the world did not have the willpower needed to meet the situation."[126]

From April to his retirement on 31 July, CINCPAC found himself in charge of a reduced military effort and with even less influence in Washington. Even though isolated in Hawaii and out of touch with developments in the United States and Vietnam, Sharp continued to press for unobtainable objectives. Rolling Thunder had dominated his life for three years, and he couldn't seem to let it go. He continued to advocate an air and naval offensive against North Vietnam, reasoning that "we now have a stronger position on the ground in South Vietnam than before the Tet offensive." He warned that if this advice were not heeded, "In the end we could lose at the conference table what the enemy could not take on the battlefield." Apparently unaware of or choosing to ignore the growing anti-war sentiment and desire for an end to the war being expressed by the leadership in Washington and many American citizens, Sharp lost sight of domestic and geopolitical realities. The admiral called for a major counteroffensive that he later believed "would have enabled us ... to win a military victory by the end of 1968."[127]

On Oley Sharp's last day in command, he once again pressed the JCS for a renewed bombing campaign against North Vietnam, but as had been the case for some time, Washington was not listening to its commander of the Pacific theater. He later characterized the era: "We were sitting back and allowing these bandits to do just as they pleased in South Vietnam . . . when we had aircraft carriers and airfields full of planes that could have gone up and blasted Hanoi and Haiphong wide open." He exclaimed that "it was the most asinine way to fight a war that could possibly be imagined."[128] Until his death on 12 December 2001, at the age of 95, the admiral spoke and published widely on how he believed Johnson, McNamara, and the other civilian leaders had lost the war in Vietnam.

Sharp found comfort with those Americans on the right of the political spectrum who lambasted the Johnson administration's strategic approach to the conflict. In April 1968, for instance, Arleigh Burke, Harry D. Felt, and other retired Army, Navy, and Air Force flag and general officers endorsed a report entitled "The Failure of Gradualism in Vietnam." Sharp agreed with these fellow officers that the graduated escalation approach was "bankrupt" and McNamara's "brainchild."[129] Indeed, Sharp and other military leaders increasingly attempted to shift blame for the failure of US policy in Southeast Asia to the civilian side of the US national security establishment. Tom Moorer later claimed that politicians made the decision to go to war in Vietnam.[130] He added that American servicemen "fought under the most severe restraints ever imposed [by the civilian leadership] on the members of the armed forces."[131]

The foreword to Sharp's *Strategy for Defeat*, written by the conservative journalist Hanson Baldwin, clearly reflected Sharp's views: "The blame for the lost war rests, not upon the men in uniform, but upon the civilian policy makers in Washington—those who evolved and developed the policies of gradualism, flexible response, off-again-on-again bombing, negotiated victory, and ultimately, one-arm-behind-the-back restraint, and scuttle-and-run."[132] This argument was also championed by Westmoreland's intelligence chief General Phillip B. Davidson in his book, *Vietnam at War*. He blamed the civilian officials in the defense and state departments for pushing a "no-win" concept on the military.[133] Richard Schreadley, a Charleston-based journalist and writer, concluded that "our political leadership never suffered from a lack of sound military advice, only from a lack of political will to follow it."[134] Even James R. Schlesinger, the defense secretary from 1977 to 1979, lamented that the military services

Sharp's post-retirement book *Strategy for Defeat* blamed the president and his civilian officials for mismanagement of the air war but excused himself and other military leaders for their equally flawed strategic and operational approaches.

were used as "a whipping boy for all the frustrations of Vietnam and all the idiocies committed by civilian leadership."[135]

Neither Sharp nor many of his military contemporaries accepted their major role in the development and execution of America's failed effort in Southeast Asia. They later denigrated flexible response, graduated escalation, military pressure, and the other political-military theories of the time. Yet, they had been strong proponents and early, eager executors of those strategic approaches.

Sharp was little different from the other American military and civilian leaders of the time. They exuded a supreme confidence in the military, diplomatic, and economic power of the United States and its ability to manage world events. Having helped fashion America's enormous contribution to victory in World War II and its dominance in the Cold War, they concluded that few international problems were beyond their scope. These men were convinced that in the nuclear age the United States had to be prepared to engage in less destructive and more focused "limited wars." Indeed, Sharp worked to moderate the calls by Air Force General Curtis LeMay and other leaders for the total devastation of North Vietnam. Sharp and other military leaders argued instead that through the flexible application and gradual increase of US military power, an adversary would ultimately have no alternative but to submit to American will. Paralleling this hubris, as it related to North Vietnam, was the almost universal assumption among American leaders that North Vietnam had neither the physical resources nor the will to oppose the United States. Moreover, they doubted that Hanoi's Soviet and Chinese allies would choose or be able to offset North Vietnam's supposed deficiencies.

There is no question, however, that the criticism by military leaders of their civilian superiors was richly deserved. The combat experience of Jim Holloway and the men of *Enterprise*, certainly not unique to that ship, revealed the dysfunctional nature of the Washington-directed air war. Lyndon Johnson proved to be an abysmal war leader and commander in chief who pursued inconsistent and ineffectual policies, micromanaged military operations, and failed to rally the country behind the war effort.[136] He placed inordinate faith in peace negotiations to resolve the Vietnam issue when North Vietnamese strength and US frustration in the combat arena boded ill for a settlement favorable to American interests. Johnson, McNamara, and their civilian subordinates compounded their ignorance of national security strategy and the operational arts by largely excluding Sharp, the JCS, and other experienced military leaders from their decision-making circles. Not only did the administration's action deny the civilians the military insight that so many of them lacked but it also discouraged initiative on the part of military leaders and staffs. Moreover, it bred resentment among the uniformed leaders that further destabilized the US approach and imperiled America's longstanding civil-military partnership.

Focusing primarily on the military mission, however, Sharp showed little understanding of the international and domestic complications that President Johnson and his administration had to deal with at the height of the conflict. The danger of full-scale Chinese intervention was real and could not be dismissed. Washington also had to weigh military actions in Southeast Asia against America's other global responsibilities and democratic values. The admiral, ensconced in his headquarters high above Pearl Harbor on the island of Oahu, increasingly failed to comprehend the vocal anti-war fervor of the demonstrators who frequently surrounded the White House and the Pentagon.

Sharp's displeasure with Washington's direction of the war can be traced to spring 1965, when Johnson made Rolling Thunder a secondary priority and placed his hopes for victory on the struggle in South Vietnam. Rolling Thunder had been Sharp's path to glory, and he and his campaign were being bypassed. The admiral's communications with his superiors became increasingly strident, personal, and ultimately unrealistic, given the course of the war. While there was much blame to go around, Washington associated Sharp with the ineffective bombing campaigns in North Vietnam and Laos.

Despite these real failings, Sharp demonstrated professional skill and balance executing his CINCPAC duties in the early, pivotal years of the war. The admiral never forgot that he had a Pacific-wide mission. His command faced heavily armed and antagonistic Soviet, Chinese, and North Korean forces across the DMZ in Korea, in the Strait of Taiwan, and throughout the region. Sharp husbanded those air and naval forces that might be called upon to uphold US interests outside of Southeast Asia. In that regard, he retained control of his Navy and Air Force components carrying out the air war against North Vietnam and the Seventh Fleet carriers, surface warships, and amphibious forces operating off South Vietnam.

At the same time, Sharp readily supported Westmoreland's need for combat support and displayed a positive capacity to compromise on key issues. He accommodated COMUSMACV's request for the control of air operations just north of the DMZ when the admiral established Route Package 1 as a MACV preserve. He gave Westmoreland great latitude in the employment of US naval forces within South Vietnam and along its coastline. Although steeped in naval doctrine established in World War II and Korea that the Navy and the Marine Corps should control their own air assets, he recognized the soundness of Westmoreland's requirement for "single management" of Marine and Air Force resources in the wake of the Tet Offensive. The practical, non-ideological flag officer displayed a balanced approach to the needs of the Army, Navy, Air Force, and Marine forces in his charge.

In short, Admiral Ulysses S. G. Sharp displayed both great strengths and great weaknesses as a leader of the US military forces fighting a complicated war during one of the most trying times in modern American history.

CHAPTER 5
NAVY TROUBLES

In August 1967, Admiral Thomas H. Moorer took the helm as the eighteenth Chief of Naval Operations, accepting responsibility for the well-being of the US Navy and its sailors. As the Navy member of the Joint Chiefs of Staff, he was also expected to provide military advice, through the chairman, to the secretary of defense and the president. The Vietnam War was only one of a number of concerns that he had to deal with as CNO. During the next three years, Moorer weighed in on many critical issues, including the Soviet Navy's growing power, the Six-Day War of 1967, and the US response to the Israeli attack on US spy ship *Liberty* (AGTR-5).[1]

Indeed, even as the Tet Offensive raged in South Vietnam during January 1968, North Korean aggression sparked a crisis that demanded Tom Moorer's attention. Kim Il-sung's navy attacked and seized the US spy ship *Pueblo* (AGER-2) and her crew in the Sea of Japan.[2] Ever the hard-bitten naval warrior, Moorer urged Johnson to threaten North Korea with war unless the communist government freed the ship and her sailors. With 500,000 men fighting in Vietnam and anti-war protests rocking the United States, however, Johnson did not heed that advice. He rightly concluded that the United States and the American people were ill-prepared and hardly eager for another conflict in Asia. In December 1968, the United States issued a statement admitting use of the ship to gather intelligence on North Korea. Only then did

An official portrait of Admiral Moorer, the Chief of Naval Operations, September 1967. The naval officer served during the war as commander of the Seventh Fleet, the Pacific and Atlantic fleets, head of the US Navy, and Chairman of the Joint Chiefs of Staff. NHHC KN-15045.

Pyongyang release the captain and eighty-one other surviving crewmen, all of whom had endured torture at the hands of their brutal captors.[3]

Moorer was unhappy not only with Johnson's capitulation to Kim Il-sung's regime but also with Navy secretary Paul Ignatius's failure to court-martial *Pueblo*'s skipper, Captain Lloyd Bucher. The admiral felt that Bucher should have battled the North Korean attacking forces and if need be gone down with his ship, despite the fact that she was virtually unarmed and her crew defenseless. Ignatius decided not to court-martial Bucher because he understood that many Americans believed that he had been made a scapegoat for the military's failure to protect the ship from attack.[4]

While global crises sometimes demanded Moorer's attention, his stewardship of the Navy was a full-time responsibility. A major issue he had to deal with was the obsolescence of the US fleet. In January 1969, the admiral testified before Congress that more than half of the ships in the Navy were twenty years old or older. During this period, the fleet declined from 900 to 760 active ships. In fiscal year 1970, the Navy suffered the biggest cut in its budget since the Korean War, receiving only $2.49 billion for new ship construction and repair. Moorer strongly opposed McNamara's plan to slash the budget for new ships, aircraft, weapons, and equipment not connected to the war. Nevertheless, McNamara carried out his severe reduction of the operating fleet. The CNO lamented that one reason the defense secretary took an axe to the Navy's budget was that "McNamara just didn't understand seapower or believe in it."[5]

The admiral resented the arrogance and inexperience of McNamara and his civilian deputies and believed that their view was, "If you didn't have a liberal arts degree, you were stupid." He concluded that McNamara was determined to "teach the admirals and the generals how to run their business." Tom Moorer remembered when McNamara went on board an aircraft carrier during the war and suggested how to fit more planes onto the flight deck. The admiral was briefly so down on his job during the McNamara reign that he once queried a trusted subordinate, Rear Admiral Jerome H. King Jr., if it "was appropriate for him to continue to be the CNO."[6]

One key issue that did not endear McNamara and Moorer to one another was the defense secretary's push for the Air Force and the Navy to accept the F-111 Aardvark as a first-line combat aircraft. A study overseen by Rear Admiral Zumwalt, then head of the Navy's Systems Analysis Office and a surface warfare officer, concluded that the F-111 was the best choice for a new combat aircraft.[7] The Navy's top admirals, including Moorer and Vice Admiral Thomas F. Connolly, and key members of Congress heatedly disagreed with those findings, considering the plane unsuitable for carrier operations. Tom Moorer characterized that fight with McNamara as a "first-class fiasco."[8] In that contretemps, Ignatius suggested that "the Navy was sure the enemy was McNamara and the Air Force."[9]

Thomas B. Hayward, a naval aviator and CNO from 1978 to 1982, considered the concept for the F-111 "a stupid one—classic McNamara, classic systems analysis." He stressed that the fight "cost the Navy a ton of money and cost the CNO [Anderson] his job."[10] Tom Moorer was sure that McNamara "wanted me to shut up and go along with the F-111." He emphasized, however, that he "wasn't frightened by them."[11] The congressional testimony of several prominent naval aviators, Tom Moorer's pledge to investigate development of a more suitable Navy plane (it later came on line as the hugely successful F-14 Tomcat fighter), and Ignatius's intercession with McNamara finally convinced the defense secretary to drop the issue. Despite McNamara's displeasure with Moorer, the admiral's steadfastness ultimately won the day.[12]

THE NEW NAVY TEAM

When Moorer became CNO, he realized that a key to his success would be his ability to work productively with the civilian leaders of the Navy. He soon established a good rapport with Paul Nitze, a legend in the national security establishment, who served during Moorer's term as secretary of the Navy and then deputy secretary of defense. Moorer was especially impressed with Nitze's firm grasp of national security and foreign policy considerations.[13] The two men were equally concerned about the growing threat from the Soviet Union's nuclear arsenal and its increasingly powerful navy. Moorer and Nitze's successor Ignatius also developed a positive working relationship. Ignatius was aware that Moorer was "an intensely conservative person and I wasn't, but we didn't let our differences get in the way" of their joint actions in support of the Navy.[14]

Conversely, Moorer considered Ignatius's successor John H. Chafee a disaster for the Navy because he thought the Rhode Islander too liberal and focused on social and political issues rather than the well-being of the naval service. Moorer also believed that Chafee felt "anyone older than he was an idiot." Even though Moorer knew that the secretary had served in combat on Guadalcanal and Okinawa during World War II, his championing of the progressive-thinking Zumwalt to be the next CNO did not endear him to Moorer.[15] Raymond Peet, who served in the Pentagon with both men, remembered that "it was like being between two tigers that are fighting." He stressed that "it's not a very good place to be."[16]

One of Moorer's star performers during his tour as CNO was Rear Admiral Jim Holloway, who proved to be a strong advocate for Moorer's favored aircraft carrier fleet.[17] Moorer understood that the catastrophic fires off North Vietnam on *Oriskany* and *Forrestal*, and Holloway's former ship *Enterprise* en route to Vietnam, put the future of the Navy's capital warship in jeopardy.[18] Critics pointed to the high-priced ships' vulnerability to operational accidents. The fires took the lives of 206 sailors, injured many more, destroyed scores of aircraft, and put *Forrestal* out of commission for seven months. Tom Moorer was also well aware of Holloway's impressive combat leadership of *Enterprise* at Yankee Station and strict adherence to shipboard safety on the nuclear-powered warship. The CNO tasked the up-and-coming naval aviator with managing a three-month study to resolve the carrier fire problem. Holloway, in charge of the Navy staff's Strike Warfare Division from 1967 to 1970, enthusiastically took up the challenge. His study recommended cost-effective measures to ensure the proper handling of fuel and explosives and to improve damage control practices. According to Holloway, Moorer was so pleased with the study that he immediately pushed implementation of the recommendations throughout the fleet.[19]

Not one to let an opportunity pass, the ambitious rear admiral seized on the success of the carrier study to recommend that Moorer establish a "Navy Carrier Program" under a single manager. No surprise, Jim Holloway considered himself the prime candidate to fill that billet. Moorer endorsed the proposal, but on the condition that Admiral Rickover agreed with it. Rickover had long recognized Holloway's stellar leadership qualities and deep understanding of nuclear technology and had mentored the young officer throughout his early career.[20] Moorer and Holloway, unlike many other naval officers, did not have major problems with the older, crankier admiral. Holloway knew that "Rickover was unpopular to the point of being despised," especially by old-school flag officers. He was conscious that the dislike of Rickover "extended to surface warfare officers, submariners, and aviators alike [that] translated into an animosity for the nuclear program itself."[21]

Tom Moorer reasoned that you had to emphasize the positive when you dealt with individuals like Rickover who could anger people. Moorer made up his mind when he became CNO that he "wasn't going to get into a big hassle" with him and he never did.[22] Holloway credited Moorer for recognizing Rickover's major contributions to the Navy and his renowned influence with Congress, because Rickover "was too valuable to needlessly antagonize."[23] For his part, Rickover thought Moorer was someone you could talk to, and according to one of his biographers, it was "an accolade he bestowed on few."[24] Already an enthusiastic backer of the hard-charging Holloway and wanting to streamline the bureaucratic process of carrier development and construction, Rickover readily concurred with many of the rear admiral's carrier improvement proposals.[25] Thereafter, any issue related to aircraft carriers was forwarded to Holloway, who became in essence the "carrier czar."[26]

One of Jim Holloway's first challenges was to respond to a campaign by Minnesota Democratic Senator Walter Mondale and others to cut the next defense budget by reducing the number of expensive nuclear-powered aircraft carriers. Holloway characterized these opponents of the big ships as "a group of liberal congressmen . . . and a determined cadre of systems analysts" in OSD who wanted to beef up the Air Force's air strike capability.[27] Counted among the opponents of more nuclear-powered carriers was the secretary of defense. Jim Holloway knew that McNamara had taken a hard stand against nuclear power and said "not only no but hell no." He didn't think the nuclear-powered carriers were cost-effective. Rickover, however, used a visit by McNamara to a nuclear facility to help change the secretary's mind. When McNamara asked if one 70,000-horsepower nuclear reactor (instead of the four required to drive *Enterprise*) could propel a carrier, Rickover said, "Oh yes, Sir. Yes, Sir." Holloway then convinced Moorer and the latter's Vice Chief of Naval Operations, Horacio Rivero, that a two-reactor propulsion plant could do the job. They so recommended that project to the defense secretary, who authorized a two-reactor carrier, commissioned in May 1975 as *Nimitz* (CVN-68), the first in her class. Holloway crowed that the arguments made by the Navy and the *Enterprise*'s performance in Vietnam gave McNamara reasons to change his mind.[28]

In April 1970, a joint congressional committee chaired by Senator Stennis and including former Air Force secretary Stuart Symington, Henry "Scoop" Jackson, Strom Thurmond, and other powerful senators and representatives held hearings focused on naval aviation. Moorer selected Holloway to serve as the Navy's principal witness and to present the Navy's case in favor of nuclear-powered carriers. Chafee, Moorer, Rickover, and General Wheeler buttressed Holloway's testimony. The upshot was that the committee, in a positive vote with only Symington abstaining, recommended continuation of the long-term carrier building program. Holloway considered the hearings a watershed moment. Never one to shy away from the spotlight, he considered his testimony as "a major factor in shaping today's carrier force" of *Nimitz*-class nuclear-powered carriers.[29]

Jim Holloway strongly believed in public relations as a tool for persuading members of Congress and the American public to support the construction of big-deck, nuclear-powered ships. His office, in consultation with Rickover and his staff, produced and distributed widely a booklet entitled *All the Questions You Had About Aircraft Carriers but Were Afraid to Ask*. Holloway related that the fact book was instrumental in solidifying support within the defense department and Congress for carrier authorization and funding. Indeed, he also grasped the importance of the Navy's Office of Legislative Affairs in providing legislators with positive information on the naval service. With that in mind, once he became CNO, Holloway ensured that Commander John McCain III, by then a returned POW and war hero, was assigned to the office, where he put in a first-rate performance.[30]

Holloway further burnished his reputation in the world of naval aviation by persuading Tom Moorer and later Bud Zumwalt to accept his idea that the air wing of each carrier should be tailored for the mission at hand. He argued in his "CV Concept" that Congress was unlikely to fund both attack aircraft carriers (CVAs) focused on strike operations and others devoted to antisubmarine warfare (CVSs). He suggested that all carriers be simply designated multipurpose aircraft carriers (CVs). Hence, carriers bombing targets in North Vietnam would operate with a wing heavy in fighter, attack, electronic, and intelligence aircraft and only a few for antisubmarine protection. Carriers deployed to the North Atlantic and Mediterranean, where the threat from Soviet submarines was greatest, would employ a wing strong in antisubmarine planes and a few fighters for air defense. Holloway capped his argument with the observation that "the dollar cost to prepare a CVA of the *Forrestal* class to operate an ASW-oriented air wing was $925,000 . . . as opposed to the price tag of about $500 million for a new CVS." Moorer was so impressed that, according to Holloway, he ordered execution of the proposal "on the spot." Zumwalt too expressed admiration for Holloway's innovative concept, which the Navy adopted.[31]

In short, as a staff officer in the Pentagon during the war, Jim Holloway gained well-deserved recognition for his efforts to institutionalize the Navy's carrier safety and damage control practices in the wake of the Vietnam-related carrier fires. Moreover, he significantly enhanced the efficiency and cost-effectiveness of the carrier force with his "CV Concept." Confident about Holloway's combat-tested expertise and bureaucratic skills, Moorer, Rickover, and other superiors considered him the carrier man on the Navy staff. With those mentors in the lead, he helped convince a dubious McNamara to support the continued construction of nuclear-powered carriers. Holloway clearly appreciated the value of publicity and favorable media coverage in support of projects he wanted endorsed by Congress, defense department officials, Navy leaders, and the public.

Like his classmate and future CNO Bud Zumwalt, Jim Holloway was no stranger to self-promotion and establishing useful connections to politically powerful individuals. Kent Lee, a longtime professional rival and no friend, suggested that Holloway "would find out which way the wind was blowing, and that's the way he'd go." Lee had to admit, however, that Holloway, like his father, had a golden tongue and was an impressive speaker. Lee recognized that to be successful in Washington, you had to have a "certain amount of political sophistication [and Holloway] had more than his share."[32]

QUALITY OF SERVICE

In addition to the challenge of bolstering the Navy's material strength, Tom Moorer focused on counteracting the growing disaffection in the ranks. When Paul Ignatius took the reins as secretary of the Navy one month after Moorer became CNO, he discovered that the Navy was the "slowest of the services to widen opportunities for black Americans."[33] Female, Hispanic, and other minority sailors increasingly protested about the harassment and discrimination they suffered in the naval service. Sailors of many different backgrounds also spoke against the Navy's participation in the unpopular war.[34]

In May 1968, with personnel troubles bubbling up in the Navy, sometimes related to differences between officers and sailors over grooming and clothing styles, CNO Moorer sent a personal letter to his commanders. He reaffirmed naval policy that permitted the wearing of sideburns, beards, and moustaches and suggested that commanding officers not attempt to regulate civilian clothing. The admiral, however, told his subordinates to refrain from announcing or highlighting the new policy, in essence giving commanders wide latitude in their interpretation of the directive. Many continued to set their own standards or disregarded the directive altogether.[35]

Concerned that the war and other issues were draining the Navy of key enlisted personnel, as early as 1964 Secretary of the Navy Nitze had established a task force to study sailor retention. One of the group's recommendations, published in SECNAV Notice 5420 of 14 February 1966, was to create a "Leading Chief Petty Officer of the Navy" billet that would facilitate direct dialogue between enlisted personnel and the Navy's top leadership. In response, on 13 January 1967, the Navy established the billet of Senior Enlisted Advisor of the Navy (soon changed to Master Chief Petty Officer of the Navy [MCPON]). A special board unanimously selected Master Chief Gunner's Mate Delbert D. Black as the first MCPON.[36] Nitze and his successor, Ignatius, as well as Congressman Mendel Rivers of South Carolina and other powerful members of the legislative branch, strongly supported the billet. According to Black, however, then-CNO McDonald was against the idea from the start. Some commanding officers and senior enlisted personnel also opposed the billet, seeing it as a threat to their authority. When Robert Nolan, head of the Fleet Reserve Association, asked Black "what the Navy was doing to help him get started," he responded that the Navy was not doing "a blessed thing." Nolan remembered that Black's office was "so small you had to step outside to change your mind."[37]

Unlike McDonald, Moorer strongly supported the new billet. The MCPON's main purpose was to provide enlisted sailors with a way to express to the CNO their grievances and suggestions for improvement. With Moorer's backing, Black also helped establish senior enlisted advisors at fleet and naval district headquarters and visited sailors in Vietnam and at naval stations around the world. Black worked hard to influence personnel policies such as designating career counselors for large ships; pushing for an increase in sea pay; and enabling sailors to keep civilian clothing on board their ships. As he informed Mobile Riverine Force sailors during a visit to the Mekong Delta, he was also working to ease "chicken regulations."[38]

Much as he supported these ideas, Moorer as CNO did not implement many of them. He rationalized that "people were too busy with the war [and] we were stretching our resources to the limit with our fleet commitments." He considered the issue a "matter of priorities." He and other leaders thought that the MCPON concept was "a good idea but the general attitude was, 'Don't bother me with it now.'"³⁹ Indeed, as Admiral Harry Train has astutely observed, Moorer "took what he inherited and made it better, but he wasn't a big innovator."⁴⁰

Dramatic changes in American society during the war influenced many sailors to leave the Navy, often after only one hitch. Tom Moorer remembered that "those were difficult times for the services." He related, "Sailors were unhappy and they were bitching." He recognized that "a sailor has to put up with hardships and sacrifices to be in the Navy [and] feels a lot better about doing that if the American public is supporting him." He had to admit that in the late 1960s, "that was not the case."⁴¹

Sailors knew that many young people like themselves were coming home from Vietnam in body bags. Between 1965 and 1968, there was nearly a ninefold increase in the number of American servicemen killed in Vietnam. They were also aware of the anti-war demonstrations, civil rights protests, and urban riots occurring throughout the nation. Propelling this social revolution were youths, many of whom disdained civilian or military authority and social conventions. In March 1969, Moorer convened a conference whose goal was to keep more sailors from leaving the service. The final report recommended increased educational opportunities, better housing and ship habitability, upgraded legal and medical services, and increasing sea pay by $15 a month. The admiral was especially proud of his support for the construction of the Navy Lodge at the Norfolk Naval Base that served sailors and their families.⁴²

Another manifestation of society's wartime dysfunction was the widespread abuse of drugs, especially in Southeast Asia. By the late 1960s, substance abuse in Vietnam began to upset the discipline and operational efficiency of the military. Investigators had to look into only forty-three cases of marijuana use in 1965 but more than 3,200 cases in 1968. A defense department task force established in November 1967 to investigate the issue documented increasing numbers of recruits disqualified for military service because of illicit drug use. In 1969, more than half of the soldiers leaving Vietnam reported having smoked marijuana during their year-long tour. Heroin overdoses increased from two a month in spring 1970 to two a day by fall of that year. Marine forces in Vietnam dealt with a marijuana problem "of epic proportions." In October 1970, the surgeon general of Army forces in Vietnam reported to Congress on a significant increase in the number of overdose deaths among soldiers in-country.[43]

General Creighton Abrams, who apparently had been unaware of the severity of the problem in his command, apologized to CINCPAC for not previously enlightening him on the issue. Indeed, many high-ranking officers appeared ignorant of the drug problem and doubted its impact on operational effectiveness. Even years later, Tom Moorer mistakenly asserted that drugs were not as much of a problem for the Navy as they were for the Army since "we didn't have too many sailors ashore [and] the confined life style on board ship doesn't lend itself to massive use of drugs."[44] That view was echoed by Admiral Hyland, in charge of the Pacific Fleet until July 1970, who "never thought it was terribly serious." He added that "it certainly was nothing to pay a lot of attention to [because] we didn't think we had an emergency on our hands."[45]

President Nixon demanded that the secretary of defense take immediate action to deal with the drug problem in the military. In spring 1970, defense secretary Melvin Laird set up a task force to suggest ways to deal with drug abusers in the services, including disciplinary action and drug education, prevention, and rehabilitation. That August, the task force recommended the establishment of an amnesty program for those service members who turned themselves in for treatment and rehabilitation. Those recommendations were formalized in an October defense department directive entitled "Illegal or Improper Use of Drugs."[46]

The upsurge in drug use also reflected a worldwide trend in the armed forces. In early 1971, Laird directed Moorer, by then JCS chairman, to look into reports of heroin use in Vietnam and, shortly afterward, the president ordered establishment of an interagency group to develop a drug prevention program. On 17 June, Nixon labeled drug abuse "America's public enemy number one." Navy secretary Chafee concluded that drug abuse in the Navy and Marine Corps was "out of control." No surprise, given Laird's focus on ending the war, that the defense secretary observed at a staff meeting that "the best way to handle the drug problem in Vietnam was to get the troops out of Vietnam." Nonetheless, the drug problem defied solution during the war and for many years afterward.[47]

Racial turmoil during the 1970s, stimulated by the war in Vietnam, caused additional problems for the armed services. Many white males secured deferments to attend college or for disabilities. Others enlisted in the Navy, the Air Force, the National Guard, and the Reserves to avoid fighting in the jungles of South Vietnam. Hence, the Army and Marine Corps had little choice but to draft men who were unemployed or had not been able to obtain significant education or technical skills. African Americans suffered disproportionately from these disadvantages. As a result, Blacks—who constituted less than 12 percent of the US population—accounted for 31 percent of all combat troops in Vietnam and suffered 24 percent of the casualties. Chronically short of the men needed to fill the ranks, McNamara instituted Project 100,000 that dramatically lowered enlistment standards. Almost half of the men brought into the services through that effort were poor, Black, high school dropouts, and some had come from dysfunctional backgrounds or had criminal records. The average inductee read at the 6.4 grade level.[48]

Compounding the problem, the civil rights and anti-war movements in the United States questioned the propriety of African Americans fighting in Vietnam when racism seriously troubled the society at home. The Black Power movement went further and denigrated their service. These influences increasingly prompted Black servicemen to greet other Blacks with Black Power salutes, engage in complex "dapping" handshakes, and congregate at clubs where whites were not welcome. Racial disturbances occurred with increasing frequency throughout the military.[49]

In August 1968, a race riot broke out at the military's Long Binh Jail (referred to by many GIs in "tribute" to the president as the LBJ) northeast of Saigon. Drugs were one of the proximate causes, but the riot "was not just about drugs. It was also a distinctly Black affair—the sum total of frustrations caused by the war, the draft, and a racially polarized military." The Long Binh Jail riot, according to one source, was "the most severe outbreak of racial unrest in the Army."[50] Throughout the last years of the Army's stay in Vietnam, racial turmoil continued to rock that service.

During 1968, racial fighting also broke out at Marine bases on Okinawa, at Camp Lejeune, North Carolina, and at the Marine air station at Kaneohe, Hawaii. Fights between Black and white Marines resulted in the death of one Marine and injury to sixteen others. The

Marine Corps identified 1,060 violent racial incidents in 1970 alone. In February of that year, at a club in Danang, a Black Marine lobbed two grenades into a crowd, killing one Marine and wounding sixteen others. The Air Force also did not escape racial turmoil. In May 1971, at Travis Air Force Base near San Francisco, 200 Black and white airmen fought it out, which led to the hospitalization of thirty men and the arrest of 135 others.[51]

Tom Moorer was hardly a social reformer, but he did take steps as CNO that reflected some understanding of the changes coursing through American society and the Navy. In May 1968, he established at predominantly Black Prairie View Agricultural and Mechanical College in Texas the first new Naval Reserve Officers Training Corps unit in twenty-two years. He also recommended that commanders establish race relations councils at their naval bases. This action contrasts with Zumwalt's later exaggerated contention that admirals Anderson, McDonald, and Moorer sought to maintain "a lily-white Navy." In his oral history, Zumwalt suggested that McDonald "had the old southern, traditional view of blacks [that] there are good niggers and bad niggers, but they were all niggers." Zumwalt added charitably that although McDonald was "not an unkind man, he clearly had the racist view, as did his successor, Tom Moorer."[52]

Discrimination against African Americans had truly limited their full or equitable integration into the Navy during the 1950s and 1960s. Laden with biases, many naval leaders doubted the ability of Black sailors to measure up in the service. Despite Wesley A. Brown in 1949 becoming the first African American to complete four years at the US Naval Academy, by 1968 only three dozen Black men had graduated from the institution. Many Black families considered the Navy as "the epitome of snobbery" because the service still assigned many Blacks to the Steward Branch to wait on white officers.[53] Admiral Charles Duncan remembered that when McNamara ordered Navy recruiting teams into big-city ghettos, they were pelted with stones. He recalled that many African Americans considered the Navy the "worst of the Services."[54] The Civil Rights Commission suggested that while the other services had made small but measured advances with regard to ending racial discrimination, the Navy had "shown little or no improvement" since President Truman's 1948 order desegregating the military. The number of Black officers in the Navy rose from 0.3 percent in 1965 to only 0.7 percent in 1970 and, by the latter date, only three Black captains served on active duty.⁵⁵ As one indication of the problem, Kent Lee later expressed his amazement about the Navy's social disruptions during the early 1970s, since "we had no problems with blacks or anyone else before the Zumwalt era."⁵⁶

Other naval leaders, however, had taken action earlier in the 1960s to improve the lot of racial and ethnic minorities. Zumwalt's mentor Secretary of the Navy Nitze had issued a "Manual on Equal Opportunity and Treatment of Military Personnel" in 1965, amended in February 1970. The latter document called for all commands to ensure "equal opportunity for career fulfillment of Negroes and other minorities" and the establishment of training and educational programs. The instruction, however, left it up to individual commands to enforce its provisions.⁵⁷

Tom Moorer was not unlike many Americans at that time who displayed prejudice toward minorities. On one occasion, for instance, Lyndon Johnson discussed with McNamara the potential impact of Project 100,000 on Blacks. He suggested that "we'll take this Nigra boy in Johnson City, Texas, and from Winder, Georgia, and we'll get rid of the tapeworms and get the ticks off of him, and teach him to get up at daylight and work till dark and shave and to bathe."⁵⁸ Vice Admiral William R. Smedberg III, who served as Chief of Naval Personnel early in the war, contended that "the colored man, basically, doesn't like the Navy. He doesn't like being at sea. He's afraid of the sea. Very few colored people could swim in those days, and they didn't like the water."⁵⁹

Moorer later exclaimed that "if you are going to be American, you've got to be an American. If you want to be a Greek, go to Greece. Or if you want to be a black, go to Africa."⁶⁰ Describing Black society in Miami, he suggested that "people are not going to hire little blacks when the Cubans will work." He contrasted Cubans with Blacks, reasoning that Cubans "won't be sassy, and they'll work twice as long, and they'll take a bath at least once a week." He regretted that "the politicians have destroyed the pride of the blacks [because] they've told them that nothing is their fault; it's because of the way they were treated; they weren't given a chance; they don't have equal opportunities. Nothing at all is their fault, and the government will correct all these things for you. Just sit and wait."⁶¹

Tom Moorer's views partly reflected the culture from which he hailed and his exposure in rural Alabama to the racial turmoil of the time. During the American Civil War, both of his grandfathers had fought for the Confederacy, whose ultimate goal was to preserve the institution of slavery. His mother was a devoted member of the United Daughters of the Confederacy. Post–World War I rural Alabama, where Moorer spent his youth, did not escape the racial troubles that rocked the nation during that turbulent period in American history. In the Naval Academy's yearbook, the *Lucky Bag*, Moorer was described as "a true Johnny Reb if ever there was one."[62]

The Navy's limited steps in the right direction did not prevent the outbreak of racial disturbances in July 1970 at the Navy's Great Lakes training center north of Chicago. Teams of Black and white personnel specialists dispatched to the base from Washington learned that there had been twenty-six race-related incidents at the facility during May, June, and early July alone. The teams also heard from hundreds of sailors in "gripe sessions" that all was not well at the base. Captain Draper L. Kauffman, Commandant of the 9th Naval District (which included the Great Lakes naval base) and the legendary father of the World War II underwater demolition teams, immediately established a program to improve race relations. His actions included creation of a committee made up of Black and white enlisted personnel; race relations seminars; the hiring of more Black hairstylists at the base exchange and Black entertainers at the enlisted club; a focus on Black issues in the base newspaper; and approval of the Afro hairstyle for Black sailors. Moreover, he put out the word that he would not allow white sailors and their families to stay in any accommodations that denied housing to minority sailors. Despite his actions and those limited measures taken by Admiral Moorer, the prospect then for improved race relations in the Navy can only be described as bleak.[63]

ON THE SIDELINES OF VIETNAM STRATEGY AND POLICY

Even as Tom Moorer coped with the Navy's myriad internal troubles, he attempted to exert influence as a member of the Joint Chiefs on the direction of the war.[64] He worked to learn as much as he could about the situation in Vietnam in order to support his deliberations with the other Joint Chiefs. What he learned firsthand from returning combat commanders was discouraging. Vice Admiral Richardson, who completed a tour in charge of the carriers at Yankee Station, told Moorer that "we simply are not winning." He lamented that the US air forces could not keep up with the enemy's increasingly lethal air defenses.[65] To gather information, Moorer also made trips to Vietnam. He met with generals Westmoreland and Abrams and visited hospitals, routinely filled with Navy and Marine casualties. He talked one on one with junior officers and enlisted sailors and Marines to learn how they were doing. On his return to the states, he made a point of contacting the families to let them know how their loved ones were faring. He especially valued the bravery and self-sacrifice of the men involved in the search-and-rescue effort. He thought it "one of the great stories of the Vietnam War, the heroics of these young people" who took great risks to rescue downed pilots.[66]

He also came away with a "very disturbed feeling" about the course of events. The fact that the infantry routinely had to fight to secure territory, abandon it, and then be compelled to return and fight for the same ground he likened pejoratively to "the ebb and flow of the tide." He sensed that the conflict was going to be a "long drawn-out affair." He was decidedly against trading an American "high school graduate . . . for one of those people" from North Vietnam.

There are numerous references in his oral history, written years after the war, that the solution to the war should have been an invasion of North Vietnam.[67] Nonetheless, even if he advanced that solution in JCS discussions it got no further, and his ideas did not seem to have had much of an impact. He considered information on the war that he received from McNamara and the White House superficial. The admiral is mentioned only once in the 250-page official JCS history or the era. Perhaps, for that reason, Tom Moorer did not relish his service on the JCS. He knew that the presidents and their secretaries of defense made the key decisions on the war.[68]

While relatively powerless to move Vietnam policy on the JCS, Moorer took one action to help influence Washington's strategic approach to the conflict. He worked to ensure that a Navy flag officer whose worldviews were similar to his would continue to lead the Pacific Command. At the end of July 1968, Admiral John S. McCain Jr., the son of a renowned World War II carrier admiral, relieved Sharp as CINCPAC. Later Navy secretary John Warner remembered that McCain's nickname was "Jumpin' Jack" because he was "a man of incredible energy." It hadn't been a foregone conclusion that the billet would be filled by McCain or even a naval officer. As always, the other services lobbied for the job. Oley Sharp recommended that McCain replace him. Given Johnson's antipathy toward Sharp, however, it was no wonder that the president considered other candidates.[69]

Moorer and the top South Vietnamese naval leader Rear Admiral Tran Van Chon inspect a unit of the Vietnam Navy. As CNO, Moorer worked to provide American sailors with the resources to fight on the jungled waterways of South Vietnam. NHHC NH 104889.

Moorer met with the president at the White House on an unrelated issue but used the opportunity to make the case for the Navy and for McCain. Johnson took the admiral aside and asked him, "Do you really think McCain should be CinCPac?" Tom Moorer assured the president that the admiral was the right man for the job. He later admitted, "I stacked the deck and I've never regretted it [because] I've never known anyone as loyal as Jack McCain was."[70] Another attendee, US Ambassador to South Vietnam Ellsworth Bunker, who had worked closely with McCain during the Dominican Republic crisis of 1965, enthusiastically seconded the nomination. According to Moorer, "Johnson went right upstairs and walked in the press room and announced McCain's appointment."[71]

McCain and Moorer clearly liked each other and shared many traits—reflexive anti-Communism, political and social conservatism, and a strong belief in duty, honor, country, and the Navy. Moorer later observed that during his term as JCS chairman, CINCPAC McCain "was a very loyal, energetic team player." Moorer tried his best to keep McCain in the loop with regard to Vietnam issues. Harry Train, then serving on Moorer's staff, believed that his boss and McCain did work especially well together. He remembered that "he'd get 15 to 20 phone calls a night, mostly from McCain."[72] Many observers remarked on their no-nonsense, fact-driven, and persuasive approaches to problem solving. While Tom Moorer exuded the aura of a ramrod-straight stately Southern gentleman, McCain took on the persona of a gruff, hard-drinking, hard-bitten combat leader. The short-statured and profane CINCPAC was rarely seen without a cigar in his hand or mouth. Henry Kissinger characterized the naval officer as a "doughty, crusty officer [who] could have passed in demeanor, appearance, pugnacity, and manner of speech for Popeye the Sailor Man."[73]

The fact that bombing operations he ordered against North Vietnam might have jeopardized McCain's son John, a Navy pilot shot down and imprisoned in Hanoi, never deterred him from his duty. Indeed, associates of McCain during those years remembered that he never brought up his son's plight and routinely changed the subject when it came up. Nonetheless, the admiral spent every Christmas for three years visiting with the Marines on the DMZ so he could be as close to his son as possible.[74]

Like Oley Sharp, McCain thought that after the Tet Offensive the war could still be won. He observed in a *Reader's Digest* interview that "we have the enemy licked now. He is beaten. The enemy cannot achieve a military victory."[75] His recommendations for stronger military action against the enemy, like Sharp's, did not win the day with his civilian superiors. According to one critic, McCain's constant communications to Washington asking for more resources were so predictable that his staff maintained one standard text and merely inserted a new date.[76] Kissinger remembered that McCain "fought for the victory that his instinct and upbringing demanded and that political reality forbade."[77]

McCain's admiring son suggested that his father was a competent and reliable leader but on occasion could be too outspoken and unpredictable. But unlike Sharp, McCain had a good relationship with his civilian superiors. Abrams and McCain also maintained a close connection "facilitated by their common penchant for cigar smoking and plain speaking." Nonetheless, Abrams, like other Army generals, considered the CINCPAC position an unnecessary link in the chain of command. Later in the war, Abrams suggested that MACV supplant CINCPAC in the control of air operations against the rail lines into North Vietnam from China. The idea never got beyond his friend and confidant Tom Moorer, then the JCS chairman.[78]

Tom Moorer's direction of the Navy as Chief of Naval Operations displayed his innate intelligence, deep understanding of the Navy and how it operated, and ability to win and keep allies. While frequently feuding with McNamara and the Whiz Kids, the admiral made it a point to improve civil-military relations and forged strong bonds with Navy secretaries Nitze and Ignatius. He was similarly successful in gaining the support of Admiral Rickover and key members of Congress for his programs. Moorer should also be credited for recognizing the talents of Jim Holloway and exploiting them to bring about the much-needed shipboard safety program, the more cost-effective employment of carrier aircraft and ships, and the debut of a new class of nuclear-powered carriers. He enthusiastically supported the mission of the new Master Chief Petty Officer of the Navy and inaugurated a number of measures to improve sailor retention, race relations, drug abuse, and other ills then besetting the Navy.

Nonetheless, the increasing cost of the war and its domestic consequences had a severe impact on the health of the Navy during Moorer's tenure. Despite his best efforts, Congress would not allocate sufficient funds for non-Vietnam-related new ship construction and repair. The fleet was in much worse shape in 1970 than it had been in 1967. The admiral was unable to significantly retard the worsening racial climate, increasing drug use, and disaffection of many sailors. Indeed, he was not fully aware of the seriousness of these problems. The war and the turmoil in American society can be blamed for many of the social ills the Navy then suffered from, but Tom Moorer was not the right man to tackle those issues head on. His cultural, political, and racial biases limited his understanding of the deep malaise then infecting the service. Hence, Moorer's leadership of the Navy during a difficult time witnessed both signal achievements and troubling developments. The full demonstration of Moorer's leadership skills would surface only when he became Chairman of the Joint Chiefs of Staff.

CHAPTER 6

WHITE KNIGHT OF THE DELTA

Even before his election as president in November 1968, Richard M. Nixon recognized that the American people wanted an end to the long, bloody, and frustrating conflict in Southeast Asia. Polls indicated that 66 percent of the electorate would vote for the candidate who would accomplish the withdrawal of US troops from Vietnam.[1] Responding to the heated demand for an immediate US pullback, Nixon announced the phased withdrawal of US troops from South Vietnam. He also made it be known that to compensate for the loss of US military strength on the ground, his administration would launch a major program to train, arm, and equip the South Vietnamese armed forces to carry on the fight against their communist antagonists.

The president-elect met with his top advisors on 28 December 1968 at Key Biscayne, Florida. At the meeting was soon-to-be secretary of defense, decorated World War II veteran, and former Wisconsin congressman Melvin Laird. He had turned against the war by 1967 and stated in the meeting that "we're going to have to de-Americanize that situation over there." Laird later simplified his views: "I never was a great supporter of the Vietnam War. I was a great supporter of getting the hell out of there." That March, Laird referred to the program to prepare the South Vietnamese to take over the war as "Vietnamization," a term widely used thereafter.[2]

Nixon secretly assured South Vietnam's President Nguyen Van Thieu that as this transition took place, US air and naval power would be prepared to punish any major North Vietnamese attempt to interfere with the process.[3] With cease-fire negotiations between US and North Vietnamese representatives ongoing in Paris, Nixon did not order a resumption of air attacks on Hanoi. But he did direct his military commanders to keep a close eye on military activity north of the DMZ. And to lessen the enemy's logistics flow into South Vietnam, Air Force units based in Thailand and Navy squadrons deployed on carriers in the Gulf of Tonkin continued interdiction operations along the Ho Chi Minh Trail. They did so in a sustained campaign known as Commando Hunt, which unloaded almost three million tons of bombs on Laos by March 1972. Nixon also ordered General Abrams to put maximum pressure in South Vietnam on enemy forces, then reeling from the bloody Tet Offensive.

ZUMWALT STORMS ONTO THE SCENE

To oversee in-country naval operations, in September 1968 CNO Moorer dispatched Rear Admiral Elmo R. Zumwalt Jr. (soon promoted to vice admiral) to Saigon to relieve Rear Admiral Kenneth L. Veth as Commander Naval Forces, Vietnam. Zumwalt, born in San Francisco on 29 November 1920, was the son of two physicians who lived and practiced in Tulare, California. He hoped to become a doctor like his parents, but his mother's terminal cancer and the family's straitened financial situation prevented him from taking that career path. As the valedictorian of his high school class, Zumwalt delivered an address that foreshadowed his later emphasis on the human condition. He bemoaned a world plagued by dictatorships, poverty, food scarcity, crime, and class struggle, and suggested that when his classmates chose a career, they should consider focusing on "humanitarian opportunities."[4] In 1939, he accepted an appointment to the tuition-free US Naval Academy. Already supremely confident in his ability at oral communication, Bud Zumwalt honed his skills as a star of the Quarterdeck Society, the academy's debate and public speaking club. He scored in other areas as well, placing first out of 719 in the midshipmen summer cruise.[5]

Commissioned ensign with his class in June 1942 (a year before the wartime class of 1943 would have graduated), Zumwalt soon found himself in the Pacific war. While serving on board attack transport

Zeilin (APA-3) off Guadalcanal in the Solomons, he witnessed the nighttime Battle of Savo Island during which the Imperial Japanese Navy sank four US and Australian cruisers, killing a number of his Naval Academy classmates and many other Allied sailors. Zumwalt spent six months during 1943 with destroyer *Phelps* (DD-360), then taking part in operations to oust Japanese forces from Attu and Kiska in the Aleutian Islands. Not unlike strategic theorist Alfred Thayer Mahan and other notables in the Navy's history, Bud Zumwalt suffered from seasickness, which at one point confined him to his shipboard berth for three months. During lulls in combat, Zumwalt read voraciously and studied the Russian language.[6]

The year 1944 found him serving on *Fletcher*-class destroyer *Robinson* (DD-562), then bombarding enemy positions on the islands of Saipan and Guam in the Marianas. Zumwalt fought in the fierce nighttime engagement in Surigao Strait during the decisive Battle of Leyte Gulf in October. Assigned to the combat information center, the ship's warfighting heart, Zumwalt coordinated the ship's maneuvers as she launched a torpedo attack against the enemy fleet. He displayed remarkable coolness under the intense pressure of battle, for which the Navy awarded him a Bronze Star Medal.[7]

Bud Zumwalt had the distinction of being the first US naval officer to conn a captured naval vessel, the Japanese gunboat *Atocha*, into the port of Shanghai at the end of the war. Shortly afterward, Zumwalt met Mouza Coutelais-du-Roche, a White Russian émigré originally from Harbin, Manchuria. Her experiences as a refugee fleeing from the Red Army reinforced his early concerns about the aggressive nature of Soviet communism. Other than to enhance their romance, the young officer asked her to teach him Russian because he thought the next war would be with the Soviet Union. Zumwalt wed Mouza only two weeks after they met—with the characteristic impulsiveness he displayed throughout his later life and Navy career—but it was a marriage bond that lasted until his death fifty-five years later.[8]

Bud Zumwalt served in the Korean War on board battleship *Wisconsin* (BB-64). During the late 1950s, he commanded destroyer *Arnold J. Isbell* (DD-869) and served as a staff officer in the Navy's Bureau of Naval Personnel (BUPERS). In the shore billet, he earned the respect of one of the Navy's most able leaders during the early Cold War, Admiral James Holloway Jr. (the father of James L. Holloway III, Zumwalt's classmate and later successor as CNO). The elder Holloway considered Zumwalt an outstanding leader.[9] Zumwalt attended the Naval War College, and he and Holloway were the first in their Naval Academy class selected to attend the National War College. During this period, Zumwalt commanded guided missile frigate *Dewey* (DLG-14).

After promotion to captain, Zumwalt worked for and became an assistant to Paul Nitze, architect of National Security Council Memorandum 68 (NSC-68), the pivotal blueprint for the US Cold War military buildup. Nitze first learned of Zumwalt's intellectual acumen when he was informed about an impressive talk the young officer had given at the National War College on leadership succession in the Soviet Union. Nitze, then Assistant Secretary of Defense for International Security Affairs (ISA), asked the head of the Navy's personnel command to assign the young officer to his staff as a naval aide. Zumwalt later observed, with characteristic aplomb, that Nitze was "the kind of guy who always was looking for talent. He's been a genius at identifying it over the years."[10] So taken was Nitze with Captain Zumwalt's grasp of nuclear weapons-related issues that he assigned Zumwalt as his director of arms control, a billet normally filled by a rear admiral. Zumwalt related that in that job he "had the opportunity to have a great deal of visibility and to operate in a manner that very, very few people, even in ISA, had the opportunity to do."[11]

While other officers generally considered such posting as "non-career enhancing," Zumwalt recognized the opportunity to learn about national strategy and political-military affairs at the top levels of government. He wanted to expand his intellectual horizons and hone his administrative skills. The officer was involved in policymaking during the Cuban Missile Crisis and nuclear arms control deliberations. Like Nitze, his primary focus was on the growing power of the Soviet Union and its nuclear-capable armed forces, not on developments in Southeast Asia. Nitze was especially taken with Bud Zumwalt's sharp mind, skill at bureaucratic maneuvering, and outgoing personality. In July 1965, Nitze suggested that the Navy should promote the forty-three-year-old officer to rear admiral, even though Zumwalt had not had a major sea command. With or without this endorsement, the selection board recognized that Zumwalt possessed superior leadership skills. He became the youngest officer to achieve that rank in the Navy's history. That would not be enough, however, for the ambitious "comer." The same night that he learned of his selection to flag rank, and after a few cocktails at a party, Bud Zumwalt prophetically confided to a small group of colleagues that by 1970 he would be the Chief of Naval Operations. He had already set his sights on the Navy's top job.[12]

For eleven months, Zumwalt commanded San Diego-based Cruiser-Destroyer Flotilla 7, a job he considered "more like running a good Boy Scout troop than running a ship."[13] He did not want to remain in that billet for long. With Nitze's intercession, the up-and-coming officer then took charge of the Navy's new systems analysis office in the Pentagon.[14] Despite later Secretary of the Navy John Lehman's strong praise for Zumwalt's leadership of the naval service, he had no use for Zumwalt's proclivity for what he called McNamara's "cult of systems analysis." Lehman emphasized that "grafting of the systems analysis cult onto the navy had a particularly unfortunate effect." He reasoned that since the Navy emphasized engineering, "the seeds of systems analysis found naval waters most hospitable, and they grew like hydrilla, choking off strategic thinking." Tom Moorer was equally disdainful of systems analysis. Lehman relates that when he served on Henry Kissinger's staff in the White House, Moorer considered him a Whiz Kid, "a status in his eyes about equivalent to a car-repossessor."[15]

Nitze then brought Captain Zumwalt with him as executive assistant and naval aide when he became secretary of the Navy in November 1963. Captain Alex A. Kerr, a legal officer for Nitze, was a friend and associate of Zumwalt's. Kerr considered Zumwalt "intellectual, open-minded, [and] decisive when he needed to be, and very much loyal to his friends [who] could do no wrong." Kerr admitted, however, that "his tendency to be uncritical [of his associates] may have worked at times to his disadvantage."[16]

William Thompson served with Zumwalt on Nitze's staff and later as Zumwalt's top public affairs officer (PAO). When Zumwalt ran for election to the Senate on Virginia's Democratic Party ticket after his retirement, Thomson acted as his campaign chairman. Discussing Zumwalt's work ethic, Thompson remembered that a common sight was the officer cradling a phone between the side of his head and his shoulder. In that way, he could talk while at the same time shuffle numberless stacks of paper on his desk or write memos. Kerr considered Zumwalt a "juggler" who could keep "more balls in the air than anyone I had ever been with and constantly maintaining a level head."[17]

Kerr remembered that Zumwalt, even though only an aide, had great influence with Nitze and that the young officer helped shape the thinking of the secretary during that period.[18] Thompson related that

Zumwalt was instrumental in helping guide Nitze "through the Navy bureaucracy, translating some of its idiosyncrasies as well as providing a good 'saltwater' approach to problem solving."[19] Bud Zumwalt recognized that while his duties involved him in political action—frowned upon by most professional military officers—he felt that his service to Nitze was worth the risk to his career.[20] Indeed, the job placed Zumwalt in close personal contact with the top figures in the national defense establishment and the Congress who would prove useful to his future prospects in the Navy.

Zumwalt characterized his mission in the systems analysis office as bringing "the Navy into the 20th century with regard to . . . the things the Whiz Kids were doing to shape the budgets." In his role as director of the Navy's office of systems analysis, Zumwalt became familiar with the war's strategic issues. He and his staff produced many statistical analyses for consumption in Saigon and Washington. One study questioned the effectiveness of the bombing campaign and another affirmed the feasibility of mining North Vietnam's ports. A third analysis concluded that because of the Market Time anti-infiltration patrol, enemy supplies were not getting through by sea but didn't have to because "you had two open-ended routes, the Ho Chi Minh Trail and the Cambodian port of Sihanoukville."[21]

Zumwalt claimed that after long debates with the defense secretary, Nitze and he had "turned McNamara around completely" to oppose Rolling Thunder. They supposedly also convinced the defense secretary that the interdiction of the Ho Chi Minh Trail was not working. Further, they argued that unless the United States invaded North Vietnam, "the war was going to go on and on and on, and the public wouldn't support it." Zumwalt later observed that despite his and Nitze's concerns about the direction of the war, the two of them concluded that "we were there and we were stuck with it." Nitze and he "wanted to make it come out right since our national honor was involved" and to avoid defeat because of the "impact it would have on our alliance structure in the Third World if we blew it."[22]

Bud Zumwalt's relationship with Paul Ignatius, who became Nitze's successor as Navy secretary, was equally positive. Zumwalt highly regarded Ignatius for his good analytical mind and thoughtfulness. Zumwalt observed that Ignatius "didn't let himself get pushed around by the brass." He was not, however—unlike McNamara and other civilian defense department leaders—"contemptuous of the military mind."

Before Zumwalt's posting to Vietnam, Ignatius sent a letter commending the naval officer to COMUSMACV. Zumwalt remembered that Ignatius "opened the door for me to General Abrams."[23]

Tom Moorer selected Zumwalt to command US naval forces in Vietnam because he did not think he had "a chance in hell of getting [another admiral] with three stars" to take the in-country billet and because he "knew Paul Nitze would promote him."[24] Indeed, Moorer considered Nitze key to the young officer's "ascendancy." Zumwalt recounted that he and his wife Mouza often stayed in a residence loaned to them by Nitze on his 2,000-acre farm in Port Tobacco, Maryland, on the Potomac River. As a result, Zumwalt saw Nitze every weekend. Bud Zumwalt considered Nitze a "dear friend" and "beloved."[25] Zumwalt equated their relationship to the Greek philosophers Plato and Socrates and later gushed that Nitze was a man of "brilliant intellect" and a patriot who "more than any other man I have ever known [was] a sincere seeker of the truth."[26] At least one perceptive critic suggested that Zumwalt got the job "not so much [because of] his brilliant service record as it was his personal relationship with Paul Nitze, and Moorer's maneuvering to create another three-star billet."[27]

Zumwalt's version of why he was picked to be the next Commander Naval Forces, Vietnam, is well known since the publication of his books *On Watch* and *My Father, My Son*, and the admiral's other copious written and oral remembrances. Zumwalt contended that his assignment to Vietnam "was Moorer's way of getting rid of me: *promote the son of a bitch and nobody will ever hear from him again*" (original italics).[28] Supposedly, a "paranoid" Moorer wanted the naval aviation community to continue controlling the Navy and he saw Zumwalt, a surface sailor, as a threat. Adding to the issue of just who selected Zumwalt for the Vietnam position, Navy secretary Ignatius claimed that he and not Moorer made the decision.[29]

As Nitze's naval aide, Bud Zumwalt gained an understanding of the decision-making relating to the Vietnam War. He contended that eventually there was little difference between Nitze's views on the conflict and his own. In hindsight, Zumwalt suggested that from the start Nitze and he shared the view that a communist conquest of South Vietnam would not constitute a direct threat to the security of the United States. Nitze and he argued strongly against fighting for the Republic of Vietnam since it was not a viable, national entity. They suggested that if the object were to fight communism in Asia, that battle

General Creighton W. Abrams, Commander US Military Assistance Command, Vietnam, and Vice Admiral Elmo R. Zumwalt Jr., Commander Naval Forces, Vietnam, at a ceremony in the Mekong Delta. The general's high regard for Zumwalt's performance did much to boost the naval officer's standing in Washington. NHHC VN Collection.

should take place in Thailand, Indonesia, Malaysia, and the Philippines. Nitze and Zumwalt also considered a decisive victory against North Vietnam unlikely and a potentially heavy drain on America's military resources. Zumwalt suggested that Nitze and he were prescient because the war from 1964 to 1968 indeed did "gobble up" many of the resources the services needed to contest Soviet global advances.[30]

Zumwalt related that Admiral Bernard A. Clarey, the Vice Chief of Naval Operations from 1968 to 1970 and one of his allies in the Navy's flag ranks, told him that "Admiral Moorer used to sit there and fret and worry about the fact that I was too close to Paul Nitze" and that "he became even more paranoid about it as Paul moved up to become Deputy Secretary of Defense." Clarey supposedly persuaded Moorer to promote Zumwalt to Vice Admiral and send him to Vietnam, "the graveyard where [he] would end up, as had every other ComNavForV [Commander, Naval Forces Vietnam]."[31]

The conventional interpretation, however, is overblown. There is little question that Moorer regarded Zumwalt's social and political liberalism and personal ties to Laird, Nitze, Chafee, Ignatius, and other like-minded defense department officials with distaste.[32] Tom Moorer, like many active and retired flag officers, did not share Bud Zumwalt's zeal as COMNAVFORV and later as CNO in pushing progressive personnel policies. But the supposed bitter animus between them was little in evidence when Moorer served as JCS chairman and Zumwalt as CNO and in their retirement years. They fought side by side during and after the war to defend the US armed forces in general and the Navy in particular from the budget-cutters in Congress and the public and to oppose what they considered to be Nixon's and Kissinger's advocacy of global détente with a resurgent Soviet Union.[33] With regard to the Vietnam posting, Moorer was sensitive to the complaints of the other services that the Navy was not fairly sharing the burden in South Vietnam. Before Zumwalt took command, his two-star predecessor was unable to make any significant impact on MACV, chockablock with three-star Army and Air Force generals. Finally, the ambitious Zumwalt did not protest an assignment that he knew would vault his rising star over the heads of many contemporaries and bring him to the attention of the top civilian and military leaders of the United States.

ZUMWALT TAKES THE FIGHT TO THE ENEMY

When Zumwalt took command of in-country naval forces in September 1968, he was in sync with the goal of the Johnson and incoming Nixon administrations to withdraw US troops and strengthen the South Vietnamese government for the continuing fight. And he did recognize that America's heavy commitment of lives and treasure and loyalty to its ally demanded that the United States "disengage honorably."[34]

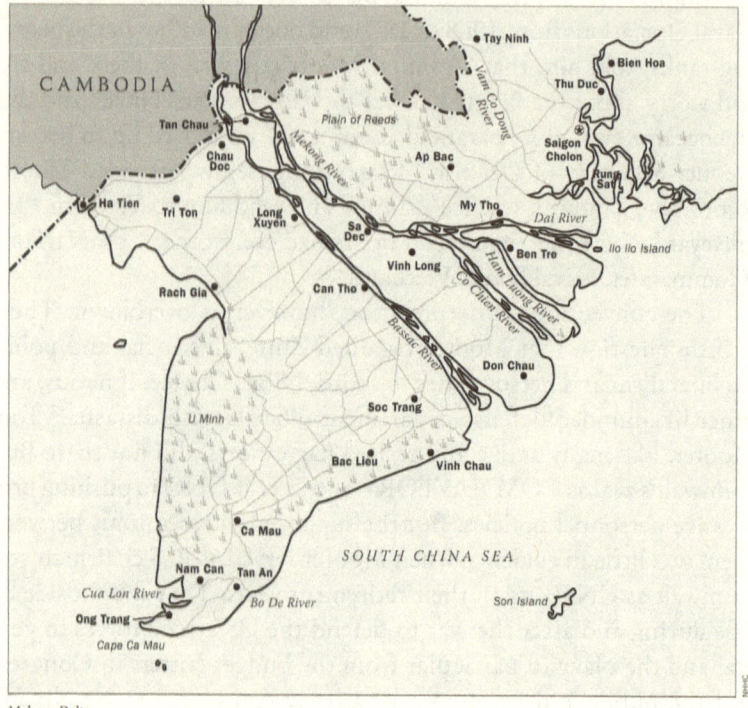

Mekong Delta.

The Mekong Delta. NHHC.

There is little question that Zumwalt's leadership had a positive impact on the US–South Vietnamese war effort during the latter stages of the conflict. Facilitating that success was the strong relationship between Zumwalt and his boss, General Abrams. Zumwalt already understood that Abrams wanted the Navy to defeat enemy forces in the Mekong Delta.[35]

The Navy had deployed a strong contingent to South Vietnam by fall 1968. The River Patrol Force (Task Force 116) operated 258 patrol and minesweeping boats. The 3,700-man Riverine Assault Force (Task Force 117) counted 184 heavily armed monitors, transports, and other craft. Helicopter Attack Light Squadron 3 (HAL-3) flew twenty-five armed helicopters. In addition, five SEAL platoons sought out the enemy and gathered intelligence in the delta. The huge naval support activities at Saigon and Danang managed the logistic effort for the Navy and Marine Corps in Vietnam. In September 1968, 38,000 US naval personnel served in South Vietnam. Complementing the American naval forces were the Vietnam Navy's 655 ships, assault craft, and patrol boats.[36]

The Coastal Surveillance Force (Task Force 115) constituted the Navy's third major formation in-country. In existence since March 1965, the command executed Operation Market Time, the anti-infiltration patrol off South Vietnam. The patrol force boasted eighty-one Swift boats, twenty-four Coast Guard WPB cutters, and thirty-nine other vessels. Market Time's first year of operation was not crowned with success. When McNamara had visited South Vietnam, Roy Johnson, the Seventh Fleet commander, asked him, "What do you think of the surveillance effort?" McNamara replied that Westmoreland told him that "it stinks."[37] Between early 1966 and 1968, however, the coastal patrol force turned things around. As one example, in a huge gamble Hanoi had sent four steel-hulled trawlers south to supply North Vietnamese and Viet Cong forces fighting for survival during the Tet Offensive of 1968. None of these ships accomplished their mission. US and South Vietnamese patrol forces destroyed three of the vessels and forced the other one to give up its infiltration attempt and return home. Between 1965 and 1968, infiltrating North Vietnamese ships accomplished at best seven missions of the twenty-eight launched, delivering only a paltry 410 tons of material to the southern battlefield.[38]

The success of Market Time ultimately compelled the North Vietnamese to redouble their infiltration efforts on the Ho Chi Minh Trail and make use of Sihanoukville on the Gulf of Thailand. From 1966 to 1970, Chinese and other communist-bloc merchant ships freely unloaded cargoes of arms and other military supplies at the port in the supposedly neutral country. Chinese ships provided communist forces in the Mekong Delta via Sihanoukville with enough weapons to arm thousands of soldiers. Companies contracted by the Cambodian government of Prince Norodom Sihanouk loaded trucks at the port with munitions and delivered the cargoes to designated locations on the border with South Vietnam. At that point, Vietnamese communist forces took charge of the stores of AK-47 assault rifles, anti-personnel mines, and rocket-propelled grenades and distributed them to enemy combat units throughout the delta. Hanoi later confirmed that "between 1966 and 1968 we shipped 21,400 tons of supplies through the port of Sihanoukville and paid the [Cambodian] government $50 million U.S. dollars in port fees and transportation charges" (and, one might add, bribes to the Cambodian military officers involved).[39]

The MACV and Naval Forces, Vietnam, commanders argued that Sihanoukville was being used for this purpose, but CIA and defense department officials disagreed. Tom Moorer related that "this was one of the big arguments [the JCS] had with McNamara," who concurred with the intelligence agencies that no supplies were coming in through the port.[40] Before the overthrow of Sihanouk's government in March 1970, however, neither the Johnson nor Nixon administrations moved to close the port since they feared being accused of spreading the war to one more nation of Indochina. Hence, the use of Sihanoukville enabled Hanoi to satisfy as much as sixty percent of its logistic needs for operations in the lower half of South Vietnam.[41]

On 5 November 1968, two months after arriving in-country, Zumwalt issued Operation Plan 111-69 that detailed a new campaign blueprint called SEALORDS (Southeast Asia Lake, Ocean, River, Delta Strategy). It called for a major offensive, led by a new Task Force 194, comprised of the bulk of River Patrol Force, Mobile Riverine Force, and Coastal Surveillance Force assets. The campaign's goals were to interdict communist infiltration into the delta, destroy enemy base camps in the Ca Mau Peninsula at the southern tip of South Vietnam, and strengthen the South Vietnamese government's authority in the region. Zumwalt's first step was to order his "First Sea Lord" (initially Captain Robert S. Salzer and after late November Rear Admiral W. H. House) to test the concept of patrolled riverine barriers on the western waterways bordering Cambodia. Abrams and his top generals liked the concept. Major General George S. Eckhardt, the senior Army advisor in the delta, concurred with the importance of cutting infiltration from Cambodia and the involvement of naval forces in that effort.[42]

Bud Zumwalt led from the front. Throughout his time in Vietnam, he visited combat hot spots, once took part in a nighttime ambush patrol, and demonstrated the physical bravery of a true warrior. Zumwalt later calculated that he visited several thousand sites and 20,000 sailors during his time in Vietnam. He often flew to the site of a previous night's action to pin medals on deserving sailors. Howard Kerr, on the NAVFORV staff, related that "going out into the field involved a lot of risk [but] I can't recall the admiral ever showing concern about his own personal safety."[43]

The men of Naval Forces, Vietnam, universally applauded Zumwalt's dynamic leadership and personal example. Lieutenant Richard McCann believed that Zumwalt "had a genuine affinity for the

Zumwalt speaks to sailors involved in Operation Sea Float deep in the heart of the Mekong Delta. He impressed many American sailors and their Vietnamese counterparts with his physical courage, dynamism, innovative thinking, and compassion for their well-being. NHHC VN Collection.

Swift boat officers [and] we didn't have any complaints about Zumwalt as our superior officer."[44] Lewis Glenn, another staffer, thought sailors recognized that Zumwalt really cared for them as individuals. He remembered that whenever a planeload of Navy casualties arrived, the admiral would visit the hospital where they were taken. Glenn observed that "we all loved him and still do . . . that great humanitarian." He added that "you would do anything for him." Still, he recognized that Zumwalt was human and subject to human foibles. He suggested that the admiral's greatest failure was that "once he embraced a [subordinate] he always kept that guy with him, and I think at times to his personal detriment."[45]

Kit Lavell was a highly decorated pilot of an OV-10 Bronco attack plane in Light Attack Squadron 4 (VAL-4), the "Black Ponies," established in Vietnam during Zumwalt's tour. Lavell related that the men of his unit idolized the boss because he "was a sailor's admiral, a pilot's admiral." Lavell characterized his leader as dashing, popular, and young. Moreover, the sailors viewed Zumwalt as approachable and genuinely interested in their situation. Whenever Bud Zumwalt visited his sailors, he gave a pep talk, "needed neither by the troops nor him, for he and they already shared an enthusiasm and optimistic view of what they could together accomplish. These were his men."[46] Lieutenant Peter M. Swartz, who served as a political warfare officer in the western delta and later on Zumwalt's staff in Saigon, shared those sentiments and observed that "Zumwalt exuded the sense that we've got to win the war; we've got to do it right; and we've got to do it now."[47]

Thomas G. Kelley, a Medal of Honor recipient severely wounded in a delta naval battle during 1969, related how Zumwalt helped him: "After I was wounded the Navy wanted to get me out. I told them I wouldn't get out." Kelley went directly to Zumwalt, then CNO, who remembered the officer from Vietnam. He told the admiral that "they are trying to kick me out." Zumwalt said, "Don't worry about that." The upshot was that Kelley stayed in the Navy for another twenty years.[48]

As another example of Bud Zumwalt's human touch, he made multiple visits to the Naval Station Saigon hospital to check in on SEAL Lieutenant (junior grade) John C. Brewton, who had earned a Silver Star Medal in combat but was dying from his wounds. The admiral arranged for Brewton's father and fiancée to fly to Vietnam and provided them with accommodations. Later, as CNO, he directed the naming and commissioning of *Brewton* (DE-1086), one of the Navy's newest destroyer escorts. Finally, Swartz provided another example of the admiral's social consciousness. On one occasion, he "hosted a Passover Seder diner with the Jews on his staff. He even flew his wife Mouza in from the Philippines to take part." Swartz remembered that "that was the sort of thing he would do."[49]

Task Force 194 inaugurated the first SEALORDS operation in November 1968. US and South Vietnamese naval units forced the enemy from several canals thirty miles south of the Cambodian border near the Gulf of Thailand and set up patrols on those waterways. That same month, Zumwalt launched a powerful effort to limit infiltration into the swampy "Parrot's Beak" salient that brought the Cambodian border uncomfortably close to Saigon. In Operation Giant Slingshot, the Navy established patrols along the rivers that the enemy had exploited to supply their attacks on the capital throughout the year. In an innovative approach, to support patrol units on the rivers Zumwalt established advanced tactical support bases close to US and

South Vietnamese army firebases whose artillery batteries could provide protection. By January 1969, the barrier interdiction line on the Cambodian border stretched from the Gulf of Thailand to the city of Tay Ninh northwest of Saigon.

Because Giant Slingshot posed the greatest threat to the enemy's logistic support of operations in the Saigon region, North Vietnamese and Viet Cong units fought hard to keep that avenue of approach free of allied forces. Intelligence revealed that during the operation the allies inflicted heavy losses on enemy units. At one point, Army Lieutenant General Julian J. Ewell, one of Abrams's primary subordinates, sent a message to the local naval commander that ended with "John Paul Jones is proud of you all."[50]

When the enemy shifted forces further east to the upper reaches of the Saigon River, Zumwalt countered in May 1969 with an innovative tactical measure. In little over three hours, Army Skycrane helicopters airlifted six river patrol boats (PBRs) of River Division 574 from the Giant Slingshot area to a point on the Saigon River sixteen miles away, a movement that would have taken many days by road-bound vehicles. The admiral used other technologies, including drone minesweepers and movement sensors developed for the "McNamara wall," to assist naval forces in their interdiction campaign on the canals. His SEALORDS units also inaugurated a different tactic, called a waterborne guard post. Around dusk, two PBRs would cut their engines and drift into the shore and its enveloping foliage, remain there silently throughout the night, and open up with their weapons only when they detected enemy movement across the waterway. This tactic took a heavy toll on enemy fighters.[51]

In December 1969, Zumwalt inaugurated one of the first Navy actions of the Vietnamization program. COMNAVFORV turned over responsibility for the operation on the Saigon River to South Vietnamese Commander Dang Trung Hieu. On the last day of 1969, Commander Hieu's PBRs and riverine assault craft, aided by US helicopter gunships, OV-10 Broncos, and artillery, fought a successful sixteen-hour battle with the enemy.

During the first six months of SEALORDS, Zumwalt's naval units also raided into the once impenetrable Cua Lon and Bo De rivers, deep in the heart of the Ca Mau Peninsula's forests, mangrove swamps, and mud flats. It was a sparsely populated region 175 miles southwest of Saigon. The Ca Mau and the U Minh Forest, the latter on the Gulf of

Thailand coast to the north, had long been communist strongholds. During Tet 1968, Viet Cong forces seized the region's major towns, compelling many of their citizens to flee to safer, government-held areas.

At one point, Zumwalt shared a helicopter flight over the Ca Mau with Tran Van Chon, the South Vietnamese chief of naval operations. The officer made a heartfelt pitch that the allies should retake the region. Zumwalt bought the argument that before the war, the Ca Mau area had been one of South Vietnam's most fertile and industrious regions.[52] Others thought differently about the area's value when woodcutting and light fishing constituted most of the economic output. SEAL Master Chief Gunner's Mate Robert H. Stoner, who fought in the Ca Mau, remembered that "this operational area was one of the most God-forsaken places anyone could imagine." He added, "I could never understand why anyone would want it."[53]

Nonetheless, Zumwalt gave the go-ahead for allied entry into the Ca Mau. During late 1968 and early 1969, the Americans killed, wounded, or captured more than 1,000 enemy combatants; destroyed huge weapons and supply caches; and established a visible, if tenuous, government presence in this part of the delta. Zumwalt and Abrams also considered it essential that US and South Vietnamese representatives negotiating with Hanoi's diplomats in Paris be able to affirm that the Republic of Vietnam controlled all of its territory.

Combat increased significantly in the Ca Mau during 1969. In April, for instance, guerrillas ambushed a force under Coast Guard Commander (later Commandant) Paul A. Yost. The devastating ambush killed five and wounded forty-six American and Vietnamese sailors and soldiers. As two participants remarked after the battle, "We got our butts kicked."[54] That same month, Navy Captain Roy F. "Latch" Hoffmann, who then ran the show in the Ca Mau, ordered Coast Guard Lieutenant Commander John C. Spence to go back to the ambush area and "get even." This time allied naval units, ground troops, helicopters, and an Air Force F-4 Phantom brought a deluge of fire down on an enemy ambush force, driving it back into the jungle with heavy loss.

Soon after taking command in Vietnam, Zumwalt had met with Hoffmann, whom Zumwalt later characterized as "the most Patton-like" of his commanders. Indeed, like Patton, Hoffmann took greater risks with his men and his boats than other officers. Zumwalt considered Hoffmann "a driver rather than a motivator."[55] The hard-charging officer, who later earned a Silver Star for his combat performance in the Ca Mau, convinced Zumwalt that the Swift boats and 82-foot Coast Guard cutters of Task Force 115 could bolster SEALORDS by deploying inland on the Cua Lon and the delta's other major rivers.

A number of his junior officers, however, considered the use of these vessels on inland waterways foolhardy. Lieutenant John Kerry, the future senator, presidential contender, and secretary of state, counted among their number. He later observed that "no one, from engineman to officer in charge, could find the rationale for letting the enemy have the first devastating shots at us in the rivers, and without exception they always did."[56] Swartz, who served early in his tour as an advisor in the region, remembered that the thin-skinned PCFs often "came back riddled and people came back dead." A major complaint was that the Swift boat had a high profile, was too noisy, and was too lengthy at 50 feet to turn around easily on the narrow jungle waterways. In short, the Swifts were not designed for inland operations. Nonetheless, Zumwalt favored their use because "the alternative was to do nothing [and] Admiral Zumwalt preferred doing something to nothing."[57]

Zumwalt and his top commanders recognized that to supply the military forces deployed in the remote Ca Mau, they needed a dedicated logistics capability. COMNAVFORV directed the construction of a floating base made up of connected barge pontoons and positioned it in the middle of the Cua Lon. The multi-barge complex, named Sea Float, eventually hosted a variety of US and Vietnamese naval vessels, SEALs, and attack helicopters that carried out combat operations throughout the Ca Mau. The admiral hoped that the base would not only supply local naval forces but also serve as a magnet to draw Vietnamese villagers back to the area.

Growing numbers of local woodcutters and fishermen visited Sea Float to have their axes sharpened and outboard motors repaired and to get treatment from US and South Vietnamese medical personnel. The allies used the opportunity to provide the visitors with food and small gifts and to inform them about their government's concern for their well-being and the communists' failings. With the larger waterways cleared of Viet Cong tax collectors by the allied forces, the region's main rivers witnessed an uptick in commercial activity.[58]

Thomas Emery, a commanding officer of Sea Float, observed that eight months after the establishment of the floating base, allied forces had killed 408 Viet Cong guerrillas, a 27 to 1 ratio of enemy to friendly losses.⁵⁹ Zumwalt's man in charge of the Navy's Vietnamization program was Captain Charles F. "Chick" Rauch, a submariner and former systems analyst. Despite Rauch's lack of an operational history relevant to Vietnam, Zumwalt prized the officer for his "people skills and his empathy for others."⁶⁰ Rauch observed that by early 1970, within five miles of Sea Float the population had grown from 0 to 10,000. Zumwalt also established a permanent South Vietnamese government presence ashore close to Sea Float. In Operation Solid Anchor, Seabees constructed an airstrip, military facilities and defenses, and schools at Old Nam Can.⁶¹ With the increased security around Sea Float and Solid Anchor, enterprising civilians opened schools, restaurants, shops, charcoal kilns, and fish markets. Bud Zumwalt later observed that Tran Van Chon was excited by the developments in the Ca Mau and felt that his earlier judgment had been vindicated. Zumwalt was similarly pleased.⁶²

In addition to Sea Float and Solid Anchor, Zumwalt championed an allied incursion into the Ong Doc, a river on the Gulf of Thailand near the U Minh Forest, and a region home to many Viet Cong guerrillas. The South Vietnamese armed forces deployed 109 river assault craft and three marine battalions into the area. Rauch observed in January 1970 that the task force had penetrated much further into the U Minh than any American unit ever had and stayed there for three months. He admitted, however, that there were command-and-control and logistics issues with the deployment. Moreover, a surprise attack on an outpost in November by one or two enemy battalions had resulted in a high loss of South Vietnamese sailors and marines.⁶³

The naval command closed down Sea Float in September 1970 and the Vietnam Navy took control of Solid Anchor in April 1971. US naval advisors continued to serve there until February 1973, one month before the withdrawal of all US military forces from South Vietnam. The Republic of Vietnam occupied Old Nam Can and the surrounding area until the end of the war in 1975, but it was a decidedly limited control.

Not a few observers of the fighting in the Ca Mau questioned SEALORDS' impact on the region. In truth, the government's control extended no more than a few thousand yards on either side of the major rivers—that is, within range of naval guns. One veteran of combat in the region contended that "we owned 500 yards of water and wasteland in the middle of nowhere. The other side owned the rest."⁶⁴ Moreover, once the enemy adjusted to the American and South Vietnamese presence, the Ca Mau increasingly turned into "a hotbed of insurgent activity." Another veteran emphasized that "the Viet Cong may have withdrawn from the Cua Lon, but they had not left the Ca Mau Peninsula."[65]

INTO THE FOREST OF ASSASSINS

Zumwalt and his staff also developed a sophisticated, multiservice, multinational campaign focused on destroying the enemy's primary fighting force operating in the Rung Sat Special Zone. The zone encompassed a mangrove swamp through which passed merchant ships loaded with war supplies heading from the South China Sea to Saigon 45 miles to the north. Earlier in the war, Viet Cong guerrillas had often mined the Long Tau River that meandered through the swamp. The enemy ambushed and sank not only the merchant vessels but also allied mine warfare and river patrol forces operating on the waterway.

In the new campaign, South Vietnamese regular and paramilitary troops and Navy SEALs increased pressure on the VC in the zone. Simultaneously, heavy Army "Rome Plow" bulldozers and aerial-sprayed herbicides denied the enemy force easy cover and concealment. In his end-of-tour report, the leader of the River Patrol Force, Captain Arthur Price, sang the praises of the Vietnamese naval commander and his US counterpart responsible for the Rung Sat. Price credited the symbiotic relationship of those leaders for enabling the responsive and coordinated employment of allied air, land, and naval resources.[66]

In late 1969 and early 1970, the enemy failed to mount a single attack on the merchant ships using the Long Tau. Zumwalt credited Commander Clarence J. "Jerry" Wages, his commander in the area, for the successful operation that the admiral said "completely eradicated" the Viet Cong presence there.[67] As US naval forces withdrew from the war, the Vietnam Navy (VNN) took over complete responsibility for the Rung Sat and kept the Long Tau open to oceangoing traffic. Hence, after years of heavy combat and a dedicated ground, naval, and air effort, the allies had finally established firm control of the crucial waterway to South Vietnam's capital.

The allied advance into Cambodia during spring 1970 demonstrated the growing capability of the VNN to conduct both allied and unilateral operations. On 9 May, more than a week after ground troops crossed the border, a Vietnamese–American naval task force under the overall command of a VNN officer steamed north on the Mekong River to take control of that key waterway to the Cambodian capital of Phnom Penh. The South Vietnamese flotilla, with American naval advisors embarked, included riverine assault craft, Swift boats, PBRs, and marines. That same day, the allied task force secured the strategically important Neak Luong ferry crossing point midway to Phnom Penh. The VNN force continued on alone to the capital and completed the mission to establish control of the river, which the Vietnam Navy and its Cambodian counterpart maintained for the next four years.

THE VIETNAM NAVY AND THE VIETNAMIZATION PROGRAM

When Zumwalt took command of Naval Forces, Vietnam, he clearly understood that his most vital responsibility would be to execute defense secretary Laird's top priority Vietnamization program. The defense secretary invariably reported to the president that the strength of the South Vietnamese armed forces was increasing daily and that the US ally ultimately could fight on alone. In December 1971, for instance, Laird informed Nixon that "it was hard not to be over-optimistic about the progress of Vietnamization."[68] Laird exuded optimism even as the 200,000-man North Vietnamese Army threatened to overwhelm the South Vietnamese armed forces in the early days of the 1972 Easter Offensive. The defense secretary, a lone voice among the administration's leaders, suggested that heavy US air and naval support would be unnecessary since "the South Vietnamese are going to come through all right" on their own.[69]

Bud Zumwalt, who thought he was the right man to implement Vietnamization, also understood that Vietnamization was Abrams's primary objective. The general convened a meeting soon after Zumwalt's arrival in-country to discuss plans for the withdrawal of US forces. An Air Force briefer detailed a program to be completed eight years later in 1976. Abrams exploded, shouting "Bullshit! Bullshit! Bullshit!" and stormed out of the room.[70] Once he had cooled down, the general reentered the room and heard Zumwalt's briefing. The admiral, who had changed his presentation after witnessing the previous tirade, offered an "accelerated" three-year plan. It entailed Naval Forces, Vietnam, integrating the VNN into US naval operations and preparing South Vietnamese sailors to operate the American ships, craft, weapons, and equipment. If Zumwalt had any doubt about COMUSMACV's demand to complete Vietnamization as soon as possible, during an April 1969 meeting the general reminded him that "the pressures [from Washington] are fantastic!"[71]

Indeed, Abrams, Moorer, and the JCS were in constant battle with the secretary of defense, who wanted a speedy withdrawal of US troops. Tom Moorer considered Laird a political animal who "would literally agree with something in the White House, although he disagreed with it, and then go over and get the Congress to stop it." Moorer suggested that even though Laird might be outwardly smiling with an opponent, inwardly he would be "on the verge of shooting you [and] he'd cut your throat for five cents."[72]

Even Bud Zumwalt understood that Laird's "intellectual frame of reference was almost totally political."[73] Laird believed that Congress and the American people would not stand for a slower pace of withdrawal and that any delay would cause Nixon trouble at the polls. Zumwalt told Howard Kerr that if Hubert Humphrey were elected, "we'd have a year, and if Nixon were elected, we'd have, maybe three years." Ironically, the admiral, who would come to despise the president, was glad Nixon won the election of 1968 because he had a more positive view than Humphrey about the pace of US withdrawal and Vietnamization.[74]

Nixon also told Abrams to complete the withdrawal as soon as possible. Indeed, the president was almost as obsessive about the speedy and total departure of US troops as Laird.[75] Zumwalt recognized that he did not have a lot of time to complete his mission. He assigned Captain Rauch as the Senior Naval Advisor and sent home his predecessor, Captain Paul Arbo, who had argued for a slower turnover pace.[76] Arbo had made the not unreasonable—and, as it turned out, accurate—observation that the VNN sailors needed to be better trained before the US naval resources were handed over to them. As Zumwalt's biographer has suggested, "Arbo's error was to keep challenging Bud on the timetable."[77]

The US Navy's part in Vietnamization was termed ACTOV (Accelerated Turnover to the Vietnamese); the Coast Guard effort was named SCATTOR (Small Craft Assets, Training, and Turnover of Resources). Soon after Zumwalt took over as COMNAVFORV, he had his staff draw up a plan to transfer the US Navy's river warfare combat vessels and support bases to the VNN by the end of 1971. A key aspect of the program entailed American naval personnel training South Vietnamese sailors in the operation, repair, and maintenance of US river warfare vessels. In early 1969, Zumwalt gave the 564-man Naval Advisory Group two years to prepare Vietnamese sailors to man an anticipated navy of 40,000 men, twice the size of the Vietnam Navy in 1968. The advisory group established recruit training centers at Saigon, Nha Trang, and Cam Ranh Bay. The Vietnamese training system, despite the receipt of US financial assistance and the dedicated work of US naval advisors, however, would be overwhelmed by the task of preparing tens of thousands of new recruits in the few years allotted for the turnover.[78]

In early 1970, Zumwalt accelerated the ACTOV program with "ACTOV-X." At one point, he informed his command that progress on the turnover program had "exceeded my fondest expectations." Still, the admiral exhorted his command to even greater effort "because we must accelerate still faster to stay ahead of the power curve. GO TEAM GO!"[79] Rauch shared his boss's optimism. He cautioned, however, that there were "some big problems." He observed that for ACTOV to succeed, a sufficient number of American sailors would have to remain in South Vietnam through fiscal year 1972. It was critical for NAVFORV to be given enough time to complete the program.[80]

Ever impatient, Zumwalt cut short the 12-week training regimen and sent Vietnamese sailors to US units for on-the-job training. The object of pairing Vietnamese with American sailors was to imbue the former with the "can do spirit" and a sense of responsibility, the assumption being that the Vietnamese, who had been fighting for decades, lacked those attributes.[81] Rauch extolled the virtues of the program even though he admitted that some of the Vietnamese sailors did not measure up. On occasion, a Vietnamese sailor had to be relieved because of "consistently hiding during combat" or took unauthorized leave to visit his family in Saigon. Sometimes, disputes between US and Vietnamese sailors ended in fistfights.[82]

Other problems included a severe shortage of skilled US instructors, inadequate barracks, and the lack of sufficient food, water, and other living essentials for the Vietnamese sailors in training. The training effort involved the integration of Vietnamese sailors into the crews of US PBRs, PCFs, and riverine assault craft. Once convinced the Vietnamese could handle the job, the US units would turn over their boats to the VNN and head home. The arrangement usually worked well enough until Vietnamese officers took command of the vessels and then operational performance often suffered.

Improving the living condition of the average South Vietnamese sailor and his family also became a priority under ACTOV. Zumwalt reasoned that a sailor living with his family in substandard housing, trying to get by on low pay, and eating poorly did little to inspire him to fight for the Republic of Vietnam. The admiral understood that pay for the Vietnamese armed forces had increased by 30 percent during the previous three years but that the cost of living had increased by nearly 300 percent. Zumwalt considered the VNN's low standard of living "a worse long-term threat than the VC."[83] Hence, he inaugurated programs to provide VNN sailors with better housing and better nutrition through animal husbandry.

The Nixon administration provided $900,000 in US Military Construction funds that enabled Navy Seabees to build 4,500 500-square-foot cinder block "dependent shelters" at naval bases throughout the country. NAVFORV also developed a "pigs and chickens" program in which the Vietnamese sailors raised farm animals on naval bases for consumption and for sale at local markets.[84] As Peter Swartz related, "NAVFORV headquarters in Saigon directed me, a Jewish city boy from Providence, Rhode Island, to establish a pig farm on Phu Quoc [an island in the Gulf of Thailand] that was to be a model for other pig farms all around South Vietnam." One object of the overall program was to reverse the VNN's high desertion rate. The thinking was that "if the sailors and their families could be co-located on the bases and provided a food source, the men would not desert."[85]

Under the direction of the Naval Advisory Group (NAG), American personnel also reorganized the inefficient VNN supply system. The NAG, with a military assistance infusion of $8 million, improved management functions, developed a more professional labor force, and modernized the industrial plant at the Saigon Naval Shipyard. By early 1973, the Vietnamese facility had improved the operational readiness of hundreds of newly acquired river craft and begun overhauling the Vietnam Navy's seagoing ships in-country. Seabees also built bases for the VNN all over the country to replace the US ships that had previously carried out the logistic support role for US naval forces. When the last US forces departed South Vietnam on 29 March 1973, the logistic establishment and the combat arms of the VNN had the material resources to continue fighting the war. The 42,000-man Vietnam Navy operated 1,500 ships and craft for warfare on the rivers and canals, in coastal waters, and far out to sea. Only time would tell if that was enough to help the armed forces preserve the Republic of Vietnam.[86]

ZUMWALT'S VIETNAM PERFORMANCE

No COMNAVFORV before or after Vice Admiral Zumwalt had as much impact on the naval war in Vietnam. When he took command, he knew that the Nixon administration intended to bring home US troops and prepare the South Vietnamese armed forces to continue the fight. One of his first significant measures was the innovative SEALORDS naval strategy that maximized allied strengths and exploited enemy weaknesses. By deploying naval forces along the Cambodian border, north of Saigon, and in the Ca Mau, he seriously degraded Hanoi's ability to reinforce and supply its forces in much of southern South Vietnam. This effort also badly hurt North Vietnamese and Viet Cong forces in the delta, the birthplace and early focus of the communist insurgency. Zumwalt contended that "we really did make what I consider to be a major contribution to the pacification of the delta."[87]

When Robert S. Salzer, who led the Navy component of the Mobile Riverine Force during the 1967–1968 period of heavy combat, returned to Vietnam in April 1971 as COMNAVFORV, he was amazed at the changed situation. He "could not believe the extent to which pacification had proceeded in the Delta." He found it remarkable that "you could drive with impunity over roads that were just an invitation to an ambush earlier." He credited Zumwalt's SEALORDS campaign and the allied invasion of Cambodia with disorganizing the enemy's efforts in the delta.[88]

Captain William J. Crowe Jr., the senior advisor to the VNN River Force, and during the 1980s Chairman of the Joint Chiefs of Staff, related that in the delta "the fighting was rarely that intense [and] the VC were there, but in small units." He added that "during my tour the VC areas of operation shrank steadily and their tax revenues dwindled." He happily observed that commercial traffic was burgeoning on the canals. He thought that "perhaps success in the Mekong Delta was not going to win the war, but at least here we had tangible achievements to point to."[89]

Bud Zumwalt's ACTOV program provided the Vietnam Navy with a powerful arsenal of ships, craft, and weapons and an advanced logistical establishment. Eventually, South Vietnamese naval officers led all coastal and riverine forces in South Vietnam, mounted successful operations into Cambodia, and sustained the government's presence in the delta until the end of the conflict in 1975. Zumwalt's bravery, innovative thinking, decisiveness, and inspiring personality helped make his tenure as COMNAVFORV the high point of the naval war for South Vietnam.

Zumwalt, however, was blessed with advantages that neither his predecessors nor his successors enjoyed. When the admiral took charge in September 1968, he found the Viet Cong in the delta devastated by casualties. The enemy had suffered more than 100,000 killed, wounded, and captured throughout South Vietnam during the Tet and follow-on attacks. Veteran Viet Cong cadres, administrators, and battlefield commanders filled the casualty lists.[90] US and Vietnamese naval forces, the Army's 9th Infantry Division, and ARVN units had driven the enemy out of all the population centers south of Saigon. Communist forces were at a disadvantage throughout South Vietnam but especially in the Mekong Delta.

As a communist deputy chief of propaganda observed, "After five fruitless attempts to capture cities in 1968 and 1969 . . . the Tet Offensive and its aftermath ushered in the darkest days of the revolution for the western Mekong Delta."[91] Washington calculated that enemy forces lost 60 percent of their manpower in the South. The Joint Chiefs reported that no major actions occurred in the latter months of 1969.[92] During this period, many of the Viet Cong's political organizations at the area and village levels were dealt a severe setback. US and South Vietnamese forces had extended government control to 9,200 hamlets and about 16 million people, out of a total of 12,395 hamlets with a population of 17,500 million.[93]

The allied incursion into Cambodia in 1970 pushed North Vietnamese combat divisions further away from South Vietnam and disrupted the enemy's logistic system in the border areas. Of even greater significance, the ascension of the Lon Nol government in Phnom Penh resulted in the closure of the port of Sihanoukville, severely hampering Hanoi's ability to supply its forces in the delta by sea. Moreover, by the end of Bud Zumwalt's term as COMNAVFORV in May 1970, the nature of the war and its geographic center had changed. North Vietnamese infantry divisions armed with heavy artillery, armored fighting vehicles, and antiaircraft defenses then operated principally in the dry lands of northern and central South Vietnam. The Mekong Delta, with only decimated and isolated bands of Viet Cong guerrillas and a few North Vietnamese regulars, became a backwater.

Especially relevant to the seeming success of Zumwalt's operations and programs was the provision by the secretary of defense of billions of dollars of military and economic assistance to the Republic of Vietnam. Laird's strong support for the Vietnamization program did much to ensure that the Vietnam Navy received more than adequate resources. Neither Zumwalt's predecessors nor his successors had access to that high level of Washington support. Tom Moorer admitted that Zumwalt "did quite well" during his time as COMNAVFORV, but suggested it was because Zumwalt "was in a position to exploit an expanding operation" that brought in an abundance of arms and equipment for the Vietnamese armed forces.[94] During Zumwalt's time, there were more US Navy personnel, ships, riverine combatants, rotary-wing aircraft, and other assets in Vietnam than at any other time of the war. The coastal, riverine, and river patrol forces had honed their skills after years of operation, maximizing their combat effectiveness. The high number of American naval personnel in South Vietnam also enabled Zumwalt to expand the program to advise and train the Vietnam Navy.

Moreover, Bud Zumwalt clearly benefitted when he gained the respect and support of General Abrams. Zumwalt understood that "the Army was the top dog in Vietnam," requiring the Navy's support and cooperation.[95] Zumwalt suggested that Army and Navy forces that operated in the delta did so as a "band of brothers."[96] Abrams's positive connection with Zumwalt differed significantly from the general's and Westmoreland's dealings with the former COMNAVORV, Rear Admiral Kenneth L. Veth. Hyland, the Pacific Fleet commander, remembered that Veth "didn't get along with Westmoreland at all."[97] Salzer remembered that the less-than-inspiring admiral "made a weak impression on the MACV hierarchy."[98] Veth remembered in his oral history that "by far the worst, most disagreeable, disruptive SOB that I came across in any [military] service was a fellow named Dutch [Walter T.] Kerwin."[99] Army Major General Kerwin served as Westmoreland's chief of staff but of greater relevance worked for Abrams, the Deputy MACV after May 1967 and later COMUSMACV. Apparently, Kerwin thought so little of Veth that he did not mention the admiral in his postwar two-volume, 524-page oral history.[100]

Before Zumwalt, Abrams and his Army subordinates criticized Veth's and the Navy's performance in Vietnam. Abrams did not invite the admiral to brief on naval operations at weekly meetings. Just before Zumwalt's departure from Washington en route to Saigon in September 1968, Westmoreland, by then the Army chief of staff, told the admiral that "the Navy's never been in a war out there." He added that "they're not giving us any help, and so I never knew much about what they were doing."[101] Zumwalt heard similar reports from Abrams. When Veth and Zumwalt visited MACV headquarters for the latter's inaugural meeting with COMUSMACV, the general kept the two admirals in a waiting room for fifty minutes. When Abrams emerged from his office, he "went over and shook Admiral Zumwalt's hand and totally ignored Admiral Veth." In fact, "he didn't even acknowledge that he was in the room."[102]

Despite Veth's real failings, Bud Zumwalt's characterization of him was inaccurate and unduly harsh. He heaped opprobrium on his predecessor as he often did on those who opposed his views or merely had a different opinion. He labeled Veth a "loser" who "was out there having a gay social time and was not invested in the war." Zumwalt added that Veth's "concept of the war was to keep his troops from getting shot at." He implied that his predecessor had failed to understand or react to the enemy's use of the smaller watercourses of the delta to transport supplies brought in from Cambodia. Zumwalt also dismissed the Navy component of the joint Mobile Riverine Force as "a sort of transportation and escort service for the Army's 9th Division."[103] He made no mention of the MRF's significant role in devastating the Viet Cong during the Tet Offensive and recapturing the delta's main population centers.

Zumwalt was equally disdainful of Veth's NAVFORV staff and by implication the mid-level officers in the field. He thought that their level of competence "hovered around zero" because Vietnam had been a "dumping ground for weak naval officers." He blamed the "second-rate Navy effort" on traditionalists who "considered Vietnam some kind of banana war, not a 'Navy' war."[104] He also faulted Tom Moorer for starving NAVFORV of resources. Zumwalt related that Moorer and Hyland cautioned him during the Vietnamization years about turning over too much US Navy material to the Vietnamese. He was being told via back channel message traffic to "take it easy; don't give away our store."[105] As a result, Zumwalt did not have a high opinion of Hyland and later as CNO ended the career of the prominent naval aviator. Zumwalt said Hyland was "a very likable and attractive person, but he just didn't seem to me to have four-star competence [and] he didn't seem to have a grasp."[106]

Zumwalt clearly understood that his ability to execute Abrams's campaign plan would determine the success or failure of his own tenure as COMNAVFORV. The seeming success of the SEALORDS campaign in interdicting enemy infiltration from Cambodia, spreading the South Vietnamese government's writ in the delta, and swiftly preparing the Vietnam Navy to continue the fight won the Army general's high praise. Abrams told the admiral that SEALORDS "was the single most important contributor to the rapid pacification of the delta." As Zumwalt remembered it, "from that point on, General Abrams was a Navy man."[107] The general told Secretary Ignatius that Zumwalt "was the best naval officer he had ever known."[108]

Abrams's high regard for Bud Zumwalt was reciprocated. The admiral considered the general "one of my true heroes" and that he never "worked for a better military boss." He rated Abrams "the number-one military superior I've ever served under." In fact, "I loved the man."[109] Zumwalt considered Abrams a "great military captain" whom the admiral compared favorably to "such historical military geniuses as MacArthur, Lee, Rommel, etc."[110] Later, when both men served on the Joint Chiefs of Staff, Zumwalt expressed "enormous respect, even veneration" for the general.[111] President Nixon was much less enamored with Abrams's performance in Vietnam, so the warm Abrams-Zumwalt connection did not enhance the admiral's popularity at the White House when he became CNO.

Evaluating Zumwalt's performance in Vietnam requires a close look at the results of the SEALORDS and ACTOV programs while the admiral served in South Vietnam and in the years afterward. One of Zumwalt's attributes was his innovative thinking and sometimes unorthodox solutions. He referred to them as his "ZWIs" (Zumwalt's Wild Ideas).[112] One of his NAVFORV staffers emphasized that Zumwalt's approach to a problem was to "shoot 1,000 arrows at the target and have ten hit [rather] than only shoot two and the two hit."[113] Captain Earl F. Rectanus, Zumwalt's chief of intelligence, related that Bud Zumwalt's "thoughts and ideas were prolific in quantity and were the epitome of originality and quality." The admiral investigated numerous measures to improve the war effort, but if he found one measure unworkable "he would readily discard it and move on."[114] Swartz remembered one of Zumwalt's more unusual ZWIs. The admiral considered depositing a herd of goats on Cu Lao Re, a deserted island southeast of Danang, so Vietnamese sailors could land there, hunt the animals, and supplement their meager diets. Only after Swartz and other subordinates had investigated the pluses and minuses of the concept and pointed out its impracticality did the admiral drop the matter. A similar use for kangaroos may also have been considered.[115]

Zumwalt's major campaign to reestablish the South Vietnamese government's presence in the Ca Mau Peninsula, one of the most inhospitable regions of Vietnam, was at best a qualified success. Air Force planes were called on frequently to defoliate the terrain surrounding allied forces with Agent Orange, later determined to be a cancer-causing substance. SEAL Robert Stoner, however, expressed confidence that defoliation saved American and South Vietnamese lives by denying the enemy cover and concealment. Zumwalt too concluded that without question, the spraying was the "single most significant factor" in reducing casualties.[116] He believed the fatal cancer contracted by his son, Swift boat officer Elmo Zumwalt III, to be the result of spraying that the admiral had personally authorized. Zumwalt judged that several hundred men might have developed malignancies from Agent Orange, but at the same time he suggested that there were "undoubtedly thousands who are alive as a result" of the spraying.[117]

Coast Guard Commander Yost led US coastal patrol forces in the Gulf of Thailand and then Operation Sea Float during the first half of 1969. He described the difficulty of winning the hearts and minds of the South Vietnamese population in the Ca Mau. Yost was uneasy when Hoffmann, his immediate superior as Commander Task Force 115, told him that "what I want out of you is body count. I want sampans. I want Viet Cong. I want pigs; I want chickens; I want farmhouses; I want water jugs. I want it [*sic*] destroyed." Yost followed orders and since "we were very effective," he turned in a significant body count. The captain sarcastically described a "relatively successful operation, if sinking dugouts, and sampans, and burning farms, and breaking water jugs, and killing chickens and chasing peasants who are supporting the Viet Cong into the hinterlands, is the measure of success." He was not convinced that was the way to win the war.[118]

Yost gave a specific example of how military necessity could work against winning hearts and minds. His Swift boats had to proceed at high speed to limit their vulnerability to enemy ambush but doing so sent waves of water into the dwellings of the very people who settled along the river to benefit from allied military protection. He recalled women standing on the banks and pleading with the Americans to slow down, as the boats' wakes hit their riverside homes, "washing right through and taking out beds [and] stoves."[119] Kerry echoed those observations. He too concluded that Swift boats speeding down the rivers "with guns blazing . . . betrayed the very reason that we were supposed to be there." He surmised that more Viet Cong recruits were enlisted by those actions than were deterred by them.[120]

Yost thought of Bud Zumwalt as "a cheerleader." He remembered that following a Zumwalt visit to Sea Float, "everybody was ready to put on a G-string and go out and find the Viet Cong themselves and win the war."[121] Yost admired the admiral's leadership, but that did not stop the commander from expressing his misgivings about the mission. Yost's reports often contradicted what Zumwalt was hearing from the "kitchen cabinet" at NAVFORV headquarters, who supposedly told the admiral what they thought he wanted to hear. Loyalty from subordinates was especially important to Zumwalt. The admiral's intelligence chief Rectanus described how his boss rewarded loyalty. He observed that "seldom does a man by intellect and force of character affect the lives of so many, and seldom does this run so deep as to give reality to the concept of complete and total loyalty." He emphasized that he and others did well with Zumwalt, "so long as you were loyal and you tried your hardest to do what he wanted."[122] Yost's truthful but negative observations almost got him fired. It didn't happen, since the NAVFORV staff knew that he was only serving a short stint at Sea Float between assignments and they did not want to create problems with Coast Guard headquarters in Washington.[123]

There was another serious problem with the Vietnamization program: the unwillingness of too many in South Vietnam's military to close with and destroy enemy forces. One VNN officer apprised Yost that if one of his boat commanders got into a firefight with the Viet Cong that resulted in damage to the boat or casualties, unlike the Americans he would not be awarded a medal but relieved of his command. Another officer explained that Americans could be brave because they only had to survive one year in combat, while the Vietnamese were in it for the duration of the long conflict. The upshot was that many Vietnam Navy leaders only reluctantly put their boats and sailors in harm's way. Yost bemoaned that "we were fighting for their country with more intensity than they were."[124]

Some observers expressed concern that the VNN would be unable to win the war on the rivers without the US forces. NAVFORV reported that by 15 March 1970, shortly before Zumwalt headed for Washington, on the barrier patrols the US Navy had killed seven times more enemy troops than had the Vietnam Navy and suffered three times the number of casualties. One Zumwalt critic concluded that the

VNN "had not a snowball's chance in hell of picking up the burden of operations" absent the US Navy.[125]

That appraisal of South Vietnamese leadership was not universal among the Americans. Crowe related that his counterpart, Captain Nguyen Thong, was a combat veteran whose riverine task force supported the ARVN 21st Infantry Division in the U Minh Forest. Crowe considered the captain a "tough, hard man [who] was a bona fide warrior who expected no quarter and gave none." Crowe remembered that Thong's men "could smell danger [since] they had been fighting guerrillas so long they just did things instinctively."[126] Swartz had a similar evaluation of Commander Do Kiem, in charge of Vietnamese coastal patrol forces in the western delta and the Gulf of Thailand. The young American officer considered Kiem "one of the finest officers of any navy that I have worked with." Swartz emphasized that he "was clearheaded; he was honest; he had impeccable judgement; and he knew how to handle Americans. I would have followed him anywhere." Swartz concluded, "If every one of the South Vietnamese and US officers had been like Kiem, we would have won the war."[127]

The South Vietnamese government, the ARVN generals in charge of the delta, and even many Vietnam Navy leaders questioned the worth of Sea Float, but that was Zumwalt's showcase of Vietnamization and he was not about to give up on the experiment. Routinely, Bud Zumwalt put visitors to Vietnam on a helicopter and whisked them to the floating barge complex for a "show and tell" by the admiral and his admiring staff. Nevertheless, Zumwalt's successes in the southern delta proved transitory. In the wake of his departure to Washington to take on the CNO billet, the situation around Sea Float and Solid Anchor slowly deteriorated from lack of military and economic support from Saigon. Capitalizing on the departure of the US 9th Infantry Division from the delta, the enemy targeted ARVN outposts throughout the region, overrunning ninety-six of them during 1971. By the end of the war, the government fully controlled no more than a few kilometers on either side of the Cua Lon.[128]

Zumwalt considered his major initiative, the Accelerated Turnover to the Vietnamese program, the "closest to my heart." He was "as proud of it as of anything I have ever done." He had a major goal for the program; it was to "obliterate an all too prevalent notion [among American sailors] that the Vietnamese were congenitally incapable of operating or maintaining mechanical equipment or mastering military tactics or preserving discipline."¹²⁹ To combat that perception, Zumwalt instituted a "sensitivity training program," also known as the Personal Response Program, for US naval personnel.¹³⁰

To improve the image of the Vietnam Navy and its leaders, Bud Zumwalt routinely engaged in public functions side by side with Admiral Chon, the South Vietnamese CNO.¹³¹ There were few change-of-command or award ceremonies, combatant craft and naval base turnover events, or visits to pigs and chickens and dependent housing program sites that did not produce numerous photos of the allied leaders together. Zumwalt suggested that he always tried not to give the impression that he rather than Chon was "running the show." Zumwalt, however, clearly dominated the relationship and made the key decisions of the naval war. Zumwalt considered Chon as "our *Ace-in-the-Hole*" (original italics) to facilitate the US withdrawal "just as rapidly as it is humanly possible."¹³²

There was no question that Bud Zumwalt had an affinity for his counterpart. He regarded the officer as brave, intelligent, a devout Buddhist, and a loyal South Vietnamese officer. Zumwalt was especially impressed that unlike many other South Vietnamese leaders, Chon "had risen on merit, not through a coup."¹³³ Zumwalt gushed about the man in his oral history. He considered the Vietnamese CNO "a magnificent individual and magnificent leader [and] a man of high ethical and moral principles." Zumwalt was impressed that Chon, unlike other Vietnamese leaders, lived a humble existence, and was revered by his officers and men. Zumwalt suggested that "there was not the slightest doubt about his incorruptibility."¹³⁴ When Chon thanked Zumwalt for facilitating his son Truc's entry and graduation in 1974 from the US Naval Academy, the American admiral, then in his last days as CNO, responded, "I felt that he was my own son, and you my brother." With Chon retiring that same year, only one year before Hanoi's conquest of the Republic of Vietnam, Zumwalt observed that "you can look on a great fighting South Vietnamese Navy which you have forged from humble beginnings." He added that "history will record you at the side of Tran Hung Dao [a great Vietnamese hero] and I am proud to be known as your friend."¹³⁵

Chon returned the compliments manyfold. In his letters, the Vietnamese leader expressed a "strong nostalgia of those cherished moments that we shared together." He exclaimed, "I came to know and greatly admire you for the distinguished demeanor, the outstanding

Secretary of Defense Melvin Laird and Zumwalt share a laugh. Laird and Navy secretary John Chafee were so impressed with Zumwalt's leadership qualities that they backed him to be the next Chief of Naval Operations. NHHC VN Collection.

capabilities and the broad knowledge that you have demonstrated."[136] Chon thanked Zumwalt for the "countless benefactions you have bestowed upon me and the Vietnamese Navy during your most laudable tour of service in Vietnam and your succeeding tenure as Chief of Naval Operations of the United States Navy."[137]

The apparent success of ACTOV, in conjunction with Laird's personal impression of the naval officer formed during the defense secretary's visit to Vietnam in early 1969, gave his career, as Zumwalt suggested, "an unexpected boost."[138] Laird had not intended to be brought up to speed about in-country naval operations, but COMNAVFORV managed to get on the briefing schedule along with Lieutenant General Ewell.

The admiral put on his usual attention-riveting performance. The general exclaimed afterward that "he had been scalped" and that it was "the last time he'd ever invite Zumwalt to participate in a briefing."[139] Since the man and his support for Vietnamization were already well known to Laird and Navy secretary Chafee, the briefing could not have come as a complete surprise. Bud Zumwalt hit a home run with his performance. Abrams suggested to Laird that the officer should be the next head of the Navy. He learned later that when the defense secretary returned to Washington, he told Chafee to make sure Zumwalt's name was on a short list for Moorer's replacement as CNO. Zumwalt remembered that his briefing resulted in "one of those pieces of luck that anyone who aspires to high position needs," but luck had little to do with his ascension to power.[140]

Laird did indeed want Zumwalt to be the next CNO because many observers considered the admiral youthful, energetic, intelligent, and a natural leader.[141] To facilitate that promotion, Laird did not stand in the way of Tom Moorer becoming Chairman of the Joint Chiefs of Staff, even though he was advised against that action. The defense secretary's military assistant, Air Force Colonel Robert Pursley, was an "old friend" of Zumwalt's. He warned Laird that Moorer was "devious" and "not to be trusted."[142] Laird sometimes butted heads with Moorer, who often helped the White House bypass the defense secretary. On the other hand, Laird and Moorer on occasion played golf and had lunch at Maryland's exclusive Burning Tree Country Club.[143]

Zumwalt later wrote that during his time in-country, he was confident that the South Vietnamese navy could ably carry on the war. The admiral had a much less rosy appraisal of the situation in Vietnam when as CNO he returned in 1972. He simply related how the VNN, on the schedule he had developed, had taken over 1,000 US naval vessels and grown from 17,000 to 40,000 officers and men. He did not address the strengths or weaknesses of the Vietnamization program or the course of the war at that point.

Other observers of ACTOV, however, were much less sanguine about the success of the program. One critic, who had served on Zumwalt's staff as the NAVFORV historian, compiled a report on the naval war. He suggested that the effort was doomed from the start. He emphasized that US naval advisors had been working since the mid-1950s to develop an efficient Vietnam navy, but that the service in the latter years of the war still suffered from many of the same ills that troubled its beginning.¹⁴⁴ Bill Crowe wrote that the Vietnam navy's dysfunction was hardly a unique phenomenon. He suggested that "the underlying corruption, thuggishness, and cronyism of the South Vietnamese government strangled the war effort in a dozen ways."¹⁴⁵

A number of key South Vietnamese naval officers also found fault with ACTOV. Hoang Co Minh was a combat veteran who would continue the fight against the Socialist Republic of Vietnam long after the fall of Saigon. In 1987, as head of the National United Front for the Liberation of Vietnam, he led 200 guerrillas from Thailand into southern Laos and toward Vietnam bent on setting up a resistance movement in the Central Highlands. Communist Laotian and Vietnamese troops intercepted the band, killing 100 of the insurgents including Minh and imprisoning the survivors. The intrepid naval officer paid with his life for his belief in a non-communist Vietnam.¹⁴⁶

Minh had served in the latter years of the war as the VNN's Deputy Chief of Staff for Political Warfare and in that capacity worked closely with the NAVFORV staff on the ACTOV program. Minh respected Zumwalt because the latter clearly wanted to help Vietnam. The officer, however, believed that the admiral misdirected ACTOV and "destroyed the [Vietnam] Navy." He concluded that the VNN "played a big part in his becoming the U.S. Navy CNO." In short, "he stepped on us to come up."¹⁴⁷ Zumwalt and his champions trumpeted the fact that the US Navy completed its objectives in the Vietnamization program before the other American services. But to Minh, that was the problem. He made an analogy: "I clean this room and you have to clean the same room, and after about five minutes I finish and I tell you that you are very slow. [However] the room is still very dirty." He concluded that "we had everything on the surface but underneath there was nothing." The "whole ACTOV program . . . was a big failure."¹⁴⁸

From the beginning, the VNN was overwhelmed by the speed with which NAVFORV developed the ACTOV program and compelled the Vietnamese to adopt it. At one point, the VNN staff was given twenty-four hours to study a plan, make comments, and reply to the Americans. The document, however, was written in English, and the Vietnamese never got a copy in their own language. Minh related that his complaints about the process got nowhere, since Zumwalt "didn't want to listen."¹⁴⁹

Minh was also in charge of the pigs-and-chickens programs. He lamented that "sometimes I could not understand what the program was, what was going on." The Americans and the Vietnamese interpreted what was required differently.[150] Ho Van Ky Thoai, commander of naval forces in northern South Vietnam from 1970 to 1975, thought raising pigs and chickens worked out all right until they emptied the warehouse that the Americans had filled with feed before they departed.[151]

Similar problems arose with the $900,000 dependent housing program. US Navy Seabees fitted each cinder block house with water, electricity, and toilet facilities—free of charge. Naval officer Nguyen Xuan Son related that the program succeeded in facilities close to large urban areas but not at remote bases.[152] Minh explained why he thought the entire program ultimately failed. Many sailors did not want to expose their families to danger by bringing them to an isolated and potentially vulnerable base. Thoai asked rhetorically, "What happens when you see your kid die in front of you; or your wife is dying right there and your kids are running around? Do you think that you would have the courage to abandon them there and go to the bunker to fight back?"[153]

Moreover, if a family occupied a house on the base, the wife and other family members would not be able to supplement family income by selling produce at a local market or be able to visit a nearby school or place of worship. The American-built houses were too small for the typical Vietnamese family. The toilets posed another problem. Unlike typical rents in the cities and towns, the cinder block houses did not have flush toilets—only fifty-five-gallon drums sawed in half. The families were expected to remove their waste daily but could not afford the fuel or odor-damping powder or the hired laborers employed by the Americans to dispose of their own offal. Few Vietnamese families chose to occupy one of the "free" houses. When Minh was told that Zumwalt planned to visit Dong Tam, the old Mobile Riverine Force base near My Tho, he learned that Chon had given him three or four days to "fill every house [400 units] to please Admiral Zumwalt." When Minh protested that he could not comply in the time allotted, Chon scrubbed the visit.[154]

Minh recommended that Chon not agree to accept former US Coast Guard cutters and Navy destroyer escorts because he thought it too difficult and expensive to man those large vessels, operate their mechanical systems, and maintain them. He felt that the time spent training Vietnamese sailors on board the larger US vessels (four or five months) was too short to prepare them to operate or maintain the vessels on their own. Zumwalt, however, had pushed the provision of these large combatants to the VNN and Chon would not cross his mentor.[155]

Still, Bud Zumwalt later remarked that "on balance I felt good about leaving" when he relinquished command of Naval Forces, Vietnam. He concluded that the allied navies were doing an "exceedingly fine job" and ACTOV was "showing results." He was also pleased that "the delta had been taken from the enemy and became a friendly area with only a few unfriendly pockets."[156]

THE IN-COUNTRY WAR AFTER ZUMWALT

Zumwalt's immediate successors as COMNAVFORV, Vice Admiral Jerome H. King Jr. and Rear Admiral Robert S. Salzer, were much less positive about the prospects of the Vietnam Navy or the Republic of Vietnam. King had been one of Tom Moorer's devoted subordinates.[157] The CNO rewarded that loyalty by facilitating King's promotion to vice admiral and dispatching the surface warfare officer to Saigon to relieve Zumwalt.[158] The prospective COMNAVFORV remembered that even though Moorer favored him, he was surprised at his selection for the billet. King admitted that he "was severely deficient in my understanding of the background of the Vietnam War, my understanding of Vietnamese culture, and my understanding of why we had so much difficulty dealing with the enemy—these little brown guys in black pajamas." Once in Saigon, he worked hard to understand his job, but progress was hard to come by.[159] Zumwalt later endorsed King's self-evaluation, observing that the officer "did a very poor job . . . primarily because he was the kind who simply never understood the Vietnamese culture."[160]

King had problems from the start. When Zumwalt departed, he took the best and the brightest members of the staff with him. Zumwalt later suggested that as CNO he "no longer involved myself in the day-to-day conduct of the Vietnam War," but King had a different appreciation. Until he put a stop to it, officers on his staff who had served under Zumwalt continued to communicate directly with their contacts in Washington without King's knowledge. King also complained about Zumwalt's micromanagement. The CNO called him once or twice a week because Zumwalt "had built NavForV and he couldn't let go."[161]

Unlike Zumwalt, King did not think highly of the VNN's leader. He considered Chon a "delightful fellow, with a nice sense of humor."

But he remembered that while Chon always agreed with his suggestions for action, he never took any. The American found it "so typically Vietnamese in character."[162] Minh was even less charitable about his compatriot. He complained that the Vietnamese CNO "was under very great pressure from Admiral Zumwalt and he wanted very much to satisfy Admiral Zumwalt." Minh felt that as the CNO, Chon "had a great responsibility to the Vietnamese [and that] to just please one man was bad" for the VNN. There is at least one indication that Zumwalt failed to accurately assess the character or loyalty of Chon and other South Vietnamese leaders. Zumwalt later related that a number of VNN officers "turned out to be a real surprise to all of us, that we would have all sworn were loyal to us . . . were actually VC agents." Swartz also related that after the war, commander Do Kiem told him "which of his fellow officers turned out to be Viet Cong; he was as surprised as I was."[163]

King railed against the infighting among the South Vietnamese military leaders. The ARVN general in charge of the Mekong Delta "didn't like anything to do with the Vietnamese Marine Corps," whose troops protected Nam Can and other naval bases. For their part, the Vietnamese marine leaders put King on their blacklist because they didn't think he allotted them enough ammunition. The admiral thought the marines didn't even expend what they had because they rarely went looking for the enemy in the jungle and swampy areas around Nam Can.[164] Dinh Manh Hung, in charge of riverine forces in the delta from 1971 to 1975, related that all the Vietnamese military services wanted to control operations in the delta. He complained that he had to be more of a diplomat than a military leader to satisfy the competing services.[165]

The upshot was that the military situation in the Ca Mau remained tenuous through the end of the war. Once the US Navy's two aviation squadrons returned to the states, the VNN had no dedicated air support. Maintaining the South Vietnamese government's presence at Nam Can was also much more difficult for the Vietnam Navy, which did not have the robust logistic support fleet that enabled Zumwalt to establish the base there.[166]

King detailed a host of problems that dogged the VNN during his time in Vietnam. Too often, the commanding officers of riverine craft would keep their vessel at anchor rather than go out on patrol. The US advisors serving with these units were sometimes concerned that if they raised an issue and it displeased the Vietnamese crew, the Americans would end up dead in the water. King explained how Vietnamization impacted the sailors of the VNN. "They were lassoing kids out of the rice paddies and bringing them in and making sailors out of them in a very big hurry." He added that "their motivation was thin [and] desertion was rampant."[167]

A special challenge of the Vietnamization program was the effort to improve the VNN's logistic establishment. King related that accounting for spare parts was "totally foreign to [the Vietnamese and] they were selling spare parts on the black market."[168] CNO Zumwalt helped overcome some problems with the logistic system by posting a flag officer logistics expert to the NAVAFORV staff. Unfortunately, Crowe found that "the Vietnamese developed the habit of letting the Americans" do everything. On one occasion he discovered a US sailor cleaning weapons on a river craft and his Vietnamese counterparts nearby fast asleep. He recognized that part of the problem was cultural, because "Vietnamese boys had not come of age driving cars [and] they didn't grow up fixing mechanical gadgets."[169]

ACTOV also entailed the turnover to the Vietnamese of all the US Navy's operational and support bases. As with the combat units, Zumwalt and his successors engineered the program so that Vietnamese officers and men ultimately replaced their American counterparts and took command of the facility. Bud Zumwalt had established the Personal Response Program to instruct American officers and men how to interact with their Vietnamese counterparts "across the cultural divide."[170] Minh argued that it looked good on paper but didn't work in practice. When NAVFORV headquarters dispatched personal response teams to straighten out troubled bases, as Minh related, "it came out very, very bad, because nobody listened." Whether you were American or Vietnamese, no one felt comfortable "under the command of a foreigner."[171] King believed that many of his sailors were distressed that the war's earlier gains were "slipping away" since the turnover process rarely achieved positive results. King implied that he felt the same as his men and considered the collapse of South Vietnam inevitable.[172]

Aside from the manifest problems associated with the Vietnamization program, King lacked his predecessor's ability to master them. Other than Tom Moorer, King did not have influential Washington supporters, a genius for innovative approaches, a close

CNO Zumwalt and Rear Admiral Robert S. Salzer, the latter then commander of US naval forces in Vietnam, confer on board a plane during Zumwalt's May 1971 visit to South Vietnam. Salzer expressed pessimism about the course of the war. NHHC USN 1148801.

rapport with his South Vietnamese counterparts, or personal magnetism. Moreover, during King's short one-year assignment as COMNAVFORV, he became so ill with back problems that at one point he could not walk and was in great physical pain. He spent the better part of three months recovering in the Philippines, and the Navy finally had to send him home. King later observed, "I don't believe I had—ever in my whole life—the sense of failure" that he had as COMNAVFORV. He recounted, "I just had a bad feeling that I had somehow been inadequate [and] the impression of a lot of people [was] that I flopped in the job." Zumwalt agreed with King's own negative assessment and "got Jerry out as soon as I reasonably could and put Bob Salzer in."[173]

In contrast to King, Robert Salzer was ideally suited to command Naval Forces, Vietnam. The officer, who filled a billet reduced from three to two stars, had earlier led riverine forces and earned the accolades of his Army and Navy superiors for tactical skill and bravery in battle. Bud Zumwalt was impressed with Salzer's straightforward manner and keen strategic sense. The senior officer characterized him as a "soldier-statesman." Zumwalt respected his judgment "most highly among all of those that were there" during Zumwalt's time as COMNAVFORV.[174] When Salzer pitched the idea of patrols to interdict enemy crossing points—the waterborne guard post tactic—it caught fire with Zumwalt, who tasked him with leading the SEALORDS campaign as First Sea Lord.[175]

Salzer was concerned about the Market Time coastal patrol when he arrived in April 1971 for his second Vietnam tour, but he soon found cause for optimism.[176] Allied patrol forces destroyed three infiltrating trawlers, compelling Hanoi to suspend their use of these ships for the rest of 1971 and early 1972.[177] Hanoi tried again in April 1972 when another trawler loaded with 400 tons of ammunition headed for the Ca Mau. Salzer remembered with distaste in his oral history that "we let this North Vietnamese trawler get in close before we challenged him."[178] He might have forgotten that in actuality nuclear-powered submarine *Sculpin* (SSN-590) and P-3 Orion patrol planes had trailed the enemy trawler all the way from the Chinese island of Hainan to the Ca Mau. US intelligence verified through communications intercepts that the ship was indeed North Vietnamese. When the trawler's captain refused to stop or alter his course away from the coast, VNN submarine chaser *Tran Khanh Do* (HQ-4) opened fire on the infiltrator. Rather than surrender, the North Vietnamese crew scuttled their vessel.[179]

Nonetheless, Salzer later characterized the Vietnam Navy's coverage of the offshore patrol sectors "totally ineffective." He contrasted the South Vietnamese sailors with the North Vietnamese trawler crewmen. He remembered admiringly how the communist sailors "blew themselves up" rather than surrender.[180] Nguyen Huu Chi, who commanded the VNN's Market Time operation from 1970 to 1972, agreed with Salzer that without the dedicated support of the American P-3s, the Vietnamese surveillance force did not have "a high level of efficiency."[181] Indeed, after the Paris Agreement, Hanoi significantly ramped up its seaborne infiltration effort. In 1973, Brigade 125 delivered 3,000 tons of munitions to South Vietnam and the following year 15,000 tons. In the pivotal year of 1975, North Vietnamese ships transported south for the final battles 17,473 personnel, 40 tanks, and 7,786 tons of arms.[182]

Salzer also considered the River Force operationally ineffective. He concluded that the South Vietnamese units in the delta would have been in deep trouble "if the Viet Cong had not become so disorganized." He found the VNN's maintenance of recently turned over US river vessels substandard and the River Force's American advisors demoralized.[183] Hoang Co Minh also found the morale of the South Vietnamese sailors especially low because they had seen too much action and too many fellow sailors killed or wounded. Complaining that their command responsibilities were "too hard," Minh's two predecessors had asked to be relieved of command.

Like King, when Salzer had completed his April 1971–June 1972 tour as COMNAVFORV he concluded that the fast pace of the US withdrawal from Vietnam "had left us with at best, a shaky foundation for the success of Vietnamization." He suggested that had the United States started the Vietnamization process earlier in the war, the VNN might have developed into a decent combat force. The American attitude toward the Vietnamese then, however, had been: "Stand aside little brother, and we will square things away and then we will hand you back your country."[184]

Salzer questioned the professionalism and courage of South Vietnamese naval officers, at various times suggesting that they were "chicken" and prone to run away at the first ambush. The navy in general he ranked "for a number of reasons, including their ineptness," fourth behind the army, air force, and marine corps.[185] Other Americans shared that view. Right after Zumwalt initiated SEALORDS, Lieutenant Don Droz, a Swift boat officer later killed in action, wrote to his wife. He told her that "we simply have to force the Vietnamese Navy to do anything—and then their performance is so half-assed and second-rate as to be a nuisance rather than a help." He lamented that "these people simply don't give a damn . . . so why should we?" Kerry was equally negative about the VNN. He complained that he and his men rarely saw the South Vietnamese-crewed patrol boats provided through ACTOV on patrol and when they did, the allied sailors were either asleep or fishing.[186]

Salzer bemoaned that in 1972 he had little time to strengthen the VNN. He doubted that the Vietnam Navy would amount to much then or for the next decade. He related that he was told the day before he left Vietnam that he was a defeatist, a sentiment repeated when he got to Washington. There he discovered "sort of a football team mentality—our team must win—without much appraising of its strengths and weaknesses."[187]

At one point, Admiral McCain suggested to Washington that the provision to the South Vietnamese armed forces of sophisticated weapons could place an unmanageable burden on them. Laird disagreed with CINCPAC, reminding the admiral that he should not underestimate the ability of the Vietnamese armed forces to do the job. In fact, for the Enhance and Enhance Plus Vietnamization-support programs, Laird accelerated the supply of advanced tanks, aircraft, and other armaments, with the entire effort costing the United States $5.3 billion. During 1972, the United States shipped to Vietnam over 105,000 tons of equipment, including 70,767 small arms, 382 artillery pieces, 622 tracked vehicles, and 2,035 wheeled vehicles.[188] Laird was impressed that of all the services, the Navy had accomplished its Vietnamization goals the fastest and had turned over 80 percent of its combat craft to the VNN by mid-1970.[189]

Early on, Salzer learned that the US-Vietnamese effort to develop a robust logistic establishment for the VNN was failing. Mountains of resources were pouring into the country with little accountability as to their distribution or use by the Vietnamese. Salzer immediately met with Abrams and did "one of those things that one should never do and walk on board and tell your boss, 'Everything is a Goddamn mess.'" But the intrepid officer explained that he had a "fetid mess in logistics."[190] Corrective measures only marginally improved the problem.

Admiral Chon, who resented Salzer's intrusion into what he considered his preserve, proved to be one of the chief obstacles to the effort to improve the VNN's logistic establishment. Like King, Salzer considered Chon a "very nice man" who was accepted by all the factions in the highly politicized Vietnam Navy. Unlike King, however, Salzer considered the Vietnamese CNO "inept and almost certainly corrupt."[191] Captain Son, who commanded the VNN's sea forces, agreed with Salzer's assessment.[192] Salzer suspected that Chon objected to the logistic system reforms because it would upset other naval officers "who aspired to be big-scale thieves." Salzer told Chon that he would withhold any new supplies of spare parts until the VNN completed an accurate account of the material it already had. Chon immediately complained to Zumwalt in Washington about Salzer's action.[193]

When the CNO visited Vietnam in February 1972, Salzer and Chon had a confrontation in his presence. Afterward, Zumwalt counseled Salzer that "you've got to be easier on Chon; he can't take that kind of pressure." The hard-nosed COMNAVFORV responded that if Chon couldn't handle that kind of pressure, how would he fare in future against North Vietnamese General Giap? Salzer suggested that Chon would be "chewed up alive." Despite being close to Chon personally from his time as COMNAVFORV and still in favor of his leadership of the VNN, Zumwalt heard Salzer's complaints and didn't countermand anything his subordinate was doing. Thereafter, Chon and Salzer established a more cooperative relationship, but Salzer felt that Chon did not have his heart in it. Salzer concluded that with the South Vietnamese, "poor leadership or no leadership was the rule of thumb." He regretted that the United States had failed to develop a professional officer corps. Before he returned to Washington, Zumwalt checked on the progress of ACTOV and, according to Salzer, "couldn't believe his eyes." The former COMNAVFORV wondered how it could have "deteriorated so much?"[194]

In his 1976 memoir, Bud Zumwalt told a different story, observing, "I found that the [ACTOV] program was right on schedule I had set for it when I initiated it." He contended that Abrams was positive, and Vietnamization was proceeding well.[195] He blamed Congress, not the failure of Vietnamization, for the final debacle in 1975. Addressing students at the Industrial College of the Armed Forces in March of that year, the former CNO expressed shock that Congress, "in what seems to be almost a death wish," had ruled out US forces coming to the assistance of South Vietnam.[196]

Several Vietnamese naval leaders argued that the military assistance provided by the United States could not solve the underlying weaknesses of the Republic of Vietnam. Ho Van Ky Thoai was convinced that sooner or later the communists would win "because you cannot get U.S. aid forever."[197] Admiral Chung Tan Cang, the CNO from 1964 to 1966 and again in the last days before the end of the war, suggested that US military assistance was "like a sick man who can only survive by daily injections."[198]

The image of Vietnamization in Washington was that the program had strengthened South Vietnam's armed forces, but that image was an illusion. Even one of Laird's biographers admitted that the "ignominious, rapid collapse of South Vietnam in 1975 brutally exposed the weaknesses of its armed forces and raised anew questions about the validity and accomplishments" of Vietnamization.[199] Signs abounded that the navy and the other armed forces, despite the infusion of US military assistance, could not stand up to a determined North Vietnamese invasion to secure victory.

Zumwalt ultimately came to recognize that despite US efforts in general, and his own in particular, the Republic of Vietnam was doomed. At one point the admiral praised the valor of the US Navy sailors killed in action because they shared the burdens of war with American soldiers and because they helped secure the Mekong Delta. He lamented in his memoir, however, that "all that was accomplished for nothing, so all these soldiers and sailors died in vain." He concluded, "I believe our effort in Vietnam was worse than futile. We would have been better off in every way never taking that stand."[200]

CHAPTER 7

FIGHTING TO RETREAT

Admiral Thomas Moorer's service as acting chairman and then chairman of the Joint Chiefs of Staff made him the central military figure in President Nixon's war on North Vietnam. In contrast to his time as the Navy member of the JCS, which the admiral dismissed as inconsequential, chairman Moorer became directly involved in Vietnam-related issues.

In 1969, Nixon contemplated a bombing campaign against North Vietnamese forces concentrated in Cambodia not many miles from South Vietnam's capital city. Enemy incursions from sanctuaries in Cambodia had long plagued allied ground operations in South Vietnam and threatened to destabilize the Vietnamization program. General Abrams believed that his staff had identified the location in Cambodia of North Vietnam's main combat headquarters, the Central Office for South Vietnam (COSVN). Nixon saw bombing in Cambodia as a way to disrupt North Vietnamese logistic operations. Most important, he wanted to let North Vietnam, China, and the Soviet Union understand "who is boss around here" and not think of him as hamstrung in international affairs by America's commitment to South Vietnam.[1] While regularly opposing US air operations external to South Vietnam, this time Secretary of Defense Laird came around to the proposal for a bombing campaign in Cambodia. He hoped to show his support of the Joint Chiefs during his first operational interaction with the group.

Laird did, however, want the operation to be acknowledged publicly. Nixon did not agree to that proposal.

Those in the know about the proposed "secret" campaign included only Laird, Secretary of State William Rogers, National Security Advisor Henry Kissinger, Tom Moorer (standing in for JCS chairman Wheeler who was ill), and several staff officers. Moorer agreed that secrecy was essential because by that time in the war leaks to Congress and the press about military operations had become commonplace. He groused that "no one can keep a secret." He felt it "a goddamn shame" that "you can't even conduct foreign policy without everyone and their mother finding out what the hell is going on."[2]

On 18 March 1969, in the first of a series of so-called Menu operations, sixty Guam-based B-52 bombers dropped their ordnance on what was suspected to be the COSVN headquarters. It turned out to be a fuel and ammunition dump, destroyed by the bombers' twenty-four tons of bombs. Over the next fourteen months, the B-52 fleet had their fill flying 3,630 sorties in the decidedly unmilitary-sounding operations Lunch, Dinner, Snack, Supper, and Dessert, unloading 100,000 tons of bombs inside Cambodia.[3]

While the operations took a toll of enemy supply caches, they did not remain secret. Within months, a military member passed information to the press that American aircraft were bombing in Cambodia. Moorer remembered that when he saw the newspaper account of the bombing in Cambodia based on leaked information, he didn't think he'd "seen Mr. Nixon as mad in my life." Moorer remembered him "stalking across the rose garden on the way to the Oval Office with the *New York Times* in his hand."[4] In an unsuccessful effort to keep the operation quiet, the military chain of command had manipulated the reporting system by identifying "fictitious" sites in South Vietnam as the targets when in fact the actual sites were in Cambodia. The full details of the operation did not surface for many more years. North Vietnamese leaders, of course, were not about to admit that they had 100,000 troops in Cambodia, so they said nothing. Prince Sihanouk of Cambodia publicly denounced the bombings but privately informed US authorities that he applauded the measure to rid his country of the ever-intrusive Vietnamese. The Menu operations ended in May 1970, but US bombing operations in Cambodia would continue to the end of the war in Southeast Asia.[5]

Frustrated by Hanoi's rejection of various proposals for a negotiated settlement of the war, Nixon decided to get tough with his adversaries.

In a secret July 1969 communication to Ho Chi Minh, Nixon threatened that the North Vietnamese government had until 1 November to agree to US terms or he would have no alternative but to adopt "measures of great consequence and force."[6] Like many in the government before him, Kissinger refused to believe that "a little fourth-rate power like North Vietnam does not have a breaking point." Like Nixon, he too wanted "a savage, decisive blow" against North Vietnam.[7]

Nixon's relationship with Secretary of Defense Laird began to fray during this period. In April 1969, little more than a year after North Korea's seizure of the US intelligence ship *Pueblo*, the North Korean air force attacked a US Navy EC-121 Warning Star intelligence-collection plane over the Sea of Japan. The attackers destroyed the aircraft, killing its entire 31-man crew. The president wanted to launch an immediate military retaliation against North Korea and ordered the deployment of naval forces to waters off Korea. But the defense secretary delayed the process until the time for effective action had passed. Nixon was furious with Laird, but he resisted chastising his subordinate for fear of antagonizing Laird's powerful friends on Capitol Hill. He did, however, vow not to let Laird hamstring his actions ever again.[8]

As a consequence of that episode, Nixon directed Kissinger to establish a liaison office to serve as a direct link, bypassing the defense secretary, between the president and the Joint Chiefs. Chairman Wheeler assigned Captain (later Rear Admiral) Rembrandt C. Robinson as head of that small office that reported to the White House. Nixon tasked Robinson and his staff with studying "brutal" military actions that the US could take to make the North Vietnamese more amenable to the president's proposals after the November deadline. The resulting study—Duck Hook—considered renewed bombing of the North, closure of that country's ports through mining, an amphibious landing in North Vietnam, and the possible employment of tactical nuclear weapons. Nixon soon realized that his chief cabinet advisors would vehemently oppose such measures, as would the powerful and growing anti-war movement. Moreover, Wheeler and the other members of the JCS considered the plan inadequate from a military standpoint. In the end, Nixon decided that the time was not right to launch such serious military actions.[9]

On 1 October 1969, Moorer forwarded to Laird a JCS-proposed operation that would accommodate Nixon's wish to strike North Vietnam with a massive air and naval assault. The objective in

Operation Pruning Knife would be to deliver a "shock" to the North Vietnamese government. US forces would neutralize North Vietnam's air defenses and airfields, close all of its ports through aerial mining and surface Navy interdiction, and destroy high-value economic and war-supporting facilities. The Joint Chiefs wanted to employ "maximum available force," including B-52 bombers and tactical aircraft. Targets would include sites in Haiphong and the North Vietnamese ministry of defense, Communist Party training centers, the telephone and telegraph office, and the railroad station in downtown Hanoi.

Still, the military leaders did not call for the overthrow of the Hanoi government or an invasion and occupation of the country. The Joint Chiefs' one caveat was that the White House had to understand that the northeast monsoon, which lasted from November through March, stood to adversely impact air operations. A week later, Laird took his own pruning knife to the JCS Concept Plan. He observed that the Joint Chiefs' scheme did not convince him that it would achieve decisive results. Instead, he felt it would inflame anti-war opinion at home and around the world, cause heavy casualties, and deplete dwindling defense department resources. It went no further.[10]

Given Nixon's animus toward Laird, the president's relationship with Moorer (as acting and then permanent chairman of the JCS) took on added importance and stood in stark contrast to the almost nonexistent connection between President Johnson and General Wheeler. Tom Moorer's influence with Nixon became so strong that he became the only JCS leader the president would go to. Moorer remembered that for major operations, "Nixon would tell me to write the order that I wanted Laird to send me, and then give it back to him, and he would send it over to Laird and say, 'Send this to the Chairman of the Joint Chiefs of Staff.'" Moorer complied with the president's wishes but being "always caught in the middle" made him uneasy.[11] One suspects, however, that the admiral was not displeased with the latitude this gave him to orchestrate operations.

Tom Moorer considered his relationship with the president "excellent." The admiral particularly liked Nixon's decisiveness because he would take action even if everyone else was opposed. Moorer affirmed that he never had a problem with Nixon, who normally approved the admiral's proposals for action. Moorer told Oley Sharp, then retired, that Nixon called him on the phone frequently and according to Sharp, the JCS chairman had no difficulty passing Sharp's views to Nixon or

Richard Nixon and Moorer confer on board aircraft carrier USS *Saratoga* (CVA-60) in May 1969. As Chairman of the Joint Chiefs of Staff, the admiral became Nixon's closest and most trusted military advisor. NHHC K-72713.

Kissinger. The former CINCPAC was pleased that the president made Moorer a member of relevant National Security Council subcommittees and frequently asked for the admiral's opinion during those meetings.[12]

The president, however, never cultivated a personal bond with the naval officer, despite Tom Moorer's close association with many of Nixon's Vietnam ventures and direct connection with the White House. Moorer, for instance, never heard Nixon use profanity in his presence; he was shocked when he later listened to the White House tapes.[13] Moorer observed that Nixon "had a very formal relationship with the man in uniform." Alexander Haig, Kissinger's deputy at the time, remembered that "the president didn't mistrust the military." Indeed, "he was very, very pro-military." He was "a Boy Scout [and] he thought the military was the cream of the crop."[14]

WAR COMES TO CAMBODIA

Nixon saw another opportunity to strike at the North Vietnamese war effort when Cambodian army chief of staff Lon Nol used Sihanouk's absence from the country in March 1970 to overthrow the government. The new leader immediately closed the port of Sihanoukville, which cut off a major supply line to Viet Cong forces in the Mekong Delta. Lon Nol also called for US and South Vietnamese help because North Vietnamese troops and Cambodian communist guerrillas—the Khmer Rouge—seemed poised to overwhelm his ill-trained and under-armed forces. In response, Nixon authorized Abrams to complement the B-52 bombing with tactical air strikes.

Nixon began to seriously consider a ground invasion of the country. He knew such a step would fire up the domestic and international anti-war movement but considered the effort worth the risk since, as he intimated to New York governor Nelson Rockefeller, "when you bite the bullet, bite it hard—go for the big play."[15] During Nixon's mid-April visit to CINCPAC headquarters in Hawaii, Admiral McCain so impressed the president about the advantages of a major ground action in Cambodia that Nixon had the officer travel to San Clemente, California, the "Western White House," to reiterate that message to Kissinger and others. McCain emphasized that if the president withdrew 150,000 troops from South Vietnam that year as planned, an invasion of the Cambodian sanctuaries would divert enemy attention from the American withdrawal operation.

Nixon, Moorer, McCain, and CIA director Richard Helms wanted not only South Vietnamese but also US forces to enter Cambodia. Laird, while fully supportive of an effort to eliminate the border sanctuaries, insisted that South Vietnamese forces were capable of handling the job alone. His view did not prevail. As noted earlier, after the EC-121 episode, Nixon did not easily accept Laird's advice. On 24 April, Nixon convened a meeting that included Kissinger, Helms, Marine Corps Commandant General Robert Cushman, and Moorer, the last filling in for the once again ailing General Wheeler. Not invited to the gathering was the secretary of defense. When Moorer asked if he should discuss planning for the ground invasion with Laird, Kissinger's staff informed the admiral that he was then acting as the president's military advisor and that "he was to tell Laird nothing."[16]

Abrams then developed a plan for a joint US–South Vietnamese advance under US command into Cambodia. Nixon recognized that the employment of American troops would inflame the anti-war movement but considered the destruction of the enemy's base areas in that part of Cambodia essential. Moorer agreed with the president and remembered Nixon saying, "If we get caught with our hand in the cookie jar, we must be sure we get the cookies."[17] Laird learned of the decision to invade Cambodia after the fact. On 27 April, Nixon telephoned Wheeler, back on the job, to emphasize that for the coming push into Cambodia, "the military is really on the spot, and if they blow this you've had it."[18] Moorer understood the president's determination to have his way in this and other White House-generated actions.

On 29 April 1970, 48,000 South Vietnamese and soon afterward 40,000 US ground forces surged into the "Parrot's Beak" and "Fishhook" areas of Cambodia north and northwest of Saigon. The goals of the operation were to seize enemy supply caches, support Lon Nol's defensive efforts against the communists, and give the Vietnamization program more time to work. On 1 May, Nixon impressed on Laird and the JCS that he considered the operation in Cambodia to be the highest priority US mission in Southeast Asia. After the meeting, Tom Moorer, again acting chairman of the JCS in Wheeler's absence, tasked Abrams with developing a comprehensive plan for US actions in Cambodia during the next thirty days.[19]

To drain some of the fierce domestic and international opposition to the US incursion into Cambodia, Nixon grudgingly and publicly promised to remove US ground forces by 30 June. Moorer, however, was not opposed to sometimes bending rules to get results. He recommended to Laird that US special forces and helicopters continue to support secret intelligence-gathering teams in Cambodia beyond the end of the month. The admiral argued that the South Vietnamese did not have the capability to handle the job alone and he feared for the limited quantity and quality of the information they could gather. Moorer recognized the political and diplomatic difficulties involved but believed the importance of the mission outweighed the risks. The secretary of defense finally had to tell Moorer that he did he not consider the proposed action in keeping with the president's pledge. In disapproving the proposal, he also correctly asserted that such a secret mission would ultimately be leaked to the world.[20]

Nixon's attempt to diminish some of the criticism he received about the operation hampered its execution. In answer to a reporter's question about how far US forces would be allowed to advance into Cambodia, Nixon offhandedly said twenty miles. Tom Moorer later remarked that if any troops had gone beyond that distance, the media would have pounced on Nixon and accused him of being a liar. The admiral lamented, however, that an incursion of even twenty-five miles would have netted twice as much of the munitions already seized. John Lehman, then an assistant to Kissinger, remembered that his boss and Haig were appalled that presidential aides John Erlichman and H. R. Haldeman, panicked over the national outcry, convinced Nixon that "he had to end the incursion before the [military] objectives were basically met."[21]

In the short run, the strategy worked. The allied push uncovered thousands of tons of enemy war materials, lent critical military support to the Cambodian armed forces, and significantly improved the Saigon government's situation in the Mekong Delta. Former NSC staffer Peter Rodman considered Nixon's decision to invade Cambodia "courageous" and observed, with exaggeration, that the "combination of the Tet Offensive, and the enemy's loss of Cambodia as a logistics base, virtually ended the war in the southern (and most populous) part of South Vietnam."[22] The operation also gave the South Vietnamese armed forces some breathing space to accommodate the Vietnamization program. Laird was so pleased with the South Vietnamese performance in Cambodia that in June 1970 he even asked an incredulous Abrams to consider reducing the number of soldiers in the South Vietnamese army.[23]

The positive results, however, did not last. Fueled by anti-war fervor, the Senate prohibited the presence of US troops in Cambodia after 30 June. By the end of the war in 1975, communist forces had driven Cambodian and South Vietnamese troops from all of the country except Phnom Penh. The North Vietnamese reestablished their base areas on South Vietnam's border, and the air war in Cambodia and elsewhere increasingly ate into diminishing US military resources. Indeed, Hanoi accurately concluded that the growing demand by the American people for the withdrawal of troops from Southeast Asia would ultimately negate any short-term US gains on the battlefield.

Impressed with Moorer's performance during the Cambodian operations, on 1 July 1970 Nixon replaced the ailing and retiring General Wheeler as Chairman of the Joint Chiefs of Staff. Nixon and Kissinger especially valued Moorer's usually sound military advice and understanding of the administration's national security and foreign policy goals. The national security advisor characterized the admiral as "a more elemental personality than Wheeler." He observed that

Tom Moorer "had spent the 1960s in command positions which . . . did not produce the physical and psychological exhaustion of high-level Washington." Kissinger, a master of palace intrigue, also found Moorer useful for his purposes and characterized him as a "canny, bureaucratic infighter." He added that the admiral "if anything . . . exaggerated the attitude of an innocent country boy caught in a jungle of sharpies." Kissinger noted that "what his views lacked in elegance they made up in explicitness."[24]

In the same breath, however, the consummate scholar sniffed that Tom Moorer "made no pretense of academic subtlety." Moorer would not have been displeased with the characterization. He later observed that "people ask me what did I learn from the Vietnam War? I say, 'Nothing.' I mean all that I saw happen proved that the principles of war are sound. They were violated and we didn't succeed." Moreover, the admiral did not highly prize non-technical academic achievement. He opposed liberal education at the US Naval Academy, considering that it was "nice to know Shakespeare [but that] there's only one priority, one reason for midshipmen existing, and that's to learn how to fight."[25] That Tom Moorer worked well with Kissinger was no doubt influenced by the latter's affinity for naval aviation. The admiral later declared that Kissinger was "an ardent supporter of aircraft carriers" because he understood their utility in international crises.[26] The national security advisor remembered that when Moorer became JCS chairman, "Vietnam had become a rearguard action [and] he conducted its heartbreaking phaseout with dignity." Kissinger emphasized that "no President could have had a more stalwart military adviser."[27] It was high praise indeed.

Tom Moorer always considered himself a nonparochial leader. After he retired, he asserted that he had been "eminently fair" and that he knew of no one who had accused him of using his "position as Chairman for the benefit of the Navy."[28] Vice Admiral King, a devoted subordinate, concurred, observing that there were "many, many officers, of the Army and the Air Force, who found that here was an admiral they really could relate to." In short, "Admiral Moorer was just perfect in that position."[29] Not everyone shared that view. One observer blamed Moorer for "his intractable all-for-the Navy position." He added that "if it hadn't been for Curtis LeMay, Moorer might well be remembered as the most partisan service leader in JCS history."[30] Moorer also thought that, unlike in World War II and the Korean War, it was rare to witness service rivalries in the Vietnam War. Close cooperation supposedly ruled the day. In his oral histories, however, Moorer characterized Air Force General Curtis LeMay as "totally parochial." He added that General John D. "Jack" Ryan, another Air Force chief of staff, "didn't like joint activities [and] was zeroed in on the Air Force."[31] Moorer certainly was a product of Navy culture and his long experience with the fleet, but he did endeavor to give the other services a fair hearing when he led the Joint Chiefs.

CONTINUING AIR OPERATIONS IN LAOS

The major operations of the Navy and the Air Force after the October 1968 bombing halt in North Vietnam took place along the Ho Chi Minh Trail. Over time, the North Vietnamese had significantly improved their ability to transport reinforcements to the southern fighting front. Conscripted Laotian laborers and North Vietnamese troops created more main roads and bypasses, many hidden from aerial observation by thick foliage or camouflage, and built submerged bridges across which trucks moved at a steady pace. Beginning in late 1968, the Chinese People's Liberation Army built six roads in Laos for the resupply of communist forces.[32]

To offset the enemy's innovative counter-tactics, US forces employed a system of sensors in a program labeled the Igloo White. In 1968 and afterward, US aircraft dropped more than 20,000 acoustic and seismic sensors along the Ho Chi Minh Trail. The sensors could detect the sound or vibration of moving vehicles and even human odors. The sensors transmitted contacts to aircraft overhead that forwarded them to an intelligence fusion center at Nakhon Phanom air base in Thailand. That command then provided relevant information to forward air controllers who directed attack aircraft against ground targets. In some instances, these aircraft were able to attack a target five minutes after the sensors picked up enemy vehicles or personnel below. One Air Force officer optimistically related that "we wired the Ho Chi Minh Trail like a drugstore pinball machine, and we plug it in every night."[33]

Buoyed by the early success of Igloo White, Washington launched a series of strike operations named Commando Hunt that functioned until April 1972. The US air forces worked to complicate the enemy's efforts to repair roads cut by bombs or washed out by monsoonal floods. Navy aircraft dropped 500-pound Mk-36 Destructor and 1,000-pound

Mk-40 magnetic or seismic mines on river fords and along the roads leading to and from them.

One object of Commando Hunt was to stymie Hanoi's attempt to replace troops and supplies depleted by Tet and the allied push into Cambodia. Proponents of the interdiction campaign claimed that these operations severely restricted the enemy's ability to transport supplies south by destroying the transport vehicles. But US military leaders and pilots, whether deliberately or based on inaccurate information, inflated the number of trucks destroyed on the trail. General Momyer, the Seventh Air Force commander, observed that "claims were exceeding the total truck inventory [of North Vietnam] by a factor of two at times."[34] The enemy learned how to quickly repair bombed roads and develop bypasses. Enemy air defenses were now a much more potent threat than they had been in earlier bombing phases. Between 1969 and 1973, for instance, 21,000 Chinese troops manned antiaircraft defenses in Laos.[35]

Laird pressed the Joint Chiefs and MACV to prepare the South Vietnamese air force to take over the interdiction campaign. Moorer and Abrams, however, argued that the South Vietnamese armed forces did not have the aircraft, weapons, or experience needed to accomplish that mission. Laird chastised his opponents for concluding that the South Vietnamese could not do the job. Moorer agreed with COMUSMACV, however, that preparing the South Vietnamese armed forces to defend the population centers and coastal resources of their own country should take priority over interdicting the trail. Finally, Laird had to accept that reality. All thoughts of Saigon's forces operating in Laos vanished forever after 1971 and especially after the disastrous experience of Operation Lam Son 719.[36]

VIETNAMIZATION'S FIRST TRIAL BY FIRE

After US and South Vietnamese troops overran North Vietnamese base areas in Cambodia in 1970, Nixon directed Abrams to prepare plans for a similar incursion into southern Laos. In December, Nixon and Kissinger concentrated on a possible allied push into that country's panhandle. In response, Tom Moorer sent Abrams a message via CINCPAC labeled, as retired Army officer Lewis Sorley has characterized as classic bureaucratic overkill, "Top Secret Sensitive Hold Extremely Close Absolutely Eyes Only."[37] Moorer told Admiral McCain to limit any discussion of plans for an incursion into Laos to a select few. He purposely excluded Laird from those discussions. Indeed, Nixon and Kissinger demanded that he do so.[38]

Despite being consistently shut out of Nixon's inner circle, Laird had multiple sources of information, including Nitze who kept him informed about impending actions. In addition, to improve his access Laird floated a proposal to establish a four-star position in the defense department that would, according to Tom Moorer, "eliminate or bypass the Joint Chiefs of Staff." When Moorer anxiously talked to Nixon about Laird's scheme, the president said, "Forget it."[39] Then Laird proposed, for "emergency and crisis situations," a shortened "chain through the Chairman representing the Chiefs." This actually approximated the existing situation, since on many Vietnam questions when time was critical, Moorer issued the orders and informed the JCS members after the fact. The admiral concluded that "personalities . . . not organization charts" were the determining factors.[40]

Unsurprisingly, the Navy member of the Joint Chiefs disapproved of Nixon's use of Moorer to bypass the defense secretary. Zumwalt, Chief of Naval Operations since July 1970, greatly respected Laird; he and Chafee had been instrumental in the admiral's promotion. Zumwalt came to loathe the Nixon-Kissinger penchant for secrecy, intrigue, and bureaucratic manipulation. The CNO considered the national security advisor "diabolical in keeping everybody uninformed—even the Secretary of State—on issues about which the Secretary of State had a constitutional need to know."[41] Even Tom Moorer was not above complaining about the White House modus operandi. He was irritated, for instance, that Kissinger kept him and the JCS members in the dark about peace negotiations with the North Vietnamese.

The objective of the proposed move into Laos, Operation Lam Son 719, was to sever the Ho Chi Minh Trail and disrupt Hanoi's plans for a major offensive in South Vietnam during 1971. Nixon considered Lam Son 719 a good opportunity not only to cut the enemy's supply jugular but also to test the mettle of the ARVN combat divisions beefed up in the Vietnamization program. Moorer fully supported Abrams's plan for a major South Vietnamese thrust into the panhandle, as did McCain. Moorer did so despite Oley Sharp's prediction two years earlier that such an operation would run into a heavy enemy concentration in hostile terrain and give the North Vietnamese a chance to inflict high allied casualties and thus gain "a major propaganda victory."[42]

The Joint Chiefs of Staff gathered for a photo on 4 January 1971. Shown (left to right) are Admiral Zumwalt, CNO; General Westmoreland, Chief of Staff, US Army; Admiral Moorer, Chairman; General John D. Ryan, Chief of Staff, US Air Force; and General Leonard F. Chapman Jr., Commandant, US Marine Corps. The US–South Vietnamese invasion of Laos took place the following month. NHHC NH 104900.

The national security advisor put a lot of faith in Moorer's professional judgment on the Laos issue. Kissinger remembered that in January meetings, the admiral stressed that if the enemy challenged the ARVN attack, "American air power would isolate the battlefield and inflict heavy losses that would be difficult [for the enemy] to recoup."[43] With justification, critics later pointed out that the admiral, a naval aviator, put too much faith in air power.

Tom Moorer dismissed an alternative proposal by Army Chief of Staff Westmoreland for short-term raids into Laos. The JCS chairman, who fully backed Abrams's plan, rebuked Westmoreland during a Pentagon meeting, observing that "a mediocre commander in the field can do much better than an expert in Washington and we should leave the operational commanders alone."[44] The admiral did not involve Westmoreland in the detailed planning for Lam Son 719 but did brief the general and the other Joint Chiefs on the outlines of the proposed venture. Kissinger related that "according to the protocol of the Joint

Chiefs, the White House was supposed to deal with the Chairman, not individual chiefs; hence, we could not have . . . approached Westmoreland directly [in the planning stage of Lam Son 719]."[45]

The same restriction applied to Bud Zumwalt, who made no mention of Lam Son 719 in his 500-page memoir. Indeed, the CNO related that he spent most of his time in 1971 working to encourage better relations between the US Navy and allied navies. Admiral James D. Ramage, the Task Force 77 commander in 1971, related that when he visited Washington, Moorer button-holed him in his office to learn about fleet activity off Vietnam. Ramage found it "kind of an unusual thing" that the JCS chairman was interested in hearing about carrier operations in the Gulf of Tonkin but the CNO was not.[46]

Moorer told Abrams that he was sold on the latter's plan. He also emphasized to subordinates that "we are going to do the Laotian operation . . . exactly like GEN ABRAMS wants to do it and *no other way*" (original emphasis).[47] General Davidson, not unlike other Army leaders, suggested that Moorer knew little of the complexities of ground combat. General Bruce Palmer also criticized Tom Moorer for not understanding Army operations and added that the admiral "could not appreciate the subtleties of the war" either.[48] These assertions were overdrawn, but Moorer did place undue faith in Abrams's understanding of the reality in South Vietnam.

Nixon and Kissinger, buoyed by reports from Haig, who had returned from a visit to Thieu and Abrams in Saigon, gushed about the Laos invasion's potential for decisive results. Nixon exclaimed that it was "about time to rip them up, finish them off."[49] Kissinger was even more supportive of the idea. Presidential assistant Haldeman recorded in his diary on 26 January that Kissinger believed the assault into Laos would succeed and would "end the war because it would totally demolish the enemy's capability."[50]

The earlier incursion into Cambodia, which had suggested to Nixon that the same action in Laos would bring success, ironically doomed Lam Son 719. The congressional Cooper–Church Amendment to a foreign military sales act, which passed in January 1971, prohibited the entry into Cambodia or Laos of US troops and advisors. Moorer wanted full US air support for Lam Son 719, including B-52 strikes in North Vietnam, but Nixon, reluctant to antagonize Congress, would not allow it. Almost as an afterthought, the White House directed Moorer to inform Laird of the impending operation. Key to Laird's approval of the proposed operation was Nixon's promise that no US ground troops would enter Laos. Laird also regarded the planned operation as a useful test of Vietnamization.[51]

The North Vietnamese recognized the vulnerability of the Ho Chi Minh Trail in this region of the panhandle, traversed each month by 6,000 communist troops on their way to the battlefields of South Vietnam. As a result, Hanoi had moved twenty air defense battalions and more than two hundred large-caliber antiaircraft guns into southern Laos. Shortly before the kickoff of Lam Son 719, Moorer reported that US intelligence had discovered that the allies had lost the element of surprise. He also suggested that the North Vietnamese would probably fight hard to defeat the allied incursion. The CIA confirmed that assessment in early February. Despite this knowledge, both Laird and Moorer continued to support the planned operation, and so did Nixon who on 3 February ordered its execution.[52]

South Vietnamese armor and infantry units, without their American advisors, moved west along Route 9 into Laos on 8 February 1971. A fleet of 600 US helicopters airlifted South Vietnamese infantrymen to fire support bases on either side of the barely passable road. Almost immediately, fog, cloudy skies, and a low overcast limited the air support provided by US fixed-wing and helicopter aircraft. Task Force 77 deployed *Ranger*, *Kitty Hawk*, and *Hancock* to the Gulf of Tonkin to support the South Vietnamese advance. Despite the foul weather, US air support inflicted heavy casualties on the enemy troops massing in Laos for counterattacks. Progress westward was slow but steady until 11 February when the ARVN offensive stalled. Seizing the initiative, the North Vietnamese rushed in troop reinforcements armed with tanks, heavy artillery, surface-to-air missiles, and heavy antiaircraft guns. The South Vietnamese president and the operation's officer in charge, Lieutenant General Hoang Xuan Lam, reacted slowly and indecisively. The enemy zeroed in on the stationary ARVN firebases and began to storm one position after another. US helicopters, ferrying in food, fuel, and ammunition and lifting out wounded troops, began to sustain heavy losses of men and machines.

Kissinger grew increasingly uneasy at the turn of events, intimating to Moorer that "if we get our pants beaten off here I tell you we have had it in Vietnam." When Kissinger asked Westmoreland to give his appraisal of the situation, the former COMUSMACV replied that Lam Son 719 was headed for defeat. He especially criticized General Lam and the commanding general of the ARVN airborne division, both of whom had performed badly when Westmoreland ran the show in South Vietnam. Despite this appraisal, with some nervousness Kissinger informed Tom Moorer that "I tell the President everything is great." The JCS chairman did the same, advising Nixon that he thought the operation was going "exactly as we expected."[53] Laird and Moorer dismissed Westmoreland's critique, with the observation that Abrams had a better understanding of the situation on the ground than the former MACV commander.[54] However, working with insufficient information he received from Abrams's staff during this time, Moorer provided answers to Nixon that, according to one source, "were overly optimistic and some were just plain wrong."[55]

Unhappily, on 26 February Moorer had to inform the commander in chief that the North Vietnamese had three times more troops in the Lam Son 719 area than the South Vietnamese. Nixon now shared Kissinger's dread. Moorer and Abrams, however, continued to give upbeat assessments of ARVN operations. In early March, the admiral asserted that the South Vietnamese "can hold their own with the best of the North Vietnamese." At President Thieu's direction, "to save face" ARVN helicopters landed troops in Tchepone, one of Lam Son 719's original objectives. The units were instructed to stay there only three days before withdrawing.[56] Meanwhile, the enemy had begun assaulting and overrunning the fire support bases behind them on Route 9. Laird and Moorer, strong supporters of Vietnamization, continued to press for an extended ARVN stay in Laos, at least into April, and suggested Abrams pressure the South Vietnamese to do so. With irony, the general responded that he had been giving the South Vietnamese "pep talks, hand-holding and whatever the situation called for and I will continue to do that, but in the end, they are running it."[57]

Between 13 and 24 March, the elite armor, infantry, and marine units of the South Vietnamese armed forces withdrew from Laos. Lam Son 719 was not the overwhelming catastrophe described in the US media, but it had witnessed the brutalization of ARVN. The South Vietnamese suffered the loss in Laos of 7,000 killed, wounded, and captured, a casualty rate of forty percent. The invading force lost 54 tanks, 87 other combat vehicles, 96 artillery pieces, and much more support equipment. US losses were equally doleful. More than 1,400 Americans were killed, wounded, or reported missing in action. Enemy defense forces caused the destruction or damage of more than 700 US helicopters and fixed-wing aircraft.[58]

The White House put a positive spin on Lam Son 719, arguing with some justification that the operation had prevented an enemy offensive into South Vietnam in 1971; disrupted the enemy's logistic pipeline in Laos; inflicted 19,000 casualties on enemy forces; gave Vietnamization more time to mature; and enabled the continued unhindered withdrawal of American troops from South Vietnam. Abrams told McCain that "Lam Son 719 may well prove to have been a pivotal point in the Indochina conflict," perhaps a true statement, but not the way the general meant it.[59]

In council, administration leaders painted a less cheery picture. Nixon told Kissinger that the ARVN could not "hack it" without continued US advisory and material support. Abrams offered that the South Vietnamese had learned hard lessons from the experience that would be of future benefit. Other civilian and military leaders, however, concluded that South Vietnamese morale had suffered a serious blow. Moreover, the president, Kissinger, and Moorer had now lost their confidence in Abrams, whom Nixon had earlier compared to World War II General George S. Patton.[60]

Disappointed with Abrams's performance, Moorer concluded that COMUSMACV and his generals "never should have let this operation be approved" if they did not think the South Vietnamese leaders could handle it. Only Laird continued to wholeheartedly support Abrams. Thereafter, Tom Moorer sought military advice not only from Abrams but also from other key leaders in-theater, especially successive commanders of the Seventh Air Force. Moorer directed them to send him daily situation reports, through Air Force channels, on the operations in South Vietnam. Neither Abrams nor McCain received copies of these assessments, while Kissinger did.[61]

After Lam Son 719, the president considered relieving Abrams but feared with good reason that that would suggest the operation had been a failure. Lam Son 719 also revealed the bankruptcy of the Nixon administration's Vietnamization program. The ARVN forces in Laos would in all likelihood have been utterly destroyed without the heavy commitment of US air support involving 160,000 helicopter sorties and more than 10,000 air strikes. As had been the case since the earliest days of US involvement in the conflict, abysmal leadership doomed the South Vietnamese cause. President Thieu's disruptive interference in decision-making, General Lam's inept handling of the operation, and the ARVN division commanders' often petty squabbling seriously compromised the mission, despite the bravery and self-sacrifice of many South Vietnamese troops. Moreover, the operation in Laos seriously degraded the morale and confidence of many ARVN officers and men who understood that their elite soldiers and marines had been badly beaten by their northern brothers.[62]

MOORER CHAMPIONS PROTECTIVE REACTION

When the Rolling Thunder bombing campaign ended on 31 October 1968, Washington leaders believed that US negotiators in Paris had achieved a certain "understanding" with Hanoi's delegates over air operations in North Vietnam. The Americans assumed that the North Vietnamese would not contest the presence of unarmed US reconnaissance planes in their air space. The North Vietnamese did not recognize the understanding and soon violated it. North Vietnamese air defense forces repeatedly attacked US aircraft in 1969, when Air Force and Navy planes carried out more than 5,000 reconnaissance missions over the North.[63]

The rules of engagement enabled US planes, if fired upon, "to destroy [the] weapons, installations and immediate supporting facilities" involved in the attack. Once the pilot received a wavering tone in his headset that indicated his plane was being tracked by radar and that a SAM firing was imminent, he could attack the relevant sites. The administration used the term "protective reaction," first coined by Secretary of Defense Laird who affirmed that US forces could defend themselves if attacked, even if it meant crossing international borders to engage the attackers. But by December 1971, the enemy had made technical advances that negated the effectiveness of the electronic warning. The Navy's Task Force 77 aircraft soon adopted the tactic of "trolling" to deal with aggressive enemy radar sites. As intelligence-gathering planes flew near known SAM sites, attack aircraft would stand by, and when the North Vietnamese radar operators began tracking the plane, the pilot would swoop in to attack with anti-radar missiles. Such trolling liberally interpreted but did not violate the rules of engagement.

Retaliatory strikes for such radar illuminations or actual antiaircraft missile and gunfire attacks became common. In one instance, North Vietnamese antiaircraft fire downed an Air Force plane, and when an HH-53 Jolly Green Giant search-and-rescue helicopter dashed to the scene a North Vietnamese MiG-21 shot it down, killing the six-man crew. The North Vietnamese took other hostile actions to gauge how the US might respond. In March 1970, for instance, a pair of MiG-21s fired at Navy planes near Thanh Hoa, North Vietnam. The F-4 Phantom flown by Lieutenant Jerome E. Beaulier and his radar intercept officer, Lieutenant (junior grade) Steven J. Barkley, took on the attackers and destroyed one of them with Sidewinder air-to-air missiles. The enemy's aggressive actions infuriated Nixon and his advisors, but the president decided against a resumption of full-scale bombing.

At Tom Moorer's urging, the president ordered one-time attacks on targets just north of the DMZ and near the Mu Gia and Ban Karai passes in Laos. During the first week of May 1970, Air Force and Navy planes carried out more than 700 sorties against targets in Laos and North Vietnam. Despite the loss of two planes, Navy attacks destroyed tons of supplies in the logistic pipeline. Admiral McCain reported that with the confusion associated with the allied advance into Cambodia, the enemy had been caught by surprise in the target areas.[64]

In October 1970, Moorer, McCain, and Abrams became especially alarmed that a buildup of supplies and air defenses south of the 20th parallel and along the approaches to the trail presaged a large-scale enemy offensive in early 1971. Moorer pressed Laird to order preemptive and retaliatory strikes on antiaircraft sites in North Vietnam able to shoot down B-52s flying over Laos. Laird refused, worried that the action would hurt the administration's peace negotiations. In November, Tom Moorer persuaded Nixon to approve a preplanned "protective reaction" strike—labeled Freedom Bait—simultaneously with a raid to free POWs from Son Tay prison west of Hanoi. The president remembered how staging such strikes in North Vietnam during the Cambodian incursion had muted criticism of those operations by the anti-war movement. On 21 November, as the Son Tay raid unfolded, Laird announced that "we are conducting limited protective reaction air strikes against missile and antiaircraft facilities in North Vietnam south of the 19th parallel."[65] Due to the limited nature of the Freedom Bait operation and seasonal heavy weather, however, the 210-plane strike accomplished little of military value.

As expected, the media's focus on the Son Tay raid deflected attention from the strike operations in North Vietnam, the first since the 1968 bombing halt. Moorer, however, suggested that such one-time strikes were not sufficient to seriously degrade the enemy's air defenses in southern North Vietnam abutting Laos and the DMZ. He continued to press Laird for "standing authority" to launch strikes when needed. Secretary Laird, however, continued to deny the admiral's requests based on his concern that Congress would cut funds for the defense department and military assistance budgets and hamper the peace negotiations in Paris.[66]

Early in 1971, Moorer informed Laird that enemy SAM sites in North Vietnam seriously threatened the B-52 bombers operating against the trail in Laos, necessitating the diversion of much-in-demand fighter and electronic jamming aircraft to protect them. This assessment prompted the defense secretary to allow sixty-seven attack sorties during three days in February against the missile sites. The operations resulted in the destruction of only three missile launchers and some supporting equipment. The loss of US planes and the concentration of enemy MiGs in southern North Vietnam during early November 1971 again prompted Moorer to call for an operation against enemy airfields. Moorer expected that the enemy would fire on the US planes, so he considered it an ideal opportunity to preplan a multi-plane bombing operation.

This approach was hardly in keeping with the earlier concept of protective reaction. Moorer, Laird, and Abrams, however, urged the commanders in the field to be more aggressive and flexible in their understanding of the rules of engagement. But the most powerful advocate for a liberal understanding of the protective reaction rules was President Nixon. His only caveat was that the strikes on North Vietnam be kept secret. Nixon also directed Moorer to deal directly with commanders in the field on protective reaction matters without going through Laird. The admiral had no serious problem with that approach since, as he told Haig, "My first loyalty is to the President and the orders he gives me are obeyed immediately."[67]

For four days after Christmas 1971, Navy and Air Force planes carried out Proud Deep Alpha, the largest bombing operation against North Vietnam since President Johnson's bombing halt in 1968. More than 200 US aircraft struck targets in North Vietnam, some within seventy-five miles of Hanoi. Poor weather limited bomb accuracy, and the Navy lost several planes.[68] Seventh Fleet surface ships armed with long-range surface-to-air missiles complemented the air strikes. Guided by ship-based radar, a warship's Terrier missiles could hit targets more than twenty miles distant. Talos missiles, with a range of sixty-five miles, were even more capable of downing enemy aircraft over land. Throughout the war, both Oley Sharp and Tom Moorer had advocated deploying Talos-equipped cruisers off North Vietnam, clearing the skies of US aircraft, and then letting Hanoi know that any aircraft coming or going into the country would be shot down. To Tom Moorer, this apparently "caused the people across the river [the White House] great heartburn." He related that "they had visions of us shooting down either a Chinese or a Russian airplane." If Moorer had had his way, the North Vietnamese wouldn't have dared to fly a single aircraft.[69]

On three occasions, however, Washington gave the Navy permission to employ Talos against enemy aircraft. On 23 May 1968, the guided missile cruiser *Long Beach* (CGN-9) fired two Talos missiles at a pair of MiG fighters sixty-five miles from the ship. The first missile obliterated an aircraft, and the second one detonated in the falling wreckage. *Long Beach* registered another shoot-down at a range of sixty-one miles in September 1968. Nonetheless, despite Moorer's support, the Nixon administration did not countermand the Johnson administration's long-range missile ban.[70]

The protective reaction approach to air operations ultimately led to the firing of Air Force General John D. Lavelle, the Seventh Air Force commander. Nixon, Moorer, and a few other key civilian and military officials in the administration orchestrated, endorsed, and indeed applauded Lavelle's liberal interpretation of the rules of engagement, and the general dutifully reported in detail to the White House what he was doing. Upon questioning by Air Force Chief of Staff Ryan, Lavelle admitted that he had "erroneously" labeled the twenty-eight missions he had launched from November 1971 to March 1972 as protective reaction strikes. Lavelle explained at a Senate Armed Services Committee hearing that he took preemptive action against the enemy sites to protect the lives of his air crews. Once Nixon's "secret" operation became public knowledge, many hostile members of Congress hammered the administration for its subterfuge. The key figures involved, including Laird and Moorer, in testimony expressed their innocence and suggested that Lavelle had exceeded his authority with regard to the protective reaction strikes. They abandoned Lavelle, who paid the price for carrying out the orders of his superiors. Melvin Laird and Tom Moorer did not cover themselves with glory in this sorry episode.[71]

MOORER AND THE WHITE HOUSE

President Nixon and Admiral Moorer hit it off because they shared many conservative political, social, and temperamental characteristics. Both men disdained the anti-war movement, "doves" in Congress and among the intelligentsia, and what they described as "the liberal media." They worried about civilian casualties in North Vietnam, but this related more to the impact on domestic and foreign opinion than a strong concern for taking the lives of noncombatants. Both men, for instance, excused the behavior of the US soldiers who perpetrated the atrocities at South Vietnam's village of My Lai. Moorer thought Army 2nd Lieutenant William Calley and the men of his infantry unit should not have been punished for their involvement in the March 1968 massacre during which American soldiers indiscriminately brutalized and killed between 300 and 500 civilians, including many women and children.[72] Soon after a court martial convicted Calley of premeditated murder and in March 1971 sentenced him to life in prison, Nixon telephoned the admiral and told him to facilitate Calley's release from jail. Moorer registered no complaint. When the president hung up the phone, he confided to his assistant H. R. Haldeman that "at least a P [president] can do something once in a while." He then said of the JCS chairman, "That's the one place where they say, 'Yes, sir,' instead of, 'Yes, but.'"[73] Indeed, Tom Moorer thought that what Calley did was correct and that he would do the same thing himself. He later observed that he "personally thought that the Mylai thing was way overplayed." The rationale for his argument was that since American soldiers found themselves "in a jungle environment where women had grenades in their brassieres and in the baby's diapers" they had to take drastic action.[74]

On other occasions, the admiral could be similarly insensitive to human suffering. Years later, he suggested that instead of fighting in South Vietnam, the United States should have invaded North Vietnam because there, unlike in South Vietnam, you could identify the enemy. Then, "every Oriental you saw" would be the enemy.[75] When Nixon wondered about the morality of bombing North Vietnam, Tom Moorer responded that it was not a factor since "they've been torturing these boys [American POWs] all this time." He added, "So far as I'm concerned I'd kill them all."[76] In the same vein, Moorer admitted that he was never able "to draw the distinction between getting stuck in the belly with a cold piece of bayonet and hit with . . . napalm." He was surprised that "apparently in some people's minds there was a moral difference."⁷⁷ Tom Moorer's political conservatism was reflected in his pessimistic and ultimately inaccurate postwar assessment of the likelihood of Asian countries adopting the democratic form of government. He concluded that democracy would never work in South Korea or the Philippines. He also predicted that the Panama Canal Treaty of 1977 would turn out to be a disaster, with the establishment in Panama of a Soviet and Cuban presence.⁷⁸ As Chairman of the Joint Chiefs of Staff, Admiral Thomas Moorer demonstrated skill as a military leader but at the same time very human prejudices.

Trouble at the White House diverted the administration's attention from the growing North Vietnamese military concentration on South Vietnam's borders. In late 1971, Yeoman 1st Class Charles E. Radford served in the White House JCS liaison office, headed then by Rear Admiral Robert O. Welander. The officer instructed the sailor to collect relevant defense and foreign policy papers that came through the office for Admiral Moorer's information. To please his superiors, the yeoman even began recovering top secret and sensitive documents from the office "burn bags" and eventually stole papers from Kissinger's briefcase during trips to Asia.

At one point, Radford became inflamed over US policy toward India. To express his displeasure at the administration's stand, he leaked classified information to sensationalist columnist and fellow Mormon Jack Anderson. The journalist and his parents had befriended the young sailor, and when Anderson discovered at dinner one night where Radford worked and the unique access he had to the administration's deepest secrets, he suddenly "began to view our dinner guest as the main course."⁷⁹ When Welander suspected that Anderson was receiving information from Radford and publishing it in *The Washington Post*, he went to Haig and Moorer. As a result, the White House launched an investigation. Under questioning, Radford told his lawyer that Moorer had instructed him to copy White House documents, an assertion that the yeoman later retracted. Tom Moorer responded, "I had never seen the guy and I didn't select him. He was there when Wheeler was the Chairman." Moorer recommended to Laird that Radford be court-martialed. Kissinger had a different target in mind. According to some accounts, he went ballistic over the spying operation and suggested that Moorer be fired.

US Attorney General John Mitchell interviewed Welander, and according to Ehrlichman told the president that Moorer "denied knowing the material he received from Welander was stolen." Moorer thought the papers were provided for his information but if they were stolen, he recommended that Welander be punished.[80] The admiral later related, "I was not in any sense involved in any kind of spying on the President. It was just ridiculous. I was the only one that supported Nixon. I supported him on everything, sometimes when I was lukewarm on the idea. . . . I supported him on Vietnam throughout."[81] Captain Harry Train, who served as Moorer's executive assistant and senior aide at the time, remembered that Moorer "really felt that he had been wronged," but he did not complain.[82] During hearings before the Senate Armed Services Committee in 1974, the admiral reiterated that he had no idea that the documents in question had been purloined. Ironically, given Kissinger's earlier expressions of outrage over Moorer's role in the affair, he testified in support of the naval leader, his partner in so much decision-making relating to the war.[83]

In his memoir, CNO Bud Zumwalt concluded that "it was clear to me that Radford had done some things he clearly should not have done and that Moorer did not know he had done them." But Zumwalt faulted Nixon and Kissinger for creating "a system in which 'leaks' and 'spying' were everyday and essential elements." Zumwalt considered the president "the most immoral participant in the affair" and expressed the view that "it wasn't easy to keep hold of your integrity or honor or pride when you worked for Richard Nixon."[84]

Nixon contended that it was no surprise that the JCS spied on the White House, because "they wanted to know what was going on." Haig understood that the president accepted the existence of the liaison office because he wanted to be sure that "the chairman of the Joint Chiefs of Staff hears every decision I make." Nixon said that he couldn't "count on the third floor of the Pentagon [office of the secretary of defense] to pass it on."[85] Nixon decided that he did not want to jeopardize his connection to Moorer. The president and Kissinger had invested much confidence in the admiral. Nixon said he feared that if he disciplined Moorer for conducting espionage activity against the president and his national security advisor, it would impair their vital "back channel" to the military. Moreover, it would give Laird "a whip hand over the Joint Chiefs." Ehrlichman and Mitchell told the president that Zumwalt was involved in the spying operation, which prompted Nixon to exclaim that the Joint Chiefs were all "a bunch of shits [and] Zumwalt was the biggest shit of all."[86] Despite these observations, it is unclear how much or how little information Moorer shared with the JCS service chiefs. The upshot of the affair was that Nixon ordered his staff to "sweep it under the rug" or, as Moorer characterized it, "keep it quiet"[87] Whether Radford spied for Tom Moorer or acted on his own was never substantiated. Moreover, Nixon and Kissinger continued to use the backchannel method to conduct business.[88]

The JCS chairman certainly accommodated Nixon's preference for secret, close-held decision-making by a small group that routinely included only the president, Alexander Haig, presidential assistants Erlichman and Haldeman, Kissinger, and himself. Tom Moorer was comfortable with that system since, like Nixon, he disdained bureaucratic foot-dragging and the premature leak of information to often unsympathetic audiences at home and abroad. Nixon saw Moorer as his indispensable link to the US military because he came to trust in the admiral's judgment. The admiral made the most of that bond, recognizing that the chairman, unlike the service members of the JCS, still had statutory authority to issue operational orders. His own experience as CNO on the Joint Chiefs had also convinced him of the group's inability to effect policy. Finally, Nixon was relieved at not having to deal directly with Zumwalt, Westmoreland, Abrams, and other flag and general officers who had earned his disfavor.

As chairman (and acting chairman) of the Joint Chiefs of Staff during 1970 and 1971, Admiral Moorer proved to be a key facilitator of Nixon's Vietnam strategies and policies. The naval leader understood that the president viewed the dolorous situation in Southeast Asia in the context of America's international objectives. A prime motive for the bombing and invasion of Cambodia, the Lam Son 719 incursion into Laos, and the "protective reaction" strikes above the DMZ was to convince the Soviet Union, China, and North Vietnam that US military power still counted. Like Nixon, Tom Moorer considered it vital that America's global allies continue to believe that the United States would help defend them from aggression. Moorer applauded Nixon's penchant for showy military measures (the 1970s version of "shock and awe") to impress adversaries and allies alike with his determination and even ruthlessness. The White House even toyed with the idea in Operation Duck Hook of employing tactical nuclear strikes against North Vietnam.

At the same time, Nixon and Moorer recognized that it was much too late in the war to risk a direct military confrontation with the USSR and the PRC by invading North Vietnam or taking similar measures to end the conflict. On numerous occasions, Nixon and Moorer each restrained the impulses of the other for serious escalatory actions. Moorer helped dissuade Nixon early in the administration from resuming the bombing of North Vietnam in response to its flaunting of the "understanding" reached at Paris in 1968. For fear of antagonizing Congress, the president rejected Moorer's call for full use of US air resources in Lam Son 719. While Nixon allowed Moorer to launch one-time strikes against North Vietnamese SAM sites, airfields, and other enemy facilities prior to the Easter Offensive, he limited the occasions and wanted them kept secret.

Tom Moorer developed a positive working relationship with the president because the admiral was comfortable with Nixon's reliance on him and the select group of White House insiders. While uneasy about bypassing Secretary of Defense Laird, Moorer did so willingly at Nixon's behest. The admiral, like his boss, was not above bending the rules and employing secrecy to achieve desired objectives, as was demonstrated in the "secret" bombing of Cambodia and the protective reaction strikes in North Vietnam.

The operations into Cambodia and Laos bought time—at a frightful cost in lives and resources—but they did not end the war nor prevent later calamities in Indochina. The JCS chairman was hardly alone in pressing for measures that held the promise of victory for US and allied arms. Many military leaders, buoyed by the seeming success of Vietnamization, called for these offensives to exploit the enemy's weakness on the battlefield after Tet 1968. Moorer can be faulted, however, for placing undo faith in military force while domestic and international pressures weighed against long-term success. He erred in crediting General Abrams's overly optimistic reports about the combat readiness of ARVN, the operational skill of South Vietnamese military leaders, and the effectiveness of the Vietnamization program. And perhaps because he was a naval aviator, he oversold the decisiveness of air power. For good or ill, however, Tom Moorer served the president loyally and worked consistently to execute the wishes of the commander in chief.

CHAPTER 8
TEST OF FIRE

In the early months of 1972, the most powerful and indeed the most feared leader in North Vietnam planned a major military campaign to destroy the Republic of Vietnam and compel a decisive and humiliating withdrawal of President Nixon's American forces from Indochina. Le Duan, General Secretary of the Communist Party of Vietnam, longtime revolutionary, and ruthless advocate of aggressive warfare throughout the region and absolute political control in North Vietnam, anticipated a final victory in the long, bloody Vietnam War.

The hardened communist leader knew that the time to strike was at hand, since his forces had embarrassed his South Vietnamese and American enemies the previous year in Operation Lam Son 719, the disastrous attempt to cut the Ho Chi Minh Trail in Laos. Le Duan considered that episode "the heaviest defeat ever ... for Nixon and Company."[1] At the same time, he knew that he had to act before Nixon's successful diplomatic overtures to Hanoi's Chinese and Soviet allies weakened communist international support for the North Vietnamese war effort.

For those reasons, in spring 1972 Le Duan concentrated his forces to launch the Nguyen Hue Offensive (better known by Americans as the Easter Offensive). A specific object of Hanoi's massive ground invasion would be to destroy Nixon's Vietnamization program that aimed to strengthen Saigon's military forces before the planned US withdrawal. With the pro- US government of President Nguyen Van Thieu in control of most population centers in South Vietnam and communist Viet Cong guerrilla forces severely depleted after the Tet Offensive of 1968, the North Vietnamese leader now looked to his conventionally armed

North Vietnamese Army for victory. As they had since the beginning of the conflict, the Soviet Union and China continued to pour prodigious amounts of war material into North Vietnam. New equipment included 130mm long-range artillery, mobile self-propelled antiaircraft guns, and shoulder-fired SA-7 Strela antiaircraft missiles.[2]

In spring 1972, Admiral Moorer focused laser-like on the impending North Vietnamese invasion of South Vietnam. He was well aware of Hanoi's major buildup of forces in the border regions of Laos and Cambodia and just above the demilitarized zone in North Vietnam. Moorer told Maine's Senator Margaret Chase Smith that we "knew where every tank and every division was."[3] The admiral concluded that prior to the start of the expected invasion, US commanders should be authorized to strike military targets in North Vietnam, including the airfields, SAM batteries, and logistic sites.

Standing in the way of Moorer's plan was Secretary of Defense Laird. The former congressional representative from Wisconsin took office determined to end America's involvement in the war and bring American forces home as soon as possible. The politically astute cabinet officer reasoned that Nixon would not win the presidential election that year if the war ground on. As the early advocate and primary cheerleader of Nixon's Vietnamization program, Laird contended that a resumption of bombing in North Vietnam would hurt the cause of Vietnamization. In a similar frame of mind, Laird dismissed the need for US Navy cruisers and destroyers to continue providing South Vietnamese ground forces with naval gunfire support. Moorer strongly protested that direction, arguing that it was vital that this assistance be provided until the South Vietnamese army's artillery arm was prepared to take over the mission and all US forces had withdrawn from Vietnam. The admiral's argument won the day on that occasion, and it paid dividends when North Vietnamese troops soon afterward stormed across the DMZ. Finally, Laird wanted defense department funds increasingly shifted away from supporting the war effort to strengthening America's other global interests.[4]

Moorer had the president's ear and Laird did not. Disappointed with the defense secretary's initial opposition to Nixon's incursion into Cambodia in 1970 and Laos in 1971 and other war-related issues, the commander in chief and Kissinger continued to systematically exclude Laird from their inner circle. At one point, Moorer observed that Laird "was really mad as hops that Kissinger had been by-passing him."[5] Moorer told CNO Zumwalt that on several occasions the president expressed the desire to fire Laird. Nixon did not, however, since as Zumwalt observed, "Laird was almost immune from reprisal for anything less than a major dereliction of duty because of his immense popularity in Congress."[6]

Despite Laird's attempt to shut down the communication channel between the White House and the JCS in the wake of the Radford affair, Nixon reestablished his direct contact with Moorer and continued to exclude the defense secretary. Moorer named flag officer-selectee Kinnaird McKee to head the White House liaison office. The JCS chairman zealously followed Nixon's direction. He did, however, sometimes express discomfort with the awkward situation and on occasion complained that both Nixon and Laird bypassed him, communicating directly with Abrams and Ambassador Ellsworth Bunker in Saigon.[7]

Nixon, like Moorer, wanted to strengthen US forces for massive retaliation if North Vietnam invaded South Vietnam. Rebuffing Laird, Nixon told the admiral, "To hell with the budget." He wanted to have plenty of resources available to respond to Hanoi. The president ordered the deployment to Southeast Asia of more B-52s—210 of the bombers would eventually be devoted to countering the Easter Offensive—and a fourth aircraft carrier. He also eliminated the ceiling on bomber and tactical aircraft sorties in Laos and South Vietnam. Finally, the president authorized preparation for air strikes north of the DMZ should North Vietnam kick off its invasion.[8]

Moorer and the military establishment did not escape unwanted White House attention. Without crediting the irony, Kissinger could not understand why "the Pacific Command [led by four-star Admiral John McCain] in Hawaii . . . four thousand miles away, was responsible for the whole [air] campaign" when the president and he stage-managed operations from Washington more than 8,000 miles away. Kissinger equally disdained the Pacific Command's division of bombing responsibilities between the Navy and the Air Force. Kissinger ascribed the set up as "institutionalized schizophrenia." Moorer argued that the military "had enough on their hands without taking on an internal row this late in the game." Moreover, Tom Moorer strongly supported the overall command authority of his close associate and friend John McCain. Nixon agreed with his military advisor and dismissed Kissinger's complaint.[9]

Nixon's primary motivation during this period was to avoid the embarrassment of a debacle in Vietnam after he had made his historic

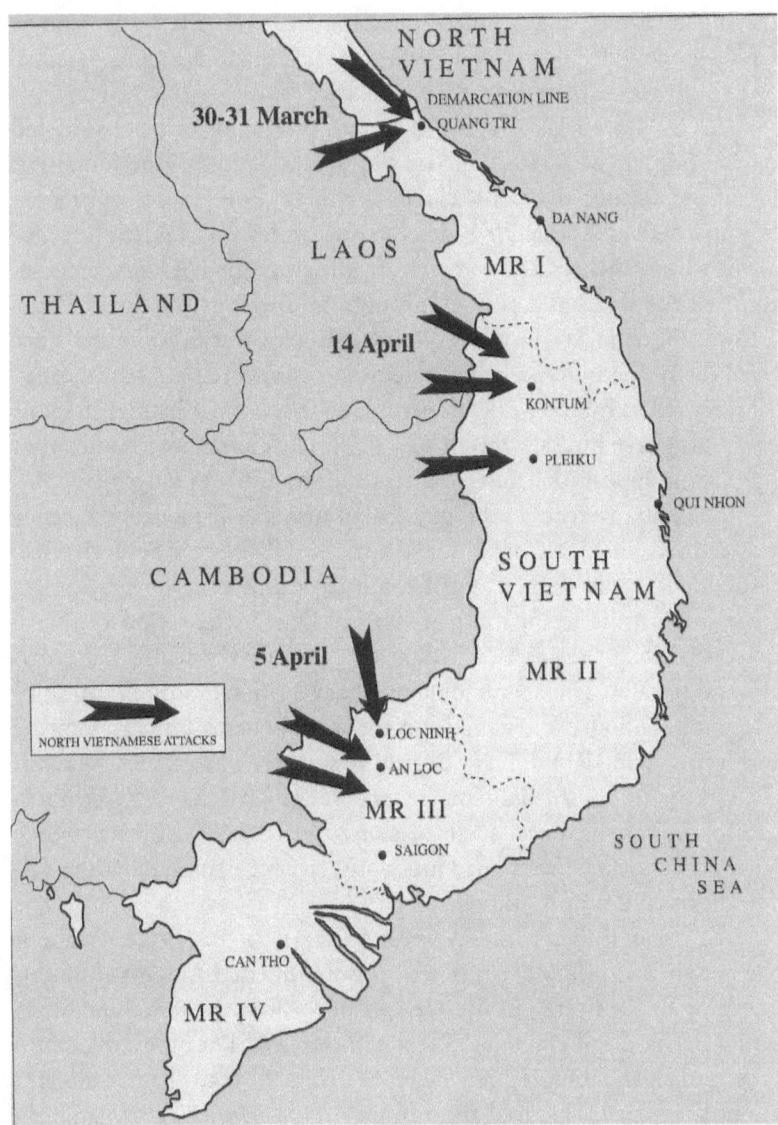

North Vietnam's main offensive thrusts during the Nguyen Hue or Easter Offensive of 1972. NHHC.

February visit to China and prepared to attend a May US-Soviet summit meeting in Moscow. If Hanoi attacked, Nixon wanted to show the Chinese and the Soviets that he was not one to be trifled with and was prepared to launch a strong military response. Nixon remarked, "We're playing a much bigger game—we're playing a Russia game [and] a China game." He added that he was also playing an "election game," so "we're not gonna have the ARVN collapse."[10]

On 30 March 1972, Hanoi's tens of thousands of troops massed on the borders of South Vietnam began the Nguyen Hue Offensive. Combat-hardened divisions stiffened with tanks and long-range artillery and defended from air attack by thousands of portable surface-to-air missile launchers and antiaircraft guns smashed ARVN defenses south of the DMZ and poured through the lowlands and down Route 1 toward Quang Tri City. Nixon now felt with justification that since the North Vietnamese had violated the supposed "understanding" with regard to military operations since the bombing halt in 1968, he could now take military action against North Vietnam without fear of significant opposition from Congress and the anti-war movement.[11]

The rain, overcast, and fog of the annual winter monsoon severely constrained allied air operations, but the US Navy's Seventh Fleet responded to the desperate call for naval gunfire support by South Vietnamese units fleeing south in disarray. During the period, the Navy deployed along the coast of Military Region I sixty cruisers, destroyers, and frigates armed with long-range naval rifles. Gunfire from ships operating off South Vietnam decimated entire enemy units attempting to advance along Route 1. Naval gunfire support was a critical factor in the successful South Vietnamese stand at the My Chanh River north of Hue. Navy ships also steamed along the coast of southern North Vietnam, blasting enemy road junctions, river crossings, defensive fortifications, and supply dumps.

American military leaders weren't always on the same page about the presence or utility of sea power. Moorer queried Abrams about his handling of the fleet's gunfire support in Military Region I and along writer Bernard Fall's famous "Street without Joy." The often blunt, profane, and cigar-chomping general replied that "he really hadn't thought about that at all." He told the admiral to check with Army subordinates in the area for details. Moorer considered Abrams outstanding in his knowledge of ground combat but deficient in his understanding of joint-service operations. He felt that the soldier-focused Abrams "had little or no comprehension . . . of the contribution that could be made by the Air Force and the Navy." The JCS chairman also thought that Abrams failed to see the big picture, especially with regard to foreign policy considerations.[12]

With South Vietnamese troops and their American advisors retreating in Military Region I, Nixon ordered an expansion of the air war into North Vietnam. In Operation Freedom Train, B-52 bombers, tactical aircraft, and Navy warships struck at targets just north of the DMZ. Nixon told Moorer that he wanted to "hit the goddamn enemy at the maximum [and] I want to give it to them ten times right in the butt."[13] Conscious of the president's determination to apply heavy force, several times a day Kissinger rang up the admiral to express his frustration over the seeming inability of the air forces to operate in the heavy weather over Vietnam. It seemed to Kissinger that "our entire Air Force consisted of delicate machines capable of flying only in the desert in July." Certainly not then, but later, Kissinger felt sorry for "poor Moorer, who was not to blame [but] endured my badgering and sarcasm."[14]

Despite Nixon's clear desire to escalate air operations against North Vietnam—he wanted among other things to impress the Soviets and the Chinese with his determination—Abrams continually argued that the B-52 fleet should be concentrated against the enemy facing his forces in South Vietnam. Abrams bridled against direction from CINCPAC, his superior in the chain of command. Indeed, control of the B-52 strikes fueled a "ferocious" confrontation between Abrams and McCain.[15] Abrams also railed against what he considered Washington's interference in his military operations. Tom Moorer remembered that the general threatened to resign if the White House tried to stage-mange the tactical employment of the B-52s. The commander in chief, however, had his way on the bombing priority, transmitting his wishes through Moorer and McCain to Abrams. Indeed, the president and Moorer, disappointed in Abrams's leadership, were already bypassing COMUSMACV and gathering information directly from some of Abrams's subordinates in South Vietnam.[16]

Laird continued to oppose the deployment to the combat arena of additional air and naval forces. He reasoned, "Jeez, you gotta win this damn thing on the ground. You can't win this damned thing just with airpower." Nixon overruled him.[17] Once the weather cleared, carrier-based squadrons, Marine air units operating from airfields in South Vietnam, and Air Force squadrons based all over Southeast Asia and on Guam added their considerable firepower to the mix.

The situation on the ground, however, only got worse as 40,000 North Vietnamese troops stormed Quang Tri City and continued to advance toward the old imperial city of Hue. Despite this calamity,

Laird told his staff not to worry because "the South Vietnamese have stood up well *in most cases*" (italics added).¹⁸ Moorer and Zumwalt considered Laird "an almost totally political man" and "from the beginning the most determined advocate of rapid disengagement from Vietnam." The defense secretary was also troubled that emergency wartime expenditures would severely deplete his department's budget, jeopardizing the US military's long-term health. Laird's stance ignited Moorer's ire, prompting him to emphasize that "the name of the game *now* is what we do *right now*" (original emphasis).¹⁹

Bud Zumwalt, although a member of the Joint Chiefs, did not take part in these deliberations over the US response to the Easter Offensive. He later related that unlike Moorer, who was in daily contact, he "did not see the President during this period." Only through Moorer were Zumwalt and the other Joint Chiefs kept informed of the president's thinking. For once distancing himself from his mentor Laird, Zumwalt supported Nixon's strong response to the North Vietnamese attack. The admiral, however, did not justify the action as the need to stand by America's ally or take a moral stand against naked aggression. He had another agenda. The CNO thought it vital that Nixon "signify unmistakably to the Soviets that he was willing and able to act."²⁰ And it would strengthen the president's hand in current negotiations for a strategic arms limitation agreement. Indeed, Bud Zumwalt thought that while the Easter Offensive was the most newsworthy event in spring 1972, the negotiations with the Soviets in preparation for the May meeting in Moscow "were probably more significant."²¹

Meanwhile, ARVN forces under General Ngo Quang Truong, one of the few gifted South Vietnamese battlefield commanders, slowed the enemy advance north of Hue and assisted by US air and naval power frustrated the North Vietnamese effort to seize the old imperial capital. During the April–August period, the US and South Vietnamese air forces conducted 18,000 tactical sorties in Military Region I. South Vietnam's air force also fought well, its attack planes carrying out an average of 150 close air support missions every day.²²

The enemy also attacked South Vietnam from another direction. In April, North Vietnamese forces crossing from Cambodia quickly seized the South Vietnamese town of Loc Ninh and shortly thereafter laid siege to An Loc further south. The road to the capital of South Vietnam seemed wide open. Only elements of the ARVN 5th Infantry Division that had been rushed to An Loc stood a chance of stopping the enemy's powerful thrust. The South Vietnamese fighting men then withstood weeks of close combat with North Vietnamese troops and endured countless bombardments by the enemy artillery batteries ringing the town. Brave government troopers used shoulder-fired M-72 anti-tank rockets to knock out a dozen enemy tanks trying to push through the rubble-strewn streets. The decisive factor at An Loc, however, was US air power. B-52 bombers and AC-130 Spectre gunships, Air Force, Navy, and Marine attack planes, and Army Cobra attack helicopters aided by forward air controllers pounded enemy formations during assaults and in the hills above town. A final, desperate enemy attack in mid-May, accompanied by a deluge of supporting artillery fire, failed to break South Vietnamese resistance, and by early June ARVN units still held the largely obliterated town.

April also witnessed a major North Vietnamese offensive from Cambodia against the city of Kontum in South Vietnam's Central Highlands. There, too, US air power made the difference between victory and defeat. That month, US aircraft, flying 3,400 sorties, bludgeoned the North Vietnamese attackers. In May, the Strategic Air Command's B-52 fleet, guided on the ground by legendary American advisor John Paul Vann, carpeted the jungle around Kontum with thousands of tons of bombs. The battered enemy forces finally gave up the assault on the city and by the end of June had withdrawn to their jungle and mountain hideaways.

Hence, at Quang Tri and the My Chanh River front in Military Region I, at An Loc north of Saigon, and at Kontum in the Central Highlands, South Vietnamese troops trained through the Vietnamization program fought bravely and with determination to repulse Hanoi's attacks, in the process killing tens of thousands of enemy troops and decimating their conventional army.[23] Nonetheless, US air power accounted for most of the 459 North Vietnamese tanks destroyed in the conflict and half of the soldiers killed in the invading army. Laird finally had to admit that "this invasion could not have been held . . . without U.S. air support."[24]

Unlike in the past, Viet Cong guerrillas did not emerge from the jungle to hit and run; in 1972, the North Vietnamese Army advanced across the battlefield with massed infantry and armored forces, which made them much more susceptible to air attack. Moreover, Hanoi's fourteen divisions in the south required many tons of supplies each day to sustain their offensive. Such demands could not be met by bicycle-mounted villagers pressed into service to move supplies down the Ho Chi Minh Trail. The trucks and trains on the line of communications in southern North Vietnam were now much more vulnerable to US air power, which took a heavy toll on the enemy transportation system.

Le Duan's assault did not bring the victory that he so ardently desired. The Nguyen Hue campaign cost the North Vietnamese close to 100,000 dead in contrast to the South Vietnamese loss of 25,000 men. Stymied on the battlefield, Le Duan then looked to negotiations to achieve his aims.[25]

ISOLATING NORTH VIETNAM BY SEA AND AIR

In early May 1972, Moorer feared the worst in the herculean struggle to stop the North Vietnamese advance. Kissinger had reported from Paris after one of the shortest negotiating sessions on record that the North Vietnamese felt they no longer needed to negotiate since Hanoi's forces were on the verge of a total victory in South Vietnam. Nixon understood that his stewardship of the war effort, the Vietnamization program, and South Vietnam's very survival were at stake. He honored his pledge to President Thieu by committing US air and naval forces and massive material resources to the fight in South Vietnam. But he recognized early that this effort could only succeed if he resumed major military operations against North Vietnam. In a memorandum to Kissinger, Nixon wrote: "I have determined that we should go for broke [and] punish the enemy."[26]

From the earliest days of the conflict in Southeast Asia and throughout the Johnson administration, the JCS and especially the Navy had pushed for the aerial mining of North Vietnam's ports. In retirement, former CINCPAC Oley Sharp emphasized that "of all the things we should have done but did not do, the most important was to neutralize Haiphong." Even Laird had once backed mining North Vietnam's ports.[27] Bud Zumwalt later related that he and the other members of the JCS believed that mining the ports of North Vietnam would not precipitate Washington's big fear: Soviet and Chinese intervention. Zumwalt believed that the "Chinese and the Soviets were gloating about their ability to force us to spend $30 billion a year, while they were spending a billion."[28] Johnson and McNamara consistently rejected calls for mining, concerned that it would provoke even greater international communist involvement or at the least torpedo peace negotiations that they naively hoped would save them from their Vietnam dilemma.

Nixon was much more inclined than his predecessor to take bold steps to resolve the conflict. The president let McCain and Abrams know that he did not think their military actions vigorous enough to impress the Soviets of how seriously he regarded Hanoi's breach of the peace. Nixon wanted his commanders to give the North Vietnamese and their allies the message that he intended to "use whatever force is necessary."[29] Moreover, he found the international situation in 1972 much more advantageous than had Johnson. Clearly, a major split had developed between the Soviet Union and the People's Republic of China, manifested in bloody fighting between the forces of the two communist nations on their common border at the Ussuri River during 1969. The Soviet Union's Leonid Brezhnev considered a strategic arms agreement with the United States and similar issues much more important to his country's interests than prolonging the Vietnam War. Hence, Nixon and Kissinger believed that Brezhnev would register only mild opposition to the US mining of Haiphong. In fact, following the mining operation, Soviet Ambassador to the United States Anatoly Dobrynin told Kissinger that the planned Moscow summit was still on and that Nixon had handled the military actions against North Vietnam "uncommonly well."[30]

The American president also doubted that China would be a problem since he knew that Mao was at odds with Hanoi over ideological issues and was fully engaged in dealing with the chaos of the Cultural Revolution. Moreover, in the wake of Nixon's pathbreaking visit to Beijing in February, whose ultimate goal was the establishment of US-PRC diplomatic relations, he considered it unlikely that Mao would react strongly to the mining. Nixon was right on that count too.[31]

From the outset of the Vietnam War and as Commander Seventh Fleet, Commander in Chief, Pacific Fleet, and as CNO, Admiral Moorer had pressed for a mining campaign. Few other naval aviators and even surface warfare officers had been exposed as much as he during his Navy career to mine warfare. During World War II, Moorer served as an observer of the Royal Navy's mine warfare activities and in the immediate postwar period prepared a report for the US Strategic Bombing Survey on Allied aerial minelaying against Japan. A significant aspect of that campaign in the Western Pacific was the mining and closure to maritime traffic of Haiphong in Japanese-occupied French Indochina.[32]

So it was no surprise that Nixon, who was familiar with his principal military advisor's background, turned to the admiral to plan and implement the mining of North Vietnam's ports. On 4 April 1972, when the North Vietnamese were storming across the DMZ in the opening round of the Easter Offensive, Nixon directed Moorer, then attending the retirement ceremony for Secretary of the Navy Chafee at the Washington Navy Yard, to rush to the White House to discuss an issue of vital importance. When Nixon asked Moorer about the efficacy of a mining operation, the enthusiastic naval officer assured him that it could be planned and executed quickly and secretly. The president, looking for a dramatic impact, planned to inform the American public of the bold operation on national television as it was being carried out.[33]

Moorer immediately contacted the acting director of the Joint Staff and the Navy's mine warfare office in the Pentagon. Since that office's staff had compiled numerous minelaying plans and gathered a mountain of information on mine warfare during the early years of the war, it basically dusted off the material and adapted it to current requirements. In his oral history, Tom Moorer made no mention of his sometimes-rival Zumwalt's involvement in the episode, and most accounts emphasize Moorer's major role. Jerome King, who had worked for Moorer on many occasions and was clearly a devotee, later suggested that the admiral personally "planned the whole thing."[34] That assertion was an exaggeration.

Bud Zumwalt, the CNO, correctly emphasized years later that he was "intimately involved" in the planning and it was "one time during the four-year period [1970–1974] when Tom Moorer had to rely totally on me." Zumwalt related that since mid-April, Moorer, McCain, and he had been in daily contact on the subject. Zumwalt also affirmed that he, Moorer, and the Director of Naval Intelligence, Rear Admiral Earl F. "Rex" Rectanus—one of Zumwalt's old Vietnam hands—crafted the plan in the CNO's office.[35] Zumwalt relished the opportunity to do this professional work, since his duties as CNO mostly involved administrative work and "paper shuffling."[36] Another source emphasized that work on the mining plan was a joint effort. Lieutenant Commander Roberta Hazard, who served on Zumwalt's staff from 1971 to 1974, remembered the evening when "Admiral Z and Admiral Moorer [were] on their knees" going over the plan in detail in the CNO's office.[37]

Nixon approved the mining operation, which he saw as a dramatic and decisive option and one that would not drain air power from

Abrams's fight to stem the enemy advance in South Vietnam. After dinner on 4 May, Nixon exclaimed that the object of the mining would be "to go all out to win the war now."[38] Kissinger also understood that Nixon's political future depended on a decisive and dramatic action. In hindsight, he considered the mining decision "one of the finest hours of Nixon's Presidency."[39] The plain-speaking Tom Moorer praised Nixon for "having the guts" to order the mining.[40]

When the chairman informed the other Joint Chiefs of the president's thinking on 5 May, the military leaders were so sold on the mining proposal that they were "ready to walk out the door unless Nixon did it." Moorer understood that "we had a real chance to break their backs [and] we weren't going to throw it away like Johnson did." The often profane Tom Moorer pressed the president to "let us make these bastards pay for the American blood they've spilled."[41] Moorer decided that the issue was "not vital to the Soviet Union," so he doubted the mining would prompt more than an official communique of displeasure.[42]

Only then was Laird fully briefed on the operation scheduled for 8 May.[43] As expected, the defense secretary considered the mining an unnecessary diversion from the conflict in South Vietnam. CIA director Richard Helms was even more negative, concluding that it was "probable" that the operation would torpedo the planned Moscow summit and prompt the Chinese to deploy tens of thousands of support troops back into North Vietnam. Tom Moorer later claimed with all-too-common exaggeration that "the President and I were the only ones in favor of mining Haiphong." The admiral observed that with regard to Soviet or Chinese intervention then or earlier in the war, "I never did think [that] was a possibility at all" and indeed was a lot of "nonsense."[44] Realizing that the president had already given the go-ahead, all of his advisors ultimately signed on to the mining operation.

Washington kept execution of the Haiphong mining so secret that even Abrams was not informed when McCain ordered a number of Seventh Fleet ships to steam from South Vietnamese waters into the Gulf of Tonkin in support. The often explosive Abrams complained during dinner at the time that he was "damned pissed off." He lambasted "this fucking Navy [for] fighting their own war, and I'm sick and tired of it."[45]

The Navy's planners determined that air-laid Mk-52 magnetic mines would work best against steel-hulled oceangoing ships. Moreover, the weapons would be easier to clear up after the war. Moorer related that "we deliberately laid it [the minefield] down so we could get it up." He emphasized that he "could have put a minefield in there they'd never get up and it would still be there."⁴⁶ The prime object of the operation, however, was not to sink ships but to close the port to maritime traffic. The Mk-52s could be set for delayed activation, which would enable Washington to warn the international shipping companies to stay away from North Vietnam and allow those ships already in Haiphong to depart. After the minelaying operation, one British and four Soviet vessels immediately sailed from Haiphong.

Roger Sheets, the commander of *Coral Sea*'s Carrier Air Wing 15, led Operation Pocket Money. He was concerned that the 8,000-pound weight of the four parachute-retarded Mk-52s to be loaded onto each Corsair and Intruder attack plane slated for the mission would slow them to a speed of 375 knots. At relatively slow speed, the aircraft would be more vulnerable to North Vietnamese MiGs, SAMs, and antiaircraft guns. And with that weight, the planes could not take on board extra fuel tanks and hence would have to launch from a carrier within a risky 100 miles of the coast.⁴⁷

At 0810 on 9 May, *Coral Sea* launched the minelaying force, three A-6A Intruders of Marine All-Weather Attack Squadron 224 and six Navy A-7E Corsairs of Attack Squadrons 92 and 94. Soon afterward, Commander Sheets's group headed for Haiphong. Beginning at 0859, the Marine planes dropped their twelve mines into the narrow inner channel and the Navy aircraft laid their weapons in the outer channel.

Even before the minelaying group had withdrawn to sea, Sheets radioed Rear Admiral Howard Greer, the commander of Carrier Division 3 on board *Coral Sea*, that the mission had been accomplished. Greer immediately communicated the news to the White House. The president had deliberately stretched out a speech broadcast nationwide to give the attack force time to reach safety. He then explained to his viewers that he had ordered the mining of Haiphong in response to North Vietnamese aggression. A Gallup poll soon established that three out of every four Americans supported his strong military stand. Tom Moorer made the insightful observation that at that time "we were flying a thousand sorties a day in Southeast Asia [but] with 25 sorties [the mining operation] we shut off the harbor indefinitely and didn't lose a man and the other side didn't lose anybody" either.⁴⁸

Despite the importance of the operation, Bud Zumwalt's assertion that "the mining of Haiphong . . . finally turned the tide" of the campaign is an exaggeration.⁴⁹ The bombing campaigns in South and North Vietnam as well as the hard fighting of the South Vietnamese armed forces were also instrumental to the success of allied arms that year. While Nixon and Moorer then and thereafter took credit for the bold mining operation, minimizing Zumwalt's involvement, Laird ensured that his loyal subordinate would not be overlooked. He arranged for Zumwalt to appear as a defense department spokesman on NBC's *Today* show and afterward telephoned the admiral to compliment him on his performance. According to Zumwalt, the White House was not similarly pleased with his appearance on the national media.⁵⁰

During the remaining months of the war, the Seventh Fleet laid more mines in the approaches to Haiphong and dropped 11,700 Mk-36 Destructor mines in North Vietnam's major ports and along inland waterways. Pocket Money idled twenty-seven foreign ships in Haiphong for the duration of the conflict. On 9 January 1973, Moorer testified before Congress that after the mining of Haiphong no vessel was detected entering or leaving the port.⁵¹ North Vietnam's total imports were decreased by thirty percent. The country's road and rail network could not compensate for the loss of the ports and became the focus of even heavier Air Force and Navy bombing. As Tom Moorer related, "When we mined Haiphong, the traffic on the railroads just mushroomed and consequently we got all kinds of wonderful targets."⁵²

Not wanting to jeopardize the budding Sino-American relationship, Mao's government registered only mild disapproval of the action and even for a time did not allow the Soviets to ship supplies by rail through China. The Soviets protested the US mining but did nothing to endanger the upcoming talks with Nixon in Moscow. They did dispatch three or four submarines toward Vietnam from their Far East naval bases at Vladivostok and Petropavlovsk. According to Moorer, US naval forces tracked the boats all the way to the South China Sea but relaxed that vigil when the Soviet vessels steamed into but did not linger in the Gulf of Tonkin. Bud Zumwalt remembered that during a Washington dinner party related to negotiations over a prospective US-Soviet Incidents at Sea Treaty much desired by Moscow, American and Russian naval officers watched Nixon on TV announce the mining of Haiphong. The Soviet political officer or "commissar" on hand suggested that "this could mean war." Zumwalt remembered that in contrast all the other Russian officers present "took it well." In fact, the senior Russian admiral at the function said that "he understood that this is what a superpower had to do."[53]

After the start of Hanoi's Nguyen Hue Offensive, Nixon believed that a majority of the American people would support a new bombing campaign against North Vietnam. He exclaimed that "the bastards have never been bombed like they're going to be bombed this time."[54] Despite Laird's efforts to slow the buildup, from January to the end of April Nixon had ordered the deployment to Southeast Asia of 139 B-52s, more than 800 Navy and Air Force tactical aircraft, and more than fifty warships.[55]

On 14 April, Laird grudgingly agreed to Tom Moorer's recommendation that US air forces carry out a one-time strike to destroy petroleum storage facilities in the North Vietnamese heartland and that the fleet's warships bombard the Do Son Peninsula that guarded the entrance to Haiphong. The Soviets complained that the attacks that occurred two days later caused damage to their ships docked in Haiphong harbor. Secretary of State William Rogers testified before the Senate Foreign Relations Committee that these operations were justified "to protect the 85,000 U.S. troops still in Vietnam, to guarantee the continuing troop withdrawal program, and to give the South Vietnamese a chance to defend themselves."[56]

Finally, by early May Nixon had decided that he needed to take even stronger actions against North Vietnam. He told Kissinger, "We have the power to destroy the enemy's war-making capacity" but asked if his administration had the will to use that power. He answered his own question by asserting that "what distinguishes me from Johnson is that I have the will in spades."[57] As the mining of Haiphong proceeded, Nixon announced the initiation of continuous bombing operations throughout North Vietnam. The campaign, initially labeled Rolling Thunder Alpha, would instead be called Linebacker, since Nixon enjoyed the use of football analogies. The program's objectives were to: 1) destroy military supplies in North Vietnam; 2) isolate North Vietnam from outside suppliers; and 3) interdict the flow of munitions to the southern battlefield. Nixon allowed military leaders and combat commanders in the theater much greater freedom to select targets, tactics, aircraft, and weapons that they considered appropriate to the mission. Avoiding civilian casualties and "collateral damage" to religious, cultural, and other sites remained an important aspect of the rules of engagement, so new precision-guided munitions and navigation systems afforded the attacking forces greater ability to destroy military targets in population centers.[58]

Nonetheless, the president did not resist directing operational matters. Like Johnson, Nixon was especially focused on limiting civilian casualties. Tom Moorer suggested that at White House meetings the issue was always "How many civilians are you going to kill?" The admiral remembered his exasperation: "Now, how in the hell did we know how many civilians we were going to kill?"[59] As an example of Nixon's direct involvement in operations, he instructed the Navy and the Air Force to carry out 1,200 combat sorties each day and increase that number when carrier *Saratoga* arrived on station. He added that a minimum of those sorties should be executed in the Hanoi–Haiphong area. As Moorer later lamented, "It was never really a hands-off bombing permission." The White House still did not allow strikes in downtown Hanoi or Haiphong or the border strip next to China. The Navy could not fire its Talos surface-to-air missiles over the capital city. Moorer complained that "it was just one damn thing after another."[60]

Laird continued to strongly oppose most actions that would widen the war and impede the speedy US withdrawal from Vietnam. In June 1972, Moorer requested authority for US air forces to hit forty-four targets previously off-limits in the restricted areas around Hanoi and Haiphong. Laird approved some of those targets but would not agree to strikes on Gia Lam airfield near Hanoi. In the opening weeks of Linebacker, Navy and Air Force planes attacked critical bridges, including the previously off-limits Paul Doumer/Long Bien Bridge in Hanoi, and the roads and railways between the North Vietnamese capital and the border with China. Linebacker, in contrast to Rolling Thunder, enabled the attacking air forces to hit a number of targets simultaneously rather than sequentially. By 30 June, the attacking forces employing laser-guided bombs, Walleye TV-guided bombs, and conventional munitions had rendered more than 400 bridges inoperable. Other Linebacker targets included POL facilities, power-generating plants, barracks, and air defense targets. Navy warships complemented the aerial blitz. During Linebacker, Navy surface ships fired over 111,000 rounds at targets along the North Vietnamese coastline.

While both the mining and the Linebacker campaign had a major impact on the final resolution of the war and its international aspects, those actions did not materially affect the success or failure of the Easter

Offensive. Hanoi had stockpiled mountains of supplies in the North Vietnamese panhandle, Laos, and Cambodia prior to the invasion that enabled the enemy to fight without major resupply from North Vietnam until the end of heavy fighting in June. In short, the mining and bombing operations in North Vietnam had had little time to significantly influence the battles in South Vietnam. Defeat of the Easter Offensive resulted from ARVN tenacity and US air power. Nonetheless, between June and the end of fighting in January 1973, the campaigns in North Vietnam significantly degraded Hanoi's ability to continue the war.[61]

HOLLOWAY GOES TO WAR AGAIN

The up-and-coming and especially talented Vice Admiral James L. Holloway III took command of the Seventh Fleet in May 1972 to lead the Navy's operations in the Linebacker campaign. Moorer and Zumwalt had been impressed not only with Holloway's performance in the Pentagon on aviation issues but also with his successful management of the Sixth Fleet carriers during a Middle East crisis over Jordan in 1970. Many observers credited the presence of Holloway's three carriers and their supporting warships in the Eastern Mediterranean with helping to peacefully resolve the international confrontation. Faced with the prospect of a US retaliatory air strike, Syrian President Hafez al Assad withdrew his troops. Kissinger asserted that the Sixth Fleet had had a "decisive impact" on the outcome of the issue. Holloway remembered that afterward "the U.S. Navy was riding high, as neither the Army nor the Air Force had been able to respond to the crisis because of the nonavailability of the NATO [North Atlantic Treaty Organization] bases." Holloway related that thereafter Kissinger "was one of my great boosters."[62] Zumwalt too was "ecstatic" over the Navy's role in the Jordanian crisis, which the CNO considered "a near perfect demonstration" of the maritime service's capabilities. When Holloway's plane touched down in Jacksonville, Florida, shortly afterward, Zumwalt had an aircraft ready to whisk the new celebrity to Washington so he could brief the Navy staff.[63]

Admiral Holloway took charge of a formidable naval force when he became Commander Seventh Fleet. In addition to the six aircraft carriers at his disposal, his fleet boasted sixty destroyers and escort ships, thirty-one amphibious ships, twelve submarines, and thirty-four tankers, supply, and ammunition ships. More than 73,000 sailors and 27,000 Marines served in the combat force. Directing the fight against North Vietnam was Jim Holloway's most immediate responsibility, but

Vice Admiral Holloway, then Commander Seventh Fleet, welcomes South Vietnamese President Nguyen Van Thieu to the naval leader's flagship during the Linebacker campaign of 1972 that helped end America's involvement in the Vietnam War. NHHC K-94833.

the Seventh Fleet commander was also expected to keep his forces and war plans in readiness for any conflict with the Sino-Soviet bloc and to support US diplomatic interests throughout the Western Pacific.[64]

Jim Holloway understood that the nature of the war had changed since his command of carrier *Enterprise* from 1965 to 1967. The Nixon administration now fully intended to turn the war over to Saigon, withdrawing US troops from South Vietnam and using military power to extract a cease-fire agreement from Hanoi. He also knew that while he would have much greater latitude than his Johnson-era predecessors in the selection of targets and the use of tactics, planes, and ordnance, the Nixon administration would be closely involved in Linebacker decision-making, sometimes even at the tactical level.

Fortunately for Holloway, the Seventh Fleet that he inherited had emerged from the Rolling Thunder campaign and subsequent operations in Indochina as an experienced and battle-ready force. The carriers and surface warships of Task Force 77 had become a potent asset for the projection of naval power ashore. Holloway later remarked that "by far, the most important single contribution of the US Navy to the conflict in Southeast Asia in 1972 was the carriers."[65] Planes from these ships mounted around-the-clock strikes against North Vietnam's supply lines in the country's panhandle. The Seventh Fleet commander put emphasis on precision strikes by technologically advanced A-6 Intruder attack planes employing laser-guided bombs, electro-optical glide bombs, and other "smart" weapons rather than the previous, multi-plane Alpha strikes with World War II–era bombs. Navy and Air Force planes knocked down bridges that had earlier proven impervious to "iron bombs."

John B. Nichols, a veteran and highly decorated naval aviator, related how the improved handling of air operations during Linebacker impacted the morale of his squadron-mates. He related that "spirits took an immediate upturn [and] we felt as though we were finally at war." He related that "more lucrative targets were opening up almost daily after four dreary years." He added, "In under eight months the war Up North [in North Vietnam] had turned around [and] fleet aviators saw the dramatic change on every trip over the beach." Nichols remembered that "SAMs became almost nonexistent, and AAA [anti-aircraft artillery] dribbled off from 85mm barrages to a token squirt here and there of 23- or maybe 37mm." Indeed, "few supplies were getting in [and] little was moving on the ground, for bridges and rail lines were shattered." He concluded that "when Air Force F-4s finally toppled Thanh Hoa Bridge [the "Dragon's Jaw"] with smart bombs, we knew we had it knocked."[66]

Rolling Thunder had encouraged the Navy to reinforce its carrier air wings with more advanced fighter, attack, and reconnaissance aircraft. F-4 Phantoms, A-6 Intruders, A-7 Corsairs, and RA-5C Vigilantes became the mainstays for operations in the lethal skies over Hanoi and Haiphong. EA-6B Prowlers jammed enemy radars so they could not track attack aircraft. By 1972, the Seventh Fleet's warships and their crews had become adept at dropping timely, accurate, and coordinated fire on targets along the North Vietnamese coast. The same day that Task Force 77 planes mined Haiphong harbor, a trio of destroyers knocked out enemy coastal batteries on the nearby Do Son Peninsula. North Vietnamese coastal guns responded in kind, damaging ships and killing American sailors. Indeed, the Seventh Fleet change of command ceremony was temporarily interrupted when enemy rounds straddled Holloway's flagship, guided missile cruiser *Oklahoma City* (CLG-5).[67]

Missions so close to the enemy's shore defenses around Haiphong were especially risky. In August 1972, when the Joint Chiefs directed a bombardment of coastal sites, Holloway requested the mission be reconsidered. He worried that if North Vietnamese gunfire immobilized one of his ships so close to Haiphong, it might not be possible to haul the damaged vessel to safety. He was particularly concerned that the loss of a ship would be a devastating propaganda blow. Despite these concerns, Admiral McCain did not want to "get in a fight with the JCS" so he told the Seventh Fleet commander to proceed with the mission.[68]

Jim Holloway faulted himself for not paying closer attention to the attack planning. His staff, overly confident since they had planned and executed numerous gunfire support missions before, failed to prepare a formal Seventh Fleet operation plan. The final product did not provide for dedicated air support or defense against torpedo boat (PT) attack. Indeed, Holloway's intelligence officer, whom he later fired, assured him that "we've seen no PT boats up there in the last three or four months and there are none there now." Holloway had to admit that on that score, the North Vietnamese "surprised the hell out of us."[69]

In Operation Lion's Den, Holloway's warships steamed into the waters off Haiphong on the night of 27 August. Heavy cruiser *Newport News* (CA-148), light guided missile cruiser *Providence* (CLG-6), and destroyers *Rowan* (DD-782) and *Robison* (DDG-12) were directed to deploy at night off the North Vietnamese coast and bombard preselected targets. As the Seventh Fleet commander, Holloway was not expected to take part in a four-ship tactical evolution, but he decided to go along on the risky raid deep into North Vietnamese waters. Jim Holloway wanted to demonstrate that he was willing to share the danger of combat with his sailors. He admitted that another reason for joining the mission was to personally witness the "fireworks up north." Holloway liked to highlight his many years of combat experience, often trumpeting the observation that "he was shot up in World War II, shot down in Korea, and shot at in Vietnam."[70]

The ships of the task unit fired 700 rounds that caused a number of explosions, while two air-launched Shrike anti-radiation missiles struck air defense radars. Enemy gunners responded with approximately 300 rounds, all of them missing their targets. The task unit then retired from the area and headed for the mouth of the Gulf of Tonkin. Holloway was pleased to feel "the rush of wind, the hot blast of the guns, and the acrid smell of gunsmoke [that] differed little from what I had experienced on board the destroyer *Bennion* (DD-662)" in the World War II Battle of Leyte Gulf.[71]

The admiral soon experienced more drama than he probably wanted. Radar operators on *Newport News* reported four high-speed contacts, later identified as Soviet-made P-6 fast patrol boats, closing on the task unit from different directions. Numerous islands, rocks, and other obstructions made it difficult for *Newport News* and the other ships to locate the boats on their radars and then fire on them. The Seventh Fleet commander finally broadcast on a special emergency frequency who he was and that he was requesting any aircraft in the vicinity to provide the task unit with high-powered flares to illuminate the scene below. Lieutenant (junior grade) William W. Pickavance of Attack Squadron 93 replied almost immediately that his and another A-7 Corsair were on hand to help out. Shortly afterward, the two attack planes illuminated the waters around the task unit and with their Rockeye cluster bombs and gunfire from the ships sank or heavily damaged three of the attackers. Jim Holloway returned from one more successful combat mission in his eventful Navy career.[72] He remembered that "the foray made page 2 of *The New York Times*." Zumwalt too was "delighted with the press coverage."[73]

The Linebacker campaign enabled the first combat test of the naval aviators who had attended the Navy's "Top Gun" school. Dissatisfied with the two-to-one ratio of Navy aerial victories-to-losses during Rolling Thunder, the Navy directed veteran pilot Captain Frank Ault to investigate the cause. His study concluded that the focus of F-4 Phantom crews before the war had been on readiness for air combat at long ranges with radar-guided missiles, a practice that had dramatically impaired their close-in dogfighting skills. Backed by Ault's report, the Navy established the Fighter Weapons School at Naval Air Station, Miramar, California. For the next three years, the school honed the skills of its students in air combat at close quarters. In addition to the Top Gun program, the Navy had also improved its aircraft, missiles, and early warning and jamming systems. As a result, by the end of Linebacker naval aircrews had registered a 13 to 1 ratio of victories to losses. In sum, the provision to the Seventh Fleet of new, advanced equipment and better trained aviators significantly strengthened its combat power. Naval personnel of all ranks had profited from Rolling Thunder and later years of combat in Vietnam to develop a superior instrument of war.

Despite the improved operational capability of the fleet, Admiral McCain had to report to his subordinate Navy and Air Force commands in August 1972 that Washington was pressing for a greater effort against the North Vietnamese heartland. CINCPAC wanted his commanders "to signal Hanoi in the strongest way possible that our air presence over their country" would only increase.[74] By mid-October, that effort had borne fruit. The US air and naval forces had severely impacted North Vietnam's ability to remain on a war footing. The Linebacker campaign reduced imports from China from 160,000 tons a month to just 30,000 tons a month. The Defense Intelligence Agency estimated that as early as June, the campaign's 14,621 Linebacker air strikes and 836 naval gunfire attacks on North Vietnam had interdicted critical rail lines from China, sunk or damaged 1,000 small craft operating on the coast, and significantly hampered road traffic. The campaign had reduced Hanoi's fuel stocks from 103,000 metric tons to 40,000 metric tons and shut down forty percent of the country's power plant capacity.

In October, Kissinger, Nixon's representative in Paris, even thought a deal was imminent that would finally end the war. Le Duc Tho, his professionally skilled and crafty North Vietnamese counterpart, had let it be known that Hanoi would allow the Thieu government to remain in place after a cease-fire and release American POWs held in Hanoi. Kissinger advised Nixon to order a bombing halt to accommodate the North Vietnamese sign of compromise. Hence, Nixon ended bombing north of the 20th parallel on 23 October. The president, however, had second thoughts about the agreement and delayed responding to the North Vietnamese. Of equal importance, President Thieu, whose government would be party to any cease-fire agreement, refused to accept the terms. He specifically wanted any final document to stipulate that all North Vietnamese forces would be withdrawn from South Vietnam. Hanoi was also having second thoughts. Two days after the bombing halt, Hanoi broadcast that American and South Vietnamese actions had spoiled the chance for peace. Kissinger tried to salvage the situation, stating to the world's press on 26 October that "we believe that peace is at hand. We believe that an agreement is within sight."[75] It was not.

While Tom Moorer understood and supported the Nixon administration's political-military objectives for ending the war with North Vietnam, there was one issue he considered nonnegotiable: the repatriation of the American prisoners of war. As a naval aviator, he considered it an article of faith that there was "nothing we won't do to rescue a pilot who goes down or any other individual who is caught in the enemy lines, regardless of the risk."[76] The JCS chairman had eagerly backed the attempted rescue in November 1970 of the POWs imprisoned at North Vietnam's Son Tay prison camp.[77] Soon after that failed operation, he reemphasized the importance of the POW issue to Lieutenant General Julian Ewell, then the military advisor to the US delegation at the Paris peace talks. The admiral had observed that he wanted it clearly understood that he considered the "early return of our men to be of paramount importance." He asserted that their release "should be an essential prelude to any further military concessions on our part."[78]

Tom Moorer's concern for the POWs had taken on a personal note when his friend and former subordinate, Commander William P. Lawrence, had been shot down and captured leading Fighter Squadron 143 in an Iron Hand anti-missile battery strike earlier in the war.[79] Moorer also remembered that Sybil Stockdale and Jan Denton, the wives of prominent Navy POWs, "never failed to goose me just as hard as they could goose me about making sure that [I knew that] the men had been in [North Vietnamese captivity] going on six, seven and eight years."[80] In his retirement years, the grizzled combat veteran declared, "If I ever had my way about it . . . I would have given an ultimatum to the North Vietnamese to release the POWs or . . . I would have demolished the whole outfit." He contended that "the only way you can make these people [communists] be less difficult is to apply brute force." The earthy admiral emphasized that "the way you talk to those little bastards" was akin to "hitting a mule with a two-by-four to get his attention."[81]

BRINGING THE WAR TO HANOI

Nixon believed that his expected November election victory over Democratic Senator George McGovern would empower him to take stronger actions to end the war in Southeast Asia. He related to Kissinger that after the election, "school's out." He promised to "take out the heart of installations in Hanoi." Moreover, "We're going to take out the whole goddamn [Haiphong] dock area, [foreign] ships or no ships."[82]

Nixon also put pressure on Thieu. He had the South Vietnamese president informed that if he wanted continued US military assistance, he would have to agree to the terms negotiated earlier by Kissinger and Le Duc Tho.

Always eager to withdraw US forces from the war, on 13 December 1972 Secretary of Defense Laird advocated an immediate signing of a cease-fire agreement with North Vietnam. Without alluding to US air power's obvious contribution during the Easter Offensive, he contended that since "Vietnamization has been successful," the Republic of Vietnam would not need US military assistance to survive another North Vietnamese onslaught.[83] That assertion would be found wanting in only a few short years.

Nixon, however, wanted desperately to end the war on his terms. A journalist who attended a dinner party with the president and Admiral Moorer on 18 December 1972 recounted two years later what Nixon said that night. Reportedly, the commander in chief "did not care if the whole world thought he was crazy in resuming the bombing and mining." He added, "If it did, so much the better; the Russians and Chinese might think they were dealing with a madman and so had better force North Vietnam into a settlement before the world was consumed in a larger war."[84] Indeed, according to one of Kissinger's subordinates, Nixon and Kissinger were later convinced that their forceful diplomacy had brought about the final cease-fire agreement.[85]

While obviously overdrawn, Tom Moorer remembered that "the President and I were the only ones in favor" of the so-called "Christmas bombing" or more formally the Linebacker II campaign. The admiral had in hand the plan for just such an effort.[86] Nixon intimated to Moorer that even though he was the commander in chief, he would not interfere in military operations and it would be Moorer's job to oversee a hard-hitting bombing campaign. Nixon told the admiral that he didn't "want any more of this crap about the fact that we couldn't hit this target or that one." He emphasized, "This is your chance to use military power effectively to win this war, and if you don't, I'll consider you responsible." Nixon remembered calling Moorer "to stiffen his back." Remarkably, given Nixon's limits on operations, he criticized the Navy and the Air Force since "at times in the past ... our political objectives had not been achieved because of too much caution on the military side."[87]

Tom Moorer needed no prodding to employ the powerful resources at his disposal. He sent a message to Air Force General

John C. Meyer, commander of the Strategic Air Command, reminding him that "I'm sure you realize that Line Backer II offers the last opportunity in Southeast Asia for USAF and USN to clearly demonstrate the full professionalism, skill, and cooperation" in the forthcoming strike operation. In his usual direct, unvarnished way, Moorer told the general, "You will be watched on a real-time basis at the highest levels here in Washington." The JCS chairman stressed that "we are counting on all hands to put forth a maximum, repeat maximum, effort in the conduct of this crucial operation."[88]

In contrast to JCS chairman General Earl Wheeler in Rolling Thunder, Tom Moorer took a direct role in the planning for Linebacker II. Initially, Moorer and Kissinger thought Air Force and Navy tactical aircraft would be the logical weapon systems to execute the campaign. It soon became clear, however, that Nixon wanted to use the B-52 strategic bomber force to achieve a strong psychological impact on Hanoi. The admiral and the other Joint Chiefs then validated targets nominated by General Meyer's B-52 fleet, but except on a few occasions the general ran the operation. Moorer explained that the SAC commander was "told what to do" but not told how to do it.[89]

Moorer directed execution of Linebacker II on 18 December. The object of this campaign was to "impose maximum damage on the enemy's war-making capability while also producing a mass shock effect in a psychological context." Moorer told Meyer that while his force was to minimize civilian casualties, he wanted the populace of Hanoi "hear the bombs."[90] The targets for the December campaign included airfields, POL storage sites, and railroad yards close enough to the centers of Hanoi and Haiphong that the cascade of bombs would be clearly heard and felt by North Vietnam's leaders and people. At the same time, planners went to extraordinary lengths to protect civilians from errant bombs; this would be no "carpet bombing" that critics of the war erroneously but routinely used to describe US air operations.[91]

At 1945 local time on 18 December, three waves of B-52s inaugurated Linebacker II when they dropped their payloads in the heart of North Vietnam. Simultaneously, Navy and Air Force tactical aircraft and Seventh Fleet warships struck targets along the coast, as they would do for the duration of the campaign, despite heavy weather. The targets included defense sites, army barracks, storage facilities, truck parks, and bridges in all weather, day and night. On the 19th near the port of Hon Gai, aircraft from carrier *Enterprise* sank a Soviet-made Komar-class missile boat and damaged two others, each of them armed with two ship-killing Styx surface-to-surface missiles.[92]

The B-52 force escaped with the relatively low figure of three bombers lost on the first two nights of the operation, but this grace period would not last. On the 20th, enemy SAM batteries knocked down six of the big bombers and damaged two others that had flown at set times and on predictable approach patterns. The loss of two more B-52s and a Navy Intruder on the 21st prompted Nixon to order a cessation of attacks on Christmas Day. The future of Linebacker II did not look promising.

Clearly under great stress during this period, Tom Moorer later gave vent to his frustrations with the US media for what he considered their often-biased coverage of the war. He remembered a B-52 crewmember who refused to fly a mission. The admiral complained that the crewman "got all the publicity [and] was the hero of the operation [while] the real heroes weren't mentioned." Never one to mince words, Moorer asserted that the recalcitrant airman "should have been shot." He suggested that many publishers and journalists didn't "care if a lot of American boys get killed or not [because] they think their right to have the news over-shadows everything else."[93] He also remembered that the editor of *The New York Times* told him that the newspaper was "opposed to the war and consequently they were going to paint it in the worst possible light." He complained about "these bitter, sarcastic, vitriolic people like Mary McCrory [*Washington Star* reporter] and that type [writing] that the generals couldn't win."[94] He thought reports about bombing North Vietnam's dikes were media "hobgoblins" and "nonsense."[95] He wrote a scathing opinion piece for *The Washington Post* rebutting an article by Marquis Childs who made the grossly inaccurate claim that "much of Hanoi was razed" during the Linebacker campaign.[96]

Before Christmas, Air Force leaders knew that they could not continue to sustain such a high loss rate, so they immediately called for operational changes. They directed the bombers to take out the SAM batteries around Hanoi and Haiphong and, beginning on 26 December, instructed the bomber crews to approach their targets from different directions and altitudes and at different times. In addition, the Air Force began employing only those bombers equipped with upgraded electronic countermeasures to foil SAM attacks. Nixon related that his major concern during that first week of bombing was not expected domestic and international criticism but the high loss of B-52s.

Hoping Nixon, under pressure from a fractious Congress, would not resume the attacks after Christmas, Hanoi continued to refuse negotiations. Nixon, however, remembered Winston Churchill's quote regarding World War I: "One can follow a policy of audacity or one can follow a policy of caution, but it is disastrous to follow a policy of audacity and caution at the same time." Nixon affirmed that he intended to stay the course.[97] Alexander Haig remembered that concern over the high bomber losses had prompted CINCPAC to call for an end to the bombing and that the JCS equivocated over the issue. Moorer, however, "remained steady." Haig suggested that the admiral's steadfastness might have resulted from a "rare exercise of personal browbeating" by the president.[98] On 26 December the B-52s began a maximum effort raid against targets in Hanoi and Haiphong. The bomber fleet struck all ten major targets around Hanoi in the same fifteen-minute period.

The post–Christmas operation represented one of the most powerful demonstrations of US conventional air power in history. In addition to the 120 B-52s bombing rail yards and POL sites, more than 100 Navy and Air Force tactical aircraft engaged air defense sites around Hanoi and Haiphong. To Tom Moorer and the other Joint Chiefs, the success of Linebacker II was the "high-water mark of the war."[99] On the 27th, North Vietnamese leaders condemned the "extermination bombing" but at the same time informed Washington of their willingness to reenter peace negotiations in Paris on 8 January. Nixon answered that he wanted the talks to begin on 2 January but, as a sign of good faith, offered to stop bombing above the 20th parallel. Following two more nights of bombing, the North Vietnamese agreed to his conditions. Nixon wrote in his diary that this was "a very stunning capitulation by the enemy to our terms."[100]

Linebacker II had achieved the immediate objective of compelling Hanoi to resume serious negotiations to end the war. And Nixon could argue from a position of strength, at least in a tactical sense. By the end of the short campaign, North Vietnam had depleted its arsenal of surface-to-air missiles. On the first day of Linebacker II, North Vietnam's air defense system had launched 200 SA-2s against the American aircraft, but by day eleven of the campaign could only put twenty-three missiles in the air.

Linebacker II also witnessed the destruction of Hanoi's SAM assembly plant and the neutralization of its airfields. Tom Moorer related that US intelligence intercepted enemy communications in which the North Vietnamese were "screaming bloody murder" about the rapid depletion of their missile inventory. The admiral later suggested, with obvious exaggeration, that you could have flown around North Vietnam in a Piper Cub plane and not heard anything "except for a rifle shot here and there."[101] Tom Moorer reached the conclusion held by many Air Force and Navy commanders that "airpower, given its day in court after almost a decade of frustration, confirmed its effectiveness as an instrument of national power—in just nine and a half flying days."[102] The JCS chairman testified before Congress on 9 January that Hanoi's ability to supply munitions to the troops in South Vietnam after the Linebacker campaigns had been reduced by half.[103]

The admiral also contended that at the start of the war had an "amphibious landing been made and the Army and Marines brought into North Vietnam and given adequate support, [and a] complete and total blockade laid on Haiphong, [the war] would have been over."[104] Later in life, Moorer repeatedly argued that the United States could have won the war. In a number of instances in his oral history he observed that "there are more people in Los Angeles and Orange counties in the state of California than there are in North Vietnam and we have 49 other states besides that and we let these lying little revolutionaries run us out of the there."[105] Defeat is a hard pill to swallow.

WAR LEADERS

Admiral Thomas H. Moorer's crowning achievement as a military leader was to oversee President Nixon's successful campaign to end America's direct involvement in the Vietnam War. He clearly sympathized with the president's determination to protect US global interests and to exploit US military power to achieve his objectives. The admiral served as the president's primary and most trusted advisor on the military campaigns and operations of the last pivotal year of the conflict. It was no easy task for a leader in uniform, who had experienced victory in battle, to oversee America's military withdrawal from the only war the nation had ever lost. Moorer's leadership was key to the defeat of the enemy's Nguyen Hue Offensive, the mining of Haiphong, and the Linebacker campaigns. He understood and supported Nixon's efforts to preserve the independence of the Republic of Vietnam. He continued to support Vietnamization. But after witnessing the disastrous result of the Lam Son 719 incursion into Laos and General Abrams's troubled leadership in that sorry episode, he developed a more realistic understanding of the South Vietnamese military's strengths and weaknesses. He recognized that only the full application of US air and naval power would make it possible for the Republic of Vietnam to survive.

Tom Moorer proved especially adept at dealing with Melvin Laird's opposition to the air and mining campaigns and the deployment of critical US forces to the combat theater. Still, he maintained a solid working relationship with Laird in spite of Nixon's exclusion of the defense secretary from the White House inner circle. Indeed, Moorer worked especially hard to repair the damage done to the civil-military relationship during the McNamara era. Unlike Johnson and his subordinates, Moorer involved CINCPAC in the war's key decisions and worked closely with the like-minded Admiral McCain. In the operational realm, the JCS chairman supported the theater-wide employment of Air Force B-52 bombers, despite Abrams's singular focus on the air operations in South Vietnam. Moorer also successfully endorsed the continued naval leadership of the Pacific Command in the predominantly maritime theater and the employment of naval gunfire ships in support of allied ground troops. He exploited his professional skill and years of service to develop the mining plan in concert with Admiral Zumwalt. Profiting from his experience fighting the North Vietnamese, the Seventh Fleet under Admiral Jim Holloway masterfully executed Tom Moorer's campaign to bring Hanoi to the peace table.

Moorer later suggested that an all-out aerial blitz and even an invasion of North Vietnam could have won the war. In 1972, however, the admiral and his commander in chief realized the impossibility of those actions due to foreign and domestic, if not moral concerns. They were compelled to adopt the "flexible response," "graduated escalation," and "tit-for-tat" approaches for which they had so heatedly condemned the Johnson administration.

The belligerents signed the peace agreement in Paris on 27 January 1973. It provided for an immediate cease-fire and the release of the 591 American POWs.[106] The Paris Agreement required negotiations between the South Vietnamese parties for a settlement that would "end hatred and enmity" and allow the people to decide their political future. The accord did not result in the removal of North Vietnamese troops from the territories they held in South Vietnam at the cessation of hostilities. Nonetheless, it enabled Nixon to extricate the United States from the war.

Jim Holloway later thought that the agreement produced positive, if short-term, results for the United States. He observed, "I spent a lot

The approaches to the port of Haiphong mined by Navy and Marine aircraft flying from Holloway's Seventh Fleet carrier USS *Coral Sea* (CVA-43). The operation closed off North Vietnam to seaborne imports of war materials. NHHC.

of time in the Vietnam War and it was a lousy war. None of us could see how the hell we were going to get out of it [and] I was sick over it." He was satisfied that the negotiated settlement brought the cease-fire and the return of the POWs. He concluded that "it was an honorable peace and it was sure better than war."[107]

Admiral Holloway had one more task as Commander Seventh Fleet: clearing the mines from North Vietnam's waters as provided for in the agreement. Operation End Sweep, conducted by the Mine Countermeasures Force (Task Force 78), led by Rear Admiral Brian McCauley, got underway on 6 February 1973. McCauley's units began airborne minesweeping with helicopters in the primary shipping channel to Haiphong on 27 February and in the ports of Hon Gai and Cam Pha on 17 March. Minesweeping operations continued in the Haiphong and the northern areas until 17 April when US leaders, concerned that the North Vietnamese were not adhering to all the terms of the Paris Agreement, temporarily withdrew the task force. Once Holloway and his superiors were convinced that Hanoi had received the intended message, he restarted End Sweep and in little more than a week declared the mission to clear the water approaches to Haiphong and the harbors of Hon Gai and Cam Pha accomplished. Finally, on 18 July 1973, the Seventh Fleet departed North Vietnamese territorial

Jim Holloway's expert handling of naval forces during the Linebacker campaigns and End Sweep did not go unnoticed by the CNO. In spring 1973, Zumwalt sent Holloway an "eyes-only" message informing him that he was recalling "Jimmy" to serve as his primary deputy, the Vice Chief of Naval Operations, a four-star billet. Holloway also understood that Zumwalt was positioning him as a nominee for the CNO billet at the end of the latter's tour. Holloway related that this action "could not have been a nicer gesture on the part of the CNO."[109] Bud Zumwalt was glad to welcome the combat-tested warrior and highly regarded leader to his team because the Chief of Naval Operations then needed all the help he could get leading the US Navy out of the doldrums of the Vietnam War.

CHAPTER 9
A NEW BROOM

On 1 July 1970, Elmo R. Zumwalt Jr. was promoted over the heads of thirty-three other admirals to become the 19th Chief of Naval Operations, then the youngest officer to have achieved four-star rank. His tumultuous four years in command would define a new era in the modern history of the US Navy.

Earlier that year, Secretary of Defense Laird had directed Navy secretary Chafee to fly Zumwalt home from South Vietnam for a job interview. During his first meeting in the Pentagon, Chafee asked the admiral to identify the Navy's most significant problems and offer solutions. Bud Zumwalt suggested that the Navy's most pressing issues were the need to enlist new sailors and retain current sailors in the service; provide the aging fleet with newer warships; and modernize the ballistic-missile-firing submarine force. The admiral remembered that Chafee was not especially interested in his views on strengthening the fleet to meet the Soviet threat because other more senior flag officers could do that. Instead, he wanted someone who could handle the Navy's personnel problems, which had put the service in "even greater immediate danger."[1]

Chafee told Zumwalt that he wanted him to bring the Navy "into the modern age."[2] Chafee, and indeed Laird, favored him over all the other flag officers because Zumwalt seemed to have the intellectual gifts, dynamism, youth, and a bond with young sailors to reinvigorate the Navy. Jim Holloway, an early supporter but later critic of Zumwalt, characterized Chafee as the "culprit" who championed Zumwalt for the CNO billet, wondering, "Why would you send a guy to be CNO who's never commanded?"[3] Indeed, the vice admiral had never led a

253

numbered fleet such as the Seventh Fleet or a geographically based command such as the Atlantic Fleet, which had been customary. Of course, Zumwalt had commanded 38,000 sailors in South Vietnam.

Laird met briefly with Zumwalt the day after Chafee did. The defense secretary then arranged for the admiral to meet with Kissinger at the White House. In the interim, Laird telephoned the national security advisor and told him that "he is the person that I lean towards for CNO." Laird considered Bud Zumwalt "the best of all the vice admirals we have."[4] Zumwalt credited Laird, "probably more than anyone," for the appointment. He knew that he had impressed Laird when the defense secretary had visited Vietnam. Abrams's strong endorsement at that time also worked in Zumwalt's favor. The meeting with Kissinger, according to Zumwalt, was "brief and . . . inconsequential."[5] Kissinger knew little about Zumwalt. Laird's blessing, however, counted with him. When Kissinger assured the president that Zumwalt was an acceptable candidate, Nixon readily concurred with the nomination. Nixon and Kissinger later regretted their offhand endorsement, coming to loathe the outspoken and often contentious Chief of Naval Operations.[6]

While Zumwalt in his memoirs emphasized that Laird and Chafee were interested in his human resources skills, several other factors certainly weighed in their selection. Laird was especially pleased that Zumwalt not only valued the secretary's Vietnamization program but implemented it with gusto in the Mekong Delta. Laird and Chafee also knew that Zumwalt shared their and his mentor Nitze's focus on meeting the Soviet threat with an improved US military establishment. And finally, Nitze and many civilian officials who had witnessed the officer's meteoric rise in the Pentagon sang his praises to whomever would listen.

Conversely, Tom Moorer and many other Navy flag officers groused, with some justification, that Zumwalt had not gained the position because of a stellar operational record but rather because of his political connections. Soon after Bud Zumwalt arrived in Washington to take up the CNO billet, Moorer asked him to visit his home, the Naval Observatory on Massachusetts Avenue, which he shared with his wife Carrie Foy Moorer. Tom Moorer told Zumwalt flat out that he "did not recommend you for this assignment" because of his lack of fleet command experience. The JCS chairman considered Zumwalt "a man of great talents" but feared the Navy would suffer the loss when Zumwalt had to retire after his tour at the relatively young age

JCS chairman Moorer and Secretary of the Navy Chafee congratulate Zumwalt as the new Chief of Naval Operations. The conservative Moorer disdained Zumwalt's and Chafee's liberalism. NHHC Vietnam Collection.

of fifty-three.[7] Laird, however, remembered Moorer reacting in a more elemental way. He recalled that Moorer "damn near went nuts" and spent two days in his office arguing that Zumwalt wasn't qualified for the job.[8] Before Zumwalt's selection, Moorer had urged Chafee to nominate instead admirals Jerome King, Bernard Clarey, or William F. Bringle. Soon-to-be Navy secretary John Warner also wanted Clarey to be the next CNO, but Laird backed Chafee. Warner lamented that the secretary of defense "let Chafee pick a liberal, and that guy . . . piled up on the rocks [and] never amounted to anything."[9]

Jim Holloway related that when he heard Zumwalt was to replace Moorer, "I could not conceive of myself serving competently as CNO at this point in my career or at my age." He could not envision himself relieving Moorer, "who was ten years older than me, at the peak of his professional career, and the epitome of experience, wisdom, and dignity." Holloway knew that Moorer had commanded the Seventh Fleet, the Pacific Fleet, and the Atlantic Fleet.[10] Admiral Richardson, who had led carrier forces at Yankee Station, sniffed that Zumwalt's operational experience had been "ashore, down in Vietnam," which most naval aviators deemed a decidedly peripheral assignment. Richardson considered it "unfortunate, because had Zumwalt been given two, three, or four years in command of operational [read major fleet] forces, he could easily have become one of the best CNO's we've known."[11]

Bud Zumwalt clearly understood Nixon's desire to end the half-million-man US military presence in South Vietnam and, despite all the negative reporting from King and Salzer, he continued to place faith in Laird's Vietnamization program. Zumwalt thought that the South Vietnamese navy and the other services could have held their own against the North Vietnamese. Zumwalt contended that Nixon, through diplomacy and the occasional use of B-52 bombers and other military forces, could have prevented Hanoi's victory in the war. He asserted that "we could have made it work," but unfortunately "history will prove that Mr. Nixon [was] castrated by the Watergate crisis." He also averred that the North Vietnamese "always knew that where they had to win the war was here in the United States."[12] The admiral castigated Congress for drastically reducing its military assistance to South Vietnam. Ironically, Zumwalt, the most impatient of the US leaders working to turn the war over to the Vietnamese, blamed Congress for pushing too hard for a fast exit.

The end of America's direct involvement in the Vietnam War did not end that conflict's impact on the United States in general and the US Navy in particular. Those members of Congress and other Americans who had railed against the war and the policies of the Johnson administration continued in the 1970s to oppose heavy commitments overseas. That reality was reflected in the Nixon Doctrine, which the president articulated during a visit to Guam on 25 July 1969. He made it clear that America's global allies might be provided naval and air support by the United States but should not count on US ground troops. Indeed, that understanding was at the heart of the Vietnamization program. The American people, angered by the war's high death toll and fiscal costs, were unlikely to support huge future outlays for the ships, planes, and troops called for by the defense department.

Nixon and Kissinger worked to lessen the Soviet threat through rapprochement or "détente" rather than confrontation. In Moscow during May 1972, the United States and the Soviet Union signed an Anti-Ballistic Missile Treaty, reached an interim agreement on the limitation of offensive weapons, and signed the Incidents at Sea Agreement to help lessen the danger of military accidents at sea and in the air.[13]

The war severely impacted the size and combat readiness of the US fleet. President Johnson had taken a "guns and butter" approach to the conflict—prosecuting the war in Vietnam while pursuing his goals for the betterment of society at home. To provide the armed services with the bombs, missiles, aircraft, ammunition, construction material, and supplies needed to fight the protracted war in faraway Southeast Asia, the Johnson administration had "stretched out" programs for the construction of new ships. Instead of building fifty ships each year, as the Navy anticipated in the early 1960s, yearly the service constructed only thirteen ships.

That development was especially troublesome because by 1969 the more than 700 ships built in World War II or just afterward, which comprised 58 percent of the fleet, were due for replacement. This "bloc obsolescence" would engage the attention of naval leaders throughout the 1970s. The Navy's antisubmarine carriers, escort ships, patrol planes, antisubmarine warfare equipment, and other sea control assets had suffered a steep decline in command attention. With few new surface ships being built and hundreds being decommissioned because of their advanced age, the US fleet was reduced from 743 vessels in 1970 to 533 in 1979. The number of combat aircraft dropped from 3,457 to 2,681 during the same years. By the end of the decade, 206,322 fewer personnel served in the fleet. The Navy's budget for 1970 was $22 billion, and it did not rise above $30 billion during the next five years. The lack of adequate funding support for the maintenance and upkeep of naval vessels and their weapon systems, training, repair parts, and supplies during the war hurt the readiness of the entire operating Navy. In the years that followed, the situation only worsened.[14]

The war's long, divisive, and ultimately unsuccessful outcome also exacerbated existing social, political, and racial tensions in American society. Many politically radical, antiestablishment, and minority citizens came to consider the nation as imperialistic, militaristic, and racist and its government unworthy of their trust. Some enlisted personnel in the armed forces were convinced that their officers and veteran noncommissioned officers were professionally incompetent, only interested in their careers, and insensitive to their lives. The upshot was that in the period from 1969 to 1973, the troops "found it even harder to understand their mission and nearly impossible to ennoble it." At the same time, during the war other Americans railed against the anti-war movement as unpatriotic, and its adherents as draft-dodging, anti-establishment, counterculture "hippies." Many urban ethnic groups, rural whites, and suburbanites of the middle class especially resented the upper middle class whose sons and daughters had secured deferments from active service and denounced the government's handling of the war.[15]

Many young Americans, rebelling against the constraints of previous decades, challenged constituted authority, adopted unconventional lifestyles, and experimented with hallucinogenic drugs and other dangerous substances. Despite the reality that more volunteers served in Vietnam than those inducted involuntarily, there was widespread opposition in the nation to continuation of the draft. Attuned to that sentiment, the same day that his representatives signed the Paris peace accords, Nixon ended the military draft. Hence, the Nixon administration needed new approaches to maintaining the material strength of the armed forces and filling its ranks with qualified volunteers to meet the challenge posed by the USSR.

In many ways, the CNO worked to distance the Navy from the Vietnam experience. When Zumwalt worked in the Pentagon before his tour in Vietnam, he and Nitze had argued against the US commitment to South Vietnam as an unnecessary diversion from the Cold War struggle with the Soviet Union. He bemoaned the fact that the war "gobbled up" the resources needed by the Navy to control the oceans of the globe. It is curious that even while championing Laird's Vietnamization program, Zumwalt later stated that he "did not consider South Vietnam to be a viable national entity capable of repelling Hanoi's aggression." Bud Zumwalt saw the Vietnam War as "the wrong war, in the wrong place, at the wrong time," using Omar Bradley's famous characterization about a potential war with China but without crediting the general for the pithy quote.[16] Peter Swartz, who served in Vietnam as an advisor and on Zumwalt's staff and helped develop the Navy's Maritime Strategy of the 1980s, has observed that "Zumwalt went over to Vietnam not thinking that counterinsurgency and in-country operations were the Navy's long-term responsibility." Swartz added that Zumwalt "knew that the effort in Vietnam was a dead end, although he never once let on. But as soon as he got back as CNO he slammed the door shut . . . on those aspects of warfare."[17]

Zumwalt considered the Navy's most vital task to be preparing for possible war with the Soviet Union and its increasingly capable navy.

He recognized the irony that he "was known mostly as the CNO who allowed sailors to grow beards, wear mod clothes, and drive motorcycles" when he "spent most of my time [on] the U.S.-Soviet maritime balance." Measures for countering the Soviet threat dominated his 500-page autobiography *On Watch*, while his Vietnam experience counted for only ten pages. He argued that the US Navy had taken sea control for granted during the early Cold War and the Korean War since the Soviet Navy had stayed close to home. America's adversaries did not sink a major US warship during the 1950s or 1960s. Zumwalt, however, contended that the US Navy could no longer expect to operate unscathed in a conflict at sea.[18]

Indeed, led by the brilliant naval leader and strategist Admiral Sergei Gorshkov, the Soviet navy had been busy during the Vietnam years deploying a powerful fleet of missile-armed cruisers and destroyers supplemented with long-range naval aircraft. From 1966 to 1970, the Soviets built 209 cruisers, destroyers, and other surface ships and submarines equipped with advanced offensive and defensive systems. In 1970, in the exercise *Okean 70*, the Soviet Navy's fleet commanders coordinated the deployment of more than 200 warships and submarines in seas distant from the USSR. By 1971, the Soviet Navy was operating fifty ballistic missile submarines and more than 300 attack boats. That same year, the Soviet Union overtook the United States in the total number of nuclear-powered submarines built or under construction.[19]

The Soviet Navy flexed its new muscles and moved aggressively into the oceans of the world, threatening America's control of the sea and its overseas interests and influence. During the Middle East crisis over Jordan in 1970, twenty Soviet ships and submarines with another fifty vessels only a day away trailed the US Sixth Fleet. In the Yom Kippur War of 1973, the Soviets clearly challenged the US Navy's historic dominance of the Eastern Mediterranean. Aircraft from airfields in Egypt, Syria, and Yugoslavia and the Soviet Union's warships and submarines faced off against their American adversaries. Soviet naval forces outnumbered US naval forces by a third during the crisis. JCS chairman Tom Moorer concluded during the episode that the side that fired first would win.[20]

In March 1971, Bud Zumwalt told the Senate Appropriations Committee that in a conventional naval war with the Soviets, "we would lose." Just before his retirement in 1974, he concluded that "we stand now at our point of greatest weakness and, in my estimate, in our greatest jeopardy." He observed years later that the odds were "that we would have lost a war with the Soviet Union if we had to fight in any year" after 1970.[21]

His one-time subordinate and successor as CNO held a contrary view. In retirement, Jim Holloway affirmed that had the US and Soviet navies gone to war it wouldn't "have been close" since "we had 18 aircraft carriers and they had none [and] we had an amphibious force second to none." Holloway, however, was "absolutely convinced" that had a war broken out with the Soviet Union, it would have escalated to a nuclear exchange almost immediately because, echoing Moorer's words, the side that took action first was the side "that's going to win." Jim Holloway thought that even though Zumwalt sincerely believed the US Navy would come out second best in a confrontation with the Soviet Navy, Bud Zumwalt "really didn't have a feel for it" since he had never commanded a fleet. Holloway revealed another reason why Zumwalt emphasized the Soviet threat. Supposedly, Zumwalt told Holloway that "that's the only way to get their attention and get increased funding" from Congress. Holloway did not favor that approach to dealing with the legislature, since "if you're not honest and you play games you're going to hurt yourself."[22]

PROJECT SIXTY AND OVERSEAS HOMEPORTING

One of Zumwalt's first acts as CNO was to order the completion of a plan in sixty days—hence the name—for the Navy's near term and even distant future composition and missions. Indeed, he later mused that by the middle of the next century, "warfare might be run on a global basis, with CINCPAC based in the Rocky Mountains and CINCLANT's [Commander in Chief, Atlantic] headquarters in the Appalachians."[23] Months before he left his command in Vietnam, he had already given serious thought to his ideas for modernizing the fleet. With time running short to complete the project, Zumwalt decided that his Office of the Chief of Naval Operations (OPNAV) staff would take too long to complete it and it would run into inevitable bureaucratic delays. Instead, as often in Vietnam, he took an ad hoc approach and tasked with the work Captain (later Admiral) Stansfield Turner, then Chafee's executive assistant. Over a six-week period, which Turner described as "the most frantic period of his entire career," he employed a systems analysis approach pioneered by McNamara's systems analyst, Alain

Zumwalt published *On Watch* shortly after his retirement to support his bid for a seat in the US Senate. The self-promoting book laid out Zumwalt's case for his leadership in the war and stewardship of the Navy.

Enthoven. Working virtually alone, Turner turned over to the CNO a list of potential projects and recommendations for action.

Rear Admiral Worth H. Bagley and Commander Henry "Hank" Mustin later took up the project but changed little of Turner's work. In Project Sixty it was clear that Zumwalt wanted to put the Vietnam

War behind. Peter Swartz, later a special assistant to JCS chairman Colin Powell, has observed that "Stan Turner, Worth Bagley, and Hank Mustin were all surface warfare officers and no friends of counterinsurgency."[24] Zumwalt also enlisted Rear Admiral Emmett Tidd, who had been his chief of staff in Vietnam, to coordinate and monitor the implementation of the program. In essence, "Tidd became Zumwalt's SOB."[25]

In the CNO's Pentagon conference room on 26 August 1970, Turner briefed the project to most of the Washington-based flag officers, including Rickover. Unsurprisingly, since few officers besides Turner knew of its contents, his briefing prompted "few questions and even fewer comments." Indeed, Zumwalt made it clear in advance that he supported the presentation, and no one wanted to challenge the new CNO.[26]

The central theme of Project Sixty was to reemphasize one of the Navy's core missions—sea control—and deemphasize what had been its function in Vietnam, the projection of naval power ashore primarily by the aircraft carrier fleet, naval bombardment ships, and in-country naval forces. In one Navy Vietnam veteran's apt words, "Let's get back to our natural habitat at sea and stop worrying about 'brown water navies,' gun line ships and that kind of thing; let's talk about fighting the Russians."[27] Bud Zumwalt felt that too much of the Navy's budget had been devoted to aircraft carriers and naval aviation at the expense of the cruisers, destroyers, and other surface navy combatants. He also bemoaned a too-generous outlay of funding for the nuclear-powered ballistic-missile and attack submarine fleet.

In Project Sixty, Zumwalt called for a more balanced Navy. Nonetheless, the words and actions of this former destroyerman clearly revealed an intention to elevate the status of the surface navy— his navy—vis-à-vis the naval aviation and submarine "unions," as he called them. Zumwalt recognized that the country's anti-war and anti-military sentiment at the time would not allow a sizeable increase in the Navy's budget. He described the constituent pressures with which some normally pro-defense congressmen labored during this post–Vietnam period. One senator told the admiral: "Look, I've got to have a 30 percent pro- and a 70 percent anti-defense voting record to get reelected in my state. You tell me which 30 percent to vote for." The cost was high for new, technologically sophisticated ships, weapons, and sensors. For instance, pre-Vietnam destroyers were built for $30 million apiece, but the new *Spruance*-class ships of the 1970s cost $120 million each.

Rather than build many 90,000-ton aircraft carriers and additional ballistic-missile and attack submarines to replace hundreds of obsolescent ships, Zumwalt recommended a "High-Low Mix" of first-line warships but also many smaller, single-purpose, inexpensive, and relatively lightly armed combatants. He tested new technologies such as "ships that rode on bubbles of air [air-cushion vehicles], hydrofoils that flew over water, cruise missiles [and] aircraft that took off and landed straight up and down."[28] He also envisioned a patrol frigate that would be half the size of an existing destroyer escort and be armed with Harpoon anti-ship missiles and helicopters. The Navy eventually brought the concept to life as the *Oliver Hazard Perry* (FFG-7) class of guided missile frigates and built fifty-five of them for convoy and battle group escort duties. John Lehman, secretary of the Navy during the 1980s, acknowledged that the *Oliver Hazard Perry* class was Zumwalt's brainchild and was "one of the most successful shipbuilding programs in the Navy's postwar history."[29] Zumwalt also called for the construction of 17,000-ton Sea Control Ships. He was especially enamored with the concept of a naval vessel that could carry helicopters and vertical/short-takeoff-and-landing planes and cost less than 15 percent of a new nuclear-powered carrier. Bud Zumwalt got Congress to accept gas-turbine engines for the surface navy's destroyers, frigates, and missile craft over the opposition of Admiral Rickover, who saw the gas-turbine engines as a threat to his goal of an all-nuclear-powered Navy.[30]

Bud Zumwalt considered the overall Vietnam venture and the employment of the Navy's projection forces in that conflict a wasteful application of naval power even though he did not explicitly push that conclusion in the project paper. As Swartz has remarked, "Vietnam was the 'dog that didn't bark' in the Project Sixty study." He added, "I think he knew that Vietnam . . . was a loser, and while basking in (and benefiting from) his past glory as a recent combat commander, conceptually and programmatically he refocused the Navy laser-like on its future as a vital anti-Soviet player."[31]

Strongly influencing Project Sixty were the Nixon Doctrine that called on allies to shoulder the burden of local defense and the growing Soviet threat. Project Sixty itemized the force levels, ship types, and weapon systems that the CNO thought the Navy should have. Zumwalt also rejected the Navy's Cold War commandment that to have a positive impact on the enemy, naval forces had to strike at the source of their power. He considered America's aircraft carriers too vulnerable to approach the Soviet heartland and instead called for what was essentially a defensive strategy. Project Sixty was highly classified at the time of its issuance, so it did not gain public notice. Admiral Turner's Naval War College *Review* article, "Missions of the U.S. Navy," that contained key aspects of Zumwalt's strategic study, however, spread the CNO's ideas throughout the national security establishment.[32]

Bud Zumwalt had too many enemies and too few friends to bring his Project Sixty and all his follow-on shipbuilding and modernization efforts to fruition. One problem was his approach to its adoption as Navy policy. Rather than develop a corps of supporters within the Office of the Chief of Naval Operations and the Navy bureaus, he exploited his political connections (as he had done often in the past), going directly to Chafee and Laird. Tom Moorer, who consistently called for a nuclear-powered, 16-carrier Navy, deplored Zumwalt's High-Low Mix, and especially his championship of low-end helicopter and V/STOL (vertical short takeoff and landing) ships. Even though Zumwalt favored construction of another large carrier, Moorer feared for the future of the large-deck ships. In his *Aircraft Carriers at War*, while Jim Holloway did not identify Zumwalt, he was clearly referring to his predecessor when he observed that little thought had been given "to the lack of battleworthiness in a carrier without the speed, armor, protection, compartmentation, and redundancy required in a warship." And he found VSTOL aircraft "by design markedly inferior to its conventional contemporaries in combat operational capabilities—speed, range, bomb load, and safety."[33]

Tom Moorer and other naval aviators argued that Bud Zumwalt, because of his lack of top-level seagoing command, failed to understand that the US Navy had a global mission—even after Vietnam—that required large carriers and other major combatants with weapon systems oriented for offensive warfare. Zumwalt's planned fighting vessels were not suited to the Navy's global responsibilities and America's maritime position. Vice Admiral Gerald Miller, one-time Sixth Fleet commander and a naval aide like Zumwalt during their Pentagon days, suggested that Zumwalt's desired force would be more appropriate to the Greek or Turkish navies, whose security responsibilities did not extend beyond the Aegean.[34]

In the end, Congress failed to approve funding for the Sea Control Ship or the air-cushion vehicle, major setbacks to Zumwalt's program. A number of his initiatives came to fruition, but long after his time in command of the Navy and largely through the efforts of his successors. The SH-60B LAMPs anti-submarine helicopter, the Harpoon ship-to-ship missile, the Trident II (D-5) intercontinental ballistic missile (ICBM) and *Ohio*-class submarine, and the Vulcan Phalanx close-in weapon system entered fleet service in the late 1970s and early 1980s.[35]

Key members of Congress opposed Zumwalt because of his personnel reforms and hesitated to fund unconventional naval vessels. At the same time, retired and active flag officers from the naval aviation and submarine communities feared that his procurement initiatives would gut their own favored projects. Zumwalt gambled that Congress would replace the ships he ordered decommissioned with his Sea Control Ship and the other naval vessels identified in Project Sixty, but he lost that bet. During Zumwalt's tenure as CNO, the active fleet declined from 769 warships to 512. Most of the ships decommissioned were in the surface force.[36]

Moreover, Bud Zumwalt's actions to promote opportunities for surface navy officers, which entailed cutting short the careers of John Hyland and other renowned naval aviators, did not endear him to that community. As Admiral Clarey told Hyland, when Moorer met with Zumwalt to learn who the soon-to-be CNO planned to promote or retire, "he had never, ever seen Tom Moorer so indignant, so angry as when he came out of that meeting." Thomas Hayward thought it "very clear that Bud Zumwalt was knocking off aviators."[37]

Zumwalt decided to demonstrate to the Navy the benefit of giving young and talented officers more responsibility. The CNO designated one destroyer squadron in which every billet was assigned to an officer one rank below what was traditional. He called it the "Mod Squad" after a TV program popular at the time and directed Captain Richard Nicholson, an old hand from Vietnam days, to head it. Vice Admiral King was typical of those naval leaders who considered the Mod Squad idea "stupid." He observed that "the selection of these people was contentious, and it made those not selected think they were somehow second-class or worse."[38] Even fervent Zumwalt supporter Howard Kerr thought the Mod Squad experiment "was something that the admiral probably shouldn't have done [because] it irritated too many people." He added that "it was one of those things where the payoff just wasn't that big for him, for the Navy [and that] the negatives kind of outweighed the positives."[39]

Another of Zumwalt's initiatives, the forward basing of major fleet units at key sites in Asia and Europe—at the time referred to as overseas homeporting—had mixed results. His goals in the effort were to improve the fleet's overseas presence, reduce costs for the resource-starved service, and improve the morale of sailors and their families. The CNO pushed the long-term stationing of aircraft carriers and their support ships at Yokosuka, Japan, and in the Mediterranean. He also improved the smaller facilities at Sasebo, Japan, La Maddalena on the Italian island of Sardinia, Rota in Spain, and Naples. He wanted to station major combat forces closer to the Soviet Union. Zumwalt also reasoned that basing ships overseas would save the Navy money otherwise spent having to return ships to the United States for repairs and overhauls after months-long cruises across the Atlantic or the Pacific. And he hoped to improve sailor morale by collocating crews and their loved ones overseas for up to three years, thus avoiding long-term family separations.

The program worked well in Japan. Japanese government officials supported the proposal because they understood that a US aircraft carrier and its support ships stationed at the Yokosuka and Sasebo naval bases would strengthen their alliance with the United States and give a boost to commercial activity around the facilities. In 1972, Prime Minister Kakuei Tanaka let it be known unofficially—since it was a sensitive domestic political issue—that if asked informally the government would support the forward-basing proposal. Then Vice Chief of Naval Operations Jim Holloway, only recently the Seventh Fleet commander, worked behind the scenes in Washington to help facilitate Congress's acceptance of the proposed action. From October 1973 on, task groups composed of carrier *Midway*, amphibious, and mine warfare ships operated out of Japan. Almost from the start, the American sailors, their families, and the Japanese people in general worked and lived in relative harmony. In short, the forward-basing of *Midway* and the other warships improved the operational readiness of the fleet, strengthened the US-Japan alliance, and stimulated the economies of Yokosuka and Sasebo. And, in general, sailors and their families were satisfied with their stay in Japan.[40]

Bud Zumwalt's overseas homeporting measure did not fare as well in Europe. In 1973, the Navy deployed Destroyer Squadron 12 to Athens, Greece. The plan was for a carrier to move to the region later. At the same time, Zumwalt's newly established and Navy-wide "intercultural relations" program was morphed into an overarching "human resources management" program for implementation in the

Greek capital. The Navy established relevant offices throughout the city and encouraged sailors and their families to find accommodations among the populace. This approach, rooted in Zumwalt's Vietnam-era Personal Response Program, and indeed overseen in Washington by old Vietnam hands Chick Rauch and his deputy John Walker, was also instituted at US naval facilities in Italy and Spain. Swartz, who helped manage the intercultural relations effort in Europe, remembered that to save money and foster good relations with the local people, the CNO suggested not building isolated and self-contained "little Americas" at these locations. Provided with ample funding, the thirteen Vietnam veterans who ran the program in Athens taught sailors the Greek language and worked to immerse the Americans in the local culture.[41]

Nonetheless, according to Zumwalt a poll of the Americans there found that only 60 percent of them considered Athens a desirable place to live. Moreover, a Government Accounting Office investigation discovered real problems. Zumwalt remembered that "some families had prepared themselves or had been prepared by the Navy badly for living in an unfamiliar culture and had been surprised or frightened or affronted by the local sanitation, cooking, shopping facilities, and manners and, particularly, by the overt anti-Americanism of some Greeks."[42] The commanders of the destroyer squadron and their subordinates, stressed to cover the costs to maintain and repair their ships and handle operational responsibilities, also complained about the seeming preference given to the intercultural relations program. Eventually, Admiral David Bagley, Commander US Naval Forces, Europe, throttled back the program. Moreover, as Swartz has related, after Zumwalt left office the Navy put much of the intercultural relations program "under the knife," using its resources to reinforce its race relations and drug and alcohol abuse education programs.[43] And finally, key members of Congress opposed stationing US warships in Greece, then experiencing political turmoil related to the repressive rule of a US-supported military junta. The Navy did not forward-deploy a carrier to the Mediterranean and eventually withdrew the destroyer squadron from Athens.

HEAD TO HEAD WITH THE OLD MAN

Bud Zumwalt picked one fight that made his tenure as CNO much more difficult and unfulfilling than it had to be. At the outset he knew that developing a productive working relationship with Admiral

Hyman G. Rickover would be one of the "toughest nuts" he would have to crack. Zumwalt admitted that "in my exuberance over being chosen to head the Navy, I believed I could do it—I was wrong."[44] Zumwalt considered Rickover, the czar of the naval nuclear-power community, a "malady that afflicted ... the whole Navy," because of his abrasive personality, too close relations with key members of Congress, and statutory independence from the Navy as Director, Naval Reactors, Atomic Energy Commission.[45] When Zumwalt first heard Rickover speak at the Naval War College years earlier, he "found him distasteful to listen to, egotistical, [and] critical." Zumwalt recalled that he learned "nothing from that lecture."[46]

Bud Zumwalt endured one of Rickover's storied and grueling interviews for the nuclear-power program. Submariner Harold E. Shear, who later served on Zumwalt's Pentagon staff, sat in on the session. As was the norm for such interviews, the admiral grilled Zumwalt mercilessly and then told him to "get out of here." Shear accompanied Zumwalt to a small, bare room to wait for Rickover's summons for another session. Shear remembered that Zumwalt "was feeling pretty bad [and that] he was upset over that interview, quite upset, much more than he should have been." That reaction prompted Shear to put his arm around Zumwalt and say, "Oh, hell, Bud, this is par for the course. Don't get too upset about this." Shear remembered that Zumwalt spoke to him about the episode a number of times in later years.[47] The experience clearly had an impact on the sensitive young officer and may partly explain his animus toward Rickover later on.

Zumwalt's reaction to the meeting with Rickover revealed a characteristic approach to adversaries. He shared his gripes with a wider audience, naturally presenting his own sometimes varnished interpretation. While having assured Rickover that he would not discuss their supposedly private interaction, Commander Zumwalt typed up a lengthy, verbatim transcript and shared it with CNO Burke, then-Secretary of the Navy Thomas S. Gates Jr., and the latter's subordinate in charge of personnel.

Despite Rickover's harsh treatment of Zumwalt during the interview process, the admiral selected the mid-level officer for the nuclear program. Zumwalt turned down the offer and instead accepted command of the conventionally powered guided missile frigate *Dewey* (DLG-14).[48] Zumwalt remembered that whenever he and Rickover encountered one another, "the hair on the backs of our necks seemed

Admiral Rickover, "Father of the Nuclear Navy," delivers a typically negative assessment of Navy shipbuilding. Zumwalt tried but failed to limit Rickover's power and influence. NHHC K-114805.

to bristle."[49] One of Zumwalt's biographers has cogently observed that "in some respects Rickover was just like [Zumwalt]—one of a kind. Brilliant, sly, tireless, blunt, devious, arrogant, farsighted, vain, [and] angry."[50] At one point, Rickover accused Zumwalt of being a political animal.[51] Frank Duncan, a long-time subordinate of the admiral, related that "Rickover considered Zumwalt a protégé of Paul H. Nitze, whom he disliked, and an advocate of systems analysis, a discipline he despised."[52]

Zumwalt devoted an entire chapter in *On Watch* to his ultimately unsuccessful effort to have his way with the redoubtable naval leader. When Zumwalt served on Navy secretary Nitze's staff, his boss had assigned him the task of finding a way to retire the admiral. Bud Zumwalt accepted the mission enthusiastically, "seeing it as his chance for ultimate payback."[53] Rickover, however, retained the support of powerful members of Congress who were hardly inclined to weaken the nation's ballistic missile submarine force, the most potent US counter to the USSR. Zumwalt fought Rickover over the design of the *Glenard P. Lipscomb* and SSN-688 *Los Angeles*-class attack submarines, but the

CNO lost those fights too. Zumwalt's method of opposing Rickover differed markedly from Moorer's. Bud Zumwalt observed that "Moorer never called Rickover and whenever Rick called him he'd say, 'Yes, Rick, Yes, Rick, Yes, Rick,' and then hang up and never do anything about it." In contrast, Zumwalt's approach was to fight Rickover. He admitted, though, that it caused "a hell of a lot more friction."[54]

Despite Rickover's negative perception of Zumwalt's intentions for the submarine arm, Zumwalt did champion the Trident ballistic missile submarine program and the fourth nuclear-powered carrier to be built, eventually named *Carl Vinson* (CVN-70).[55] Zumwalt credited Rickover for getting congressional support by naming the carrier after retired Congressman Vinson, an ardent and long-time supporter of the Navy. Zumwalt was undeterred by the fact that the ship was named for a living person, contrary to tradition, admitting that he got criticism from naval buffs but that "tradition is there to be broken for the right reasons." Howard Kerr affirmed that Zumwalt's mindset was "always on tomorrow and not yesterday."[56]

In retirement, Zumwalt's opposition to Rickover became even more bitter and personal. He told Rickover's biographers that he considered the man "paranoid" and one who "had turned the world into his asylum." He considered Rickover an enemy of the United States second only to the Soviet Union and ranted that "the force of Admiral Rickover's out-of-channel, executive branch-unsupervised, Byzantine, bureaucratic operation has perverted" the Navy's development.[57] Bud Zumwalt's loathing of Rickover was only equaled by that of former Secretary of the Navy John Lehman, who ultimately fired the aging officer. Lehman related that "four chiefs of naval operations (Moorer, Zumwalt, Holloway, and Hayward) and six former secretaries of the navy (Anderson, Nitze, Korth, Claytor, Hidalgo, and Chafee)" told him that they were "routinely ignored by Rickover and, whenever it suited him, he simply flatly disobeyed direct orders or instructions."[58]

A NEW LOOK AT NAVY HEADQUARTERS AND THE NAVAL WAR COLLEGE

Zumwalt launched an effort to streamline the Office of the Chief of Naval Operations. To satisfy the submarine, surface, and aviation communities, he established separate staff organizations, but to acquire tighter control of policy and budgetary matters he also created systems analysis and resource directorates—a "staff within a staff"—that reported directly to his Vice Chief of Naval Operations and hence to him. Rickover disapproved of the action, which he thought destabilized the Navy's headquarters. He complained that under Zumwalt, the Navy's mission was confused by too much organizational complexity. He asserted that there were too many managers and administrators between the decision-makers and "the people who are doing the actual work—the hewers of wood and drawers of water."[59] The staff reorganization did not succeed, partly because Zumwalt did not get the resources he needed to sustain it. Moreover, his policy initiatives often denied him the sympathy that he needed for a successful reorganization. Bud Zumwalt's favoring of young, talented officers "undermined the tradition of seniority, thereby robbing himself (and his office) of some of the support he might otherwise have had from the officer corps." By the end of his term as CNO, Zumwalt did not have the clout to push through further internal reforms.[60]

In 1972, Zumwalt also set his sights on reforming the Naval War College, from which he had graduated in 1953. The CNO and many other naval officers had come to regard the war college as a "gentlemen's club where students could relax" between demanding overseas and stateside tours. Zumwalt concluded that the curriculum there lacked intellectual rigor and did not arm an officer with an understanding of grand strategy, the operational arts, or international relations. The courses of instruction had revolved around lectures by visiting scholars, with little interaction or intense study required from the students. Bud Zumwalt's approach to problems was often revolutionary rather than evolutionary, and the changes that occurred at the Naval War College fit the mold.[61]

To execute his revolution, the CNO selected junior Rear Admiral Stansfield Turner, who like Zumwalt had headed the Navy's Systems Analysis Division in OPNAV and who had crafted much of Project Sixty. The officer, who later served as the director of the Central Intelligence Agency, had attended Oxford University as a Rhodes Scholar and was considered a likely candidate for fleet command. Zumwalt gave Turner almost complete latitude in how he would reform the curriculum and overall academic approach at the college. The CNO only emphasized that Turner was to "broaden officers who are often preoccupied with their area of specialty [that is air, surface, submarine, and support operations] and help them to learn to analyze problems."[62]

Even before he took the helm as president of the Naval War College (as a vice admiral), Stan Turner had developed a new curriculum that stressed the study of strategy based on in-depth analyses of historical cases. One of those cases was *The Peloponnesian War* by the Greek historian Thucydides that detailed the conflict between Athens and Sparta from 431 to 404 BCE. The object of the instruction was to learn about the "Athenian government's attempt to conduct an ever more expensive, protracted, overseas war in the face of political disaffection at home." Of course, that long-ago war had many similarities to the nation's contemporary struggle in Vietnam. Hence, the students could discuss the "basic and recurring problems in strategy while avoiding the passions of current political views" and the personal experience of the students, many of them Vietnam veterans.[63]

Under Stan Turner's plan, the students would be responsible for completing term papers and special studies, take an active part in seminars, and read 1,000 pages a week in required texts. Their work would now be graded. Turner, in an approach similar to that of his mentor, turned to outside experts rather than the leaders and faculty at the war college to develop his concept. Like Zumwalt, the handsome, charming, and erudite Turner skillfully exploited the informational media and delivered speeches in support of his program to many groups nationwide.[64]

And like Zumwalt, Turner's actions generated intense opposition from many Navy quarters. One scholar has compared Stan Turner to Admiral William S. Sims, an early twentieth century Navy reformer, but Zumwalt fits the characterization as well: "Each held values in professional education similar to the other's and each had an exceptionally strong personality. Both were controversial; both had devoted admirers and ardent detractors; both were abrasive in doing exactly what they thought was right; both equated opposition to their positions with error; both thought their opponents were hopelessly wrong and misguided."[65] When Vice Admiral Julien J. LeBourgeois succeeded Turner as president in August 1974, he understood that there was little appetite at the war college for further reform of the institution. He announced that he would focus on "consolidating and refining the innovations" initiated by Turner. Secretary of the Navy J. William Middendorf and then CNO Holloway, as they were doing with the service at large, endorsed LeBourgeois's emphasis on stability at the Navy's institution of higher learning.

In July 1970, Bud Zumwalt, the young, dynamic, politically savvy, and combat-tested admiral tapped by Secretary of Defense Laird and

Secretary of the Navy Chafee to be the next Chief of Naval Operations, stormed into Washington to remake the Navy. In a typical approach, he immediately launched multiple projects, fully expecting that some would succeed and others would not. His primary effort, Project Sixty, conformed to the Nixon administration's post–Vietnam worldview of avoiding heavy commitments overseas. The White House wanted the Navy to focus on protecting the sea lanes to America's European allies—a defensive approach—rather than plan for potential offensive operations against the Soviet Union. Reduced funding support of the armed services further limited the ships, planes, and weapons that Zumwalt believed Congress would support. His High-Low Mix approach reflected that perception.

He did, however, continue to support construction of limited numbers of nuclear-powered aircraft carriers and submarines, F-14 Tomcat fighters, and other ships and weapon systems. At the same time, the new CNO advanced many innovative and indeed revolutionary concepts for the fleet of the future that would put to sea hydrofoils, surface effect ships, surface-to-surface missiles, and small carriers able to operate V/STOL aircraft. Zumwalt, however, failed to bring much of Project Sixty to fruition. Congress rejected what Zumwalt considered his most important innovation, the Sea Control Ship. Only through the patient advocacy of admirals Jim Holloway and Tom Hayward did many of the ships and weapons systems identified in Project Sixty enter the fleet years later.

Zumwalt's other initiatives registered mixed success. The homeporting of Seventh Fleet ships in Japan proved to be a long-term benefit to the US-Japan alliance, but similar measures in the Mediterranean fared badly. His support for revitalization of the Naval War College's program boosted that institution's reputation as the Navy's primary center for the analysis and dissemination of naval strategy. Conversely, his measures to streamline the management of the Office of the Chief of Naval Operations and his Mod Squad experiment did not outlast his time as CNO.

Several factors worked against Bud Zumwalt's initial efforts to remake the Navy in line with his vision. His ad hoc approach to problem-solving, impatience to proceed with and complete projects, and reliance on a few individuals to carry the load did him no favors. Instead of enlisting allies to his cause, he alienated many of those people he needed most. Bypassing subordinate flag officers and their staffs in the Pentagon to develop Project Sixty and the reorganization of

OPNAV denied him their expertise and support. In truth, his lack of fleet command experience showed in his unfamiliarity with the support that subordinate organizations and staffs could provide. He never gained the backing of those aviators who continued to value the utility of large-deck carriers in the projection of naval power ashore. His public and personality-driven feud with Admiral Rickover turned many leaders in Congress, the shipbuilding industry, and the submarine and aviation arms of the Navy against him. Admiral Tom Moorer and other naval leaders agreed with Zumwalt's highlighting of the Soviet threat, but they were not comfortable with his "the sky is falling" approach. And one cannot discount the personal resentment of those flag officers bypassed when the political leadership favored Zumwalt for the CNO billet. Finally, Bud Zumwalt's efforts to modernize the fleet suffered from the dearth of resources available to him as a result of the seemingly endless and costly war in Vietnam. The conflict's doleful effects on the men and women of the Navy would present him with an even greater challenge.

CHAPTER 10

REVOLUTION IN THE NAVY

Bud Zumwalt's greatest challenge by far as the Chief of Naval Operations was to improve the quality of service of Navy men and women in the wake of a war that had opened serious and longstanding social wounds. At stake was the future health of the Navy.

One of his most immediate concerns was to retain in service experienced sailors, many of them veterans of combat in Vietnam, and to enlist the new men and women he needed to sustain the postwar Navy. At the start of the 1970s, only 9.5 percent of the men were reenlisting after their first hitch when that figure had traditionally been 35 percent. Zumwalt recognized that the fleet he intended building for the global confrontation with the Soviet Navy would be impotent if it could not retain a core of highly trained and motivated sailors. When he became CNO, the US Navy was hemorrhaging sailors. AWOL and desertion rates were high. Moreover, the future looked bleak. With the end of the war and the end of the draft approaching, he realized that the Navy could not count on enlisting the most highly educated and technically skilled young Americans, many of whom had joined the naval service to avoid combat in the jungle. He understood that the Navy was in a "catastrophic situation" owing to the anti-war and anti-military mood of the country. He realized that "we had to shock the system."[1]

Zumwalt's command experience in Vietnam had alerted him to the social pressures affecting his young sailors. Stanley R. Arthur, the future leader of US and allied naval forces in the Persian Gulf War and ultimately Vice Chief of Naval Operations, was a mid-level officer during Zumwalt's tour of duty as CNO. Arthur thought that "Zumwalt understood way before his time that there was a transformation going on in society." Arthur recognized that if the Navy didn't deal with it, the service would be in trouble. He observed that when he was the Vice Chief, it dawned on him that "Admiral Zumwalt saw this coming." Zumwalt knew that commanders would need to take a different approach to the new generation.[2]

The Navy had a drug problem. In 1969 and 1970, the Navy discharged 3,800 sailors for drug pushing or using, both in Vietnam and at other global locations. Zumwalt said that the issuance of his directive, "Navy Drug Exemption and Rehabilitation Program," was prompted by reports from Vice Admiral Salzer, then the naval commander in Vietnam, who reported the sudden appearance of "large quantities of high quality, low cost heroin."[3] Salzer related that when he took over as COMNAVFORV in April 1971, he was "hit in the face" with the drug abuse issue "like a pail of ice-cold water." He added that the drug scene was "the part of the tour there that I disliked the most."[4]

Salzer complained that during Bud Zumwalt's February 1972 visit to Vietnam, the CNO made an all-too-typical snap decision with regard to a Navy in-country amnesty program. When Zumwalt met with a group of sailors, he told one man that his staff would urgently look into the drug issue. The sailor, however, responded that "urgently isn't fast enough; we need amnesty now!" Zumwalt then turned to Salzer and told him to formulate a program and relevant regulations "within twenty-four hours." Salzer complied and kept "that god-damn rehabilitation center open." He observed though that his main objective in the amnesty program was to get the drug abusers out of his units and send them home. He asserted that he would not permit any sailor detected using heroin to remain in his command. He wanted them "out of our brotherhood" of warriors.[5]

The Navy also had a race problem. In October 1971, Lieutenant Commander William S. Norman, special assistant to the CNO for minority affairs, prepared a report concluding that any Navy commander 'who assumes he has no racial problem is making a mistake."[6] Stanley Arthur recounted that many Black sailors from Detroit who joined his squadron off Vietnam "were hard core antiestablishment" and had a "me-against-the world type mentality." On a later visit to the city, he discovered that one cause was the "us-against-the-blacks" attitude of Detroit cops who had previously served as military policemen.[7] Salzer remembered that "we had a lot of not-very-well-concealed bigots particularly among the Senior Petty Officers—as well as in the Officer Corps." He added that the Navy chain of command had not nourished the concept of equal opportunity, so it had not taken root.[8]

Indeed, at the time many Navy officers considered racial differences in their command a minor problem, if it existed at all. Ironically, African American Samuel Gravely, the commanding officer of guided missile frigate *Jouett* (DLG-29) during 1970 and 1971, later asserted, "I didn't have any racial problems on board my ship."[9] Arthur remembered that "we did not have any real racial incidents that I can recall on *Hancock*." He did, however, relate that working conditions on his ship created great stress. He remembered that his ship was a really "tired old lady" with the crew working in "just horrendous conditions." He had "the crew berthing in the expansion joints, and anytime it rained, which it rained a lot out there, water was just streaming through those expansion joints." The result was that "the kids were living in those berthing areas with water sloshing around [and] it was really, really tough."[10]

Jim Holloway, then vice chief of the Navy, remembered that he received few reports of racial or substance abuse troubles because, as he thought, many commanders believed they could handle the problems before the "CNO got wind of it." Holloway admitted that his administrative responsibilities severely limited his worldview and kept him "cloistered" in his Pentagon office. He complained, "I didn't even go to the football games in Annapolis."[11]

As he had in Vietnam, Bud Zumwalt exploited various media to highlight his social programs and not secondarily his qualities of leadership. One of Holloway's first surprises as VCNO was "how much Bud relied on his chief of information." Holloway considered the chief public affairs officer, Rear Admiral William Thompson, Zumwalt's "image maker." The vice chief related that Zumwalt connected with naval personnel through the medium of "Z-Grams," 120 subject-focused electronic communications to Navy commands worldwide.

The CNO also reached out to naval personnel through "rap sessions," focus groups, all-hands gatherings in the base auditorium, and visual media. Quarterly, Thompson produced a sophisticated half-hour movie entitled *The CNO Report*. The film consisted mainly of clips of Zumwalt visiting the fleet, awarding medals, meeting with Navy families, and digging the first spade of dirt in a new housing project. He also broadcast more intimate scenes of his daily routine, including his exercise workout in gym clothes. The films were done skillfully and professionally. Holloway stressed that Bud Zumwalt could pull it off because "he was photogenic, bright, articulate, and above all, passionate about his role as the personal head of the U.S. Navy." *The CNO Report* was distributed throughout the Navy and shown to all ranks. At the same time that Zumwalt was purging many older admirals from the ranks, he established for the first time in the Navy's history a flag-level public affairs specialist—Rear Admiral Thompson.[12]

Zumwalt also brought on board his staff Peter Hackes, a highly regarded Pentagon reporter for NBC. Hackes, a commander in the Naval Reserve, came away from his first visit to the CNO with stars in his eyes. He told Thompson that the meeting with Zumwalt was great because "that guy is so handsome, so smart, so charismatic, so knowledgeable, so articulate that he will make any PAO look good."[13] Other observers remarked on Zumwalt's "bushy eyebrows and an aquiline nose [that] gave him a dashing appearance." Bud Zumwalt often enhanced his visual presence during visits to the fleet by wearing a flight jacket emblazoned with a large Z on the back. No surprise, "the News media found him fascinating."[14]

One of Zumwalt's first actions as CNO was a communication with the fleet that established study groups to find ways to encourage sailors to stay in the service. He asserted that "no other problem concerns me as deeply as reversing the downward trend of Navy retention rates."[15] In Z-Gram 2 he announced that a small group of Washington-based junior officers and enlisted personnel would study the retention issue and report directly to him with suggested solutions. He specifically wanted the group to investigate quality of life issues and how to restore "the fun and zest of going to sea."[16] Indeed, "fun" and "zest" became common words to describe Zumwalt's hopes for improved quality of service for his sailors. The use of Z-Grams in a direct approach to sailors contrasted with the previous, well-established procedure in which the CNO tasked flag officers and others in the chain of command to address personnel problems.[17]

This new approach, heartily endorsed by Zumwalt's sponsor Laird, was not unlike that launched by 48-year-old Army General Bernard Rogers in 1969 to persuade soldiers to remain in the service. In short order, Rogers significantly improved performance and morale at racially and discipline-troubled Fort Carson, Colorado, home base of the 5th Infantry Division (Mechanized). He described the American service member of the time: "They are interested in 'why' we do certain things in certain ways. Answers based on faith, 'just believe me'; or authority, 'it's so because I say it's so'; or custom, 'we've always done it this way,' were not good enough." Laird was especially impressed with Rogers's establishment of "Enlisted Men's Councils" made up of unit representatives and "Racial Harmony Councils" that enabled Black soldiers to voice their concerns. Rogers ended make-work projects, early-morning reveille, and weekend inspections.

The general also had barracks reconfigured to afford soldiers more privacy, broadened opportunities for recreation, and improved food service in the mess halls. As a result of his efforts, the division increased its reenlistment rate by 45 percent and doubled the junior officer retention rate. AWOLs and disciplinary problems declined dramatically. Laird was overjoyed with the "media blitz" that followed an article in *The New York Times* that portrayed Fort Carson as "the most progressive troop-oriented base in the U.S. military."[18] Rogers's accomplishments did not go unrewarded. The forward-looking general served as Army chief of staff from 1976 to 1979. It was unlikely that Zumwalt remained unaware of Rogers's innovations.

Between late July and early December 1970, the CNO dispatched a veritable flood of sixty-four Z-Grams that focused on retention-related policies such as liberty and leave, civilian clothing on board ships and at shore stations, sea/shore rotation, enlisted selection boards, extended commissary hours, lockers and wash facilities, shore establishment habitability, reenlistment ceremonies, long lines at service facilities, independent study opportunities for officers, and action line telephones to enable sailors to receive answers to their concerns directly from commanders. Admiral James Holloway Jr., an early Zumwalt mentor, reassured the CNO during this period that "you are doing so many things for our Navy . . . that had to be done." The vice chief's father emphasized that those things "would never have been done without your perception, and the power and prestige of the Chief of Naval Operations in directing and underwriting them."[19]

Zumwalt's vice chief later observed that before the Z-Grams, the Navy had increased leave between duty stations and taken other steps to improve the quality of life for sailors. The younger Holloway recognized, however, that Bud Zumwalt's skillful use of information media brought much more positive attention to his personnel reform efforts.[20] Zumwalt realized that some observers viewed the way he mandated these changes as "theatrical" and overly showy, but he did so deliberately. He argued that the Navy had to change fast the widespread opinion among sailors and civilians that the Navy was "a humorless, tradition-bound, starchy institution owned by and operated for the benefit of white males."[21]

Stan Arthur, serving with Attack Squadron 122 on board *Hancock* when the first Z-Grams went out, remembered that at first he couldn't understand their purpose. He asked, "Why are we doing this?" He wondered why it wasn't being done in the traditional way. He reasoned that the chain of command was the usual means for transmitting information from the top. He complained about "this little short Z-gram that... left to all of us to figure out how to interpret it." However, he realized that he had to figure it out because he had 1,000 sailors who would soon want to wear beards, long hair, and civilian clothes to work.[22]

Many commanding officers were irked with the manner in which these messages came to them, so they did not comply with the directives. Master Chief Petty Officer of the Navy Delbert Black related that the Z-Grams were reaching the fleet as message traffic, so the sailor in the communication center would know the content of the Z-Gram before the skipper did. With understatement, Black suggested that "that created a bit of heartburn in the chain of command."[23] Admiral Charles Duncan was less circumspect. He remembered that "a Commanding Officer was really afraid to discipline people, because he knew they could write direct to Washington." He contended that commanding officers "were especially afraid to even say 'Boo' to a black or bring one to mast [non-judicial punishment], even though it was a clear-cut case."[24]

In Z-Gram 52, Zumwalt chastised those commanders who proved resistant to his efforts to improve sailor retention. Indeed, Salzer remembered that "most of the senior officers were fighting the CNO [and] were not carrying out his instructions."[25] Gravely, who served under Zumwalt as head of naval communications in OPNAV, liked and admired his boss, but also thought that the "COs were being trampled on a little bit." He understood that Zumwalt was "instituting some new policies, which a lot of people felt they could drag their feet on." He added that "if you as a four-star can't get three stars to carry out your orders, you're in trouble."[26]

Secretary of the Navy John Warner interacted with many active and retired flag officers concerned over the fast pace and unsettling nature of Bud Zumwalt's personnel actions. Gravely suggested that Warner was no obstructionist with regard to Black advancement, but he was "trying to do it cautiously." As Gravely knew, however, "caution was not the name of the game in those days" with Zumwalt.[27] Indeed, Bud Zumwalt contended that "going fast was essential." The admiral related that Laird and Chafee supported his approach, so "Warner's attempts to slow me down went for naught." Zumwalt understood that Laird and Chafee had selected him to be CNO primarily so he would institute personnel reforms.[28]

Z-Gram 57, "Elimination of Demeaning or Degrading Regulations," which most sailors referred to as "Mickey Mouse" regulations, generated the most heat from senior officers and senior enlisted personnel. The intent of the Z-Gram was to liberalize regulations on sideburns, moustaches, beards, civilian clothing, hairstyles, dungaree uniforms, and similar issues. In the message, Zumwalt took a swipe at Tom Moorer—without naming him—stating that he was issuing the Z-Gram because his predecessor's directives were "insufficiently understood." Zumwalt asserted that he would "not countenance any personnel being in any way penalized during the time they are growing beards, moustaches, or sideburns."[29] He later explained that "at a time when they were risking their lives" in Vietnam, it was asking too much to "fly in the face of their generation's style of life."[30] As always, Chafee supported his favored naval officer's liberalization efforts. The Navy secretary opined that "one's ability to fight isn't affected by the length of his hair."[31]

By spring 1971, the service experience for many officers and enlisted sailors differed sharply from that of previous years. Now, officers and petty officers could keep civilian clothing on board ship. Sailors could wear their dungarees to and from work. Senior enlisted barracks now boasted beer machines and sailors could keep their motorcycles on base. Commissaries stayed open longer so sailors would have more time to shop after duty hours. Regulations limited inspections before and after ship deployments and established more lenient leave policies. Finally, sailors were allowed to grow longer hair and beards.

Zumwalt, buoyed by a December 1970 Navy-wide survey that found 80 percent of those enlisted sailors polled in favor, directed the transition from the traditional "cracker jack" bell-bottoms to a double-breasted uniform similar to that worn by chief petty officers and commissioned officers. Warner thought the new enlisted uniforms "looked like bus driver suits."[32] Tom Moorer later complained that after the uniform change, he couldn't "tell a chief petty officer from a third class petty officer." The uniform change ushered in more than a decade of turmoil in uniform guidance.[33]

Roberta Hazard, who served as a lieutenant commander on Zumwalt's staff for most of his tour, observed that the CNO "had captured the affection of junior officers and junior and mid-grade enlisted personnel, probably as no other CNO at least since Arleigh Burke." She remembered that often when she accompanied the admiral as he exited the Pentagon, groups of enlisted sailors and junior officers were waiting to "thank him for what he was trying to do for them and to relate how much they appreciated it." She added that this was a time when "this man was being beaten about the head and shoulders by a whole host of people," including other naval leaders.[34]

Many of Bud Zumwalt's Z-Grams had a positive impact on the average sailor's quality of life and experience in the service and in many ways changed the Navy's attitude toward the enlisted ranks forever. Nonetheless, the detailed and seemingly endless stream of communications emanating from Washington generated heated opposition from senior officer and senior enlisted personnel. Many of those leaders concluded that Zumwalt was deliberately bypassing them—the chain of command—in order to reach the sailors. Moorer understood that "the chiefs are the backbone [of the Navy] and many chiefs are unhappy over actions that degrade their authority."[35]

TROUBLE IN THE WARDROOMS AND IN THE RANKS

The inclusion of more and more minority sailors brought unsettling change to the Navy's ranks. The Navy focused so strongly on accommodating the new enlistees that discipline suffered, to the chagrin of the service's petty officers—its "lifers." These men were traditionalists. Tom Moorer related that before Zumwalt's CNO tour, American sailors looked sharp. He remembered that "no one was allowed ashore unless every button was in place, their shoes shined, their hair was cut, and they were clean-shaven." Moorer emphasized that the petty officers ensured that the sailors' appearance was correct.[36] In retirement, he stressed that when he was in command of the Atlantic and Pacific fleets he always relied on the chain of command and the chief petty officers to communicate with the sailors. One senior enlisted sailor later observed that the Z-Gram approach "caused a great deal of negative reaction, negative feedback, which caused a very serious breakdown in the chain of command."[37] As a result of all this, retention rates for the highest ratings plummeted. These were the men who because of their years of experience and training were best able to operate the Navy's increasingly advanced weapon systems.

The list of those admirals who railed against Zumwalt's personnel reforms is long. Oral histories with many of those officers reflect widespread dissatisfaction with what they considered Zumwalt's hasty and ill-thought-out social changes.[38] Zumwalt and his supporters routinely likened those flag officers who opposed his personnel and social reforms as tired, old-guard retired white men set in their ways and resisting innovation and enlightenment—just so many "ancient sons of Neptune."[39] Thompson, Zumwalt's chief of information, considered the opposition of the Navy's retired officers to the CNO's policies as simple jealousy. He opined that "along comes a young whippersnapper who in a short time had become the most popular flag officer in the public eye since Admiral Nimitz of World War II." Thompson observed that *"Time* magazine had Bud Zumwalt on its cover hailing him as the most innovative leader in [the] Navy's history, a breath of fresh air, eons ahead of the 'stodgy old Navy.'" The exciting admiral had become "the darling of the media."[40]

Many of the flag officers who opposed Zumwalt's progressive actions were perhaps less photogenic and charismatic than he, but they had achieved their high rank based on courage, steadfastness, and skill in battle and inspired leadership of the Navy throughout the Cold War and the Vietnam War. In a common complaint, James D. "Jig Dog" Ramage, a combat-tested naval aviator, contended that the Z-Grams "generated an air of permissiveness, led to the deterioration of smartness, and the denigration of the CNO's authority."[41] Tom Moorer suggested what image a US Navy sailor should project: "There is nothing as smart looking as a muscular young American in a sailor's uniform, clean and pressed." When Moorer visited MACV headquarters in 1972, he found that "the Navy was by far the worst looking group there," with one sailor "walking around with no laces in his shoes and his hair down over his back."

The JCS chairman received letters from all over the world deploring the appearance of Zumwalt's sailors. He later lamented that the

Navy had "gone to the dogs."[42] Admiral Anderson, the US ambassador to Portugal after his term as CNO, told journalist Hanson Baldwin that he was "shocked" at the appearance of American sailors in the Mediterranean.[43] Gerald Miller, then the Sixth Fleet commander, related that the Greek authorities complained to him about the unkempt look of his men, "particularly the blacks."[44] Bud Zumwalt remembered that all of his CNO predecessors called on him "to remonstrate with me on the beards."[45]

Salzer empathized with those in the chain of command who wondered, how can I "tell how long a man's hair should be" and "can I tell them to put in their shirttails? Is it inappropriate for them to wear sandals [on] the quarterdeck?" The result was that, while the leaders equivocated, the ships were falling apart, and the sailors were looking "like a bunch of disreputable tramps." Salzer noted that Bud Zumwalt contributed to this problem by letting his own hair grow too long.[46] Miller asserted that Zumwalt wrecked the chain of command. He considered Zumwalt "a great builder and a great destroyer," but in essence "a tragedy—for him and the Navy."[47] Some of Zumwalt's critics compared his personnel reform efforts to the cartoon of an officer hurrying after his men saying, 'Wait for me, I'm your leader.'"[48] Tom Hayward, the CNO from 1978 to 1982, contended that "the Z-grams were always a big problem with me and with most of us," so when he became CNO, he "reversed a lot of them."[49]

Zumwalt is justly renowned for his pioneering efforts to change the Navy's relationship with its serving and future African American sailors. Howard Kerr observed that Zumwalt led the Navy "out of the dark ages of racial injustice . . . to a higher form of interpersonal relations, to greater sensitivity."[50] From the earliest days of his service in the Navy, Zumwalt had sympathized with the plight of Black sailors and their struggle for respect and fair treatment. During his posting to the Bureau of Naval Personnel, he found that a "relatively racist system . . . was in vogue." He remembered that the bureau routinely detailed Black officers to low-priority recruiting jobs or to broken-down supply ships and tankers. It was expected that most Black officers would become frustrated and leave the service.[51]

One officer who had a significant influence on Bud Zumwalt's growing awareness of the Navy's racial problem was Lieutenant Commander William "Bill" Norman, an African American officer. He had served for six years as a minority affairs advocate on one human relations council after another. When he spoke with Zumwalt in November 1970, Norman was close to resigning his commission since he did not want to deal with "the unceasing strain of the conflict between being black and being Navy."[52] Norman agreed to stay on once Zumwalt pledged to make the racial issue one of his top priorities. In weekly meetings thereafter, Norman presented Zumwalt with detailed lists of measures that promised to alleviate some of the problems. The two officers also developed a close working relationship, and "from those experiences Zumwalt began to develop a true personal consciousness of the issue."[53]

Zumwalt, however, focused on quality of service and personnel retention issues during his first five months of the job—not racial equity. His assertion in *On Watch* that one of his immediate objectives was to "throw overboard once and for all the Navy's silent but real and persistent discrimination against minorities—not only black, the chief victims, but Puerto Ricans, American Indians, Chicanos, Filipinos, orientals, and, indeed, women as well" is patently overblown. In the same work he admitted that when he became CNO, he saw the racial issue through a managerial rather than a humanitarian lens. He was then focused on recruiting and retaining sailors of whatever personal characteristics.[54] Indeed, even after Zumwalt took command, defense secretary Laird had to "lean on the Navy . . . the service with the fewest number of blacks eligible for flag rank," to promote one. Hence, in June 1971 Zumwalt endorsed rather than championed the promotion of Captain Gravely to rear admiral. The officer was already the first African American to command a US warship.[55]

Bud Zumwalt did not specifically address discrimination against the Navy's "minorities" until mid-December 1970 with the issuance of Z-Gram 66. Holloway observed that before he became CNO, Zumwalt "was not a crusader in the area of race relations or minority affairs."[56] Indeed, in Z-Gram 66 Zumwalt suggested that before its issuance, he was convinced that "we had relatively few racial problems in the Navy" but added that "I was wrong." He came to understand "the depth of feeling of our black personnel that there is significant discrimination in the Navy."[57] Admiral Draper Kauffman confided to Zumwalt that during his career he too "hardly ever thought" of race relations. He added, however, that the young Blacks of the 1970s thought about it all the time because it affected "his life, his family, his self-respect, his dignity."[58] Kerr was another one of the self-described "dumb bastards who

Zumwalt discusses racial issues with a group of mostly African American sailors. One of the admiral's greatest successes was to improve the Navy's treatment of its minority sailors. NHHC USN 114844.

didn't think he had a racial problem" on his ship but, "Sure enough, I did."[59] Salzer too "had no idea as to the depth of feeling [of] inequality of opportunity . . . perceived by the blacks." Holloway remembered that "Zumwalt was so overwhelmed by the reports of discrimination, harassment, and downright brutality [that he learned about from various sources] that as he told me later, it left an indelible scar on his consciousness."[60]

Z-Gram 66 mandated that by 15 January 1971—that is, one month after issuance of the directive—the commander of every ship, naval base, shore station, and aircraft squadron "shall appoint an aware minority group officer or senior petty officer as his special assistant for minority affairs." The message also tasked relevant commands to stock ship stores, Navy exchanges, and commissaries with food, grooming, and other products sought by Black sailors; increase the number of Black barbers and beauticians; and stock wardrooms, libraries, and other reading areas with materials focused on the Black experience.

In Z-Gram 66, Zumwalt identified Lieutenant Commander Norman as his special assistant for minority affairs. Soon afterward, the

CNO established the CNO Advisory Committee on Race Relations and Minority Affairs that included Rear Admiral David Bagley from the Navy's personnel command and Rear Admiral William A. Greene, the Navy's head recruiter. In March 1971, with Zumwalt's blessing the committee issued a report that affirmed that a vital Navy objective would be to "increase and intensify the Navy's efforts to attain and retain the highest quality officer and enlisted volunteers from the minority community." Hence, "affirmative action" had become a top Navy goal. The committee's report was a building block for the Navy's 1973 Human Goals Program, which comprehensively addressed the Navy's equal opportunity, human resource management, and drug and alcohol abuse policies.[61]

Following on Army General Rogers's "racial harmony councils" and Captain Kauffman's "gripe sessions" at Great Lakes, Zumwalt encouraged commanders to allow "rap sessions" and systematic racial awareness training where Black and white sailors discussed their grievances. The CNO set in motion a host of other actions to increase the percentage of Black officers and enlisted personnel in the Navy, including enhanced recruiting and educational, training, and public relations programs. Under his leadership, the Navy also took steps to spread knowledge about the historical accomplishments of African Americans, such as the naming of destroyer escorts *Doris Miller* (DE-1091) and *Jesse Brown* (DE-1089) after heroic Black naval personnel.

Critics, however, charged that Zumwalt and Norman pushed a multitude of programs on the Navy instead of focusing on a few critical areas such as officer recruitment. Indeed, the Navy's effort to commission Black officers fell flat. During the period from July 1971 to January 1972, for instance, in contrast to more than 16,000 white Americans, the Navy commissioned only eighty-four African Americans. The situation for enlisted sailors was brighter. During the last six months of 1971, the percentage of Black men and women enlisted in the Navy (12 percent) approximated the number of African Americans in the US population. On the negative side, during 1971 and 1972, 50 percent of the African American recruits brought into the service were from test category IV, the lowest test category. Many of the new sailors were high school dropouts and lacked the skills needed in the technology-intensive Navy.[62]

Many of the Navy's bases around the world and ships in the fleet experienced racial tension and hostility by sailors, Black and white. A 1971 report by the Naval Investigative Service on the situation at the large Subic Bay naval base in the Philippines characterized many of the new Black enlistees as "militant and uncompromising" and many of the white sailors as racists. Both groups segregated themselves at clubs and other gathering places. Moreover, both Blacks and whites were stressed by the need to carry out their duties with fewer shipmates. In early 1971, Navy recruiters met their quotas by 102 percent, but by that December the number had fallen to 50 percent, "the worst percentage of all four services."[63]

In spring 1972, the Vietnam War once again shot holes in Zumwalt's plans for the Navy's future. In response to the enemy's massive Easter Offensive against South Vietnam, Nixon directed fleet units based in the Atlantic and the eastern Pacific to converge on the Gulf of Tonkin. The president then ordered a renewed air campaign against North Vietnam. Since many Air Force planes had been withdrawn from South Vietnam and Thailand after 1969, the Navy's role in the early stages of Linebacker was even more critical than before. One out of every four ships in the Navy, including one-fourth to one-half of the carriers, cruisers, destroyers, logistic ships, and aircraft squadrons soon operated off Vietnam.

The heavy demands of combat lengthened overseas tours and subjected sailors to long, hot, exhausting days and nights at work on crowded vessels in dire need of repair. Sixteen- to eighteen-hour workdays on line off Vietnam were not uncommon. Overseas deployments went from six to nine months, with abbreviated times ashore between deployments. Many of the men had been continuously at sea for up to four years. And approximately 77 percent of the men in the Seventh Fleet off Vietnam were on their first enlistment.[64]

Hardly surprising, the Navy's racial problem came to a boil in connection with the war. As John Lehman has observed, "The racial tensions in American society, when placed in the crucible of a naval ship at war, created a special devil's brew." He remembered serving on active duty for training on board carrier *Saratoga* on Yankee Station in 1972. He related that no white officer could walk near the enlisted men's mess. That location on the ship often witnessed racially inspired muggings and beatings involving both Blacks and whites. His ship was "totally polarized."[65]

Sailors of two ships operating off Vietnam and another due for a combat deployment to the Western Pacific vented their pent-up frustrations. By October 1972, carrier *Kitty Hawk* and her crew had spent 164 days arming, repairing, and launching combat aircraft for bombing missions, and those aircraft had set a record of the most sorties flown on a single deployment during the war. Race-related fighting ashore in Subic Bay during a liberty period, fueled by drug and alcohol use on board, finally sparked a riot. Clearly, fatigue and stress also played a part in the outbreak of violence that occurred on 7 October, as did African Americans' perceptions that they were assigned the most menial jobs on board. Before the ship's officers and senior enlisted men brought the fighting under control, white and Black sailors had exchanged punches, heaped verbal abuse on one another, and defied orders by their superiors, the great majority of whom were white. That same month, Black and white sailors fought and injured one another in oiler *Hassayampa* (AO-145), then tied up to the pier at Subic Bay. The crewmen were exhausted, and they grew restive when they learned that their ten-month-long cruise had been extended indefinitely. The outbreak of violence on board the oiler showed that personnel unrest might not be unique to one type of ship and indeed might be fleetwide.[66]

In November, 144 *Constellation* sailors, mostly Black but a few white and Hispanic men, staged sit-downs, refused to obey superiors, and proclaimed their defiance to the national and international news media in San Diego. The causes of the disturbance on board the carrier preparing for a Vietnam deployment were many and included opposition to the war and *Constellation*'s role in it; the heated racial atmosphere on board; and dissatisfaction with the quality of life for sailors.[67] The carrier's commanding officer, his staff, and spokesmen for the militants failed to reach agreement on how to resolve their differences. Secretary of the Navy Warner and Zumwalt also made speedy resolution of the disturbance difficult by attempting to manage the crisis from Washington.

To make matters worse, there was bad blood between the Navy secretary and the CNO. Warner was sympathetic with those in the Navy who thought Bud Zumwalt was going way too far with his revolutionary personnel programs. According to Zumwalt, Warner ordered an end to the Z-Grams, but the CNO promised to resign if he had to follow through on that order. The Navy secretary and later long-term senator from Virginia did not press the issue. As was often the case with those who opposed or displeased Zumwalt, he resorted to character assassination and innuendo, describing Warner as a "dilettante [who] conducted his professional career somewhat along the lines of his marital career, that is, totally without integrity. He had the backbone of a jellyfish and great vanity which was stroked by those who thought to use him."[68]

The CNO's objective in the *Constellation* matter was to end the affair before the November presidential election and thus take away ammunition from the "ideologues and rabble-rousers on both sides of the racial issue." Ultimately, the Navy removed 120 sailors from the crew, transferred seventy-four of the men to new assignments, and discharged from the service forty-six others (ten dishonorably). In January 1973, *Constellation* finally reached Yankee Station off North Vietnam—but the war was almost over. Lehman later bemoaned that during the period, "the navy suffered its first real mutinies since the nineteenth century."[69]

THE HICKS HEARINGS

By fall 1972, Zumwalt realized that he had a public relations disaster on his hands and feared that the disturbances on *Constellation* and *Kitty Hawk* would endanger his equality and personnel programs. As a result, on 10 November Zumwalt gathered Washington-based flag officers for a speech on his policies. He expected his words to be passed on to other commanders Navy-wide, telling his chief of information that "it was probably the most important speech of his life."[70] Zumwalt focused on the issue of racial discrimination in the Navy, which he stressed "must be faced openly and fully." He added, in the way of clarification, that "these current racial incidents are not the results of lowered standards but are clearly due to failure of commands to implement those programs with a whole heart" and a failure of "leadership." The CNO demanded that his subordinates implement his equal opportunity programs comprehensively and without delay. To ensure that his directives were carried out, Zumwalt indicated that he intended to "use the Inspector General of the Navy as an 'on-the-scene' examiner of these problems on a continuing basis."[71] Although Zumwalt later disagreed, it is clear from various sources that many senior officers saw the speech as a dressing-down. Indeed, Gravely sat in the meeting and wondered "what the hell I did to rate this kind of whipping?"[72]

The legendary Admiral Arleigh Burke, while impressed by the intellectual brilliance of the younger leader, characterized Bud Zumwalt as one who became "impatient with other people who were not so brilliant." Burke believed that Zumwalt got "his personal ambitions confused with his obligations to the service."[73] Other retired flag officers went further. According to Zumwalt, retired Admiral George Anderson, the CNO who had run afoul of McNamara and Zumwalt's idol Nitze during the Cuban Missile Crisis, became the "ringleader" of those who vehemently opposed the CNO's progressive policies and constituted a "right wing racist reaction."[74] As a member of the president's Foreign Intelligence Advisory Board, Anderson had direct access to the White House and Nixon's ear. As he sometimes did with opponents, Zumwalt attacked the moral character of the decorated World War II combat veteran and Navy leader during the early years of the Vietnam War. He described Anderson as "by nature shallow, vain, [and] egotistical." He added that the former CNO was "a back-biter, and quite two-faced."[75]

President Nixon, who had served as a naval officer during World War II, exploded in fury when he watched media coverage of the *Constellation* disturbance. H. R. Haldeman recorded in his diary that Nixon was especially upset that rather than disciplining the protesting sailors, Zumwalt "gave them active shore stations with Coca-Colas and ice cream." The president railed against what he described as "a service without discipline." It did not help Zumwalt's case that, in Nixon's eyes, the admiral was a "McNamara man."[76]

At Nixon's direction, Kissinger had phoned Zumwalt during the disturbance and threatened to fire him unless the CNO dismissed the protestors from the Navy with dishonorable discharges. According to Hazard, who monitored the phone call in Zumwalt's office, Kissinger "sounded like he was outside his own skin, he was so angry over this thing."[77] While such an action could not occur without a court-martial proceeding, it revealed Nixon's and Kissinger's strong distaste for Zumwalt's reformist approach. As many times in his career, Zumwalt's political connections once again proved invaluable. Laird, who had strong support in Congress and whom Nixon had previously assured would have the last word on defense department appointments, ignored Kissinger's demand to fire the CNO and later assured Zumwalt that "you have my full confidence and backing."[78]

There was so much dissatisfaction with Bud Zumwalt among the flag officer community that former CNOs had delegated Anderson to tell the president that "we've got to get rid of Zumwalt [because] he's just tearing the Navy apart." Jim Holloway speculated that had Nixon's attention not been diverted by Watergate, he would have fired Zumwalt.[79] Hazard remembered that after the shipboard disturbances and the strained relations with the administration and Congress, Zumwalt was "besieged and beset." He was "exhausted and was as focused or over focused as I saw him in all my time with him."[80]

The *Constellation* and *Kitty Hawk* disturbances and the CNO's speech brought to a head the growing dissatisfaction with Zumwalt's leadership. In Zumwalt's memoirs and in histories written by others covering the tumultuous CNO years, the events of November 1972 are often described as the result of the Navy's "institutional racism." He dismissed or downplayed the issue of "permissiveness," a weakening of discipline in the service, as "an obvious buzz word" for racial integration.[81] There is no question that the Navy had a major and longstanding problem with discrimination against Blacks and other minority sailors, and it certainly was a contributing factor in the shipboard disturbances.

But by November 1972, Zumwalt's dictates with regard to "Mickey Mouse" regulations; leave and liberty, uniform and civilian clothing, and grooming policies; and issue groups composed of junior officers and sailors had irked many commanders and senior enlisted sailors, prompting many of the latter to leave the Navy prematurely. Moreover, Zumwalt's championship of the High-Low Mix, which entailed a diminished reliance on nuclear-powered ships, his assignment of surface warfare officers instead of aviators or submariners to key commands, and his reliance on a limited number of favored subordinates for major decision-making had earned him few friends among the admirals and key members of Congress. Indeed, Salzer concluded that Zumwalt hurt himself by getting "talked into too many abrasive little things by his damned 'kitchen cabinet' of very bright, young, eager beavers who had little experience at sea but great experience at buttering up the boss."[82] Gravely imagined Bud Zumwalt sitting "in a little corner someplace with some junior advisors, who gave him advice contrary to the way these old sea lords had been doing things for years" and then just sending out an implementing message.[83]

Hazard described the group, which she called the "mini-staff." It was made up of twenty to twenty-five officers, "hand-picked by the Admiral to move ideas and initiatives along through the often dilatory bureaucratic maze." She explained that "we were a tight group of totally dedicated, loyal, and proactive team members who were supportive of what the Admiral was trying to accomplish." But even Hazard, who idolized the admiral, recognized that the mini-staff approach had problems. She related, "If I found a trait, some would say weakness, in senior leaders, with whom I worked including Admiral Zumwalt, it was their need for a group of extremely loyal staffers on whom they could depend." She suggested that there were probably loyalists whom "he could have cut off at the knees much earlier and to the advantage of his mission accomplishment." She also admitted that Zumwalt failed to enlist more senior and middle-grade officers to his cause. Instead, Duncan, Zumwalt's personnel chief, remembered that the senior admirals were screened out. Harry Train suggested that Bud Zumwalt "could build a palace guard, but he couldn't build a constituency."[84]

On 13 November 1972, Louisiana's F. Edward Hébert, chairman of the House Armed Services Committee (HASC), announced that a special subcommittee would look into Zumwalt's personnel reforms and their relationship to the *Constellation* and *Kitty Hawk* incidents. Hébert had supported Senator Strom Thurmond's States Rights Party in 1948, opposed the Civil Rights Act of 1964, and in general disdained the civil rights movement. At the same time, he was an ardent champion in Congress of the US Navy and was concerned about the current state of the service.[85] Hébert was especially upset at Zumwalt's speech upbraiding the Navy's flag officers for their lack of attention to the race issue. Moreover, he related to Zumwalt that Congressman Carl Vinson of Georgia, a renowned Navy supporter, called him and said "get rid of Zumwalt."[86] Admiral Ramage remembered that during his visit to Hébert's New Orleans office, the congressman complained that the CNO was doing the Navy a lot of harm.[87] To Zumwalt, Hébert was not so much concerned about discipline in the fleet as he was with Blacks in the Navy.[88] Nonetheless, much about Hébert's true leanings is based only on Zumwalt's recollections, decidedly self-serving, of his personal visits and private telephone conversations with the congressman.

Hébert's 450-page autobiography *"Last of the Titans"* devotes an entire chapter to the My Lai massacre but not a word about the subcommittee hearings conducted by his subordinate, Congressman Floyd Hicks, a Democrat from Washington state.[89] Zumwalt considered Hicks his "only potential friend" on the subcommittee.[90] Hicks did in fact approach the hearings in a nonpartisan manner and not as Hébert's cat's-paw. Another of the three members of the subcommittee was Wilbur C. Daniel, a Democrat from Virginia who had chaired another subcommittee on Navy recruiting and retention. Zumwalt granted that Daniel was "genuinely concerned about the welfare of the Navy's people" but whom the admiral thought had a hidden agenda. The admiral suspected that Daniel feared enlisting too many Blacks into the Navy. The third member of the subcommittee was Alexander Pirnie, a Republican from New York. Zumwalt considered him a "straight law and order man" whose main goal was to ensure that the *Constellation* protesters were punished for their acts of disobedience. A decade later, however, Zumwalt denigrated the contribution of these members, suggesting that "the politicians on the subcommittee, torn between racist and liberal pressures, cooked up a compromise report."[91]

On 20 November, Zumwalt appeared before the Hicks subcommittee and observed that despite the hardships imposed by the war, the officers and enlisted personnel in the fleet were carrying out their duties with exemplary professionalism. He pointed out that by 1972 the enlistment rate had more than doubled since he became CNO. The CNO admitted, however, that the need to take in a significant number of mostly Black sailors from the lowest test categories contributed to the shipboard personnel problems. In his testimony, former CINCPAC Oley Sharp praised Zumwalt's equal opportunity programs. Admiral Bernard Clarey, then Commander in Chief, Pacific Fleet, addressed the issue of discipline in the ranks. He testified that he "saw no evidence of a breakdown in good order and discipline." But he exaggerated the point with the observation that "the overall level of discipline in the fleet is as high as at any point in history."[92] When, however, Congressman Hicks asked him if the actions taken by some of the *Constellation*'s crew constituted "mutiny," the admiral answered, "Yes, sir, certainly that was collective insubordination in my view."[93]

In his testimony, Zumwalt blamed the Vietnam War and extended deployments for the problems in the Navy. He observed that the racial and disciplinary disturbances occurred only in the Pacific Fleet. Racial troubles, however, were even then occurring in the Sixth Fleet in the Mediterranean and would occur worldwide ashore and afloat in 1973 and 1974. Captain J. D. Ward, the skipper of *Constellation*, and Commander John Schaub, the ship's executive officer, did not buttress Zumwalt's contention that the Navy's "institutional racism" drove sailors to riot and disobey orders. Ward observed that most of the trouble was caused by "a group of young men who you might describe as militants or agitators." Schaub suggested that one could assume that some crewmen had "criminal intent." On the other hand, Commander Benjamin W. Cloud, a combat veteran, African American, and executive officer of *Kitty Hawk*, testified that there was a perception among

Black people that the Navy was the most biased, segregated branch of the military.[94] Zumwalt's sympathetic biographer suggested that the witnesses who appeared before the subcommittee, many combat veterans and accomplished naval leaders, were led like sheep by their interrogators: "Witness after witness, through a tangle of badgering and leading questions, was directed toward the committee's conclusions.[95]

Roger Kelley, the assistant secretary of defense for manpower and reserve affairs and an authority on race relations, concluded that racism was a serious problem in the Navy, but so too was the general breakdown in shipboard order. His testimony followed an official October 1972 tour of military facilities and ships worldwide, including aircraft carrier *Forrestal* in the Mediterranean. Kelley "identified the senior noncommissioned officer as a sort of forgotten man [who] perceived that he had lost control over his own units of people." Kelley added that some of the junior officers he observed seemed "untrained and undisciplined." He concluded his testimony by observing, "If I have failed to convey strongly here the point that race relations is only one of several reflections of breakdown in discipline and authority [in the Navy], then I have been a poor communicator."[96]

The subcommittee's final report, which the Navy did not disseminate, dismissed Bud Zumwalt's argument that "institutional racism" fueled much of the discontent in the naval service. The subcommittee found, with regard to *Kitty Hawk* and by implication *Constellation*, that "not only was there not one case wherein racial discrimination could be pinpointed, but there is no evidence which indicated that the blacks who participated in that incident perceived racial discrimination . . . of such a nature as to justify belief that violent reaction was required."[97] The subcommittee registered strong objection not only to Zumwalt's negotiation with the *Constellation*'s dissidents but also to his attempt to appease them by "meting out minor non-judicial punishment for what was a major affront to good order and discipline."[98]

Moreover, the subcommittee report criticized leaders at the lower level—junior officers and senior enlisted personnel—for not enforcing discipline in the ranks, especially with dissident crewman. The report cited the poor personal grooming of the crew, the poor standards of cleanliness on at least one of the ships, the failure to take corrective action when corrective action was warranted, and the failure to demand an immediate response to lawful orders.[99]

Whether or not the Hicks subcommittee sought to torpedo Zumwalt's equal opportunity programs, as the admiral averred, the final report did not bring that result about. The disturbances in the fleet and the Hicks subcommittee hearings did highlight to the nation that the Navy had a serious racial problem that demanded correction. For the remainder of Zumwalt's tour as CNO, hundreds of racial incidents occurred on board naval vessels and at naval bases around the world. The same month as the Hicks hearing, white and Black sailors and Marines battled on board amphibious transport dock *Trenton* (LPD-14) at Brindisi, Italy. The episode revealed that the mostly white officers and senior petty officers in the crew had great difficulty understanding and dealing with the grievances of Black sailors. Jerry Miller, the Sixth Fleet commander, observed that as protests against leadership developed, "race became the focal point." But he added that the "problem is bigger than the *Trenton* incident and involves complex sociological aspects."[100] Similar violent episodes occurred in the 1972–1974 period on board aircraft carriers *Ticonderoga* (CVS-14), *Intrepid* (CVS-11), and *John F. Kennedy* (CVA-67) and amphibious assault ship *Inchon* (LPH-12). While a few of the Black dissidents in these encounters resorted to violence for violence's sake, many others were outraged over discrimination against them in terms of promotions, job assignments, and disciplinary actions and the scarcity of Black officers and senior enlisted personnel. Whites routinely reacted in kind to Black demonstrations and physical attacks.[101] Nonetheless, racial trouble was only one of a number of serious problems affecting the Navy during the Vietnam years.

LUKEWARM SUPPORT FOR NAVY WOMEN

In his memoirs, Bud Zumwalt suggested that he fought discrimination against Navy women almost from day one as CNO, but the record does not support that contention. Indeed, he later admitted that because of the Navy's pressing needs at the end of the Vietnam War, redressing the inequities suffered by women in the Navy "could not be the highest immediate priority."[102] During his service as COMNAVFORV and in his first year as CNO, he was certainly aware of the Navy's policy that only two non-nurse Navy women could serve in Vietnam at one time, but he took no action to redress what some Navy women clearly considered discriminatory. In contrast, 7,500 Army, Air Force, and Marine Corps women and 425 female Navy nurses served in-country or just offshore on hospital ships during the war. The women from the other services carried out headquarters, communications, logistical, and other functions and shared the danger with men from enemy rocket, mortar, and sabotage attacks, and some made the ultimate sacrifice.[103]

Captain Rita Lenihan, the Assistant to the Chief of Naval Personnel for Women (ACNP (W)) was a traditionalist with regard to female roles in the military. Commissioned in World War II, she considered it inappropriate and improper for women to serve in proximity to men in a combat environment. Captain Robin Quigley, who succeeded Lenihan in January 1971, espoused a similar conservative social philosophy. Both leaders enforced the near-total ban on Navy women serving in the combat zone. Lieutenant Elizabeth G. Wylie represented many more Navy women who fervently desired to serve their country in Vietnam, gain operational experience, and enhance their qualifications for promotion. Only after persistent entreaties to BUPERS, no doubt aided by the fact that her father was an admiral, a respected naval strategist, and a vocal Zumwalt critic, did she succeed in her quest. She and eight other non-nurse officers ultimately deployed to South Vietnam, but the Navy gave no enlisted female sailors that opportunity. CNO Zumwalt, who certainly had the authority to act and who proclaimed himself a champion of women's equality, never reversed the policy insisted on by Lenihan and Quigley.[104]

Bud Zumwalt's views on the role of women in the military did not differ significantly from those held by Lenihan and Quigley and many other senior Navy leaders. Tom Moorer's views were not atypical. When interviewed in retirement about "the new adjunct to the Navy— the ladies," he responded that when "I see movies of them climbing in and out of trucks and airplanes . . . I'm opposed to the whole idea." He added, "I think the girls in uniform do some very fine work at many activities ashore, but I don't buy for one second the idea that they can enter into combat." He felt that "it just goes against the grain across the board" because "in wartime in real fighting, the kind that I've seen, I think they would be a burden." Sensing the admiral's discomfort that the issue had even been raised, the interviewer apologized that he "just threw it in—a bit of whimsy, actually."[105]

With his superior political instincts, Bud Zumwalt eventually realized that societal changes would demand better treatment for women in the naval service. He was keenly aware of the strength of the American feminist movement in the early 1970s, whose adherents called for greater equity and nondiscrimination in the Navy and the other armed services. Even though it was never ratified by the states, the Equal Rights Amendment to the Constitution reflected strong support among the electorate for a change to the status of women. Another prod to action was the Equal Employment Opportunity Act of 1972.[106]

Zumwalt also came to understand that following the abolition of the draft in 1973 American women could fill many billets in the forthcoming all-volunteer force. As Stan Arthur, who served a tour in the Bureau of Naval Personnel during the mid-1970s, has observed, "The needs of the service were starting to dictate, because of demographics, that if we were going to have a viable force, and we could only use the males in combat, then there were lots of roles for the females."[107] Hazard contended that Zumwalt was getting the Navy ready for the coming of the all-volunteer force. He recognized that the service's attitudes, traditions, and policies had to change to attract volunteers at a time when the Navy "was still wallowing in post–Vietnam trauma and related anti-military [and] civilian media criticisms."[108] Congress had already taken steps to improve opportunities for women in the services. Public Law 90-130, passed in 1967, ended the cap on the number of women in the military branches and enabled women officers to compete with their male peers for promotion to captain (O-6). Previously, only the woman filling the (ACNP (W)) billet was entitled to hold the rank of captain.[109]

But many Americans, male and female, opposed changing the status of women in the Navy. Bud Zumwalt made light of those antagonists, characterizing them as "folk who feared unisex showers and floating orgies." He also castigated high military and civilian officials from whom "it was maddeningly difficult to elicit more than locker-room jocularity." In that group he included Nixon, who according to the admiral once told him, "I guess I can put up with this race thing, but don't push too hard for women."[110]

Nonetheless, the CNO and the secretary of the Navy did not move out smartly on the issue of women in the service. The first retention study group did not meet until March 1971. Moreover, the CNO did not communicate Z-Gram 116, on the "Rights and Opportunities for Women," until August 1972, more than two years into his tour.[111] A further complication was that John Warner was not as keen as his predecessor Chafee with regard to women in the service. The secretary of defense had to repeatedly prompt Warner to include women on promotion lists for flag rank.[112]

The other services had already taken the first steps toward promoting women to flag/general rank. The Army and the Air Force promoted four female officers to brigadier general in 1970 and 1971. Not until June 1972 did the Navy follow suit. The defense secretary had to "force the Navy's hand" to get a female flag officer, even though Warner later claimed that "he made that decision."[113] In any case, on 1 June, the Navy "shook off the barnacles" and promoted Captain Alene B. Duerk, head of the Navy Nurse Corps, to rear admiral. The Navy did not oppose raising nurses to flag rank, but it was another matter to consider a woman in charge of an operational command. In his memoir, Zumwalt could only observe that "a woman finally made admiral during my watch."[114]

In January 1971, Zumwalt brought Lieutenant Commander Hazard into his immediate staff. She was a graduate of Boston College (magna cum laude) and the Navy's Officer Candidate School and a rising star among Navy women. She worked for Zumwalt as a protocol officer and in other capacities until the admiral's retirement in July 1974. While her duties did not entail it, she related that "the admiral used me as a sounding board" with regard to women in the service. She revered her boss because "he had a vision, and he was a wonderfully clear articulator of that vision." One of the things that impressed her about him was his "deep and abiding belief in the average American" learning and doing the job with dedication. She related that she had never known a man with a more "visceral commitment to equality and decency and hope for the future." She added that his was "the best mind I ever worked with in my 32 years of military service."[115]

When Captain Quigley took the helm as ACNP (W), the young, energetic, and forthright leader conceived a new approach to the connection of women to the Navy. When Zumwalt invited Quigley to join him and Hazard for lunch, the captain immediately broached the subject. According to Hazard, Quigley stated forcefully that Navy women were already "convinced that they should not be a separate entity" and that "they *are* [original italics] equal." Hence, Quigley recommended abolition of the widely popular acronym WAVES (Women Accepted for Volunteer Emergency Service—the women's branch of the United States Naval Reserve), since, she said, that title had had no official standing since 1948. In reaction to that bold assertion, Hazard "nearly fell off my chair" and she remembered the meeting as "one of the most vexing occasions that I had yet encountered in my Navy career." As was true for many Navy women, even the young, intelligent, and progressive junior officer was not yet prepared for such changes. Hazard had had enough exposure to officers and enlisted women "not to delude myself that there was equality or even remotely felt or perceived equality between men and women." In short, she was "horrified" with the direction the talk between Zumwalt and Quigley had taken.[116]

Zumwalt, however, was persuaded by the advice of his senior Navy woman. Quigley fueled her argument with information on the low morale in the ranks and abysmal retention rates for women. After a tour of bases worldwide, Quigley had discovered that over the previous ten years, between 88 and 96 percent of Navy women had failed to complete their first enlistment. She called for action to reverse that trend. Retention rates were certainly high on Zumwalt's list of concerns. As a result, and with her approval, he disestablished the billet of ACNP (W)—Quigley's own position. He also abolished each Navy command's special advisor for women's concerns. Quigley persuaded the CNO that commanding officers should rightly handle all such issues. There would no longer be a WAVES detailer in the Navy's personnel command for enlisted women or officers and no separate women's policy developer.[117]

Quigley's vision and zeal to institute these changes seemed in line with Zumwalt's reformist approach. One would have thought Zumwalt and Quigley "were in full harmony [but] in fact, they were not."[118] Quigley remained a staunch conservative with regard to the role of women in the service. She objected when Zumwalt set up the retention study group on women's issues whose recommendations she was not allowed to influence. When the CNO set up a committee to draft what became Z-Gram 116, he nominated her to chair it. But she knew that he wanted the committee to recommend sending women to sea, an action she strongly opposed. She also did not favor women taking flight training or attending the US Naval Academy. As a result, Quigley refused to attend the committee's meetings and sent a deputy in her stead. She was now on the outs with the Zumwalt team.

In *On Watch*, Bud Zumwalt suggested that Quigley was fired because she lost favor with Secretary of Defense Laird over the elimination of the ACNP (W) billet. Quigley later declared, however, that "that is an unbelievably preposterous misrepresentation of the facts." She asserted that Laird didn't have "the foggiest thing to do with anything [regarding Navy women] until 1972, after I had told the Chief of Naval Operations I could not and would not endorse his program."[119]

Zumwalt lost confidence in her because he finally realized that aside from a few actions, she was not prepared to endorse his increasingly radical and wide-ranging measures. According to Quigley, the CNO was displeased with her philosophy; she alluded to the "hypocrisy of Admiral Zumwalt's purported interest in women." It was clear to Quigley that she was persona non grata with the CNO and that "they had to find out what to do with the squirrely lady." She understood that "her next assignment needed to be something with a certain degree of high visibility, so that it would not look as though I had been fired or quit."[120] Recognizing that her ability to work in Washington would be limited, Quigley agreed to accept command of the naval schools in San Diego, and despite her differences with the CNO, thus became the first woman to lead a major Navy command.

Facing opposition from Quigley, Zumwalt turned to a few other female officers and Rear Admiral Rauch, his Senior Naval Advisor in Vietnam and then head of the Bureau of Naval Personnel's human resources management efforts, to develop what became Z-Gram 116. Commander Fran McKee, later the first female line admiral, Commander Barbara Nyce, and Lieutenant Commander Hazard formed the core group. Hazard considered the most important part of Z-Gram 116 to be the philosophical statement of equality of women within the Navy and the commitment to equal opportunity for women.[121] Specifically, the purpose of Z-Gram 116, a reflection of Zumwalt's new "one-Navy concept," was to eliminate legal or attitudinal restrictions on women.[122] The communication authorized the entry of enlisted women into all ratings. It assigned women to the (non-nurse) crew of hospital ship *Sanctuary* (AH-17) as a pilot program whose ultimate goal was to open shipboard duty to Navy females; opened attendance of female officers at the National War College and the Industrial College of the Armed Forces; opened midshipmen programs to women at all NROTC campuses; and stated the Navy's intention to promote women to flag rank and to command of shore-based units.

Key provisions of Z-Gram 116 proved to be premature and ill-conceived. The states did not pass the Equal Rights Amendment, and the Combat Exclusion Law would continue to bar women from serving not only on board warships but also on other ships operating in a war zone or piloting combat aircraft. Hence, many of the billets ostensibly opened up to women by the Z-Gram could not be filled. In addition, more women serving in shore billets made it much more difficult for male sailors to follow their arduous tours at sea with assignments ashore close to their families. As Hazard related, with Z-Gram 116 the Navy took "one giant step forward to change a policy, and months later discovered that it didn't work, and so we took one giant step back, reversing the policy."[123]

And even Hazard, a strong supporter of Zumwalt's personnel policies with regard to women and one of the crafters of Z-Gram 116, expressed views not atypical of men and women in the Navy. She was dubious about women going to sea. She knew women "who had not been brought into the Navy with the understanding that they would have to go to sea." She understood that many women were concerned that they would "have to perform at sea a variety of jobs that were physically very demanding of strength, endurance, etc." Finally, Hazard was worried about the unknown impact on operational readiness of pregnant women serving at sea.[124] Many of these problems defied solution during Bud Zumwalt's time as CNO, but he had begun the worthy and long-overdue process of improving the service of women in the United States Navy.

THE SAILORS' ADMIRAL

Elmo Zumwalt's most pressing challenge when he took the helm as Chief of Naval Operations was to stabilize the Navy's personnel base in the last years of the war and into the postwar period. He realized that because of the conflict's debilitating effects on the sailors of the fleet and the end of the draft, he needed to take extraordinary and immediate steps to keep the Navy afloat. The first Z-Grams went out less than a month after he started work in the Pentagon. Those early communications focused on basic but to sailors especially relevant quality-of-life issues. The establishment of programs to deal with drug and alcohol abuse soon followed. He employed *The CNO Report* and similar media efforts to reintroduce "fun and zest" to Navy life and to dispel the common image of a "stodgy old Navy." His focus groups and other ad hoc measures went to the heart of what he considered the major obstacles to recruiting and retention. Only well into the process did he zero in on the discrimination and denied opportunity of the Navy's minority sailors, especially women. He did realize, however, that once Blacks and women were confident of equal treatment and a chance to prosper in the service, they could significantly strengthen the Navy's personnel base. At the same time, he came to understand in a personal and introspective way the Navy's long-term and serious neglect of its minority sailors. He then energetically moved to correct those injustices in affirmative action, human goals, and similar efforts.

Zumwalt's task was made especially difficult by the war's continuing drain on resources, the operational pressure on sailors resulting in AWOLs and desertions, the loss of skilled sailors, and the enlistment of less technically qualified and sometimes trouble-plagued Americans. Moreover, he had to cope with anti-war and anti-military sentiment, drug abuse, and racial turmoil that affected American society and the naval service. The nation's failure to pass the Equal Rights Amendment and continued enforcement of the Combat Exclusion law complicated his ability to widen opportunities for women in the service.

His own actions, or inactions, added to his problems. The stimulus to promote the first Black and female admirals originated in the office of the secretary of defense, not the office of the Chief of Naval Operations. While wishing to do good by women, he either acceded to impractical, ill-thought-out proposals for change by the Navy's female leaders or failed to take obvious measures for fear of alienating them. On the plus side, he did enable women to join NROTC detachments and to attend national security institutions of higher learning.

Zumwalt erred in seeming to sideline his admirals, commanding officers, and senior petty officers by communicating directly with sailors. His resorting to focus groups made up of a small number of junior officers and enlisted sailors and his "kitchen cabinet" of star-struck subordinates necessarily excluded participation by other ranks. His elimination of the traditional "Cracker Jack" uniform and similar measures did not sit well with many traditionalists. While his measures to enhance the retention of sailors successfully addressed longstanding grievances, they also often eroded discipline in the service. Despite Bud Zumwalt's implication that the members of the Hicks subcommittee were racists, it is clear that they were much more concerned about the overall personnel turmoil in the Navy. Zumwalt's policies did not cause the disturbances on board *Constellation* or the other ships and shore stations around the world, as President Nixon and some Navy leaders asserted. Rather, they were the result of a host of ills then affecting American society and the Navy.

There is no doubt that Bud Zumwalt's personnel reforms changed for the better the Navy's treatment of Black, female, and other minority sailors. The reforms also encouraged naval leaders to improve the quality of service for all sailors. The Navy at the time of his death in 2000, while certainly not free from personnel problems, bore little resemblance to the Vietnam-era service. Women, African Americans, Asian Americans, and all ranks had much greater opportunity for self-improvement and advancement. Admiral Zumwalt, despite a number of programmatic failures, changed for good how the service accommodated the quest for dignity, equality, and opportunity of its men and women.

CHAPTER 11

FIGHTING WASHINGTON

As Chief of Naval Operations, Zumwalt served as the Navy member of the Joint Chiefs of Staff. In that capacity, he expected to influence strategy and policy on key national security concerns. At the outset of his term, he prepared to take part in deliberations at the highest levels with regard to the war, nuclear arms control, and other key international and domestic issues. Since he had interacted with Paul Nitze earlier in his career on these very subjects, he anticipated doing the same on the JCS. It was not to be.[1]

Part of the problem was that professional and personal differences with the other JCS members often stymied cooperation. Zumwalt's relations with the other Joint Chiefs were personality driven. He liked and worked well with the other naval officer on the JCS, Marine Commandant General Leonard F. Chapman Jr. He had a mixed view of Air Force General John D. "Jack" Ryan, thinking him practical and forthright but "evidently more at home as an operational commander than engaged in the kind of wide-ranging speculation and analysis that is required of members of the Joint Chiefs." He had even less regard for Westmoreland, the Army chief of staff, with whom he "never became close and often disagreed." On one occasion, Zumwalt complained that an unidentified action proposed by Westmoreland subjected the admiral to "the most intensely embarrassing experience of my four years in the Tank [JCS conference room]."[2] Jerry Miller remembered Zumwalt denigrating Westmoreland. Miller was shocked, thinking that the Joint Chiefs were "supposed to stick together and work together [but] they're down there fighting one against the other [and] Zumwalt above all."[3]

This relationship contrasted markedly with Bud Zumwalt's connection to Westmoreland's successor, Creighton Abrams. Based on his close association with Abrams in Vietnam, Zumwalt expressed great respect, "even veneration," for the former COMUSMACV. While Abrams favored Zumwalt, other Army generals did not. General Bruce Palmer, the Army vice chief of staff, conceded that the admiral was intelligent and dynamic and that his naval service and "systems analysis background were plusses in dealing with the civilian bureaucracy." Nonetheless, Palmer thought that Zumwalt was "relatively very junior and lacked major command experience." He remembered that at meetings of the JCS, "he was sometimes naïve (particularly with respect to the conduct of the war) and often an irritant."[4]

Vice chief Jim Holloway sometimes stood in for Zumwalt when the latter was away. He related that the other Joint Chiefs were put off by Zumwalt's preoccupation with abstract nuclear warfare and strategic arms control theories. Although not uncommon among the other members of the JCS, Zumwalt did not shy away from a parochial approach to a subject. Indeed, Vice Admiral Donald D. Engen, at the time the head of OPNAV's Strategic Plans Branch, remembered that Zumwalt "was too parochially Navy" and that he "really didn't understand the other services [and] didn't really understand his role as one of the Joint Chiefs of Staff."[5]

Bud Zumwalt and JCS chairman Tom Moorer had a complicated relationship. The younger officer was well aware of Moorer's opposition to Zumwalt's social reform policies. But in addition to both men pronouncing Vietnam as "Veetnaam," the naval leaders "almost always saw eye to eye on matters of [Cold War] strategy." The two leaders consistently warned of the growing danger from Soviet nuclear and naval power and bemoaned the parlous state of the US fleet. Zumwalt expressed a positive view of Moorer's character, finding him "a cheerful and gregarious man, a good raconteur, a dedicated golfer [and] a mighty fisherman and hunter."[6] During much of Zumwalt's term in office, he and Moorer privately conferred about the declining strength of the US Navy in relation to the Soviet Navy and their opposition to the administration's arms control strategy.[7] In his 1986 book, Bud Zumwalt was less charitable toward Moorer, suggesting that the older admiral became chairman of the JCS because it was "the Navy's turn to assume that post" rather than because he merited the promotion. Zumwalt also related that during meetings of the Joint Chiefs, "Moorer, who is from Alabama, wasted few opportunities to comment sarcastically on my 'blackening' of the Navy."[8]

It was unsurprising that Moorer and Zumwalt worked together on the JCS to protect mutual interests. In late 1971, Moorer butted heads with the deputy secretary of defense, David Packard, over the control of US nuclear forces. The JCS chairman noted in his diary that he considered Packard "rather boyish" in that "if he does not get his own way he would pack up his toys and go home." Moorer recorded the observation by another Navy flag officer that Packard "puts out fires that he creates in a face-saving way because he is very petulant and hates to be wrong." Moorer noted that Packard did not understand the nuclear-control system. The JCS chairman and Zumwalt expressed concern that Packard intended to eliminate the JCS and the Navy from the nuclear weapon control process. The senior officer concluded that instead, the office of the secretary of defense should be cut out of the process. On several occasions, Zumwalt suggested to Moorer that the former contact the president with advice about Navy issues, but the JCS chairman declined the offers. Moorer was determined to be the president's primary—and only—naval advisor.[9]

The signal difference between the two naval leaders was the approach they took to Nixon and Kissinger. Tom Moorer used his almost daily contact with the White House to argue his case in a non-public, fact-based, and nonconfrontational manner. In contrast, Bud Zumwalt trumpeted his views before Congress and in the media and did so in a manner that challenged not only the administration's wisdom but also that of influential members of Congress. As an example, early in his term Zumwalt threw caution to the winds by publicly warning that unless Congress increased successive defense budgets, the US Navy would lose in a fight with the Soviets for control of the sea. He emphasized that "as of 1 July 1970 the United States had a 55 percent chance of winning a major conventional war at sea, was heading toward a 45 percent chance as of 1 July 1971, and a considerably smaller one than that by 1 July 1972." In March 1971, he stated that US naval forces had only a 35 percent chance of winning a fight with the Soviet Navy. In his later pronouncements he did not give percentages but said flatly that the United States would lose a conventional war with the USSR.

Initially, Zumwalt's lobbying efforts with the president and Kissinger produced positive results. According to the admiral, in the Fiscal Year '72 budget the Navy got "almost a billion more in expenditure than it had in FY '71," which meant a "saving of seventy-seven ships" that would have been decommissioned otherwise. Nonetheless, by the end of his tour as CNO, the Navy had in operation only 512 ships, many of them in poor physical condition.[10]

Zumwalt lamented that only he and General Chapman were willing to publicly say "what all of us said so emphatically so often to each other inside: that . . . the U.S. would lose a conventional war with Russia." Zumwalt decided that even though the other Joint Chiefs opposed his use of percentages to magnify the growing disparity between US and Soviet naval power, "I would go it alone." He recognized that this approach differed from that of Moorer, who believed that "the JCS must not only be strictly subject to civilian authority [but] that our official expressions must conform to the views of our civilian superiors." Bud Zumwalt admitted that "this difference between Admiral Moorer and me never was resolved, and it diluted our influence."[11]

Zumwalt observed that many defense department officials, even including deputy defense secretary Packard, Navy secretary Chafee, and other supporters, "balked at even mentioning the possibility that America might lose a war."[12] In early 1972, during a hearing on the hill, John Stennis, chairman of the Senate Armed Services Committee, asked Laird if he agreed with Zumwalt's previous assertions about losing a war. Laird, Bud Zumwalt's mentor and political backer, felt compelled to disagree vehemently with the admiral's stance.[13] Even Jim Holloway felt that Zumwalt's assertion that the US Navy would lose in a fight with the Soviets was overblown. Holloway was not able to determine "whether Bud really believed that we were number two or whether he was just saying this . . . in an effort to persuade the White House, the DoD, and the Congress to provide greater support for his shipbuilding programs." When he later became CNO, Holloway made it clear to his sailors that the US Navy was still number one.[14]

Moorer and Zumwalt complained that US negotiators were too willing to offer their Soviet counterparts easy terms in order to reach agreement on strategic arms limitation. Laird, Nitze, Moorer, and Zumwalt stood together to ensure that the proposed Trident ICBM (intercontinental ballistic missile)-launching submarine program and the Tomahawk cruise missile program were not subverted in the

Strategic Arms Limitation Talks (SALT).[15] Lehman asserted Kissinger "became an enthusiastic booster of both systems and pledged his undying support [for them] to Tom Moorer and Mel Laird."[16]

One of the Nixon administration's primary goals was to achieve "détente" between the United States and the Soviet Union. Nixon and Kissinger believed that the United States needed a cooling off period with the Soviets to give the White House time to repair the problems created by the war and the civil rights disturbances. They wanted the SALT negotiations to result in both sides freezing their arsenals of nuclear-armed missiles and giving up anti-missile defensive systems. Kissinger also wanted the détente process to mute Moscow's opposition to the US bombing campaign against North Vietnam. Kissinger worked to ensure that the competition with the Soviets did not get dangerously out of hand. He helped establish a new global balance that preserved American influence after the Vietnam War and America's drawback from heavy overseas commitments.[17]

Zumwalt vehemently disagreed with the policy of détente and what he considered Nixon's and Kissinger's acceptance of the global decline of American power. The admiral came to that conclusion when he and Kissinger shared a ride returning from an Army-Navy football game in Philadelphia. In his notes from that day's events, Zumwalt recorded that Kissinger "believes that the U.S. is on the downhill and cannot be roused by political challenge."[18] The admiral related that all his instincts "rejected [Kissinger's] prophecy of American decline." He added that "my mind was as intolerant of Kissinger's intimations of American decay as my stomach was." From that point on, in JCS and defense department meetings Bud Zumwalt insisted that the military should demand that their views be incorporated in Kissinger's national security studies and aired at the White House. The admiral ruefully admitted, however, that "my success in this endeavor was limited indeed."[19]

One reason Zumwalt used a public and inflammatory approach to problem-solving was his exclusion from the strategic arms decision-making process. A subordinate once half in jest suggested that Zumwalt wanted to be "CinC World [commander in chief of the world]."[20] Earlier in his career, Zumwalt had worked closely with Nitze in drafting arms limitation position papers and considered himself an expert on the arcane subject. Nitze's biographer has concluded that both he and Zumwalt "loved details as much as grand theories [and] they complemented each other."[21] Zumwalt began his term as the Navy member of the JCS expecting to make a strong impact on nuclear policymaking and working with Nitze, one of the administration's chief SALT negotiators in Vienna. On Zumwalt's first day in office, he approved a tasker to the staff to study strategic arms limitations and their relation to the Navy. But when Zumwalt expressed a desire to confer with Nitze in Vienna, Chafee turned him down. Apparently, the Navy secretary did not want to antagonize JCS chairman Moorer with a rejuvenated Zumwalt-Nitze connection.[22]

What Zumwalt soon discovered was that the president and his national security advisor, and not Secretary of Defense Laird or Secretary of State Rogers, dominated the decision-making process with regard to the strategic arms negotiations with the Soviets and the diplomacy ending the Vietnam War. While bemoaning that fact, Zumwalt had to admit that "the Kissinger team with a compact organization . . . was in a better field position than [the JCS] even if it hadn't been sitting right outside the Oval Office of the Umpire."[23]

Zumwalt also discovered with dismay that when the White House needed military advice or buy-in for a policy option, it called on Tom Moorer and not individual service representatives. Routinely, Moorer briefed the other JCS members only after the White House had taken or was about to take an action. During negotiations with the Soviets over strategic arms control, Bud Zumwalt complained that Moorer "dispensed in the Tank [what] was at best peripheral to the day-to-day substance of the negotiations." As a result, "we could not affect those negotiations, which was precisely what Kissinger and Dobrynin [Soviet Ambassador to the United States] intended." Despite his obvious discomfort at not being privy to key deliberations, Zumwalt understood that "Congress had intended a somewhat different kind of service from the Chairman than from the service Chiefs." He grudgingly observed that the JCS chairman "serves only two years but is eligible for reappointment, a clear indication that Congress intended him to be the President's man."[24]

Nixon spoke to the Joint Chiefs as a body only once during Zumwalt's four-year term as CNO and Navy member of the JCS. On 18 August 1970, the military heads participated in a meeting at the White House along with Laird, Rogers, Kissinger, Haig, and a few other officials. Both Zumwalt and Moorer once again stressed the fleet's weakened state and the chairman suggested, as he often did, that the Navy might soon find itself in the same inferior position as the Soviet Navy had during the Cuban Missile Crisis. Their briefings persuaded the president that the Navy needed additional resources. Nonetheless, under pressure from the anti-military and anti-Vietnam War factions in Congress, Nixon approved only a marginal increase in the Navy's budget.[25]

IN THE DARK ON NATIONAL SECURITY AFFAIRS

Not only was Bud Zumwalt outside the loop on Vietnam and arms control policymaking, he also found himself a secondary figure with regard to other global issues, such as crises in the Middle East. He bemoaned the fact that during a September 1970 crisis involving Jordan, on key issues the JCS were not consulted. Nixon, Kissinger, and Moorer successfully managed the crisis by bolstering the strength of the Navy's Sixth Fleet and deploying it to the Eastern Mediterranean. Zumwalt suggested that "the American forces may have been sufficient for the occasion, but they were far from formidable." He conceded, however, that "the successful Presidential bluff in the Mediterranean... had been a notable piece of statesmanship."[26]

Nixon used his 1970 tour of allied European countries to visit the Sixth Fleet at sea. Zumwalt, present during the event, exploited the opportunity to express his concern again about the Navy's shortfalls. According to Zumwalt, Nixon understood the admiral's view that the Soviets seriously jeopardized US maritime dominance. The president, however, told the admiral flatly that Congress and the American people would not support more than marginal defense spending. In early October and back in Washington, Nixon hosted a visit by Zumwalt and Laird to discuss operational measures for improving the Sixth Fleet's capability in the Mediterranean. This proved to be only one of the few times during Zumwalt's four-year tour that they met. Nixon pledged support for the Navy but took little action to address Zumwalt's concerns.[27]

Nixon had even less use for Zumwalt in the development of strategic arms control policies. Zumwalt complained that he and the other chiefs did not contribute to the discussions leading to the final SALT agreement, which he considered a dereliction of duty as military advisors. What really steamed the CNO, however, was the fact that Nixon did not "seek the counsel of the 'principal Naval advisor to the President' about something that is so clearly within the boundaries of that naval advisor's expertise and responsibility." Early on in his term as CNO, Zumwalt had looked forward to direct interaction with the commander in chief. Zumwalt considered Nixon's failure to consult the CNO "a poor way for a President to arrive at a decision that vitally affects national security."²⁸

The admiral acknowledged that Nixon was not the only administration official who did not heed his advice. The CNO's suggestions "never got far" because even if they emerged from the JCS they "sank without a trace" in the office of Secretary of Defense James Schlesinger. In addition, "more often than not Navy or JCS positions, even when they got as far as Kissinger's office, were simply ignored." In the latter regard, Bud Zumwalt complained that "most of the country's national security eggs were in one unelected, unaccountable basket."²⁹ Zumwalt considered Kissinger and Alexander Haig "masters of deceit and disingenuousness." The admiral derided Haig's towering ambition and his promotion from colonel to four-star general after his tour in the White House. But Haig's accomplishment mirrored the admiral's equally stunning ascendancy. Just before his retirement, Zumwalt bemoaned the loss of a naval officer's traditional ability to make decisions independently. He observed that that was "before we had instant communications [and] now all a naval leader has to be able to do is put the rudder over 15% when the White House tells him to."³⁰

The admiral butted heads often with Kissinger, the second most powerful figure in the US national security establishment.³¹ When Zumwalt first had contact with Kissinger, the admiral was charmed by the latter's intellectual skill, wit, and "powers of seduction." But his view of the national security advisor soured when he realized that Nixon's and Kissinger's method of operation excluded not only Laird, Zumwalt's mentor, from the policy formulation process but also the admiral. Bud Zumwalt refused to take part in "the secret world of Henry Kissinger" and "concluded that professional ethics compelled me to pass along the substance of our conversations to Tom Moorer and to Mel Laird."³² Zumwalt later confided, "I had my own spies" in the Navy liaison office of the National Security Council who reported to him regularly on White House activities.³³

During a war between India and Pakistan that broke out in December 1971, the Soviet Union sided with India, with which country it had earlier that year signed a treaty of peace and friendship. Moscow twice vetoed US-sponsored UN resolutions calling for a cease-fire. The Soviets then reinforced two warships in the Indian Ocean with two more, then transiting the Strait of Malacca. On the 6th and the 16th, the Soviet Pacific Fleet dispatched toward the crisis area two separate task groups comprising two missile cruisers and five other combatants. Nixon and Kissinger feared that if the war continued, and Pakistan was at the point of losing, that country would demand a US commitment to defend its SEATO ally. Moreover, the White House was concerned that if the United States did nothing to counter the Soviet actions, Beijing, which supported Pakistan, would think twice about Nixon's and Kissinger's diplomatic efforts to establish a rapprochement with the People's Republic of China.

Despite opposition from some members of the National Security Council, Nixon decided to buttress the US naval presence in the region. Tom Moorer remembered that Nixon emerged from the NSC meeting and pointing a finger at the admiral, saying that "he wanted that ship [aircraft carrier *Enterprise*] to go to the Indian Ocean now." The admiral responded with an "Aye, aye, Sir." The JCS chairman directed McCain's Pacific Command to dispatch Task Force 74, eventually comprising aircraft carrier *Enterprise*, an amphibious assault ship, ten destroyer types, a submarine, and five logistic support ships from the Gulf of Tonkin to the Bay of Bengal in the Indian Ocean. Washington wanted a visible show of force, so the task force's movements were not kept secret. Moorer characterized the deployment as "a classic use of naval power in the interest of supporting the overall U.S. objectives" without infringing "in any way on any nation's sovereignty."[34] The crisis ended when Pakistani forces in East Pakistan surrendered and India established a unilateral cease-fire. The confrontation resulted in the creation of the independent country of Bangladesh and the strengthening of the Indian-Soviet connection. Nevertheless, the administration believed that the dispatch of the task group had reassured both Pakistan and China of US reliability.[35]

Zumwalt later complained that the White House kept him, the head of the US Navy, in the dark about the reasons for the deployment. Nixon and his national security advisor managed the crisis through the Washington Special Action Group, chaired by Kissinger and whose members included defense department, state department, and CIA representatives and Admiral Moorer, or occasionally one member of the Joint Chiefs. Zumwalt attended one of the meetings and according to the admiral expressed his opposition to the administration's "tilt" toward Pakistan. He later concluded that his comment had not even been recorded in the meeting's minutes, which he suggested had been "laundered," presumably by Kissinger or his staff. At one point, Kissinger subjected the admiral to a verbal tirade. Zumwalt suggested that "a statesman shouldn't take his failures . . . personally, but Henry" does.[36] This is a curious statement indeed, as Bud Zumwalt clearly took his differences with Nixon, Rickover, Moorer, and a host of other leaders "personally."

Zumwalt, in keeping with his concern over the inferiority of the US Navy with regard to the Soviet Navy, had feared during the India-Pakistan crisis that the US task force would be endangered by the Soviet naval concentration. He admitted, however, that only after a second Soviet task force from Vladivostok had arrived in the Indian Ocean and the crisis was over were the US ships put at a disadvantage. Zumwalt later suggested that Nixon and Kissinger had acted "impulsively" by deploying *Enterprise* to the hotspot and denigrated their "effort to show the world that America was not to be taken lightly."[37] The admiral should not have been surprised by the move, since deploying naval task forces during overseas crises was a trademark of Nixon and Kissinger.[38] Moreover, the CNO no longer had the authority to direct fleet actions. The chain of command went from the White House to the secretary of defense, the JCS chairman, and finally to the combatant commands, in this case the Pacific Command. That understanding did not satisfy Zumwalt, who thought he should have been cut in on the action.[39]

An emotional exchange between Zumwalt and Kissinger in spring 1972 further inflamed their relationship. It resulted from direct complaints to the admiral by Sybil Stockdale and Jane Denton, leaders of the National League of Families of American Prisoners and Missing in Southeast Asia and other wives of POWs then imprisoned in Hanoi. They argued that the Nixon administration was not doing enough for them or their husbands. Emotionally charged, Bud Zumwalt went straight from the group's meeting in Arlington, Virginia, to the White House on a Sunday morning in May and "walked into Henry's office uninvited." He told the surprised national security advisor "bluntly that the White House had let the POW/MIA families down." As Zumwalt related, Kissinger responded in kind, getting "red in the face and . . . shouting." According to the admiral, before they parted company Kissinger threatened Zumwalt with actions of "revenge against 'my' Navy." Unsurprisingly, Zumwalt found that during the last two years of his term, his relationship with Kissinger "was almost entirely adversary."[40]

This episode is a good example of the fundamental difference between Kissinger and Zumwalt and their approach to matters of state. Kissinger was a foreign policy realist who believed in spheres of influence and the global balance of power. He strove for a balance between America's ideals and interests achieved without sentimentality. On the other hand, Zumwalt, "a true humanist and ethically grounded leader, saw America's global struggle in crusading, values-based, moral, and sentimental terms."[41]

Strengthening his ability to deal with adversaries in Washington, in July 1973 Zumwalt named Jim Holloway as his Vice Chief of Naval Operations. The newly minted four-star admiral understood that the CNO appointed him because of his successful command of the Seventh Fleet during the Linebacker campaign and the fact that the VCNO billet was normally occupied by a flag officer from another warfare community. Since Zumwalt was a surface warfare officer it was appropriate for Holloway, a naval aviator and an ardent supporter of Rickover's nuclear-powered submarine force, to take up that billet. Holloway also had a well-known reputation for working easily with a wide range of military and political leaders. Moreover, Zumwalt personally liked his Naval Academy classmate. In addition, the two men had studied together at the National War College in 1962. While there, the Zumwalt and Holloway families had forged a close relationship, so when Jim Holloway became VCNO, "Bud and Mouza Zumwalt were effusive in their welcome to Dabney and me."[42]

There were, however, significant differences between Zumwalt and Holloway over the composition of the fleet, nuclear power for warships, social changes in the Navy, and other key issues. Zumwalt was the poster child of the surface Navy while Holloway was a favorite of the naval aviation community that felt aggrieved under Zumwalt's command. The latter officer had experienced combat in Vietnam along the jungle rivers of the Mekong Delta while Holloway had fought his battles from the South China Sea. In contrast to Zumwalt, Holloway did not despise Nixon and admired Kissinger. While the CNO came to view Kissinger as "duplicitous, intellectually arrogant, and dangerously elitist," Holloway extolled the national security advisor's global vision and support for carrier aviation.[43] Jim Holloway especially valued his relationship with Rickover and considered Moorer and other leading naval aviators "family." They reciprocated those sentiments. Zumwalt detested Rickover and was decidedly ambivalent about Moorer.[44]

CNO Zumwalt swears in Holloway as his next Vice Chief of Naval Operations, August 1973. Holloway proved to be a loyal subordinate but later questioned Zumwalt's policy decisions.

Despite their professional differences, Zumwalt and Holloway enjoyed an amicable working and personal relationship, and Holloway proved to be a loyal, energetic subordinate. Well into his tenure as CNO, Zumwalt sent an "eyes only" memo to Holloway saying that he wanted his vice chief "to know how impressed I've been (but not surprised) to see how fast you have gotten up to speed."[45] The controversies surrounding Zumwalt's Z-Grams and the shipboard racial incidents had lessened by the time Holloway teamed up with Zumwalt. The CNO supported the development of the F-14 Tomcat fighter and construction of the nuclear-powered carrier *Nimitz*, projects favored by the naval aviation community that one might have expected this CNO to oppose. Holloway, however, credited Zumwalt with personally taking the lead to generate support for those programs in the office of the secretary of defense and in Congress. Moreover, in keeping with Navy tradition, Holloway served like an executive officer of an operational command and acted as "the CNO's alter ego, with no agenda or initiatives" of his own. As VCNO, Holloway handled a heavy load of Navy administrative and organizational matters and thus rarely had the time to leave his desk in the Pentagon or visit the fleet.[46]

Tom Hayward considered Holloway an outstanding vice chief. He remembered that the desks in the offices of all the previous VCNOs had been stacked high with papers that would not be processed in a timely fashion. Hayward recounted that you couldn't find any papers stacked up on Holloway's desk. He observed that Holloway had a good perspective on "all the political shenanigans" that were going on in the Joint Chiefs of Staff and Navy headquarters.[47] Jim Holloway, for instance, opposed Zumwalt's proposal that Army and Air Force aviation squadrons operate from Navy carriers and opposed the development of a fleet of catamaran troop transports to be propelled by gas-cooled nuclear reactors. Holloway related that with the CNO out of town, the Air Force chief of staff had contacted him and asked the vice chief to inform Zumwalt that, with regard to the offer of space on board Navy carriers for Air Force squadrons, "we're not interested."[48] The catamaran idea did not get beyond the conceptual stage, so Holloway did not have to press that case with his boss.

Zumwalt's fight with Rickover was another subject that might have caused friction between the CNO and his deputy but, as Holloway related, to avoid that he "simply steered completely clear of Admiral Rickover" during that period. While recognizing Rickover's well-known disdain for the Navy's chain of command and his grating personality, Holloway faulted Zumwalt for worsening the animus between the two men. He remembered that Zumwalt "really detested Rickover [while] I was very fond of him." Holloway observed that, unlike Zumwalt, former CNOs Burke, McDonald, and Moorer favored nuclear power in submarines and aircraft carriers and were okay with Rickover selling the program and managing it, "as long as he didn't make mistakes." Holloway added, "and Rickover didn't make mistakes." Zumwalt never persuaded Rickover to serve in a clearly subordinate role. Unlike the former CNOs, Bud Zumwalt had not had much exposure during his career to engineering or related technology, especially nuclear propulsion.[49] Hence, certain defense contractors, characterized by Holloway as "hustlers" and "charlatans," were able to sell the CNO on questionable nuclear power concepts.[50]

ON THE OUTS

Zumwalt's opposition to the policies of the Nixon administration and his isolation from the president and his national security advisor grew even more intense in 1973.[51] The CNO, like many other American leaders, understood that Nixon's involvement in the Watergate scandal was having a deleterious impact on the Vietnamization program at the same time that Hanoi was flagrantly violating the terms of the Paris Agreement and launching military operations in Laos, Cambodia, and even South Vietnam. In his memoir, Zumwalt made the suggestion, overly optimistic in retrospect, that Congress and the American people could have supported the Nixon-Kissinger promise to President Thieu of US military support if North Vietnam violated the Paris Agreement and that that public support might have deterred Hanoi. He blamed the Nixon-Kissinger penchant for secrecy in their hidden deal with Thieu as the reason for the failure of Vietnamization and America's final defeat in the war. According to Bud Zumwalt, Richard Nixon, hamstrung by Watergate, was forced to meekly accede to Congress's passage of legislation that forbade future US military action in Indochina.[52]

Zumwalt also blamed Kissinger for what the admiral considered the tardy US resupply of weapons to Israel during the Yom Kippur War of October 1973. At a time when Nixon was transfixed by Watergate, Kissinger managed the US response to the crisis in the Middle East. The admiral, a strong supporter of Israel, speculated that Kissinger "wanted Israel to bleed just enough to soften it up for the post–war diplomacy he was planning."[53] Kissinger, however, did not want to rearm Israel to such an extent that its army would rout the Egyptians on the battlefield. He later observed that "we did not think that turning an Arab setback into a debacle represented a vital interest" of the United States.[54] Moreover, Egypt had expelled Soviet troops the year before and seemed inclined to replace them with American military support. Kissinger wanted a cease-fire that would lead to negotiations.

Unlike Zumwalt, Tom Moorer understood that the administration's objectives during the Yom Kippur crisis were to "not permit the Arabs to push Israel into the sea and not permit the Israelis to humiliate the Arabs." The admiral was concerned that if the latter situation unfolded, America's petroleum supply would be imperiled. He stressed the importance of stabilizing the Arab-Israeli confrontation. Moorer also considered it vital to prevent another Vietnam-like commitment ashore. He emphasized that the United States had finally gotten the POWs out of North Vietnam only months before.[55]

Soviet Premier Leonid Brezhnev then announced that he was considering the airlift of Soviet troops into Egypt. In response, Kissinger ordered a global state of alert for US nuclear and conventional forces.

His object was to signal the Soviets that the US was serious about its opposition to the proposed Soviet move. Moorer approved of Kissinger's worldwide alert and restraint of the Israelis, but he cautioned Nixon and Kissinger that "the Middle East would be the worst place to fight a war with the Soviet Union."⁵⁶ In contrast to Zumwalt, however, Moorer assured Congress that the Sixth Fleet would be a match for Soviet forces in the Mediterranean.

Kissinger was dismissive of Zumwalt's leadership qualities. Kissinger knew that even though the admiral was "later a vocal opponent of such diplomacy," he facilitated the establishment of a secret Navy back-channel communication process to facilitate Kissinger's negotiations over a Berlin issue. In his 1,476-page *White House Years*, the former national security advisor and secretary of state mentioned Zumwalt only three times. In contrast, Kissinger alluded to Moorer 37 times.⁵⁷ Kissinger made no mention of Zumwalt in his 563-page work *Ending the Vietnam War* and only remembered the admiral's parochialism in his *Years of Upheaval*.⁵⁸ Kissinger considered Zumwalt "the most obsequious in the extreme of all the Chiefs [and] he was also the most dovish." Kissinger suggested that before their relationship became strained, the admiral "would bootleg to me all of the briefings of the Joint Chiefs and their preparations for discussions with the president. He was desperate to curry favor with me."⁵⁹

Schlesinger, who became the secretary of defense in May 1973, opposed public opposition to the president's foreign policies by members of his department. He told Zumwalt, for instance, that US policy was to "maintain a low profile and avoid visible involvement" in the Arab-Israeli conflict. Zumwalt discounted the argument that the US didn't want to inflame Arab opinion by seeming to side with the Israelis. He countered that Israel was vital because it served as a buffer between the United States and the Soviet Union, the latter seeking domination of the Middle East.⁶⁰ Disregarding Schlesinger's wishes, Bud Zumwalt went outside the chain of command and "told a tale out of school" to inform Senator Henry "Scoop" Jackson about Kissinger's supposed perfidy in holding back the US airlift during the Yom Kippur War. Zumwalt often provided the senator with confidential information on Kissinger's contacts, bureaucratic maneuverings, and thinking on national security issues.⁶¹ The upshot of the Yom Kippur War was that the Soviets did not intervene militarily, the cease-fire held, and Kissinger's management of the crisis paved the way for a later Israeli-Egyptian rapprochement.

Zumwalt's appeal to Congress for support on contentious subjects did not sit well with either Schlesinger or Moorer, who thought involving the legislature would only embarrass the administration and complicate the resolution of issues.[62] Schlesinger established a working relationship with Zumwalt, who considered him a superior "strategic theorist." But Zumwalt no longer had Laird to shield him from the increasing wrath of the White House. Zumwalt observed that Kissinger, "the superior bureaucrat," was "able to impose his policy positions on [Schlesinger] most of the time." Through much of his term as secretary of defense, Schlesinger worked to prevent his inflammatory subordinate from further angering the White House. The briefing Zumwalt planned to deliver on 22 December 1973 at a meeting between the president and the JCS was so incendiary that Schlesinger vehemently urged Zumwalt not to give it. According to Zumwalt, Schlesinger said that presenting such a briefing in the current climate at the White House would be just "shooting yourself in the foot." The defense secretary added that "the President is paranoid. Kissinger is paranoid. Haig is Paranoid. They're down on the Navy and to present facts like these to them will drive them up the wall." Schlesinger feared that White House ire would adversely impact Navy and defense department budgets. For once, Bud Zumwalt decided to tone down his remarks. In any case, the admiral never had a chance to voice his views since the president rambled on through most of the meeting.[63]

Zumwalt related that "my frustration impelled me in spring 1973 to initiate one last large-scale effort to get the facts out" through Congress and the White House about the growing disparity between the US and Soviet navies. He tasked Rear Admiral Train and his staff with developing a net assessment of the relative strengths of the navies, looking at the previous five years and into the next five years. The resulting report convinced Zumwalt that it was clear that US military capability was on the wane and Soviet capability was on the rise, which would be made worse by congressional parsimony. Later that year, Zumwalt emphasized that if Congress fully funded the Navy's programs, this would be "the last year when our chances of winning would be as low as 30 percent." Even though Bud Zumwalt's evaluation made it to key Congressional committees, that was as far as it got. Surprisingly, Zumwalt credits the net assessment with convincing Nixon to send to Congress the "best naval budget of my four years, albeit still inadequate."[64]

A more likely stimulus for the Navy budget increase was the 1973 report of the specially created President's Foreign Intelligence Advisory Board (PFIAB). Former CNO George Anderson, held in high regard by the White House and the JCS chairman, and the leader of the traditionalists who had wanted Zumwalt fired over personnel and social issues, headed the board. As instructed by now chief of staff Haig, the board worked "independently of Navy channels"—Zumwalt's Office of the Chief of Naval Operations. For various reasons, the final report died in the White House. Zumwalt blamed "Watergate, Haig's hostility toward the Navy [or] a conviction that it was impossible to sway an anti-military Congress." He might have added another factor, the bitter estrangement between the president, his immediate staff, and himself.[65]

As later related by his son, Zumwalt had been "appalled by the Nixon administration, and had said publicly and privately that the final Nixon years were as close as this country has ever come to a fascist dictatorship."[66] The embittered CNO railed against "a wrecked President and an unprincipled Secretary of State" who ruined "my last month as a sailor." Zumwalt found himself "awash in controversy and the target of recriminations that were not only acrimonious but personal." At the US Naval Academy's graduation ceremony on 5 June 1974, attended by the president, Bud Zumwalt made light of "long hair" in the Navy and the fact that the institution was getting "blacker and blacker" and would soon "be truly representative of the Nation at large." He also alluded to "those barebones defense budgets which *you* [italics added] have submitted to the Congress." Nixon was not pleased with the speech; Schlesinger told Zumwalt that he was "in the doghouse again." Zumwalt also did not endear himself to the White House when as acting chairman of the JCS in Moorer's absence he expressed opposition to a Soviet proposal for a nuclear weapons test ban agreement that Kissinger favored. Long before that, Zumwalt had decided he didn't want to be "Kissinger's whore."[67]

During Zumwalt's last months as CNO, he again focused, as "the principal naval advisor to the president," on his favorite subject, nuclear arms limitation. Believing that he had finished his work on the Navy's budget, he considered himself "pretty much a lame duck as far as running the Navy was concerned." Those months witnessed intense debate within the US national security establishment over the terms of the SALT treaty being negotiated. As with many other issues, Bud Zumwalt considered Kissinger his nemesis, but he was not alone in that regard. Zumwalt's mentor Nitze, serving as the secretary of defense's representative on the US delegation, opposed what he considered Kissinger's push to have a treaty signed at any cost—or, as Zumwalt characterized it, a "disaster Kissinger was cooking up for America in Moscow." Zumwalt complained that Kissinger's actions had caused Nitze, "the finest flower of his generation in public service, a quiet, brilliant, deeply patriotic, and sensitive man," to resign from his post in May. In addition to Nitze, arms negotiator Gerard Smith, Tom Moorer, and Senators Henry Jackson and Barry Goldwater opposed Kissinger's objectives.[68]

Zumwalt and the other JCS members were against the draft terms of the treaty, but many of their protestations got no further than the desk of the secretary of defense. Zumwalt speculated that Schlesinger feared for his job, or more charitably that he felt the JCS proposals would do more harm than good to the military. Zumwalt was less forgiving of the defense secretary in a private conversation with admirals Holloway and Bagley. The CNO related that Schlesinger "had gotten his ass chewed out several times from Kissinger and Haig" and that the president had "accused him of disloyalty and not keeping the Pentagon in line."[69] Zumwalt also related that Schlesinger believed that "whenever the Russians press too hard Mr. Nixon shows flashes of instinctive patriotism but that Kissinger starts backpedaling immediately and then adroitly charms the President and Haig into going along."[70] The close hold by the White House over the SALT process continued to frustrate Bud Zumwalt's desire to participate in the arms limitation process.

Zumwalt found himself isolated within the defense department bureaucracy since individual JCS members reported first to the chairman and then to the secretary, both of whom jealously guarded their access to the White House. Zumwalt was not alone in his detachment from operational matters. As a former Army vice chief of staff related, "The other chiefs found themselves less and less informed, if not isolated, on operational matters. It put the onus on each individual chief to keep himself up to speed, but this is difficult when the Joint Staff works exclusively for the chairman with respect to current operations."[71]

Bud Zumwalt was not bereft of insight on the doings in the White House. He had a source of information in the president's inner circle: Howard Kerr, then assigned as an aide to Vice President Spiro Agnew and after the latter's forced resignation, Gerald Ford. Kerr later asserted, "I was not Zumwalt's man in the White House." But he did provide a service "in terms of describing the atmosphere, the flavor of things, the pressure points, who was on the rise, who was on the fall [and] he would pass those things on to the admiral."⁷² Bud Zumwalt and his wife Mouza also periodically sponsored teas at the CNO's residence to counteract the anti-war impression then being made by John Kerry and to emphasize the positive aspects of the war effort. Invited to these gatherings were the wives of congressmen and White House staffers, including on occasion Mrs. John Erlichman and Mrs. H. R. Haldeman.[73]

In mid-June, Zumwalt got around Kissinger's embargo of information intended for the president. Understanding that the last thirteen JCS memos on SALT had not made it beyond the national security advisor's desk, Zumwalt bypassed Kissinger by secreting a letter to Nixon via Kerr and hence the vice president. Bud Zumwalt's communication, according to Kerr, was "very critical of the President and the President's handling of the whole nuclear balance issue." Kerr added, "By implication, he basically said that the President wasn't executing his responsibilities under the Constitution, which requires the President, by law [to] seek the input" of his military advisors. Kerr understood that the other Joint Chiefs agreed with some of Zumwalt's views but that "the letter was a little too strident, that it had too much of a cutting edge on it, and it overstated the situation."[74]

Nixon was livid and considered cashiering the intrepid admiral, but with the president only two months away from resigning over Watergate, he did not need another fight over the firing of the head of the Navy. Nixon ultimately decided against signing the proposed agreement, not based so much on Zumwalt's opposition but rather that of key members of Congress, the JCS chairman, influential retired military leaders, and national security experts.[75]

Nixon's animus toward Zumwalt only increased in the remaining days of the admiral's tour as CNO. The White House refused Zumwalt permission to speak on the nationally televised program *Meet the Press* scheduled for the admiral's last day in office. They feared he would air his opposition to the SALT negotiations. Schlesinger told him that he was persona non grata at the White House, and the defense secretary thought that anything Bud Zumwalt said would be anathema to Nixon and Kissinger and would hurt the defense department, the Navy, and "me." The White House told Schlesinger that they could court-martial Zumwalt if he went on *Meet the Press* and "destroy" him. Schlesinger later told Zumwalt that on 26 June the White House told him to fire the admiral. Zumwalt did in fact appear on the program, but he did not discuss details of the SALT negotiations.[76]

Gathered at Annapolis for the Navy's change of command on 29 June 1974 are (right to left) admirals Holloway, Zumwalt, and Moorer, Secretary of Defense James R. Schlesinger, and Vice Admiral William P. Mack, Superintendent of the US Naval Academy. NHHC NH 103813.

Incensed with Zumwalt's behavior throughout his last months as CNO, the White House told Vice President Ford and Schlesinger that they could not attend Zumwalt's retirement ceremony and denied the admiral an already approved Department of Defense Distinguished Service Medal. In tacit defiance, both men attended the ceremony and Zumwalt was awarded the approved medal, although unlike all previous awards given to retiring Joint Chiefs the citation did not bear the president's signature. To his credit, and despite the ill-will coursing through the White House, Ford spoke at Zumwalt's farewell.[77]

Before the ceremony, the attendees had met at the Naval Academy superintendent's house for refreshments. Present were Tom Moorer and the other Joint Chiefs. Kerr remembered that the men "were all gathered around in little groups, and standing all by himself over in a corner was Bud Zumwalt, the outsider, the guy who had ended his brilliant, spectacular Navy career with no one talking to him."[78] So ended the tumultuous and historic four-year term of the Vietnam hero and nineteenth US Chief of Naval Operations.

In contrast to Admiral Zumwalt's generally positive impact on the Navy's social development, his service on the Joint Chiefs of Staff had little impact on decision-making related to the Vietnam War, the management of global crises, or nuclear arms deliberations. The real power of the JCS resided in the chairman, who jealously guarded his access to the commander in chief. The defense secretaries, especially James Schlesinger, also filtered recommendations from the JCS members. Unable to deploy fleets and other forces during international crises, Zumwalt and his counterparts were reduced to competing among themselves for their service's share of much-diminished military budgets. Clashing personalities further limited their influence. Compounding Zumwalt's isolation, President Nixon restricted the decision-making process to a small coterie of trusted subordinates, including Henry Kissinger, Al Haig, and Tom Moorer.

Non-organizational factors also erected a barrier between the White House and the Chief of Naval Operations. Zumwalt's close association with Secretary of Defense Laird, excluded from Nixon's inner circle, and General Abrams, in disfavor after Lam Son 719, did not endear him to the president. Neither did Zumwalt's identification with what Nixon considered a Navy overrun with miscreants. Bud Zumwalt's appearances before Congress and in the media decrying the administration's détente policy, what he considered the failure to address the Soviet threat, opposition to nuclear arms negotiations, and the management of foreign crises further enraged Nixon and Kissinger. Zumwalt failed to comprehend that administration actions during the India-Pakistan War and the Yom Kippur War helped bring about Nixon's rapprochement with China and an eventual cease-fire in the Arab-Israeli conflict. The admiral's surrender to vitriolic and emotionally charged attacks against the national security advisor did not benefit the Navy or his own legacy. The president's desire to fire his Chief of Naval Operations during the admiral's last days in office, in part because Zumwalt had disobeyed a direct order not to appear on national television, reflected the parlous state of White House-Navy affairs. It was a sad end to Admiral Zumwalt's four turbulent years leading the US Navy.

CHAPTER 12

THE END GAME

When Admiral James L. Holloway III became the Chief of Naval Operations on 29 June 1974, like Zumwalt he had to deal with the consequences of the Vietnam War. He also had to contend with Zumwalt's stewardship of the Navy, which many believed had strengthened the service and many others that it had damaged it. President Nixon was among the latter group. When he nominated Holloway as the next CNO, with Moorer's strong endorsement, the president told Holloway, "Admiral, get some discipline back in the Navy. I'm an old Navy man and very proud of my service, and I don't like what I see going on in the Navy today."[1] Secretary of Defense Schlesinger, who later headed the Department of Energy, also favored Holloway because of the latter's experience with nuclear power. Schlesinger told Holloway, "There's an old adage in show business [that] you don't follow one tap dancer with another tap dancer." Jim Holloway understood that the secretary was telling him to avoid emulating Zumwalt.[2]

As an indication of the respect many leaders had for Holloway's credentials, he was the first vice chief promoted directly to the Chief of Naval Operations billet. Above all, Jim Holloway wanted to bring stability and balance to the post–Zumwalt Navy. In a private conversation with the chief of information, Holloway told him that "I'm just a smooth-bore gunner." Bill Thompson explained that "in layman's language that means a traditionalist who isn't looking to change the world."[3]

Holloway, in response to a request from Secretary of the Navy Warner, had earlier laid out in a "personal and private" letter what his goals would be if he were selected as the next CNO. He observed that he completely and energetically supported Zumwalt's programs but would "slow down the rate of change." In elaboration, Holloway wrote that Admiral Zumwalt's reforms were marked by innovation and imagination and routinely resulted in "drastic changes to the traditional 'old Navy' way of doing things." He recognized that "shock tactics were required to defeat the resistance to change inherent in the institutionalized Navy." He added, however, that he thought it was time for the Navy to go slower and concentrate on incorporating the changes. He promised to give the highest priority to seven areas, and his top three were personnel stability, discipline and human goals, and military standards.[4]

Like Zumwalt, Jim Holloway put primary emphasis on stabilizing the Navy's manpower base. He asserted that the CNO had to focus on the recruitment and retention of high-caliber people. He also observed that "the human goals program and the exercise of good order and discipline are mutually supporting" but the latter aspect was "an absolute requirement in a military organization." He reinforced that point by suggesting that "a disciplined Navy must have a well-defined and clearly understood set of standards for appearance, dress, and conduct." In a nod to his mentor Rickover, Holloway observed that exposure to engineering or scientific disciplines should enable officers to achieve an adequate understanding of technical naval warfare factors. The prospective CNO also wanted a balance of youth and experience in the officer corps that would provide the best officers with the background needed to prepare them for high levels of responsibility. While he would eventually change his mind, he then concluded that "our naval construction policies, such as the high-low mix, are heading the Navy in the proper direction." In closing his missive to the Navy secretary, Jim Holloway observed that he did not "advocate any major changes in direction" but called for a slower pace to consolidate progress.[5]

Admiral Harold E. Shear, who served as Holloway's third vice chief, later remarked that what Zumwalt did "with regard to racism, to blacks, and to women . . . was absolutely positive. All the other things he did were not good for the Navy." Shear suggested that he and Holloway had to "quietly and firmly get the Navy back to battery" which he believed was accomplished.[6] Tom Hayward credited Jerry Miller with the observation that "when Admiral Zumwalt was CNO, every sailor could tell you who the CNO was." Holloway, on the other hand, saw

President Nixon congratulates Holloway on his selection as Chief of Naval Operations while Secretary of the Navy John Warner looks on approvingly. Nixon and Warner hoped Holloway would bring greater social stability to the Navy after the unsettling tour of his predecessor, Zumwalt. NHHC NH 103851.

his job as ensuring that every sailor knew who his commanding officer was, "and could care less about who the CNO was."[7]

Zumwalt had favored Worth Bagley to be the next CNO, even though according to one close observer Bagley "probably had the least flag officer experience in the Fleet of any 4-star unrestricted line officer in modern history."[8] But Zumwalt wanted to ensure that his successor continued his personnel reforms and advocacy of the High-Low Mix for naval construction. Another requirement was that the individual had to have the strength and wisdom to protect the programs "from the stratagems of Admiral Rickover" and be able to sell them to Congress. Above all, he wanted someone with the "integrity and strength of character to keep the Navy from being suffocated in the political miasma that was enveloping ever more closely the Nixon-Kissinger-Haig White House."[9] Bud Zumwalt's high regard for Bagley was mutual. Bagley valued Zumwalt's honesty, forthrightness, and the "courage of a lion." He was also impressed with Zumwalt's intellectual brilliance. He opined that there hadn't been "his kind of brains in the Navy in a very long time." Bagley contrasted Zumwalt with the Navy's "many small people, too many independent people, and too many dumb people who react only from the gut."[10]

Zumwalt ruled out recommending one possible successor, Admiral Isaac Kidd, because he perceived him as someone who would reverse his personnel reforms. He also denigrated Kidd because he was Warner's favorite. Zumwalt considered Warner "unhelpful to me in just about every way a Secretary of the Navy could be unhelpful to the Chief of Naval Operations." And Zumwalt characterized Kidd as "a very devious man," one who had "overriding ambition with no ethical limits" and who displayed "absolute unctuousness" toward him.[11]

Zumwalt found his vice chief, Holloway, less objectionable, even though he was a Rickover favorite and wanted more nuclear-powered aircraft carriers. Moorer, John Warner, and the White House staff were positively inclined toward Holloway, as were a plurality of Navy flag officers. Jim Holloway recalled that Moorer called him up and said he was recommending him for the job. Even though Zumwalt reminded readers in his autobiography that "the racial disturbances in the Seventh Fleet occurred when he [Holloway] was in command," the CNO also told Secretary of Defense Schlesinger that he would endorse Holloway.[12]

The one caveat was that Bagley would have to be the next VCNO. Zumwalt confided to Bagley that "you are going to have to help him [Holloway] enlarge his horizons . . . because he tends to think in terms of the narrow interpretation." Zumwalt wanted Holloway to be more like Admiral McDonald, whom he found to be wise and mature, but many others considered a disaster as CNO.[13] Holloway accepted Bagley as his deputy but came to consider him too academically inclined, "not a guy with thorny hands from handling lines and things like that." On one occasion, Holloway needed Bagley to stand in for him, but his deputy "was nowhere to be found." When he discovered that Bagley was attending an academic meeting away from the Pentagon, Holloway admonished the officer, telling him to "forget about this theoretical crap about studies." He stressed that he wanted him "to be in this office acting as CNO" when he was absent.[14] Later, when Holloway offered Bagley the CINCPAC billet after his time as vice chief, his deputy instead retired from the Navy. Bagley was disappointed that Holloway did things differently than his idol Zumwalt. His biggest complaint was that Holloway didn't try to get Rickover under control. When Bagley retired in mid-1975, Holloway replaced him with a nuclear submarine and pro-Rickover officer, Admiral Robert L. J. Long. The latter remembered that when he took the job, Holloway told him that the two of them had to "bend over backwards so that we do not appear to be parochial."[15]

Not only did Jim Holloway reject Bagley's advice about controlling Rickover, he refused a suggestion by his immediate boss, Deputy Secretary of Defense William P. Clements Jr., that the CNO "fire Rickover. Fire him today. Get him out of here." According to Holloway, Clements's friends in the shipbuilding industry were upset that Rickover, in the name of shipboard safety, was overly demanding with regard to the quality of the materials used in carrier and submarine construction. Holloway told Clements that Rickover was responsible for the Navy's stellar record of nuclear safety. The CNO predicted that if he fired Rickover, "I'll give you three weeks before there's an incident, because he's the guy that's being tough and holds it all together."[16]

As CNO, Jim Holloway increasingly found fault with Zumwalt's leadership of the Navy. About a year after Holloway became CNO, he related that "the fallout from many of his policies began to emerge and reveal the damage that had been done to the military cohesion and character of our Navy." He blamed Zumwalt for "forcing people in the Navy to take sides: were you for human rights or for discipline?" Holloway found this "a very foolish characterization of our two philosophies, but unfortunately [it] came to be a perspective in which our two tours of duty as CNO were being compared." Holloway later admitted that over the years he had become "one of Bud's severest critics."[17]

Holloway did not blame Zumwalt for his failure to live up to his potential, concluding that he had been pushed into the job by Chafee who "totally disregarded the considered advice of every senior naval officer on active duty and the retired CNOs." Holloway contended that Zumwalt was "too immature and professionally unprepared to be an effective CNO." Holloway felt that Zumwalt did not qualify as a great leader because "his command philosophy was not to lead but to accede to the wishes of the subordinate levels of the Navy." Jim Holloway thought that his Naval Academy classmate "was a dashing figure, articulate and immensely popular with the junior officers and younger sailors" who constituted the majority of the Navy. He added, however, that *"we must not confuse popularity with leadership, and a military organization is not a democracy"* (original italics). Holloway concluded that overall, his predecessor's work was not helpful to the Navy except for his accomplishments on race relations. And even on that score, Holloway considered Zumwalt's goals admirable but his implementing actions "not well conceived." He offered that "the Navy does not need another Zumwalt in its foreseeable future."[18]

ADAPTING THE ZUMWALT REFORMS

Shortly after he took the oath of office at the Naval Academy as the new CNO, Holloway described his initial approach to the job: "There is a traditional expression from the sailing Navy that an oncoming officer of the deck should not change the set of the sails in the first fifteen minutes of his watch." He decided that he was "going to wait a while before [he considered] changing the set of the sails." The Navy was still suffering from the aftereffects of the Vietnam War and dealing with Zumwalt's social revolution. He understood that there were many in the service who applauded Zumwalt's programs, but there were also many who did not. Holloway was determined "to get these differences under control, to heal and unify the Navy."[19]

That approach especially related to the Navy's racial issue. He did not want "race relations to be an abnormality or a unique problem we have in the Navy" but instead he wanted "one big happy family." He asked the rhetorical question, "If I am for the Blacks, then how would the White guys feel?"[20] When Robert J. Walker became the new MCPON in September 1975, Holloway told the senior enlisted sailor that he intended to bring the Navy back to a "middle of the road policy." Walker considered Holloway's approach "absolutely brilliant." He explained that the four-star admirals were putting a lot of pressure on the CNO to "go out there and really hammer" those who had supported Zumwalt's personnel policies. Walker remembered that Holloway and he decided that that approach would have been "totally wrong" because sentiment in the Navy and indeed in American society had changed. So, instead Holloway "did the right thing" and promoted discipline and "enlightened leadership."[21]

With Congress loath to increase defense spending, the Navy had to maintain its global commitments with fewer personnel. Between 1973 and 1980, at a time when the national inflation rate rose to nearly 20 percent, the Navy was unable to afford raises in basic pay. Despite Bud Zumwalt's valiant efforts, complemented by Jim Holloway's actions, enlisted retention rates dropped in 1979 to new lows. Lehman, reflecting on the era preceding his tour as Navy secretary, observed half in jest that the Navy almost had to resort to "press-gangs." Speaking seriously, he related that many of the new recruits continued to be "illiterate, convicted felons, drug users, and worse."[22]

Holloway noted that when he served under Zumwalt as the vice chief and carried out the CNO's directives, he recognized that they had basic differences with regard to service in the Navy. He suggested that "Bud's premise was that Navy life should be fun, and his policies were to restore this element to the Navy." Holloway reflected, however, that "we were living through the cold war and Vietnam [in which] the Navy's purpose was to fight and win wars." He added that, unlike Zumwalt, he "believed that the military career is a demanding profession and a tough life."[23]

Admiral James D. Watkins, Holloway's Chief of Naval Personnel and a later CNO, reported that because of Zumwalt's efforts to communicate directly with sailors, the chief petty officers felt stripped of power. These experienced "lifers," the mainstay of the Navy, had left the service in droves or just gave up on the job. Bud Zumwalt later admitted that his one regret with regard to the personnel program was that he didn't connect with the senior chiefs to get their input on his plans. In contrast, Holloway and his successor, Hayward, reaffirmed the relevance of the Navy's traditional approach to communication. They worked to reintegrate the chief petty officers in the chain of command.[24]

Jim Holloway recognized that many of his sailors lacked the leadership abilities, technical skills, or motivation needed for the upkeep of the vessels. He testified before Congress that the Navy was experiencing a shortage of petty officers skilled in maintenance and repair since many of the best sailors failed to reenlist. He remembered that Zumwalt told sailors, "You don't have to chip paint" anymore because contractors could do the work. But problems ensued when a ship with a repair problem docked in a remote place like Bermuda devoid of a contractor. He also observed that at the end of a typical six-month cruise, "a U.S. Navy cruiser now looked like a rust-bucket." As a result, observers overseas wrote to the Navy Department and complained that US ships that they saw in foreign ports were an embarrassment.[25]

Holloway understood that the Vietnam War had negatively impacted the social mores of many young Americans. He bemoaned "a palpable diminution of the characteristic American work ethic in this postwar generation." He implied that to get young people to enlist, his predecessor had his recruiters make "promises of good pay, fun cruises, rapid promotion, and the opportunity to learn a marketable trade." Sadly, according to Holloway, "the Navy couldn't deliver, especially to the young people who had been underachievers on the civilian side, both in high school education and in the job market." Many new recruits expecting "instant gratification" couldn't comprehend "why they had to start at the bottom of the ladder chipping paint." Unfortunately, these new sailors weren't trained to handle the "more glamorous careers in electronics and computers." He concluded that their disenchantment led to "a lack of motivation for the menial tasks of keeping their vessel shipshape [and] up to man-of-war standards."[26]

There continued to be widespread complaints about a lack of discipline in the Navy. When General Alexander Haig became Supreme Allied Commander, Europe, in December 1974, he visited Sixth Fleet units in the Mediterranean. There he found "ill-disciplined, ill-trained, sometimes disoriented sailors operating some of the most sensitive and powerful technology in the American arsenal."[27] After serving under Zumwalt in Vietnam and on Project Sixty, Captain Henry Mustin commanded Destroyer Squadron 12 based in Athens, Greece. When Mustin arrived at his new command, he recalled that the engineering plant of one ship "was in shambles" with equipment parts strewn all around the deck. When he passed by some compartments, "the smell of pot coming up out of the hatches was enough to give you a high." He also learned that some of the unit's sailors had gone AWOL and ended up "somewhere in Greece." Despite the captain's best efforts, "morale had deteriorated to the point that sailors were deserting or committing crimes like robbing Greek taxi drivers."[28]

Jim Holloway was shocked to discover that measures Zumwalt had taken in hopes of reversing downward reenlistment trends were severely impacting operational efficiency and the work ethic. When he visited the Norfolk naval base, he witnessed hundreds of sailors during the lunch hour heading for enlisted clubs which offered "a martini happy hour, two drinks for the price of one . . . [and] topless go-go dancers too." After such lunch breaks, many of the same sailors fell asleep at their shipboard tasks or skirted them altogether. This observation tied in with his discovery that his Navy had a serious problem with alcohol, as well as drug abuse. He suggested that his ignorance might have been because "as vice chief I had stayed in the Pentagon while Bud visited the fleet." In any case, acting decisively, Holloway put out a Navy-wide order banning the service of alcohol at all enlisted and officer clubs during working hours.[29] Holloway and his chief subordinates also acted quickly to relieve from command an officer who, in an effort to introduce more "fun and zest" to shipboard life, permitted a stripper who went by the name Cat Futch to dance topless on the deck of *Finback* (SSN-670), an attack submarine heading out to sea.[30]

One of Jim Holloway's significant changes to Zumwalt's policies was to do away with the chief-like uniform for enlisted personnel and return the Navy to the traditional dark blue bell-bottomed pants—the "Cracker Jack" uniform—and unique circular white hat. Holloway related that during his visits to ships, once the ice was broken sailors would invariably want to discuss the uniform issue. They emphasized that they "wanted to look like sailors [because] they were sailors, and very proud of it."[31] Noted military writer Paul Fussell, in his chapter "Zumwalt's Big Mistake," also understood that sailors "thoroughly hated" the new uniform.[32] Like Holloway, MCPON Walker wanted to see sailors who "had respect for themselves because they were proud of what they were doing." He especially wanted to ditch what he called the new "funeral director's uniform" and replace it with the traditional Cracker Jack uniform. While sharing Walker's view, Holloway reasoned that they had to proceed deliberately. He told MCPON that "the change was too far along to reverse it [and] if we tried to go back too quickly, we'd be investigated for fraud and abuse because so much money was already invested" in the new uniform. But Holloway promised that before he left office the change would be made, and he kept his word.[33]

Jim Holloway had decidedly mixed feelings about Bud Zumwalt's approach to the problem of race relations. He believed that the Navy benefitted from Zumwalt's actions to improve the quality of life for African American sailors because "it highlighted a problem." His disagreement about the program, however, was the way Zumwalt administered it. Holloway felt that Zumwalt's racial awareness program was amateurish and conducted unprofessionally. Indeed, one sailor complained that he was "more prejudiced *after* [original italics] I attended that damned UPWARD [racial awareness] program than I was before."[34] Gravely found the sensitivity training sessions "pretty hard to swallow" because young counselors were "telling me that I [a flag officer] was to blame for all the Navy's problems."[35] Salzer expressed similar views, observing that the sensitivity training was being "left to all of those Goddamn little special staff people that BuPers had, running around instigating trouble between blacks and whites." He emphasized that "they were not solving any problems; they were creating problems."[36]

Stan Arthur also complained about the Zumwalt-initiated sensitivity training sessions. He understood the need for greater understanding among racial groups, but the programs would "sometimes go awry."[37] Salzer remembered when an equal opportunity advisor, "a bright abrasive young black lieutenant commander," had led a discussion on race relations at the admiral's Saigon headquarters. During that session, the officer told his African American listeners that "your first responsibility is to your fellow blacks, not to the Navy." Salzer "blew up like a geyser" and dispatched a complaint that reached the CNO.[38] Rickover found another Zumwalt initiative, the Navy Human Goals Program, "amateurish" because it had been "poorly conceived, poorly executed, is a joke in the fleet, and is inimical to building a strong fighting force."[39] A poll of the Naval War College class of 1974 found that 68.5 percent of captains / commanders and 50 percent of lieutenant commanders / lieutenants agreed with Rickover. As a result, Jim Holloway reduced much of the racial awareness training.[40]

With the support of Secretary of Defense Donald Rumsfeld, in 1976 Holloway assigned Samuel Gravely to command of the Pearl Harbor-based Third Fleet. The vice admiral was the first African American to command a US fleet. Still more effort was required, however, to eradicate prejudice from the service. Gravely related that on one occasion, he drove onto the grounds of the Naval Observatory in civilian clothes to attend an evening function. A white sailor at the entrance told him to park his car in the rear of the CNO's house. When informed that the driver was a Navy flag officer, the young man apologized profusely, explaining that he "didn't know you were Admiral Gravely. I thought you were a chauffeur." Gravely excused the faux pas but counseled the sailor to "always remember—chauffeurs wear caps."[41]

Despite Zumwalt's well-meaning and Navy-wide approach to improving race relations and other measures to retain sailors in the service, much work remained to be done when he retired from the service. By 1974, only 36 percent of African American sailors who joined the Navy attended advanced specialty training, compared with 60 percent of whites. The recruitment picture was equally dire. In 1974, Black officers still represented only 1.24 percent of the Navy's officer corps. During the same year, minorities represented 7.4 percent of the Navy, not even close to the goal of 11.9 percent.[42]

Nonetheless, by improving the image of the Navy in the African American community, Zumwalt and Holloway helped transform the service "into one of the best employers in the nation for minorities—a workplace often cited later as a model of racial harmony."[43] Holloway continued a number of Zumwalt's programs and established his own Navy Affirmative Action Plan (NAAP). By 1977, every major naval command had created an affirmative action plan. Despite setbacks, the racial climate in the Navy had improved significantly by the late 1970s.

Hayward praised Zumwalt's and Holloway's efforts to broaden opportunities for African Americans and other minorities. He observed that "once the policies were clearly understood, it was just a matter of time for minorities to advance into new and better positions of leadership and skill levels." He remembered that "you started seeing black first class [petty officers], chief petty officers, and officers in certain positions." He related that "by the time I became CNO [in 1978], the minority policies had a lot of momentum to them, and I don't remember any significant problems I had to deal with."[44]

The decade also witnessed significant advances for Navy women. In 1970, 6,633 women (.95 percent of all naval personnel) served on active duty, but by 1979 that figure had risen to 24,644 (4.7 percent of those in service). Holloway continued the effort to broaden opportunities for women. By 1979, out of 102 enlisted ratings, ninety-one (including fifteen combat-related billets) were open to women. But at the same time, responding to complaints from male sailors and their wives, the service closed other shore billets to women in order to facilitate a reasonable sea/shore rotation for male sailors.[45] In 1972, the first females entered naval aviation training, and by the end of the decade many of them piloted helicopters and fixed-wing aircraft. In 1978, Lieutenant Barbara Allen became the first woman to qualify in jet aircraft. The Navy ended the practice of separating from the service pregnant women or women with dependents under 18, which had long been the norm. Holloway was fully supportive when Congress opened the US Naval Academy to women in 1976. And in 1978, Jim Holloway authorized females to serve on board naval vessels other than hospital ships and transports.[46]

REBUILDING THE FLEET

In many ways, Jim Holloway bore little resemblance to his predecessor. As a naval aviator who had commanded and executed combat operations from aircraft carriers in Korea and Vietnam, he showed little

Holloway speaks with Chief Machinist's Mate Lilton Davis during a fleet tour in March 1976. Holloway dispensed with some Zumwalt social reforms but also established the Navy Affirmative Action Plan. NHHC NH 103818.

enthusiasm for Zumwalt's "High-Low Mix" to the detriment of large, nuclear-powered aircraft carriers. Indeed, Holloway would be comfortable with a description of the nuclear-powered aircraft carrier as "the Navy's most versatile instrument" whose missions included overseas presence, coercive diplomacy, sea control, power projection, nuclear deterrence, crisis management, and humanitarian relief.[47] Holloway pressed his case, even though Schlesinger initially found the prospect of building less expensive warships enticing. Holloway considered the Navy's nuclear carrier force to be indispensable. Naval aviator Stan Arthur felt that Holloway "put the nuclear carrier on the map." Arthur explained that without the need for nuclear carriers to operate in conjunction with much slower tankers and ammunition ships, a carrier could speed to a crisis and be ready for action when it arrived. Nonetheless, Jim Holloway, like Bud Zumwalt, also understood that the Navy needed a balanced and affordable fleet of non-nuclear-powered cruisers and destroyers.[48]

Holloway recognized the need to replace some existing combat vessels since, as he explained, "The ships in the fleet had simply been run to death in Vietnam operations."[49] He added that by the end of the war, the fallacy of "guns and butter" had become evident. He emphasized that during the war, resources to repair and maintain ships, aircraft, and equipment were hard to come by. In short, after the war "the cupboard was bare [and] our military forces were worn out."[50] The Navy had delayed or cancelled ship overhauls and shortened in-port stays for maintenance and repair. The crews had neither energy nor enough time during combat cruises or short port visits to upgrade equipment or their ships. The fleet that had suffered from the lack of new naval vessels and the delayed maintenance of obsolescent warships got little more respite during Holloway's tenure than it had during Zumwalt's. Even Rickover, a strong Holloway supporter, testified before Congress shortly after Holloway became CNO that "in my opinion there has been no point in the last fifty years where the fleet has been in as poor condition as it is today."[51]

Holloway knew that after Vietnam the American people were not inclined to support robust defense spending. And with little public support, few members of Congress chose to beef up the armed forces. Despite continuing resistance to military spending, during Holloway's term in command Congress favored the Navy over the Air Force and the Army. Indeed, Jim Holloway was "an intransigent defender of the Navy's claim to a greater share of the budget than the other services, a position he proudly defended as in the national interest."[52]

To highlight his fleet's dilemma, Holloway frequently told the story of four ships that deployed to the Mediterranean from Norfolk and only one got there on its own. The other three ships had to be towed into port. Holloway also recognized that despite the fact that

Zumwalt came from the surface warfare side of the Navy, many ship commanding officers lacked the engineering skills to recognize or correct propulsion system casualties. To tackle the problem, he made a tour as chief engineer mandatory for all officers who aspired to command of a naval vessel. According to Holloway, it was an overnight success. He observed, "We put top notch people into engineering spaces and then moved them up into command where they understood taking care" of the ship's machinery.[53]

Like Zumwalt, Jim Holloway endeavored to put the Vietnam War behind in order to meet the threat posed by a resurgent, technologically advanced, and globally deployed Soviet Navy. During much of the Vietnam War period, American leaders had been assured that the US Navy had absolute control of the world's oceans. By 1975, however, that control was widely questioned. Holloway understood that "we were faced by a Russian navy twice the size of our own in numbers, if not in capabilities, but constructed and organized specifically for contesting U.S. maritime superiority." *Okean* 75, a Soviet naval exercise in 1975 that involved 220 ships, was a masterful exhibition of the USSR's new global presence. The drill included mock strikes against the continental United States and its sea lines of communication. Thereafter, Russian ships continued to operate in all the world's major bodies of water and close to African hot spots. The change in the naval balance was highlighted at the end of Zumwalt's tour when Soviet naval units began operating from the base at Cam Ranh Bay in Vietnam, built with great care and expense by American taxpayers.[54]

Holloway took concrete action to reorganize the fleet in response to the Soviet threat. He considered his "Battle Force Fleet" organization "probably my most significant contribution to the U.S. Navy in my tour as CNO."[55] Through this measure, battle groups were formed consisting of an aircraft carrier, two cruisers, four destroyers, and a nuclear submarine. Two or more battle groups constituted a battle force. Holloway incorporated the battle force concept and his overall strategic vision in *Naval Warfare Publication No. 1: Strategic Concepts of the U.S. Navy*, issued Navy-wide in May 1978.[56] Strategic analyst Peter Swartz considered NWP-1 "a repudiation of some of the overarching concepts put forth in [Zumwalt's] Project Sixty."[57]

Moreover, while Zumwalt worked to break down barriers between the surface, aviation, and submarine communities—but antagonized many of their number—Holloway largely succeeded in that effort. He established that the commander of a battle group could be a qualified surface ship, submarine, or aviation flag officer. He later concluded that "the elimination of the parochial boundaries in the fleet operating forces ... significantly expanded the support for the aircraft carrier's position as the capital ship of today's Navy." The Battle Force remained the Navy's central organizational tool well into the twenty-first century.[58]

Jim Holloway reemphasized experience over youth in regard to naval aviation leadership. Zumwalt, in an effort to open up opportunities for young officers, had enabled commanders to lead carrier air wings and lieutenant commanders to command aviation squadrons. Holloway related that one of the first things he did was to reverse those actions because "there's no substitute for experience." He asked rhetorically, "Why [would you] take this captain with all of that experience, all of that background, and put him in a desk when he can still fly? He can still lead."[59]

Despite their close professional and personal relationship, Jim Holloway was not Rickover's toady. The two officers sparred over the latter's championship of nuclear propulsion for cruisers, destroyers, and frigates. Holloway agreed that carriers needed nuclear propulsion systems because that freed up space on board for aviation fuel and bombs, but he also believed that "the little [antisubmarine] frigate could do almost as good a job as the 10,000-ton displacement nuclear cruiser." Rickover and other antagonists argued that every nuclear-powered carrier needed four nuclear-powered escorts. The CNO countered that "this was clearly an extravagance." He emphasized that after serving two years in command of *Enterprise* and its task group in combat off Vietnam, he could not justify the need to build additional nuclear-powered escorts for twice the cost of oil-fired ships. Secretary of the Navy Middendorf reinforced the CNO's position when he testified before Congress. He offered that "we should have an all-nuclear Navy—but I suspect it would be a pretty small Navy" because of the cost.[60]

The representatives of the nuclear shipbuilding lobby had a lot of clout with Congress, which they used to make their case. So did Rickover, whose biographers nicknamed him "Admiral of the Hill" and suggested that by the 1970s he "was practically an honorary member of Congress." He courted and won the support of key senators and representatives, who eagerly sought his appearances before them. From the 1950s to the 1970s, Rickover testified before Congress 150 times. Rickover used his support from Congress and the shipbuilding industry to directly challenge Jim Holloway's opposition to the all-nuclear Navy.

The CNO, however, did not hesitate to shoot back. He provided key senators with a statement in which he suggested that "the issue is which advice should the Congress follow: the advice of the CNO, the senior uniformed official responsible for the readiness of naval forces now and in the future—and whose views are supported by the Secretary of the Navy and Secretary of Defense and presidential decision—or the advice of Adm. Rickover."[61] Holloway's views prevailed, and the policy of limiting nuclear power to carriers and submarines became firmly established. By the late 1970s, the Navy had plans for the fleet of the 1980s and 1990s to operate fifty oil-fired destroyers.

Despite their public disagreements, Jim Holloway and Hyman Rickover continued to enjoy a strong personal and professional relationship. Indeed, Holloway observed that he was "enormously grateful" to Rickover for his management of the "technical side of the nuclear navy." Holloway wondered how much time and energy "it would have taken a CNO who did not have a person of Rickover's mind, dedication and guts running this nuclear component of our Navy."[62] Neither did Holloway shy away from opposing some actions proposed by Secretary of Defense Schlesinger. In 1974, when military officers overthrew the government of Archbishop Makarios on the island of Cyprus, Schlesinger considered removing US nuclear weapons from Greece. According to Harry Train, then director of the Joint Staff, Holloway argued against the proposed action because "not only would it be breaking faith with Greece" but perhaps also would prompt the Greek government to stop the removal operation. It would be "turning a bad situation into a much worse situation." As Train related, "Eventually, that logic prevailed, and that intransigence really prevailed" since Schlesinger backed down.[63]

Holloway had both an ally and an adversary in the secretary of state. Kissinger especially valued the admiral's leadership and the utility of naval power. He remembered Jim Holloway's contribution to the resolution of the Jordan crisis of 1970 and championship of carrier aviation. In various crises, Kissinger's first words were often, "Where are the carriers?"[64] Lehman, who served on Kissinger's staff in one capacity or another from 1969 to 1972, observed that "from the shooting down of the EC-121 in 1969 to the 1973 Yom Kippur War, time and time again the principal military tools used by the President were the Navy and

Holloway, popular in Congress, testifies before a committee. He stressed the vital necessity of the fleet's large aircraft carriers and the importance of the Navy's global mission. NHHC NH 103811.

the Marine Corps."[65] On one occasion, Kissinger spied Holloway, put his arm around him, and exclaimed to others in the party, "This is the greatest admiral in the world."[66]

When Holloway commanded the Seventh Fleet in 1972, Nixon had directed Kissinger to investigate the effectiveness of naval operations against North Vietnam. Holloway later suggested that Army and Air Force partisans had worked to plant doubts in Nixon's mind about the Navy's contribution to the war effort. An equally plausible reason was the president's desire to document what he considered the demise of the Navy under Zumwalt, even then under fire for the racial troubles.

Kissinger dispatched one of his staff members, Lieutenant (junior grade) John Lehman, to Holloway's fleet to comply with the president's wishes. Eschewing the usual practice of subjecting officials visiting from Washington to information-packed briefings, Holloway suggested that the Naval Reserve aviator fly as a bombardier/navigator on board an A-6 Intruder and take part in a bombing strike. Holloway, however, intended that Lehman's plane not enter the potentially lethal air space over North Vietnam with the rest of the flight. The admiral explained to Kissinger's assistant that "it would certainly be embarrassing if he were captured and had his fingernails slowly pulled out with pliers."

Holloway later learned that the young officer had disregarded that cautionary directive and proceeded with the other planes in harm's way.

Holloway was pleased when Lehman had informed the Seventh Fleet commander that his report to Kissinger was a positive one and that he found "little to criticize in the Navy's operations." Jim Holloway found it apparent "that John Lehman was an exceptional young man with an enormous amount of common sense to go along with his sharp intellect."[67] When he was the CNO, Holloway brought Lehman on board as a personal consultant. Holloway also considered Lehman "one of the most active and productive secretaries of the navy in its long history of distinguished public servants."[68]

Jim Holloway respected Kissinger's many skills and often found common cause with him, but the admiral didn't hesitate to oppose the towering figure of American foreign and national security policy. By implication, he blamed Kissinger, the chief US negotiator for the Paris Agreement, because "our terms for the cease-fire were inadequate to eliminate the Communist threat inside South Vietnam."[69] Another example was Holloway's determined stand, backed up by the other members of the JCS, to block the signing of SALT II. Kissinger, directly involved in US-Soviet negotiations in Vienna, was prepared to restrict the deployment of revolutionary Tomahawk cruise missiles to only ten Navy cruisers in exchange for a Soviet pledge to limit the capability of their intercontinental ballistic missiles. Holloway understood that cruise missiles enabled the fleet's surface ships and submarines to attack enemy targets hundreds of miles away with great precision and without risking aircraft and aircrews on those missions. The Navy was also concerned that the Soviets' Backfire bomber, which was a long-range threat to the fleet, would not be prohibited by the treaty.

President Gerald R. Ford, running hard for election in November 1976, Secretary of Defense Rumsfeld, and Chairman of the JCS General George S. Brown were inclined to approve the draft treaty language. Holloway, acting chairman in Brown's absence, argued before the National Security Council against what he considered "an unbalanced agreement." When Ford turned to Holloway, the admiral replied, "You're not going to like this, Mr. President, but we cannot agree" with giving up the cruise missile.[70] After consultation with the other JCS members, Holloway informed the president that "the chiefs were unanimous in recommending in the strongest terms that the president not agree to this proposal."[71] Ford was especially displeased with Holloway's position. According to the admiral, only Fred Iklé, head of the Arms Control and Disarmament Agency, and his deputy John Lehman sided with Holloway and the chiefs. The president, unwilling to proceed without the endorsement of the uniformed heads of the armed services, overruled his secretary of state. Kissinger later admitted to Holloway that at the time he was "very mad" at the admiral over the issue but came to recognize the great value of the revolutionary weapon system to America's warfighting capability. Despite Jim Holloway's determined stand, the newly elected Carter administration signed a SALT II agreement on 18 June 1979, but neither the US nor the Soviet legislatures ratified it.

HOLLOWAY VS. CARTER

Jim Holloway had little positive to say about President Jimmy Carter, even though the Georgian had graduated from the US Naval Academy and served in the submarine fleet. Holloway observed that although Carter considered himself an expert on naval matters, he had had only limited experience at sea. During the presidential election of 1976, Carter told Soviet premier Brezhnev that "if elected he would take steps to eliminate all nuclear weapons in the United States's arsenal by the end of his first four-year term," assuming the Soviet Union would do the same. Holloway thought "Carter rather naïve in his simplistic approach to an impossibly complex issue."[72]

Holloway was equally dismissive of Carter's secretary of defense, Harold Brown, who discounted the need for sea power. Holloway lamented that Brown never failed to "make life difficult for me." During one meeting, the defense secretary blurted out that "the trouble with the Navy is that you have no imagination." He suggested that if the Navy "had smaller planes and smaller carriers, you could buy more of them." He complained, "You don't even try; you just stick with the big nuclear carriers."[73] Jim Holloway felt that Brown was "absolutely committed, as was the President, not to do anything that would justify the Navy carrier force."[74] Lehman too found that Brown "made no bones about his belief that the Navy was of quite secondary utility."[75] At one point, the Carter administration cut the Navy's five-year shipbuilding program from 159 ships to seventy. Holloway considered Carter's opposition as an example of what career military officers often had to cope with in their work with their civilian superiors. He concluded, "After the initial shock at some impracticality proposed by the civilian leadership, there is usually a period of education and reflection, and then more reasonable courses of action evolve, usually without any further reference to the bizarre opening postulation."[76]

The Navy's post-Vietnam fortunes did not get a boost from Carter. When retired Admiral Zumwalt met with Carter, the former CNO related that the commander in chief was "literally contemptuous of the military point of view."[77] In January 1978, when Holloway and the other Joint Chiefs met with the president at the White House to discuss the defense department budget, Carter announced that he planned to cut $9 billion from the military budget (including three-and a-half billion from the Navy). Holloway told the president that he would support the decision but explained that if questioned by Congress he would have to say that that action would have a severe impact on the Navy, which was already woefully short of funds for its operational commitments. But the other Joint Chiefs said little, so the cuts came to pass. They resulted in "a reduction in training, in flying hours, in ship steaming days, in practice ammunition fired, in technical training school quotas, and in the essential spare parts to keep our aircraft and ships operating." Holloway had to testify before Congress that the United States "no longer [had] a two-ocean navy" and if a war broke out with the Soviets, the Navy could not control the Pacific. Holloway's principled stand did not endear him to the president, and thereafter he "never enjoyed a cordial relationship with President Carter" or easy access to the White House.[78]

Carter also endeavored throughout Holloway's term to delay or kill funding for nuclear-powered carriers. Despite a determined stand by the CNO, Carter dropped the carrier itemized in the fiscal year 1978 budget and did not include a carrier in the fiscal year 1979 budget. Holloway and Rickover had powerful friends in Congress who did not take kindly to the president's moves to limit the carrier force. Nevertheless, when the legislature put a flattop back in the 1979 budget, Carter vetoed the entire defense budget. He took the same action the following year. But this time, once again persuaded by Jim Holloway's fact-filled testimony and aggressive Soviet moves at the time, Congress overrode the president's veto so the appropriation and authorization of funds for the construction of the carrier remained in the budget. This nuclear-powered ship, later named *Theodore Roosevelt* (CVN-71), entered the fleet in 1986.[79] Lehman has concluded that because of Holloway's powers of persuasion before Congress "during the Carter years, the navy lost many battles in the corridors of the Pentagon, then won most back in the halls of Congress."[80]

Soured by the Vietnam experience and opposed to future overseas interventions, Carter and Brown believed that the only US commitment that really mattered was that in support of NATO. They believed that the US focus should be on strengthening NATO's central front in Germany, not on the maritime flanks of the alliance. Hence, they directed that the Navy's primary, if not exclusive, mission should be to control the Atlantic so troop reinforcements and supplies could reach Europe in a war with the Soviet Union. Indeed, the Carter administration's "Swing Strategy" was based on the assumption that in a war with the USSR, the US Pacific Fleet would dispatch most of its warships to the Atlantic. Acceptance of that strategy implied a much smaller Navy and a reduced presence in the Pacific and East Asia.

Unlike Zumwalt, who overemphasized the sea control mission, Jim Holloway reaffirmed the importance of projecting naval power ashore and deploying warships around the globe to deter potential enemies and to reassure allies. Indeed, Japan and America's other Asian allies worried that Carter's strategy would "sacrifice the East to save the West."[81] Holloway testified before Congress that if the size of the fleet were reduced, it would be unable to help Japan. Hence, the US-Japan Security Treaty would be meaningless for America's faithful post–World War II ally.[82]

He also stressed the importance of the Pacific theater to US global interests and encouraged the study of strategic concepts in that regard. Lehman lauded the CNO as a stalwart advocate of "maritime superiority." He observed that the admiral continued to argue forcefully against the kind of downgrading and cuts that were underway in the Carter administration. Lehman considered Holloway "not the average, docile peacetime chief" but a leader "who never trimmed his sails to [the] prevailing winds."[83] Lehman remembered that "a number of aggressive navy strategic thinkers kept the flame alive during the Carter years [and] Admiral Holloway was, of course, first among them."[84] Unfortunately, he paid a price for his stand. Holloway was convinced that because of his uncompromising position in support of the large-deck carrier, Carter and Brown did not select him to succeed Air Force General Brown as chairman of the JCS.[85]

Holloway was prescient in assigning Tom Hayward to command of the Seventh Fleet and then the Pacific Fleet because that officer reinforced the effort to revise the Carter administration's Euro-focused strategy and diminution of the Navy's overseas role. Hayward argued that in a major war, the US Navy should be empowered to attack the Soviet Union all around its vast empire, especially in the Far East and the waters of Northeast Asia. Secretary of the Navy Graham Claytor Jr. and Under Secretary of the Navy R. James Woolsey shared many of Hayward's views and, with Holloway's strong endorsement, in August 1977 persuaded the defense department to authorize a study of Navy missions through the end of the century. Holloway's second vice chief, Bob Long, a former CINCPAC, represented the CNO in the development of the study which also involved Lehman and the Naval War College's Francis "Bing" West.

The resulting work, Sea Plan 2000, completed in March 1978, called for a forward-deployed Navy prepared to execute offensive operations, including in the Pacific, with powerful carrier and battleship battle forces. Sea Plan 2000's most optimistic scenario suggested that to carry out that global strategy, the Navy would require fifteen carrier battle groups and close to 600 ships. The advent of the high-performance F-14 Tomcat fighter armed with Phoenix long-range air-to-air missiles and the Aegis air defense system promised a strong defense of these forward forces.[86] At one point, both Holloway and Navy secretary Middendorf opposed Aegis as too expensive. But, persuaded about the radar system's potential, the CNO changed course and began lobbying Congress for it. Harry Train has suggested that "the guy who really sold the Aegis cruiser was not Zumwalt but rather Holloway."[87]

Carter and Brown did not endorse Sea Plan 2000, since neither they nor Congress were prepared to pay for it. Lehman remembered that it was "received with such hostility by Harold Brown and his staff."[88] As many naval historians have observed, however, Sea Plan 2000 did provide a credible mission statement for the Navy of the future. Moreover, it served as the intellectual underpinning for the Reagan administration's naval buildup and the Maritime Strategy of the 1980s. Lehman, as a reflection of his high regard for the former CNO, concluded that "the success of the 600-ship Navy in the Reagan years owes more to Holloway than any other person."[89]

THE END IN SOUTHEAST ASIA

The Paris Agreement of January 1973 between the United States and the warring Vietnamese parties did not inaugurate a new era of peace in Indochina. Bent on the eventual destruction of the Republic of Vietnam and domination over Laos and Cambodia, Le Duan's communist government disregarded the terms of the agreement almost from the start. Kissinger, Nixon's chief negotiator of the Paris accords, recalled that as early as his visit to Hanoi in February 1973 he had a foreboding that North Vietnam would not abide by the provisions of the agreement. He suggested that the greatest flaw of the pact was not that it tacitly accepted the presence of 160,000 North Vietnamese troops in South Vietnam and 100,000 more in Laos and Cambodia but that it compelled the withdrawal from South Vietnam of all US forces within sixty days. Kissinger would have preferred to have kept some US forces in the region as a deterrent to bad behavior by Hanoi, but Nixon suspected that the American people would not countenance that action. Instead, Nixon assured President Thieu that he would use force if necessary to stop flagrant North Vietnamese abuse of the Paris Agreement.[90]

Before his retirement from office, Zumwalt most objected to the fact that neither Congress nor the American people were told of these understandings. He complained that "not even the JCS were informed that written commitments were made to Thieu." Bud Zumwalt said with regard to the agreement that "there are at least two words no one can use to characterize the outcome of that two-faced policy. One is 'peace.' The other is 'honor.'"[91] According to Kissinger, the anti-war movement, the adversarial media, and an unsympathetic Congress moved from the partial withdrawal of US forces to eventually total and unilateral withdrawal with short timelines.

In contrast, the North Vietnamese pushed more and more troops into Laos, Cambodia, and South Vietnam and improved the Ho Chi Minh Trail. By the middle of April 1973, the North Vietnamese had infiltrated 35,000 more troops into South Vietnam or its border reaches in a buildup more sizeable than before the 1972 Easter Offensive. Kissinger concluded that "Congress paralyzed enforcement when, in June 1973, it proscribed enforcing the [North Vietnamese] withdrawal from Laos or the ban on infiltration." He emphasized that those actions "ensured the collapse of Indochina." That act by Congress in summer 1973 prohibited the use of military force in Indochina. He bemoaned that it invalidated "an agreement for which over 55,000 Americans and hundreds of thousands of Vietnamese had given their lives."[92] Kissinger was on the mark when he concluded that "liberals were losing interest because they had little commitment to the survival of South Vietnam [and] the conservatives believed that they had discharged their obligations by supporting the war to an honorable conclusion." These considerations were reflected in the military assistance provided to Thieu's government. Congress reduced appropriations for Vietnam by 50 percent each year after the signing of the Paris Agreement, from $2.1 billion in 1973 to $1.4 billion in 1974 and to $700 million for fiscal year 1975.[93]

Watergate truly doomed US efforts to preserve the independence of the Republic of Vietnam and the other Indochinese states. Not only did the scandal further alienate Congress but it also diverted Nixon's attention and weakened his resolve to stand up to North Vietnamese transgressions. At the same time, Tom Moorer, who considered the return of the American POWs the only substantial issue, did not strongly counsel Nixon to press Hanoi over an upsurge in infiltration. When Ford succeeded Nixon as president in August 1974, there was little he could do to avoid defeat in Indochina, but he believed the United States owed its ally a last try.[94]

While the military sympathized with that view, "the Joint Chiefs had no concrete plans to deploy U.S. forces back into Southeast Asia on behalf of the Saigon government."[95] Indeed, the same month of the signing of the Paris Agreement, defense secretary Laird appeared before the House Armed Services Committee and asserted that Vietnamization had been successfully completed, the implication being that the South Vietnamese were on their own. By January 1975, many in the military had all but written off Indochina in hopes of concentrating most defense spending on rejuvenation of the US armed forces. As Kissinger observed, "The Pentagon was in no mood to expend any more capital on Vietnam." A proposed deployment of carrier *Independence* (CV-62) to the Gulf of Tonkin in reaction to North Vietnamese violations of the Paris Agreement never took place.[96]

By early 1975, the North Vietnamese army was poised to launch another massive assault on South Vietnam via the Ho Chi Minh Trail. Hanoi had built a network of strategic roads totaling 12,000 miles, some paved and suitable for trucks. The enemy had also constructed 3,000 miles of oil pipeline to fuel the armored vehicles and trucks deployed in Laos and Cambodia and all along South Vietnam's border.

As a member of the JCS from mid-1974, Jim Holloway took part in the final effort to provide the South Vietnamese government and armed forces with the weapons and supplies they needed to continue the ongoing conflict with North Vietnam. The admiral did not give American leaders, including military leaders, a pass for failing to abide by America's promise to prevent South Vietnam's defeat. He concluded, "The national leadership and the American people looked the other way while our former ally was overwhelmed and occupied by a veteran and professional North Vietnamese army, fully modernized with Communist bloc weapons and logistical support." In short, "We turned our backs and allowed South Vietnam, Laos, and Cambodia to fall."[97]

In his 2012 oral history and after years of reflection, however, the admiral had a different perspective. He suggested that "it wasn't so much the [lack of] funding and the equipment, it was that the Vietnamese panicked." He asserted that the commanders "wanted to get out of town before the Commies showed up." He bemoaned that "we were asking the Vietnamese [military] to do things that they really were not equipped to do." He admitted, "I think we made a mistake." Much like Bud Zumwalt, Jim Holloway had come to question the wisdom of deploying an American expeditionary force ashore in Asia because it became a war of attrition and the Vietnamese communists were "breeding faster than we could kill them." He speculated that had the United States been willing to make a supreme effort and "gone in there from the beginning and said, 'We're going to win [and] we're going to knock their socks off,'" that result might have come to pass. He regretted that "nobody wanted to make the commitment" and besides, "We were scared to death that the Chinese, if they saw [that] we might win they would have entered the war."[98]

Holloway, however, concluded that because of changing global conditions, in the long run the United States benefitted from the fight in Southeast Asia. In a speech at Washington's Metropolitan Club in 1996, he stressed that the Korean and Vietnam wars "were essential to the ultimate [Cold War] objective of demonstrating to the world, ally and adversary alike, that the United States would go to war and fight in support of allies and to protect its own national interests." He asserted that the war "established beyond question the credibility of our commitment [that] convinced the Russians that America would fight if threatened."[99] The admiral also suggested that the US strategy of détente with the Soviet Union, combined with the containment strategy of the 1970s, "made holding South Vietnam no longer critical as the containment line of the Soviet Union" had moved to the northern border of post-Mao China. In short, the Americans fighting in Vietnam had held communism in check "until the firmness of our military posture and the adroitness of our diplomacy had exploited the endemic fissures in the Communist hegemony and shifted the world's balance of power in our favor."[100]

The final act in the long Vietnam War occurred in spring 1975, when communist forces launched an offensive in the Central Highlands of South Vietnam that soon developed into the rout of Army of Vietnam forces north of Saigon. In March, the Navy's Military Sealift Command (MSC) dispatched merchant ships and large tugs pulling barges to Danang, Qui Nhon, and other ports of northern and central South Vietnam. The vessels evacuated thousands of retreating South Vietnamese troops and civilian refugees from those and other sites. At the same time, the Seventh Fleet deployed elements of Amphibious Task Force 76 off Nha Trang. Since the Paris Agreement restricted the use of US military forces in South Vietnam, however, Washington maintained the naval contingent in a noncombat supporting role.[101]

Vice Admiral George P. Steele, the Seventh Fleet commander, then focused his efforts on Cambodia, which he knew was expected to fall soon to the radical communist Khmer Rouge guerrillas. Since 1970 and the US incursion into that country, Washington had supported President Lon Nol and his armed forces fighting against Khmer Rouge and North Vietnamese forces along the border with South Vietnam and further inland. By early 1975 and despite major US military assistance to government forces, the Khmer Rouge guerrillas had seized every population center except Phnom Penh and were closing in on the capital.

Steele prepared his forces for the evacuation of Phnom Penh—Operation Eagle Pull. On 3 March 1975, Amphibious Ready Group Alpha and the 31st Marine Amphibious Unit deployed to a staging area off Kompong Som (formerly Sihanoukville) in the Gulf of Thailand. The contingent consisted of the carrier *Hancock*, three amphibious ships, and four destroyer types. Embarked were Marine and Navy helicopters. Early on the morning of 12 April, President Ford ordered the execution of the evacuation. At 0745, the ships began launching helicopters in three waves that deployed the 360-man Marine ground security force to embassy grounds in Phnom Penh. In an orderly fashion, the 276 evacuees, including US Ambassador John Gunther Dean and members of his staff, the acting president of Cambodia, senior Cambodian government leaders and their families, and journalists boarded the waiting Marine helicopters. A little after noon, all helicopters, evacuees, and military personnel were safely on board the ships of the amphibious group. The Navy-Marine Corps team executed the mission without the loss of life.

With little time to spare, Steele prepared for an even greater challenge: the evacuation from the Republic of Vietnam. The Seventh Fleet commander had already deployed MSC vessels off Vung Tau southeast of Saigon and reinforced them with Marine security detachments. Sailors and Marines loaded the ships with food, water, and medicine. Also concentrated at Vung Tau, under Commander Task Force 76, Rear Admiral Donald Whitmire, were command ship *Blue Ridge* (LCC-19) and fourteen amphibious ships. Aircraft carriers *Hancock* and *Midway*, embarking Navy, Marine, and Air Force helicopters, joined the flotilla, as did the Seventh Fleet flagship *Oklahoma City* and eight destroyer types. The carriers *Enterprise* and *Coral Sea* steamed over the horizon to provide air cover for the operation. The 9th Marine Amphibious Brigade, slated to carry out the evacuation, consisted of three battalion landing teams and four helicopter squadrons.

South Vietnamese troops fighting to defend the approaches to Saigon finally collapsed on 21 April, and South Vietnamese President Thieu resigned his office. On the 29th, Vietnamese communist forces surrounding Saigon began infiltrating the city. At that point, Ford ordered the evacuation of Saigon—Operation Frequent Wind. Rear Admiral Whitmire began executing the evacuation plan as soon as he received the order at 1108 local time on 29 April. At 1244, *Hancock* launched the first wave of helicopters that headed for the primary landing zone in the US Defense Attaché Office (DAO) compound in Saigon. There, the 2nd Battalion, 4th Marines established a defensive perimeter and Task Force 76 helicopters began lifting out American, Vietnamese, and third-country nationals. Earlier, enemy shelling of the compound killed two Marines. During the operation, two helicopters and their crews were lost at sea. By 2100, the evacuation force had transported from the site 5,000 evacuees and the Marine security force.

Pandemonium ruled at the US Embassy. Many desperate evacuees pushed against the Marine security force and tried to climb over the perimeter fence to board departing aircraft. Marine and Air Force helicopters flew all night, sometimes dodging fire from the ground to transport evacuees from the dangerous landing zones. By 0500 on 30 April,

US Ambassador Graham Martin and the last of thousands of evacuees had been rescued from the closing enemy army. By the time North Vietnamese tanks smashed down the gates to the Presidential Palace, Task Force 76 had rescued more than 7,000 Americans and Vietnamese.

During the evacuation, not only US but South Vietnamese helicopters and even fixed-wing aircraft loaded with refugees headed for the flotilla offshore. Task force ships recovered forty-one Vietnamese aircraft, while American Sailors pushed another fifty-four over the side to make room on deck. Navy small craft worked to rescue Vietnamese military personnel and civilian refugees who bailed out of aircraft that ditched alongside the evacuation ships. Simultaneously with the US-led evacuation operation, an array of junks, sampans, and other vessels fully loaded with people headed for the American fleet. MSC tugs pulling barges brought more refugees from Saigon port down the Long Tau River and out to the ships offshore. There, American sailors helped the evacuees to board and after a check for weapons provided them with food, water, and medical care. The Seventh Fleet units eventually transferred most of the Vietnamese refugees they had embarked to the MSC ships. Another flotilla, this one consisting of twenty-six Vietnam Navy warships and support vessels loaded with 30,000 sailors and their families, gathered off the southern coast of the Mekong Delta.

Task Force 76 and the MSC ships steamed from the coast of South Vietnam on the afternoon of 30 April, but for the next day and night continued to pick up refugees fleeing in sometimes unseaworthy vessels. At dusk on 2 May, the amphibious task force, carrying 6,000 passengers; the MSC flotilla with 44,000 refugees; and the Vietnam Navy group set sail for reception centers in the Philippines and Guam.

By 13 May, the refugee camp on Guam accommodated 50,430 refugees. The US government, however, regarded Guam only as a way station. The final destination for most of the refugees was the continental United States. The defense department opened many bases to accommodate the human tide. Retired Admiral Zumwalt was representative of the many Americans who literally opened their homes to the refugees from Southeast Asia once they had passed through reception centers nationwide. The admiral invited the nephew of Chung Tan Cang, a former VNN chief of naval operations, and his family to stay in the Zumwalt home and helped them find permanent shelter and employment in the United States. Bud Zumwalt worked tirelessly during the decade after the war to convince the authorities in Hanoi to release from a "reeducation" camp his fellow naval officer and close friend, Tran Van Chon.

The admiral was sincere in his lifelong compassion for the Vietnamese and American veterans of the war. He lent significant support to the establishment and development of the Vietnam Archive at Texas Tech University and spoke frequently at conferences there long after the conflict. He was even more vital to the education of the American public about the serious health risks incurred by those soldiers, sailors, airmen, Marines, and coastguardsmen exposed to Agent Orange. The admiral was convinced that his son Elmo's contact with the sprayed toxin in the Mekong Delta had led to his death. Zumwalt also worked to provide prostheses and wheelchairs to those needing them in post–war Vietnam, founded The Marrow Foundation (now The Match Foundation), and worked with President Bill Clinton to pass the Chemical Weapons Convention.[102]

HOLLOWAY AND POST-VIETNAM CRISES IN ASIA

Even after the evacuations from Phnom Penh and Saigon, events in Southeast Asia continued to demand the attention of naval leaders. Jim Holloway believed his duty on the JCS to be his primary responsibility and his leadership of the Navy of secondary importance.[103] Indeed, Harry Train considered Holloway, unlike Moorer and Zumwalt, "enthusiastically a participant in JCS matters."[104]

Holloway gave full attention to his JCS responsibilities when communist Khmer Rouge forces seized US container ship SS *Mayaguez* and her crew off Cambodia on 12 May 1975.[105] Working with his National Security Council, President Ford kept a tight rein on the decision-making process throughout the 12–15 May crisis. The president made the major decisions, although he sought advice from Secretary of State Kissinger, Secretary of Defense Schlesinger, Deputy National Security Advisor Brent Scowcroft, Vice President Nelson Rockefeller, and Air Force General David C. Jones, who acted for the JCS chairman, Air Force General Brown, the latter out of the country for most of the period.[106]

Ford was especially dissatisfied with the support he received from Schlesinger, later firing him for what he considered the defense secretary's failure to execute the president's directives in a complete and timely fashion. He even determined that Schlesinger had been insubordinate. After one NSC meeting, Ford exclaimed, "I am disturbed at the lack of carrying out orders. I can give all the orders, but if they [defense department] don't carry them out—." He added, "I was mad yesterday."[107] Schlesinger, however, can be credited with slowing the president's and Kissinger's push for quick and potentially heavy-handed military action against the Khmer Rouge for their seizure of *Mayaguez* and her crew. Early in the crisis, the White House considered sinking Cambodian vessels that might have held the ship's crewmen on board. Ford and other principals were also unimpressed with General Jones's contribution to crisis management. At one point, Kissinger, who said he had no expertise in military matters, asked for Jones's recommendations, which Kissinger did not think were forthcoming. Holloway was similarly dissatisfied with Jones and like Zumwalt not above character assassination; he later remembered that "the guy was an idiot. I mean he really was."[108]

Jim Holloway joined the management team for the last of four NSC sessions during the crisis. In that meeting, he answered naval-related questions and departed to convey the president's decisions to the command centers. Hence, he played an important if decidedly secondary role in the planning and execution of the military operations to resolve the crisis. Schlesinger, Holloway, and Admiral Train's Joint Staff worked to organize the military reaction. CINCPAC Admiral Noel Gayler, in Washington on other business, also was a participant in the planning process.[109] These leaders in Washington persuaded the president that bombing the airfield at Kompong Som with planes from aircraft carrier *Coral Sea*, rather than B-52 bombers, would have the greatest effect on Khmer Rouge perceptions of US resolve without inflaming the situation through overkill. Moreover, Schlesinger, following the advice of JCS chairman Brown, by then returned to Washington, redirected the last of four planned carrier strikes against Kompong Som to close air support of the embattled Marines on Koh Tang, an island where the Americans thought the Khmer Rouge were holding the *Mayaguez* crewmen. Unfortunately for Schlesinger, the president believed he had not authorized that changed mission.[110]

The military action unfolded on 15 May. Destroyer escort *Harold E. Holt* (DE-1074) intercepted *Mayaguez* and a boarding party of Marines and sailors recaptured the ship, which the Khmer Rouge had abandoned earlier. Some of Ford's civilian and military advisors, despite the lack of solid information on the enemy's strength on Koh Tang, had pressed for swift action to liberate the *Mayaguez* crew. In fact, the mariners had been held briefly ashore in Cambodia by their captors and then put on a boat and released in the Gulf of Thailand. The National Security Council did not seriously pursue a diplomatic solution, and as one source concluded, Secretary of State Kissinger "was the biggest advocate for the use of force."[111] Holloway related that during the *Mayaguez* affair, he had "very good rapport with Kissinger" and when the admiral was exiting a meeting of the National Security Council, Kissinger suggested the need to "bomb those God damn bums back into the stone age!"[112]

Air Force Lieutenant General John J. Burns, in charge of the operation, deployed from Thailand a contingent of assault helicopters and Marines. Guided missile destroyer *Henry B. Wilson* (DDG-7) also closed on Koh Tang. Complicated command-and-control measures, faulty intelligence, interservice differences, and other factors spelled trouble for the assault force.[113] A hail of enemy ground fire laced the helicopter landing force, destroying three of the aircraft and pinning down the Marine troops ashore. Gunfire support by *Henry B. Wilson* and combat aircraft prevented the enemy from overrunning the landing force, which was then extracted. The operation had been costly, with the death or wounding of seventy servicemen and the destruction or severe damaging of most of the helicopters involved. Disaster was only narrowly averted.[114]

The *Mayaguez* operation demonstrated that even in the wake of the Vietnam disaster, the United States was still ready and able to take decisive military action to support its global interests. Indeed, deterring potential North Korean aggression had been a major factor in the administration's swift military action to recover *Mayaguez* and her crew. Scowcroft later commented that the administration's focus at that time was not Southeast Asia but Korea.[115]

Holloway further burnished his crisis management credentials in August 1976 when North Korean soldiers brutally murdered two US Army officers who had been involved in pruning a tree in the demilitarized zone (DMZ) between North and South Korea. Kim Il-sung's government was well aware that Washington had not retaliated when North Korean forces seized the US intelligence ship *Pueblo* (AGER-2) and crew and shot down a Navy EC-121 patrol plane during the Vietnam War. Nor had Washington responded with force to Hanoi's invasion of South Vietnam in 1975. One may speculate that the North Korean leader believed that there would be no US retaliation for the unprovoked murders in the DMZ, but this time they had misjudged their adversary. President Ford was determined to make a strong response.

Secretary of State Kissinger, with memories of the US defeat in Vietnam still fresh, warned of the danger of inaction. He concluded that if the United States did not act, the North Koreans "will think of us as the paper tigers of Saigon." He added, "We have to make it clear that we will not be pushed around and that we are not afraid of the North Koreans." He predicted that "if we let this incident go then there will be other incidents."[116] He championed an immediate and robust military response to the aggressive North Korean action. The secretary of state, in words reminiscent of Nixon's approach to Hanoi, observed that "it will be useful for us to generate enough activity so that the North Koreans begin to wonder what those crazy American bastards are doing or are capable of doing in this election year."[117]

Although he was in Kansas City for the Republican National Convention, Ford called for an 18 August meeting of the Washington Special Action Group (WSAG). The group, chaired in the nation's capital by Kissinger, included CIA director George H. W. Bush, deputy national security advisor Scowcroft, the State Department's Philip Habib, and Jim Holloway, acting chairman of the JCS. Before attending the meeting, the admiral briefed the Joint Chiefs on the situation and raised the defense condition (DEFCON) in the Pacific from 5 to 3 and worldwide to DEFCON 4. He also gained the approval of deputy defense secretary Clements, despite his and Habib's fear of provoking Pyongyang, to direct the deployment of relevant US forces to the crisis area.[118] CINCPAC dispatched the Seventh Fleet's *Midway* carrier task force into the Sea of Japan ready to launch strikes against North Korea. Admiral Gayler also deployed B-52s in proximity to North Korean air space as a visible deterrent and dispatched Air Force tactical aircraft to South Korean airfields.

Army General Richard Stilwell, commander of United Nations and US forces in Korea, also raised the DEFCON in Korea to 3 and readied allied infantry divisions for action. According to Major General John Singlaub, the chief of staff of US Forces, Korea, "nuclear and conventional artillery and missiles . . . were carried forward by road and helicopter to prepared concrete bunkers." Stilwell later observed that "it was my estimate, shared by many of the staff, that the operation stood a fifty-fifty chance of starting a war."[119] Jim Holloway considered Stilwell a "tough, combat-hardened army general whom I personally knew and professionally admired."[120] With the Vietnam War finally over, both military leaders understood that the United States had strong forces available in Asia for military action. They also recognized that world opinion was solidly against North Korea for its government-sanctioned killings. Holloway and Stilwell considered it vital to demonstrate to Kim that the United States would not tolerate such hostile actions by his soldiers.

Clements and Habib, however, continued to fear that the proposed action was too "risky." Clements told Holloway, "You're going to start World War III."[121] At the 19 August WSAG meeting, Clements suggested that the plan to send a small force of US and South Korean soldiers into the contested area to cut down the tree "nonsense." He added, "It will lead to a confrontation and may get a bunch of [soldiers] killed. What for? A tree? . . . Why risk a bunch of people for a tree? I don't like it at all. It makes no sense."[122] Jim Holloway later suggested that "we could not afford to lose this confrontation since our reputation and our credibility depended upon our being resolute and unafraid to assert our rights." Finally, Kissinger informed Holloway that he would recommend to the president that he send US and South Korean troops into the DMZ to cut down the relevant tree.[123] Shortly after being contacted, Ford ordered the measure.

On 21 August 1976, helicopter gunships and engineers armed with chain saws and axes and defended by infantrymen skilled in martial arts entered the DMZ and reduced the tree to a stump. Faced with the resolve of the United States and the Republic of Korea, the North Koreans did nothing to bring on an armed conflict. Indeed, the only action taken by Kim Il-sung was to release a personal statement expressing regret that "an incident occurred in the Joint Security Area." The crisis ended almost as quickly as it had begun.

IN THE COCKPIT

Jim Holloway became the Chief of Naval Operations at a time when the US Navy continued to suffer from the consequences of the war and his predecessor's missteps. Congress, reflecting the nation's opposition to further overseas commitments, starved the Navy of the new ships, aircraft, and weapons it needed to counter a surging Soviet Navy. Anti-military and antiestablishment sentiment, racial conflict, drug abuse, and a host of other societal ills continued to trouble the Navy's personnel base. Bud Zumwalt's social reforms did set the Navy on the right course to eliminate racial and gender discrimination and to improve sailors' quality of service. Holloway recognized, however, that Zumwalt's corrective measures, well-meaning but too often haphazardly administered, had seriously unsettled the service and disoriented leaders and sailors of all ranks.

Jim Holloway's primary accomplishment as CNO was to bring stability to the Navy. He took a measured, common sense approach that reemphasized tradition, experience, and practicality. As an example, while realizing that many sailors wanted to reverse Zumwalt's uniform changes, Holloway delayed that action to limit related costs. He dropped some of Zumwalt's personnel programs, kept others that worked, and introduced his own more mature measures, including the Navy Affirmative Action Program. He accommodated some of the younger generation's desires for free expression but insisted on greater discipline and order in shipboard life. He endorsed the promotion of Blacks to flag rank and the attendance of women at the Naval Academy and opened up many more aviation and other billets to women. Eschewing parochialism, he enabled surface warfare officers and submariners to lead naval aviation commands.

What set Jim Holloway apart from his predecessor was his extraordinary ability to win and keep allies who could help rebuild and strengthen the Navy of the future. His nonconfrontational, facts-based, and civil approach charmed President Ford, Kissinger, successive secretaries of defense and secretaries of the Navy, key members of Congress, the ever-powerful Admiral Rickover, many fellow flag officers, MCPON Walker, and legions of sailors. At the same time, he stood up to many of those same individuals who opposed his recommendations for improving the service. He had a running fight with President Carter over new nuclear-powered carriers; with Rickover over nuclear power for every ship in the fleet; and with Kissinger over the terms of the SALT treaty.

He understood intrinsically that Carter's "raise the drawbridge" defensive strategy and Zumwalt's associated High-Low Mix would not work in the face of the Soviet Union's global threat. Instead, he reaffirmed the central role of America's aircraft carriers and battle fleets based in Europe and Asia in deterring Soviet aggression. He promoted Tom Hayward's vision of a two-ocean counter to Soviet military power. Holloway's NWP-1 and Sea Plan 2000, while opposed by the Carter administration, solidified thinking in strategic circles about the optimum naval approach to the Soviet Union. These ideas formed the core of the Reagan administration's 600-ship Navy and the Maritime Strategy of the 1980s that witnessed the demise of the Soviet Union and the end of the Cold War.

Holloway's connection to the Vietnam War extended from 1965, when he led carrier *Enterprise* into battle, to 1975 when as a member of the Joint Chiefs of Staff he helped manage the US withdrawal from Cambodia and South Vietnam. Moreover, he helped reaffirm America's postwar commitment to its Asian allies in the *Mayaguez* and Korean axe murder crises. In short, James Holloway, who passed away at the age of 97 on 26 November 2019, exhibited the vision, balance, and professionalism characteristic of a true naval leader.

CHAPTER 13

CONCLUSION

The Vietnam War and the challenges of the era seriously tested the leadership skills of admirals Harry D. Felt, U. S. G. Sharp, Thomas H. Moorer, Elmo R. Zumwalt Jr., and James L. Holloway III. They were closely associated with the conflict from beginning to end and with its consequences. Their greatest hurdle was to adapt their combat and command experiences and strategic understanding to the demands of civilian leaders convinced of their own geopolitical wisdom and ability to manage conflict from afar. Presidents Kennedy, Johnson, Nixon, and Ford and their top civilian officials largely shaped the strategic, operational, and often tactical direction of the war. Changes in the national security establishment and advances in communications greatly enhanced their capability to do so. After passage of the Department of Defense Reorganization Act of 1958, the service chiefs in Washington lost the ability to deploy combat forces and the legislation limited the authority of the Joint Chiefs of Staff. At the same time, it significantly enhanced the power of the secretary of defense, his civilian staff, and the JCS chairman to deal directly with CINCPAC and the other global combatant commanders.

As always, personalities played a major role in the interaction of these leaders. Kennedy, Johnson, and to some extent Nixon and Ford thought that their military subordinates lacked a broad, sophisticated understanding of the intricacies of US national security and foreign policy. Kennedy and Johnson and Secretary of Defense McNamara routinely ignored or discounted the advice provided them by the JCS and bypassed their commander of the Pacific theater. Nixon had greater faith in the advice of his favored military subordinate, Tom Moorer, but had little use for Bud Zumwalt and the other Joint Chiefs. President Ford was especially displeased with the advice he received from his Defense Department advisors during the postwar *Mayaguez* crisis. He did, however, credit Jim Holloway's contribution as acting JCS chairman during the axe murder incident of 1976.

Determined to serve their civilian superiors loyally, the five officers adapted to the new political-military dynamic. Don Felt, Oley Sharp, and Tom Moorer fully embraced the limited war, flexible response, and graduated escalation approaches and helped develop associated military campaign plans. Felt ably handled the crises in Laos and championed counterinsurgency as the Kennedy administration's solution to the conflict in South Vietnam. He delayed as long as he could the introduction there of US regular forces. He understood the potential pitfalls of that commitment ashore. In 1964 and early 1965, Sharp had some influence in crafting the escalatory Rolling Thunder bombing campaign against North Vietnam. He and Moorer pushed for air strikes and other measures to deter Hanoi from its aggressive behavior in Indochina. Despite later assertions to the contrary, these officers, like their civilian superiors in Washington, did not call for an invasion or complete destruction of North Vietnam's economy or the overthrow of its communist government. They adhered closely to President Johnson's policies.

The naval leaders shared the fairly universal misunderstanding of those in the US national security establishment that American military power would overwhelm North Vietnam despite whatever support that nation might get from its Chinese and Soviet allies. When that early appraisal proved false, Johnson and McNamara retreated to military half-measures against Hanoi and pushed the deployment of ground, air, and naval forces to South Vietnam. The primary US objective then became preventing the defeat of the Saigon government and its armed forces rather than victory. Felt, Sharp, and Moorer helped craft and execute those decisions. Contrary to their postwar assertions, they too came to understand that Beijing and possibly Moscow would oppose with force a US attempt to defeat their Marxist-Leninist ally.

The five admirals experienced varying degrees of success dealing with their civilian superiors and executing Washington's plans and policies. Don Felt proved to be an influential figure with regard to the early crises in Laos and the first stages of the Kennedy administration's counterinsurgency approach in South Vietnam. By the time he retired in mid-1964, however, the admiral had become completely isolated from the Johnson administration's decision-making process. Johnson and McNamara routinely ignored Felt to deal directly with Westmoreland. In the end, the commander in chief of the Pacific Command was totally out of touch with the true situation in South Vietnam. Dispirited and disillusioned by the turn of events at the end of his tour, Harry D. Felt headed for home and retirement, having been unable to avert the coming catastrophe in Southeast Asia.

Oley Sharp, his successor, then took up the challenge of executing the Johnson administration's war effort. That was no easy task since the president, his secretary of defense, and their civilian advisors badly handled their wartime responsibilities. Johnson placed inordinate faith in the diplomatic process to resolve the conflict when the situation on the battlefields of Indochina hardly warranted it. Johnson's reluctant decision-making with regard to Vietnam, micromanagement of military operations, and strong focus on US domestic affairs seriously impaired his wartime leadership. McNamara's supersized ego mixed with contempt for military experience and advice further troubled the war effort. These leaders did serious damage to the civil-military relationship.

In many ways, Oley Sharp proved to be an able theater commander. He consistently affirmed his responsibility for the defense of US interests and allies in the vast Pacific in the face of the military threat from the Sino-Soviet bloc. He wisely maintained central control of the air and naval forces operating against North Vietnam, although he gave General Westmoreland great latitude in the conduct of operations in and around South Vietnam. When appropriate to the situation, Sharp supported the specific needs of the Air Force, Marine Corps, and Army commands fighting in Vietnam.

Sharp's main objective, however, was to carry out a successful air war in North Vietnam and Laos. As a commander with the responsibility for the lives of his men and America's military resources, he rightly condemned Washington's overly restrictive rules of engagement and the misuse of air power during Rolling Thunder. But Sharp erred in failing to understand the commander in chief's determination to avoid overt Chinese or Soviet military intervention, hopes for a negotiated settlement, and desire not to inflame international and domestic opinion. It was admirable for Sharp to call attention to the failings of the campaign, but he did so in such a persistent and caustic manner that it negated whatever influence he had with the administration.

By the time he retired in mid-1968, Sharp—like Felt—was being bypassed by his civilian superiors and excluded from the strategy and policy-making process. Moreover, like Felt he had lost touch with the reality of the situation in Indochina, in the United States, and on the international scene. It was patently clear by then that the bombing campaign in North Vietnam and the aerial interdiction effort in Laos had failed to break Hanoi's will or prevent the enemy's reinforcement and resupply of communist forces throughout the region. Moreover, he refused to acknowledge that millions of Americans and others then doubted the possibility of a US victory and clamored for an end to the long, bloody conflict.

As the war reached a crescendo in 1967, Tom Moorer, Jim Holloway, and Bud Zumwalt applied their considerable leadership skills in Washington to support the war effort. As CNO after August 1967, Moorer emphasized providing the Navy with the sailors and resources it needed to prosecute the war, since his service on the Joint Chiefs did not allow much impact on Vietnam decision-making. Holloway, following his two combat tours on Yankee Station, applied himself to improving carrier safety and helping ensure a solid future for naval aviation. Zumwalt provided his mentor Paul Nitze with informed military advice on the Navy and helped McNamara improve the Pentagon's budgetary system. Moorer and Holloway worked at overcoming the McNamara-inspired civil-military divide, and they became especially adept at winning support for Navy programs from members of Congress and the administration.

By 1968, it was clear that there would be no victory for the United States in the Vietnam War. The Tet Offensive and subsequent attacks convinced many Americans, including the president, that his administration's policies had failed to achieve even its limited objectives. At the end of March, Johnson halted the bombing campaign in most of North Vietnam, called for negotiations with Hanoi, and announced his withdrawal from politics. In November, Americans elected Richard M. Nixon to the presidency based on his pledge to take a different approach to the conflict. He promised to withdraw American troops from the war and better prepare the South Vietnamese armed forces to defend their country. Bud Zumwalt, Jim Holloway, and Tom Moorer, each in his own way, took on board that new strategic appreciation and focused on how they would exercise their leadership to implement it.

After he took the helm as Commander Naval Forces, Vietnam, in September 1968, Zumwalt became the Navy's most well-known and successful combat leader of the war. Despite his conviction that the war ashore in South Vietnam had been ill-advised from the start, Zumwalt set out to execute the post–Tet SEALORDS campaign and faithfully execute the administration's Vietnamization program. As a result of his innovative and energetic leadership, strong support from General Abrams and supporters in Washington, increased material resources, the enemy's temporarily dire situation, and the changing character of the war, Naval Forces, Vietnam, and the Vietnam Navy made great gains on the battlefield during his near two-year tour. Zumwalt inspired the men in his command with his physical courage, passion for their well-being, and dynamic leadership. He made the Navy a vital component of the allied war effort during the post–Tet years. ACTOV, the Navy's Vietnamization program, resulted in a Vietnam Navy of 42,000 sailors and 1,500 naval vessels. In the process, Zumwalt enthusiastically followed the lead of Secretary of Defense Laird and Abrams, both of whom sang his praises, as did Secretary of the Navy Chafee.

Nonetheless, the success of both SEALORDS and ACTOV proved ephemeral. Following Zumwalt's departure to Washington, Vietnamization suffered setbacks in the Mekong Delta and in Laos. ACTOV had been implemented too hastily and with insufficient thought given to future resource support. The latter years of the war found the VNN barely able to operate the naval vessels, logistics establishment, and equipment it had been provided during Zumwalt's tenure and afterward. Finally, the Vietnam Navy could do little to prevent Hanoi's victory in 1975, especially since the conflict had become a ground battle for control of the country far from the river and canal-laced Mekong Delta.

Bud Zumwalt was an outstanding combat leader, although a lot of what we have learned about his performance comes from his own pen. His *On Watch*, published shortly after the war as a political manifesto, and the follow-on *My Father, My Son* established them as the starting point for the study and interpretation of the in-country naval war. Having early seized the literary high ground, Zumwalt amplified his successes and denigrated those who doubted his vision. The admiral was a master of self-promotion throughout his career. More contemporary scholarship on the war has called into question his accomplishments in Vietnam.

Jim Holloway's signal achievement during the Nixon administration was to lead the Seventh Fleet in its most successful air and sea campaign of the Vietnam War. His six-carrier, multi-surface warship force employed America's most advanced and combat-tested aircraft, weapon systems, and equipment in a hard-hitting assault on North Vietnam's air defenses and war-related facilities during 1972. The sailors of his fleet, many of whom had honed their skills after years of combat in Southeast Asia, turned in a thoroughly professional performance. The operations mounted by Holloway's command, including the Linebacker strikes and the mining of Haiphong, along with the Air Force B-52 and tactical air attacks, were instrumental in prompting Hanoi to sign the Paris Agreement and securing the repatriation of American POWs. The fleet's End Sweep mine clearance operation enhanced Nixon's diplomatic endeavors with regard to Indochina. Holloway was a brave, combat-tested, and successful operational commander.

In the four years after Tom Moorer became Chairman of the Joint Chiefs of Staff, only the second naval officer to hold that billet since the end of World War II, he exploited his considerable leadership skills to ably serve his commander in chief. He became the president's most valued military advisor. He understood Nixon's desire to reaffirm US global power, maintain the independence of the Republic of Vietnam, and bring American troops home. His professional experience in command of the Navy and its regional and numbered fleets significantly enhanced the credibility, if not always the soundness, of his military advice to the president. He proved to be a key figure in the administration's military operations in Cambodia, Laos, and South Vietnam; the mining of North Vietnam's ports; and the Linebacker strikes.

However, like others in the US national security establishment, he put more faith in the Vietnamization program than was warranted. Moorer often mouthed the desire for drastic military action against North Vietnam but, like Nixon and Kissinger, recognized that the objectives of those actions were unachievable. International and domestic realities would not allow it. The admiral understood that like Johnson, Nixon was compelled to adopt military half-measures. Moorer was much more effective as JCS chairman than his predecessor General Wheeler in bridging the gap between civilian leaders and the military establishment, and he strengthened the link between Washington, Pearl Harbor, and Saigon. In short, from July 1970 to July 1974, JCS chairman Tom Moorer served as a dedicated and successful military advisor to the commander in chief during one of the nation's most trying times.[1]

The challenges faced by Bud Zumwalt and Jim Holloway coping with the impact of the war on the US Navy in many ways proved far more difficult to manage than their responsibilities during the conflict. This was a time when the nation and the Navy were confronted with a failed war and a host of social ills that defied easy solution. Zumwalt's seemingly successful operational tour in Vietnam propelled the vice admiral to the top command of the US Navy. While in Vietnam, Zumwalt had employed personal contacts and a friendly press to ensure that top-ranking US national leaders knew of his and his command's accomplishments. His long-time or newly established relationships with the secretary of defense, the secretary of the Navy, and other prominent civilian decision-makers in the government helped pave the way. Laird, Chafee, and Nitze were especially keen on Zumwalt's image as a sailor's admiral with liberal social views.

Zumwalt's revolutionary personnel reforms, stimulated by the Vietnam War and the social turmoil in American society, improved the Navy's treatment of its minority and other sailors and the quality of their service. All ranks, but especially women and African Americans, found greater opportunities for promotion and career enhancement. Not all of Zumwalt's programs succeeded, but his personnel reform campaign strongly influenced the way the Navy would respond in future to its sailors' demand for dignity and equality. John Lehman observed that Bud Zumwalt and his successor Jim Holloway "transformed the attitudes and practices within the navy [and] moved dramatically and at great political expense to themselves to rid the navy of the ingrained practices that were inherently prejudicial to minorities." The former Navy secretary asserted that the Navy he inherited in 1981 "had as healthy racial attitudes as any organization in the United States."[2] In his eulogy of Zumwalt in 2000, President Bill Clinton observed that the admiral "worked in the face of wilting criticism and a highly resistant institutional culture to make the Navy do the right thing and make the Navy one of the most colorblind institutions in our entire nation." He added that Zumwalt "had the vision to see a great future for the Navy" and that "the changes he brought about [would] continue to shape the character and culture of our Navy for a long time in the 21st century."[3]

Zumwalt's successors eliminated or revised a number of his personnel initiatives, but they continued with their own programs to further his goal of ridding the service of discriminatory policies and practices. While not all of Zumwalt's personnel actions succeeded, they must be understood in the context of the times. He had to lead the Navy when it was still fighting a war in Southeast Asia, supporting US interests all around the world, operating with battered ships and aircraft, and enduring deep budget cuts, all in the face of surging Soviet naval power. A host of other problems at home and in Vietnam affected all American institutions, including the Navy.

On the negative side, Bud Zumwalt's method of operations first witnessed in Vietnam often caused him difficulties. His ad hoc approach to problem-solving, reliance on a small coterie of old Vietnam hands and junior personnel, adoption of some ill-thought-out ZWIs (Zumwalt's Wild Ideas), and preference for quick fixes confused and troubled many officers and sailors. His Z-Gram method of communication did highlight problems that needed to be addressed Navy-wide, but by skirting the chain of command he needlessly antagonized senior officers and senior enlisted personnel.

His goal of improving the balance between the surface navy and the aviation and submarine communities was a worthy one. The cruiser and destroyermen deserved more attention, and they got it during Zumwalt's tenure. But the measures he took to implement that vision revealed the favoritism of his own surface ship community over the others. While Bud Zumwalt did not consider his lack of fleet command a drawback, that dearth of experience was a major deficiency. His promotion of junior officers to billets of greater responsibility and creation of the "Mod Squad" demonstrated that he considered youthful energy and innovation more relevant than many years of operational experience. Zumwalt changed the assignment, promotion, and retirement of flag officers to cull the ranks of experienced but older flag officers in favor of less experienced but more youthful mid-level officers.[4]

Despite Bud Zumwalt's exceptional service in South Vietnam, his impact as Chief of Naval Operations and as a member of the Joint Chiefs on the development and execution of US strategy for the war proved nil. Nixon, working with Henry Kissinger and Tom Moorer, essentially ran the war from the White House. Only when it suited him did the JCS chairman inform the service chiefs of planned operations, and then often after the fact. Zumwalt's isolation from Vietnam-related decision-making was an irritant, but the war had never been the prime focus of his service in the Navy. His two-year stint in Southeast Asia was an interlude. On the other hand, since the admiral's early and close association with Paul Nitze, Bud Zumwalt had considered himself an expert on nuclear weapons and the global competition with the Soviet Union. What especially rankled him were Nixon's and Kissinger's actions to exclude him from strategic arms control deliberations and their determination to limit the confrontation with the USSR through their détente policy, which he opposed.

Even if the constraints of the national security bureaucracy hadn't prevented Bud Zumwalt from making a great impact on the main issues of the day, the admiral's outspoken and abrasive approach to his leadership responsibilities surely would have. Zumwalt not only failed to remove Rickover from office but in his feud with the influential leader he antagonized a host of powerful members of Congress and Navy flag officers who supported nuclear propulsion for warships. Nixon blamed Zumwalt for the Navy's racial disturbances and for introducing what the president considered radical social experimentation. Zumwalt's public utterances and repeated testimony before Congress that the Soviet Navy would win a war at sea against the US Navy further estranged him from his commander in chief.

Kissinger shared his boss's view that Zumwalt was not a team player. The national security advisor, himself a master of behind-the-scenes intrigue and bureaucratic secrecy, took personal umbrage at Zumwalt's similar actions. The latter's revolutionary measures to improve the lot of America's sailors marked him as one of the nation's most influential naval leaders of the twentieth century. But his heated public feuds with the White House, members of Congress, key naval officers, and various communities in the Navy detracted from that legacy. One questions a recent conclusion that Zumwalt's championship of change was "something he did better than any other flag officer in the Navy's history."[5]

When Zumwalt retired in 1974, he was not highly regarded by many senior and mid-level officers of the Navy. By the time of his death in January 2000, however, he had become a legend. In retirement, he had made frequent public appearances at home and abroad and continued to weigh in on defense and nuclear issues. He was a founding member, along with Tom Moorer, of the conservative and pro-defense Committee on the Present Danger. Other members included Nitze, George Shultz, and Ronald Reagan. In December 1975, Zumwalt pressed his case with President Ford on the SALT negotiations. In December 1978, he blamed President Carter for weakening the US military's posture in the face of the Soviet challenge.[6]

Bud Zumwalt conducted a highly publicized post-retirement run for office in Virginia on the Democratic Party ticket that emphasized his time as CNO. He got sidetracked, however, by his personal obsession with Henry Kissinger. The admiral even believed that the secretary of state was bugging his home and tape-recording his phone calls. Another negative aspect of the campaign was the admiral's impatience to proceed. Instead of waiting for the election of 1978 against a weak opponent, Zumwalt decided to run in 1976 against Senator Robert Byrd, a powerful figure on the national and Virginia stages and heir to a decades-old political dynasty. Not for the first time, Zumwalt made a petty response to a Byrd comment on the campaign trail by alluding to the senator's Revolutionary War ancestor as a "Tory." Byrd trounced the admiral that November by a margin of 57 to 38 percent.[7]

Nonetheless, that campaign and the book *On Watch* published to promote that run for office, his long-time championship of Vietnam veterans, and the heartrending story of his son Elmo's death from Agent Orange exposure kept him in the public eye throughout the late twentieth century. President Clinton's eulogy for the admiral at the Naval Academy drew national interest. Obituaries and op-ed pieces in *The Washington Post* and *The New York Times* further burnished Zumwalt's image. On the Fourth of July in 2000, the Navy announced plans to build a new, revolutionary class of guided missile destroyers that would bear the name of the illustrious naval leader. By 2012 and the publication of Larry Berman's hagiographic tome *Zumwalt*, the admiral's star had risen to new heights. As his biographer gushed, "He was the iconoclastic admiral who brought a navy drifting toward the shoals back into the channel of the twentieth century and prepared it for the new millennium." He was like "Zorro, fighting for the rights of oppressed navy men and women."[8] Zumwalt would have been pleased with that characterization.

While certainly less well known than Bud Zumwalt, Jim Holloway, the Chief of Naval Operations from 1974 to 1978, in many ways proved to be a more effective and successful leader of the Navy. Like Zumwalt, Holloway had to contend with the deleterious impact of the war on the naval service. Throughout his term the American people, their representatives in Congress, and the Carter administration failed to adequately resource the Navy even though it had a global presence and vital responsibilities at the height of the Cold War. Defense budget outlays proved insufficient for the replacement, maintenance, and repair of obsolete ships or the enlistment and retention of qualified sailors.

Despite these impediments, Jim Holloway reaffirmed the importance of strengthening the fleet for its missions, including the projection of naval power ashore. He produced Naval Warfare Publication 1 (NWP-1) and oversaw Seaplan 2000 that became building blocks for the Reagan/Lehman 600-ship Navy and the Maritime Strategy of the 1980s. Holloway understood that while the Soviet Navy posed a serious threat to the US Navy, the professional skill of America's leaders and sailors and technologically advanced air, surface, and submarine forces would win in a fight for control of the sea with the Soviet Navy. Holloway reaffirmed the understanding that the full-sized aircraft carrier was the fleet's capital ship. With the help of influential legislators, he eroded the opposition of President Carter to the construction of new nuclear-powered carriers. He improved the combat power and versatility of the service by instituting the Fleet Battle Force concept and championed Rickover's nuclear-powered attack and ballistic missile submarines, the F-14 Tomcat fighter, and the Aegis battle management system. When Jim Holloway acted in his capacity as a member of the JCS or as acting chairman, he demonstrated superior leadership at the highest levels of the military. He served as an advisor to President Gerald Ford during the evacuations from Cambodia and South Vietnam in 1975, the *Mayaguez* crisis, and the axe murder episode on the Korean peninsula in 1976.

One of Holloway's most significant accomplishments was to bring stability to a Navy reeling from the effects of the war and adjusting to Admiral Zumwalt's progressive social programs. Holloway recognized that the Navy for far too long had discriminated against Black, female, and other minority sailors and turned a blind eye to the quality of service of all ranks. He applauded Zumwalt's revolutionary programs to right those wrongs and to convince America's youth that the Navy welcomed their enlistment and retention in the service. Indeed, Holloway continued many of those efforts with his Navy Affirmative Action Plan and by opening naval aviation and many more operational billets afloat and ashore to women. Following through on Zumwalt's organizational balancing efforts, Holloway broadened the opportunities for surface warfare and submarine officers on board the fleet's aircraft carriers.

Holloway, however, did not applaud all of Zumwalt's social programs nor the way in which many of them were designed and administered. He considered many projects as not well thought out and hastily adopted. He came to believe that the functioning of the chain of command, the morale of mid-level officers and senior enlisted personnel, shipboard discipline and upkeep, the value of experience in command, and personal grooming had suffered under his predecessor. Holloway was especially taken aback by what he considered Zumwalt's pandering to enlisted personnel and the national media to enhance his popularity. Holloway took both immediate and long-term measures to rectify those problems that, by the end of his tour, had borne fruit.

One of Holloway's greatest strengths was his ability to win allies for the programs he considered vital. Like Zumwalt, he was politically savvy. His straightforward, facts-based, and thoroughly considered approach to problem-solving as well as his engaging personality won him many friends and supporters. He avoided antagonizing others and taking hard-edged, abrasive public stands on key issues and displayed a willingness to compromise to accomplish his objectives. He cultivated positive relationships with presidents Nixon and Ford, Scoop Jackson and other key senators, and Moorer, Rickover, and a host of other flag officers and civilian officials, including Schlesinger, Warner, and Middendorf. He generally worked well with Kissinger, who appreciated Holloway's handling of the Seventh Fleet during 1972 and the value of the Navy's carriers in international crises. While Jim Holloway understood that Rickover antagonized legions of people, he knew that the cantankerous but brilliant admiral was the key to America's dominance of the nuclear-power world. Despite significant reservations about some of Zumwalt's social programs, Holloway served his Naval Academy classmate loyally as VCNO. For the rest of Zumwalt's life, the two remained friends.

At the same time, Holloway did not hesitate to mount a vigorous opposition to those individuals who threatened what he considered to be important issues. He fought and won the dispute with Rickover over the issue of nuclear-powered cruisers and destroyers. In the National Security Council, he did not hesitate to oppose President Ford's and Henry Kissinger's positions on issues related to the SALT negotiations. He refused to comply with Deputy Secretary of Defense Clements's demand that he fire Rickover.

Less creditable, Holloway was not above harshly denigrating admirals Anderson and McDonald, Army General David Jones, and others with whom he disagreed or personally disliked. While skillfully exploiting the informational media to achieve professional objectives, he also trumpeted his personal successes and often exaggerated his contribution to mission accomplishment. Holloway's *Aircraft Carriers at War*, while insightful in many ways, should be considered in that light.

Jim Holloway's experience in the Vietnam War was not unlike that of many other leaders of the era. When he brought carrier *Enterprise* to the waters off Vietnam in 1965, he exuded optimism that in short order the military power of the United States would prevail against North Vietnam. He saw it as a righteous fight to hold back global communism and to defend a friendly country under attack. Despite knowing full well that the Rolling Thunder campaign was not succeeding while he served in the Pentagon, he redoubled his efforts to provide the fleet with the best ships and aircraft needed to prosecute the war.

Although dubious of victory, he did not hesitate to carry out the Nixon administration's war aims as commander of the Seventh Fleet in 1972. Like many of his military colleagues, Holloway periodically expressed a desire for an all-out attack against North Vietnam but also like them understood that domestic and international considerations forbade it. By the time of the Paris Agreement, he was tired of the war and wanted the United States out of it as soon as the POWS were repatriated. In the end he regretted that the American people had turned against the war and that the South Vietnamese were not up to the task of preserving their country. Nonetheless, throughout the conflict, Holloway demonstrated the attributes of a superlative wartime commander and top-rank Navy leader.

The naval leaders who commanded and fought in Vietnam exploited that hard-earned experience to end the Cold War on US terms, reassert America's control of the sea, and defeat aggression in the Middle East. Long into their retirements, Felt, Sharp, Moorer, Zumwalt, and Holloway pressed for the modernization and strengthening of the fleet to counter the Soviet Union's military power and global presence.

CNO Tom Hayward, who had flown multiple combat missions over North Vietnam, continued his predecessor's rebuilding efforts. He worked to scrap the old strategy of protecting the sea lines of communication to Europe and the Far East—a defensive approach—in favor of an offensive "Maritime Strategy." He and other naval leaders wanted to exploit the fleet's inherent flexibility and mobility to strike where the enemy was most vulnerable. If war broke out with the Soviet Union, strategists expected the enemy to launch a massive assault in Europe, hoping to win a quick, decisive, and one-front victory against the NATO allies. Hayward and fellow Vietnam veteran Bob Long,

Commander in Chief, Pacific, pushed for the adoption of a strategic approach that would deny the Soviet Union a one-front war. The naval leaders concluded that if the Soviets opened an offensive in Europe, the fleet should attack enemy military concentrations not only from the waters of northeast Asia but also from the Barents, Baltic, and Black Seas.

Vietnam veteran John Lehman understood that one of President Reagan's primary goals was to put military pressure on the Soviet Union. The navy secretary also realized that for the fleet to successfully execute the Maritime Strategy, it needed significant strengthening after the Vietnam drawdown. He led the charge to put to sea a "600-ship Navy." With Reagan's support, Lehman waged and won a national campaign to sell the idea. He missed his target by two dozen ships, but by 1990 the Navy operated a powerful force of fifteen carrier battle groups, four battleship surface action groups, 100 attack submarines, and scores more cruisers, destroyers, frigates, amphibious ships, and auxiliaries. Moreover, with programs to combat drug abuse and racial discrimination registering greater success, sailors once again prized their service and indeed exuded optimism about their future in the Navy.

The Navy's Vietnam veterans also put to sea a fleet possessing the most technologically advanced and combat-ready ships, planes, and weapons. Tom Hayward ensured that the large-deck, 90,000-ton *Nimitz*-class ships would be the only major combatants to slide off the building ways in the 1980s. Provided ample resources by the Reagan administration, the Navy armed the fleet with nuclear and conventionally armed Tomahawk land attack missiles that could be launched from surface ships, submarines, and aircraft. The Navy also put into service advanced versions of the all-weather, day-night A-6 Intruder attack plane, the new F/A-18 Hornet strike fighter, the EA-6B Prowler electronic countermeasures aircraft, and high-speed anti-radiation missiles (HARMs). Anticipating the need to launch amphibious operations on the periphery of the Soviet Union, the Navy commissioned the *Whidbey Island* (LSD-41) and *Wasp* (LHD-1) classes of amphibious ships and landing craft air-cushion vehicles (LCAC). Finally, John Lehman fought for and won the fight to reactivate the four *Iowa*-class battleships with their long-range 16-inch guns and new Tomahawk batteries.

Naval leaders also realized that the deployment of the fleet along the margins of the Soviet Union demanded robust defensive weapons systems. Hence, they integrated into the fleet advanced aircraft like the F-14 Tomcat armed with AIM-54C Phoenix air-to-air missiles capable of destroying attacking aerial forces hundreds of miles from the fleet. With their new SPY-1A phased array and other radars in the 1980s, the Aegis guided missile cruisers served as the battle group's principal antiair warfare ships. The Phalanx close-in weapons system (CIWS) gave the fleet the ability to stop incoming aircraft and missiles with a high volume of fire. To deal with Soviet attack submarines, the fleet deployed the 3,650-ton *Oliver Hazard Perry* (FFG-7)-class guided missile frigate. The ship operated the especially capable SH-60B Seahawk Light Airborne Multipurpose System (LAMPS) helicopters. Also key to the antisubmarine mission was the two-seat, carrier-based, jet-powered S-3 Viking. The plane could launch bombs, naval mines, Harpoon missiles, and torpedoes.

Admiral Holloway exploited his combat and leadership experience during the Vietnam War to improve military readiness in later years. Following the failed US military operation in April 1980 to free fifty-two Americans held hostage by Ayatollah Ruhollah Khomeini's Iranian regime, President Reagan named the admiral to lead an investigation. The resulting Holloway Report determined that poor interservice planning, command and control, and execution doomed the mission. It resulted in major improvements to the planning and conduct of joint operations.

Admiral Bill Crowe, who had served as the senior advisor in the Mekong Delta during the war, significantly influenced postwar developments as Commander in Chief, Pacific, and then as JCS chairman. He reacted with dispatch to reports of serious US military deficiencies during the Grenada and Lebanon crises of the mid-1980s. His advocacy helped prompt Congress's passage of the Goldwater–Nichols Department of Defense Reorganization Act of 1986. That act enhanced the power of the JCS chairman, like that exercised by Tom Moorer and Holloway during and immediately after the war, and further empowered the operational flexibility of the Commander in Chief, Pacific, and the other combatant commanders worldwide. And Goldwater–Nichols, heavily influenced by the Vietnam experience, limited the responsibility of individual military members of the JCS to managing and arming their respective services.

The post–Vietnam rebuilding and reorganization of the military establishment paid dividends when Reagan called on the Navy to uphold US interests in the Persian Gulf during the late 1980s. By 1987, Iran and Iraq had fought a seven-year (and seemingly endless) war. To achieve victory, the armed forces of both nations began to target petroleum storage sites ashore, oil platforms in the Persian Gulf, and international tankers plying their trade. These attacks threatened the US and global economies, heavily dependent on Middle Eastern oil. In January 1987, President Reagan authorized eleven of Kuwait's tankers to fly the American flag and hence entitled them to protection by the US Navy. Remembering the Johnson administration's half-measures approach to the Vietnam War, JCS chairman Crowe and other US leaders deployed a substantial naval force to the gulf to ensure US interests. By the end of 1987, thirteen warships patrolled inside the gulf to carry out the tanker-escort mission, Operation Earnest Will. The Navy also deployed battleship *Missouri* (BB-63) to the Strait of Hormuz. Finally, steaming in the Gulf of Oman as backup for the other contingents was a US carrier battle group.

The seriousness of the threat became clear when an Iraqi Mirage F-1 mistakenly identified US frigate *Stark* (FFG-31) as an Iranian vessel and struck her with two air-to-surface missiles, killing thirty-seven American sailors. It was no accident, however, when Iran sowed mines in the gulf that damaged US-flagged tanker *Bridgeton* and frigate *Samuel B. Roberts* (FFG-58). In Operation Praying Mantis, the US naval forces in the gulf responded by destroying two Iranian-occupied platforms and sinking or damaging half of the ships in the Iranian navy. When guided missile cruiser *Vincennes* (CG-49) accidentally shot down an Iranian airliner on 3 July 1988, the leaders in Tehran realized that they could not accomplish their war aims. On the 18th, Iran accepted a UN cease-fire proposal. Under the direction of Admiral Crowe and other Vietnam veterans, the Navy strengthened by the Reagan buildup brought the conflict in the gulf to a speedy and successful conclusion. US naval forces had accomplished the mission of securing the international tanker route through the gulf.

The experience and wisdom gained by the Vietnam-era leaders truly came to the fore in the Persian Gulf War of 1990–1991. General Colin Powell, chairman of the JCS, General Norman H. Schwarzkopf, Commander in Chief, Central Command, and the other old Vietnam hands followed the "Weinberger Doctrine" first enunciated by Secretary of Defense Caspar Weinberger in 1984. It asserted that in any conflict, the commitment of US troops should be considered only as a last resort;

that any commitment should have the support of Congress and the American people; that US political and military goals should be clearly defined; and that US forces should only be committed to combat with the clear intention to win.

Soon after Saddam Hussein's 150,000 Iraqi troops invaded the neighboring nation of Kuwait on 2 August 1990, President George H. W. Bush launched a diplomatic effort in the United Nations to settle the conflict, gathered an international coalition of thirty-five nations determined to oppose Iraq's aggression, and restricted US objectives to compelling the withdrawal of Saddam Hussein's forces and the return of Kuwait to its people. Americans rallied around the government and roundly condemned the Iraqi invasion. Finally, as the diplomatic process unfolded, the United States and its allies gathered in the Persian Gulf region a massive and militarily powerful combat force.

Vice Admiral Henry H. Mauz Jr., a veteran of riverine operations in the Mekong Delta, and Vice Admiral Stanley R. Arthur, who flew 514 combat missions over North Vietnam, oversaw US and allied naval forces in Desert Shield and the follow-on Desert Storm operations. Before sending 80,000 American sailors and Marines into harm's way, they marshalled a US and allied armada of 120 ships, including six carriers with more than 400 aircraft, two battleships, thirteen submarines, and forty-three amphibious combat vessels. One of the Navy's first actions, unlike in the Vietnam War, was to isolate Iraq from seaborne supplies of tanks, artillery, and other munitions. In the maritime interception phase, US and allied warships challenged, boarded, or diverted more than 8,500 merchant ships suspected of carrying war materials. To degrade Saddam's air defenses and continue building up ground and naval forces, on 17 January 1991 Stan Arthur's carriers with their F-14s and F/A-18s and his Tomahawk-firing surface ships and submarines launched a devastating air assault on Iraq, executing more than 18,000 sorties. Arthur mounted a masterful deception campaign to fool Saddam into thinking that an amphibious invasion of Kuwait was in the offing. He did not intend to repeat the Vietnam experience of sending American and allied forces against hardened enemy defenses when alternatives existed.

Only on 24 February, when Saddam's forces had been seriously degraded by the air campaign, did the US leaders kick off a massive allied ground invasion that within 100 hours had liberated Kuwait and compelled Saddam to sue for peace. Benefitting from their Vietnam experience, US military leaders had planned and executed one of the most masterful campaigns in American military history. Moreover, at the end of the conflict, President Bush could accurately proclaim that "the ghosts of Vietnam have been laid to rest beneath the sands of the Arabian desert."[9]

When Stan Arthur returned to Washington, DC, after leading US and allied naval forces to victory in the Persian Gulf War, he decided that "it was time to go face . . . The Wall," the hallowed memorial bearing the names of the 58,000 Americans who had died in Vietnam. He did not go there easily even after two decades, since he "had a lot of friends on that wall, some very close friends."[10] It was a moving experience, as he knew it would be. But he chose to honor those men and women who had given their all. Indeed, Stan Arthur's leadership and that of the other Navy flag officers who fought in and commanded US forces in the Vietnam War and worked to restore the health of the Navy afterward reflected an abiding faith in service and sacrifice for the nation they so ably served.

NOTES

INTRODUCTION
1. H. R. McMaster, *Dereliction of Duty: Lyndon Johnson, Robert McNamara, the Joint Chiefs of Staff, and the Lies that Led to Vietnam* (New York: Harper Collins, 1997), x, 333.
2. See Jeffrey Record, "Why We Lost in Vietnam," in Thomas Cutler, ed., *Vietnam: A Retrospective*: (Annapolis: Naval Institute Press, 2016), 37–39.

CHAPTER 1
1. US Naval Academy *Lucky Bag*, 1923.
2. "Pacific Commander, Harry Felt," *Time*, 6 January 1961, 20. See also Eric W. Osborne, "People Come First—Harry Donald Felt (1902–1992)," in *Nineteen-Gun Salute: Case Studies of Operational, Strategic, and Diplomatic Naval Leadership during the 20th and Early 21st Centuries*, John B. Hattendorf and Bruce A. Elleman, eds. (Newport, RI: Naval War College Press, 2002); Harry D. Felt interview with John T. Mason, March 1972, US Naval Institute (USNI), 40.
3. Harry D. Felt Biography File, Naval History and Heritage Command (hereafter NHHC); Samuel Eliot Morison, *The Two-Ocean War: A Short History of the United States Navy in the Second World War* (Boston: Little, Brown and Co., 1963), 180; Clark G. Reynolds, *Famous American Admirals* (New York: Van Nostrand Reinhold Co., 1978), 115–17.
4. "Pacific Commander, Harry Felt," *Time*, 6 January 1961, 20. See also Felt USNI OH, 1, 15, 30, 153, 161, 176.
5. Felt USNI OH, 257. See also Harry D. Felt Biography File, NHHC. As related by David C. Richardson, who served on the Navy's Pentagon staff during the late 1950s, "Arleigh Burke thought the world [of Felt]." David Richardson interview with Paul Stillwell, March-April 1992, USNI OH, 157.
6. Felt USNI OH, 273, 285, 297.
7. Quoted in Edgar F. Puryear Jr., *American Admiralship: The Moral Imperatives of Naval Command* (Annapolis: Naval Institute Press, 2005), 104.
8. "Pacific Commander, Harry Felt," *Time*, 6 January 1961, 20, and Lawson P. Ramage, 1975, USNI OH, 289–99. See also Charles K. Duncan interview with John T. Mason, 1978, USNI OH, 528; William D. Irvin interview with John T. Mason, 1980, USNI OH, 437–40; Henry L. Miller interview with John T. Mason, March–May 1971, USNI OH, 274; Aide Ebby Bell, as recounted

in Thomas R. Weschler interview with Paul Stillwell, 1995, USNI OH, 327; Raymond E. Peet interview, USNI OH, 122; David L. McDonald interview with John T. Mason, 1974–1976, USNI OH, 219; Floyd D. Kennedy Jr., "David Lamar McDonald: 1 August 1963–1 August 1967," in Robert William Love Jr., ed., *The Chiefs of Naval Operations* (Annapolis: Naval Institute Press, 1980), 333. On the other hand, Admiral Robert L. J. Long remembered that "when I became CinCpac, Admiral Felt was living in Hawaii, and he was the sweetest, gentlest, kindest person you could ever imagine. So people change." Robert L. J. Long interview with Paul Stillwell, 1995, USNI OH, 175.

9. Edward J. Marolda, *Ready Seapower: A History of the U.S. Seventh Fleet* (Washington, DC: Naval History and Heritage Command, 2012), 40–41; Felt USNI OH, 268–69.

10. Marolda, *Ready Seapower*, 41–42.

11. Ltr., Burke to Mountbatten, 15 May 1958. Unless otherwise indicated, this source and the primary documents cited below can be found in the source notes, held in the Naval History and Heritage Command's archives, of Edward J. Marolda and Oscar P. Fitzgerald, *From Military Assistance to Combat*, Vol. II in the series The United States Navy and the Vietnam Conflict (Washington, DC: Naval Historical Center, 1986).

12. Maxwell Taylor, *Swords and Plowshares* (New York: W.W. Norton & Co., 1972), 169; Ingo Trauschweizer, "Cautious Hawk: Maxwell Taylor and the Path to War in Vietnam," *Journal of Military History* (July 2019): 835; OP-93, ltr, ser 000P93, 3 December 1957; CNO, Annual Report, FY 1958, 1–3; Arleigh Burke, "The Sea Carries Security on its Back," *Navy-Magazine of Seapower* 1, no. 1 (May 1958): 9–10; Malcolm W. Cagle, "Sea Power and Limited War," US Naval Institute *Proceedings* 85, no. 5 (May 1959): 34–42; CINCPAC, "CINCPAC's Evaluation of Capabilities and Major Deficiencies in His Command," (early) 1958; memo, DCNO (Plans and Policy) to ASD (ISA), ser 00099P60, 19 March 1959; David Halberstam, *The Best and the Brightest* (New York: Random House, 1972), 162–80, 269, 279. Taylor related that soon after publication of his *The Uncertain Trumpet* (New York: Harper, 1960), presidential candidate Kennedy sent him a note observing that the general's views on strategic matters were "most persuasive [and helpful] to shape my own thinking." Taylor later asserted that Kennedy "was a sincere convert to the need for a strategy of Flexible Response." Taylor, *Swords and Plowshares*, 180, 204, 253. See also *U.S.-V.N. Relations*, bk. 11, 400; Taylor interview with Dorothy Pierce, 9 January 1969, LBJ Oral Histories, LBJ Library, 2, 3; Ingo Trauschweizer, *Maxwell Taylor's Cold War: From Berlin to Vietnam* (Lexington: University of Kentucky Press, 2019).

13. Quoted in Puryear, *American Admiralship*, 246. See also Felt USNI OH, 358–59.

14. Peter M. Swartz, "Drawing Lines on the Sea: The U.S. Navy Confronts the Unified Command Plan, 1946–1998," in proceedings of *Fourteenth Naval History Symposium* (Annapolis: US Naval Academy), 25 September 1999.

15. CINCPAC, Command History, 1959, 39. See also ltr, Felt to Burke, 29 January 1959; Felt USNI OH, 396.

16. CNO, "Statement before the Senate Armed Services Committee, regarding the Military Posture of the United States Navy," 24 January 1959. See also

memo, CNO to Frankel, No. 89-59, 2 March 1959; Naval Long Range Studies Project (Naval War College), "Long Range Estimate of the Situation," 1 August 1960.
17. Msg, CPFLT 042155Z November 1959.
18. Felt USNI OH, 451, 508.
19. Felt USNI OH, 636; as reported in CNO, memo for record, ser 0007-60, 7 January 1960.
20. OP-60, briefing memo, No. 414-59, 4 September 1959. See also ltr, Burke to Felt, ser 00301P60, 11 August 1959; JCS Paper 1992/643, 1129; 1992/649; 1992/652; *U.S.-VN Relations*, bk 10, 1092; Ronald H. Spector, *Advice and Support: The Early Years, 1941-1960*, in series United States Army in Vietnam (Washington, DC: Center of Military History, 1983), 359-60; Arthur J. Dommen, *Conflict in Laos: The Politics of Neutralization* (New York: Praeger, 1971), 94-111; Bernard B. Fall, *Anatomy of a Crisis: The Laotian Crisis of 1960-1961* (Garden City, NY: Doubleday, 1961), 80-81, 162-72.
21. Msg, CP 050232Z September 1959.
22. Msg, CP 081004Z September 1959.
23. Msg, CP 022040Z October 1960.
24. Msg, CP 282347Z December 1960.
25. Msg, CNO 311849Z December 1960. For an easily understood explanation of the escalation theory, see Edwin E. Moise, *Tonkin Gulf and the Escalation of the Vietnam War* (Annapolis: Naval Institute Press, 2019), 35-38.
26. M. G. Weiner, J. R. Brom, and R. E. Koon, *Infiltration of Personnel from North Vietnam: 1959-1967* (Santa Monica, CA: Rand Corp., 1968), vi, 7, 39, 41, 53; *U.S.-V.N. Relations*, bk. 2, pt. IV.A.5, tab 3, 55-60; "Aggression from the North: The Record of North Vietnam's Campaign to Conquer South Vietnam," The Department of State Bulletin (22 March 1965), 407; Paul F. Langer and Joseph J. Zasloff, *North Vietnam and the Pathet Lao: Partners in the Struggle for Laos* (Cambridge, MA: Harvard University Press, 1970), 71-72, 80, 116, 167-68, 173, 226, 237.
27. Jack Shulimson, *The Joint Chiefs of Staff and the War in Vietnam, 1960-1968*, pt. 1 (Washington, DC: Office of Joint History, 2009), 83, 61-87. See also David K. Hall, "The Laos Crisis, 1960-61," in Alexander L. George, David K. Hall, and William E. Simons, eds., *The Limits of Coercive Diplomacy: Laos, Cuba, Vietnam* (Boston: Little Brown, 1971), 42-51; Martin E. Goldstein, *American Policy Toward Laos* (Cranbury, NJ: Associated University Presses, 1973), 236-44; Roger Hilsman, *To Move a Nation: The Politics of Foreign Policy in the Administration of John F. Kennedy* (Garden City, NY: Doubleday, 1967), 127-33; Steven L. Rearden, *Council of War: A History of the Joint Chiefs of Staff, 1942-1991* (Washington, DC: Joint History Office, 2012), 223; Fredrik Logevall, *Embers of War: The Fall of an Empire and the Making of America's Vietnam* (New York: Penguin Random House, 2012.
28. The disdain of Kennedy and his civilian advisors for the military was clear in McGeorge Bundy's recounting of the reaction to Burke's support for intervention in Laos. Even though the admiral was acting as a member of the Joint Chiefs and focusing on strategic-level issues, Bundy snidely remarked that Kennedy "did not miss the irony that among his chief military advisors one energetic supporter of a large operation in Laos—which is landlocked—was

the Chief of Naval Operations, who had nothing to fear from the Laotian navy." Gordon M. Goldstein, *Lessons in Disaster: McGeorge Bundy and the Path to War in Vietnam* (New York: Times Books, 2008), 46. See also Noam Kochavi, "Limited Accommodation, Perpetuated Conflict: Kennedy, China, and the Laos Crisis, 1961–1963, *Diplomatic History* (Winter 2002): 107–8.

29. Maxwell Taylor interview with Dorothy Pierce, 9 January 1969, LBJ Oral Histories, LBJ Library, 5. See also Shulimson, *The Joint Chiefs of Staff and the War in Vietnam, 1960–1968*, pt. 1, 395; Rearden, *Council of War*, 223–24, 279; Goldstein, *Lessons in Disaster*, 42.
30. Halberstam, *The Best and the Brightest*, 162, 465–89.
31. Robert S. McNamara with Brian VanDeMark, *In Retrospect: The Tragedy and Lessons of Vietnam* (New York: Times Books, 1995), 6, 54.
32. Halberstam, *The Best and the Brightest*, 347.
33. McNamara, *In Retrospect*, 6.
34. Halberstam, *The Best and the Brightest*, chap. 12. Elmo R. Zumwalt Jr., who as a mid-level officer heard McNamara speak, considered him "shallow with regard to geopolitical thinking." See Zumwalt USNI OH, 346.
35. Quoted in Lawrence S. Kaplan, Ronald D. Landa, and Edward J. Drea, *The McNamara Ascendancy, 1961–1965* (Washington, DC: Historical Office of the Secretary of Defense, 2006), 535. See also McNamara, *In Retrospect*, 1.
36. Taylor, *Swords and Plowshares*, 253. See also John M. Taylor, *General Maxwell Taylor: The Sword and the Pen* (New York: Doubleday, 1989); Douglas C. Kinnard, *The Certain Trumpet: Maxwell Taylor and the American Experience in Vietnam* (Washington, DC: Brassey's, 1991); Trauschweizer, "Cautious Hawk."
37. Nitze interview with Dorothy Pierce, 10 January 1969, LBJ Oral Histories, LBJ Library, 5. See also Rearden, *Council of War*, 81.
38. McNamara, *In Retrospect*, 32, 39, 117. See also Kaplan et al., *The McNamara Ascendancy*, 291.
39. Zumwalt USNI OH, 371–72. See also Paul H. Nitze, *From Hiroshima to Glasnost: At the Center of Decision* (New York: Grove Weidenfeld, 1989), 230; Larry Berman, *Zumwalt: The Life and Times of Admiral Elmo Russell "Bud" Zumwalt Jr.* (New York: Harper Collins, 2012), 134–36.
40. Nitze, *From Hiroshima to Glasnost*, 230–31.
41. George W. Anderson interview with Joseph E. O'Connor, 25 April 1967, JFK Library, 6, 17, 19–24. A recent study by Dan Martins, incorporating information from McNamara's 1986 oral history, provides a more balanced account of the incident, depicting "a calmer encounter, with the meeting focussed on suspected Soviet submarine positions and the Secretary of Defense directing Navy ships to positions intended to force the interdiction of specific Soviet ships." He added that "while the Secretary of Defense's oral history makes for a great 'sea story,' the presidential recordings of the ExComm [Executive Committee of the National Security Council] meetings reveal a nuanced understanding of the difficulties the Navy could anticipate in upholding the quarantine." Martins observed that "McNamara's oral history cast Admiral Anderson as a naval officer who would have preferred to blow the Soviets out of the water at first light. The truth is just not that simple." Dan Martins, "The Cuban Missile Crisis and the Joint Chiefs of Staff: Military Operations

to Meet Political Ends," *Naval War College Review* (Autumn 2018): 105–6, 192. See also William H. J. Manthorpe, "The Secretary and CNO on 23–24 October 1962: Setting the Historical Record Straight," Naval War College *Review* (Winter 2013): 21–22.
42. Thomas H. Moorer USNI OH, 1299.
43. Moorer jested that "perhaps it would be a good idea to pass a law forbidding the mothers to buy tin soldiers for the kids because they never get over that." Moorer USNI OH, 1302. See also 10, 478, 1301; Halberstam, *The Best and the Brightest*, 399, 515; McNamara, *In Retrospect*, 14, 26. Nitze, who favored McNamara's tight control of the military, however, later suggested that the key decisions during the missile crisis "were made with the best inputs from the joint chiefs of staff and the military services." See Nitze interview with Dorothy Pierce, LBJ Oral Histories, LBJ Library, 10 January 1969, 2.
44. Quoted in Halberstam, *The Best and the Brightest*, 89–90. See also Shulimson, *The Joint Chiefs of Staff and the War in Vietnam, 1960–1968*, pt. 1, 205–6. As related in Walter S. Poole, *The Joint Chiefs of Staff and National Policy, 1961–1964*, vol. VII, 1961–1964 (Washington, DC: Office of Joint History, 2011), 135, China dispatched 2,149 soldiers, 1,771 civilian workers, 203 vehicles, and 609 horses and mules to Laos in support of the Pathet Lao.
45. Shulimson, *The Joint Chiefs of Staff and the War in Vietnam, 1960–1968*, pt. 1, *205–6*, 219–32; Nicholas Khoo, *Collateral Damage: Sino-Soviet Rivalry and the Termination of the Sino-Vietnamese Alliance* (New York: Columbia University Press, 2011), 42; Xiaoming Zhang, "China's Involvement in Laos During the Vietnam War, 1963–1975," *Journal of Military History* (October 2002): 1145, 1158; Rearden, *Council of War*, 222.
46. Moorer USNI OH, 1227.
47. Rearden, *Council of War*, 224; McNamara, *In Retrospect*, 55; Robert D. Sander, *Invasion of Laos 1971: Lam Son 719* (Norman: University of Oklahoma Press, 2014), 7.
48. CNO, "Terminology for Counterinsurgency Matters," ser 361P60, 29 March 1962.
49. CINCPAC OPLAN 32-59, ser 000253, 16 December 1959. See also ltr, Felt to Draper, 28 December 1958; Felt USNI OH, 422; Harry D. Felt Biography File, NHHC.
50. Felt USNI OH, 421. See also Ang Cheng Guan, *The Vietnam War from the Other Side: The Vietnamese Communists' Perspective* (New York: Routledge Curzon, 2002), 7.
51. Felt USNI OH, 576–78. See also Robert Buzzanco, *Masters of War: Military Dissent and Politics in the Vietnam Era* (Cambridge, MA: Cambridge University Press, 1996), 7–72; msg, CP 272243Z April 1960; Shulimson, *The Joint Chiefs of Staff and the War in Vietnam, 1960–1968*, pt. 1, 25; CINCPAC, "Counter-Insurgency Operations in South Vietnam and Laos," 26 April 1960, 3–4; msg, AMEMB Saigon, 7 March 1960 in *U.S.-V.N. Relations*, bk. 10, 1254–75; bk. 2 pt. IV.A.5, 43–48; msg, CP 142351Z March 1960; CINCPAC Command History, 1960, 162–63.
52. CINCPAC, "Counter-Insurgency Operations in South Vietnam and Laos," 14–15.
53. Felt USNI OH, 425.

54. Memo, CNO to OP-03, 12 September 1960. See also CNO, memo for record, ser 00389-60, 11 July 1960.
55. John F. Kennedy, *Strategy of Peace* (New York: Harper and Brothers, 1960), 37–38, 184.
56. Quoted in Richard P. Stebbins, *The United States in World Affairs, 1961* (New York: Harper, 1962), 64.
57. Msg, CNO 240133Z, February 1961.
58. Quoted in James Wright, *Enduring Vietnam: An American Generation and Its War* (New York: St. Martin's Press, 2017), 85.
59. CNO, memo for record, ser 000221-61, 21 April 1961. With regard to Kennedy's emphasis, see Richard H. Shultz Jr., *The Secret War Against Hanoi* (New York: Harper Collins, 1999), 3–8.
60. Memo, OP-06 to OP-60, ser BM0098-61, 29 April 1961.
61. Memo, OP-60 to CNO, ser BM00286-61, 10 March 1961.
62. Henry L. Miller interview with USNI, 1971, 327.
63. Memo, OP-60 to CNO, ser BM000511-61, 9 May 1961; see also Buzzanco, *Masters of War*, 9, 83, 97, 99. Felt was also concerned that a major deployment of troops ashore would detract from the Pacific Command's ability to counteract Soviet, Chinese, and North Korean threats elsewhere in the theater.
64. JCS Paper 1992/978.
65. Junk Force Advisor, Fact Sheet, "Support of the Junk Force by the VN Navy," 21 August 1962; CINCPAC, Third Secretary of Defense Conference, 19 February 1962. See also Shulimson, *The Joint Chiefs of Staff and the War in Vietnam, 1960–1968*, pt. 1, 33–36; Kaplan et al., *The McNamara Ascendancy*, 262.
66. Memo, CNO to OP-61, ser 00242-61, 3 May 1961.
67. Memo, OP-40 to OP-60, ser 003107P40, 16 May 1961; CNO to OP-01, ser 00242-61, 3 May 1961; Paul H. Nitze interview with Dorothy Fosdick, 22 May 1964, JFK Library, tape 1, 7–9.
68. Msg, CP 022210Z August 1961.
69. As reported in memo, OP-04B to CNO, ser 003233P40, 1 September 1961.
70. Taylor, *Swords and Plowshares*, 228.
71. Msg, CP 200401Z October 1961. See also Shulimson, *The Joint Chiefs of Staff and the War in Vietnam, 1960–1968*, pt. 1, 109–40; Buzzanco, *Masters of War*, 107–8.
72. *U.S.-V.N. Relations*, bk. 2, pt. IV B.1, 102.
73. *U.S.-V.N. Relations*, bk. 2, pt. IV B.1, 96–97.
74. Ltr, OP-61 to COM7FLT, ser 00225P61, 22 December 1961. See also Shulimson, *The Joint Chiefs of Staff and the War in Vietnam, 1960–1968*, pt. 1, 166–68.
75. SECDEF, "Record of Third Secretary of Defense Conference," 19 February 1962, 1–10, 1–5; Shulimson, *The Joint Chiefs of Staff and the War in Vietnam, 1960–1968*, pt. 1, 181–85.
76. Henry L. Miller USNI OH, 325–26.
77. SECDEF, "Record, Fourth Secretary of Defense Conference, 21 March 1962, 1-5, 1-1. See also Felt USNI OH, 477; Shulimson, *The Joint Chiefs of Staff and the War in Vietnam, 1960–1968*, pt. 1, 189–90.
78. Anderson Diary, 6 August 1962; OP-09, memo, ser 00133P09, 10 August

1962.
79. Msg, CP 011034Z December 1961.
80. Joseph Drachnik interview with William M. Moss, NHHC, 8. See also Philip H. Bucklew interview with John T. Mason, March–June 1980, USNI OH, 345; Marolda and Fitzgerald, *From Military Assistance to Combat*, 168–77; Moise, *Tonkin Gulf and the Escalation of the Vietnam War*, 49. Admiral Hyland, who served as either Commander Seventh Fleet or Commander in Chief, Pacific Fleet from 1965 to 1970, related years afterward that he "didn't think there was very much infiltration by sea from north to south." Hyland USNI OH, 347.
81. Christopher E. Goscha's "The Maritime Nature of the Wars for Vietnam (1945–1975): A Geo-Historical Reflection," *War and Society* (2005): 76–79, is an authoritative work in English but based on deep research in Vietnamese sources; Socialist Republic of Vietnam, *Vietnam: The Anti-U.S. Resistance War*, 32; NAVFORV, "Maritime Infiltration into the Republic of Vietnam," 4 March 1967; CINCPAC, "CINCPAC/COMPONENTS Assessment of Sea Infiltration, Committee B," July 1967; CINCPAC, "Infiltration Study," 1 May 1968; Judith Erdheim, *Market Time*, study CRC 280 (Washington, DC: Center for Naval Analyses, 1975); Christopher B. Havern Sr., "The U.S. Coast Guard in the Vietnam War," presentation, 29 March 2019, Washington Navy Yard.
82. CNO, Minutes of Meeting, 5 January 1962.
83. CNO, OPNAV Instruction 01500.17, ser 01666P10, 19 July 1962. See also OP-09A, memo for record, ser 0037P09, 9 March 1962.
84. Ltr, Anderson to Admiral John H. Sides, 30 January 1962.
85. Memo, Kennedy to Nitze/McDonald, 7 November 1963. See also Nicholas Thompson, *The Hawk and the Dove: Paul Nitze, George Kennan, and the History of the Cold War* (New York: Henry Holt and Co., 2009), 197–98.
86. Ltr, Anderson to Sides, 11 September 1962.
87. CINCPAC, Command History, 1963, 236, 247; COMCBPAC, "Helping Others Help Themselves," 35; SEAL Team 1, Command History, 1966; SEAL Team 2, Command History, 1962–1966, ser 019, 31 May 1967; Bucklew USNI OH, 360–65; Charles D. Griffen interview with John T. Mason, January–June 1980, USNI OH, 522–24; Hamilton/Marcinko interview with Marolda, NHHC; Lionel Kriesel, "Special Maritime Operations in Vietnam, 1961–1972," unpublished history in NHHC, 1973, 73–75.
88. Marolda and Fitzgerald, *From Military Assistance to Combat*, 219–20.
89. Msg, CP, 2 November 1960.
90. Shulimson, *The Joint Chiefs of Staff and the War in Vietnam, 1960–1968*, pt. 1, 188; Walter S. Poole, *Adapting to Flexible Response, 1960–1968* (Washington, DC: Historical Office, Office of the Secretary of Defense, 2013), 136.
91. Msg, CP 250501Z April 1962. See also CINCPAC, Command History, 1962, 48.
92. Memo, CNO to JCS, ser 000762P60, 13 July 1962.
93. George W. Anderson Jr. interview with John T. Mason, June–November 1980, USNI OH, 1983, 492 (see also 694). Ironically, given his later opposition to US military operations against North Vietnam, Melvin Laird in *A House Divided: America's Strategy Gap* (New York: H. Regnery, 1962) concluded

that the struggle in Indochina could not be won "unless the war was taken into North Vietnam." Dale Van Atta, *With Honor: Melvin Laird in War, Peace, and Politics* (Madison: University of Wisconsin Press, 2008), 61.

94. Msg, CP 040745Z September 1962. See also Colby Interview with Marolda, NHHC, 1–10; William Colby, *Honorable Men: My Life in the CIA* (New York: Simon and Schuster, 1978), 172–75, 219; Kriesel, "Special Maritime Operations in Vietnam," 55, 58–62, 66–67.

95. Felt USNI OH, 467. With the support of his mentor and former boss Arleigh Burke, in 1959 Felt had launched a CINCPAC study of Norwegian-built "Nasty"-class motor torpedo boats for possible use in special missions along the coast of Vietnam. Memo, SECDEF to SECNAV, 12 October 1962.

96. Memo, McNamara to President, 21 December 1963, in Gareth Porter, ed., *Vietnam: The Definitive Documentation of Human Decisions*, vol. II (Stanfordville, NY: Early M. Coleman Enterprises Inc., 1979), 232. See also msg, CP 182345Z November 1963; Colby, *Honorable Men*, 219–20; Colby interview with Marolda, 10–12; Kriesel, "Special Maritime Operations in Vietnam," 72–79; Shultz, *The Secret War Against Hanoi*, 31–40; Graham A. Cosmas, *The Joint Chiefs of Staff and the War in Vietnam, 1960–1968*, pt. 2 (Washington, DC: Office of Joint History, 2012), 8–10, 13–14; Moise, *Tonkin Gulf and the Escalation of the Vietnam War*, 1–21; Jacob Van Staaveren, *Gradual Failure: The Air War over North Vietnam, 1965–1966* (Washington, DC: Air Force History and Museums Program, 2002), 35; Kaplan et al., *The McNamara Ascendancy*, 501; McMaster, *Dereliction of Duty*, 120. McNamara later disingenuously distanced himself from 34A even though he was an early and eager champion of the program as a useful means for putting pressure on North Vietnam. See McNamara, *In Retrospect*, 103, 120, 129, 130, 137. As observed by Thomas Hughes, McNamara was one of those men who "exhibited the greatest elasticity when it came to truth-shading, truth-shaping, and truth-creating inevitably convinced observers that they loved power more than the truth." Thomas L. Hughes, "Experiencing McNamara," *Foreign Policy* no. 100 (Autumn 1995): 171.

97. Msgs, CPFLT 190259Z May 1964; CP 272258Z; CP 250741Z. See also Kaplan et al., *The McNamara Ascendancy*, 507; William P. Bundy, memo for record, 27 April 1964; Michael L. Mulford (who had served as an advisor to the 34A group at Danang) interview with Marolda, NHHC, 20 April 1983, accession no. 887187, NHHC.

98. MACV, Command History, 1964, Ann. A. IV-2; msgs, MACSOG 041100Z; 081215Z July 1964, Kriesel, "Special Maritime Operations in Vietnam," 116–18.

99. Ltr, Miller to Stroh, 30 July 1963; Felt USNI OH; Shulimson, *The Joint Chiefs of Staff and the War in Vietnam, 1960–1968*, pt. 1, 277–79; Kaplan et al., *The McNamara Ascendancy*, 282; Rufus Phillips, *Why Vietnam Matters: An Eyewitness Account of Lessons Not Learned* (Annapolis: Naval Institute Press, 2008), 141–42.

100. Felt USNI OH, 400. See also Halberstam, *The Best and the Brightest*, 205; Robert T. S. Keith interview with Paul Stillwell, USNI, 1996, 127–28. Hanson Baldwin, the conservative *New York Times* military analyst, sympathized with Felt's query to the media, "Whose side are you on?" Baldwin believed that

"there is a higher loyalty on the part of the press than the public's 'right to know.'" Baldwin USNI OH, 651–52.
101. CINCPAC News Release No. 12263, 30 January 1963, NHHC Bio Files.
102. "Felt details Free Vietnam gains in past six months," May 1963, Douglas Pike Collection, acc. no. 2120211030, Texas Tech Vietnam Archive. See also *The Washington Post*, 31 January 1963, Ralph F. Turner Papers, acc. no. 1781248001, Texas Tech Vietnam Archives.
103. Memo for the record by the Director of the Bureau of Intelligence and Research, Department of State, Saigon, January 1963, "Conversation with Major General Edward L. Rowney, *Foreign Relations of the United States, 1961–1963*, Vol. III, *Vietnam: January–August 1963*, 7–11.
104. Graham A. Cosmas, *MACV: The Joint Command in the Years of Escalation, 1962–1967* (Washington, DC: U.S. Army Center of Military History, 2006), 41.
105. William C. Westmoreland, *A Soldier Reports* (New York: Doubleday and Co., 1976), 76. John Prados in his *Vietnam: The History of an Unwinnable War, 1945–1975* (Lawrence, KS: University Press of Kansas, 2009) and Gregory A. Daddis, in his *Westmoreland's War: Reassessing American Strategy in Vietnam* (New York: Oxford University Press, 2014), apparently had even less regard for Felt. The admiral does not appear once in their 600-page and 248-page tomes. See also Halberstam, *The Best and the Brightest*, 539, 543.
106. Bucklew USNI OH, 323.
107. Felt USNI OH, 475, 482–83, 587–88.
108. Felt USNI OH, 611, 615. See also Phillips, *Why Vietnam Matters*, 202, 195–207; Shulimson, *The Joint Chiefs of Staff and the War in Vietnam, 1960–1968*, pt. 1, 329–60. Suggesting that Kennedy had nothing to do with Diem's assassination, Roger Hilsman observed that "if we had had any ideas that there was a coup scheduled for the first of November, we sure as hell wouldn't have let Don Felt go to Vietnam, much less go into Diem's office." Roger Hilsman interview with Dennis J. Obrien, 14 August 1970, JFK Library, 30–34.
109. Moorer USNI OH, 469. See also Shulimson, *The Joint Chiefs of Staff and the War in Vietnam, 1960–1968*, pt. 1, 383–94.
110. Lien-Hang T. Nguyen, *Hanoi's War: An International History of the War for Peace in Vietnam* (Chapel Hill: University of North Carolina Press, 2012), 66. See also 64–65; Guan, *The Vietnam War from the Other Side*, 8, 73, 75; Fredrik Logevall, *Choosing War: The Lost Chance for Peace and the Escalation of War in Vietnam* (Berkeley: University of California Press, 1999); Paul Thomas Chamberlin, *The Cold War's Killing Fields: Rethinking the Long Peace* (New York: Harper, 2018).
111. Edward J. Marolda, "Troubled Assignment: The U.S. Navy's Advisory Mission in Vietnam, 1954–1973," in Donald Stoker and Michael T. McMaster, eds., *Naval Advising and Assistance: History, Challenges, and Analysis* (West Midlands, UK: Helion & Company, 2017), 243–48.
112. Quoted in Nicholas J. Schlosser, ed, *The Greene Papers: General Wallace M. Greene Jr. and the Escalation of the Vietnam War* (Quantico, VA: History Division USMC, 2015), 63, 65. See also Senior Member, Vietnam Delta Infiltration Study Group, "Report of Recommendations Pertaining to Infiltration into South Vietnam of Viet Cong Personnel, Supporting

Materials, Weapons and Ammunition," ser 0076, 15 February 1964, p. 2.
113. Bucklew USNI OH, 202. See also 338–39, 354, 355; Rivero USNI OH, 443.
114. Van Staaveren, *Gradual Failure*, 34; Van Staaveren, *Interdiction in Southern Laos, 1960-1968* (Washington, DC: Air Force History and Museums Division, 1993), 20.
115. Memo, CNO to JCS, CNOM 59–64, 24 February 1964. See also Cosmas, *The Joint Chiefs of Staff and the War in Vietnam, 1960-1968*, pt. 2, 31–32; Marolda and Fitzgerald, *From Military Assistance to Combat*, 19–20.
116. Schlosser, *The Greene Papers*, 32. See also Kaplan et al., *The McNamara Ascendancy*, 506, 509.
117. Quoted in Cosmas, *The Joint Chiefs of Staff and the War in Vietnam, 1960-1968*, pt. 2, 82. Edwin Moise, in *Tonkin Gulf and the Escalation of the Vietnam War*, 30, speculates that Felt even considered the possibility of having to use nuclear weapons against the North Vietnamese Army.
118. Quoted in Robert Dallek, *Flawed Giant: Lyndon Johnson and His Times, 1961-1973* (New York: Oxford University Press, 1998), 254, and Halberstam, *The Best and the Brightest*, 512, 564. Moise, in *Tonkin Gulf and the Escalation of the Vietnam War*, 34, observed that US leaders at the time thought six US divisions could handle the North Vietnamese army.
119. Memo, SECNAV to SECDEF (transmitted orally on 12 June 1964) encl. in memo, OP-60 to SECNAV, ser 000493P60, 12 June 1964. Zumwalt later affirmed that he "advocated through Paul Nitze, *who agreed with me* [italics added], that the U.S. position should be one of Air Force and Navy heavy against North Vietnam, and [in South Vietnam] advisory light." Zumwalt, USNI OH, 559. According to his biographer, Zumwalt wrote a paper heavily influenced by his mentor Nitze that suggested "U.S. forces should be brought to bear only by air and naval surface-ship bombardment and by a blockade of North Vietnam." Zumwalt suggested, according to Larry Berman, that if those actions did not prompt the North Vietnamese to stop infiltrating South Vietnam, there would have to be "amphibious landings to seize Haiphong and Hanoi." One is left wondering how the United States would have avoided being embroiled in the conflict ashore in Asia after having occupied the capital of North Vietnam not far from the southern border of the People's Republic of China. Zumwalt did not think the PRC would "challenge these actions." Berman, *Zumwalt*, 131–32. On the other hand, Marine General Greene thought that by March 1964 "it was clearly evident that [Nitze] did not favor military action against the Hanoi Government." Schlosser, *The Greene Papers*, 54. See also Thompson, *The Hawk and the Dove*, 176–78, 200.
120. Memo, OP-92 to CNO, 27 January 1965.
121. McDonald USNI OH, 361.
122. Moorer USNI OH, 11, 551. See also Nitze interview with Dorothy Pierce, 10 January 1969, LBJ Library Oral Histories, LBJ Library, 8.
123. McNamara, *In Retrospect*, 107. See also Victor H. Krulak, "A Conflict of Strategies," in Thomas Cutler, ed., *Vietnam: A Retrospective* (Annapolis: Naval Institute Press, 2016), 71–72; Memo, CNO to JCS, CNOM 59–64, 24 February 1964; Edward J. Drea, *McNamara, Clifford, and the Burdens of Vietnam, 1965-1969* (Washington, DC: Historical Office, Office of the Secretary of Defense, 2011), 43; Halberstam, *The Best and the Brightest*, 577;

Trauschweizer, "Cautious Hawk," 853.
124. Rearden, *Council of War*, 282. See also Msg, CP 280311Z February 1964; Felt USNI OH, 627–28, 638–39; CINCPAC, Command History, 1964, 361; Halberstam, *The Best and the Brightest*, 242; U. S. G. Sharp, *Strategy for Defeat* (Novato, CA: Presidio, 1978), 34; Westmoreland, *A Soldier Reports*, 105–9. Ingo Trauschweizer, in "Cautious Hawk," 837, 844, 846, relates that Taylor had an "unhealthy faith in airpower," convinced as he was that at the end of the Korean War the "Americans had impressed on Chinese and North Korean leaders that they had no choice but to enter into a compromise agreement on terms palatable to the United States."
125. Felt USNI OH, 631, 633. See also Msg, CP 250022Z February 1964; Shultz, *The Secret War Against Hanoi*, 174–92.
126. Quoted in Schlosser, *The Greene Papers*, 157.
127. MACV History, 1964, 360–61; memo, SECDEF to President, 16 March; Sharp, *Strategy for Defeat*, 4, 31–34; memo, OP-60 to CNO, ser BM000579-64, 14 May; Lyndon B. Johnson, *The Vantage Point: Perspectives of the Presidency, 1963–1969* (New York: Holt, Rinehart, Winston, 1971), 65–67; Van Staaveren, *Gradual Failure*, 41–45; Cosmas, *The Joint Chiefs of Staff and the War in Vietnam, 1960–1968*, pt. 2, 25–50; Kaplan et al., *The McNamara Ascendancy*, 512.
128. CINCPAC, Command History, 1964, 52–54; MACV, Command History, 1964, 160–65; Sharp, *Strategy for Defeat*, 46–48; Cosmas, *The Joint Chiefs of Staff and the War in Vietnam, 1960–1968*, pt. 2, 45–46; Marolda and Fitzgerald, *From Military Assistance to Combat*, 373n16.
129. And just two months before, communist representatives from China, North Vietnam, Laos, and Indonesia secretly met near Guangzhou where Zhou Enlai assured the attendees that the PRC "would serve as a reliable rear echelon for their revolution and would help them drive the Americans out of Southeast Asia." Ziaoming Zhang, "China's Involvement in Laos During the Vietnam War," 1146 (see also 1147–50).
130. CINCPAC, Command History, 1964, 269; msg, CNO 171439Z May 1964; memo, OP-60 to CNO, ser BM000584-64, 18 May; Cosmas, *The Joint Chiefs of Staff and the War in Vietnam, 1960–1968*, pt. 2, 134–35.
131. Pathet Lao guerrillas captured the naval aviator and marched him off to captivity in a rude hut already occupied by Thai and Laotian prisoners. Almost three months later, Klusmann escaped from his prison and made his way through the jungle to friendly lines. "Klusmann Debriefing Report," encl. in ltr, COMNAVAIRPAC, ser 36/0150, 12 February 1965; msgs, CTG77.4 061415Z June 1964; CHINFO 301548Z June 1964.
132. Quoted in Kaplan et al., *The McNamara Ascendancy*, 516.
133. Ltr, Moorer to McDonald, 2 June 1964. See also Moorer USNI OH, 507. Later in the war, McDonald sponsored a report that documented frequent complaints by Navy pilots that they were bombing targets of little value over and over again. Sharp disagreed with the conclusion of the CNO's study. See Van Staaveren, *Gradual Failure*, 187.
134. Quoted in McMaster, *Dereliction of Duty*, 233.
135. Msg, CP 122146Z June 1964. See also msg, JCS 061632Z June 1964.
136. Memo, SECNAV Aide to CNO, 9 June 1964. See also Kaplan et al., *The*

McNamara Ascendancy, 516–17.
137. Schlosser, *The Greene Papers*, 129, 132, 136.
138. McNamara, *In Retrospect*, 40.
139. Felt's association with the Vietnam War would continue in a personal way. His only son, Donald L. Felt, who retired as a rear admiral, completed 240 combat missions while in command of Navy Attack Squadron (VA-27) and other units and flying A-4 Skyhawk and A-7 Corsairs during Operation Rolling Thunder. Donald L. Felt obituary, *The Virginian Pilot* (23 April 2011).

CHAPTER 2

1. Ulysses S. G. Sharp Biography, Bio Files, Navy Department Library, NHHC; "Frustrated Warrior: Admiral Ulysses S. Grant Sharp Jr.," in Norman Polmar and Edward J. Marolda, *Naval Air War: The Rolling Thunder Campaign*, in series The U.S. Navy and the Vietnam War, Edward J. Marolda and Sandra Doyle, eds. (Washington, DC: Naval History and Heritage Command, 2015), 47; Glenn Helm, "Ulysses S. Grant Sharp: Courage," in *Leadership Embodied: The Secrets to Success of the Most Effective Navy and Marine Corps Leaders*, 2nd ed., Joseph J. Thomas, ed. (Annapolis: Naval Institute Press, 2013), 172–74; Reynolds, *Famous American Admirals*, 303–4.
2. US Naval Academy *Lucky Bag*, 1927.
3. Ulysses S. G. Sharp Biography, Bio Files, Navy Department Library, NHHC; "Frustrated Warrior."
4. Moorer USNI OH, 28, 1537–38; John J. Hyland Jr. interviews with John T. Mason/Paul Stillwell, March 1972, May 1984, USNI OH, 208, 213.
5. Ulysses S. G. Sharp Biography, Bio Files, Navy Department Library, NHHC; "Man in the News: No-Nonsense Admiral Ulysses Simpson Grant Sharp Jr.," *New York Times*, 28 February 1964.
6. Msg, CP 240124Z January 1964. The following sources treat the Desoto Patrol and the Gulf of Tonkin crisis: Moise, *Tonkin Gulf and the Escalation of the Vietnam War*; Tonkin Gulf Collection, Naval History and Heritage Command; Marolda and Fitzgerald, *From Military Assistance to Combat*; McNamara, *In Retrospect*; Sharp, *Strategy for Defeat*; Robert J. Hanyok, "Skunks, Bogies, Silent Hounds, and Flying Fish: The Gulf of Tonkin Mystery, 2–4 August 1964, *Cryptologic Quarterly* (Winter 2000/Spring 2001); US Congress, Senate, Committee on Foreign Relations, *Hearings on the Gulf of Tonkin, the 1964 Incidents* (90th Cong., 2nd Sess.) (Washington, DC: US Government Printing Office, 1968); US Congress, Senate. Committee on Armed Services, *Nomination of Admiral Thomas H. Moorer, USN, to be Chairman, Joint Chiefs of Staff* (91st Cong., 2nd Sess.) (Washington, DC: US Government Printing Office, 1970; John Prados, "Essay: 40th Anniversary of the Gulf of Tonkin Incident," 4 August 2004, National Security Archive; Marolda, "Grand Delusion: U.S. Strategy and the Tonkin Gulf Incident," *Naval History* (August 2014): 24–31.
7. Memo, Office of the Judge Advocate General to SECNAV, 1 February 1968.
8. Msgs, CP 010022Z February 1964; 010308Z; ADMIN CPFLT 120142Z; 120143Z; COM7FLT 140200Z; 291015Z; 051132Z; Fitzwater, JRC (JCS), memo for record, 13 August 1964.
9. Msg, COMUSMACV 192241Z July 1964.

10. Quoted in memo, OP-002 to OP-03/OP-06/OP-92, ser 00197-64, 18 July 1964.
11. Msg, CPFLT 302237Z July 1964. Moise, in *Tonkin Gulf and the Escalation of the Vietnam War*, 60, has concluded that "after August 2 the mission of the patrol was substantially altered. 'Showing the flag,' demonstrating that the US Navy had the ability and the will to patrol in the Gulf of Tonkin, took precedence over intelligence gathering of all sorts." But Moorer, at least, had stressed that point even before the attack.
12. US Naval Academy *Lucky Bag*, 1933.
13. Quoted in J. Kenneth McDonald, "Thomas Hinman Moorer, 1 August 1967–1 July 1970," in Robert William Love Jr., ed., *The Chiefs of Naval Operations* (Annapolis: Naval Institute Press, 1980), 352. See also Reynolds, *Famous American Admirals*," 227–28.
14. Moorer USNI OH, 1221.
15. Quoted in McDonald, "Thomas Hinman Moorer, 355. See also Edward J. Marolda, "Admiral Thomas H. Moorer: Conviction," in *Leadership Embodied: The Secrets to Success of the Most Effective Navy and Marine Corps Leaders*, 2nd ed., Joseph J. Thomas, ed. (Annapolis: Naval Institute Press, 2013), 168–71; Moorer Biography, Naval History and Heritage Command, https://www.history.navy.mil/research/library/research-guides/modern-biographical-files-ndl/modern-bios-m/moorer-thomas-h.html; John Darrell Sherwood, "Admiral Thomas Hinman Moorer," in *Nixon's Trident: Naval Power in Southeast Asia, 1968–1972*, 28–29, in series The U.S. Navy and the Vietnam War, Edward J. Marolda and Sandra J. Doyle, eds. (Washington, DC: NHHC/NHF, 2009); Willard J. Webb and Ronald H. Cole, *The Chairmen of the Joint Chiefs of Staff* (Washington, DC: Historical Division, JCS, 1989); Ronald H. Cole, Lorna S. Jaffe, Walter S. Poole, and Willard J. Webb, *The Chairmanship of the Joint Chiefs of Staff* (Washington, DC: Joint History Office, 1995).
16. Special Operations Division, SACSA, Talking Paper, "Operation Plan 34A Maritime Operations in the Gulf of Tonkin, July/August"; SACSA, "Description of South Vietnamese Operations on 30/31 July 1964"; SACSA, Chart of 30/31 July 1964 34A operation; MACV, Command History, 1964, Ann. A, IV-2-IV-4; Kriesel, "Special Maritime Operations in Vietnam," 120–21; U.S.-V.N. Relations, bk. 4, pt. IVC.2(b), 5, 11; Bucklew USNI OH, 366–79; Mulford interview with Marolda; Cosmas, *The Joint Chiefs of Staff and the War in Vietnam, 1960–1968*, pt. 2, 104.
17. Msg, CTU72.1.2 011954Z August 1964.
18. Msg, CTU72.1.2 012245Z August 1964.
19. The North Vietnamese, in their history of the war, confirmed the ample evidence that they ordered the torpedo boats to attack the American destroyer. See Socialist Republic of Vietnam, *Vietnam: The Anti-U.S. Resistance War*, 60. Moise, in *Tonkin Gulf and the Escalation of the Vietnam War*, 79–82, has concluded with strong evidence that naval leaders in the chain of command planned and ordered the attack. He disputes Bui Tin's and Lien-Hang Nguyen's contention that Le Duan was the initiator. The latter suggests, based on Vietnamese sources, that Ho Chi Minh and NVA General Vo Nguyen Giap were surprised when they learned of the attack and discovered that party secretary Le Duan had approved the attack order. Nguyen email to Marolda,

11 January 2019.

20. Hanyok, "Skunks, Bogies, Silent Hounds, and the Flying Fish," 4–10. See also Richard A. Mobley and Edward J. Marolda, *Knowing the Enemy: Naval Intelligence in Southeast Asia*, in series The U.S. Navy and the Vietnam War, Edward J. Marolda and Sandra Doyle, eds. (Washington, DC: NHHC, 2015), 21.

21. Msg, CTG 77.5 021008Z August 1964. See also *Maddox*, Action Report, ser 003, 24 August; *Maddox*, Patrol Report, ser 002, 24 August; *Maddox*, Deck Log, 1–31 August.

22. Msg, CPFLT 021104Z August 1964. Moorer frequently stressed the importance of upholding the concept of freedom of the seas. See, for instance, Moorer interview with Ted Gittinger, 16 September 1981, LBJ Oral Histories, LBJ Library, 8.

23. Quoted in Puryear, *American Admiralship*, 253. See also Naoyuki Agawa, *Friendship Across the Seas: The US Navy and the Japan Maritime Self-Defense Force* (Tokyo: Japan Publishing Industry Foundation for Culture, 2019), 152.

24. Hanoi did not share Johnson's view, considering all the US-led operations of the previous months in North Vietnam and along its coastline as pre-planned, coordinated, and especially provocative. See Moise, *Tonkin Gulf and the Escalation of the Vietnam War*, 66, 76.

25. Johnson, *The Vantage Point*, 113.

26. Msg, JCS 021725Z August 1964; "Statement by the President Upon Instructing the Navy to Take Retaliatory Action in the Gulf of Tonkin, August 3, 1964," in *Public Papers of the Presidents of the United States, Lyndon Johnson: 1963–64* (Washington, DC: US Government Printing Office, 1965), bk. II, 926–27.

27. Msg, CTG72.1 021443Z August 1964.

28. Msg, CPFLT 032259Z August 1964. See also Sharp USNI OH, 222–23, 226.

29. Msg, CP 032353Z August 1964.

30. Michael R. Beschloss, *Taking Charge: The Johnson White House Tapes, 1963–1964* (New York: Simon & Schuster, 1997), 496–97.

31. Msg, CTG72.1 041240Z August 1964.

32. Msg, COM7FLT 041540Z August 1964.

33. Msg, CP 041657Z August 1964.

34. Msg, CP 041718Z August 1964.

35. Joint Staff, JCS, Tonkin Gulf Composite Diary; Outline Chronology of Washington Actions, tab B; msgs, CP 041547Z August 1964; 051840Z; CPFLT 130059Z; CP 280350Z October; CPFLT 140403Z November; CP 240042Z; COM7FLT 311102Z March 1965; memo, OP-601 to CNO, ser BM0001780-64, 15 December 1964.

36. Msg, CTG72.1 041727Z August 1964.

37. Msg, CTG72.1 041754Z August 1964.

38. Msg, CTG72.1 041848Z August 1964.

39. Roy L. Johnson interview with John T. Mason, December 1980, USNI OH, 238.

40. Moorer USNI OH, 526.

41. Joint Staff, JCS, Tonkin Gulf Composite Diary. See also Outline Chronology of Washington Actions, tab B; Shulimson, *The Joint Chiefs of Staff and the*

War in Vietnam, 1960–1968, pt. 1, 11–22.

42. Pierre Asselin, *Hanoi's Road to the Vietnam War, 1954–1965* (Berkeley, CA: University of California Press, 2013), 196–97. One of the few voices still asserting that North Vietnamese naval forces attacked *Maddox* and *Turner Joy* on 4 August belongs to retired Rear Admiral Lloyd R. Vasey, in August 1964 the Seventh Fleet chief of staff. See Lloyd R. Vasey, "Tonkin: Setting the Record Straight," in *Vietnam: A Retrospective*, Thomas J. Cutler, ed., 12–23 (Annapolis: Naval Institute Press, 2016).
43. Joint Staff, JCS, Outline Chronology of Washington Actions, tab B; Sharp USNI OH, 230, 250–51; Sharp, *Strategy for Defeat*, 44; Johnson, *The Vantage Point*, 115; JCS, *History*, pt. 1, 11–22.
44. Johnson, *The Vantage Point*, 117. See also msgs, JCS 042119Z August 1964; CP 042153Z; JCS 042157Z.
45. For a detailed account of the Pierce Arrow strikes, see Moise, *Tonkin Gulf and the Escalation of the Vietnam War*, 220–40.
46. Despite later stating that "I was never a great supporter of the Vietnam War," Congressman Melvin Laird, a future secretary of defense, opined at the time that it was necessary to take "whatever steps are necessary to win the war . . . within a reasonable period of time." The United States had to follow a "winning policy in Vietnam, or get out." Quoted in Van Atta, *With Honor*, 96 (see also 173).
47. Msg, CTG72.1 042002Z August 1964. See also Johnson USNI OH, 184.
48. Msg, CP 170530Z August 1964. Indeed, Moise has cogently observed that "if . . . the actual reason that PT boats had come out to fight an American destroyer on August 2—that the coastal defense forces were unwilling to tolerate the presence of hostile warships near their territory after the OPLAN 34A attacks against DRV coastal facilities—it would have been hard to avoid noticing that the DRV had to a significant extent achieved its goal. Washington kept U.S. Navy destroyers much farther from the coast after August 2 than before." Moise, *Tonkin Gulf and the Escalation of the Vietnam War*, 258.
49. Van Staaveren, *Interdiction in Southern Laos*, 35. See also Kaplan et al., *The McNamara Ascendancy*, 525.
50. Marolda and Fitzgerald, *From Military Assistance to Combat*, 453–62; Cosmas, *The Joint Chiefs of Staff and the War in Vietnam, 1960–1968*, pt. 2, 133–34; Schlosser, *The Greene Papers*, 202–9; Moise, *Tonkin Gulf and the Escalation of the Vietnam War*, 266–69.
51. Msg, CP 210025Z September 1964.
52. Msg, CPFLT 230639Z September 1964. President Eisenhower first referred to the Domino Effect in 1954. He suggested that if one country (such as Vietnam) fell to communist aggression, its neighbors would fall one after another like stacked dominoes.
53. Quoted in Schlosser, *The Greene Papers*, 215. See also Marolda and Fitzgerald, *From Military Assistance to Combat*, 466–69; Cosmas, *The Joint Chiefs of Staff and the War in* Vietnam, *1960–1968*, pt. 2, 187–88; Kaplan et al., *The McNamara Ascendancy*, 525–26.
54. Quoted in Van Staaveren, *Gradual Failure*, 103 (see also 57, 219). One Air Force general suggested that in implementing OPLAN 39-65, the Air Force and Navy could bomb "highly selective" targets in China that would convince

Mao of the folly of his aggressive behavior.

55. Marolda and Fitzgerald, *From Military Assistance to Combat*, 452–53, 460; Van Staaveren, *Gradual Failure*, 97–99.

56. John Fass Morton, *Mustin: A Naval Family of the Twentieth Century* (Annapolis: Naval Institute Press, 2003), 283. See also McDonald USNI OH, 393; Doris Kearns Goodwin, *Lyndon Johnson and the American Dream: The Most Revealing Portrait of a President and Presidential Power Ever Written* (New York: St. Martin's Press, 1991), 256, 282; Dallek, *Flawed Giant*, 242, 249, 276, 344.

57. Halberstam, *The Best and the Brightest*, 298. See also George C. Herring, "*Cold Blood*": *LBJ's Conduct of Limited War in Vietnam*, The Harmon Memorial Lectures in Military History, U.S. Air Force Academy, CO, 1991, 2–3, 22; Wright, *Enduring Vietnam*, 88–89.

58. The sources differ on the total number of MiGs delivered to North Vietnam in late 1964. See Asselin, *Hanoi's Road to the Vietnam War*, 201, and Zhang, "The Vietnam War: A Chinese Perspective," 741. See also Van Staaveren, *Gradual Failure*, 52; Schlosser, *The Greene Papers*, 166; Khoo, *Collateral Damage*, 19; Marolda and Fitzgerald, *From Military Assistance to Combat*, 470.

59. Qiang Zhai, *China and the Vietnam Wars, 1950–1975* (Chapel Hill: University of North Carolina Press, 2000), 10–33, 43–64, 92–111; Peter Worthing, *A Military History of Modern China: From the Manchu Conquest to Tian'anmen Square* (Westport, CT: Praeger Security International, 2007), 174–76. Between 1950 and 1956, the PRC provided North Vietnam with 155,000 small arms, 58 million rounds of ammunition, 3,600 artillery pieces, 1.08 million artillery shells, 1,200 vehicles, and 26,000 tons of fuel. Xiaobing Li, *A History of the Modern Chinese Army* (Lexington: University Press of Kentucky, 2007), 208–15. See also Xiaobing Li, *Building Ho's Army: Chinese Military Assistance to North Vietnam* (Lexington, KT: University Press of Kentucky, 2019), 3, 112-14, 134.

60. Zhai, *China and the Vietnam Wars*, 112–29. See also Kochavi, "Limited Accommodation, Perpetuated Conflict," 132–33.

61. Information from Chinese sources in John W. Garver, "The Chinese Threat in the Vietnam War," *Parameters* (Spring 1992): 76; Xiaoming Zhang, "The Vietnam War, 1964-1969: A Chinese Perspective," in *Readings in American Military History*, James M. Morris (Upper Saddle River, NJ: Pearson/Prentice Hall, 2004), 323, 734, 736, 748; Nguyen, *Hanoi's War*, 66, 75; Chen Jian, *Mao's China and the Cold War* (Chapel Hill: University of North Carolina Press, 2001), 207; Kochavi, "Limited Accommodation, Perpetuated Conflict," 134; Li, *A History of the Modern Chinese Army*, 215. See also Guan, *The Vietnam War from the Other Side*, 39–40, 46; Mobley and Marolda, *Knowing the Enemy*, 25.

62. Quoted in Zhai, *China and the Vietnam Wars*, 131. See also Jian, *Mao's China and the Cold War*, 208–15.

63. Quoted in Jung Chang and Jon Halliday, *Mao: The Unknown Story* (New York: Anchor Books, 2006), 472.

64. Quoted in Ilya V. Gaiduk, *The Soviet Union and the Vietnam War* (Chicago: Ivan R. Dee, 1996), 14.

65. Chang and Halliday, *Mao*, 473. M. Taylor Fravel, in his *Active Defense: China's*

Military Strategy since 1949 (Princeton: Princeton University Press, 2019), 113–15, 127–28, disagrees with this interpretation, contending that Mao launched the Third Front program to disarm opponents to his domestic policies in the Chinese Communist Party rather than as a reaction to an external threat.

66. Zhai, *China and the Vietnam Wars*, 132–33; Defense Intelligence Agency, Special Report, "The Chinese Communist Navy, August 1965; Mobley and Marolda, *Knowing the Enemy*, 41; Gaiduk, *The Soviet Union and the Vietnam War*, 16.
67. Zhai, *China and the Vietnam Wars*, 138–39; Khoo, *Collateral Damage*, 22.
68. Nguyen, *Hanoi's War*, 75.
69. Zhai, *China and the Vietnam Wars*, 135, 139; Xiaoming Zhang, "The Vietnam War, 1964–1969," 742, 743, 750.
70. Hyland USNI OH, 385; Xiaoming Zhang, "The Vietnam War, 1964–1969," 743, 745. See also Polmar and Marolda, *Naval Air War*, 16; Zhai, *China & the Vietnam Wars*, 143.
71. Li, *A History of the Modern Chinese Army*, 219, 215–26; Xiaobing Li, "The Dragon's Eyes in the Ocean: Chinese Naval Intelligence and the Cold War," paper presented at the 2013 Naval History Symposium, US Naval Academy, 10–11, 13, 15, 22–26; Zhai, *China and the Vietnam Wars*, 134–35; Worthing, *A Military History of Modern China*, 176–78; Khoo, *Collateral Damage*, 29, 74; Garver, "The Chinese Threat in the Vietnam War," 77–78; Xiaoming Zhang, "China's Involvement in Laos During the Vietnam War," 1157; Jian, *Mao's China and the Cold War*, 215–29; Xiaobing Li, *Voices from the Vietnam War: Stories from American, Asian, and Russian Veterans* (Lexington: University of Kentucky Press, 2005), 5, chap 22, 237–38; Xiaobing Li, *The Dragon in the Jungle: The Chinese Army in the Vietnam War* (New York: Oxford University Press, 2020), 8, 232, 245.
72. Between 1968 and 1975, China sent North Vietnam 233,000 rifles, 9,000 artillery pieces and other guns, and thousands of tons of ammunition each year. During the same period, the PRC sent to Vietnam 518 tanks, 106 naval vessels, and 74 aircraft. Zhihua Shen and Danhui Li, *After Leaning to One Side: China and Its Allies in the Cold War* (Stanford, CA: Stanford University Press, 2011), 226, 229, 234–35, 239, 243.
73. Douglas Pike, *Vietnam and the Soviet Union: Anatomy of an Alliance* (Boulder, CO: Westview Press, 1987), 60, 73.
74. Zhai, *China and the Vietnam Wars*, 149–50; Nguyen, *Hanoi's War*, 75.
75. Gaiduk, *The Soviet Union and the Vietnam War*, 24, 40, 58–59, 60–61, 70–72; CIA, "Soviet and Chinese Aid to North Vietnam 1965 and 1966," CIA Online Library, FOIA.CIA.GOV; Khoo, *Collateral Damage*, 27; Mobley and Marolda, *Knowing the Enemy*, 43.
76. Asselin, *Hanoi's Road to the Vietnam War*, 175, 198, 199, 200; Guan, *The Vietnam War from the Other Side*, 80–82.
77. Msg, CP 170530Z August 1964; Van Staaveren, *Gradual Failure*, 55, 57.
78. Msg, CPFLT 290418Z September 1964; Cosmas, *The Joint Chiefs of Staff and the War in Vietnam, 1960–1968*, pt. 2, 543.
79. Msg, CPFLT 290418Z September 1964.
80. Schlosser, *The Greene Papers*; Van Staaveren, *Gradual Failure*, 59; Cosmas,

The Joint Chiefs of Staff and the War in Vietnam, 1960–1968, pt. 2, 149–55.

81. Msg, CPFLT 012131Z November 1964. See also Sharp, *Strategy for Defeat,* 49; Trauschweizer, "Cautious Hawk," 833; Mark Perry, *Four Stars* (Boston: Houghton Mifflin Co., 1989), 142, 144.
82. Quoted in Goodwin, *Lyndon Johnson and the American Dream,* 270 (see also 282). In his memoir, Johnson disingenuously implied that his advisors and Congress were more concerned about Chinese intervention than he. Johnson, *The Vantage Point,* 119, 131.
83. Quoted in Mark Clodfelter, *The Limits of Air Power: The American Bombing of North Vietnam* (Lincoln: University of Nebraska Press, 1989), 43.
84. McNamara, *In Retrospect,* 109, 160, 526; Schlosser, *The Greene Papers,* 248–52; Kaplan et al., *The McNamara Ascendancy,* 526.
85. Morton, *Mustin,* 274; Van Staaveren, *Gradual Failure,* 62, 65–66.
86. Sharp, *Strategy for Defeat,* 4.
87. Msg, CP 230555Z November 1964.
88. Msg, CP 230515Z November 1964. Sharp got support for his graduated approach from his primary contact in Washington, Vice Admiral Lloyd Mustin, the JCS representative to the National Security Council's working group looking at the Vietnam problem. Mustin suggested that "a program of progressively increasing squeeze" on North Vietnam to limit infiltration "*may* [original emphasis] be enough to turn the tide" in favor of the South Vietnamese war effort. Pentagon Papers, Gravel Edition, III: 213–14, quoted in Clodfelter, *The Limits of Air Power,* 78. See also msg, CP Command History, 1964, 384–85.
89. Sharp, *Strategy for Defeat,* 52 (see also 61). Sharp was certainly in line with the thinking of William Bundy, the State Department official responsible for East Asian and Pacific affairs. Bundy recommended "focusing at length on low-key targets not so much for the sake of damage [to the enemy] as to show how hopeless the DRV is." He added that the "undramatic 'water drip' technique" would have greater impact on Hanoi than "more dramatic attacks" as championed by the JCS. Quoted in McMaster, *Dereliction of Duty,* 187.
90. Quoted in Shulimson, *The Joint Chiefs of Staff and the War in Vietnam, 1960–1968,* pt. 1, 14–27.
91. As is clear from the preceding discussion, and in contrast to Thomas Ricks's assertions, the key US military leaders were instrumental to the development and execution of the "graduated escalation" approach to the problem in Southeast Asia. Thomas Ricks, *The Generals: American Military Command from World War II to Today* (New York: The Penguin Press, 2012), 255–57.

CHAPTER 3

1. Quoted in Shulimson, *The Joint Chiefs of Staff and the War in Vietnam, 1960–1968,* pt. 1, 15–22.
2. Moorer USNI OH, 509 (see also 545, 810). Shortly after the Soviets deployed SA-2 surface-to-air missiles (SAM) to North Vietnam, McNaughton suggested that the objective was to stiffen North Vietnamese morale and not to shoot down US aircraft. See Van Staaveren, *Gradual Failure,* 114. For a detailed account of the deployment and operation of Soviet-manned SAM batteries during Rolling Thunder, see Merle L. Pribbenow II, "The -Ology

War: Technology and Ideology in the Vietnamese Defense of Hanoi, 1967," *Journal of Military History* (January 2003), 175–99.
3. Moorer USNI OH, 808. Alex Kerr, a legal officer who worked with McNaughton, acknowledged that he "was very abrupt and some people thought quite arrogant, but he was so smart that his arrogance, or apparent arrogance, was mainly impatience toward people who didn't seem to know what they were doing." Alex Kerr USNI OH, 488. See also Halberstam, *The Best and the Brightest*, 362–65, 501; Duncan USNI OH, 733, 763.
4. Zumwalt USNI OH, 384–85.
5. CINCPAC, *Command History*, 1965, 393.
6. Msg, CP 050207Z February 1965.
7. CINCPAC, Command History, 1965, Vol. II, 395.
8. Sharp, *Strategy for Defeat*, 67.
9. Msg, CPFLT 010109Z March 1965.
10. Msg, CINCPAC 050253Z March 1965; msg, AMEMBVT 060215Z March 1965.
11. Quoted in Schlosser, *The Greene Papers*, 323. See also Van Staaveren, *Gradual Failure*, 78.
12. Sharp, *Strategy for Defeat*, 57; CINCPACFLT, "The United States Navy in the Pacific, 1965," ser 1/00847, 18 July 1967, 21. See also Van Staaveren, *Gradual Failure*, 12; Moorer USNI OH, 508; Cosmas, *The Joint Chiefs of Staff and the War in Vietnam, 1960–1968*, pt. 2, 213–18; Kaplan et al., *The McNamara Ascendancy*, 530.
13. Schlosser, *The Greene Papers*, 346.
14. Moorer USNI OH, 510.
15. Kaplan et al., *The McNamara Ascendancy*, 531; Van Staaveren, *Gradual Failure*, 81.
16. Dennis Chamberland, "Interview: Westmoreland," in Thomas J. Cutler, ed. *Vietnam: A Retrospective* (Annapolis: Naval Institute Press, 2016), 59.
17. Msg, CP 130356Z February 1965. See also Cosmas, *MACV: The Joint Command in the Years of Escalation, 1962–1967* (Washington, DC: U.S. Army Center of Military History, 2006), 166, 174.
18. Quoted in Cosmas, *MACV: The Joint Command in the Years of Escalation, 1962–1967*, 175. See also 323–24; Moorer USNI OH, 788.
19. U. S. G. Sharp, *Strategic Direction of the Armed Forces* (Newport, RI: Naval War College Press), 1977), 48. See also William W. Momyer, *Airpower in Three Wars* (Washington, DC: US Government Printing Office, 1983), 79.
20. Many Air Force leaders, however, steeped in the doctrine of the "centralization of air power," sided with Westmoreland. Historian Mark Clodfelter concluded that the absence of a single air commander for Indochina "produced chaos." Clodfelter, *The Limits of Air Power*, 128. See also John Schlight, *The War in South Vietnam: The Years of the Offensive, 1965–1968* (Washington, DC: Office of Air Force History, 1986), 130; Van Staaveren, *Gradual Failure*, 245.
21. Chamberland, "Interview: Westmoreland," 59. See also Cosmas, *MACV, 1962–1967*, 385; Jack Shulimson, *U.S. Marines in Vietnam: An Expanding War, 1966* (Washington, DC: History and Museums Division, 1982), 272; Van Staaveren, *Gradual Failure*, 243–47, 319; Ronald B. Frankum Jr., *Like*

Rolling Thunder: The Air War in Vietnam, 1964–1975 (Lanham, MD: Rowman & Littlefield, 2005), 43.

22. Schlight, *The War in South Vietnam*, 120. See also 58, 119, 121; Wayne Thompson, *To Hanoi and Back: The U.S. Air Force and North Vietnam* (Washington, DC: Smithsonian Institution Press, 2000), 18; Clodfelter, *The Limits of Air Power*, 129; Momyer, *Airpower in Three Wars*, 102; Van Staaveren, *Gradual Failure*, 209, 228–29, 247–48; James D. Ramage interview with Robert Lawson and Barrett Tillman, 1999, USNI OH, 289.
23. Thompson, *To Hanoi and Back*, 29; Johnson USNI OH, 309.
24. Quoted in Drea, *McNamara, Clifford, and the Burdens of Vietnam*, 12.
25. Quoted in Kaplan et al., *The McNamara Ascendancy*, 548.
26. Memo, SECDEF to Chairman JCS, 17 February 1965.
27. Msg, CPFLT 031912Z March 1965.
28. Msg, CP 271945Z February 1965.
29. CINCPAC, "Statement before the House Foreign Affairs Committee," 23 March 1965, 9.
30. Schlosser, *The Greene Papers*, 25, 330.
31. W. Hays Parks, "Rolling Thunder and the Law of War," *Air University Review* (January–February 1982).
32. Msg, CP 271945Z February 1965. See also Van Staaveren, *Gradual Failure*, 90, 129. Contrast that recommendation with Sharp's post–retirement article in *Reader's Digest* in which he said the United States should have embarked on a "sustained, maximum-effort attack on *all* [italics added] of the enemy's war-supporting industries, transportation facilities, military complexes, [and] petroleum-storage depots." U. S. Grant Sharp, "We Could Have Won in Vietnam Long Ago," *Reader's Digest* (May 1969): 121.
33. Johnson, *The Vantage Point*, 140.
34. Quoted in Van Staaveren, *Gradual Failure*, 25.
35. Quoted in Cosmas, *The Joint Chiefs of Staff and the War in Vietnam, 1960–1968*, pt. 2, 18-16, 225–35.
36. Moorer interview with Ted Gittinger, 16 September 1981, LBJ Oral Histories, LBJ Library, 30. See also Richard P. Hallion, *Rolling Thunder: 1965–1968* (Oxford, UK: Osprey Publishing, 2018), 4–5; Van Staaveren, *Interdiction in Southern Laos*, 54; Marolda and Fitzgerald, *From Military Assistance to Combat*, 506.
37. Msg, COM7FLT 141500Z March 1965. Goscha, "The Maritime Nature of the Wars for Vietnam," 80; Guan, *The Vietnam War from the Other Side*, 35.
38. Msg, CPFLT 100023Z March 1965.
39. Ibid.
40. Harry Train, then administrative aide to Navy secretary Nitze, later observed that McNamara "placed Nitze virtually in the chain of command as the guy to set up the Market Time operation" but that Navy leaders objected to "a civilian authority, the Secretary of the Navy . . . getting into the operational chain of command and he shouldn't be there." Train USNI OH, 147–48. Zumwalt related that he facilitated McNamara's desire to have the Coast Guard take part in the coastal patrol off South Vietnam. See Zumwalt USNI OH, 410; see also Berman, *Zumwalt*, 178. Of course, there were many more Navy and Coast Guard officials and military leaders involved in the Coast Guard's early

NOTES FOR CHAPTER 3   399

involvement in Market Time. See Alex Larzelere, *The Coast Guard at War: Vietnam 1965–1975* (Annapolis: Naval Institute Press, 1997), xix–8. See also Goscha, "The Maritime Nature of the Wars for Vietnam," 81–83.

41. Cosmas, *The Joint Chiefs of Staff and the War in Vietnam, 1960–1968*, pt. 2, 253–56. See also Havern, "The U.S. Coast Guard in the Vietnam War."
42. Quoted in Marolda and Fitzgerald, *From Military Assistance to Combat*, 519. Admiral Hyland, who served as Commander Seventh Fleet and Commander in Chief, Pacific Fleet, later complained that Westmoreland routinely tried to get operational control of the Seventh Fleet's carrier, amphibious, and naval gunfire forces. See Hyland USNI OH, 379–80.
43. Kochavi, "Limited Accommodation, Perpetuated Conflict," 107.
44. Quoted in Kaplan et al., *The McNamara Ascendancy*, 527.
45. Msg, CP 020400Z November 1964; Jack Shulimson and Charles M. Johnson, *U.S. Marines in Vietnam: The Landing and the Buildup, 1965* (History and Museums Division, USMC, 1978), xii; Sharp USNI OH, 234, 235, 242; msg, COMUSMACV 150123Z November 1964.
46. Msg, CPFLT 070647Z October 1965. This author disagrees with Halberstam's observation in *The Best and the Brightest*, 544, that Sharp "was far more aggressive than Westmoreland in the early days" with regard to deploying troops to South Vietnam.
47. Kaplan et al., *The McNamara Ascendancy*, 529, 533.
48. Marolda and Fitzgerald, *From Military Assistance to Combat*, 523; Nguyen, *Hanoi's War*, 65–66. Westmoreland later observed that "nobody was happy about committing U.S. troops, neither I nor [Maxwell] Taylor, but it simply came down to doing it or losing South Vietnam." Westmoreland interview with Charles B. MacDonald, 25 July 1985, LBJ Oral Histories, LBJ Library.
49. Msg, JCS 070001Z March 1965; msg, CP 240315Z February 1965; Kaplan et al., *The McNamara Ascendancy*, 532; Shulimson and Johnson, *U.S. Marines in Vietnam: The Landing and the Buildup, 1965*, 7.
50. Westmoreland, *A Soldier Reports*, 124.
51. Taylor, *Swords and Plowshares*, 316.
52. Quoted in Rearden, *Council of War*, 290–91.
53. Kaplan et al., *The McNamara Ascendancy*, 26. See also Schlight, *The War in South Vietnam*, 58; Shulimson and Johnson, *U.S. Marines in Vietnam: The Landing and the Buildup, 1965*, 53; Drea, *McNamara, Clifford, and the Burdens of Vietnam*, 26.
54. Quoted in McMaster, *Dereliction of Duty*, 233. See also Sharp, *Strategy for Defeat*, 70–71, 91; McNamara, *In Retrospect*, 183.
55. CFT76, report, "History of Amphibious Operations in South Vietnam, March 1965–December 1966," 8; McNamara, *In Retrospect*, 211; Shulimson and Johnson, *U.S. Marines in Vietnam: The Landing and the Buildup, 1965*, 3–27; COM7FLT, Command History, 1965; CINCPACFLT, "The United States Navy in the Pacific, 1965," 23–25; CINCPAC, Command History, 1965, Vol. II, 277–84, 452–53; MACV, Command History, 1965, 30–32, 99; Westmoreland, *A Soldier Reports*, 113–14, 123–31; Sharp, *Strategy for Defeat*, 69–74; Sharp USNI OH, 258–61, 272–73; Johnson, *The Vantage Point*, 138–41.
56. Quoted in CINCPACFLT, "The United States Navy in the Pacific, 1965," 57.

57. Westmoreland too bemoaned micromanagement of the air war from Washington. He later observed that McNamara's "views on the war—including how it was to be fought and the sources to be provided—were paramount." He added, "I do not recall that Washington ever specifically asked for my advice on the bombing, but in many cables I supported CINCPAC's position." Westmoreland interview with Charles B. MacDonald, 25 July 1985, LBJ Oral Histories, LBJ Library, 5, 8.

CHAPTER 4
1. CP msg 040304Z April 1965, quoted in Clodfelter, *The Limits of Air Power*, 81.
2. McNamara, *In Retrospect*, 153.
3. Quoted in Rearden, *Council of War*, 294. See also Cosmas, *The Joint Chiefs of Staff and the War in Vietnam, 1960–1968*, pt. 2, 283–86. Later that year, McNamara reiterated that conclusion, stating, "We don't believe today that bombing in the north will drive the North Vietnamese to the bargaining table or force them to cease their terror tactics" in South Vietnam. Van Staaveren, *Gradual Failure*, 191.
4. Sharp, *Strategy for Defeat*, 80, 96.
5. Quoted in Prados, *Vietnam*, 580n72.
6. Sharp, *Strategy for Defeat*, 80. See also Kaplan et al., *The McNamara Ascendancy*, 59–60; McMaster, *Dereliction of Duty*, 280.
7. Hughes, "Experiencing McNamara," 165.
8. CP msg 120314Z May 1965, quoted in Clodfelter, *The Limits of Air Power*, 83. See also Van Staaveren, *Gradual Failure*, 92–93, 130; Momyer, *Airpower in Three Wars*.
9. Sharp, *Strategy for Defeat*, 94–95; Johnson, *The Vantage Point*, 234, 35; Van Staaveren, *Gradual Failure*, 6; Jeffrey Record, "Why We Lost in Vietnam," in Thomas J. Cutler, ed., *Vietnam: A Retrospective* (Annapolis: Naval Institute Press, 2016), 24–41; McNamara, *In Retrospect*, 181.
10. Moorer later related that when he was the Pacific Fleet commander in early 1965, he flew to Washington "and talked to . . . everyone I could get to listen to me about mining Haiphong," but to no avail. Moorer USNI OH, 778.
11. Quoted in Van Staaveren, *Gradual Failure*, 189. See also Clodfelter, *The Limits of Air Power*, 83–84.
12. Cosmas, *The Joint Chiefs of Staff and the War in Vietnam, 1960–1968*, pt. 2, 520–22. See also Lawson Ramage USNI OH, 487–89; Edward J. Marolda, *By Sea, Air, and Land: An Illustrated History of the U.S. Navy and the War in Southeast Asia* (Washington, DC: Naval Historical Center, 1994), 113, 137, 141; Edward J. Marolda, ed. *Combat at Close Quarters: An Illustrated History of the U.S. Navy in the Vietnam War* (Annapolis: Naval Institute Press, 208), 15.
13. Krulak, "A Conflict of Strategies," 76; Cosmas, *The Joint Chiefs of Staff and the War in Vietnam, 1960–1968*, pt. 2, 19, 522; Marolda, *By Sea, Air, and Land*, 113, 137, 141.
14. Sharp, *Strategy for Defeat*, 85, 103.
15. Rearden, *Council of War*, 297; Herbert Y. Schandler, *The Unmaking of a President: Lyndon Johnson and Vietnam* (Princeton, NJ: Princeton University Press, 1977), 333; Westmoreland, *A Soldier Reports*, 76; J. D. Lawson USNI

OH, 308–9.
16. Quoted in Goodwin, *Lyndon Johnson and the American Dream*, 264 (see also 269).
17. Quoted in Goodwin, *Lyndon Johnson and the American Dream*, 331. See also Rearden, *Council of War*, 295; Thompson, *To Hanoi and Back*, vii.
18. Sharp, *Strategic Direction of the Armed Forces*, 3.
19. McNamara, *In Retrospect*, 294.
20. Sharp, *Strategy for Defeat*, 87. See also Clodfelter, *The Limits of Air Power*, 120, 122, 125; Goodwin, *Lyndon Johnson and the American Dream*, 321.
21. Quoted in Dallek, *Flawed Giant*, 244.
22. Quoted in Goodwin, *Lyndon Johnson and the American Dream*, 252, 331. See also Ricks, *The Generals*, 13, 202, 252–53. Tom Moorer remembered that Johnson was uncomfortable in the presence of military leaders. See Moorer USNI OH, 14, 660.
23. Nitze, *From Hiroshima to Glasnost*, 228. See also Zumwalt USNI OH, 369; Berman, *Zumwalt*, 134–35.
24. Zumwalt USNI OH, 405–6; Nitze interview with Dorothy Pierce, 20 November 1968, LBJ Oral Histories, LBJ Library.
25. Berman, *Zumwalt*, 458n11; Drea, *McNamara, Clifford, and the Burdens of Vietnam*, 12; Rearden, *Council of War*, 327–28.
26. Moorer USNI OH, 29, 1556–57. See also Halberstam, *The Best and the Brightest*, 600.
27. Moorer USNI OH, 1178, 1557.
28. McNamara, *In Retrospect*, 291. See also Thompson, *To Hanoi and Back*, 81.
29. McDonald USNI OH, 321, 323.
30. Holloway interview with Marolda, 39–40. See also Zumwalt USNI OH, 395; Thomas C. Hone and Curtis A. Utz, *History of the Office of the Chief of Naval Operations, 1915–2015* (Washington, DC: Naval History and Heritage Command, 2018), 248.
31. Quoted in McMaster, *Dereliction of Duty*, 83. See also Drea, *McNamara, Clifford, and the Burdens of Vietnam*, 67, 107–8; Moorer USNI OH, 15, 741.
32. McDonald USNI OH, 353–55. See also 389, 410.
33. McDonald USNI OH, 368. See also 323, 373; Berman, *Zumwalt*, 148; Nitze interview with Dorothy Pierce, 10 December 1968, LBJ Oral Histories, LBJ Library, 13–14; Drea, *McNamara, Clifford, and the Burdens of Vietnam*, 67.
34. McDonald USNI OH, 378 (see also 408).
35. Ibid., 410. William Mack observed that McNamara was "an intelligent and extremely well-informed person and yet [could] make an asinine argument [which] he did a lot." At another time, Mack concluded that McNamara was a "jackass and the group working for him were jackasses." Mack USNI OH, 328, 411. Thomas Hayward considered the Whiz Kids "very, very stupid." Thomas B. Hayward interview with Paul Stillwell, 2009, USNI OH, 80, 145.
36. McDonald USNI OH, 139, 388, 396. Not all naval officers disparaged McNamara and his civilian staff, however. Vice Admiral Gerald Miller, who spent many years in the Pentagon, credited "McNamara and his people with a lot of wisdom, good objective looks at things, and rational actions, decisions to clean up and improve our capabilities to do the job." Miller USNI OH, 311. See also Peet USNI OH, 267.

37. McDonald USNI OH, 390–91 (see also 388). Vice Admiral Lloyd Mustin, J-3 for Operations on the Joint Staff, claimed that once the JCS members considered resigning in protest over administration policies. See Morton, *Mustin*, 275. Many other sources, including Moorer, Greene, and Wheeler, contest his conclusion. Indeed, the JCS chairman suggested the rumor was "bullshit!" Drea, *McNamara, Clifford, and the Burdens of Vietnam*, 217.
38. McDonald USNI OH, 393, 396.
39. Quoted in Kaplan et al., *The McNamara Ascendancy*, 55.
40. Hyland USNI OH, 338 (see also 308, 416, 570). This conclusion was shared by Lawson Ramage, who served under Hyland as his deputy and chief of staff. Ramage observed that "there was absolutely no discretion left to the Commander in Chief Pacific, not to Commander in Chief, Pacific Fleet . . . nor anybody down the line." Ramage USNI OH, 474.
41. Parks, "Rolling Thunder and the Law of War," 3; Sharp, *Strategy for Defeat*, 85.
42. Clodfelter, *The Limits of Air Power*, 86–87; Hyland USNI OH, 308.
43. Sharp, *Strategy for Defeat*, 104.
44. Quoted in Clodfelter, *The Limits of Air Power*, 90.
45. Halberstam, *The Best and the Brightest*, 439; Davidson, "Senior Officers and Vietnam Policymaking," 59; Buzzanco, *Masters of War*, 244.
46. Johnson, *The Vantage Point*, 241, 250. See also Clodfelter, *The Limits of Air Power*, 91–92.
47. Quoted in Clodfelter, *The Limits of Air Power*, 93. Johnson never approved the mining operation. In an exchange with General Wheeler, the president asked the JCS chairman, "Do you think [a mining campaign] will involve the Chinese Communists and the Soviets?" Wheeler responded, "No sir," prompting Johnson, with Chinese intervention in the Korean War clearly in mind, to ask rhetorically, "Are you more sure than MacArthur was?" Quoted in Clodfelter, *The Limits of Air Power*, 97. See also Dallek, *Flawed Giant*, 373; Johnson, *The Vantage Point*, 369; McNamara, *In Retrospect*, 163.
48. Morton, *Mustin*, 280.
49. Sharp, *Strategy for Defeat*, 141, 149; Lawson Ramage USNI OH, 477.
50. Van Staaveren, *Gradual Failure*, 249–51, 279–86.
51. Ibid., 288.
52. Quoted in Van Staaveren, *Gradual Failure*, 286. See also 287–89; Clodfelter, *The Limits of Air Power*, 96; Kaplan et al., *The McNamara Ascendancy*, 69, 74–77; Prados, *Vietnam*, 159–62.
53. Polmar and Marolda, *Naval Air War*, 41.
54. Clodfelter, *The Limits of Air Power*, 98–99.
55. Richardson USNI OH, 197; Sharp, *Strategy for Defeat*, 118; Van Staaveren, *Gradual Failure*, 297–307, 323; Frankum, *Like Rolling Thunder*, 51.
56. Sharp, "We Could Have Won in Vietnam," *Air Force Magazine* (September 1971), 83.
57. Morton, *Mustin*, 282. See also Sharp, "We Could Have Won in Vietnam," *Air Force Magazine* (September 1971), 83; Kaplan et al., *The McNamara Ascendancy*, 179; Shulimson, *U.S. Marines in Vietnam: 1966*, 314–18, 319; Jack Shulimson, Leonard A. Blasiol, Charles R. Smith, and David A. Dawson, *U.S. Marines in Vietnam: The Defining Year, 1968* (Washington, DC: History

and Museums Division, USMC, 1997), 21–23, 31; Graham A. Cosmas, *The Joint Chiefs of Staff and the War in Vietnam, 1960–1968*, pt. 3 (Washington, DC: Office of Joint History, 2009), 38–43; Van Staaveren, *Interdiction in Southern Laos*, 257; Sharp, *Strategy for Defeat*, 137; Van Staaveren, *Gradual Failure*, 324.

58. Sharp, *Strategy for Defeat*, 124, 126, 134.
59. Ibid., 127.
60. CINCPAC Command Histories, 1967, 1968. The USNI interviews with top admirals David L. McDonald, Horacio Rivero, and Roy Johnson make no mention of the Mobile Riverine Force or the Navy's combat leaders involved in in-country operations.
61. See Edward J. Marolda, "Orphan of the Mekong Delta: The Army-Navy Riverine Force," *Journal of Military History* (October 2016). For additional information on Army-Navy riverine operations, see Marolda, *By Sea, Air, and Land*; John Darrell Sherwood, *War in the Shallows: U.S. Navy Coastal and Riverine Warfare in Vietnam, 1965–1968* (Washington, DC: Naval History and Heritage Command, 2015); William B. Fulton, *Riverine Operations, 1966–1969* (Washington, DC: Department of the Army, 1972); Edward J. Marolda and R. Blake Dunnavent, *Combat at Close Quarters: Warfare on the Rivers and Canals of Vietnam*, in series The U.S. Navy in the Vietnam War, Edward J. Marolda and Sandra K. Doyle, eds. (Washington, DC: Naval History and Heritage Command, 2015); Cosmas, *The Joint Chiefs of Staff and the War in Vietnam, 1960–1968*, pt. 2, 473–74; William C. McQuilkin, "Operation SEALORDS: A Front in a Frontless War: An Analysis of the Brown Water Navy in Vietnam," MA thesis, U.S. Army Command and General Staff College, Fort Leavenworth, KS, 1997.
62. Robert S. Salzer interview with John T. Mason, 1977, USNI, 327, quoted in Marolda, "Orphan of the Delta," 1160.
63. For a comprehensive description of the MRF's operations during the Tet Offensive, see Erik V. Villard, *Staying the Course: October 1967 to September 1968*, in series The United States Army in Vietnam: Combat Operations (Washington, DC: Center of Military History, US Army, 2017), 367–79, 468–71, 632–36; Sherwood, *War in the Shallows*, 275–311; ltr, Salzer to Zumwalt, 17 October 1969, NFV Records, NHHC, Lessons Learned, Box 543.
64. George C. O'Connor, Senior Officers Debriefing Report, 14 March 1968, 7–8, HRC 314.82 Debriefs, U.S. Army Center of Military History.
65. Marolda, "Orphan of the Delta," 1158, 1160, 1166. See also James H. Willbanks, *The Tet Offensive: A Concise History* (New York: Columbia University Press, 2007), 41.
66. Introductory remarks by Rear Admiral Arthur W. Price Jr., in Norvell Ward interview with Price, April 1983, Rancho Santa Fe, CA, NHHC, 1. See also Marolda, "Orphan of the Delta," 1168, 1177; Norvell Ward interview with E. J. Marolda, NHHC, 6 September 1983, acc. no. 887076, NHHC. Vice Admiral James D. Ramage, on the CINCPACFLT staff from 1967 to 1970, remembered Sharp telling a book writer that "he didn't think that the riverine operations were of any value." James D. Ramage, USNI OH, 316.
67. Shulimson and Johnson, *U.S. Marines in Vietnam: The Landing and the Buildup, 1965*, 70 (see also 70–83).

68. Chamberland, "Interview: Westmoreland," 58.
69. Quoted in Shulimson and Johnson, *U.S. Marines in Vietnam: The Landing and the Buildup, 1965*, 203. See also Chamberland, "Interview: Westmoreland," 57; Westmoreland interview with Charles B. MacDonald, 25 July 1985, LBJ Oral Histories, LBJ Library, 6.
70. Shulimson and Johnson, *U.S. Marines in Vietnam: The Landing and the Buildup, 1965*, 304–6; Jack Shulimson, Gary L. Telfer, Lane Rogers, and V. Keith Fleming Jr., *The U.S. Marines in Vietnam: Fighting the North Vietnamese, 1967* ((Washington, DC: HQ, USMC, 1984), 150; Marolda, *By Sea, Air, and Land*, 133–34.
71. Shulimson et al., *U.S. Marines in Vietnam: The Defining Year, 1968*, 631–36.
72. Ibid., 636–39.
73. Shulimson and Johnson, *U.S. Marines in Vietnam: The Landing and the Buildup, 1965*, 151–52; Shulimson et al., *U.S. Marines in Vietnam: The Defining Year, 1968*, 472–73.
74. Quoted in Graham A. Cosmas, *MACV: The Joint Command in the Years of Withdrawal, 1968–'73* (Washington, DC: Center of Military History, US Army, 2007), 42–43.
75. Quoted in Cosmas, *MACV, 1962–'67*, 330. See also 328–29; Shulimson et al., *U.S. Marines in Vietnam, 1968*, 466.
76. Bernard C. Nalty, *Air War over South Vietnam, 1968–1975* (Washington, DC: Air Force History and Museums Program, 2000), 95.
77. Shulimson et al., *U.S. Marines in Vietnam, 1968*, 255; Thompson, *To Hanoi and Back*, 125.
78. Westmoreland, *A Soldier Reports*, 344. Years earlier, Sharp told General Greene that "General Westmoreland and Ambassador Taylor do not like Marines and will do everything they can to prevent the Marine Corps from getting credit for their accomplishments in South Vietnam." Quoted in McMaster, *Dereliction of Duty*, 304. See also Shulimson et al., *U.S. Marines in Vietnam, 1968*, 487; Nalty, *Air War over South Vietnam*, 93–96; Chamberland, "Interview: Westmoreland," 60.
79. Cosmas, *MACV, 1968–'73*, 43, 77–82; Nalty, *Air War over South Vietnam*, 114; Shulimson et al., *U.S. Marines in Vietnam, 1968*, 492; Schlight, *The War in South Vietnam*, 286; Bernard C. Nalty, *Air Power and the Fight for Khe Sanh* (Washington, DC: Office of Air Force History, 1973), 68–81.
80. Shulimson et al., *U.S. Marines in Vietnam, 1968*, 495–96; Sharp, *Strategic Direction of the Armed Forces*, 51.
81. Cosmas, *MACV 1968–'73*, 188; Nalty, *Air War over South Vietnam*, 96, 103, 116; Shulimson et al., *U.S. Marines in Vietnam, 1968*, 504–15.
82. Westmoreland, *A Soldier Reports*, 76, 318.
83. Admiral James L. Holloway III, Obituary, *The Washington Post*, 1 December 2019, C8; *20th Chief of Naval Operations Leaves Behind a Legacy of Service*, 27 November 2019, NHHC; James L. Holloway III Funeral Service Program, US Naval Academy Chapel, 18 December 2019.
84. James L. Holloway III, *Aircraft Carriers at War: A Personal Retrospective of Korea, Vietnam, and the Soviet Confrontation* (Annapolis: Naval Institute Press, 2007), 147; Puryear, *American Admiralship*, 205–7.
85. Elmo R. Zumwalt Jr. and Elmo Zumwalt III, *My Father, My Son* (New York:

Macmillan Publishers, 1986), 38.
86. Van Staaveren, *Gradual Failure*, 230.
87. Holloway interview with Marolda, pt. 1, 7.
88. Richardson USNI OH, 214. See also 209; Holloway interview with Marolda, 1, 7.
89. Holloway interview with Marolda, pt. 1, 6.
90. Richardson USNI OH, 193–94.
91. Holloway interview with Marolda, 1, 2.
92. Ibid., 3. See also Richardson USNI OH, 193.
93. Holloway interview with Marolda, 32.
94. Ibid., 27. McNamara wanted the next carrier built to be conventionally powered. When asked if the defense secretary was impressed by the combat record and operational efficiency of *Enterprise*, Moorer related that "they didn't know a damned thing about the performance of the ship." He marveled at their [McNamara's and Enthoven's] ability to come up with these decisions on programs while they didn't know a damned thing about what they were saying.... It was something like getting a hairdresser to remove your appendix." Moorer USNI OH, 672, 695. Admiral Charles K. Duncan had a similar appraisal of McNamara, whom he observed "made statements that would make one wonder if he'd been to high school" such as 'Why did we need more than one type of a plane on a carrier?'" Duncan USNI OH, 656.
95. Quoted in Puryear, *American Admiralship*, 356–58.
96. Holloway related that Rickover paid close attention to Holloway's command of *Enterprise* during the war but that "he left me alone." Holloway observed, "I had a wonderful relationship with Rickover. It was just super.... He'd tell me things and I usually didn't disagree with him because he was right [and] when I did disagree [with him] he would listen because he accepted the fact that I knew tactics." Holloway interview with Marolda, 14–16.
97. Tragically, Admiral Holloway's son, in 1964 a student at the University of Virginia, was killed in an automobile accident.
98. Holloway, *Aircraft Carriers at War*, 215, 220. See also Puryear, *American Admiralship*, 393–95.
99. Holloway, *Aircraft Carriers at War*, 214, 215, 221, 232.
100. Ibid., 234–35, 237, 239.
101. Ibid., 240–41.
102. McNamara, *In Retrospect*, 234.
103. Sharp, *Strategy for Defeat*, 167; Thompson, *To Hanoi and Back*, 19.
104. Morton, *Mustin*, 326. See also Moorer USNI OH, pt. 28, 1537; Cosmas, *MACV, 1962–'67*, 308–9; Schandler, *The Unmaking of a President*, 111; Westmoreland, *A Soldier Reports*, 190; Kaplan et al., *The McNamara Ascendancy*, 60, 61.
105. Gerald Miller USNI OH, 352.
106. Sharp, *Strategy for Defeat*, 180, 184. See also Thompson, *To Hanoi and Back*, 76; Kaplan et al., *The McNamara Ascendancy*, 54.
107. McNamara, *In Retrospect*, 176n, 245n.
108. US Congress, Senate, Preparedness Investigating Subcommittee of the Committee on the Armed Services, *Air War Against North Vietnam*. 90th Cong., 1st Sess. Washington, DC: US Government Printing Office, 1967, 75

(hereafter Stennis hearings). See also Cosmas, *The Joint Chiefs of Staff and the War in Vietnam, 1960–1968*, pt. 3, 70–72, 25; Morton, *Mustin*, 326; Ronald H. Spector, *After Tet: The Bloodiest Year in Vietnam* (New York: Free Press, 1993), 18.

109. Sharp, *Strategy for Defeat*, 193. See also Cosmas, *The Joint Chiefs of Staff and the War in Vietnam, 1960–1968*, pt. 3, 70–71.
110. Stennis Hearings pt. 2, 213. Nitze affirmed that the military "never recommended bombing the dikes; they did not think that would be militarily effective." Nitze interview with Dorothy Pierce, 10 December 1968, LBJ Oral Histories, LBJ Library, 12.
111. Quoted in Cosmas, *The Joint Chiefs of Staff and the War in Vietnam, 1960–1968*, pt. 3, 73.
112. Quoted in Sharp, *Strategy for Defeat*, 197. See also Rearden, *Council of War*, 310; Kaplan et al., *The McNamara Ascendancy*, 217.
113. Clodfelter, *The Limits of Air Power*, 109–10.
114. Kaplan et al., *The McNamara Ascendancy*, 203. See also Halberstam, *The Best and the Brightest*, 645.
115. Sharp, *Strategy for Defeat*, 201, 204; Kaplan et al., *The McNamara Ascendancy*, 213.
116. Msg, CINCPAC to CJCS, 261858Z December 1967, quoted in Schandler, *The Unmaking of a President*, 70.
117. Quoted in Van Staaveren, *Interdiction in Southern Laos*, 288. See also Clodfelter, *The Limits of Air Power*, 112.
118. Sharp, "We Could Have Won in Vietnam Long Ago," *Reader's Digest* (May 1969): 118. See also Buzzanco, *Masters of War*, 295.
119. Sharp, *Strategy for Defeat*, 216; Westmoreland, *A Soldier Reports*, 357.
120. Quotes from Dallek, *Flawed Giant*, x, 283, 390. See also Goodwin, *Lyndon Johnson and the American Dream*, 251; Wright, *Enduring Vietnam*, 99.
121. Moorer USNI OH, 31. See also Clark M. Clifford, "A Viet Nam Reappraisal: The Personal History of One Man's View and How It Evolved," *Foreign Affairs* (July 1969): 601–22.
122. Elmo R. Zumwalt Jr. interviews with Paul Stillwell, 1982–1986, USNI OH, 486; Thompson, *The Hawk and the Dove*, 217. Indeed, Nitze later applauded Johnson's decision to halt the bombing, which he thought could have been done sooner than 31 March. Nitze interview with Dorothy Pierce, 10 December 1968, LBJ Oral Histories, LBJ Library, 6.
123. Quoted in Thompson, *The Hawk and the Dove*, 217.
124. Cosmas, *The Joint Chiefs of Staff and the War in Vietnam, 1960–1968*, pt. 3, 255. Air Force General Momyer concurred, observing that "most of the top military commanders thought a halt to the bombing above the 20th parallel would be militarily acceptable." Momyer, *Airpower in Three Wars*, 27.
125. See Moorer USNI OH, 835–36. See also Cosmas, *The Joint Chiefs of Staff and the War in Vietnam, 1960–1968*, pt. 3, 171–72.
126. Sharp, *Strategy for Defeat*, 218, 225; Goodwin, *Lyndon Johnson and the American Dream*, 345; Drea, *McNamara, Clifford, and the Burdens of Vietnam*, 225; Clodfelter, *The Limits of Air Power*, 113–15.
127. Sharp, *Strategy for Defeat*, 228–29, 232 (see also 236).
128. Ibid., 233.

129. Ibid., 230. See also Moorer interview with Ted Gittinger, 16 September 1981, LBJ Oral Histories, LBJ Library, 16–19.
130. Moorer USNI OH, 534–35.
131. Moorer speech, 17 March 1973, Pittston, PA, quoted in Richard L. Schreadley, *From the Rivers to the Sea: The United States Navy in Vietnam* (Annapolis: Naval Institute Press, 1992), 361.
132. Sharp, *Strategy for Defeat*, xvii. See also Prados, *Vietnam*, 580n72.
133. Phillip B. Davidson, *Vietnam at War: The History: 1946–1975* (Novato, CA: Presidio, 1988), 515.
134. Schreadley, *From the Rivers to the Sea*, xii–xiii.
135. Quoted in Perry, *Four Stars*, 249.
136. Curiously, in his 1969 article in *Reader's Digest*, Sharp blamed McNamara, who "consistently discarded the advice of his military advisors," for the failure of the administration's Vietnam policies. However, he absolves Johnson, whom Sharp thought "was receptive to the arguments of our military leadership, but [that the opinion of] the Secretary of Defense seems always to have prevailed." Sharp, "We Could Have Won Long Ago in Vietnam," 119–20. See also Sharp, "Airpower Could Have Won in Vietnam," *Air Force Magazine* (September 1971): 82–83.

CHAPTER 5

1. McDonald, "Thomas Hinman Moorer," 357. See also US Congress, Senate. "Nomination of Admiral Thomas H. Moorer to be Chief of Naval Operations." Hearings before the Committee on Armed Services. 90th Cong., 1st Sess. Washington, DC: US Government Printing Office, 1967.
2. James Zumwalt, the son of Admiral Elmo R. Zumwalt Jr. and a Marine veteran of the Vietnam War, learned from a North Korean defector that Pyongyang might have attacked *Pueblo* to avenge the loss of face when US aviators shot down every North Korean MiG pilot flying in North Vietnam during 1967. James Zumwalt, "Was Frustration the Motivation?" *Navy Times* (23 November 2006), 46. See also Merle L. Pribbenow II, "The -Ology War: Technology and Ideology in the Vietnamese Defense of Hanoi, 1967," *Journal of Military History* (January 2003): 185.
3. McDonald, "Thomas Hinman Moorer," 357–58; Richard A. Mobley, *Flash Point North Korea: The Pueblo and EC-121 Crises* (Annapolis: Naval Institute Press, 2003); Moorer USNI OH, 704–9, 848; Paul R. Ignatius, *On Board: My Life in the Navy, Government, and Business* (Annapolis: Naval Institute Press, 2006), 150; Perry, *Four Stars*, 238.
4. Zumwalt shared Moorer's disdain for Bucher's leadership. During a meeting with Abrams in October 1969, Zumwalt compared Bucher to the captain of a Soviet spy ship who refused to stop for a search when confronted by a South Vietnamese naval vessel. Zumwalt was "full of admiration for the skipper of the *Guidrifon*. I wish the commanding officer of *Pueblo* had behaved half so well." Lewis Sorley, ed., *Vietnam Chronicles: The Abrams Tapes, 1968–1972* (Lubbock: Texas Tech University Press, 2004), 281. On the other hand, in a conversation between this author and Captain Lloyd Bucher at the Naval Historical Center, 27 March 1989, he related that after returning from captivity in North Korea, when many US naval leaders shunned him, Zumwalt got

him a staff job in appreciation for his years of creditable service in the Navy. William J. Crowe Jr. and David Chanoff, *The Line of Fire: From Washington to the Gulf, the Politics and Battles of the New Military* (New York: Simon & Schuster, 1993), 73, 57–74; Crowe interview with Paul Stillwell, Naval Historical Foundation, 2009.

5. Moorer USNI OH, 1152. See also McDonald, "Thomas Hinman Moorer," 358–70; Frederick H. Hartmann, *Naval Renaissance: The U.S. Navy in the 1980s* (Annapolis: Naval Institute Press, 1990), 11. Moorer late observed that Clark Clifford was "totally engrossed with getting out of the Vietnam War" and left "the technical problems [related to Navy ships, aircraft, and weapons] almost entirely up to Paul Nitze [Deputy Secretary of Defense]." Moorer USNI OH, 721.

6. King USNI OH, 330, 327, 329. See also Moorer USNI OH, 67–68, 70, 244, 248; Perry, *Four Stars*, 162.

7. Poole, *Adapting to Flexible Response*, 239. See also 240–42; Hone and Utz, *History of the Office of the Chief of Naval Operations*, 254. Berman, *Zumwalt*, 158–59, argues that even though Zumwalt's study supported acquisition of the F-111B, he and Moorer convinced McNamara to set aside funds for an alternative aircraft (later the F-14) if the Navy's version of the plane did not pan out.

8. Quoted in Perry, *Four Stars*, 172.

9. Ignatius, *On Board*, 162. Gerald Miller remarked that McNamara "never fought an airplane, never designed an airplane, never built an airplane, [and] never managed an airplane company [but] he can't be wrong because he is McNamara." Gerald Miller USNI OH, 491. See also Peet USNI OH, 268.

10. Hayward USNI OH, 150–51.

11. Quoted in Perry, *Four Stars*, 172.

12. Ignatius, *On Board*, 162.

13. Moorer USNI OH, 1571.

14. Ignatius, *On Board*, 152, 179. Zumwalt, from his vantage point in the systems analysis office, agreed that Ignatius and Moorer worked well together and shared a mutual respect. See Zumwalt USNI OH, 469; Moorer USNI OH, 840. William Thompson, who worked under Ignatius on the SECNAV staff, considered him "one of the most outstanding bosses I have ever had. He was a straight shooter, tough, a decision maker and not overly impressed with the ranks of admirals surrounding him. Additionally, he was cordial and communicative." William Thompson, *Gumption: My Life – My Words* (self-published, 2010), 288.

15. McDonald, "Thomas Hinman Moorer," 362; Moorer USNI OH, 357, 672, 738, 840, 1603. See also Van Atta, *With Honor*, 424; Zumwalt and Zumwalt, *My Father, My Son*, 102.

16. Peet USNI OH, 345, 349.

17. The feeling was mutual. Holloway related that he was "a great admirer of Admiral Tom Moorer" who "called on me quite often for specific jobs, and of course, I was flattered." Quoted in Puryear, *American Admiralship*, 205.

18. Holloway implicitly blamed the *Enterprise* fire, which killed twenty-eight sailors, seriously injured sixty-two others, and destroyed fifteen aircraft, on the ship's leaders, including the commanding officer, his long-time rival Kent L.

Lee, who "cut corners because they weren't getting the sorties out and they were being graded.... And that's what happens when you cut corners." He alluded to Rickover's "Rules of Engagement" that said "Do not cut corners" with safety. Holloway interview with Marolda, 36–37. See also Polmar and Marolda, *Naval Air War*, 43; Peter Fey, *Bloody Sixteen: The USS Oriskany and Air Wing 16 during the Vietnam War* (Lincoln, NE: Potomac Books, 2018), 5–25.

19. Holloway, *Aircraft Carriers at War*, 250–56. A film captured by one of *Forrestal*'s flight deck cameras of the July 1967 conflagration served for many years as a training tool that demonstrated the dire results of poor damage control practices.

20. Holloway interview with Marolda. Apparently, Rickover had a direct phone line established on the bridge of *Enterprise* so he could personally monitor how his first nuclear-powered carrier was faring in battle, but Holloway never used it; he communicated with the admiral through the traditional message system. Curiously, Francis Duncan's *Rickover: The Struggle for Excellence* (Annapolis: Naval Institute Press, 2001), a comprehensive and balanced biography, makes only passing reference to Holloway. Kent L. Lee, a classmate of Holloway's at the Naval Academy, frequent competitor for higher rank, and often an antagonist, credited the senior Holloway's fair treatment of Rickover to the latter's support for the junior Holloway. Kent L. Lee, USNI OH, 310.

21. Holloway, *Aircraft Carriers at War*, 269. See also Moorer USNI OH, 1574. John Lehman clearly loathed Rickover, observing that the admiral "had disdain for the Navy and many in the Navy had disdain for him.... Too many good men could [not] stomach Rickover's egotistical rages and rules." John Lehman, *On Seas of Glory: Heroic Men, Great Ships, and Epic Battles of the American Navy* (New York: The Free Press, 2001), 315.

22. Quoted in Puryear, *American Admiralship*, 391. Harry Train related that Moorer and Rickover had "a very good relationship" and that "they talked to each other frequently, they understood each other thoroughly, and there was no stress at all." Train USNI OH, 243.

23. Quoted in Puryear, *American Admiralship*, 397.

24. Duncan, *Rickover*, 228.

25. One source suggests that Holloway's father, then the chief of naval personnel, was instrumental in getting Rickover made captain when prejudice against the Jewish officer had threatened to prevent that promotion. Supposedly, "Rickover never forgot the kindness of the Holloway clan." See Perry, *Four Stars*, 255.

26. With his experience as a former commanding officer of *Enterprise*, Holloway became the point man on the Navy staff dealing with the heated opposition of many Japanese to the nuclear-powered ship's January 1968 visit to the naval base at Sasebo, Japan. As related by a Japanese scholar, the Japanese Maritime Self-Defense Force "cooperated fully" with Holloway in a successful effort to ease citizens' concerns. Agawa, *Friendship Across the Seas*, 179. See also Marolda, *Ready Seapower*, 73–74; Holloway, *Aircraft Carriers at War*, 256; Holloway interview with Marolda, 18.

27. Holloway, *Aircraft Carriers at War*, 262.

28. Holloway interview with Marolda. See also Puryear, *American Admiralship*,

396–99; Norman Polmar and Thomas B. Allen, *Rickover: Controversy and Genius* (New York: Simon and Schuster, 1982), 346–47.
29. Holloway, *Aircraft Carriers at War*, 257–58.
30. Ibid., 259, 373–74.
31. Ibid., 263, 264; Elmo R. Zumwalt Jr., *On Watch: A Memoir* (New York: Quadrangle/New York Times Book Co., 1976), 77; Holloway interview with Marolda, 22, 42.
32. Lee USNI OH, 315.
33. Ignatius, *On Board*, 159.
34. McDonald, "Thomas Hinman Moorer," 360–61; Gwendolyn Frazier Hall, "Managing Interservice Competition: The Relationship between the Secretary of Defense and the Joint Chiefs of Staff," PhD dissertation, University of Maryland, 1992, 160, 165. For greater detail on the Navy's personnel problems during this period, see Edward J. Marolda, "The Social History of the U.S. Navy, 1945–Present," in Michael J. Crawford, ed. *Needs and Opportunities in the Modern History of the U.S. Navy* (Washington, DC: Naval History and Heritage Command, 2018). Oral Presentation: http://www.youtube.com/watch?v=aIIB6V07jK8
35. McDonald, "Thomas Hinman Moorer," 361; Zumwalt, *On Watch*, 191.
36. Charlotte D. Crist, *Winds of Change: The History of the Office of the Master Chief Petty Officer of the Navy: 1967–1972* (Washington, DC: Office of MCPON/Naval Historical Center, 1972), 2–4, 14, 16–19. See also Jim Leuci, "Delbert Black: More Than Just a Gunner's Mate," Naval Historical Foundation "Thursday's Tidings," 1 October 2020.
37. Quoted in Crist, *Winds of Change*, 14–15, 17. See also Leuci, "Delbert Black: More Than Just a Gunner's Mate."
38. Crist, *Winds of Change*, 23.
39. Quoted in Crist, *Winds of Change*, 24. See also Puryear, *American Admiralship*, 250.
40. Train USNI OH, 215.
41. Quoted in Crist, *Winds of Change*, 3–4.
42. Wright, *Enduring Vietnam*, 168.
43. John Darrell Sherwood, *Black Sailor, White Navy: Racial Unrest in the Fleet During the Vietnam War Era* (New York: New York University Press, 2007), 22; Spector, *After Tet*, 273–78; Gregory A. Daddis, *Withdrawal: Reassessing America's Final Years in Vietnam* (Oxford, UK: Oxford University Press, 2017), 153.
44. Moorer USNI OH, 842. See also Richard A. Hunt, *Melvin Laird and the Foundation of the Post–Vietnam Military, 1969–1973*, in Secretaries of Defense Historical Series (Washington, DC: Historical Office, Office of the Secretary of Defense, 2015), 520.
45. Hyland USNI OH, 557–58.
46. Hunt, *Melvin Laird*, 521.
47. Ibid., 522–24; Van Atta, *With Honor*, 336–37; Nathan R. Packard, "Repairing the Wreckage of Vietnam: The Marine Corps' Great Personnel Campaign, 1975–1979," in Lori Lyn Bogle and James C. Rentfrow, *New Interpretations in Naval History: Selected Papers from the Eighteenth McMullen Naval History Symposium Held at the U.S. Naval Academy, 19–20 September 2013* (Newport,

RI: Naval War College Press, 2018), 257, 264.

This author, a 1st Lieutenant serving with the US Army at Long Binh, Republic of Vietnam, during 1970 was involved in the confiscation of marijuana from unit personnel.

48. Sherwood, *Black Sailor, White Navy*, 16–17; Wright, *Enduring Vietnam*, 120–22. See also Hayward USNI OH, 483. For a comprehensive look at all the social problems plaguing the US armed forces during this period of the war, see Daddis, *Withdrawal*; Packard, "Repairing the Wreckage of Vietnam," 254.
49. Sherwood, *Black Sailor, White Navy*, 18–22; Charles R. Smith, *High Mobility and Standdown, 1969*, in series U.S. Marines in Vietnam (Washington, DC: Histories and Museums Division, HQ USMC, 1988), 156–57.
50. Sherwood, *Black Sailor, White Navy*, 25, 27. See also Spector, *After Tet*, 242–59; Andrew J. Birtle and John R. Maass, *The Drawdown, 1970–1971*, in series The U.S. Army Campaigns of the Vietnam War. Washington, DC: U.S. Army Center of Military History, 2019, 46–47.
51. Sherwood, *Black Sailor, White Navy*, 26–29; Smith, *High Mobility and Standdown*, 156–57. See also Daddis, *Withdrawal*, 151.
52. Zumwalt USNI OH, 291, 421.
53. Robert J. Schneller, *Blue & Gold and Black: Racial Integration of the U.S. Naval Academy* (College Station: Texas A&M University Press, 2008), 117.
54. Duncan USNI OH, 1877.
55. Marolda, "The Social History of the U.S. Navy," 17.
56. Lee USNI OH, 437.
57. Quoted in Sherwood, *Black Sailor, White Navy*, 45.
58. Quoted in Wright, *Enduring Vietnam*, 121.
59. William R. Smedberg III, interview with USNI, July 1979, 745.
60. Moorer, USNI OH, 1264.
61. Moorer, USNI OH, 1483–84.
62. Quoted in McDonald, "Thomas Hinman Moorer," 351–52.
63. Zumwalt, *On Watch*, 268; Sherwood, *Black Sailor, White Navy*, 41–42; ltr, Kauffman to Zumwalt, 4 November 1972, Peter M. Swartz Papers.
64. One reflection of the civilian choke hold over strategy and policymaking during the war and the impotence of the JCS can be seen in Robert S. McNamara, James G. Blight, and Robert K. Brigham's *Argument Without End: In Search of Answers to the Vietnam Tragedy* (New York: Public Affairs, 1999). In the 450-page work documenting a series of meetings between American and Vietnamese connected to the war, McNamara dominates the proceedings, and the US military leaders get scant or no mention. The JCS are referred to collectively, and there are no more than one or two references to generals Earl Wheeler and Curtis LeMay. Absent from the narrative are admirals McDonald and Moorer as well as CINCPACs Felt, McCain, and Gaylor. Only generals Westmoreland and Taylor receive any coverage.
65. Richardson USNI OH, 207, 223.
66. Quoted in Puryear, *American Admiralship*, 251 (see also 61). Harry Train related that "the OpNav staff adored [Moorer because he was] a very, very authoritative figure [and] made decisions very, very easily." He added that "no one really argued with the decisions he made." Train USNI OH, 212, 215.

67. Moorer USNI OH, 664–66, 1194.
68. Moorer USNI OH, 94. Nonetheless, as Moorer discovered when he fleeted up to chairman of the JCS, Johnson was not a unique commander in chief in that regard. Nixon did not shy away from giving rudder orders to the admirals and generals executing operations in Southeast Asia. Cosmas, *The Joint Chiefs of Staff and the War in Vietnam, 1960–1968*, pt. 2; Train USNI OH, 217; McDonald, "Thomas Hinman Moorer," 356.
69. Warner USNI OH, 135. See also Drea, *McNamara, Clifford, and the Burdens of Vietnam*, 194; Reynolds, *Famous American Admirals*, 208–9.
70. Quoted in John McCain (with Mark Salter), *Faith of My Fathers* (New York: Random House, 1999), 260 (see also 258–59).
71. Moorer USNI OH, 785 (see also 1443–46).
72. Ibid., 786. See also 1447; Train USNI OH, 226, 230–31.
73. Henry A. Kissinger, *Ending the Vietnam War: A History of America's Involvement in and Extraction from the Vietnam War* (New York: Simon & Schuster, 2003), 145.
74. Robert Timberg, *The Nightingale's Song* (New York: Simon & Schuster, 1995), 137; McCain, *Faith of My Fathers*, 266, 287; John S. McCain Jr. interview with John T. Mason Jr., 1999, USNI OH, 20.
75. Quoted in Van Atta, *With Honor*, 153 (see also 178).
76. William Shawcross, *Sideshow: Kissinger, Nixon, and the Destruction of Cambodia* (New York: Simon and Schuster, 1979), 191 (see also 192–94).
77. Kissinger, *Ending the Vietnam War*, 145.
78. Cosmas, *MACV: The Joint Command in the Years of Withdrawal, 1968–'73*, 194–96, 370, 388.

CHAPTER 6

1. Wright, *Enduring Vietnam*, 195–96.
2. Quoted in Van Atta, *With Honor*, 124, 158, 173. See also Hunt, *Melvin Laird*, 104, 115; Van Atta, *With Honor*, 133, 182; Warner USNI OH, 65–66.
3. Zumwalt later related that the JCS were not informed of Nixon's promises to Thieu. Berman, *Zumwalt*, 306.
4. Berman, *Zumwalt*, 38. For a comprehensive account of Zumwalt's early life and education, see 27–40. The Zumwalt family granted Berman access to many personal documents and provided him with insight on the admiral's social and intellectual development. There are a number of other biographical treatments of Zumwalt, including the following: Dean C. Allard, "Elmo R. Zumwalt Jr.," in *Dictionary of American Military Biography*, Roger J. Spiller, Joseph G. Dawson III, T. Harry Williams, eds. (Westport, CT: Greenwood Press, 1984); Thomas J. Cutler, "Elmo R. Zumwalt Jr.: Hero or Heretic?" in *Quarterdeck & Bridge: Two Centuries of American Naval Leaders*, James Bradford, ed. (Annapolis: Naval Institute Press, 1997), 415–19; Norman Friedman, "Elmo Russell Zumwalt Jr.: 1 July 1970–1 July 1974," in Robert William Love Jr., *The Chiefs of Naval Operations* (Annapolis: Naval Institute Press, 1980); Thomas J. Cutler, "Elmo R. Zumwalt Jr.: Innovation," in *Leadership Embodied: The Secrets to Success of the Most Effective Navy and Marine Corps Leaders*, 2nd ed., Joseph J. Thomas, ed. (Annapolis: Naval Institute Press, 2013); R. Blake Dunnavent, "Maverick: Elmo Russell

Zumwalt Jr. (1920–2000)," in Hattendorf and Elleman, eds, *Nineteen-Gun Salute: Case Studies of Operational, Strategic, and Diplomatic Naval Leadership during the 20th and Early 21st Centuries*, John B. Hattendorf and Bruce A. Elleman, eds. (Newport, RI: Naval War College Press, 2010).

5. Berman, *Zumwalt*, 50–52, 56, 67.
6. Ibid., 75–78.
7. Ibid., 78–83.
8. Ibid., 73, 76, 85–93. Elmo and Mouza raised three children: Elmo R. III, James G., and Mouzetta.
9. Ibid., 116 (see also 94–115).
10. Zumwalt USNI OH, 349. See also Berman, *Zumwalt*, 129.
11. Zumwalt USNI OH, 353. See also Thompson, *The Hawk and the Dove*, 243. George W. Anderson, the CNO at the time, was equally impressed with Captain Zumwalt's presentation, which he thought reflected "broad intellectual capability . . . and high-quality professional competence." Ltr, Anderson to Zumwalt, 20 July 1962, Anderson Papers, NHHC, Box 48.
12. Thompson, *Gumption*, 262; Berman, *Zumwalt*, 130–31, 150–52; Zumwalt and Zumwalt, *My Father, My Son*, 38–39.
13. Quoted in Berman, *Zumwalt*, 154.
14. Cutler, "Elmo R. Zumwalt Jr.: Hero or Heretic?" 415–19; Friedman, "Elmo Russell Zumwalt Jr.: 1 July 1970–1 July 1974," 365–67; Zumwalt USNI OH, 449–50; Puryear, *American Admiralship*, 454.
15. John F. Lehman Jr., *Command of the Seas* (New York: Charles Scribner's Sons, 1988), 96, 107. Alain Enthoven, one of McNamara's "Whiz Kids," later observed that "we did try to encourage the military to do some systematic analysis and evaluation of the effectiveness of alternative kinds of operations." He admitted, however, that "we were much less successful than we would have liked to have been." Alain C. Enthoven interview with William W. Moss, 4 June 1971, JFK Library, 21.
16. Alex A. Kerr interview with Paul Stillwell, 1984, USNI OH, 450–51. Zumwalt provided materials for the preparation of Nitze's memoir that had the latter saying, "I needed someone on my staff to keep me alert on what was going on among uniformed Admirals. [Zumwalt] was my eyes and ears on uniformed Navy." Berman, *Zumwalt*, 139.
17. Thompson, *Gumption*, 247–48, 256, 264.
18. Alex Kerr USNI OH, 450. In contrast to assertions that Zumwalt had a significant influence on Nitze, in his 475-page *Hiroshima to Glasnost*, Nitze mentioned Zumwalt briefly and only with regard to Zumwalt serving as his assistant or naval aide. Nitze says nothing about their interaction on the Vietnam War, the admiral's stewardship of the Navy, or Strategic Arms Limitation Talks (SALT) deliberations.
19. Thompson, *Gumption*, 251.
20. Zumwalt, *On Watch*, 32.
21. Zumwalt USNI OH, 394, 467.
22. Ibid., 410, 411.
23. Ibid., 469. See also Berman, *Zumwalt*, 170, 462n35.
24. Moorer USNI OH, pt. 28, 1533.
25. Zumwalt USNI OH, 411, 469, 481.

26. Quoted in Berman, *Zumwalt*, 150.
27. Schreadley, *From the Rivers to the Sea*, 146.
28. Zumwalt and Zumwalt, *My Father, My Son*, 41. See also Zumwalt, *On Watch*, 41; Cutler, "Elmo R. Zumwalt Jr.,"419; Zumwalt USNI OH, 470, 482; Berman, *Zumwalt*, 7. Relying solely on Zumwalt's *On Watch* and Berman's *Zumwalt*, James Stavridis in *Sailing True North: Ten Admirals and the Voyage of Character* (New York: Penguin Press, 2019), 204, 206, repeats this tired and inaccurate story.
29. Ignatius, *On Board*, 152, 153, 160.
30. Zumwalt, *On Watch*, 35; Zumwalt and Zumwalt, *My Father, My Son*, 39; Zumwalt USNI OH, 559.
31. Zumwalt USNI OH, 481. See also Van Atta, *With Honor*, 142–44, 232–33; Berman, *Zumwalt*, 162–64.
32. Harry Train, who served under Moorer and truly admired him, once characterized the admiral's views as "a little bit to the right of Attila the Hun." Train USNI OH, 215.
33. Indeed, even Berman, who is familiar with the "get the son-of-a-bitch out of Washington" story, has observed that "for the next four years [of their tours of duty], Bud Zumwalt and Tom Moorer were able to forge a solid although rocky relationship. They were in general agreement on navy issues and budgets" and the Soviet threat. Nonetheless, Berman is on shaky ground when he suggests that Zumwalt and Moorer stood together against Nixon, Rickover, and Kissinger. Moorer did not take on Rickover, and he had close relationships with the president and Kissinger, unlike Zumwalt. Berman, *Zumwalt*, 218.
34. Zumwalt, *On Watch*, 35.
35. Marolda and Dunnavent, *Combat at Close Quarters*, 45. See also Marolda, *By Sea, Air, and Land*; Zumwalt USNI OH, 467; Moorer USNI OH, 768.
36. Marolda, *By Sea, Air, and Land*, 268–69.
37. Johnson USNI OH, 291. See also Goscha, "The Maritime Nature of the Wars for Vietnam," 82; Cosmas, *The Joint Chiefs of Staff and the War in Vietnam, 1960–1968*, pt. 2, 349–51.
38. Goscha, "The Maritime Nature of the Wars for Vietnam," 83; Havern, "The U.S. Coast Guard in the Vietnam War."
39. Sander, *Invasion of Laos 1971*, 72; Goscha, "The Maritime Nature of the Wars for Vietnam," 85–90; Kenneth Conboy. *The Cambodian Wars: Clashing Armies and CIA Covert Operations* (Lawrence: University Press of Kansas, 2013), 4–5; Wilfred P. Deac, *Road to the Killing Fields: The Cambodian War of 1970–1975* (College Station: Texas A&M University Press, 1997), 44, 52, 57.
40. Moorer USNI OH, 17, 914–15, 924. See also Zumwalt and Zumwalt, *My Father, My Son*, 88.
41. Mobley and Marolda, *Knowing the Enemy*, chapter 4. See also Sander, *Invasion of Laos 1971*, 71.
42. Eckhardt, Senior Officer Debriefing Report, 1 July 1969, HRC 314.82, U.S. Army Center of Military History. See also Marolda, *By Sea, Air, and Land*, 263–73; Willbanks, *Tet*; Berman, *Zumwalt*, 178–82.
43. Zumwalt and Zumwalt, *My Father, My Son*, 50. See also W. Lewis Glenn Jr. interview with Paul Stillwell, 1989, USNI OH, 176, 187, 195; Jackson K. Parker, 1987 interview, USNI OH, 283–85; Francis R. Kaine interview with

Etta-Bell Kitchen, 1991, USNI OH, 295; Schreadley, *From the Rivers to the Sea*, 146–47; Kit Lavell, *Flying Black Ponies: The Navy's Close Air Support Squadron in Vietnam* (Annapolis: Naval Institute Press, 2000), 91; Berman, *Zumwalt*, 195–96; Zumwalt USNI OH, 498.

44. Quoted in Douglas Brinkley, *Tour of Duty: John Kerry and the Vietnam War* (New York: William Morrow, 2004), 255.
45. Glenn USNI OH, 179, 186–87, 217. See also Berman, *Zumwalt*, 16, 196–97.
46. Lavell, *Flying Black Ponies*, 31. See also Berman, *Zumwalt*, 17. Lavell was not similarly pleased with Navy secretary John Chafee who, when he visited Binh Thuy in the Mekong Delta, stayed in his air-conditioned limousine as he "looked through the tinted, rolled-up windows at an ordnance display neatly arranged for him in front of an OV-10 in the hangar, and without stopping, motored on."
47. Peter M. Swartz interview with Marolda at Center for Naval Analyses, 20 February 2017.
48. Naval Station Newport, RI, Public Affairs release, 17 February 2017. For Kelley's Medal of Honor citation and his photograph, see Marolda, *By Sea, Air, and Land*, 374; Berman, *Zumwalt*, 17.
49. Swartz interview with Marolda 2017. See also Zumwalt USNI OH, 498; Berman, *Zumwalt*, 16.
50. Quoted in Schreadley, *From the Rivers to the Sea*, 198. See also Zumwalt USNI OH, 492; Jackson K. Parker USNI OH, 256, 330.
51. Arthur Price, End of Tour Report, January 1970, Price Collection, Texas Tech Vietnam Archive, acc. no. 162001030003, 4; ltr, Faulk to Zumwalt, 31 December 1969, NFV Records, NHHC, Lessons Learned, Box 543.
52. Zumwalt and Zumwalt, *My Father, My Son*, 63; Zumwalt USNI OH, 502.
53. Robert H. Stoner, "SEAL/MST Operations from Sea Float/Solid Anchor in 1970," 2008, unpublished mss, acc. no. 22360101004, Burton Brooks Williams Jr. Coll., Texas Tech Vietnam Archive, 13.
54. Virgil Erwin and Peter N. Upton, "Duong Keo," in Guy Gugliotta, John Yeoman, and Neva Sullaway, *Swift Boats at War in Vietnam* (Guilford, CT: Stackpole Books, 2017), 157.
55. Zumwalt USNI OH, 523–24. John Kerry was less charitable, suggesting that Hoffmann was after "splashy victories" in SEALORDS in order to get promoted. See Brinkley, *Tour of Duty*, 177.
56. Quoted in Brinkley, *Tour of Duty*, 296.
57. Peter M. Swartz interview with Marolda, Naval Historical Center, 21 July 1982, 77–78. acc. no. 887154.
58. Jim Corrigan, "Seafloat," in Gugliotta et al., *Swift Boats at War in Vietnam*, 165–69; 175–83.
59. Thomas Emery, "Sea Float," Naval Institute *Proceedings*. See also memo, Emery to Deputy COMNAVFORV, 30 March 1970, NFV Records, Lessons Learned, NHHC, Box 543.
60. Swartz interview with Marolda 2017.
61. Rauch, draft ltr, 1 January 1970, Charles F. Rauch Collection, acc. no. 4820104005, Texas Tech Vietnam Archive, 6. See also Berman, *Zumwalt*, 174; Swartz interview with Marolda 2017.
62. Zumwalt USNI OH, 543; Schreadley, *From the Rivers to the Sea*, 229.

63. Rauch, draft ltr, 1 January 1970, Charles F. Rauch Collection, acc. no. 4820104005, Texas Tech Vietnam Archive, 6.
64. Ted Kenny, "What the Hell Am I Doing Here," in Gugliotta et al., *Swift Boats at War in Vietnam*, 225.
65. Gugliotta et al., *Swift Boats at War in Vietnam*, 203.
66. Arthur Price End of Tour Report, January 1970, Price Collection, Texas Tech Vietnam Archive, acc. no. 162001030003, 2–3. For a detailed study of the fight to secure the Rung Sat and the primary river route to Saigon, see Salvatore R. Mercogliano, *Fourth Arm of Defense: Sealift and Maritime Logistics in the Vietnam War*, in series The U.S. Navy and the Vietnam War, Edward J. Marolda and Sandra J. Doyle, eds. (Naval History and Heritage Command, 2015), 43–48. See also Berman, *Zumwalt*, 203–4.
67. Zumwalt USNI OH, 495, 544. See also msg, Zumwalt to Ewell, 130914Z August 1969, NFV Records, NHHC, Box 416; memo, Assistant Chief of Staff for Operations, 1 September 1969, NFV Records, NHHC, Box 416.
68. Hunt, *Melvin Laird*, 212. Nixon was equally optimistic. In September, Moorer recorded that the president felt the South Vietnamese "are reaching a point where they can defend themselves." Moorer Diary, September 1971, Documents 9, NARA RG 218, Records of the JCS, Chairman JCS Admiral Moorer History File, Admiral Moorer Diaries, box 3, folder 17, September 1971, obtained by National Security Archive.
69. Quoted in Hunt, *Melvin Laird*, 231 (see also 553).
70. Zumwalt and Zumwalt, *My Father, My Son*, 43. See also Howard Kerr USNI OH, 46–47; Schreadley, *From the Rivers to the Sea*, 164; Zumwalt, *On Watch*, 36.
71. Sorley, *Vietnam Chronicles*, 236.
72. Moorer USNI OH, 1461, 1462.
73. Zumwalt, *On Watch*, 383.
74. Zumwalt USNI OH, 482–83. See also Hunt, *Melvin Laird*, 199–202. Kerr has a somewhat different recollection. He remembered Zumwalt stating "that if Nixon won the election [of 1968], we probably would have 18 months. If Humphrey won the election, we might only have six months." Howard Kerr USNI OH, 33, 47.
75. Van Atta, *With Honor*, 201–3, 244, 338–39, 367. At one point, presidential assistant H. R. Haldeman recorded in his diary that the administration could "announce [a] massive withdrawal right after the Vietnamese elections, and this is the P's [president's] present plan." H. R. Haldeman, *The Haldeman Diaries: Inside the Nixon White House* (New York: Berkley, 1994), 282.
76. Ltr, Rauch to Bill [unnamed], 12 July 1969, Charles F. Rauch Collection, Texas Tech Vietnam Archive, acc. no. 4820104003. Rauch admitted that he had little background for this assignment: "For a person who only recently recognized that there was a part of the Navy outside the submarine force it has been a new and somewhat traumatic experience." Ltr, Rauch to James V. Galloway, 28 August 1969, Rauch Collection, acc. no. 4820102090, Texas Tech Vietnam Archive. But Zumwalt prized him. Kerr related that Zumwalt found in Rauch "a person that was as loyal and supportive as any person that he had in Vietnam." Kerr USNI OH, 66. See also Glenn USNI OH, 183.
77. Berman, *Zumwalt*, 205.

78. Ltr, Rauch to Bill [unnamed], 12 July 1969, Charles F. Rauch Collection, Texas Tech Vietnam Archive, acc. no. 4820104003.
79. Msg 280121Z January 1970, COMNAVFORV to NAVFORV, Zumwalt Collection, Texas Tech Vietnam Archive, acc. no. 16200103004.
80. Rauch, draft ltr, 1 January 1970, Charles F. Rauch Collection, acc. no. 4820104005, Texas Tech Vietnam Archive, 6.
81. Ltr, Rauch to Bill [unnamed], 12 July 1969, Charles F. Rauch Collection, Texas Tech Vietnam Archive, acc. no. 4820104003, 5. See also Marolda, "Troubled Assignment," 249–57; Schreadley, *From the Rivers to the Sea*, 333–39.
82. Ltr, Rauch to Bill [unnamed], 12 July 1969, Charles F. Rauch Collection, Texas Tech Vietnam Archive, acc. no. 4820104003, 7. See also Arthur Price, End of Tour Report, January 1970, acc. no. 162001030003, Texas Tech Archive, 3–4.
83. Msg 280121Z January 1970, COMNAVFORV to NAVFORV, Zumwalt Collection, Texas Tech Vietnam Archive, acc. no. 16200103004.
84. Marolda, "Troubled Assignment," 249–57; Schreadley, *From the Rivers to the Sea*, 359–60; Berman, *Zumwalt*, 209.
85. As a NAVFORV staff officer, Swartz was also involved in the establishment and development of the non-profit Helping Hand Foundation, whose object was to see to the welfare of Vietnam Navy dependents and disabled veterans. Swartz interview with Marolda 2017. See also memo, CNO to President, Board of Directors, Helping Hand Foundation, Ser 3357P61, 27 December 1972, Peter M. Swartz Papers.
86. Marolda, "Troubled Assignment," 249–57.
87. Zumwalt USNI OH, 547.
88. Salzer USNI OH, 495, 596, 624. See also Spector, *After Tet*, xvi, 290. This author, a 1st Lieutenant in the US Army's 538th Transportation Company throughout 1970, operated resupply convoys all over III Corps from the Cambodian border in the north to Vung Tau in the south and into IV Corps as far as Dong Tam. During daylight, the roads (mostly asphalted) were thronged with commercial traffic and the roadside markets were bustling. Farmers operating US-supplied tillers and other equipment were exploiting the country's rich land all around. The enemy's presence along these transportation routes seemed minimal and consisted of ineffectual sniper fire and the occasional road mining or ambush.
89. Crowe and Chanoff, *The Line of Fire*, 83. See also Crowe interview with Paul Stillwell, Naval Historical Foundation, 2009.
90. Spector, *After Tet*, 282. See also 289, 312; Jayne S. Warner and Luu Doan Huynh, eds., *The Vietnam War: Vietnamese and American Perspectives* (Armonk NY: M.E. Sharpe, 1993), 49–50.
91. Nguyen, *Hanoi's War*, 130.
92. Willard J. Webb, *The Joint Chiefs of Staff and the War in Vietnam, 1969–1970* (Washington, DC: Office of Joint History, 2002), 102. See also Daddis, *Withdrawal*, 110; Hunt, *Melvin Laird*, 91.
93. Guan, *The Vietnam War from the Other Side*, 134. See also Nguyen, *Hanoi's War*, 112.
94. Moorer USNI OH, 945.
95. Glenn USNI OH, 206. Gerald Miller related that Zumwalt was "very popular

with the Army. . . . A lot of people on the Army staff told me how much they all admired Zumwalt." Gerald Miller USNI OH, 551.

96. "Admiral Zumwalt's address at the Industrial War College, Fort McNair, Washington, DC," 26 March 1975, Zumwalt Coll., acc. no. 6230606007, Texas Tech Vietnam Archive, 1.

97. Hyland USNI OH, 395. See also Marolda, "Orphan of the Mekong Delta," 1169–71. Nonetheless, Berman's assertion that "Bud Zumwalt was going into an area in which the two flag officers preceding him [rear admirals Norvell Ward and Kenneth L. Veth] had not been able to achieve anything significant" does a great disservice to two leaders who were in charge when the Navy essentially stymied the enemy's seaborne infiltration effort, secured the country's main rivers, and joined with the Army to devastate Viet Cong forces in the Mekong Delta during Tet. He is also far off base when he asserts that "until Bud arrived, the navy got little respect in Vietnam" where sailors remained in "well-protected areas." See Berman, *Zumwalt*, 169, 192.

98. Salzer USNI OH, 474. Westmoreland's attitude might have reflected his ignorance of naval history. In a post–war interview, he related that he didn't think the Navy did riverine operations during the Civil War. "I think they were done by the U.S. Army Engineers as General U. S. Grant operated along the Mississippi and the Cumberland rivers. There were some naval operations during the course of the Civil War, but they were mostly warfare at sea." Chamberland, "Interview: Westmoreland," 61.

99. Kenneth K. Veth interview with John T. Mason, July, August 1997, USNI OH, 403.

100. General Walter T. Kerwin Jr., USA Retired, Senior Officers Oral History Program, Project 80-2, Vol. II, U.S. Army Military History Institute, archived at U.S. Army Center of Military History.

101. Zumwalt USNI OH, 484.

102. Howard Kerr interview with Paul Stillwell, September 1982, USNI OH, 16, 32. See also Zumwalt and Zumwalt, *My Father, My Son*, 42; Zumwalt USNI OH, 490.

103. Quoted in Berman, *Zumwalt*, 171, 192. See also Zumwalt, *On Watch*, 37.

104. Zumwalt and Zumwalt, *My Father, My Son*, 77. See also Zumwalt USNI OH, 493.

105. Zumwalt and Zumwalt, *My Father, My Son*, 44. There is support for this view. See Marolda, "Orphan of the Mekong Delta." Zumwalt also faulted his administrative superior in the chain of command, CINCPACFLT, Admiral John J. Hyland, who "when he came out to Vietnam [did not] express any interest in what was going on there." Zumwalt USNI OH, 488, 509. Vice Admiral James D. Ramage, then on the CINCPACFLT staff, recalled that Hyland was concerned that Zumwalt was "operating beyond his authority." He "was doing things in the way of Vietnamization and giving away stuff that had never been cleared with us [which] was quite a problem." Ramage suggested that that episode later influenced Zumwalt's forced retirement of Hyland. Ramage USNI OH, 316.

106. Zumwalt USNI OH, 488. See also Berman, *Zumwalt*, 250–51. Gerald Miller did not agree that Hyland was incompetent but that he had made a speech in which he averred that only an aviator should command the Seventh Fleet.

Miller and many other naval aviators had "great reverence" for Hyland, a "highly respected naval aviator." Gerald Miller USNI OH, 586, 592.
107. Zumwalt USNI OH, 501, 510. See also Sorley, *Vietnam Chronicles*, 275.
108. Ignatius, *On Board*, 160.
109. Zumwalt USNI OH, 505, 507.
110. Quoted in Berman, *Zumwalt*, 191, 219.
111. Zumwalt, *On Watch*, 277.
112. Zumwalt, *On Watch*, 39–40.
113. W. Lewis Glenn Jr. USNI OH.
114. Earl F. Rectanus, "The Naval Intelligence Organization Vietnam," 3 March 2008, Zumwalt Collection, acc. no. 1955010200, Texas Tech Vietnam Archive, 5. Berman credits many of the Navy's accomplishments of the SEALORDS program to the corps of Naval Intelligence Liaison Officers, which is an overstatement. While the twenty to twenty-five NILOs routinely did good work, they were too few in number to seriously affect the strategic or operational situation. See Berman, *Zumwalt*, 184–87.
115. Swartz interview with Marolda 2017. Perhaps in jest, Commander John A. Walker Jr., the Assistant Chief of Staff for Psychological Warfare and VNN Welfare, in memo 45-70, 8 March 1970, Peter M. Swartz Papers, recommended that a Navy team be dispatched to Australia for a "kangaroo round-up." He observed that "kangaroos are reported to be proficient in hand-to-hand combat. [His staff was] attempting to identify funds for a comprehensive feasibility study of [a] dual purpose program to include training of kangaroo guerrillas in addition to meat production. Such a program should accelerate U.S. troop redeployment."
116. Stoner, "SEAL/MST Operations from Sea Float/Solid Anchor in 1970," 10.
117. Zumwalt USNI OH, 500. See also Zumwalt and Zumwalt, *My Father, My Son*, 163; Schreadley, *From the Rivers to the Sea*, 227; Berman, *Zumwalt*, 203; Paul Stillwell, "Looking Back: Death of a Family Man," Naval Institute *Proceedings* (April 2000): 4.
118. Paul A. Yost Jr. interviews with Paul Stillwell, May–November 2001, USNI, 230, 240, 255, 282. See also Spector, *After Tet*, 221, who quotes Salzer describing a 9th Infantry Division brigade commander who was a "super fanatic on body count." Ewell, the division commander, was referred to by some as the "Butcher of the Mekong Delta." Daddis, *Withdrawal*, 54, 95. Hugh Highland, who served as a young officer in river units, remembered that "everybody was looking for bodies.... There is no doubt... they wanted dead bodies, so you reported dead bodies." He also related that "I had the feeling that those things were not very reliable." Hugh Highland interview with Marolda, 10 August 1982, NHHC.
119. Yost USNI OH, 269.
120. Quoted in Brinkley, *Tour of Duty*, 286. Carvel Blair, who commanded riverine forces earlier in the war, related to Zumwalt that the "Viet Cong often gain propaganda value" from short-term raids because they could point to "death and destruction resulting from U.S./GVN operations." Ltr, Blair to Zumwalt, 20 June 1969, NVF Records, NHHC, Lessons Learned, Box 543.
121. Yost USNI OH, 258. In a similar vein, Swartz observed that "in Vietnam we were working for a guy, Zumwalt, who wanted to win the war so badly that he

could taste it." Swartz interview with Marolda 2017.
122. Quoted in Berman, *Zumwalt*, 166, 174.
123. Yost USNI OH, 239–40. Schreadley, *From the Rivers to the Sea*, 327, observed that like other charismatic leaders Zumwalt "collected more than a few self-serving sycophants in their train. From only being told what one wants to be told, to seeing things not as they are but as they are wished to be, is a small but fatal step."
124. Yost USNI OH, 246, 281. See also 222–23, 228–30; Daddis, *Withdrawal*, 71.
125. Schreadley, *From the Rivers to the Sea*, 328.
126. Crowe and Chanoff, *The Line of Fire*, 77. From December 1970 to November 1971, South Vietnamese forces, while losing 490 men, killed 4,900 Viet Cong troops. Birtle and Maass, *The Drawdown*, 64.
127. Swartz interview with Marolda 2017.
128. Schreadley, *From the Rivers to the Sea*, 227, 238; Willard J. Webb and Walter S. Poole, *The Joint Chiefs of Staff and the War in Vietnam, 1971-1973* (Washington, DC: Office of Joint History, 2007, 85.
129. Zumwalt, *On Watch*, 39–40. Apparently, CNO Moorer only grudgingly approved ACTOV (which entailed the transfer of Navy equipment to a foreign navy), but since he was responsible for that material that is no surprise. See Berman, *Zumwalt*, 191.
130. Ltr, Rauch to Bill [unidentified], 12 July 1969, Charles F. Rauch Coll., acc. no. 44820104003, Texas Tech Vietnam Archive, 4–5.
131. Born in Vung Tau, Chon studied at the French Maritime Navigation School in Saigon and then sailed in the merchant marine. He served in the French Navy and was one of the first nine Vietnamese naval officers in that service. He also graduated from the US Naval War College. After his return to Vietnam, he served in various military capacities until being named on 1 November 1966 the Chief of Naval Operations of the VNN. He retired from the navy on 1 November 1974 and died on 2 May 2019.
132. Quoted in Berman, *Zumwalt*, 210. See also Zumwalt and Zumwalt, *My Father, My Son*, 65. This was hardly the "brilliantly effective command team" that Stavridis refers to in *Sailing True North*, 206.
133. Zumwalt and Zumwalt, *My Father, My Son*, 63, 65, 77, 106, 123, 130–31; Zumwalt, *On Watch*, 494. Rauch shared the admiration of his boss for Chon, whose "wisdom, foresight, common sense and leadership ability" made him "one of the finest Naval officers I have known." Rauch, draft ltr, 1 January 1970, Charles F. Rauch Collection, acc. no. 4820104005, Texas Tech Vietnam Archive, 6. Berman also refers to the "remarkable" Chon. See Berman, *Zumwalt*, 205–6.
134. Zumwalt USNI OH, 510.
135. Ltr, Zumwalt to Chon, 12 July 1974, Zumwalt Coll., acc. no. 6210206081, Texas Tech Vietnam Archive.
136. Ltr, Chon to Zumwalt, 21 June 1974, Zumwalt Coll., acc. no. 6210206082, Texas Tech Vietnam Archive.
137. Ltr, Chon to Zumwalt, 10 November 1974, Zumwalt Coll., acc. no. 6210206005, Texas Tech Vietnam Archive. See also Chon to Zumwalt, 21 November 1974, Zumwalt Coll., acc. no. 6210206006. Refusing Zumwalt's offer to spirit the admiral and his family from Saigon in April 1975, Chon

bravely remained in Vietnam to care for his family and because he believed in the "highly respected tradition that the captain will not abandon his ship unless she is completely sunk." The officer paid a price for his self-sacrifice, spending the next twelve years in a communist "reeducation" camp and enduring brutal treatment by his captors. Zumwalt worked for many years to secure Chon's release from imprisonment. When Chon came to the United States in 1992, he and Zumwalt met in San Francisco and "tears trickled down their faces." Ltr, Chon to Zumwalt, 25 February 1993, Zumwalt Coll., acc. no. 6230115004, Texas Tech Vietnam Archive; Berman, *Zumwalt*, 420.

138. Zumwalt, *On Watch*, 41. See also Berman, *Zumwalt*, 207.
139. Zumwalt USNI OH, 516; Howard Kerr USNI OH, 135, 136.
140. Zumwalt, *On Watch*, 41. See also Berman, *Zumwalt*, 207; Zumwalt and Zumwalt, *My Father, My Son*, 40; Zumwalt USNI OH, 516.
141. Thomas C. Hone, *Power and Change: The Administrative History of the Office of the Chief of Naval Operations, 1946–1986* (Washington, DC: Naval Historical Center, 1989), 85.
142. Quoted in Van Atta, *With Honor*, 270. See also Zumwalt, *On Watch*, 47.
143. Moorer Diary, September 1971, Document7, NARA RG 218, Records of the JCS, Chairman JCS Admiral Moorer History File, Admiral Moorer Diaries, box 3, folder 17, September 1971, obtained by National Security Archive.
144. Schreadley, *From the Rivers to the Sea*, 166 (see also xii–xiv). Commander Schreadley produced a draft work in 1970 that revealed so many problems with ACTOV that the admiral refused to distribute a finished copy. Indeed, the manuscript and an accompanying lessons-learned study were deposited in the Operational Archives of the Naval Historical Center, in much the same way as the Ark of the Covenant was archived in the last scene of the 1981 film *Raiders of the Lost Ark*. R. L. Schreadley, *From the Rivers to the Sea*, xii, lumped Zumwalt with Kennedy, Johnson, Nixon, and other "fatally flawed" American leaders of the Vietnam War. See also ltr, Norvell Ward to Zumwalt, 14 January 1970, NFV Records, NHHC, Lessons Learned, Box 543.
145. Crowe and Chanoff, *The Line of Fire*, 81, 85.
146. "Vietnamese Court Sentences Rebels," *The Washington Post* (4 December 1987), A31.
147. Hoang Co Minh interview with Oscar Fitzgerald, Naval History Division, 8, 18 September 1975, acc. no. NHHC, 4, 44.
148. Minh interview, 44, 59.
149. Ibid., 33, 41 (see also 46–47).
150. Ibid., 34–35.
151. Ho Van Ky Thoai interview with Oscar Fitzgerald, Naval History Division, 20 September 1975, acc. no. 88916, NHHC, 38.
152. Nguyen Xuan Son interview with Oscar Fitzgerald, Naval History Division, 16 July 1975, acc. no. 887180, NHHC, 15–16.
153. Thoai interview.
154. Minh interview, 35–39.
155. Ibid., 29–30; Schreadley, *From the Rivers to the Sea*, 332–33.
156. Zumwalt and Zumwalt, *My Father, My Son*, 105.
157. King USNI OH, 222–23, 238.
158. During his change of command ceremony in Saigon prior to taking on the

CNO job, Zumwalt related that he had had "the good fortune to participate" in King's selection. Zumwalt gave Moorer a short list of four or five people he had a high regard for, and understanding Moorer's affinity for King, his former aide, included his name. But Zumwalt's first choice to replace him was Salzer. Zumwalt USNI OH, 519, 550; Schreadley, *From the Rivers to the Sea*, 325.

159. King USNI OH, 377, 79, 399.
160. Zumwalt USNI OH, 550. See also Berman, *Zumwalt*, 222–23.
161. King USNI OH, 388, 390. See also Salzer USNI OH, 543.
162. King USNI OH, 398.
163. Zumwalt USNI OH, 502. Swartz interview with Marolda 2017.
164. King USNI OH, 395–96. ARVN leaders' dislike of Vietnamese marines operating in the delta had a long history. Zumwalt complained to Abrams during a meeting in March 1969 that the IV Corps commander would not accept two marine battalions as replacement for departing US 9th Infantry Division troops. Salzer complained that he got little support in the delta from either the South Vietnamese army or the marines. See Sorley, *Vietnam Chronicles*, 236; Salzer USNI OH, 612–13.
165. Dinh Manh Hung interview with Oscar Fitzgerald, Naval History Division, 19, 21 August 1975, acc. no. 887169, NHHC, 11–12.
166. Assistant Chief of Staff to COMNAVFORV, 3 July 1970, NFV Records, NHHC, Box 415; memoir for the record, Report of Field Trip to SEAFLOAT/Operation Tran Hung Dao III on 31 July 1970, 5 August 1970, NFV Records, NHHC, Box 415; memo, King to Chon, 12 August 1970, NFV Records, NHHC, Box 415; Assistant Chief of Staff to COMNAVFORV, 31 October 1970, NFV Records, NHHC, Box 417; Schreadley, *From the Rivers to the Sea*, 224–25.
167. King USNI OH, 397, 398.
168. Ibid., 391. See also Salzer USNI OH, 543.
169. Crowe and Chanoff, *The Line of Fire*, 78, 80. See also Salzer USNI OH, 572; Minh interview, 28.
170. Peter M. Swartz email to Marolda, 22 February 2017.
171. Minh interview, 57, 61–64.
172. King USNI OH, 392, 401, 405, 408, 411, 412. When Medal of Honor recipient Captain Thomas G. Kelley visited South Vietnam in 1971, he found many of the VNN ships and craft "in terrible shape, inoperable, and rusty." Kelley conversation with this author, Naval Historical Center, 14 December 1989.
173. Quotes from King USNI OH, 404–6 and Zumwalt USNI OH, 550. See also Moorer USNI OH, 938. King served under CNO Zumwalt after the former's return from Vietnam, "chafing every moment under that regime." He added, "It was a very strained relationship we had, and I was working directly for him—very uncomfortable." Moorer came to the rescue, assigning King to the Joint Staff. King USNI OH, 238, 418, 426.
174. Zumwalt USNI OH, 519, 523.
175. Salzer USNI OH, 480. See also 530; Schreadley, *From the Rivers to the Sea*, 363–75; Zumwalt USNI OH, 522.
176. Moorer also recognized that under Vietnam Navy control the effectiveness of the Market Time patrol during 1971 had suffered. See Webb and Poole, *The*

Joint Chiefs of Staff and the War in Vietnam, 99.
177. Goscha, "The Maritime Nature of the Wars for Vietnam," 84.
178. Salzer USNI OH, 598.
179. Mobley and Marolda, *Knowing the Enemy*, 68–70.
180. Salzer USNI OH, 546, 603 (see also 607–8).
181. Nguyen Huu Chi interview with Oscar Fitzgerald, Naval History Division, 21 August 1975, NHHC, 15–16. Captain Son made a similar observation that once the American air support was withdrawn, the coastal patrol was much less effective. See Son interview, 4.
182. Goscha, "The Maritime Nature of the Wars for Vietnam," 91.
183. Salzer USNI OH, 550, 552, 596.
184. Salzer USNI OH, 217.
185. Salzer USNI OH, 380, 442, 448, 490. He also disdained the South Vietnamese army's leaders. He condemned the actions of an ARVN division commander during the Tet Offensive of 1968: "That son of a bitch . . . was about to bug out. All he was doing was packing his car and wailing 'my city has gone; my city has gone.'" Salzer remarked sarcastically when the South Vietnamese Joint General Staff promoted a general, that "he had all . . . the right attributes to be a Vietnamese corps commander." Salzer USNI OH, 405 (see also 380). Willbanks, in his *The Tet Offensive*, 41, relates that "the ARVN colonel commanding at Vinh Long cracked under the stress of the situation." He added that a "provincial adviser found his province chief wearing civilian clothes under his military uniform—just in case he had to make a quick escape."
186. Quote from Brinkley, *Tour of Duty*, 143 (see also 203, 296–97).
187. Salzer USNI OH, 7, 321, 448–49, 498, 554, 618, 638.
188. Hunt, *Melvin Laird*, 207. See also 551; Mercogliano, *Fourth Arm of Defense*, 65.
189. Van Atta, *With Honor*, 270. Knowing the end of the story, Berman blames "political authority" for not giving Vietnamization the time it needed to properly prepare the South Vietnamese to take over the war, but Zumwalt was the most impatient of all the service leaders, wanting to quickly end the US commitment. Berman, *Zumwalt*, 210.
190. Salzer USNI OH, 545–46.
191. Minh, who professed being "clean," believed that "many of the high ranking [VNN] officers were corrupt" and the ARVN leaders were "all corrupt." See Minh interview, 67.
192. Son interview, 61. Laird's biographer, in discussing the weaknesses in the South Vietnamese leadership, observed that the defense secretary considered "corruption . . . one of the enemies of Vietnamization that [he] had not been able to defeat." Quoted in Van Atta, *With Honor*, 406.
193. Salzer USNI OH, 547–48, 553, 621.
194. Salzer USNI OH, 553, 554, 569–70, 617, 693.
195. Zumwalt, *On Watch*, 377–78.
196. "Admiral Zumwalt's address at the Industrial War College, Fort McNair, Washington, DC," 26 March 1975, Zumwalt Coll., Vietnam Archive, acc. no. 6230606007, 8.
197. Thoai interview, 13.
198. Chung Tan Cang interview with Oscar Fitzgerald, 31 July 1975, Naval History

Division, NHHC, 57.
199. Quoted in Hunt, *Melvin Laird*, 552. See also 557; Spector, *After Tet*, xvii, 116, 313; David L. Anderson, *Vietnamization: Politics, Strategy, Legacy* (Lanham, MD: Rowan & Littlefield, 2019), 1–10.
200. Zumwalt and Zumwalt, *My Father, My Son*, 134, 163.

CHAPTER 7

1. Quoted in Hunt, *Melvin Laird*, 147. See also Moorer USNI OH, 625; Rearden, *Council of War*, 317. William Burr and Jeffrey P. Kimball, in *Nixon's Nuclear Specter: The Secret Alert of 1969, Madman Diplomacy, and the Vietnam War* (Lawrence: University Press of Kansas, 2015), 106–12, 134–35, 150–51, relate that the administration considered, in the effort to increase Soviet pressure on Hanoi's peace negotiators, mining and blockading North Vietnam as an alternative to bombing in Cambodia. Nixon also ordered an October 1969 nuclear alert exercise for the same purpose.
2. Quoted in Perry, *Four Stars*, 205. See also Moorer USNI OH, 86–87; 918–19.
3. Hunt, *Melvin Laird*, 144–52; Van Atta, *With Honor*, 179–80; David P. Chandler, *The Tragedy of Cambodian History: Politics, War, and Revolution since 1945* (New Haven: Yale University Press, 1991), 184.
4. Moorer USNI OH, 865.
5. John Morrocco, *Rain of Fire: Air War, 1969–1973*, in series The Vietnam Experience (Boston: Boston Publishing Co., 1986), 11–14. See also Hunt, *Melvin Laird*, 151–52; Moorer USNI OH, 918.
6. Quoted in Morrocco, *Rain of Fire*, 15. Whether Nixon knew it or not, the real power in the North Vietnamese government was actually in the hands of Le Duan, the hardest of the hard-liners in Hanoi. Moreover, Ho Chi Minh was ill and would die that September.
7. Wright, *Enduring Vietnam*, 288, quoting from David F. Schmitz, *Richard Nixon and the Vietnam War: The End of the American Century* (Lanham, MD: Rowman & Littlefield, 2014), 62.
8. Alexander M. Haig interview with Naftali/Powers, 30 November 2007, Nixon Library, 11. See also James Duermeyer, *The Capture of the USS Pueblo: The Incident, the Aftermath and the Motives of North Korea* (Jefferson, NC: McFarland & Co., 2018; Bill Streifer and Irek Sabitov, "Improbable Allies: The North Korean Downing of a U.S. Navy EC-121 and U.S.-Soviet Cooperation during the Cold War," *Naval War College Review* (Spring 2020): 104–40.
9. In line with consideration of mining North Vietnam's ports, in May 1969 Commander Task Force 77 directed his subordinate command in the Philippines to train selected air squadrons from *Enterprise* for offensive mine warfare. Msg, CTF 77 to CTG 77.4 131602Z May 1969, National Security Archive. See also "Memorandum From the President's Assistant for National Security Affairs (Kissinger) to President Nixon (Duck Hook Plan)," 2 October 1969, in *Foreign Relations of the United States, 1969–1976*, Vol. VI, *Vietnam, January 1969–July 1970* (Washington, DC: US Government Printing Office, 2006), 418–23; Moorer USNI OH, 1317; Rearden, *Council of War*, 322; Morrocco, *Rain of Fire*, 14–15; Burr and Kimball, *Nixon's Nuclear Specter*, 187–90, 202, 310–12; Seymour M. Hersh, *The Price of Power: Kissinger in the Nixon White House* (New York: Summit Books, 1983), 120; Prados, *Vietnam*,

311, 471–72; Rearden, *Council of War*, 317; Hunt, *Melvin Laird*, 157; Jeffrey Kimball, *Nixon's Vietnam War* (Lawrence: University Press of Kansas, 1998), 159–60, 202; Van Atta, *With Honor*, 259–60; Shawcross, *Sideshow*, 180; Daddis, *Withdrawal*, 52, 72, 106.

10. Memo for the President, 8 October 1969, inclosing JCS Memo for the Secretary of Defense, "Air and Naval Operations Against North Vietnam (Operation Pruning Knife), 1 October 1969, National Security Archive.
11. Moorer USNI OH, 1175, 1457; Alexander M. Haig Jr., *Inner Circles: How America Changed the World: A Memoir* (New York: Warner Books, 1992), 245n.
12. Moorer USNI OH, 751, 1178. See also Perry, *Four Stars*, 236; Sharp, *Strategic Direction of the Armed Forces*, 36.
13. Moorer USNI OH, 1456. Rearden's assertion in *Council of War*, 313, that Nixon thought "that military people had mediocre minds because intelligent people would never contemplate a military career," is not persuasive in light of Moorer's observation.
14. Haig interview with Naftali/Powers, 30 November 2007, Nixon Library, 20. Harry Train remembered that Moorer "had a good relationship with Nixon" and that the president "really respected him." Train USNI OH, 231.
15. Quoted in Morrocco, *Rain of Fire*, 82.
16. Quoted in Shawcross, *Sideshow*, 140. See also John Erlichman, *Witness to Power: The Nixon Years* (New York: Pocket Books, 1982), 75. While Nixon and Kissinger endeavored to bypass Laird, the defense secretary reportedly employed the directors of the National Security Agency and the Defense Intelligence Agency to monitor White House communications to and from the National Command Authority. Peter Rodman, *Presidential Command: Power, Leadership, and the Making of Foreign Policy from Richard Nixon to George Bush* (New York: Random House, 2010), 66.
17. Quoted in Nalty, *Air War over South Vietnam*, 187. See also 203; Henry Kissinger, *White House Years* (Boston: Little, Brown and Co., 1979), 495; Birtle and Maass, *The Drawdown*, 12–13.
18. Quoted in Hunt, *Melvin Laird*, 160. See also Schmitz, *Richard Nixon and the Vietnam War*, 87.
19. Webb, *The Joint Chiefs of Staff and the Vietnam War*, 155, 165; Birtle and Maass, *The Drawdown*, 18–24; Deac, *Road to the Killing Fields*, 70–95.
20. Webb, *The Joint Chiefs of Staff and the Vietnam War*, 187.
21. Lehman interview with Naftali, 30 November 2007, Nixon Library, 11. See also Moorer USNI OH, 868.
22. Rodman, *Presidential Command*, 65. See also Birtle and Maass, *The Drawdown*, 24, 51.
23. Van Atta, *With Honor*, 258.
24. Kissinger, *White House Years*, 35–36.
25. Moorer USNI OH, 326, 506. Moorer's remarks were not unlike those of Rickover and other naval officers who denigrated the Naval Academy's teaching the humanities. The admiral contended that it had "done serious harm to its young graduates." He added that "we cannot afford to penalize men who are working hard to learn atomic power plant technology by wasting our resources on individuals who have been taught the easy social science courses."

Admiral H. G. Rickover speech to National Society of Former Special Agents of the Federal Bureau of Investigation, Seattle, Washington, August 30, 1974, 10, 11; copy courtesy of David A. Rosenberg.

26. Moorer USNI OH, 747, 1184–85, 1258. See also Willbanks, *Abandoning Vietnam*, 99; Davidson, *Vietnam at War*, 640. Memo of conversation, 22 December 1970, FRUS, 1969–1976, VII, 233–35, quoted in Daddis, *Withdrawal*, 170.
27. Kissinger, *White House Years*, 35–36.
28. Moorer USNI OH, 909.
29. King USNI OH, 430.
30. Perry, *Four Stars*, 208.
31. Moorer USNI OH, 818, 909.
32. Xiaoming Zhang, "China's Involvement in Laos During the Vietnam War," 1160.
33. Quoted in Sherwood, *Nixon's Trident*, 8.
34. Quoted in Sherwood, *Nixon's Trident*, 17.
35. Xiaoming Zhang, "China's Involvement in Laos during the Vietnam War," 1162.
36. Bernard C. Nalty, *The War Against Trucks: Aerial Interdiction in Southern Laos, 1968–1972* (Washington, DC: Air Force History and Museums Division, 2005), 260–66; Hunt, *Melvin Laird*, 203.
37. Lewis Sorley, *A Better War: The Unexamined Victories and Final Tragedy of America's Last Years in Vietnam* (New York: Harcourt Inc., 1999), 233. See also Kissinger, *Ending the Vietnam War*, 193; Prados, *Vietnam*, 407–19.
38. Hunt, *Melvin Laird*, 177. Dale Van Atta is off the mark when he concludes that "Moorer would manipulate the liaison office to spy on the president, using a military aide to surreptitiously photocopy and steal White House national security documents." Van Atta, *With Honor*, 157.
39. Moorer USNI OH.
40. Quoted in Webb and Cole, *The Chairmen of the Joint Chiefs of Staff*, 86. See also Cole et al., *The Chairmanship of the Joint Chiefs of Staff*, 99; Van Atta, *With Honor*, 342–53; Thompson, *The Hawk and the Dove*, 233; Rodman, *Presidential Command*, 61–62.
41. Zumwalt USNI OH, 557.
42. Quoted in Cosmas, *MACV: The Joint Command in the Years of Withdrawal, 1968–'73*, 325. See also Birtle and Maass, *The Drawdown*, 51.
43. Kissinger, *Ending the Vietnam War*, 194, 196.
44. Quoted in Webb and Poole, *The Joint Chiefs of Staff and the War in Vietnam, 1971–1973*, 9–10.
45. Kissinger, *White House Years*, 1004. See also Davidson, *Vietnam at War*, 641; Willbanks, *Abandoning Vietnam*, 303n20.
46. Ramage USNI OH, 322, 330. See also Zumwalt, *On Watch*, 356.
47. Quoted in Hunt, *Melvin Laird*, 177. See also Sander, *Invasion of Laos 1971*, 89; Kissinger, *Ending the Vietnam War*, 201–2; Moorer USNI OH, 1238; Rearden, *Council of War*, 320.
48. Bruce Palmer, *The 25-Year War: America's Military Role in Vietnam* (Lexington: University of Kentucky Press, 1984), 90–91; Davidson, *Vietnam at War*, 640.

49. Quoted in Hunt, *Melvin Laird*, 177. See also Kissinger, *White House Years*, 994, 996; Schmitz, *Richard Nixon and the Vietnam War*, 119; Kimball, *Nixon's Vietnam War*, 244.
50. Haldeman, *The Haldeman Diaries*, 287.
51. Moorer condemned the Cooper–Church Amendment for enabling the North Vietnamese to "move right into South Vietnam" and for "the bloodbath in Cambodia." He suggested that rather than the military, it was "the Senate that really was responsible for the bloodbath by prohibiting any kind of air support for those poor people down there." Moorer USNI OH.
52. Hunt, *Melvin Laird*, 181.
53. Quoted in Hunt, *Melvin Laird*, 184–85.
54. Westmoreland, then the Army Chief of Staff, had minimal influence on the course of the war, and his counterparts on the Joint Chiefs did not consider him a strong figure in their deliberations. Van Atta, *With Honor*, 151; Kissinger, *White House Years*, 1004–5.
55. Sander, *Invasion of Laos 1971*, 141. See also Daddis, *Withdrawal*, 174; Van Atta, *With Honor*, 151; Kissinger, *White House Years*, 1004–5.
56. Birtle and Maass, *The Drawdown*, 54–55.
57. Quoted in Hunt, *Melvin Laird*, 189.
58. James H. Willbanks, *A Raid Too Far: Operation Lam Son 719 and Vietnamization in Laos* (College Station: Texas A&M University Press, 2014), 162. Detailed accounts of Lam Son 719 can also be found in Sander, *Invasion of Laos 1971*; Nguyen Duy Hinh, *Lam Son 719*, in series Indochina Monographs (Washington, DC: U.S. Army Center of Military History, 1979; Birtle and Maass, *The Drawdown*, 55.
59. Quoted in Birtle and Maass, *The Drawdown*, 56. See also Willbanks, *A Raid Too Far*, 158–59, 163; Cosmas, *MACV: The Joint Command in the Years of Withdrawal, 1968–'73*, 337; Robert Dallek, *Nixon and Kissinger: Partners in Power* (New York: HarperCollins, 2007), 258–61.
60. Hunt, *Melvin Laird*, 194. See also Van Atta, *With Honor*, 351.
61. Quoted in Willbanks, *A Raid Too Far*, 176. See also Hunt, *Melvin Laird*, 198; Daddis, *Withdrawal*, 174; Cosmas, *MACV: The Joint Command in the Years of Withdrawal, 1968–'73*, 337–38; 366.
62. Willbanks, *A Raid Too Far*, 163, 169, 170.
63. An insightful, balanced, and impressively documented study of the protective reaction controversy and Air Force General John D. Lavelle's role in it can be found in Mark Clodfelter, *Violating Reality: The Lavelle Affair, Nixon, and the Parsing of the Truth* (Washington, DC: National Defense University Press, 2016). See also Thompson, *To Hanoi and Back*, 199 ff; Van Atta, *With Honor*, 134; Cosmas, *The Joint Chiefs of Staff and the War in Vietnam, 1960–1968*, pt. 3, 254.
64. Sherwood, *Nixon's Trident*, 26; Webb, *The Joint Chiefs of Staff and the Vietnam War*, 220; Van Atta, *With Honor*, 177.
65. Quoted in Webb, *The Joint Chiefs of Staff and the Vietnam War*, 224. Harry Train later related that Moorer received intelligence before the operation that the POWs were not then at Son Tay, but for various reasons Laird let the operation proceed. Train USNI OH, 220–22. See also Benjamin F. Schemmer, *The Raid* (New York: Harper & Row, 1976), 2–3.

66. Webb, *The Joint Chiefs of Staff and the Vietnam War*, 225; Van Atta, *With Honor*, 206, 212–13, 383–88; Rearden, *Council of War*, 321; Webb and Poole, *The Joint Chiefs of Staff and the War in Vietnam*, 94–95; Sherwood, *Nixon's Trident*, 27.
67. Quoted in Clodfelter, *Violating Reality*.
68. Sherwood, *Nixon's Trident*, 30–31; Van Atta, *With Honor*, 386.
69. Moorer USNI OH, 728–29. See also Moorer interview with Ted Gittinger, 16 September 1981, LBJ Oral Histories, LBJ Library, 22; Lawson Ramage USNI OH, 476.
70. Polmar and Marolda, *Naval Air War*. Malcolm Muir Jr., *Black Shoes and Blue Water: Surface Warfare in the United States Navy, 1945–1975* (Washington, DC: Naval Historical Center, 1996), 158.
71. Clodfelter, *Violating Reality*. See also Thompson, *To Hanoi and Back*, 204; Morrocco, *Rain of Fire*, 104–5; Rearden, *Council of War*, 322; Moorer USNI OH, 1295; Daddis, *Withdrawal*, 190–91. Clodfelter has suggested that, during the hearings on Lavelle, Moorer was up for another two-year term as chairman and that might have influenced his testimony. See Clodfelter, *Violating Reality*, 57–58.
72. Spector, *After Tet*, 203–4; Daddis, *Withdrawal*, 5.
73. Haldeman, *The Haldeman Diaries*, 321. For a comprehensive account of the My Lai massacre, see Howard Jones, *My Lai: Vietnam, 1968, and the Descent into Darkness* (New York: Oxford University Press, 2017); Wright, *Enduring Vietnam*, 299–301.
74. Moorer USNI OH, 521, 1531. The admiral's views about My Lai and Calley's role in it were shared by many other Americans. Indeed, even the politically liberal Jimmy Carter, then the governor of Georgia, proclaimed an "American Fighting Men's Day" and urged citizens to "drive with their headlights on to honor the flag as 'Rusty' [Calley's nickname] had done." Quoted in Christian G. Appy, *American Reckoning: The Vietnam War and Our National Identity* (New York: Penguin, 2016).
75. Moorer interview with Ted Gittinger, 16 September 1981, LBJ Oral Histories, LBJ Library, 20.
76. Ibid., 42.
77. Moorer USNI OH, 533.
78. McDonald, "Thomas Hinman Moorer," 363; Moorer USNI OH, 857, 1394.
79. Quoted in Mark Feldstein, *Poisoning the Press: Richard Nixon, Jack Anderson, and the Rise of Washington's Scandal Culture* (New York: Farrar, Straus and Giroux, 2010), 177.
80. Ehrlichman, *Witness to Power*, 278.
81. Moorer USNI OH, 1115; 1320–28. See also Ehrlichman, *Witness to Power*, 275–81; Haldeman, *The Haldeman Diaries*, 470–71; Zumwalt, *On Watch*, 369–70; Berman, *Zumwalt*, 325–44; Dallek, *Nixon and Kissinger*, 350–51. Moorer consistently supported Nixon's actions, so Stephen Ambrose's assertion in *Nixon: The Triumph of a Politician, 1962–1972* (New York: Simon and Schuster, 1987), 488, and *Nixon: Ruin and Recovery, 1973–1990* (New York: Simon & Schuster, 1987), 488, that "Yeoman Radford had rendered his President a great service by making it possible for the commander in chief to blackmail his military high command into supporting his policies" clearly is

an exaggeration.
82. Train USNI OH, 234.
83. Feldstein, *Poisoning the Press*, 330.
84. Zumwalt, *On Watch*, 375–76.
85. Haig interview with Naftali/Powers, 30 November 2007, Nixon Library, 15. See also Roger Morris, *HAIG: The General's Progress* (Chicago: Playboy Press, 1982), 131–32, 187, 210, 236, 256–57, 268, 272–73, 308, which relies heavily on Zumwalt's recollections of White House affairs under Nixon.
86. Quoted in Feldstein, *Poisoning the Press*, 189.
87. Nixon quoted in Walter Isaacson, *Kissinger: A Biography* (New York: Simon & Schuster, 1992), 380–85; Moorer USNI OH, 1323; John A. Farrell, *Richard Nixon: The Life* (New York: Doubleday, 2017), 459–60; Ehrlichman, *Witness to Power*, 277.
88. Rearden, *Council of War*, 316. For a detailed, if largely speculative and skewed, interpretation of the Radford affair, see Hersh, *The Price of Power*, 465–74. See also Rodman, *Presidential Command*, 66–67; Feldstein, *Poisoning the Press*, 175–98.

CHAPTER 8

1. Willbanks, *A Raid Too Far*, 719. See also Nguyen, *Hanoi's War*, 233, 242; Daddis, *Withdrawal*, 183–89.
2. Gaiduk, *The Soviet Union and the Vietnam War*, 215; Zhang, "The Vietnam War, 1964–1969," 738; John Darrell Sherwood, *Afterburner: Naval Aviators and the Vietnam War* (New York: New York University Press, 2004), 251–61.
3. Moorer USNI OH, 64 (see also 1237).
4. Hunt, *Melvin Laird*, 223, 229; Van Atta, *With Honor*, 403; Webb and Poole, *The Joint Chiefs of Staff and the War in Vietnam*, 100.
5. Memo for the record, "Sensitive-Eyes Only," Secure Voice Call between Admirals Zumwalt and Moorer at 1755 this date," 24 July 1972, Zumwalt Coll., acc. no. 6230407034, Texas Tech Vietnam Archive.
6. Zumwalt, *On Watch*, 335, 380.
7. Hunt, *Melvin Laird*, 226–27, 241, 550; Van Atta, *With Honor*, 223.
8. Quoted in Hunt, *Melvin Laird*, 217.
9. Kissinger, *White House Years*, 1112.
10. Quoted in Wright, *Enduring Vietnam*, 294. See also Hunt, *Melvin Laird*, 223.
11. Moorer USNI OH, 1267.
12. Moorer USNI OH, 1559, 1561; Cosmas, *MACV: The Joint Command in the Years of Withdrawal, 1968–'73*, 365–67.
13. Conversation, Nixon, Kissinger, Laird, and Moorer, 17 April 1972, *FRUS, 1969–1976*, VIII, 272–73, quoted in Daddis, *Withdrawal*, 186.
14. Kissinger, *White House Years*, 1098. See also Haldeman, *The Haldeman Diaries*, 529. Apparently, this was a recurring theme of Kissinger's. In September 1971, Moorer recorded in his diary that Kissinger wondered if the Air Force could only operate in the desert. At one point, the admiral said, "Come on, Henry, you are being unfair." Moorer Diary, September 1971, Document 8, NARA RG 218, Records of the JCS, Chairman JCS Admiral Moorer History File, Admiral Moorer Diaries, box 3, folder 17, September 1971, obtained by National Security Archive.

15. Lewis Sorley, *Thunderbolt: General Creighton Abrams and the Army of His Times* (New York: Simon & Schuster, 1992), 324, 326.
16. Rearden, *Council of War*, 323; Hunt, *Melvin Laird*, 227, 228; Daddis, *Withdrawal*, 187.
17. Quotes in *Melvin Laird*, 240 and Van Atta, *With Honor*, 404. See also 403; Sherwood, *Afterburner*, 262–70.
18. Quoted in Van Atta, *With Honor*, 417.
19. Zumwalt, *On Watch*, 380, 384.
20. Ibid., 379, 381.
21. Ibid., 382, 391 (see also 386).
22. Morrocco, *Rain of Fire*, 108.
23. John Lehman, who served as an observer in South Vietnam during 1972, later remarked that Vietnamization had succeeded because the RVNAF (Republic of Vietnam Armed Forces) had fought so well, with US air support, throwing back the North Vietnamese offensive. Lehman interview with Timothy Naftali, 4 October 2007, Nixon Library, 6–7.
24. Quoted in Van Atta, *With Honor*, 405.
25. Nguyen, *Hanoi's War*, 255. See also 254–56, 259; Gaiduk, *The Soviet Union and the Vietnam War*, 233–34.
26. Quoted in Sherwood, *Nixon's Trident*, 45. See also Clodfelter, *The Limits of Air Power*, 156.
27. Quoted in Sherwood, *Afterburner*, 208. See also Van Atta, *With Honor*, 97, 101, 105, 119, 406–7; Burr and Kimball, *Nixon's Nuclear Specter*, 106–24.
28. Zumwalt USNI OH, 412.
29. Quoted in Hunt, *Melvin Laird*, 230.
30. Quoted in Clodfelter, *The Limits of Air Power*, 157.
31. Nguyen, *Hanoi's War*, 256.
32. Sherwood, *Afterburner*, 208.
33. Sherwood, *Nixon's Trident*, 209; Moorer USNI OH, 986; Kissinger, *Ending the Vietnam War*, 272; Hunt, *Melvin Laird*, 229; Prados, *Vietnam*, 473–74; Isaacson, *Kissinger*, 419.
34. King USNI OH, 429. See also Webb and Poole, *The Joint Chiefs of Staff and the War in Vietnam*, 161.
35. Rectanus also had served for two years as the Chief of Current Intelligence on Admiral Sharp's CINCPAC staff.
36. Zumwalt USNI OH, 554; Zumwalt, *On Watch*, 384–89; Hunt, *Melvin Laird*, 241–42; Prados, *Vietnam*, 473.
37. Hazard interview with Akers, Naval Historical Center, 35. See also Berman, *Zumwalt*, 273. Hazard became the Navy's third line officer to achieve the rank of rear admiral, at that time the highest-ranking woman in the military.
38. Haldeman, *The Haldeman Diaries*, 553.
39. Kissinger, *White House Years*, 1179. See also 1180, 1184–86; Kimball, *Nixon's Vietnam War*, 303, 314.
40. Moorer interview with Ted Gittinger, 16 September 1981, LBJ Oral Histories, LBJ Library, 26.
41. Quoted in Perry, *Four Stars*, 237.
42. Memo for the record "Secure Voice Call between Admiral Zumwalt and Admiral Moorer, Sensitive—No Eyes Only," 5 May 1972, Zumwalt Coll., acc.

no. 6230407032, Texas Tech Vietnam Archive.
43. Laird was not alone. According to Abrams's biographer, the reaction of Laird's staff to the information was, "Oh, shit! We forgot to tell Abe about the mining of Haiphong." Sorley, *Thunderbolt*, 325.
44. Moorer interview with Ted Gittinger, 16 September 1981, LBJ Oral Histories, LBJ Library, 21; Moorer USNI OH, 977, 1284, 1636. Moorer bemoaned Washington's prohibition, for fear of triggering Chinese intervention in North Vietnam, against US forces entering the territorial waters of China to rescue pilots shot down off Hainan Island.
45. Quoted in Marolda, "Orphan of the Mekong Delta," 1170. Sorley, *Thunderbolt*, 323, presents a slightly different version, observing that Abrams said, "Goddamn it. ... The Navy runs its own goddamn war."
46. Quoted in Sherwood, *Nixon's Trident*, 47. See also Sherwood, *Afterburner*, 209–10.
47. Sherwood, *Afterburner*, 211–18.
48. Moorer USNI OH, 442.
49. Zumwalt, *On Watch*, 389.
50. Ibid., 388.
51. Eduard Mark, in his *Aerial Interdiction: Air Power and the Land Battle in Three American Wars* (Washington, DC: Center for Air Force History, 2009), 375, relates that thirty-one ships remained trapped in Haiphong for the duration of the campaign.
52. Quoted in Sherwood, *Nixon's Trident*, 51.
53. Zumwalt USNI OH, 555. See also Moorer USNI OH, 647; Nguyen, *Hanoi's War*, 254; Khoo, *Collateral Damage*, 75.
54. Quoted in Morrocco, *Rain of Fire*, 102.
55. Hunt, *Melvin Laird*, 235, 223, 231, 234, 236.
56. Quoted in Sherwood, *Nixon's Trident*, 61.
57. Quoted in Thompson, *To Hanoi and Back*, 232. See also Morrocco, *Rain of Fire*, 130; Farrell, *Richard Nixon*, 491–92.
58. W. Hays Parks, "Linebacker and the Law of War," *Air University Review* (January–February 1983): 3–6.
59. Moorer USNI OH, 755.
60. Moorer USNI OH, 1000; Hunt, *Melvin Laird*, 245. Hays Parks supports Moorer's conclusion, observing that, "Like Rolling Thunder, neither Linebacker I nor II was intended to destroy the Hanoi regime, compel the North Vietnamese people to adopt another form of government, or devastate North Vietnam. If thoughts of ground invasion were remote during Rolling Thunder, they were nonexistent during Linebacker I and II." Parks, "Linebacker and the Law of War," 3.
61. Mark, *Aerial Interdiction*, 399–400. Parks, in "Linebacker and the Law of War," 6, disagrees with Mark's conclusion. Parks avers that as a result of Linebacker I, "the North Vietnamese invasion of South Vietnam rapidly lost momentum."
62. Quotes from Holloway, *Aircraft Carriers at War*, 286; Puryear, *American Admiralship*, 456; Holloway interview with Marolda, 82.
63. Holloway, *Aircraft Carriers at War*, 286.
64. Ibid., 299.

65. Ibid., 296 (see also 297–99).
66. Quoted in Polmar and Marolda, *Naval Air War*, 62. See also Arthur interview with Marolda, 176–77.
67. Holloway, *Aircraft Carriers at War*, 290–93.
68. Holloway interview with Marolda, 60–67.
69. Ibid.
70. Quotes from Holloway, *Aircraft Carriers at War*, 312; Holloway conversation with the author, Naval Historical Foundation, 13 February 1987.
71. Quoted in Sherwood, *Nixon's Trident*, 69.
72. Holloway, *Aircraft Carriers at War*, 308–24; Sherwood, *Nixon's Trident*, 68–69. A little over a month later off South Vietnam, an 8-inch gun on *Newport News* exploded. The mishap killed twenty sailors and injured another thirty-six. The accident, caused by a faulty detonating fuse, represented the single largest loss of life to the naval gunfire support force during the war.
73. Quoted in Puryear, *American Admiralship*, 456.
74. Quoted in Clodfelter, *The Limits of Air Power*, 161.
75. Quoted in Sherwood, *Nixon's Trident*, 70.
76. Quoted in Puryear, *American Admiralship*, 251.
77. Schemmer, *The Raid*, 65.
78. Quoted in Webb, *The Joint Chiefs of Staff and the Vietnam War, 1969–1970*, 312–13. See also Daddis, *Withdrawal*, 108.
79. Schemmer, *The Raid*, 66.
80. Moorer USNI OH, 911–12. Heath Hardage Lee, in *The League of Wives: The Untold Story of the Women Who Took on the U.S. Government to Bring Their Husbands Home* (New York: St. Martin's Press, 2019), 92, indicates that early in his term as CNO, Moorer listened to the concerns of the wives of the POWs. Moorer's focus on the return of the POWs was also in line with Nixon's policy. The president "embraced the cause" of the POWs since "in a war with few, if any, heroes, POWs [could] afford the president breathing room by challenging the antiwar movement's demands for a rapid, unconditional retreat."
81. Quoted in Sorley, *A Better War*, 369. See also Moorer USNI OH, 39, 794–95, 977, 1019, 1039; Zumwalt, *On Watch*, 417; Rearden, *Council of War*, 325; Kissinger, *White House Years*, 1448. In the early months of 1973, Hanoi released 591 American POWs. See Wright, *Enduring Vietnam*, 279.
82. Quoted in Nguyen, *Hanoi's War*, 266.
83. Memo, Laird to Nixon, 13 December 1972, in Jeffrey Kimball, *The Vietnam War Files* (Lawrence: University Press of Kansas, 2004), 271.
84. Richard Wilson, "The Unbelievable Scene," *Washington Star-News*, 12 August 1974, in Kimball, *The Vietnam War Files*, 274.
85. Winston Lord, interview with Kimball, Washington DC, 5 December 1994, 43, in Kimball, *The Vietnam War Files*, 282.
86. Quoted in Muir, *Black Shoes and Blue Water*, 158. See also Moorer USNI OH, 977, 1248, 1271, 1282; Perry, *Four Stars*, 137–38.
87. Richard Nixon, *RN: The Memoirs of Richard Nixon* (New York: Grosset & Dunlap, 1978), 734, 736. See also Sherwood, *Nixon's Trident*, 70–71; Clodfelter, *The Limits of Air Power*, 190; Sherwood, *Afterburner*, 282–87; Stephen Ambrose, *Nixon: Ruin and Recovery, 1973–1990*, Vol. 3 (New York: Simon & Schuster), 1987, 42.

88. Msg 5829, CJCS to CINCPAC, 180015Z December 1972, Records of Thomas Moorer, Box 71, Linebacker II Messages, December 1972, FRUS Vol IX, *Vietnam*, October 1972–January 1973.
89. Quoted in Clodfelter, *The Limits of Air Power*, 190; Rearden, *Council of War*, 325.
90. Quotes from Sherwood, *Nixon's Trident*, 70–71; Clodfelter, *The Limits of Air Power*, 184. See also Rearden, *Council of War*, 325; Marshall L. Michel III, *The Eleven Days of Christmas: America's Last Vietnam Battle* (San Francisco: Encounter Books, 2002).
91. Hanoi later announced that during the eleven-day operation, US bombing had killed 1,612 people in Hanoi and Haiphong, a total substantially lower than major bombing operations in previous wars.
92. Zumwalt interview with Malcolm Muir, 20 April 1988, quoted in Muir, *Black Shoes and Blue Water*, 169. Zumwalt considered the threat of these missiles to the Seventh Fleet as "his worst nightmare."
93. Moorer USNI OH, 293, 294, 387.
94. Ibid., 522, 567, 802, 1000.
95. Ibid., 1014, 1072. See also W. Hays Parks, "Linebacker and the Law of War," *Air University Review* (January–February 1983): 6–7.
96. Quoted in Parks, "Linebacker and the Law of War," 12, 14, 19. Parks concluded that "measured against the only standard accepted in principle by nations—the law of war—and accepting Hanoi's casualty figure [of 1,318 civilians killed] without qualification, Linebacker II is unprecedented in its minimization of collateral damage and collateral civilian casualties when compared to the intensity of effort against legitimate targets."
97. Quoted in Parks, "Linebacker and the Law of War," 73.
98. Haig, *Inner Circles*, 311.
99. Rearden, *Council of War*, 326; Momyer, *Airpower in Three Wars*, 107.
100. Quoted in Sherwood, *Nixon's Trident*, 73.
101. Moorer USNI OH, 1019.
102. Quoted in Clodfelter, *The Limits of Air Power*, 201. Burr and Kimball, in *Nixon's Nuclear Specter*, 326, disagree with that interpretation. They opine that "one of the enduring myths about Nixon's and Kissinger's handling of the war ... is the claim that US mining and bombing in 1972, coupled with their masterful management of war and diplomacy, had made it possible to bring US POWs home and honorably end a long and tortuous American war against a devious and determined enemy." See also Sherwood, *Nixon's Trident*, 51; Prados, *Vietnam*, 510–11; Daddis, *Withdrawal*, 193–94.
103. "Bombing of North Vietnam," Hearings before Subcommittee of the Committee on Appropriations House of Representatives, 93rd Cong., 1st Sess., January 9, 1973, in Kimball, *The Vietnam War Files*, 280.
104. Moorer USNI OH, 762. See also 757, 1529, 1535. Captain Wayne P. Hughes Jr., a prominent analyst and scholar on the subject of naval operations and tactics, also suggested that had the United States employed the same level of force in 1965 as it did in 1972, the war might have been won. See Wayne P. Hughes Jr., "Vietnam: Winnable War?" in Cutler, ed., *Vietnam: A Retrospective*, 5–6.
105. Moorer USNI OH, 597–98, 752.
106. For the full text of the Agreement on Ending the War and Restoring Peace

in Vietnam (the Paris Agreement), see App. C in Allan E. Goodman, *The Lost Peace: America's Search for a Negotiated Settlement of the Vietnam War* (Stanford, CA: Hoover Institution Press, 1978), 188–97.
107. Holloway interview with Marolda, 72.
108. Marolda, *By Sea, Air, and Land*, 349–50; Edward J. Marolda, ed., *Operation End Sweep: A History of Minesweeping Operations in North Vietnam* (Washington, DC: Naval Historical Center/Tensor Industries Inc., 1993); Holloway, *Aircraft Carriers at War*, 327–32.
109. Holloway, *Aircraft Carriers at War*, 337. See also Puryear, *American Admiralship*, 457.

CHAPTER 9
1. Quoted in Zumwalt, *On Watch*, 167. See also 168; Zumwalt and Zumwalt, *My Father, My Son*, 102–3; Berman, *Zumwalt*, 211.
2. Quoted in Zumwalt and Zumwalt, *My Father, My Son*, 103. See also Zumwalt, *On Watch*, 45–46; Sherwood, *Black Sailor, White Navy*, 40. Shortly after Zumwalt's retirement, Chafee told the admiral that "there has been no CNO in modern times who has made as deep an impression on the Navy as you have. Your actions are going to help the Navy, not only in the Seventies but also in the balance of this century. In personnel policies as well as the imaginative development of new ships and weapons, your mark will be felt for years to come." Ltr, Chafee to Zumwalt, 15 August 1974, Zumwalt Coll., acc. no. 6210206003, Texas Tech Vietnam Archive.
3. Holloway interview with Marolda, 57. According to Charles Duncan, Chafee fully embraced the youth factor and wanted to "have every flag officer in their forties." Duncan USNI OH, 1375.
4. Quoted in Berman, *Zumwalt*, 212. Admiral Peet later observed that while playing golf at the La Jolla Country Club with Laird, the latter told him that helping get Zumwalt the CNO billet was a mistake. The politically and socially conservative Peet, however, was especially antagonistic toward his Naval Academy classmate. Zumwalt opposed Peet being promoted to full admiral. Peet USNI OH, 356, 472.
5. Quoted in Zumwalt and Zumwalt, *My Father, My Son*, 103. Hence, Laird rather than Chafee, as Stavridis asserts in *Sailing True North*, 207, was chiefly responsible for Zumwalt's nomination to be CNO.
6. Berman, *Zumwalt*, 212, but based on telecons Laird to Kissinger, 10, 13 March 1970.
7. Moorer USNI OH, 740. See also Berman, *Zumwalt*, 218. Charles K. Duncan, a former Chief of Naval Personnel, concurred that to lose a talented officer in his fifties after a tour as CNO was a "waste" of precious talent. Charles K. Duncan interview with Paul Stillwell, 1978, USNI OH, 421–23, 1857.
8. Quoted in Van Atta, *With Honor*, 270. In contrast, Harry Train, Moorer's staff assistant and a close friend of Zumwalt's, observed that when hearing of Zumwalt's selection as CNO he was "shocked" but that "when the decision was made, he supported it." Train USNI OH, 238.
9. Warner USNI OH, 69–70. See also Berman, *Zumwalt*, 214–15; Train USNI OH, 237; Zumwalt USNI OH, 470.
10. Quoted in Puryear, *American Admiralship*, 455.

11. David C. Richardson interview with Paul Stillwell, 1998, USNI OH, 273. Richardson might have had an axe to grind, however. He believed that he would have been selected to be the vice chief had Admiral Clarey been chosen as CNO instead of Zumwalt. Admiral Duncan agreed with Moorer that "it is... important for the four-star officer to have occupied progressively responsible and broadening positions as a flag officer." Duncan USNI OH, 412.

12. Zumwalt USNI OH, 551, 554, 558, 559. See also Farrell, *Richard Nixon*, 500–501.

13. John B. Hattendorf, ed., *U.S. Naval Strategy in the 1970s: Selected Documents* (Newport: Naval War College Press, 2007), x–xi; George W. Baer, *One Hundred Years of Sea Power: The U.S. Navy, 1890–1990* (Stanford, CA: Stanford University Press, 1994), 414-15; David F. Winkler, *Cold War at Sea* (Annapolis: Naval Institute Press, 2000).

14. Hattendorf, *U.S. Naval Strategy in the 1970s*, xiii, xiv, xv.

15. Quotes from David W. Hogan Jr., "Head and Heart: The Dilemmas of American Attitudes Toward War," *The Journal of Military History* (October 2011): 1046, 1048. See also Wright, *Enduring Vietnam*, 12; Packard, "Repairing the Wreckage of Vietnam," 252.

16. Zumwalt and Zumwalt, *My Father, My Son*, 39.

17. Swartz interview with Marolda 2017.

18. Zumwalt, *On Watch*, 182–83.

19. Baer, *One Hundred Years of Sea Power*, 397. See also 399–411; Norman Polmar, Thomas A. Brooks, and George E. Federoff, *Admiral Gorshkov: The Man Who Challenged the U.S. Navy* (Annapolis: Naval Institute Press, 2019).

20. Baer, *One Hundred Years of Sea Power*, 401 (see also 400).

21. Quoted in Hartmann, *Naval Renaissance*, 15.

22. Holloway interview with Marolda, 10–14, 17. Navy secretary Warner remembered that technologically the Soviet Navy had made a "progression of improvements [but] they were still far from being a first-class navy." Warner USNI OH, 89. Malcolm Muir, in *Black Shoes and Blue Water*, 200, concluded that "the threat from Soviet surface warships, serious as it was in reality, was overstated during the Zumwalt years."

23. Zumwalt interview with David A. Rosenberg, July 1982. See also Rosenberg, "Project 60: Twelve Years Later," Study for the Systems Analysis Division (OP-96), 1982, Courtesy of David A. Rosenberg.

24. Quotes from Swartz interview with Marolda 2017; Hattendorf, *U.S. Naval Strategy in the 1970s*, 2. Like Zumwalt, Bagley had served as executive assistant to secretary of the Navy Paul Nitze. See Worth H. Bagley interview with Paul Stillwell, 1982–1984, USNI OH, 239. See also Peter M. Swartz, *U.S. Navy Capstone Strategies and Concepts (1970–2010): Strategy, Policy, Concept, and Vision Documents* (Center for Naval Analyses, December 2011); Peter M. Swartz, *The U.S. Navy in the World (1970–1980): Context for U.S. Navy Capstone Strategies and Concepts*. Center for Naval Analyses, December 2011; Morton, *Mustin*, 339; Jeffrey I. Sands, *On His Watch: Admiral Zumwalt's Efforts to Institutionalize Strategic Change* (Alexandria, VA: Center for Naval Analyses, 1993), 19–33; John Lehman, *Oceans Ventured: Winning the Cold War at Sea* (New York: W.W. Norton, 2018), 75; David A. Rosenberg, "Project 60: Twelve Years Later," Study for the Systems Analysis Division (OP-96), 1982, courtesy

of David A. Rosenberg; Peter D. Haynes, "Elmo Zumwalt's Project SIXTY: Driving Institutional Change in an Era of Great Power Competition at Sea," in *Conceptualizing Maritime & Naval Strategy: Festschrift for Captain M. Swartz, United States Navy (ret.)*, Sebastian Bruns and Sarandis Papadopoulos, eds. (Baden-Baden, Germany: Nomos Verlagsgesellschaft, 2020); Peter M. Swartz, "The Maritime Strategy," interview with Ryan Peeks and Justin Blanton, Naval History and Heritage Command, 2019 https://www.history.navy.mil/research/library/oral-histories/navy-strategy.html

25. Berman, *Zumwalt*, 233. Swartz, who had served under Tidd in Vietnam and in Washington, observed that Tidd could "translate Zumwalt's histrionics into actions." Swartz interview with Marolda 2017.

26. David A. Rosenberg, "Project 60: Twelve Years Later," Study for the Systems Analysis Division (OP-96), 1982, courtesy of David A. Rosenberg.

27. Salzer USNI OH, 521. See also Zumwalt, *On Watch*, 67; Baer, *One Hundred Years of Sea Power*, 402. Roberta Hazard's contention that Zumwalt focused on modernizing and diversifying the fleet and establishing sea control as the Navy's primary mission only after dealing with the naval service's personnel issues is not an accurate appraisal. See Hazard interview with Akers, Naval Historical Center, 26.

28. Polmar and Allen, *Rickover*, 478.

29. Lehman, *Command of the Seas*, 392. Harry Train related that Moorer also favored the FFGs (Train USNI OH, 240), as did Harold Shear in his USNI OH, 255, 257.

30. Zumwalt, *On Watch*, 74–76.; Baer, *One Hundred Years of Sea Power*, 403–6; Polmar and Allen, *Rickover*, 228–29, 233–34.

31. Peter M. Swartz emails to Marolda, 22 February 2017.

32. Baer, *One Hundred Years of Sea Power*, 407; Stansfield Turner, "Missions of the U.S. Navy," *Naval War College Review* (March–April 1974).

33. Holloway, *Aircraft Carriers at War*, 269. See also Baer, *One Hundred Years of Sea Power*, 402.

34. Baer, *One Hundred Years of Sea Power*, 406–8; Hone, *Power and Change*, 86–87.

35. David A. Rosenberg, "Project 60: Twelve Years Later," Study for the Systems Analysis Division (OP-96), 1982, courtesy of David A. Rosenberg. See also Joel Holwitt, "Lessons from Admiral Elmo," *Naval History* (December 2020): 37–38.

36. Sands, *On His Watch*, 2, 405, 410; Peter D. Haynes, *Toward a New Maritime Strategy: American Naval Thinking in the Post–Cold War Era* (Annapolis: Naval Institute Press, 2015), 28–31. Holloway considered the Sea Control Ship "essentially a merchant ship" that lacked compartmentation, critical for the survivability of a warship. See Holloway interview with Marolda, 29. See also Muir, *Black Shoes and Blue Water*, 206; Berman, *Zumwalt*, 236.

37. Hyland USNI OH, 517; Hayward USNI OH, 259–60.

38. King USNI OH, 419.

39. Howard Kerr USNI OH, 152. Jackson K. Parker was another officer who was inspired by Zumwalt but who was especially critical of the Mod Squad experiment. See Parker USNI OH, 325–27.

40. Zumwalt, *On Watch*, 129, 132; Marolda, *Ready Sea Power*, 83; Agawa,

NOTES FOR CHAPTER 9   437

Friendship Across the Seas, 153–55.

41. Swartz interview with Marolda 2017. In September 1970, Zumwalt wrote that he was "convinced from my experiences in Vietnam that the Personal Response Program as we knew it should be modified or combined with other programs to produce a Navy-wide application." CNO Memo for the Chief of Naval Personnel, Ser 331-70, 15 September 1970, Peter M. Swartz Papers. See also BUPERS Notice 5400, 22 October 1970, Peter M. Swartz Papers; Human Relations Training and Development Department, Learning Resources Bulletin, Vol. 1, 1973; Assistant Chief of Naval Personnel for Human Goals, "Guidelines for United States Navy Overseas Diplomacy," Peter M. Swartz Papers.
42. Zumwalt, *On Watch*, 132–33 (see also 126–36).
43. Swartz interview with Marolda 2017.
44. Zumwalt, *On Watch*, 85. For an extended discussion of the relationship between Rickover and Zumwalt, see also Puryear, *American Admiralship*, 381–480.
45. Zumwalt, *On Watch*, 64, 100.
46. Zumwalt USNI OH, 233.
47. Harold E. Shear interview with Stillwell, USNI, 159–60.
48. For a full recreation of the Rickover-Zumwalt interview, as remembered by Zumwalt, see Polmar and Allen, *Rickover*, 276–85. Duncan, in his *Rickover*, 229, affirms that Zumwalt's transcript of the interview "gives a fair picture." See also Lehman, *Command of the Seas*, 20; Berman, *Zumwalt*, 118–23.
49. Quoted in Puryear, *American Admiralship*, 400.
50. Berman, *Zumwalt*, 143.
51. Hone, *Power and Change*, 89. After his retirement, Zumwalt related that journalist William Anderson told him that "whenever he wrote favorable articles on Zumwalt he could always count on Admiral Rickover calling up to remonstrate along with a few other active-duty types and several retired." Memo for the record, "Bill Anderson concerning Adm Rickover and others," 9 August 1974, Zumwalt Coll., acc. no. 6210613007, Texas Tech VN Archive.
52. Duncan, *Rickover*, 228–29.
53. Berman, *Zumwalt*, 144.
54. Quoted in Berman, *Zumwalt*, 234.
55. Zumwalt, *On Watch*, 104; Baer, *One Hundred Years of Sea Power*, 410; Polmar and Allen, *Rickover*, 569; Duncan, *Rickover*, 229–30; Berman, *Zumwalt*, 160. The observation by Holloway, then ninety years old, that Zumwalt was against "all aircraft carriers" is clearly overblown. See Holloway interview with Marolda, 45.
56. Quotes from Zumwalt USNI OH, 259; Howard Kerr USNI OH, 154.
57. Quoted in Polmar and Allen, *Rickover*, 479.
58. Lehman, *Command of the Seas*, 27.
59. Quotes from Hone, *Power and Change*, 99; Admiral H. G. Rickover speech to National Society of Former Special Agents of the Federal Bureau of Investigation, Seattle, Washington, August 30, 1974, 10. See also Polmar and Allen, *Rickover*, 480.
60. Hone, *Power and Change*, 96–97; Hone and Utz, *History of the Office of the Chief of Naval Operations*, 282–97. See also Peter M. Swartz and Michael

C. Markowitz, "Organizing OPNAV (1970–2009)," study prepared by the Center for Naval Analyses (CAB D0020997.A5/2Rev, January 2010) for the Naval History and Heritage Command.
61. John B. Hattendorf, B. Mitchell Simpson III, and John R. Wadleigh, *Sailors and Scholars: The Centennial History of the Naval War College* (Newport, RI: Naval War College Press, 1984), 275.
62. Ibid., 276 (see also 275–301).
63. Ibid., 285.
64. Ibid., 281.
65. Ibid., 295.

CHAPTER 10
1. Hartmann interview with Zumwalt, quoted in Hartmann, *Naval Renaissance*, 18.
2. Stanley R. Arthur, interview with Marolda, 2015–2016, USNI OH, 201.
3. Zumwalt, *On Watch*, 269.
4. Salzer USNI OH, 557.
5. Ibid., 557. See also 374, 381; Hunt, *Melvin Laird*, 520; Crist, *Winds of Change*, 41; Lavell, *Flying Black Ponies*, 160. Charles K. Duncan, who was Zumwalt's naval personnel chief, later observed that "the idea of setting aside large rehabilitation places in the Service for drug users and for chronic alcoholics seems to me to be a mistake [since] it interferes with the military mission." He also remembered that "the men were very antagonistic to the idea that drug addicts, alcoholics or homosexuals would get the same type of discharge as the man who was working hard and had a good record." Duncan USNI OH, 1304, 1308–9, 1879.
6. Quoted in Sherwood, *Black Sailor, White Navy*, 29. See also Berman, *Zumwalt*, 13–14.
7. Arthur USNI OH, 190–91.
8. Salzer USNI OH, 565.
9. Samuel L. Gravely Jr. interview with Paul Stillwell, USNI, 1986, 298.
10. Arthur USNI OH, 197.
11. Holloway interview with Marolda, 44–45.
12. Quoted in Puryear, *American Admiralship*, 458–59. See also Thompson, *Gumption*, 339.
13. Quoted in Thompson, *Gumption*, 335.
14. Jean Ebbert and Marie-Beth Hall, *Crossed Currents: Navy Women in a Century of Change* (Washington, DC: Brassey's, 1999), 181.
15. https://www.history.navy.mil/research/library/online-reading-room/title-list-alphabetically/z/list-z-grams/z-gram-2.html
16. https://www.history.navy.mil/research/library/online-reading-room/title-list-alphabetically/z/list-z-grams/z-gram-2.html
17. Berman, *Zumwalt*, 244, 252.
18. Quoted in Van Atta, *With Honor*, 252, 254.
19. Quoted in Berman, *Zumwalt*, 250.
20. Holloway interview with Marolda, 45. For a detailed discussion of the Z-Gram program, for the most part from Zumwalt's perspective, see Puryear, *American Admiralship*, 428–38, 459.

21. Zumwalt, *On Watch*, 178.
22. Arthur USNI OH, 199. Kerr, who had served on Zumwalt's staff in Vietnam, also thought the Z-Gram approach "wasn't the best way to establish policy." Kerr USNI OH, 148–50. Vice Admiral Thomas Weschler shared that negative assessment of the Z-Gram approach. Weschler USNI OH, 678–79, 684.
23. Crist, *Winds of Change*, 26. See also Salzer USNI OH, 527–28; Robert L. J. Long USNI, OH, 283; Leuci, "Delbert Black: More Than Just a Gunner's Mate."
24. Duncan USNI OH, 1863.
25. Salzer USNI OH, 527 (see also 528–29).
26. Gravely USNI OH, 299 (see also 298).
27. Gravely USNI OH, 330. Indeed, Warner remembered that he gave Zumwalt "a lot of rough treatment as he tried to shoulder the Navy" because "he was trying to push it too far too fast." John W. Warner interview with David Winkler, USNI OH, October 2017–September 2019, 161.
28. Zumwalt, *On Watch*, 228, 239.
29. https://www.history.navy.mil/research/library/online-reading-room/title-list-alphabetically/z/list-z-grams/z-gram-57.html
30. Zumwalt, *On Watch*, 169, 17–72. See also Thompson, *Gumption*, 390–91.
31. Quoted in Berman, *Zumwalt*, 248.
32. Warner USNI OH, 207–8.
33. Quotes from Moorer USNI OH, 841; Crist, *Winds of Change*, 35 (see also 33–34). Harry Train later observed that "the uniform change was a disaster, an absolute disaster." Train USNI OH, 170.
34. Hazard interview with Akers, NHHC, 32–33. Around this time, Albert K. Murray, a noted artist, painted a portrait of the CNO that the admiral and Mrs. Zumwalt thought made him look too sad. Murray explained that he did that deliberately to depict a man who was under great pressure from the war, the Navy's social upheaval, and the criticism he was receiving from many quarters. See Albert K. Murray, interview with John T. Mason, USNI, 1994, 36–39.
35. Moorer USNI OH, 845 (see also 106).
36. Quoted in Puryear, *American Admiralship*, 60, 224.
37. Quoted in Crist, *Winds of Change*, 53. See also Beshany USNI OH, 795–96.
38. Moorer, Kent L. Lee, Robert L. J. Long, Raymond E. Peet, interviews with John T. Mason and Paul Stillwell, USNI OHs; Moorer, Holloway, Lee interviews with Edgar Puryear (2002, 2003), in Puryear, *American Admiralship*.
39. Berman quotes a Zumwalt supporter who thought the admiral's detractors were "old, fat, retired Army [but Navy too] officers [who tended] to become Colonel Blimps." Berman, *Zumwalt*, 249 (see also 2, 13, 27).
40. Thompson, *Gumption*, 365.
41. James D. Ramage interviews with Barrett Tillman/Robert Lawson, February–March 1985, USNI OH, 343.
42. Moorer USNI OH, 841, 1145. See also Holwitt, "Lessons from Admiral Elmo," 39.
43. Quoted in Berman, *Zumwalt*, 478n84.
44. Gerald Miller USNI OH, 696.
45. Quoted in Crist, *Winds of Change*, 36.

46. Salzer USNI OH, 649–50.
47. Gerald E. Miller interviews with John T. Mason, January–April 1976, USNI OH, 735.
48. Hartmann, *Naval Renaissance*, 19.
49. Thomas B. Hayward interviews with Paul Stillwell, May 1989–June 2002, USNI OH, 247.
50. Kerr USNI OH, 151.
51. Zumwalt USNI OH, 285. See also Sherwood, *Black Sailor, White Navy*, 35.
52. Quoted in Sherwood, *Black Sailor, White Navy*, 43.
53. Sherwood, *Black Sailor, White Navy*, 44–45. Samuel Gravely, who served on the OPNAV staff and later commanded the Third Fleet, related that Zumwalt never called on him to discuss racial matters because "I was there as a Navy communicator, and not as the Navy's racial expert, which I simply wasn't anyway." Gravely USNI OH, 327.
54. Zumwalt, *On Watch*, 168, 198.
55. Hunt, *Melvin Laird*, 536; Berman, *Zumwalt*, 263.
56. Quoted in Puryear, *American Admiralship*, 461.
57. https://www.history.navy.mil/research/library/online-reading-room/title-list-alphabetically/z/list-z-grams/z-gram-66.html; see also Sherwood, *Black Sailor, White Navy*, 43; Berman, *Zumwalt*, 259–62.
58. Ltr, Kauffman to Zumwalt, 4 November 1972, Peter M. Swartz Papers.
59. Kerr USNI OH, 150–52.
60. Quotes from Salzer USNI OH, 645; Sherwood, *Black Sailor, White Navy*, 47.
61. Sherwood, *Black Sailor, White Navy*, 47–48.
62. Ibid., 38–39, 50–54.
63. Quoted in ibid., 52.
64. Quoted in Crist, *Winds of Change*, 38. See also Thompson, *Gumption*, 385–87.
65. Lehman, *Command of the Seas*, 97.
66. Sherwood, *Black Sailor, White Navy*, 55–102, 103 (see also 104–29). Perhaps as an indication that the Navy's leaders were not aware of nor sufficiently concerned that there was racial trouble in the service, Holloway, the Seventh Fleet commander at the time of the *Kitty Hawk* and *Hassayampa* incidents, during a 2012 interview did not remember that the incidents happened on his ships.
67. Hazard suggested that Zumwalt's personnel changes stimulated a desire, as yet unfulfilled, among Black sailors for even more positive measures. She also suggested that Black "troublemakers . . . misinterpreted changing regulations for elimination of regulations." Hazard interview with Akers, Naval Historical Center, 3, 27.
68. Quoted in Berman, *Zumwalt*, 284.
69. Lehman, *Command of the Seas*, 97. See also Sherwood, *Black Sailor, White Navy*, 158, 163, 30–66; Holloway interview with Marolda, 51.
70. Thompson, *Gumption*, 388.
71. Quoted in Zumwalt, *On Watch*, 236–38. However, when the Inspector General's report was issued and it blamed the Z-Grams for bypassing the chain of command, Zumwalt couldn't understand why that approach was destabilizing. See Berman, *Zumwalt*, 299.
72. Gravely USNI OH, 328. See also Sherwood, *Black Navy, White Sailor*, 168; Berman, *Zumwalt*, 287–91.

73. Quoted in Berman, *Zumwalt*, 291.
74. Berman, *Zumwalt*, 298. Admiral McCain, for instance, observed that Zumwalt lowered "the standards of personal appearance and other matters, and with that went a let-down in the standards in the discipline, [and] the standards of the upkeep of machinery.... It hurt the Navy considerably." John S. McCain Jr., interview with John T. Mason Jr., 1999, USNI OH, 18. See also Ramage USNI OH, 342–43.
75. Quoted in Berman, *Zumwalt*, 293.
76. Haldeman, *The Haldeman Diaries*, 649. Indeed, in the wake of the Hicks subcommittee hearings of late 1972, Zumwalt thanked the former defense secretary for his support: "Now that the shot and shell of reaction to Navy's racial episodes have been left astern and with the failure of the effort to convert the word 'integration' into a synonym of 'permissiveness,' I wanted to let you know again how much I appreciated your thoughtful telephone message of support during the height of the action. I have thought of it, often." Quoted in Berman, *Zumwalt*, 311.
77. Quoted in Hazard interview with Akers, NHHC, 3, 28. Later that year, Kissinger suggested to Nixon that Zumwalt's "lack of intelligence has dropped on his lack of character." Berman, *Zumwalt*, 296. See also Sherwood, *Black Navy, White Sailor*, 170; Zumwalt, *On Watch*, 240–41.
78. Quoted in Berman, *Zumwalt*, 305 (see also 288–89); Sherwood, *Black Navy, White Sailor*, 170.
79. Holloway interview with Marolda, 58–59. Holloway repeated that story in his 2001 interviews with Edgar F. Puryear in *American Admiralship*, 448. For elaboration on Holloway's evaluation of Zumwalt's leadership and activist programs, see 454–78. According to Worth Bagley, in a private conversation Arleigh Burke complained that "Zumwalt used 'I' too much." Bagley admitted that "that sort of perception has had some effect on the way people evaluate what Zumwalt did." Zumwalt later learned from journalist William Anderson, who had interviewed Admiral Anderson, that the latter "launched into a 30- or 40-minute tirade against 'Zumwalt's policies.'" Journalist Anderson related to Zumwalt that Admiral Anderson "was in total opposition to and working against Zumwalt." Memo for the record, "Bill Anderson's report on interview with Admiral George Anderson," 9 August 1974, Zumwalt Coll., acc. no. 6210613006, Texas Tech Vietnam Archive.
80. Hazard interview with Akers, NHHC, 3, 33.
81. Quoted in Sherwood, *Black Sailor, White Navy*, 177; Zumwalt, *On Watch*, 233.
82. Salzer USNI OH, 528. See also 549; Beshany USNI OH, 794. Even Train, who was an enthusiastic Zumwalt supporter, criticized the CNO's reliance on what he called the "palace guard." Train USNI OH, 241.
83. Gravely USNI OH, 328.
84. Quotes from Train USNI OH, 176; Hazard interview with Akers, NHHC, 22–23, 45; Duncan USNI OH, 1376.
85. For relevant excerpts from the Hicks report, see Puryear, *American Admiralship*, 438–48.
86. Berman, *Zumwalt*, 296–97.
87. Ramage USNI OH, 344.

88. Zumwalt, *On Watch*, 257.
89. F. Edward Hébert, with John McMillan, *"Last of the Titans": The Life and Times of Congressman F. Edward Hébert of Louisiana* (Lafayette: Center for Louisiana Studies, University of Southwestern Louisiana, 1976).
90. Zumwalt, *On Watch*, 252.
91. Quotes from Zumwalt, *On Watch*, 252; Zumwalt and Zumwalt, *My Father, My Son*, 118.
92. Quoted in Sherwood, *Black Sailor, White Navy*, 177 (see also 175–77). Clarey was certainly in a position to gauge morale in the fleet. John Warner related that he and Clarey visited twenty-two ships in a 72-hour span during the Linebacker campaign off Vietnam. Warner USNI OH, 74.
93. Quoted in Berman, *Zumwalt*, 303.
94. Quoted in Sherwood, *Black Sailor, White Navy*, 179, 182.
95. Berman, *Zumwalt*, 309.
96. Quoted in ibid., 188 (see also 189). Sherwood's conclusion that Kelley's testimony was driven by the need to appease Hébert and induce the congressman to support the all-volunteer force is not persuasive. *New York Times* journalist Hanson Baldwin also went to the Mediterranean theater during this period and reported that the Sixth Fleet was plagued with disciplinary problems, rampant drug use, racial trouble, and overall poor morale. He found the officers "tense" and "frightened" and believing that "they were sitting on a volcano; something could break out at any time." He also noted that the chief petty officers were "bitter and frustrated." Hanson W. Baldwin interview with John T. Mason, 1976, USNI OH, 760–63.
97. Report by the Special Subcommittee on Disciplinary Problems in the U.S. Navy of the Committee on Armed Forces, House of Representatives, 92 Cong., 2nd Sess., January 2, 1973 (hereafter Hicks Report), 17668.
98. Hicks Report, 17669–70.
99. Quoted in Sherwood, *Black Sailor, White Navy*, 190. Holloway later claimed that "Admiral Zumwalt saw that this [Hicks report] was suppressed in the Navy. Nobody in the Navy had a chance to see it." See Holloway interview with Marolda, 44.
100. Quoted in Sherwood, *Black Sailor, White Navy*, 199 (see also 193–200).
101. Ibid., 200–226. See also Train USNI OH, 249–50. According to Hanson Baldwin, Gerald Miller, then Commander Sixth Fleet, and William F. Bringle, Commander Naval Forces, Europe, objected to Zumwalt's decision to reassign supposed Black agitators from the *Intrepid* disturbances throughout the fleet rather than return them to the United States for discharge proceedings. Baldwin USNI OH, 759–60; Gerald Miller USNI OH, 710–28.
102. Zumwalt, *On Watch*, 262 (see also 168).
103. Wright, *Enduring Vietnam*, 259; Marolda, *By Sea, Air, and Land*, 136.
104. Ebbert and Hall, *Crossed Currents*, 174–78.
105. Moorer USNI OH, 880–81.
106. Ebbert and Hall, *Crossed Currents*, 182.
107. Arthur USNI OH, 202.
108. Hazard interview with Akers, NHHC, 3, 25.
109. Ibid., 2, 3.
110. Zumwalt, *On Watch*, 264–65.

111. Even Hazard observed that it was significant that 115 Z-Grams preceded the first effort in regard to women and only another six Z-Grams followed it. Hazard interview with Akers, NHHC, 8. See also Ebbert and Hall, *Crossed Currents*, 182; https://www.history.navy.mil/research/library/online-reading-room/title-list-alphabetically/z/list-z-grams/z-gram-116.html
112. Hunt, *Melvin Laird*, 539–40; Van Atta, *With Honor*, 535–36; Zumwalt, *On Watch*, 266–67, 419.
113. Hunt, *Melvin Laird*, 540; Van Atta, *With Honor*, 335–36; Warner USNI OH, 57.
114. Zumwalt, *On Watch*, 265; Susan H. Godson, *Serving Proudly: A History of Women in the U.S. Navy* (Annapolis: Naval Institute Press, 2001), 243.
115. Hazard interview with Akers, NHHC, 4, 15–16.
116. Ibid., 5.
117. Ibid., 6.
118. Ebbert and Hall, *Crossed Currents*, 187.
119. Quigley USNI OH. See also Zumwalt, *On Watch*, 262–64. Of note, Quigley is mentioned nowhere in Berman's *Zumwalt*.
120. Zumwalt, *On Watch*, 236, 274, 296, 305, 308.
121. Hazard interview with Akers, NHHC, 7.
122. http://www.history.navy.mil/research/library/online-reading-room/title-list-alphabetically/z/z-grams-list-policy-directives-issued-admiral-zumwalt/z-gram-116.html
123. Hazard interview with Akers, 10–11.
124. Ibid., 26–27.

CHAPTER 11

1. Zumwalt, *On Watch*, 275.
2. Ibid., 275–77.
3. Gerald Miller USNI OH, 344–45.
4. Zumwalt, *On Watch*, 277, 296; Palmer, *The 25-Year War*, 91, 124.
5. Donald D. Engen USNI OH, 408–9.
6. Zumwalt, *On Watch*, 277, 279–98, 348. At one point long after their retirements, Moorer and Zumwalt happened to visit the Operational Archives of the Naval Historical Center on the same day to look into their archived papers. Staffers observed the two of them in one of the small offices smoking cigars and discussing old times.
7. Memo for the record, "Phone conversation between Admiral Zumwalt and Admiral Moorer at 0940 this date," Sensitive-No Eyes, 26 July 1972, Zumwalt Coll., acc. no. 6230407033, Texas Tech Vietnam Archive; memo for the record, "Telcon between CNO and CJCS," Sensitive, 11 May 1973, Zumwalt Coll., acc. no. 6230407019, Texas Tech Vietnam Archive; memo for the record, "Telcon between John Lehman and 002," Sensitive-Eyes Only, 20 November 1973, Zumwalt Coll., acc. no. 6230407035, Texas Tech Vietnam Archive; Moorer Diary, September 1971, Document 10, NARA RG 218, Records of the JCS, Chairman JCS Admiral Moorer History File, Admiral Moorer Diaries, box 3, folder 17, September 1971, obtained by National Security Archive.
8. Zumwalt and Zumwalt, *My Father, My Son*, 117. See also Hall, "Managing

Interservice Competition," 274.

9. Moorer Diary, September 1971, Documents 3, 4, 6, 11, 12, NARA RG 218, Records of the JCS, Chairman JCS Admiral Moorer History File, Admiral Moorer Diaries, box 3, folder 17, September 1971, obtained by National Security Archive.
10. Hartmann, *Naval Renaissance*, 14–15; Berman, *Zumwalt*, 238–40; Zumwalt, *On Watch*, 316.
11. Zumwalt, *On Watch*, 294–95, 315.
12. Ibid., 281. Zumwalt disapproved of Chafee's call for "the U.S. to reduce its overseas commitments to fit the [bare-bones] budget" (see 289).
13. Zumwalt, *On Watch*, 382–83.
14. Quoted in Puryear, *American Admiralship*, 470–71.
15. Kissinger, *White House Years*, 1130–31; Henry Kissinger, *Years of Upheaval* (Boston: Little, Brown, 1982). Despite their disagreements while on duty over a host of issues, Moorer and Zumwalt found common cause in the Soviet threat. They met in 1976 to form the Committee on the Present Danger. The committee was a conservative but bipartisan group of retired military officers and civilian defense analysts. Counted among their number were Ronald Reagan, former deputy defense secretary David Packard, former Secretary of State Dean Rusk, and strategic analysts Paul Nitze, Eugene Rostow, Jeane Kirkpatrick, Kenneth Adelman, Richard Perle, Richard Pipes, Norman Podhoretz, and George Shultz. During Reagan's first term, the committee proved to be a formidable pro-defense lobbying group.
16. Lehman, *Command of the Seas*, 166. See also Lehman interview with Naftali, 30 November 2007, Nixon Library, 15.
17. Isaacson, *Kissinger*, 764–67 (see also 9–12).
18. Quoted in Berman, *Zumwalt*, 316.
19. Zumwalt, *On Watch*, 320–21. See also Zumwalt USNI OH, 552.
20. Zumwalt, *On Watch*, 278. Indeed, despite evidence to the contrary, Zumwalt persuaded subordinates that he was a major player in the SALT negotiations. Hazard, for instance, observed that Zumwalt "became the center point of the effort to keep the State Department and the negotiations informed and on track, so that we would not give, wittingly or unwittingly, inappropriate advantage to the Soviets." Hazard interview with Akers, NHHC, 26.
21. Thompson, *The Hawk and the Dove*, 243.
22. Berman, *Zumwalt*, 226; Zumwalt, *On Watch*, 283.
23. Zumwalt, *On Watch*, 284.
24. Ibid., 348–49, 371.
25. Ibid., 290–91 (see also 293).
26. Ibid., 292, 300, 307 (see also 298–304, 319).
27. Ibid., 303–4, 307.
28. Berman, *Zumwalt*, 217, 312.
29. Zumwalt, *On Watch*, 402–3, 421, 422.
30. Memo for the Record, "Sensitive-Eyes Only," telecom with the Chief of Naval Personnel," 17 June 1974, Zumwalt Coll., acc. no. 6210709004, Texas Tech Vietnam Archive. See also Berman, *Zumwalt*, 322.
31. This contrasted with Moorer's relationship with Kissinger. King, a Moorer subordinate, related that "even though we had a lot of problems with Kissinger

... Admiral Moorer had Kissinger's confidence." King USNI OH, 431.

32. Zumwalt, *On Watch*, 310 (see also 308–11). Thompson's assertion in *The Hawk and the Dove*, 243, that "Zumwalt clashed with Kissinger from the very beginning" is not supported by Zumwalt's own remembrances.
33. Quoted in Rodman, *Presidential Command*, 67–68. See also Berman, *Zumwalt*, 318–19.
34. Moorer USNI OH, 1113–15.
35. Marolda, *Ready Seapower*, 80–81.
36. Zumwalt, *On Watch*, 365–66.
37. Ibid., *368*.
38. Kissinger in particular valued the use of Navy carriers in the management of overseas crises, but that was not always the case. In September 1971, Moorer recorded in his diary that Kissinger said "that maybe we should just build submarines and not carriers." Moorer responded to Kissinger that "the nuclear submarine program is certainly vital, but we have not had one submarine to speak of in Vietnam in 5 years." He added that "there is no way that you can handle the crisis in the small countries around the world with submarines." Moorer Diary, September 1971, Document 7, NARA RG 218, Records of the JCS, Chairman JCS Admiral Moorer History File, Admiral Moorer Diaries, box 3, folder 17, September 1971, obtained by National Security Archive.
39. Berman is incorrect in his assertion that "Bud was ordered to assemble a task force from the Seventh Fleet" for the Indian Ocean deployment. The CNO lost the authority to deploy forces in 1958. See Berman, *Zumwalt*, 331.
40. Zumwalt, *On Watch*, 389–91, 397. See also Zumwalt and Zumwalt, *My Father, My Son*, 139; memo for the record, "Sensitive," phone conversation between Admiral Zumwalt and H. K., 31 March 1972, Zumwalt Coll., acc. no. 6230407031, Texas Tech Vietnam Archive; Lee, *The League of Wives*, 222–24.
41. Isaacson, *Kissinger*, 10–11.
42. Holloway, *Aircraft Carriers at War*, 339 (see also 340–44); Holloway interview with Marolda, 43; Puryear, *American Admiralship*, 458.
43. Van Atta, *With Honor*, 155.
44. When Holloway retired as CNO, Admirals Burke, Anderson, and Moorer facilitated Holloway's selection as president of the Naval Historical Foundation and president of the Association of Naval Aviation. Holloway, *Aircraft Carriers at War*, 420–21. Holloway also served as president of the Council of American-flag Ship Operators; executive director of the President's Task Force on Combating Terrorism; Special Envoy to the Middle East; commissioner on the President's Blue Ribbon (Packard) Commission for Defense Management; the Commission for the Merchant Marine and Defense; and the Department of Defense Commission for a Long Term Strategy; president/chairman of the Naval Academy Academic Advisory Board; the Naval Academy Foundation; and Saint James School.
45. Memo, CNO 09 "Eyes Only," 7 December 1973, Zumwalt Coll., acc. no. 6210709001, Texas Tech Vietnam Archive.
46. Holloway, *Aircraft Carriers at War*, 340.
47. Hayward, USNI OH, 281.
48. Holloway interview with Marolda, 46.

49. Holloway's observation echoed Rickover's remarks in a speech to retired FBI agents in which the latter averred that "since World War II, the Navy has ignored the need for line officers to acquire operating experience in engineering.... The result is that many [ship] captains have little knowledge, respect, or regard for their engineering plants.... Is it any wonder that ships—even new ones—are frequently found in poor material condition by outside inspectors?" Admiral H. G. Rickover speech to National Society of Former Special Agents of the Federal Bureau of Investigation, Seattle, Washington, August 30, 1974, 6.
50. Holloway, *Aircraft Carriers at War*, 342–43; Holloway interview with Marolda, 46–47.
51. Indeed, it is difficult to accept the conclusion by Polmar and Allen in *Rickover*, 478, that "Zumwalt was a key player" in the 1973 Middle East crisis and SALT negotiations.
52. Zumwalt, *On Watch*, 424–26.
53. Ibid., 433. See also Isaacson, *Kissinger*, 524–38. Moorer was decidedly less enamored with Israel. He emphasized that he was "in no way anti-Semitic, but, on the other hand, there's no question about it that the Israeli lobby controls foreign policy in the Middle East." He added, "Israel is a burden to the United States when you look at the money we've supplied to them per capita. Our children will have to pay it." He didn't think, however, that it was "a criticism to be a burden" since our babies are burdens that we willingly take on. Moorer USNI OH, 1623.
54. Quoted in Isaacson, *Kissinger*, 527.
55. Moorer USNI OH, 1075, 1077, 1088, 1562.
56. Webb and Cole, *The Chairmen of the Joint Chiefs of Staff*, 84. See also Berman, *Zumwalt*, 240, 473n82.
57. Kissinger, *White House Years*, 722, 810. See also Isaacson, *Kissinger*, 204.
58. Kissinger, *Ending the Vietnam War*; Kissinger, *Years of Upheaval*, 1017.
59. Quoted in Isaacson, *Kissinger*, 623–24.
60. Zumwalt, *On Watch*, 442.
61. Isaacson, *Kissinger*, 623. According to Berman, in *Zumwalt*, 141, when Zumwalt served as Nitze's assistant and interacted with Jackson, the senator "took an immediate liking to Nitze's protégé."
62. Zumwalt, *On Watch*, 273, 435; Hall, "Managing Interservice Competition."
63. Zumwalt, *On Watch*, 432, 459. See also Dallek, *Nixon and Kissinger*, 545–46.
64. Zumwalt, *On Watch*, 462–64.
65. Ibid., 464–65.
66. Zumwalt and Zumwalt, *My Father, My Son*, 139.
67. Zumwalt, *On Watch*, 492–507. See also Berman, *Zumwalt*, 363.
68. Isaacson, *Kissinger*, 429. See also Berman, *Zumwalt*, 346; Zumwalt and Zumwalt, *My Father, My Son*, 48, 353.
69. Memo for the record, "Conversation with Admiral Holloway and Admiral Bagley with Admiral Zumwalt following line-up this date," 24 June 1974, Zumwalt Coll., acc. no. 6230407027, Texas Tech Vietnam Archive.
70. Memo for the record, "Meeting with SECDEF this date," 15 July 1974, Zumwalt Coll., acc. no. 6210613004, Texas Tech Vietnam Archive.
71. Palmer, *The 25-Year War*, 90. Until passage of the Goldwater–Nichols

Department of Defense Reorganization Act of October 4, 1986, the Joint Staff was formally tasked with serving the Joint Chiefs as a body but in practice, the chairman exerted significant influence on their support activities.
72. Kerr USNI OH, 155.
73. Swartz interview with Marolda 2017.
74. Ibid. See also Berman, *Zumwalt*, 367.
75. Kerr USNI OH, 156–57. See also Zumwalt, *On Watch*, 492–507; Berman, *Zumwalt*, 364–67.
76. Zumwalt received praise for that performance from at least one former CNO. Arleigh Burke wrote Zumwalt on 8 July that "Bobbie [his wife] and I heard your excellent interview by [Lawrence E.] Spivak" and "your answers were clear, concise and correct." Ltr, Burke to Zumwalt, 8 July 1974, Zumwalt Coll., acc. no. 6210117009, Texas Tech Vietnam Archive. Secretary of the Navy Middendorf related that during the last months of Zumwalt's time in command, when Nixon was "hunkered down in the bunker, [we got] no help from the White House on any of the programs we were working." J. William Middendorf II, *Potomac Fever: A Memoir of Politics and Public Service* (Annapolis: Naval Institute Press, 2011), 110.
77. Berman, *Zumwalt*, 368, 371–74.
78. Kerr USNI OH, 159. See also Zumwalt, *On Watch*, 508–11; Kerr USNI OH, 157–58; Berman, *Zumwalt*, 368.

CHAPTER 12

1. Holloway, *Aircraft Carriers at War*, 338. See also Puryear, *American Admiralship*, 472–73.
2. Holloway interview with Marolda, 52. See also Perry, *Four Stars*, 254.
3. Quoted in Thompson, *Gumption*, 400.
4. The remaining four were organization of the Navy, officer professionalism, age-in-grade levels, and fleet operations. Memorandum to the Secretary of the Navy, "personal and private," Goals for the Next CNO, December 1973, Zumwalt Coll., acc. no. 6210709005, Texas Tech Vietnam Archive.
5. Memorandum to the Secretary of the Navy, "personal and private," Goals for the Next CNO, December 1973, Zumwalt Coll., acc. no. 6210709005, Texas Tech Vietnam Archive. In response to a letter from Admiral James Ramage, Holloway assured him that "I will try to do things the Navy way, but effecting policy from the top is a slow process, and I ask your continued understanding and support." Even though Ramage wanted faster action in that regard, he admitted that Holloway largely succeeded in his efforts and "probably went along at just about the right pace." Ramage USNI OH, 368.
6. Shear USNI OH, 322–13.
7. Hayward USNI OH, 281.
8. Duncan USNI OH, 1320, 1783. Donald Engen had a similarly negative appraisal of Bagley's qualities and suggested Zumwalt "was building a coterie of friends around him" and was guilty of "cronyism." Donald D. Engen interview with Stillwell, USNI OH, 406–7, 442–43. Harold Shear considered Bagley "Zumwalt's boy. Hands down, he was Zumwalt's boy." Shear USNI OH, 311.
9. Zumwalt, *On Watch*, 474.

10. Bagley USNI OH, 323.
11. Quoted in Berman, *Zumwalt*, 355–58. These sentiments were shared by Kent L. Lee, who remembered Kidd as "the number one horse's ass I've met in the Navy." Lee USNI OH, 347, 581.
12. Zumwalt, *On Watch*, 474–78. See also Berman, *Zumwalt*, 355, 358–59; Holloway interview with Marolda, 47–49; Warner USNI OH, 80.
13. Quoted in Berman, *Zumwalt*, 360.
14. Holloway, *Aircraft Carriers at War*, 345. See also Holloway interview with Marolda, 61. William Thompson, who worked with Bagley on the SECNAV staff, observed that Bagley was "quiet, reserved, serious and enjoyed deep strategic discussions." Thompson, *Gumption*, 270.
15. Robert L. J. Long USNI OH, 304, 319. Long later remarked that "as much as I admire my good friend Admiral Zumwalt, he left some scars, primarily in the chain of command and in the attitude from juniors to seniors [and that] Jim Holloway did a masterful job in healing those and bringing the Navy back into a more cohesive force." See also Holloway interview with Marolda, 49–50; Polmar and Allen, *Rickover*, 337.
16. Holloway interview with Marolda, 51–52.
17. Quoted in Puryear, *American Admiralship*, 458.
18. Quoted in ibid., 453, 454. See also Shear USNI OH, 257.
19. Holloway, *Aircraft Carriers at War*, 345–46.
20. Holloway interview with Marolda, 53.
21. Quoted in Crist, *Winds of Change*, 52–53.
22. Lehman, *Command of the Seas*, 99.
23. Quoted in Puryear, *American Admiralship*, 462–63.
24. Hayward USNI OH, 405; Holloway interview with Marolda, 53; Zumwalt, *On Watch*, 180; Hartmann, *Naval Renaissance*, 19.
25. Quoted in Puryear, *American Admiralship*, 465. Holloway interview with Marolda, 19–20; Holloway, *Aircraft Carriers at War*, 349; Hartmann, *Naval Renaissance*, 21–23.
26. Holloway, *Aircraft Carriers at War*, 351.
27. Haig, *Inner Circles*, 521.
28. Morton, *Mustin*, 350–51. Robert Dunn, the Sixth Fleet's operations officer during this period, considered that statement an exaggeration but did acknowledge that many Greeks were opposed to the homeporting of a destroyer squadron in their country. Dunn email to Marolda, 27 October 2018.
29. Holloway, *Aircraft Carriers at War*, 352–53. See also Puryear, *American Admiralship*, 475; Sherwood, *Black Sailor, White Navy*, 23; Duncan USNI OH, 1868–69.
30. Shear USNI OH, 314–15.
31. Quoted in Puryear, *American Admiralship*, 477–78.
32. Paul Fussell, *Uniforms: Why We Are What We Wear* (Boston: Houghton Mifflin, 2002), 31. See also Holloway interview with Marolda, 17–18, 59.
33. Quoted in Crist, *Winds of Change*, 53–54. In August 1977, the Navy announced plans to return the enlisted uniform to the bell-bottom trousers, jumpers, and white hats, and the change was implemented under Hayward.
34. Quoted in Sherwood, *Black Sailor, White Navy*, 239. See also Puryear, *American Admiralship*, 462.

NOTES FOR CHAPTER 12

35. Gravely USNI OH, 328.
36. Salzer USNI OH, 646.
37. Arthur USNI OH, 227.
38. Salzer USNI OH, 645.
39. Quote in Sherwood, *Black Sailor, White Navy*, 239.
40. Holloway interview with Marolda, 54–55; Sherwood, *Black Sailor, White Navy*, 230, 240.
41. Gravely USNI OH, 320–21, 357–58.
42. Sherwood, *Black Sailor, White* Navy, 242.
43. Ibid., xvii, 265.
44. Hayward USNI OH, 482.
45. Crist, *Winds of Change*, 41. See also Marolda, "The Social History of the U.S. Navy"; Sherwood, *Black Sailor, White Navy*, 192; Godson, *Serving Proudly*, 227.
46. Godson, *Serving Proudly*, 240.
47. Haynes, *Toward a New Maritime Strategy*, 29.
48. Holloway interview with Marolda, 27–28, 214; Perry, *Four Stars*, 257.
49. Holloway, *Aircraft Carriers at War*, 350.
50. James L. Holloway III, "The Military Defeat of the Soviet Union," lecture at Metropolitan Club, Washington, DC, 3 June 1996, 12.
51. Perry, *Four Stars*, 244, 256.
52. Perry, *Four Stars*, 256. See also Hone, *Power and Change*, 99.
53. Holloway interview with Marolda, 22. See also 20–21; Hartmann, *Naval Renaissance*, 23; Holwitt, "Lessons from Admiral Elmo," 39.
54. Hattendorf, *U.S. Naval Strategy in the 1970s*, xi; Marolda, *Ready Seapower*, 84.
55. Holloway, *Aircraft Carriers at War*, 348. See also Hattendorf, *U.S. Naval Strategy in the 1970s*, xvi–xvii; Swartz, *U.S. Navy Capstone Strategies and Concepts (1970–2010)*; Swartz, *The U.S. Navy in the World (1970–1980)*, December 2011.
56. Holloway, *Aircraft Carriers at War*, 392–93; Hattendorf, *U.S. Naval Strategy in the 1970s*.
57. Swartz interview with Marolda 2017.
58. Holloway, *Aircraft Carriers at War*, 385–90. See also Holloway interview with Marolda, 60; Puryear, *American Admiralship*, 467.
59. Holloway interview with Marolda, 63. See also Puryear, *American Admiralship*, 467.
60. Quoted in Polmar and Allen, *Rickover*, 398. See also Hartmann, *Naval Renaissance*, 21; Puryear, *American Admiralship*, 401.
61. Quoted in Polmar and Allen, *Rickover*, 223–24, 244–45, 481.
62. Quoted in Puryear, *American Admiralship*, 401–3. See also Holloway, *Aircraft Carriers at War*, 375–79; Holloway interview with Marolda, 30, 79; Polmar and Allen, *Rickover*, 399.
63. Train USNI OH, 311.
64. Even though Zumwalt came to loathe Kissinger, the admiral appreciated that Kissinger recognized the benefits of naval power: "It was not surprising for Kissinger to lean in the direction of the Navy. The swift, sudden move is a part of his diplomatic repertoire that he places much reliance on, and the Navy is the Service most capable of moving swiftly and suddenly in parts of the world

far from home. He often has told me that he regards carriers as probably the most important of our non-strategic weapons." Zumwalt, *On Watch*, 340–41.
65. Lehman, *Command of the Seas*, 98.
66. Holloway interview with Marolda, 86.
67. Holloway, *Aircraft Carriers at War*, 305, 306.
68. Holloway, *Aircraft Carriers at War*, 306–7. Lehman related that when he was appointed deputy director of the Arms Control and Disarmament Agency, he and Holloway "worked closely together on SALT policy and became good friends." And "when President Carter was elected in 1976 and I resigned, Holloway made me a consultant to his office. During the 1980 transition Admiral Holloway became my chief strategist and worked tirelessly and with great effect to build support." Lehman, *Command of the Seas*, 107.
69. Holloway, *Aircraft Carriers at War*, 333. See also Arthur USNI OH, 330–31.
70. Holloway interview with Marolda, 33. See also Puryear, *American Admiralship*, 136–38; memo, Brent Scowcroft to President, "Kissinger Report re SALT," 21 January 1976, Ford Library; memo, Brent Scowcroft to the President, "Talking Points for Today's NSC Meeting on SALT," 21 January 1976, Ford Library; Minutes of National Security Council Meeting, 21 January 1976, Ford Library.
71. Holloway, *Aircraft Carriers at War*, 412–13. See also 411–14; Lehman, *Command of the Seas*, 166–68; Lehman interview with Naftali, 30 November 2007, Nixon Library, 20.
72. Holloway, *Aircraft Carriers at War*, 414–17. See also Hone and Utz, *History of the Office of the Chief of Naval Operations*, 310–12.
73. Quoted in Puryear, *American Admiralship*, 534.
74. Holloway interview with Marolda, 37.
75. Lehman, *Command of the Seas*, 99. Lehman, in *Oceans Ventured*, 59, presents a more moderate view of Brown's influence on the Navy's development of new weapon systems.
76. Holloway, *Aircraft Carriers at War*, 418. See also Haynes, *Toward a New Maritime Strategy*, 30.
77. Quoted in Hartmann, *Naval Renaissance*, 25.
78. Quoted in Puryear, *American Admiralship*, 138–41.
79. Holloway, *Aircraft Carriers at War*, 383–85; Perry, *Four Stars*, 270; Puryear, *American Admiralship*, 141–43.
80. Lehman, *Oceans Ventured*, 38, 59.
81. Quoted in Marolda, *Ready Seapower*, 91. See also Lehman, *Oceans Ventured*, 53; Holloway, "The Military Defeat of the Soviet Union," 13; Holloway interview with David Winkler, 21 May 1997, Naval Historical Foundation, 9–10.
82. Quoted in Agawa, *Friendship Across the Seas*, 181–82.
83. Lehman, *On Seas of Glory*, 346, 348, 367. It heightened Lehman's esteem for Holloway when the admiral, along with Zumwalt, prevented the scrapping of Lehman's favored *Iowa*-class battleships during the 1970s.
84. Lehman, *Oceans Ventured*, 48.
85. See Holloway, *Aircraft Carriers at War*, 391.
86. Ibid., 47, 52, 54. Sands's conclusion, in *On His Watch*, 73, that "Zumwalt's tour as CNO provided a necessary incremental step in the ultimately successful shift in the Navy's strategic focus from power projection to sea control" is

not persuasive. See also Hattendorf, *U.S. Naval Strategy in the 1970s*.

87. Train USNI OH, 177. The day that Hayward relieved Holloway, the new CNO was surprised that his predecessor did not attend the following reception. Hayward, however, understood that that was "classic Holloway" because he was saying, "Okay, Tom, it's all yours. . . . I've got to get out of the way." Hayward added, "I love that guy." Hayward USNI OH, 370.
88. Lehman, *Command of the Seas*, 129.
89. Lehman, *On Seas of Glory*, 349. See also Hartmann, *Naval Renaissance*, 30. See also 31–33; Baer, *One Hundred Years of Sea Power*, 424–26; Hattendorf, *U.S. Naval Strategy in the 1970s*, "Sea Plan 2000"; Paul B. Ryan, *First Line of Defense: The U.S. Navy Since 1945* (Stanford, CA: Hoover Institution Press, 1981), 128–34; Marolda, *Ready Seapower*, 90–92.
90. Kissinger, *Ending the Vietnam War*, 454. See also 433; Rearden, *Council of War*, 324.
91. Zumwalt, *On Watch*, 413.
92. Kissinger, *Ending the Vietnam War*, 455, 463–67, 469.
93. Ibid., 457, 462, 463, 471–72, 493.
94. Ibid., 463–69, 484, 492, 504.
95. Rearden, *Council of War*, 327.
96. Kissinger, *Ending the Vietnam War*, 505–6. See also 498, 516; Van Atta, *With Honor*, 431.
97. Holloway, *Aircraft Carriers at War*, 333–35.
98. Holloway interview with Marolda, 6–7.
99. James L. Holloway III, "The Military Defeat of the Soviet Union," lecture at Metropolitan Club, Washington, DC, 3 June 1996, 15–16.
100. Holloway, *Aircraft Carriers at War*, 336.
101. Arnold R. Isaacs, *Without Honor: Defeat in Vietnam and Cambodia* (Baltimore: Johns Hopkins University Press, 1983); Marolda, *By Sea, Air, and Land*; Mercogliano, *Fourth Arm of Defense*; Frank Snepp, *Decent Interval* (New York: Vintage Books, 1977); Olivier Todd, *Cruel April: The Fall of Saigon* (New York: W.W. Norton & Company, Inc., 1990); Patrick Urey, "U.S. Marine Corps Participation in the Emergency Evacuations of Phnom Penh and Saigon: Operations Eagle Pull and Frequent Wind" (Alexandria, VA: Center for Naval Analyses, Study 1089, June 1977); George J. Veith, *Black April: The Fall of South Vietnam, 1973–1975* (New York: Encounter Books, 2012); Cao Van Vien, *The Final Collapse* (Washington, DC: U.S. Army Center of Military History/US Government Printing Office, 1983); Willbanks, *Abandoning Vietnam*; Marolda, Ready *Seapower*; George R. Dunham and David A. Quinlan, *U.S. Marines in Vietnam: The Bitter End, 1973–1975* (Washington, DC: History and Museums Division, U.S. Marine Corps, 1990); John F. Guilmartin Jr., *A Very Short War: The Mayaguez and the Battle of Koh Tang* (College Station: Texas A&M University Press, 1995); Jan K. Herman, *Navy Medicine in Vietnam: Oral Histories from Dien Bien Phu to the Fall of Saigon* (Jefferson, NC: McFarland, 2009); Gerald R. Ford, *A Time to Heal: The Autobiography of Gerald R. Ford* (New York: Harper & Row, 1979), 275–84; Thurston Clarke, *Honorable Exit: How a Few Brave Americans Risked All to Save Our Vietnamese Allies at the End of the War* (New York: Doubleday, 2019).

102. Berman, *Zumwalt*, 3, 7–11, 21, 25, 403–8, 412–18.
103. Holloway, *Aircraft Carriers at War*, 394.
104. Train USNI OH, 323.
105. Useful works on the *Mayaguez* incident are Christopher J. Lamb, *The Mayaguez Crisis, Mission Command, and Civil-Military Relations* (Washington, DC: JCS History Office, Office of the Chairman of the Joint Chiefs of Staff, 2018); Dunham and Quinlan, *U.S. Marines in Vietnam: The Bitter End, 1973–1975*; Guilmartin, *A Very Short War*; Ralph Wetterhahn, *The Last Battle: The Mayaguez Incident and the End of the Vietnam War* (New York: Carroll & Graf, 2001); Richard G. Head, Frisco W. Short, and Robert C. McFarlane, *Crisis Resolution: Presidential Decision Making in the Mayaguez and Korean Confrontations* (Boulder, CO: Westview Press, 1978); Malcolm Muir Jr., *End of the Saga: The Maritime Evacuation of South Vietnam and Cambodia* (Washington, DC: Naval History and Heritage Command, 2017); Richard B. Hughes, "Abandon Ship: Interagency Decisionmaking during the *Mayaguez* Incident," National Defense University, 1 July 2015; Minutes of National Security Council Meeting re "Seizure of American Ship by Cambodian Authorities," 12 May 1975, Ford Library.
106. Lamb, *The* Mayaguez *Crisis*, xix, xx.
107. Quoted in ibid., 83. See also 142, 148.
108. Holloway interview with Marolda, pt. 1, 70 (see also 67–69). In his *Aircraft Carriers at War*, 398, 402, Holloway suggested that the president was so displeased with Jones that he called the admiral back from Newport, Rhode Island, and made him acting chairman of the JCS. He added that Ford was so pleased with Holloway's contribution that after the *Mayaguez* crisis, "I was always acting chairman when General Brown was out of town." Perhaps reflecting Holloway's view, Harold Shear, his vice chief, considered Jones a "disaster" when the general served as JCS chairman under Carter. See Shear USNI OH, 312. Others had the impression that more than one individual served as acting JCS chairman during the crisis. In his oral history, then Director of the Joint Staff Harry Train observed that "we ended up with five acting chairmen in the course of those 72 hours." Those accounts and Holloway's accounts were wrong. As related in the Minutes of National Security Council Meetings, 12–15 May 1975, Ford Library, Jones served as acting chair throughout the crisis. See also Lamb, *The* Mayaguez *Crisis*, 16, 33, 79, 167.
109. Gayler, a fighter ace and the recipient of three Navy Crosses for combat valor in World War II, led the Pacific Command from August 1972 to August 1976. In that capacity he was involved in the execution of Linebacker II, the release and recovery of American POWs held in North Vietnam, and Operation End Sweep.
110. Minutes of National Security Council Meetings re "Seizure of American Ship by Cambodian Authorities," 14 May 1975, NSC Meeting File, Box 1, Ford Library; Lamb, *The* Mayaguez *Crisis*, 14, 40, 41, 50–51, 93–101, 150.
111. Hughes, "Abandon Ship: Interagency Decisionmaking during the Mayaguez Incident," 7. See also Lamb, *The* Mayaguez *Crisis*, 7, 55.
112. Holloway interview with Marolda, 69, 72.
113. Guilmartin related that Seventh Fleet commander Vice Admiral George P. Steele criticized Air Force helicopter tactics but concluded that even though

114. Lamb, *The* Mayaguez Crisis, 196 (see also 195).
115. Ibid., 2, 4, 6, 13, 70, 79, 136, 172, 177–179, 214.
116. Minutes of Washington Special Actions Group Meeting, White House, 19 August 1976, Ford Library, National Security Adviser, NSC Staff for East Asia and Pacific Affairs, Convenience Files, box 27, WSAG Meeting, Korean Incident, 4, 10. See also Richard A. Mobley, "Revisiting the Korean Tree-Cutting Incident," *Joint Force Quarterly* (No. 35): 112.
117. 18 August WSAG Minutes of Washington Special Actions Group Meeting, White House, Ford Library, National Security Adviser, NSC Staff for East Asia and Pacific Affairs, Convenience Files, box 27, WSAG Meeting, Korean Incident, 8.
118. Holloway, in his *Aircraft Carriers at War*, 402–11, and in Puryear, *American Admiralship*, 38–44, is incorrect in his assertion that Kissinger was in Kansas City with the president during the crisis and that the DEFCON in Korea was raised to 2. See 18 and 19 August WSAG Minutes of Washington Special Actions Group Meeting, White House, Ford Library, National Security Adviser, NSC Staff for East Asia and Pacific Affairs, Convenience Files, box 27, WSAG Meeting, Korean Incident. See also Marolda, *Ready Seapower*, 77–78.
119. Quoted in Mobley, "Revisiting the Korean Tree-Cutting Incident," 111, 113.
120. Holloway, *Aircraft Carriers at War*, 405.
121. Ibid., 407.
122. 19 August WSAG Minutes of Washington Special Actions Group Meeting, White House, Ford Library, National Security Adviser, NSC Staff for East Asia and Pacific Affairs, Convenience Files, box 27, WSAG Meeting, Korean Incident, 7.
123. Holloway, *Aircraft Carriers at War*, 407, 408. Holloway interview with Marolda, 83–84.

CHAPTER 13

1. From the time of his retirement until his death on 5 February 2004, Moorer lived in McLean, Virginia, and provided advice on national security matters at the Center for Strategic and International Studies and served on the boards of the Texaco, Fairchild Industries, and Alabama Dry Dock and Shipbuilding Company. He testified before Congress to oppose the SALT II and Panama Canal treaties. The admiral was survived by his wife of sixty-eight years, Carrie Foy Moorer; four children, Thomas R. Moorer, Ellen Butcher, Richard F. Moorer, and Robert H. Moorer; two brothers; ten grandchildren; and two great-grandchildren. McDonald, "Thomas Hinman Moorer," 363; "Admiral Thomas Moorer Dies; Chaired Joint Chiefs of Staff," *The Washington Post*, 5 February 2004.
2. Lehman, *Command of the Seas*, 97. See also Kerr USNI OH, 163.
3. William J. Clinton, "Remarks at Funeral Services for Elmo R. Zumwalt Jr., in Annapolis, Maryland," http://www.presidency.ucsb.edu/ws/?pid=58232. In attendance were Mrs. Zumwalt, President Clinton and First Lady Hillary Rodham Clinton, Paul Nitze, Chairman of the Joint Chiefs of Staff, Admiral

Michael Mullen, and members of the Zumwalt family. Many of the sailors and others who had served under the admiral and who held him in high regard attended the ceremony. Among the pallbearers were admirals Emmett Tidd, Charles Rauch, William Norman, Jerry Wages, Roberta Hazard, the first Black female flag officer Lilian E. Fishburne, and former members of Zumwalt's Pentagon mini-staff. This author also saw many Black, female, and Vietnamese individuals, either in uniform or civilian attire, in the audience. The heavens always seemed to favor Zumwalt, so soon after the service began the day's cloudy and rainy sky cleared and a bright sun shone through the chapel's stained-glass window above the altar. Author's notes of the Zumwalt funeral. See also Berman, *Zumwalt*, 1–8, 21–26; Thompson, *Gumption*, 519.

4. CNO, Memo for All Flag Officers and All Flag Selectees, OP-00 Memo 292-71, 24 April 1971, Zumwalt Coll., acc. no. 6210709009, Texas Tech Vietnam Archive. See also Memo for All Flag Officers and All Flag Selectees, OP-00 Memo, 8 October 1970, Zumwalt Coll., acc. no. 6210709008, Texas Tech Vietnam Archive.

5. Stavridis, *Sailing True North*, 197.

6. Ltr, Zumwalt to Carter, 6 April 1978, Zumwalt Coll., acc. no. 6210214001, Texas Tech Vietnam Archive; ltr, Zumwalt to Ford, 12 December 1975, Zumwalt Coll., acc. no. 6210401001, Texas Tech Vietnam Archive; "First Year Program, Committee on the Present Danger," 11 May 1976, Zumwalt Coll., acc. no. 6230208011, Texas Tech Vietnam Archive; "Admiral Zumwalt's address at the Industrial War College, Fort McNair, Washington, DC," 26 March 1975, Zumwalt Coll., acc. no. 6230606007; Berman, *Zumwalt*, 409.

7. Berman, *Zumwalt*, 381, 387–89. John Warner, Secretary of the Navy from 1972 to 1979 and a senator from Virginia from 1979 to 2009, remembered that Zumwalt knew little about politics or Virginia and was "not cut out for the job." Warner USNI OH, 161–62.

8. Berman, in *Zumwalt*, 1, 14, does a disservice to the 1.8 million men and women of the US Navy who served in Southeast Asia during the war and the 2,565 who did not come home from that long conflict. Berman quotes former senior defense department official and Professor Dov Zakheim: "There was nothing in the Navy of 1970, when Bud became its highest-ranking officer that pointed to the Navy of today. Nothing. It was a troubled force consisting of demoralized men and aging ships, plagued by bitterness, discrimination and hatred. Zumwalt turned the Navy around." The Navy of 1970, however, certainly did not fit that unfair characterization. The service was then operating over, under, and on the sea and sacrificing lives all over the world to protect the United States and the American people. That same Navy was fighting skillfully and professionally with the other US armed forces to honor the US commitment to the Republic of Vietnam. It was no wonder that when Admiral Moorer heard similar words at Zumwalt's funeral about how the latter had "saved the Navy," according to JCS chairman Admiral William Crowe, [Moorer] got "madder and madder and madder." Crowe, NHF OH, 612.

9. Quoted in George C. Herring, *From Colony to Superpower: U.S. Foreign Relations Since 1776* (New York: Oxford University Press, 2008), 912.

10. Arthur USNI OH, 501–2.

BIBLIOGRAPHY

NOTE ON SOURCES

Much of the information for this book was derived from the archival holdings of the Naval Historical Center (now Naval History and Heritage Command) employed in this author's research and writing of a number of histories on the US Navy and the Vietnam War. Those unclassified or declassified documents are maintained in the following record groups: Post–1946 Command, Report, and Plan files that contain materials originated by the Office of the Secretary of Defense, Defense Intelligence Agency, Joint Chiefs of Staff, the unified commands such as CINCPAC and MACV, and other government agencies. By far the largest portions of these groups are materials generated by the Office of the Chief of Naval Operations, the Pacific Fleet, the numbered fleets, naval operating forces, shore-based commands, and individual ships and aircraft squadrons. Of particular worth are separate collections in the archives accessioned from the Navy Secretariat of the JCS; the Office of the Chief of Naval Operations; Seventh Fleet; Naval Forces, Vietnam; and Naval Advisory Group, Vietnam. This documentation is supported by the message traffic of the Pacific Command, Pacific Fleet, and Naval Forces, Vietnam. Specialized groups include the CNO Flag Plot, Tonkin Gulf, Vietnam Subject File, NAVFORV Lessons Learned and End of Tour Reports, and Biographies collections. NAVFORV monthly historical summaries may be found at https://www.history.navy.mil/research/archives/digitized-collections/commander-naval-forces-vietnam.html. The papers or interviews accessed at the NHHC include the following: G. W. Anderson, W. M. Beakley, P. H. Bucklew, A. A. Burke, W. Colby, J. B. Drachnik, W. H. Hamilton, R. Hazard, J. L. Holloway, W. D Irvin, D. L. McDonald, R. Marcinko, H. L. Miller, T. H. Moorer, M. L. Mulford, C. Ricketts, H. Rivero,

P. M. Swartz, N. Ward, and E. R. Zumwalt. This history also made extensive use of the interviews with Chung Tan Cang, Nguyen Huu Chi, Dinh Manh Hung, Hoang Co Minh, Nguyen Xuan Son, and Ho Van Ky Thoai, Vietnam Navy officers interviewed after their arrival in the United States in 1975, by the Naval Historical Center. Especially valuable to this work were the oral histories conducted by the US Naval Institute, copies of which can be found in the Navy Department Library, and include the following: G. W. Anderson, S. R. Arthur, H. Baldwin, P. A. Beshany, P. H. Bucklew, A. A. Burke, J. T. Burke, C. K. Duncan, D. D. Engen, H. D. Felt, W. D. Irvin, D. L. McDonald, U. S. G. Sharp, R. L. Johnson, J. B. Colwell, J. W. Cooper, W. L. Glenn Jr., C. D. Griffin, T. B. Hayward, E. B. Hooper, J. J. Hyland, F. R. Kaine, A. Kerr, H. Kerr, J. H. King, K. L. Lee, R. L. J. Long, W. P. Mack, J. S. McCain, G. E. Miller, H. L. Miller, T. H. Moorer, J. K. Parker, R. E. Peet, J. W. Prueher, J. D. Ramage, D. Richardson, H. H. Rivero, R. Salzer, W. R. Smedberg, H. D. Train, K. K. Veth, A. G. Ward, T. R. Weschler, P. A. Yost, and E. R. Zumwalt. Use was also made of the Naval Historical Foundation's interviews with W. Crowe, J. L. Holloway, and J. Warner and the interview with P. M. Swartz at the Center for Naval Analyses. Access to the personal papers of Peter M. Swartz was especially rewarding and appreciated.

Research for this book was also conducted in the documentary records, papers, and oral history interviews, either in person or online, of the following repositories: National Archives II; John F. Kennedy, Lyndon B. Johnson, Richard M. Nixon, and Gerald R. Ford presidential libraries; Texas Tech Vietnam Archive; National Security Archive; and the U.S. Army Center of Military History.

EXECUTIVE AND CONGRESSIONAL DOCUMENTS

Department of Defense, *United States-Vietnam Relations: 1945–1967* (Washington, DC: US Government Printing Office, 1971); and the companion *Senator Gravel Edition of the Pentagon Papers* (Boston: Beacon Press, 1971).

Foreign Relations of the United States, 1961–1963, Vol. III, *Vietnam: January–August 1963*. Washington, DC: Department of State History Office, 1991.

Foreign Relations of the United States, 1969–1976, Vol. VI, *Vietnam, January 1969–July 1970*. Washington, DC: US Government Printing Office, 2006.

Public Papers of the Presidents of the United States, Lyndon Johnson: 1963–64. Washington, DC: US Government Printing Office, 1965.

Report by the Special Subcommittee on Disciplinary Problems in the US Navy of the Committee on Armed Forces. House of Representatives. 92 Cong., 2nd Sess., January 2, 1973.

US Congress, Senate. Preparedness Investigating Subcommittee of the Committee on the Armed Services. *Air War Against North Vietnam*. 90th Cong., 1st Sess. Washington, DC: US Government Printing Office, 1967.

US Congress, Senate. Committee on Armed Services. *Nomination of Admiral Thomas H. Moorer, USN, to be Chairman, Joint Chiefs of Staff*. 91st Cong., 2nd Sess. Washington, DC: US Government Printing Office, 1970.

US Congress, Senate. Committee on Foreign Relations. *Hearings on the Gulf of Tonkin, the 1964 Incidents*. 90th Cong., 2nd Sess. Washington, DC: US Government Printing Office, 1968.

US Congress, Senate. "Nomination of Admiral Thomas H. Moorer to be Chief of Naval Operations." Hearings before the Committee on Armed Services. 90th Cong., 1st Sess. Washington, DC: US Government Printing Office, 1967.

SECONDARY WORKS

Agawa, Naoyuki. *Friendship Across the Seas: The US Navy and the Japan Maritime Self-Defense Force*. Tokyo: Japan Publishing Industry Foundation for Culture, 2019.

Allard, Dean C. "Elmo R. Zumwalt Jr." In *Dictionary of American Military Biography*, edited by Roger J. Spiller, Joseph G. Dawson

III, and T. Harry Williams. Westport, CT: Greenwood Press, 1984.

Ambrose, Stephen. *Nixon: Ruin and Recovery, 1973–1990*, Vol. 3. New York: Simon & Schuster, 1987.

———. *Nixon: The Triumph of a Politician, 1962–1972*. New York: Simon and Schuster, 1987.

Anderson, David L. *Vietnamization: Politics, Strategy, Legacy*. Lanham, MD: Rowan & Littlefield, 2019.

Appy, Christian G. *American Reckoning: The Vietnam War and Our National Identity*. New York: Penguin, 2016.

Asselin, Pierre. *Hanoi's Road to the Vietnam War, 1954–1965*. Berkeley, CA: University of California Press, 2013.

Baer, George W. *One Hundred Years of Sea Power: The U.S. Navy, 1890–1990*. Stanford, CA: Stanford University Press, 1994.

Berman, Larry. *Zumwalt: The Life and Times of Admiral Elmo Russell "Bud" Zumwalt Jr.* New York: Harper Collins, 2012.

Beschloss, Michael R. *Taking Charge: The Johnson White House Tapes, 1963–1964*. New York: Simon & Schuster, 1997.

Birtle, Andrew J., and John R. Maass. *The Drawdown, 1970–1971*. In series The U.S. Army Campaigns of the Vietnam War. Washington, DC: U.S. Army Center of Military History, 2019.

Brinkley, Douglas. *Tour of Duty: John Kerry and the Vietnam War*. New York: William Morrow, 2004.

Burr, William, and Jeffrey P. Kimball. *Nixon's Nuclear Specter: The Secret Alert of 1969, Madman Diplomacy, and the Vietnam War*. Lawrence: University Press of Kansas, 2015.

Buzzanco, Robert. *Masters of War: Military Dissent and Politics in the Vietnam Era*. Cambridge, MA: Cambridge University Press, 1996.

Chamberland, Dennis. "Interview: Westmoreland." In *Vietnam: A Retrospective*, edited by Thomas J. Cutler. Annapolis: Naval Institute Press, 2016.

Chamberlin, Paul Thomas. *The Cold War's Killing Fields: Rethinking the Long Peace*. New York: Harper, 2018.

Chandler, David P. *The Tragedy of Cambodian History: Politics, War, and Revolution since 1945*. New Haven: Yale University Press, 1991.

Chang, Jung, and Jon Halliday. *Mao: The Unknown Story*. New York: Anchor Books, 2006.

Clarke, Thurston. *Honorable Exit: How a Few Brave Americans Risked All to Save Our Vietnamese Allies at the End of the War*. New York: Doubleday, 2019.

Clodfelter, Mark. *The Limits of Air Power: The American Bombing of North Vietnam*. Lincoln: University of Nebraska Press, 1989.

———. *Violating Reality: The Lavelle Affair, Nixon, and the Parsing of the Truth*. Washington, DC: National Defense University Press, 2016.

Colby, William. *Honorable Men: My Life in the CIA*. New York: Simon and Schuster, 1978.

Cole, Ronald H., Lorna S. Jaffe, Walter S. Poole, and Willard J. Webb. *The Chairmanship of the Joint Chiefs of Staff*. Washington, DC: Joint History Office, 1995.

Conboy, Kenneth. *The Cambodian Wars: Clashing Armies and CIA Covert Operations*. Lawrence: University Press of Kansas, 2013.

Cosmas, Graham A. *The Joint Chiefs of Staff and the War in Vietnam, 1960–1968*, pt. 2. Washington, DC: Office of Joint History, 2012.

———. *The Joint Chiefs of Staff and the War in Vietnam, 1960–1968*, pt. 3. Washington, DC: Office of Joint History, 2009.

———. *MACV: The Joint Command in the Years of Escalation, 1962–1967*. Washington, DC: U.S. Army Center of Military History, 2006.

———. *MACV: The Joint Command in the Years of Withdrawal, 1968–'73*. Washington, DC: U.S. Army Center of Military History, 2007.

Crist, Charlotte D. *Winds of Change: The History of the Office of the Master Chief Petty Officer of the Navy: 1967–1972*. Washington, DC: Office of the Master Chief Petty Officer of the Navy/Naval Historical Center, 1972.

Crowe, William J., Jr., and David Chanoff. *The Line of Fire: From Washington to the Gulf, the Politics and Battles of the New Military*. New York: Simon & Schuster, 1993.

Cutler, Thomas J. "Elmo R. Zumwalt Jr.: Hero or Heretic?" In *Quarterdeck & Bridge: Two Centuries of American Naval Leaders*, edited by James Bradford, 415–32. Annapolis: Naval Institute Press, 1997.

———. "Elmo R. Zumwalt Jr.: Innovation." In *Leadership Embodied: The Secrets to Success of the Most Effective Navy and Marine Corps Leaders*, 2nd ed., edited by Joseph J. Thomas. Annapolis: Naval Institute Press, 2013.

Daddis, Gregory A. *Westmoreland's War: Reassessing American Strategy in Vietnam*. New York: Oxford University Press, 2014.

———. *Withdrawal: Reassessing America's Final Years in Vietnam*.

Oxford, UK: Oxford University Press, 2017.

Dallek, Robert. *Flawed Giant: Lyndon Johnson and His Times, 1961–1973*. New York: Oxford University Press, 1998.

———. *Nixon and Kissinger: Partners in Power*. New York: HarperCollins, 2007.

Davidson, Phillip B. *Vietnam at War: The History: 1946–1975*. Novato, CA: Presidio, 1988.

Deac, Wilfred P. *Road to the Killing Fields: The Cambodian War of 1970–1975*. College Station: Texas A&M University Press, 1997.

Dommen, Arthur J. *Conflict in Laos: The Politics of Neutralization*. New York: Praeger, 1971.

Drea, Edward J. *McNamara, Clifford, and the Burdens of Vietnam, 1965–1969*. Washington, DC: Historical Office, Office of the Secretary of Defense, 2011.

Duermeyer, James. *The Capture of the USS* Pueblo*: The Incident, the Aftermath and the Motives of North Korea*. Jefferson, NC: McFarland & Co., 2018.

Duncan, Francis. *Rickover: The Struggle for Excellence*. Annapolis: Naval Institute Press, 2001.

Dunham, George R., and David A. Quinlan. *U.S. Marines in Vietnam: The Bitter End, 1973–1975*. Washington, DC: History and Museums Division, U.S. Marine Corps, 1990.

Dunnavent, R. Blake. "Maverick: Elmo Russell Zumwalt Jr. (1920–2000)." In *Nineteen-Gun Salute: Case Studies of Operational, Strategic, and Diplomatic Naval Leadership during the 20th and Early 21st Centuries*, edited by John B. Hattendorf and Bruce A. Elleman. Newport, RI: Naval War College Press, 2010.

Ebbert, Jean, and Marie-Beth Hall. *Crossed Currents: Navy Women in a Century of Change*. Washington, DC: Brassey's, 1999.

Erdheim, Judith. *Market Time*, study CRC 280. Washington, DC: Center for Naval Analyses, 1975.

Erlichman, John. *Witness to Power: The Nixon Years*. New York: Pocket Books, 1982.

Fall, Bernard B. *Anatomy of a Crisis: The Laotian Crisis of 1960–1961*. Garden City, NY: Doubleday, 1961.

Farrell, John A. *Richard Nixon: The Life*. New York: Doubleday, 2017.

Feldstein, Mark. *Poisoning the Press: Richard Nixon, Jack Anderson, and the Rise of Washington's Scandal Culture*. New York: Farrar, Straus and Giroux, 2010.

Fey, Peter. *Bloody Sixteen: The USS* Oriskany *and Air Wing 16 during the Vietnam War*. Lincoln, NE: Potomac Books, 2018.

Ford, Gerald R. *A Time to Heal: The Autobiography of Gerald R. Ford*. New York: Harper & Row, 1979.

Frankum, Ronald B., Jr. *Like Rolling Thunder: The Air War in Vietnam, 1964–1975*. Lanham, MD: Rowman & Littlefield, 2005.

Fravel, M. Taylor. *Active Defense: China's Military Strategy since 1949*. Princeton, NJ: Princeton University Press, 2019.

Friedman, Norman. "Elmo Russell Zumwalt Jr.: 1 July 1970–1 July 1974." In *The Chiefs of Naval Operations*, edited by Robert William Love Jr., 365–79. Annapolis: Naval Institute Press, 1980.

Fulton, William B. *Riverine Operations, 1966–1969*. Washington, DC: Department of the Army, 1972.

Fussell, Paul. *Uniforms: Why We Are What We Wear*. Boston: Houghton Mifflin, 2002.

Gaiduk, Ilya V. *The Soviet Union and the Vietnam War*. Chicago: Ivan R. Dee, 1996.

Godson, Susan H. *Serving Proudly: A History of Women in the U.S. Navy*. Annapolis: Naval Institute Press, 2001.

Goldstein, Gordon M. *Lessons in Disaster: McGeorge Bundy and the Path to War in Vietnam*. New York: Times Books, 2008.

Goldstein, Martin E. *American Policy Toward Laos*. Cranbury, NJ: Associated University Presses, 1973.

Goodman, Allan E. *The Lost Peace: America's Search for a Negotiated Settlement of the Vietnam War*. Stanford, CA: Hoover Institution Press, 1978.

Goodwin, Doris Kearns. *Lyndon Johnson and the American Dream: The Most Revealing Portrait of a President and Presidential Power Ever Written*. New York: St. Martin's Press, 1991.

Guan, Ang Cheng. *The Vietnam War from the Other Side: The Vietnamese Communists' Perspective*. New York: Routledge Curzon, 2002.

Gugliotta, Guy, John Yeoman, and Neva Sullaway. *Swift Boats at War in Vietnam*. Guilford, CT: Stackpole Books, 2017.

Guilmartin, John F., Jr. *A Very Short War: The Mayaguez and the Battle of Koh Tang*. College Station: Texas A&M University Press, 1995.

Haig, Alexander M., Jr. *Inner Circles: How America Changed the World: A Memoir*. New York: Warner Books, 1992.

Halberstam, David. *The Best and the Brightest*. New York: Random

House, 1972.

Haldeman, H. R. *The Haldeman Diaries: Inside the Nixon White House.* New York: Berkley, 1994.

Hall, David K. "The Laos Crisis, 1960–61." In *The Limits of Coercive Diplomacy: Laos, Cuba, Vietnam*, edited by Alexander L. George, David K. Hall, and William E. Simons. Boston: Little Brown, 1971.

Hall, Gwendolyn Frazier. "Managing Interservice Competition: The Relationship between the Secretary of Defense and the Joint Chiefs of Staff." PhD dissertation, University of Maryland, 1992.

Hallion, Richard P. *Rolling Thunder: 1965–1968.* Oxford, UK: Osprey Publishing, 2018.

Hartmann, Frederick H. *Naval Renaissance: The U.S. Navy in the 1980s.* Annapolis: Naval Institute Press, 1990.

Hattendorf, John B., ed. *U.S. Naval Strategy in the 1970s: Selected Documents.* Newport: Naval War College Press, 2007.

Hattendorf, John, B., Mitchell Simpson III, and John R. Wadleigh. *Sailors and Scholars: The Centennial History of the Naval War College.* Newport, RI: Naval War College Press, 1984.

Haynes, Peter D. "Elmo Zumwalt's Project SIXTY: Driving Institutional Change in an Era of Great Power Competition at Sea." In *Conceptualizing Maritime & Naval Strategy: Festschrift for Captain M. Swartz, United States Navy (ret.).* Edited by Sebastian Bruns and Sarandis Papadopoulos. Baden-Baden, Germany: Nomos Verlagsgesellschaft, 2020.

———. *Toward a New Maritime Strategy: American Naval Thinking in the Post–Cold War Era.* Annapolis: Naval Institute Press, 2015.

Head, Richard G., Frisco W. Short, and Robert C. McFarlane. *Crisis Resolution: Presidential Decision Making in the Mayaguez and Korean Confrontations.* Boulder, CO: Westview Press, 1978.

Hébert, F. Edward, with John McMillan. *"Last of the Titans": The Life and Times of Congressman F. Edward Hébert of Louisiana.* Lafayette: Center for Louisiana Studies, University of Southwestern Louisiana, 1976.

Helm, Glenn. "Ulysses S. Grant Sharp: Courage." In *Leadership Embodied: The Secrets to Success of the Most Effective Navy and Marine Corps Leaders*, 2nd ed., edited by Joseph J. Thomas. Annapolis: Naval Institute Press, 2013.

Herman, Jan K. *Navy Medicine in Vietnam: Oral Histories from Dien Bien Phu to the Fall of Saigon.* Jefferson, NC: McFarland, 2009.

Herring, George C. *From Colony to Superpower: U.S. Foreign Relations Since 1776*. New York: Oxford University Press, 2008.

Hersh, Seymour M. *The Price of Power: Kissinger in the Nixon White House*. New York: Summit Books, 1983.

Hilsman, Roger. *To Move a Nation: The Politics of Foreign Policy in the Administration of John F. Kennedy*. Garden City, NY: Doubleday, 1967.

Holloway, James L., III. *Aircraft Carriers at War: A Personal Retrospective of Korea, Vietnam, and the Soviet Confrontation*. Annapolis: Naval Institute Press, 2007.

Hone, Thomas C. *Power and Change: The Administrative History of the Office of the Chief of Naval Operations, 1946–1986*. Washington, DC: Naval Historical Center, 1989.

Hone, Thomas C., and Curtis A. Utz. *History of the Office of the Chief of Naval Operations, 1915–2015*. Washington, DC: Naval History and Heritage Command, 2018.

Hughes, Thomas L. "Experiencing McNamara. *Foreign Policy* no. 100 (Autumn 1995).

Hughes, Wayne P., Jr. "Vietnam: Winnable War?" In *Vietnam: A Retrospective*, edited by Thomas Cutler, 3–11. Annapolis: Naval Institute Press, 2016.

Hunt, Richard A. *Melvin Laird and the Foundation of the Post-Vietnam Military, 1969–1973*. In Secretaries of Defense Historical Series. Washington, DC: Historical Office, Office of the Secretary of Defense, 2015.

Ignatius, Paul R. *On Board: My Life in the Navy, Government, and Business*. Annapolis: Naval Institute Press, 2006.

Isaacs, Arnold R. *Without Honor: Defeat in Vietnam and Cambodia*. Baltimore: Johns Hopkins University Press, 1983.

Isaacson, Walter. *Kissinger: A Biography*. New York: Simon & Schuster, 1992.

Jian, Chen. *Mao's China and the Cold War*. Chapel Hill: University of North Carolina Press, 2001.

Johnson, Lyndon B. *The Vantage Point: Perspectives of the Presidency, 1963–1969*. New York: Holt, Rinehart, Winston, 1971.

Jones, Howard. *My Lai: Vietnam, 1968, and the Descent into Darkness*. New York: Oxford University Press, 2017.

Kaplan, Lawrence S., Ronald D. Landa, and Edward J. Drea. *The McNamara Ascendancy, 1961–1965*. Washington, DC: Historical

Office of the Secretary of Defense, 2006.

Kennedy, Floyd D., Jr. "David Lamar McDonald: 1 August 1963–1 August 1967." In *The Chiefs of Naval Operations*, edited by Robert William Love Jr., 333–49. Annapolis: Naval Institute Press, 1980.

Kennedy, John F. *Strategy of Peace*. New York: Harper and Brothers, 1960.

Khoo, Nicholas. *Collateral Damage: Sino-Soviet Rivalry and the Termination of the Sino-Vietnamese Alliance*. New York: Columbia University Press, 2011.

Kimball, Jeffrey. *Nixon's Vietnam War*. Lawrence: University Press of Kansas, 1998.

———. *The Vietnam War Files*. Lawrence: University Press of Kansas, 2004.

Kinnard, Douglas C. *The Certain Trumpet: Maxwell Taylor and the American Experience in Vietnam*. Washington, DC: Brassey's, 1991.

Kissinger, Henry. *Ending the Vietnam War: A History of America's Involvement in and Extraction from the Vietnam War*. New York: Simon & Schuster, 2003.

———. *White House Years*. Boston: Little, Brown and Co., 1979.

———. *Years of Upheaval*. Boston: Little, Brown, 1982.

Krulak, Victor H. "A Conflict of Strategies." In *Vietnam: A Retrospective*, edited by Thomas Cutler, 64–77. Annapolis: Naval Institute Press, 2016.

Laird, Melvin. *A House Divided: America's Strategy Gap*. New York: H. Regnery, 1962.

Lamb, Christopher J. *The Mayaguez Crisis, Mission Command, and Civil-Military Relations*. Washington, DC: JCS History Office, Office of the Chairman of the Joint Chiefs of Staff, 2018.

Langer, Paul F., and Joseph J. Zasloff. *North Vietnam and the Pathet Lao: Partners in the Struggle for Laos*. Cambridge, MA: Harvard University Press, 1970.

Larzelere, Alex. *The Coast Guard at War: Vietnam 1965–1975*. Annapolis: Naval Institute Press, 1997.

Lavell, Kit. *Flying Black Ponies: The Navy's Close Air Support Squadron in Vietnam*. Annapolis: Naval Institute Press, 2000.

Lee, Heath Hardage. *The League of Wives: The Untold Story of the Women Who Took on the U.S. Government to Bring Their Husbands Home*. New York: St. Martin's Press, 2019.

Lehman, John F., Jr. *Command of the Seas*. New York: Charles Scribner's

Sons, 1988.

———. *Oceans Ventured: Winning the Cold War at Sea*. New York: W.W. Norton, 2018.

———. *On Seas of Glory: Heroic Men, Great Ships, and Epic Battles of the American Navy*. New York: The Free Press, 2001.

Leuci, Jim. "Delbert Black: More Than Just a Gunner's Mate." Naval Historical Foundation "Thursday's Tidings," 1 October 2020.

Li, Xiaobing. *Building Ho's Army: Chinese Military Assistance to North Vietnam*. Lexington. University Press of Kentucky, 2019.

———. *The Dragon in the Jungle: The Chinese Army in the Vietnam War*. New York: Oxford University Press, 2020.

———. *A History of the Modern Chinese Army*. Lexington: University Press of Kentucky, 2007.

———. *Voices from the Vietnam War: Stories from American, Asian, and Russian Veterans*. Lexington: University of Kentucky Press, 2005.

Logevall, Fredrik. *Choosing War: The Lost Chance for Peace and the Escalation of War in Vietnam*. Berkeley: University of California Press, 1999.

———. *Embers of War: The Fall of an Empire and the Making of America's Vietnam*. New York: Penguin Random House, 2012.

Love, Robert William, Jr., ed. *The Chiefs of Naval Operations*. Annapolis: Naval Institute Press, 1980.

Mark, Eduard. *Aerial Interdiction: Air Power and the Land Battle in Three American Wars*. Washington, DC: Center for Air Force History, 2009.

Marolda, Edward J. *By Sea, Air, and Land: An Illustrated History of the U.S. Navy and the War in Southeast Asia*. Washington, DC: Naval Historical Center, 1994.

———, ed. *Combat at Close Quarters: An Illustrated History of the U.S. Navy in the Vietnam War*. Annapolis: Naval Institute Press, 2018.

———, ed. *Operation End Sweep: A History of Minesweeping Operations in North Vietnam*. Washington, DC: Naval Historical Center/ Tensor Industries Inc., 1993.

———. *Ready Seapower: A History of the U.S. Seventh Fleet*. Washington, DC: Naval History and Heritage Command, 2012.

———. "The Social History of the U.S. Navy, 1945–Present." In *Needs and Opportunities in the Modern History of the U.S. Navy*, edited by Michael J. Crawford, 221–69. Washington, DC: Naval History and Heritage Command, 2018.

———. "Troubled Assignment: The U.S. Navy's Advisory Mission in Vietnam, 1954–1973." In *Naval Advising and Assistance: History, Challenges, and Analysis*, edited by Donald Stoker and Michael T. McMaster, 243–64. UK: Helion & Company, Ltd., 2017.

Marolda, Edward J., and R. Blake Dunnavent. *Combat at Close Quarters: Warfare on the Rivers and Canals of Vietnam*. In series The U.S. Navy and the Vietnam War, Edward J. Marolda and Sandra K. Doyle, eds. Washington, DC: Naval History and Heritage Command, 2015.

Marolda, Edward J., and Oscar P. Fitzgerald. *From Military Assistance to Combat, 1959–1965*, Vol. II. In series The United States Navy and the Vietnam Conflict. Washington, DC: Naval Historical Center, 1986.

McCain, John, with Mark Salter. *Faith of My Fathers*. New York: Random House, 1999.

McMaster, H. R. *Dereliction of Duty: Lyndon Johnson, Robert McNamara, the Joint Chiefs of Staff, and the Lies that Led to Vietnam*. New York: Harper Collins, 1997.

McNamara, Robert S., with Brian VanDeMark. *In Retrospect: The Tragedy and Lessons of Vietnam*. New York: Times Books, 1995.

McNamara, Robert S., James G. Blight, and Robert K. Brigham. *Argument Without End: In Search of Answers to the Vietnam Tragedy*. New York: Public Affairs, 1999.

McQuilkin, William C. "Operation SEALORDS: A Front in a Frontless War: An Analysis of the Brown Water Navy in Vietnam." MA thesis, U.S. Army Command and General Staff College, Fort Leavenworth, KS, 1997.

Mercogliano, Salvatore R. *Fourth Arm of Defense: Sealift and Maritime Logistics in the Vietnam War*. In series The U.S. Navy and the Vietnam War, Edward J. Marolda and Sandra J. Doyle, eds. Naval History and Heritage Command, 2015.

Michel, Marshall L., III. *The Eleven Days of Christmas: America's Last Vietnam Battle*. San Francisco: Encounter Books, 2002.

Middendorf, J. William, II. *Potomac Fever: A Memoir of Politics and Public Service*. Annapolis: Naval Institute Press, 2011.

Mobley, Richard A. *Flash Point North Korea: The Pueblo and EC-121 Crises*. Annapolis: Naval Institute Press, 2003.

Mobley, Richard A., and Edward J. Marolda. *Knowing the Enemy: Naval Intelligence in Southeast Asia*. In series The U.S. Navy and the Vietnam War. Edward J. Marolda and Sandra Doyle, eds. Washington, DC: Naval History and Heritage Command, 2015.

Moise, Edwin E. *Tonkin Gulf and the Escalation of the Vietnam War*. Annapolis: Naval Institute Press, 2019.

Momyer, William W. *Airpower in Three Wars*. Washington, DC: US Government Printing Office, 1983.

Morison, Samuel Eliot. *The Two-Ocean War: A Short History of the United States Navy in the Second World War*. Boston: Little, Brown and Co., 1963.

Morris, Roger. *HAIG: The General's* Progress. Chicago: Playboy Press, 1982.

Morrocco, John. *Rain of Fire: Air War, 1969–1973*. In series The Vietnam Experience. Boston: Boston Publishing Co., 1986.

Morton, John Fass. *Mustin: A Naval Family of the Twentieth Century*. Annapolis: Naval Institute Press, 2003.

Muir, Malcolm, Jr. *Black Shoes and Blue Water: Surface Warfare in the United States Navy, 1945–1975*. Washington, DC: Naval Historical Center, 1996.

———. *End of the Saga: The Maritime Evacuation of South Vietnam and Cambodia*. In series The U.S. Navy and the Vietnam War, Edward J. Marolda and Sandra Doyle, eds. Washington, DC: Naval History and Heritage Command, 2017.

Nalty, Bernard C. *Air Power and the Fight for Khe Sanh*. Washington, DC: Office of Air Force History, 1973.

———. *Air War over South Vietnam, 1968–1975*. Washington, DC: Air Force History and Museums Program, 2000.

———. *The War Against Trucks: Aerial Interdiction in Southern Laos, 1968–1972*. Washington, DC: Air Force History and Museums Division, 2005.

Nguyen, Duy Hinh. *Lam Son 719*. In series Indochina Monographs. Washington, DC: U.S. Army Center of Military History, 1979.

Nguyen, Lien-Hang T. *Hanoi's War: An International History of the War for Peace in Vietnam*. Chapel Hill: University of North Carolina Press, 2012.

Nitze, Paul H. *From Hiroshima to Glasnost: At the Center of Decision*. New York: Grove Weidenfeld, 1989.

Nixon, Richard. *RN: The Memoirs of Richard Nixon*. New York: Grosset & Dunlap, 1978.

Osborne, Eric W. "People Come First—Harry Donald Felt

(1902–1992)." In *Nineteen-Gun Salute: Case Studies of Operational, Strategic, and Diplomatic Naval Leadership during the 20th and Early 21st Centuries*, edited by John B. Hattendorf and Bruce A. Elleman. Newport, RI: Naval War College Press, 2002.

Packard, Nathan R. "Repairing the Wreckage of Vietnam: The Marine Corps' Great Personnel Campaign, 1975–1979." In Lori Lyn Bogle and James C. Rentfrow, *New Interpretations in Naval History: Selected Papers from the Eighteenth McMullen Naval History Symposium Held at the U.S. Naval Academy, 19–20 September 2013*, 251–69. Newport, RI: Naval War College Press, 2018.

Palmer, Bruce. *The 25-Year War: America's Military Role in Vietnam*. Lexington: University of Press of Kentucky, 1984.

Perry, Mark. *Four Stars*. Boston: Houghton Mifflin Co., 1989.

Phillips, Rufus. *Why Vietnam Matters: An Eyewitness Account of Lessons Not Learned*. Annapolis: Naval Institute Press, 2008.

Pike, Douglas. *Vietnam and the Soviet Union: Anatomy of an Alliance*. Boulder, CO: Westview Press, 1987.

Polmar, Norman, and Thomas B. Allen. *Rickover: Controversy and Genius*. New York: Simon and Schuster, 1982.

Polmar, Norman, Thomas A. Brooks, and George E. Federoff. *Admiral Gorshkov: The Man Who Challenged the U.S. Navy*. Annapolis: Naval Institute Press, 2019.

Polmar, Norman, and Edward J. Marolda. *Naval Air War: The Rolling Thunder Campaign*. Monograph in series The U.S. Navy and the Vietnam War, edited by Edward J. Marolda and Sandra Doyle. Washington, DC: Naval History and Heritage Command, 2015.

Poole, Walter S. *Adapting to Flexible Response, 1960–1968*. Washington, DC: Historical Office, Office of the Secretary of Defense, 2013.

———. *The Joint Chiefs of Staff and National Policy, 1961–1964*, vol. VII, 1961–1964. Washington, DC: Office of Joint History, 2011.

Porter, Gareth, ed. *Vietnam: The Definitive Documentation of Human Decisions*, vol. II. Stanfordville, NY: Early M. Coleman Enterprises Inc., 1979.

Prados, John. *Vietnam: The History of an Unwinnable War, 1945–1975*. Lawrence: University Press of Kansas, 2009.

Puryear, Edgar F., Jr. *American Admiralship: The Moral Imperatives of Naval Command*. Annapolis: Naval Institute Press, 2005.

Rearden, Steven L. *Council of War: A History of the Joint Chiefs of Staff, 1942–1991*. Washington, DC: Joint History Office, 2012.

Record, Jeffrey. "Why We Lost in Vietnam." In *Vietnam: A Retrospective*, edited by Thomas Cutler, 24–41. Annapolis: Naval Institute Press, 2016.

Reynolds, Clark G. *Famous American Admirals*. New York: Van Nostrand Reinhold Co., 1978.

Ricks, Thomas. *The Generals: American Military Command from World War II to Today*. New York: The Penguin Press, 2012.

Rodman, Peter. *Presidential Command: Power, Leadership, and the Making of Foreign Policy from Richard Nixon to George Bush*. New York: Random House, 2010.

Ryan, Paul B. *First Line of Defense: The U.S. Navy Since 1945*. Stanford, CA: Hoover Institution Press, 1981.

Sander, Robert D. *Invasion of Laos 1971: Lam Son 719*. Norman: University of Oklahoma Press, 2014.

Sands, Jeffrey I. *On His Watch: Admiral Zumwalt's Efforts to Institutionalize Strategic Change*. Alexandria, VA: Center for Naval Analyses, 1993.

Schandler, Herbert Y. *The Unmaking of a President: Lyndon Johnson and Vietnam*. Princeton, NJ: Princeton University Press, 1977.

Schemmer, Benjamin F. *The Raid*. New York: Harper & Row, 1976.

Schlight, John. *The War in South Vietnam: The Years of the Offensive, 1965–1968*. Washington, DC: Office of Air Force History, 1986.

Schlosser, Nicholas J., ed. *The Greene Papers: General Wallace M. Greene Jr. and the Escalation of the Vietnam War*. Quantico, VA: History Division USMC, 2015.

Schmitz, David F. *Richard Nixon and the Vietnam War: The End of the American Century*. Lanham, MD: Rowman & Littlefield, 2014.

Schneller, Robert J. *Blue & Gold and Black: Racial Integration of the U.S. Naval Academy*. College Station: Texas A&M University Press, 2008.

Schreadley, Richard L. *From the Rivers to the Sea: The United States Navy in Vietnam*. Annapolis: Naval Institute Press, 1992.

Sharp, U. S. G. *Strategy for Defeat*. Novato, CA: Presidio Press, 1978.

———. *Strategic Direction of the Armed Forces*. Newport, RI: Naval War College Press, 1977.

Shawcross, William. *Sideshow: Kissinger, Nixon, and the Destruction of Cambodia*. New York: Simon and Schuster, 1979.

Shen, Zhihua, and Danhui Li. *After Leaning to One Side: China and Its*

Allies in the Cold War. Stanford, CA: Stanford University Press, 2011.

Sherwood, John Darrell. "Admiral Thomas Hinman Moorer." In *Nixon's Trident: Naval Power in Southeast Asia, 1968–1972*, 28–29. In series The U.S. Navy and the Vietnam War, edited by Edward J. Marolda and Sandra J. Doyle. Washington, DC: Naval History and Heritage Command, 2009.

———. *Afterburner: Naval Aviators and the Vietnam War*. New York: New York University Press, 2004.

———. *Black Sailor, White Navy: Racial Unrest in the Fleet During the Vietnam War Era*. New York: New York University Press, 2007.

———. *War in the Shallows: U.S. Navy Coastal and Riverine Warfare in Vietnam, 1965–1968*. Washington, DC: Naval History and Heritage Command, 2015.

Shulimson, Jack. *The Joint Chiefs of Staff and the War in Vietnam, 1960–1968*, pt. 1. Washington, DC: Office of Joint History, 2009.

———. *U.S. Marines in Vietnam: An Expanding War, 1966*. Washington, DC: History and Museums Division, USMC, 1982.

Shulimson, Jack, Leonard A. Blasiol, Charles R. Smith, and David A. Dawson. *U.S. Marines in Vietnam: The Defining Year, 1968*. Washington, DC: History and Museums Division, USMC, 1997.

Shulimson, Jack, and Charles M. Johnson. *U.S. Marines in Vietnam: The Landing and the Buildup, 1965*. History and Museums Division, USMC, 1978.

Shulimson, Jack, Gary L. Telfer, Lane Rogers, and V. Keith Fleming Jr. *The U.S. Marines in Vietnam: Fighting the North Vietnamese: 1967*. Washington, DC: Headquarters, USMC, 1984.

Shultz, Richard H., Jr. *The Secret War Against Hanoi*. New York: Harper Collins, 1999.

Smith, Charles R. *High Mobility and Standdown, 1969*. In series U.S. Marines in Vietnam. Washington, DC: Histories and Museums Division, Headquarters USMC, 1988.

Snepp, Frank. *Decent Interval*. New York: Vintage Books, 1977.

Sorley, Lewis. *A Better War: The Unexamined Victories and Final Tragedy of America's Last Years in Vietnam*. New York: Harcourt Inc., 1999.

———. *Thunderbolt: General Creighton Abrams and the Army of His Times*. New York: Simon & Schuster, 1992.

———. ed. *Vietnam Chronicles: The Abrams Tapes, 1968–1972*.

Lubbock: Texas Tech University Press, 2004.

Spector, Ronald H. *Advice and Support: The Early Years, 1941-1960.* In series The United States Army in Vietnam. Washington, DC: U.S. Army Center of Military History, 1983.

———. *After Tet: The Bloodiest Year in Vietnam.* New York: Free Press, 1993.

Stavridis, James. *Sailing True North: Ten Admirals and the Voyage of Character.* New York: Penguin Press, 2019.

Stebbins, Richard P. *The United States in World Affairs, 1961.* New York: Harper, 1962.

Swartz, Peter M. "Drawing Lines on the Sea: The U.S. Navy Confronts the Unified Command Plan, 1946-1998." In proceedings of *Fourteenth Naval History Symposium.* Annapolis: US Naval Academy, 25 September 1999.

———. *U.S. Navy Capstone Strategies and Concepts (1970-2010): Strategy, Policy, Concept, and Vision Documents.* Center for Naval Analyses, December 2011.

———. *The U.S. Navy in the World (1970-1980): Context for U.S. Navy Capstone Strategies and Concepts.* Center for Naval Analyses, December 2011.

Taylor, John M. *General Maxwell Taylor: The Sword and the Pen.* New York: Doubleday, 1989.

Taylor, Maxwell. *Swords and Plowshares.* New York: W.W. Norton & Co., 1972.

Thomas, Joseph J., ed. *Leadership Embodied: The Secrets to Success of the Most Effective Navy and Marine Corps Leaders,* 2nd ed. Annapolis: Naval Institute Press, 2013.

Thompson, Nicholas. *The Hawk and the Dove: Paul Nitze, George Kennan, and the History of the Cold War.* New York: Henry Holt and Co., 2009.

Thompson, Wayne. *To Hanoi and Back: The U.S. Air Force and North Vietnam.* Washington, DC: Smithsonian Institution Press, 2000.

Thompson, William. *Gumption: My Life - My Words.* Self-published, 2010.

Timberg, Robert. *The Nightingale's Song.* New York: Simon & Schuster, 1995.

Todd, Olivier. *Cruel April: The Fall of Saigon.* New York: W.W. Norton & Company, Inc., 1990.

Trauschweizer, Ingo. *Maxwell Taylor's Cold War: From Berlin to*

Vietnam. Lexington: University of Kentucky Press, 2019.
Urey, Patrick. "U.S. Marine Corps Participation in the Emergency Evacuations of Phnom Penh and Saigon: Operations Eagle Pull and Frequent Wind." Alexandria, VA: Center for Naval Analyses, Study 1089, June 1977.
Van Atta, Dale. *With Honor: Melvin Laird in War, Peace, and Politics*. Madison: University of Wisconsin Press, 2008.
Van Staaveren, Jacob. *Gradual Failure: The Air War over North Vietnam, 1965–1966*. Washington, DC: Air Force History and Museums Program, 2002.
———. *Interdiction in Southern Laos, 1960–1968*. Washington, DC: Air Force History and Museums Division, 1993.
Vasey, Lloyd R. "Tonkin: Setting the Record Straight." In *Vietnam: A Retrospective*, edited by Thomas J. Cutler, 12–23. Annapolis: Naval Institute Press, 2016.
Veith, George J. *Black April: The Fall of South Vietnam, 1973–1975*. New York: Encounter Books, 2012.
Vien, Cao Van. *The Final Collapse*. Washington, DC: U.S. Army Center of Military History/US Government Printing Office, 1983.
Villard, Erik V. *Staying the Course: October 1967 to September 1968*. In series The United States Army in Vietnam: Combat Operations. Washington, DC: U.S. Army Center of Military History, 2017.
Warner, Jayne S., and Luu Doan Huynh, eds. *The Vietnam War: Vietnamese and American Perspectives*. Armonk NY: M.E. Sharpe, 1993.
Webb, Willard J. *The Joint Chiefs of Staff and the War in Vietnam, 1969–1970*. Washington, DC: Office of Joint History, 2002.
Webb, Willard J., and Ronald H. Cole. *The Chairmen of the Joint Chiefs of Staff*. Washington, DC: Historical Division, JCS, 1989.
Webb, Willard J., and Walter S. Poole. *The Joint Chiefs of Staff and the War in Vietnam, 1971–1973*. Washington, DC: Office of Joint History, 2007.
Weiner, M. G., J. R. Brom, and R. E. Koon. *Infiltration of Personnel from North Vietnam: 1959–1967*. Santa Monica, CA: Rand Corp., 1968.
Westmoreland, William C. *A Soldier Reports*. New York: Doubleday and Co., 1976.
Wetterhahn, Ralph. *The Last Battle: The Mayaguez Incident and the End of the Vietnam War*. New York: Carroll & Graf, 2001.

Willbanks, James H. *A Raid Too Far: Operation Lam Son 719 and Vietnamization in Laos*. College Station: Texas A&M University Press, 2014.

———. *The Tet Offensive: A Concise History*. New York: Columbia University Press, 2007.

Winkler, David F. *Cold War at Sea*. Annapolis: Naval Institute Press, 2000.

Worthing, Peter. *A Military History of Modern China: From the Manchu Conquest to Tian'anmen Square*. Westport, CT: Praeger Security International, 2007.

Wright, James. *Enduring Vietnam: An American Generation and Its War*. New York: St. Martin's Press, 2017.

Zhai, Qiang. *China and the Vietnam Wars, 1950–1975*. Chapel Hill: University of North Carolina Press, 2000.

Zumwalt, Elmo R., Jr. *On Watch: A Memoir*. New York: Quadrangle/New York Times Book Co., 1976.

Zumwalt, Elmo, Jr., and Elmo Zumwalt III. *My Father, My Son*. New York: Macmillan Publishers, 1986.

INDEX

Note: Entry numbers referring to images are in italics.

1st Viet Cong Regiment, 107
2nd Battalion, 4th Marines, 352
5th Infantry Division, ARVN, 228
5th Infantry Division, US Army (Mechanized), 279
9th Infantry Division, US Army, 106, 175, 180, 419n118, 422n164
9th Marine Amphibious Brigade, 352
9th Marine Expeditionary Brigade, 86
31st Marine Amphibious Unit, 351
538th Transportation Company, 417n88
600-ship Navy, 347, 360, 371, 374

A-1/AD Skyraider attack aircraft, 7
A-4C Skyhawk attack aircraft, 114, 119, 390n139
A-6 Intruder attack aircraft, 119, 234, 240, 247, 342, 374
Abrams, Creighton W., 110, 113, 142, 149, 152, *158*, 215, 224, 407n4, 422n164, 220
    Cambodian incursion, 196, 201–6
    connection to Zumwalt, xxii, 22, 157–58, 160, 176, 178, 254, 306, 365
    Lam Son 719, 206–14, 227, 231, 249–50, 325
    Nixon's disfavor, 220, 227, 231, 325, 431n45
    support for SEALORDS, 162, 166, 178, 184
    Vietnamization, 170–71, 176–78, 193–94
    view of sea power, 226, 233
absent without leave (AWOL), 275, 279, 303, 333
AC-130 Spectre gunships, 229
Accelerated Turnover to the Vietnamese (ACTOV), 171, 181, 365
Acheson, Dean, 123

active duty, 288, 330
ad hoc problem-solving, 260, 273, 309, 368
Adelman, Kenneth, 444n15
Admiral of the Hill, 340
Admiral of the Navy, 16
advanced tactical support bases, 164
advisors, xix, 6, 12–13, 23, 31–32, 35, 41–42, 55, 57, 61, 66, 87, 103, 140, 151, 162, 214, 229, 244, 300, 335, 371, 396n82
    Bundy, McGeorge, 77, 95
    civilian, xv, 11, 61, 74, 76, 80, 84, 92, 97, 120, 198, 355, 362–63, 381n28
    Kissinger, 197, 203–4, 207–8, 219, 254, 310, 312–14, 317, 319, 325, 369
    McNaughton, 72, 81
    military, 11, 15, 21, 61, 74, 80, 82, 85, 101, 120, 125, 188, 209–10, 227, 233, 323, 355, 362, 407n136
    Moorer, xxi, 200–201, 224, 249, 307, 366
    naval, 25, 27, 167–68, 170–72, 174, 184, 192, 258, 292, 301, 375, 386n97
    Scowcroft, 354, 357
    Zumwalt, 311, 321
Aegean Sea, 264
Aegis air defense system, 347, 371, 375
affirmative action, 336–37, 359, 372
Africa, 145
African Americans, 143–44, 287, 289, 304, 336, 367
Afro hairstyle, 146
Agent Orange, xxii, 179, 354, 370
agents, 28, 34, 65, 188, 426n25, 437, 446n49
aggression, 19, 35, 41, 220, 228, 359, 373, 377
    communist, 8, 10, 68, 393n52
    North Korean, 132, 356
    North Vietnamese, 68, 73, 234, 258
AGM-45 Shrike anti-radiation missiles, 241

Agnew, Spiro, 322
AH-1 Cobra attack helicopter, 229
AIM-7 Sparrow air-to-air missiles 119
AIM-9 Sidewinder air-to-air missiles, 119, 214
AIM-54C Phoenix air-to-air missiles, 347, 375
air defense battalions, 210
air defenses, xiii, 64, 66, 81, 104, 116, 146, 199, 206, 214, 366, 377
air forces
    Chinese, 63
    North Korean, 198
    South Vietnamese, 38, 49, 74–76, 81, 192, 206, 228
    US, xiv, 12, 41, 60, 69, 73, 75, 80–81, 104, 146, 205, 227–28, 236–37
Air Force, US, 3, 8–9, 12, 84, 101, 105, 108, 137, 239, 338, 388n119, 393n54
    CINCPAC, 130–31, 224, 363
    Easter Offensive, 228–29, 235, 430n23
    F-111 controversy, 134–35
    Ho Minh Trail interdiction, 152, 205
    Holloway, 317, 342
    Kissinger, 227, 429n14
    leaders, 12, 37, 40, 59, 68, 79, 91–92, 110, 114, 122, 127, 129, 159, 184, 205–6, 208, 216, 226, 246, 305, 346, 406n124, 427n63
    Linebacker, 236–38, 240, 243, 245, 247–50, 366
    Mayaguez, 354, 356, 453n113
    Moorer, 204, 212
    Operation Barrel Roll, 72–73
    Operation Flaming Dart, 74–76
    Operation Frequent Wind, 352
    Operation Proud Deep Alpha, 215
    Operation Rolling Thunder, 81, 103
    Operation Yankee Team, 38–39

INDEX

protective reaction, 213–14
racial turmoil, 143–44
route packages, 77–78, *78*
rules of engagement, 119
single management of air power, 111–13, 397n20
support of riverine operations, 166, 179
Vietnamization, 170
women, 296, 299
air medals, 113
air patrols, 25, 83
air strikes, xv, xxi, 28
  Cambodia, 201
  Laos, 34, 69, 82, 212
  North Vietnam, 35–37, 54, 69, 82, 86–87, 100, 214–15, 224, 243, 362
air support, 64, 86, 111–12, 256, 427n51
  Easter Offensive, 228–29, 430n23
  Lam Son 719, 209–10, 212
  Linebacker, 241
  Mayaguez, 355
  Tonkin Gulf incident, 47, 50
  Vietnam Navy, 188, 423n181
air wings, 15, 38, 56, 76, 114–20, 138, 234, 240, 340
airborne division, South Vietnamese, 211
aircraft carriers, 5, 7, 34, 45, 48, 69, 74, 88, 134, 136, 138, 200, 262, 264, 342, 371
  Battle Force Fleet, 339–40
  construction, 98, 137, 273
  Enterprise experience, xxii, 113–17, 127, 313, 336
  High-Low Mix, 263, 337
  Kissinger support for, 204
  Korean War, 336
  nuclear-powered, 317, 329
  operational control of, 110–11
  social disturbances, xxi, 295–96
  Soviet threat, 22, 260, 359, 373
  Vietnam War operations, 38, 50, 224, 238, 352, 355
Aircraft Carriers at War (Holloway), 373
aircraft squadrons, 286, 288, 455
air-cushion vehicles, 263–64, 374
airfields, 10, 259, 357
  China, 60, 63
  South Vietnam, 27, 57, 84, 114, 127, 227
  North Vietnam, 68, 92, 100, 14, 199, 215, 221, 223, 248
air–ground team, 110–11
airlift, 10, 54, 165, 210, 318–19
airmen, 3, 53, 144, 354
AK-47 assault rifles, 161
Alabama, 48, 145–46, 307
Alabama Dry Dock and Shipbuilding Company, 453n1
Alaska Command, 8
alcohol abuse, 267, 287, 302

Aleutian Islands, 3, 153
All the Questions You Had About Aircraft Carriers but Were Afraid to Ask (Holloway), 138
Allen, Barbara, 336
all-hands gatherings, 277
allied forces, 125, 165, 167, 179, 377
allies, 5, 15, 19, 27, 59, 120, 150, 159, 165–69, 220, 256, 263, 273, 351, 372–73
  communist, 11, 36, 43, 65, 129, 222, 231, 362
  global, 346, 350, 359–60, 362–63, 373, 377
  South Vietnamese, 25
all-nuclear-powered Navy, 263, 340
all-volunteer force, 298, 442n96
Alpha multi-plane air strikes, 74, 215, 240
Alvarez, Everett, Jr., 56
ambassador to Portugal, US, 284
ambush, 31, 55, 61, 100, 110, 162, 166, 169, 174, 179, 192, 417n88
American Indians, 285
American people, 31, 151, 236, 370, 377, 454n8
  demand for withdrawal of US forces, 171, 203, 348
  lukewarm to defense spending, 256, 338
  support, non-support for war effort, xv, xx, 132, 350, 373
American public, 79, 138, 141, 232, 354
American society, xx, 141, 144, 150, 257, 288, 303, 331, 367
amnesty programs, 142, 276
Amphibious Ready Group Alpha, 107, 351
Amphibious Task Force 76, 86, 351, 353
amphibious warfare, xv, 28, 68, 80, 83, 111–12
  ARG/SLF, 107–9, 351
  forces, 59, 86, 130, 260, 351
  invasion of North Vietnam, 69, 110, 198, 249, 388n119
  ships, 25, 238, 266, 296, 313, 374, 377
  Vietnam operations, 107–9, 351–53
An Loc, South Vietnam, 228–29
Anderson, George W., xiv, 25, 144, 372
  harassment of North Vietnam, 28
  and Holloway, 445n44
  and McNamara, 13, 14, 98, 135, 382n41
  naval special warfare, 22, 26
  and Rickover, 270
  and Zumwalt, 284, 291, 321, 413n11, 441n79
Anderson, Jack, 218
Anderson, William, 437n51, 441n79

animal husbandry, 173
Annapolis, Maryland, 48, 277, 324
antiaircraft artillery, 64, 66, 119
antiaircraft missiles, 223
antiaircraft suppression, 39
anti-Americanism, 267
Anti-Ballistic Missile Treaty, 256
anti-communism, 148
anti-infiltration patrol, 25, 80, 89, 108, 156, 161
anti-ship missiles, 102, 263
antisubmarine aircraft carriers, 59, 257
antisubmarine frigate, 340
antisubmarine protection, 59, 138
antisubmarine warfare, 138, 375
anti-war movement, 120, 125, 198, 201, 214, 217, 226, 348
anti-war sentiment, 95, 126
Ap Bac, South Vietnam, 31
Appalachian Mountains, 260
Appropriations Committee, US Senate, 259
Arab-Israeli conflict, 319, 325
Arab-Israeli Six-Day War, 96
Arabs, 318
Arbo, Paul, 171
Archbishop Makarios, 341
Ark of the Covenant, 421n144
Arlington, Virginia, 314
armed forces, Cambodia, 201, 203
armed forces, Iran. 376
armed forces, Iraq, 376
armed forces, Laos, 10
armed forces, South Vietnam, 27, 168
  communist threat to, 67
  Easter Offensive, 235
  Lam Son 719, 211
  strengthening, 19, 21, 23, 33, 151, 170, 176
  Vietnamization, 174, 193–94, 364
  weaknesses, 37, 173, 206
armed forces, Soviet, 154
armed forces, US, xxiii, 82, 257, 349–50, 454n8
  air operations, Laos, South Vietnam, 84
  budgets, 159, 338
  civilian leadership, 95, 127
  the draft, 258
  Gulf of Tonkin incident, 57
  McNamara, 12, 14
  social problems, 142, 411n48
armed route reconnaissance, 72
Armed Services Committee, US House of Representatives, 77, 122, 293, 349
Armed Services Committee, US Senate, 60, 122, 216, 219, 308
armored fighting vehicles, 97, 175, 349
arms control, 154, 305–6, 310–11, 369
Arms Control and Disarmament

INDEX 477

Agency, 344, 450n68
Army Air Forces, US, 12, 60
Army, Cambodian, 200
Army, Chinese, 61, 63, 64, 65, 205
Army, Israeli, 318
Army and Navy Country Club, 45
Army-Navy football game, 309
Army, North Vietnamese, 7, 64, 67, 170, 223, 229, 246, 349, 350, 388n117
Army of the Republic of Vietnam (ARVN), 83, 87, 109, 165, 423n191
  Binh Gia battle, 85, 88
  combat successes, 31, 175, 203
  Easter Offensive, 226, 228–29, 238
  enemy attacks on, 17, 32, 41
  Lam Son 719, 207–8, 210–13
  Mekong Delta operations, 181, 188, 422n164, 423n185
  Vietnamization, 221, 223
Army, US, xiv, xix, 9, 34, 63, 84–85, 109, 249, 296, 338, 342, 418n95, 418n98
  aviation, 12, 60, 82, 165, 229, 317
  commands, 8, 108, 363
  forces, 3, 10, 15, 44, 80, 87–89, 106, 110–12, 131, 142, 169, 418n97
  Green Berets, 17, 22, 27
  leaders, 32–33, 86, 92, 106, 121, 127, 149, 159, 162, 165, 176, 178–79, 190, 204, 206, 208, 217, 226, 278–79, 287, 299, 305–6, 322, 356–58, 372, 411n47, 417n88, 427n54, 439n39
Arnold, Henry, 97
Arnold J. Isbell (DD-869), 153
Arthur, Stanley R., 275–77, 280, 298, 335, 338, 377–78
artillery, 31, 62, 85, 93, 165, 175, 210–11, 223, 229, 357, 377, 394n59, 395n72
ARVN 5th Infantry Division, 228
ARVN 21st Infantry Division, 181
Asia, 7, 265, 350, 354, 358–59, 388n119
Asian allies, 346, 360
Asian Americans, 304
Asian communists, 7, 8
Asia-Pacific region, 3
Assad, Hafez al, 238
assassination, xxi, 17, 26, 33, 38
assistant chief of staff for psychological warfare and VNN welfare, 419n115
assistant for national security affairs, xxi, 424n9
assistant secretary of defense for int'l security affairs, 154

assistant secretary of defense for manpower and reserve affairs, 295
assistant secretary of state for Far Eastern affairs, 64
assistant to the chief of naval personnel for women, 297
Association of Naval Aviation, 445n44
Athens, Greece, 266–67, 272, 333
Atlantic Fleet, US, 26, 81, 88, 96, 133, 254, 255
Atocha (Japanese gunboat), 153
Atomic Energy Commission, 118, 268
atrocities, 217
Attack Carrier Striking Force (Task Force 77), 81, 116
Attack Squadron 83, 113
Attack Squadron 92, 234
Attack Squadron 94, 234
Attack Squadron 122, 280
attack transport, 152
Attila the Hun, 414n32
attorney general, US, 218
attrition, xix, 88, 350
Attu, Aleutian Islands, 153
Ault, Frank, 242
Australia, 3, 9, 153, 419n115
autobiographies, 114, 259, 293, 329
axe murders, Korea, 360, 362, 371
Axis nations, xx

B-26 bomber, 60
B-52 bombers, 63, 122, 256, 357, 214
  Cambodia bombing, 197, 201
  Easter Offensive, 224, 229
  Lam Son 719, 209
  Linebacker, 246–48, 366
  Mayaguez, 355
  in North Vietnam, 199, 215, 227, 236, 250
  in South Vietnam, 227, 250
Bac Giang, North Vietnam, 104
Backfire bomber, Soviet, 343
Bagley, David, 267, 287
Bagley, Worth H., 261–62, 322, 328–30, 435n24, 441n79, 442n96, 447n8, 448n14
Baldwin, Hanson, 127, 284, 386n100, 442n96, 442n101
banana war, 177
band of brothers, 176
Bangkok, Thailand, 7
barbers, 286
barges, 351, 353
Barkley, Steven J., 214
barracks, 74–76, 172, 237, 246, 279, 281
bases, 66, 77, 143, 235, 238, 353
  in Lam Son 719, 210–11
  Navy, 83, 144, 164, 171, 189, 266, 287, 296, 300
  North Vietnamese, xiii, 54

South Vietnamese, 21, 173, 186–88
Battle Force Fleet, 339
battle forces and groups, 263, 339–40, 347, 374–76
Battle of Dien Bien Phu, 61, 111
Battle of Leyte Gulf, 113, 153, 242
Battle of Manila Bay, 16
Battle of Okinawa, 5, 135
Battle of Savo Island, 153
Battle of Surigao Strait, 153
Battle of the Philippine Sea, 45
battleships, 16, 45, 153, 347, 374, 377, 450n83
Bay of Bengal, 313
Bay of Pigs, Cuba, 11, 19
bayonet, 217
beards, 139, 259, 280–81, 284
Beaulier, Jerome E., 214
beauticians, 286
beer machines, 281
Ben Thuy, North Vietnam, 56
Bennington (CVS-20), 88
Bennion (DD-662), 242
Berlin, West Germany, 319
Berman, Larry, 370, 388n119, 412n4, 414n33, 418n97, 419n114, 420n133, 423n189, 439n39, 445n39, 454n8
Bermuda, 332
biases, 144, 150
Bien Hoa, South Vietnam, 68, 84–85, 114
Biet Hai commandos, South Vietnamese, 27
Binh Gia, South Vietnam, 85, 88
Binh Thuy, South Vietnam, 415n46
Black Americans, 139
Black hairstylists, 146
black market, 189
Black Power "dapping," 143
Black Power movement, 143
Black, Delbert D., 140, 280
Blackburn, Paul P., Jr., 82
Blair, Carvel, 419n120
Blake, Nina, 45
Blandford, John, 77
bloc obsolescence, 257
blockade, xv, 14, 35, 68–69, 249, 388n119
Blue Ridge (LCC-19), 352
Bo De River, South Vietnam, 165
boarding parties, 355
body bags, 141
body count, 179, 419n118
bombing halts, 101–3, 125–26, 205, 214–15, 226, 243, 364, 406n122
Bon Homme Richard (CVA-31), 38
Boston College, 299
Boy Scouts, 155, 200
Boyd (DD-544), 45
Bradley, Omar, 258
bravery, 45, 49, 147, 162, 174, 190, 213
Brewton (DE-1086), 164

Brewton, John C., 164
Brezhnev, Leonid, 231, 318, 344
bridges, xiii, 27–28, 90, 103, 205, 237, 240, 246
Bridgeton, 376
briefings, 39, 310, 319, 342
Brigade 125 (Group 759), 25–26, 191
brigade of midshipmen, US Naval Academy, 5
Brindisi, Italy, 296
Bringle, William F., 255, 442n101
Brinks Hotel, Saigon, 85
British Air Cathay Airlines, 7
British Consul, Hanoi, 67
British First Sea Lord, 8
Bronze star medals, 113, 153
Brown, George S., 343, 354–55, 452n108
Brown, Harold, 344, 346–47, 450n75
Brown, Wesley A., 144
brushfire wars, 8, 19
Bucher, Lloyd, 134, 407n4
Bucklew, Phil, 32, 34
Bucklew Report, 34
Buddhists, 33
budgets, 156, 215, 307, 320–21, 325
bulldozers, 169
Bundy, McGeorge, 59, 77, 84, 95, 381n28
Bundy, William P., 64, 90, 396n89
Bunker, Ellsworth, 148, 224
Bureau of Naval Personnel, 153, 284, 298, 301
bureaucracy, 12, 18, 91, 156, 306, 322, 369
Burke, Arleigh, xiv, 8, 21, 49, 121, 127, 268, 282, 317, 445n44
  Laos intervention, 11, 381n28
  naval special forces, 19–20
  support of Felt, 6–7, 9–10, 40, 379n5
  and Zumwalt, 290, 441n79, 447n76
Burning Tree Country Club, Maryland, 184
Burns, John J., 356
Burns, Ken, xiii
Bush, George H. W., 377–78
Butcher of the Mekong Delta, 419n118
bypassing, 198, 221, 227, 273, 282, 440n71
Byrd, Robert, 370

Ca Mau Peninsula, South Vietnam, 162, 165–69, 174, 179, 188, 191
caches, 11, 166, 197, 202
cadres, 26, 175
Calley, William, 217, 428n74
Cam Pha, North Vietnam, 251–52
Cam Ranh Bay, South Vietnam, 114, 172, 339
Cambodia, 27, 83, 348–50, 360, 427n51
  bombing, xxi, 197, 220–21, 318, 424n1
  Easter Offensive, 228–29, 238
  incursion, 169–70, 174–75, 196, 200, 203, 206, 209, 214, 220–23, 318
  infiltration, 25, 33, 67, 156, 161–62, 176–78
  Mayaguez, 353–55, 366, 371
  Operation Eagle Pull, xxii, 351–52
camouflage, 82, 205
Camp Lejeune, North Carolina, 143
campaigns, 8, 10, 40, 77, 130, 235, 238, 249–50, 252
Canadian government, 103
canals, 22, 106, 164–65, 173–74
cancer, 152, 179
Cang, Chung Tan, 194, 353
Cape Ron, North Vietnam, 30
career counselors, 140
Caribbean Sea, 45
Carl Vinson (CVN-70), 270
carpet bombing, 246
Carrier Air Wing 9, 114
Carrier Air Wing 14, 56
Carrier Air Wing 15, 234
carrier battle group, 374, 376
carrier czar, 137
Carrier Division 3, 234
carrier fires, 139
carrier safety, 139, 364
Carroll, Lewis, 95
Carter, Jimmy, 344–47, 359, 369–71, 450n68
casualties
  enemy military, 175, 210, 212
  North Vietnamese civilian, 100, 217, 236–37, 246, 433n96
  South Vietnamese military, 85, 180, 207
  US military, 75, 84, 143, 147, 163, 179, 199
Cat Futch, 334
catamaran troop transports, 317
Catholic minority, 19
cease-fires, 105, 124, 152, 239, 243–45, 250–51, 312–13, 318–19, 325, 343, 376
Center for Strategic and International Studies, 453
central coast, South Vietnam, 82, 108
Central High School, Washington, DC, 4
Central Highlands, South Vietnam, 74, 87, 185, 229, 351
Central Intelligence Agency, 271
Central Office for South Vietnam (COSVN), 196
ceremonies, 182, 279
Chafee, John H., 137, 142, 232, 254, *255*, 260, 270, 298, 308, 310, 330, 415n, 46434n2, 434n3, 434n5
  championship of Zumwalt, 73, 183–84, 207, 253, 264, 273, 281, 365, 367
  Moorer's opinion of, 135, 159, 255
chain of command, 55, 197, 277, 314, 317, 332, 391n19, 398n40, 418n105
  Abrams, Sharp, McCain, 149, 227
  Defense Reorganization Act of 1958, 8, 14
  Westmoreland, Felt, 32, 94
  Zumwalt, 278, 282–84, 319, 368, 440n71, 448n158
Chairman, Joint Chiefs of Staff, 14, 74, 123, 132, 361, 402n37, 447n71, 454n3
  Brown, 343, 346, 354–55
  Crowe, xiv, 174, 375–76
  Holloway, xxii, 343, 357, 362, 371, 452n108
  Moorer, xx, 133, 142, 148, 150, 159, 184, 196–97, 199–200, 202, 204, 207–9, 211, 217–24, 226, 233, 244, 246, 249–50, 254–55, 259, 283, 306–7, 310, 313–14, 321–22, 325, 366, 368, 412n68, 445n38
  Powell, 262, 376
  Taylor, 12–13, 97
  Wheeler, 36, 59, 81, 92, 96–97, 99, 100, 198, 203, 246, 402n47
Chanh Hoa, North Vietnam, 76
Chap Le, North Vietnam, 76
Chapman, Leonard F., Jr., 112, 208, 305, 308
Charleston, South Carolina, 113, 127
Chemical Weapons Convention, 354
Chenango (CVE-28), 5
Chi, Nguyen Huu, 191
Chiang Kai-shek, 7
Chicago, Illinois, 146
chicken regulations, 140
Chief, Military Assistance Advisory Group, Vietnam, 17, 22
chief of current intelligence, 430n35
chief of Far Eastern Operations, CIA, 29
chief of information, 277, 283, 290, 326
Chief of Naval Operations, 8
  Anderson and McDonald, 13, 22, 98
  Burke, 6, 382n28
  Holloway, xx, 113–14, 326, 328, 358, 370
  Moorer, xx, 49, 132–33, 150
  Zumwalt, xx, xxii, 155, 183, 207, 252–55, 273, 275, 279, 300, 302–5, 324–25,

INDEX   479

329, 368
chief of operations, Joint Staff, JCS, 402n37
chief of staff, Cambodian Army, 200
chief of staff, North Vietnamese Army, 62
chief of staff, Royal Navy, 8
chief of staff, US Air Force, 76, 79, 216, 317
chief of Staff, US Army, 8, 86, 106, 208, 279
Chien Thang (Victory Plan), 34
Childs, Marquis, 247
China, xv, 7, 9, 13, 74, 351, 388n119
  assistance to North Vietnam, 26, 60–63, 67, 223, 389n129, 395n72
  deterrence of, 196, 220, 226, 393n54
  ideological conflict with USSR, 66, 231
  interdiction, 101, 150, 235, 237, 243
  intervention threat, 35, 47, 56, 59, 62–64, 69, 84, 104, 431n44
  and Laos, 11, 383n44
  Nixon visit to China, 65, 225, 313, 325
  nuclear warfare, 41, 80
  war with, 23, 35–36, 66, 68–69, 92, 258
Chinese Military Advisory Group, 61
Chinese Nationalists, 7
Chinook, Montana, 44
chokepoints, 73
Chon, Tran Van, *148*, 420n131, 420n133
  Ca Mau region, 166, 168
  close connection to Zumwalt, 182–83, 354, 420n137
  opposition to, 186–88, 193–94
Chon, Truc, 182
Christmas, xxi, 117, 149, 215, 245, 247, 248
Christmas bombing. *See* Linebacker campaign
churches, 102, 116
Churchill, Winston, 248
civic action, 16, 20
Civil Rights Act, 59, 293
Civil Rights Commission, 144
Civil Rights movement, 293
Civil War, US, 44, 146, 418n98
civilian control of the military, 14
civil-military relationship, xxiii, 95, 129, 150, 250, 363–64
Clarey, Bernard A., 159, 255, 265, 294, 435n11, 442n92
Clausewitz, Karl von, 13
Claytor, Graham, Jr., 270, 347
Clements, William P., Jr., 330, 357–58, 372
Clifford, Clark M., 125, 408n5
Clinton, Hillary Rodham,

454n3
Clinton, William, 354, 367, 370, 453n3
close air support, 111, 228, 355
clothing, 139–40, 279, 281, 292
Cloud, Benjamin W., 294
Cloverdale High School, Montgomery, Alabama, 48
CNO Advisory Committee on Race Relations and Minority Affairs, 287
CNO Report, The, 277–78
coalition government, 15
Coast Guard, US, 83, 161, 166–67, 171, 179–80, 186, 398–99n40
Coastal Force, Vietnam Navy, 21, 41
coastal operations, xxi, 22, 41, 33, 174, 176, 179, 181
  North Vietnam, 46–50, 93–94, 240–41, 393n48
  patrols, 25, 41, 82–84, 173, 191, 398n40, 423n181
  vessels, xv, 83, 93
Coastal Surveillance Force (Task Force 115), US, 84, 161–62
Coca-Cola, 291
Cold War, xv, 129, 153, 263, 283, 332, 350, 370, 373
  Nitze, 154, 258
  Soviet Union, 96, 259, 360
  strategy, 41, 306
  US policies, 12, 60
collateral damage, 236, 433n96
combat, xiii, xiv, xv, xxi, 180, 209, 288, 297–98
  allied forces, 30, 44, 192, 207, 229
  enemy forces, 17, 62, 67, 161, 175
  Gulf War, xix, 113
  leaders, xxii, 5, 12, 77, 104, 115–16, 118–19, 129, 135–36, 146, 164, 167, 174, 226, 236, 241–42, 263, 294, 315, 336, 340, 358, 361, 365–66, 373, 375, 377
  in South Vietnam, 107–12, 143, 166, 168–69, 172, 275
  US forces, 15, 22–23, 40, 68, 84–85, 87, 89, 105, 238, 266
Combat Exclusion Law, 301, 303
combat information center, 153
command and control, 82, 87, 375
command centers, 14, 28
Commandant, 9th Naval District, US, 146
Commander in Chief (president of the United States), 325, 428n81
  Johnson, 86, 89, 95, 345, 412n68
  Nixon, 211, 221, 223, 227, 245, 250, 312, 366, 369, 412n68
Commander in Chief, Central Command, 376

Commander in Chief, Pacific Command, xx, 8, 40, 44, 53, 120, 374–75, 380n8
Commander in Chief, Pacific Fleet, 9, 107, 402n40, 403n66
  Clarey, 294
  Hyland, 100, 385n80, 399n42, 418n105
  Johnson, Roy L., 77
  Moorer, 83, 231
  Sharp, 30, 44
Commander Sixth Fleet, 6, 442n101
Commander Task Force 77, 117
Commander, US Military Assistance Command, Vietnam
  Abrams, 157–58, 176–77, 206, 212, 227, 306
  Harkins, 24–25
  Westmoreland, 58, 76, 82, 84, 88, 94, 110, 125, 130, 210
Commander, US Naval Forces, Eastern Atlantic and Mediterranean, 114
Commander, US Naval Forces, Europe, 267
Commander, US Naval Forces, Vietnam, 159, 165, 167, 171, 174–77, 183, 187, 190–94, 276, 296
commanding officers, 55, 140, 188, 280, 300, 303, 328, 339
  Attack Squadron 83, 113
  Constellation (CVA-64), 289
  Enterprise (CVAN-65), xxii, 115–18, 409n18, 409n26
  Jouett (DLG-29), 277
  Operation Sea Float, 167
  Pueblo (AGER-2), 407n4
commandos, 27, 29
commissaries, 281, 286
Commission for the Merchant Marine and Defense, 445n44
Committee on the Present Danger, 369, 444n15
communications, 13, 21, 55, 66, 277, 280, 297, 425n16
communications intercepts, 50, 191, 248
communist bloc, 350
communists, 7, 9–10, 16, 36, 38, 47, 167, 194, 202, 244, 350, 402n47
Confederacy, 146
conflict resolution, 9, 41
Congress, US, xv, xxiii, 79, 137, 142, 156, 197, 267, 293, 310, 316, 318, 321, 322–23, 325, 340, 358, 370, 375, 377, 396n82, 453n1
  blame for lost war, 194, 256, 348–49
  budget cutting, 159, 215
  Holloway re: fleet strength, 338, 341–42, 345–47
  Johnson and "hawks," 124
  Moorer testimony, 134, 150,

235, 248–49
Moorer, Zumwalt re: Soviet fleet, 319–20
Nixon, 209, 216–17, 221, 226
opposition to Zumwalt, 274, 292, 311, 369
support of Holloway, 138–39, 359, 364
support of Laird, 171, 224, 291
support for Navy women, 298, 336
support of Rickover, 268–69
Zumwalt re: fleet strength, 260–65, 273, 307–8, 328, 331–32
Connolly, Thomas F., 134
conservatism, 148, 218
Constellation (CVA-64), xxii, 38, 56–57, 69, 103, 289–95, 303
Constitution, US, 298, 323
construction
 ships and craft, 21, 98, 118, 134, 137–39, 150, 259, 263–64, 273, 316, 327–30, 345, 371
 South Vietnam projects, 20, 22, 105, 114, 141, 167, 173
consulates, 100
containment strategy, 350–51
Continental United States, 339
control of air operations, 82, 88, 113, 149
conventional forces and operations, 7, 9, 16, 34, 40, 229, 248, 259, 307–8, 318
convoys, 417n88
Cooper–Church Amendment, 427n51
Coral Sea (CVA-43), 73–74, 76, 234, *251*, 355
cost of living, 173
Council of American-flag Ship Operators, 445n44
counter-guerrilla warfare, 20, 87
counter-infiltration measures, 67
counterinsurgency, xxi, 10, 16–22, 26, 29–32, 36–37, 41, 44, 258, 362
Counterinsurgency Education and Training Program, 26
Counter-Insurgency Operations in South Vietnam and Laos, 17
Counterinsurgency Plan, 21
courts martial, 217
Coutelais-du-Roche, Mouza, 153
covert operations, 29–30, 44, 80
Cowley, Kathryn, 5
Cracker Jack uniform, 281, 303, 334
crises, 8, 134, 204, 314, 324–25, 372, 445n38
 axe murders, Korea, 360
 Bay of Pigs, 20
 Cuban Missile, 42
 EC-121, 341
 Grenada, 375
 Laos, 20, 28, 40, 362
 Lebanon, 1958, 35, 113

Lebanon, 1985, 375
 Mayaguez, 354
 Middle East, 311
 Taiwan Strait, 16, 35, 42,13
 Yom Kippur War, 318
crisis management, 337, 355–56
Crowe, William J., Jr., 375–76, 454n8
cruise missiles, 263, 343
Cruiser-Destroyer Flotilla 7, 155
Cu Lao Re, South Vietnam, 178
Cua Lon River, South Vietnam, 165, 167, 169, 181
Cuba, 11, 14, 19, 218
Cuban Missile Crisis, 13, 15, 35, 42, 45, 291, 310
Cubans, 145
Cultural Revolution, 104, 231
Cumberland River, Tennessee, 418n98
Cushman, Robert E., 110–11, 201
customs agents, 34
cutters, US Coast Guard, 83, 161, 167, 186
CV Concept, 138–39
Cyprus, 341

Dachen (Tachen) Islands, China, 7
damage control, 136, 139
dams, 105
Danang, South Vietnam, 28–30, 47, 65, 68, 84–89, 144, 160, 178, 351
Daniel, Wilbur C., 293–94
Davidson, Philip B., 127, 209
Davis, Lilton, *337*
Dean, John Gunther, 351
decision-making, xxiii, 129, 239, 354, 363
 Felt, xxiii, 40
 McNamara, McDonald, Wheeler, Thieu, 39, 99, 100, 123, 213
 Moorer, 219–20, 364
 Zumwalt, 157, 292, 309–10, 324–25, 368
Defense Attaché Office, Saigon, 352
defense conditions, 357, 453n118
Defense Intelligence Agency, 243, 425n16
Defense Reorganization Act, 1958, 8, 40, 361, 375, 447n71
deferments, 143
defoliation, 179
demilitarized zone, Korea, 130, 356–58
demilitarized zone, Vietnam, 17, 30, 83, 105, 109, 149
 bombing near, 74, 77, 88, 130, 214–15, 220, 224, 227
 buildup of enemy forces near, 93, 152, 223, 226, 232
democracy, 218, 330
Democratic Party, 379
Democratic Republic of Vietnam (North Vietnam), 11,

28, 50, 52, 57, 61–62, 66, 101, 393n48, 396n89
Denton, Jane, 244
Department of Defense, 13, 29–30, 138, 199, 207, 235, 291, 309, 323, 347, 353
 budgets, 215, 223, 256, 320, 345
 drug abuse, 41–42
 leaders, 98, 159,
 Mayaguez, 355, 362
 McNamara, 122, 156
 officials, 40, 72, 76, 139, 162, 308, 321, 454n8
 Washington Special Action Group, 313
Department of Defense Commission for a Long-Term Strategy, 445n44
Department of Energy, 326
Department of State, 23, 29, 32, 37, 69, 74, 91, 101, 127, 313, 357, 396n89
dependent shelters, 173
deployments, 98, 281, 288, 294
depots, 101, 114, 398n32
depth charges, 54
Deputy Chief of Naval Operations (Air Warfare), 113
deputy chief of propaganda, 175
Deputy Chief of Staff for Political Warfare, Republic of Vietnam, 185
Deputy Director, Arms Control and Disarmament Agency, 450n68
deputy secretary of defense, 13, 99, 102, 112, 135, 159, 307, 330, 372, 408n5
dereliction of duty, 224, 311
Dereliction of Duty (McMaster), xix
desertion, 173, 275, 303
Desoto Patrol, xxi, 46–47, 50, 52, 57–58, 67, 70–71
Destroyer Squadron 12, 333
destroyers, destroyer escorts, 83, 93, 155, 164, 186, 259, 262–65, 287–88, 313
 Desoto Patrol, xxi, 30, 45–47, 50–51, 54–56, 58, 391n19, 393n48
 fleet component, 338–41, 368, 370, 372, 374
 in Greece, 266–67, 333, 448n28
 in Linebacker, 238, 240–41
 Mayaguez, 355–56
 naval gunfire support, 223, 226
 1975 Cambodia, South Vietnam evacuations, 351–52
 in World War II, 45, 153, 242
détente, 159, 256, 309, 325, 350, 369
deterrence, 79, 84, 337
Detroit, Michigan, 276
Dewey (DLG-14), 154

INDEX   481

Dewey, George, 16
dictatorships, 152
Diem, Ngo Dinh, xxi, 19, 21–25, 31–33, 38, 41–42, 59, 387n108
dikes, 123, 247, 406n110
dinners, 6, 118, 197, 218, 233, 235, 245
diplomacy, 15–16, 92, 101–2, 245, 318–19, 337, 351, 433n102
Director of the Joint Staff, JCS, 232, 341, 452n108
Director, Naval Reactors, Atomic Energy Commission, 268
discipline and concern with operational efficiency, 4, 141, 182, 279, 282, 291–95, 303, 326–27, 330–31, 333, 359, 372, 441n74
discrimination, 139, 144, 285–86, 290, 292, 295–96, 302, 359, 374, 454n8
dishonorable discharges, 291
Distinguished Flying Cross medals, 5, 49, 113
Distinguished Service Medals, 45, 324
Dixie Station, 114
Do Son Peninsula, North Vietnam, 236, 240
Dobrynin, Anatoly, 101, 231, 310
doctrine, 109, 111, 130, 256, 263, 376, 397n20
dogfighting, 242
domestic social programs, 95
Dominican Republic intervention, 1965, 95, 148
Domino Effect, 58, 393n52
Dong Ha–Saigon railroad, South Vietnam, 28
Dong Hoi, North Vietnam, 74
Dong Nham, North Vietnam, 104
Dong Tam, South Vietnam, 186, 417n88
Doris Miller (DE-1091), 287
doves, 217
Drachnik, Joseph B., 25–26
draft, 143, 258, 275, 298, 300, 302
Dragon's Jaw Bridge, North Vietnam, 240
Droz, Don, 192
drug abuse, xx, xxii, 142, 150, 276, 303, 333, 358, 374
drug education, prevention, and rehabilitation, 142
Duerk, Alene B., 299
Duncan, Charles K., 144, 280, 293, 405n94, 435n11, 437n48, 438n5
Duncan, Frank, 269
Dung, Van Tien, 62
Dunn, Robert, 448n28
duty, honor, country, 148

EA-6B Prowler electronic warfare aircraft, 240, 374
early warning and jamming systems, 242
East Asia, 13, 346, 396n89, 453n116
East Pakistan, 313
Easter Offensive, 170, 221–25, *225*, 228, 232, 238, 245, 288, 348
Eastern Mediterranean, 238, 259, 311
EC-121 Warning Star electronic intelligence aircraft, 198, 201, 341, 356
Eckhardt, George S., 162
economic assistance, 65–66, 176
Edsel Line, 105
educational opportunities and programs, 145
Egypt, 63, 259, 318–19
Eisenhower administration, 7–8, 18, 40
Eisenhower, Dwight D., 42, 76, 80, 84, 393n52
elections, 416n75
electronic countermeasures, 114, 247, 374
electro-optical glide bombs, 240
Elimination of Demeaning or Degrading Regulations, 281
embassies, 351–52
Emery, Thomas, 167
Ending the Vietnam War (Kissinger), 319
Engen, Donald, 306, 447n8
engineering, 118, 155, 317, 333, 339, 446n49
Enhance Plus Program, 193
Enhance Program, 193
enlisted clubs, 333
Enlisted Men's Councils, 279
enlisted personnel, 140, 146, 257, 278, 281–82, 287, 294–96, 368, 372
enlisted ratings, 336
enlistment, 143, 288, 294, 300, 303, 370–71
Enterprise (CV-6), 48
Enterprise (CVAN-65), xxi, 129, 137, 313–14, 246, 352, 405n96, 409n20, 424n9
 fire, 136, 408n18
 Rolling Thunder, 113–20, 239–40, 360
Enthoven, Alain C., 73, 261, 405n94, 413n15
Equal Employment Opportunity Act, 298
Equal Rights Amendment to the Constitution, 298, 301, 303
Erlichman, John, 203, 220
Erlichman, Mrs. John, 323
ethnic groups, 258
Europe, 265–67, 273, 311, 333, 346, 359, 373–74
evacuees from South Vietnam, 352–53
Ewell, Julian J., 165, 183–84, 244, 419n118
exchanges, 286
executive assistants, 219, 260

Executive Committee (EXCOM), 382n41
executive officers, 6, 115, 294, 316
expenditures, 18, 228
explosives, 82, 136
eyes-only memos, 206, 316

F/A-18 Hornet strike fighters, 374, 377
F-4B Phantom fighters, 114
F-8D Crusader fighters, 39
F-14 Tomcat fighters, 135, 273, 316, 347, 371, 375, 377, 408n7
F-111B Aardvark attack aircraft, 134–35, 408n7
factories, 63
"Failure of Gradualism in Vietnam, The" 127
Fairchild Industries, 453n1
Fall, Bernard, 226
families, 141, 144–47, 173, 186, 266–67, 278, 302, 314–15, 352
Far East, 235, 347
Far East Command, 8
fast attack craft, 50–51
fast patrol craft, 29, 242
Father of the Nuclear Navy, xxii, 117, *269*
Fegan, Ronald, 64
Felt, Harry D., xiv, xv, xx, xxi, xxiii, *4*, *24*, 44, 89, 98, 127, 361–64, 373, 380n8, 386n95, 387n108, 388n117, 390n139, 411n64
 actions to deter the DRV's support for insurgency in the South, 28–31
 actions to influence communist behavior in Indochina, 35–37
 counterinsurgency in South Vietnam and naval special forces, 16–25
 deterioration of allied war effort in South Vietnam, 31–34
 early life and career, 3–8
 Kennedy, McNamara, and civil-military relations, 12–15
 response to crises in Laos, 1959–1961, 9–11, 15–16
 seaborne infiltration, SEALs, and STATs, 25–27
 successes and failures of Felt's tenure as CINCPAC, 40–43
 support for flexible response, counterinsurgency theories, 8–9
 Yankee Team reconnaissance in Laos, 38–40
female sailors, 297
feminist movement, 297
field marshals, 15
Fighter Squadron 94, 120
Fighter Squadron 143, 244
Fighter Weapons School, 242

Filipinos, 285
films, 277–78, 409n19, 421n144
financial assistance, 62, 172
Finback (SSN-670), 334
firebases, 165, 210
First Fleet, US, 45
First Indochina War, 7, 111
First Sea Lord, 8, 162, 191
Fishburne, Lilian E., 454n3
fishermen, 30, 167
Fishhook, South Vietnam, 202
Flag Plot, 14
flagships, 16, 239, 241, 352
flak suppression, 119
flash precedence message, 50
fleet command, 254, 271, 274, 368
Fleet Marine Force, Pacific, 93, 108
Fleet Reserve Association, 140
fleet, US, xxii, 98, 136, 205, 266, 280, 315, 359, 366
  rebuilding, 253, 260, 273–75, 371, 373–75, 436n27
  reduction in strength, 134, 150, 257, 265, 306
  social tensions, 293–94, 296, 302
  Zumwalt and Holloway efforts to improve, 328–46
  Zumwalt visits, 277–78, 287
Fletcher-class destroyer, 153
flexible response, 16, 28–29, 36–37, 41, 60, 127–28, 250, 362, 380n12
Florida, 5, 48, 151, 238
focus groups, 277, 302–3
fog of war, 13
football, 48, 192, 236, 277, 309
Ford Motor Company, 12, 105
Ford, Gerald R., 324, 343, 349, 351–62, 369, 371, 452n108
Ford, Henry, 12
Foreign Affairs Committee, US House of Representatives, 31
foreign assistance, 65
foreign intelligence advisory board, 291, 321
foreign military sales act, 209
foreign minister, 124
foreign policy, 60, 70, 135, 197, 203, 218, 226, 315, 446n53
Forest of Assassins. *See* Rung Sat Special Zone
Forrestal (CVA-59), 136, 295, 409n19
Forrestal, Michael, 32
Fort Bragg, North Carolina, 22
Fort Carson, Colorado, 279
fortifications, 27
forward air controllers, 205, 229
forward basing, 265
forward presence, xiv
IV Corps, South Vietnam, 417n88, 422n164
Foy, Carrie Ellen. *See* Moorer, Carrie Ellen Foy
France, 61, 111
free use of int'l waters, 47

freedom of the seas, 51, 58, 70, 392n22
freighter, 122
French forces, 7, 61
French Maritime Navigation School, Saigon, 420n131
French Navy, 420n131
frigates, 226, 263, 340, 374
fuel, 54, 56, 104, 136, 186, 197, 210, 234, 243, 340, 394n59
Fussell, Paul, 334

Galbraith, John Kenneth, 20
Gallup poll, 234
gas-turbine engines, 263
Gates, Thomas S., Jr., 268
Gayler, Noel A. M., 355, 357, 452n109
general officers, 9, 26, 127, 220
General Quarters, 58
General Secretary of the Communist Party of Vietnam, 33, 222
Geneva Agreement, 1962, 15
Geneva Conference, 1954, 61
Geneva Declaration and Protocol on Neutrality of Laos, 15
Geneva, Switzerland, 15, 61
Geng, Chen, 61
Georgia, 145, 293, 344, 428n74
Germany, 346
Gia Lam airfield, North Vietnam, 237
Giap, Vo Nguyen, 193, 391n19
Gilbert Islands, 45
Gilpatrick, Roswell, 13
Glenard P. Lipscomb-class, 269
Glenn, Lewis, 163
global balance of power, 309, 315
goats, 178
gold wings, 48
Golden Gate Bridge, San Francisco Bay, 119
Goldwater, Barry, 322
Goldwater–Nichols Department of Defense Reorganization Act, 375, 447n71
Goodpaster, Andrew, 121
Gorshkov, Sergei, 259
Government Accounting Office, 26
gradualism, 28, 37, 127
graduated escalation, xxi, 28, 37, 41, 43, 61, 70, 75, 104, 127, 250, 362, 396n91
Gravely, Samuel, 277, 280–81 285, 290, 292, 334–35, 440n53
Great Lakes Naval Training Center, Chicago, 146, 287
Great Society presidential program, 60
Greece, 145, 266–67, 333, 341
Greek Navy, 264
Green Berets, xxi, 17, 19, 27, 41
Greene, Wallace, 34–39, 68–69, 79, 388n119, 402n37, 404n78
Greene, William A., 287
Greer, Howard, 234
Grenada crisis, 375

grenades, 82, 144, 217
gripe sessions, 146, 287
grooming, 139, 286, 292, 295, 372
ground security force, 351
Group 759 (Brigade 125), 25
Guadalcanal, Solomon Islands, 5, 135, 153
Guam, Mariana Islands, 153, 227, 256, 353
Guangzhou, China, 389n129
guerrilla warfare, 7, 19–20, 62, 85
guerrillas, 26, 31, 82–85, 166–67, 169, 175, 185, 201, 229, 351, 389n131, 419n115
guided missile frigates, 154, 216, 241, 263, 268, 277, 356, 375
Guidrifon (Soviet ship), 407n4
Gulf of Oman, 376
Gulf of Thailand, 25, 161, 164–65, 168, 173, 179, 181, 351, 356
Gulf of Tonkin, 57, 122, 235
  August 1964 incident, 51, 54, 59, 63, 68, 84
  Desoto Patrol in, 46–47, 58
  fleet operations in, 38, 77, 114, 152, 209–10, 242, 288, 313, 349, 391n11
Gulf of Tonkin Resolution, 57
gunboats, 25, 81, 83
guns, 26, 29, 51, 66, 93, 179, 210, 226, 240, 374
guns and butter, 257, 338

Habib, Philip, 357–58
Hackes, Peter, 278
Hagerstown, Maryland, 113
Haig, Alexander, 200, 203, 209, 215, 218–20, 248, 310, 312, 320–22, 325
Hainan Island, China, 56, 64, 191, 431n44
Haiphong, North Vietnam, 7, 249, 388n119
  bombing, 103, 122, 199, 244, 246–48, 433n91
  minesweeping of, 251–52
  mining of, xxi, 28, 35–36, 102, 121, 230–36, 366, 400n10, 431n43
  naval bombardment, 240–41
  port, *251*
  off-limits to bombing, 100, 127, 237
hair, 33, 268, 281–84
HAL-3 (Helicopter Attack Light Squadron) Seawolves, 160
Haldeman, H. R., 203, 209, 217, 220, 291, 416n75
Haldeman, Mrs. H. R., 323
Halsey, William F., xx
Hancock (CVA-19), 76, 210, 277, 280, 351–52
Hanoi Hilton, 57
Hanoi, North Vietnam, 7, 62, 67, 70, 103, 152, 214, 314, 348, 388n119

INDEX 483

bombing, 117, 119, 123, 149, 237, 240, 243, 433n91, 433n96
Linebacker, 244, 246–48
off-limits to bombing, 100, 124, 127, 215
Hao Mon Dong, North Vietnam, 30
Harbin, Manchuria, 153
Harkins, Paul D., 24, 28–32, 40, 42
Harold E. Holt (DE-1074), 355
Harris, Hunter J., 77
Harvard Law School, 72
Hassayampa (AO-145), 289, 440n66
Hawaii, 3, 21, 23, 37, 40, 43, 107, 119, 126, 143, 201, 224, 380n8
hawks, 124
Hayward, Thomas B., 135, 270, 374, 401n35, 448n33
and Holloway, 317, 332, 336, 346, 451n87
Maritime Strategy, 347, 359, 373
and Zumwalt, 265, 273, 284, 327, 336
Hazard, Roberta, 232, 282, 291–92, 298–302, 430n37, 436n27, 440n67, 443n111, 444n20, 454n3
headquarters, 50, 61, 76, 88, 140, 180, 260, 297
CINCPAC, 3, 23–24, 42–43, 100, 107, 130, 201
enemy, 196–97
MACV, 177, 283
NAVFORV, 173, 180, 189, 335
Navy, 270–71, 317
hearings before Congress, 97–98, 122–23, 137–38, 219, 290, 293, 296, 428n71
hearts and minds, 41, 65, 179
heavy cruisers, 48
Hébert, F. Edward, 293, 442n96
Heflin, James T., 48
helicopters, 31, 122, 165–66, 181, 202, 211–12, 264, 357–58, 375
Air Force, 213, 356
Army, 82, 210, 229
Marine, 86, 107, 351–52
Navy, 114, 160, 167, 251, 263, 265, 336, 351
Helms, Richard, 201, 233
Helping Hand Foundation, 417n85
Henry B. Wilson (DDG-7), 357
herbicides, 169
heroin, 141–42, 276
Herrick, John J., 50–57
HH-53 Super Jolly Green Giant helicopters, 213
Hicks, Floyd, 290, 293–96, 303, 441n76, 442n99
Hidalgo, Edward, 270
Hieu, Dang Trung, 165
High-Low Mix, 263–64, 273,

292, 327–28, 337, 359
Hilsman, Roger, 32, 387n108
hippies, 258
Hispanics, 139, 289
historians, xiv, 184, 272, 347–48, 397n20
Ho Chi Minh, 7, 33, 61, 101, 198, 391n19, 424n6
Ho Chi Minh Trail, 15, 65, 74, 80, 92, 104, 161, 230, 348–49
early use, 11, 17, 38–39, 61, 85
air interdiction, 105, 152, 156, 205
Lam Son 719, 207, 210, 222
Hoa Lo Prison, North Vietnam. *See* Hanoi Hilton
Hoffmann, Roy F., 166, 179, 415n55
Holloway, Dabney Rawlings, 118
Holloway, James L., Jr., 113, 153–54, 279, 409n25
Holloway, James L., III, xiv, xv, xx, xxii, xxiii, 98, *115*, *118*, 150, *239*, *316*, 322, 324, *328*, 333, *337*, *342*, 361, 364, 366–67, 370–75, 445n44
carrier fires, Carrier Program, Moorer, McNamara, Rickover, CV Concept, 136–39, 408n17, 409n18
Carter, Harold Brown, defense budgets, Swing Strategy, Hayward, Sea Plan 2000, Maritime Strategy, 344–47, 451n87
and Chafee, 137, 253, 255
Chief of Naval Operations, retention, Hayward, Bagley, 326–31
and Clements, 330, 357–58
Enterprise in Operation Rolling Thunder, 113–20, 129, 137, 405n96, 409n26
and Ford, 324, 343, 354–55, 357–59, 361, 371–72
and James L. Holloway Jr., 153–54, 279, 409n25
and Kissinger, 238, 315, 341–44, 354–59, 372, 453n118
Linebacker, 238–42, 250
and Long, 330, 448n15
Mayaguez crisis, axe murders in Korea, WSAG, 354–58, 452n108
Middendorf, Naval War College, 272, 340, 347, 372, 447n76
military assistance to RVN, Cambodia, Frequent Wind, refugees, 348–54
a new course, MCPON, retention, Watkins, race, women, 331–36, 447n5
overseas homeporting, Japan, Greece, 266, 333
Paris Agreement, Operation End Sweep, 250–52

Project Sixty, 264, 273, 436n36
racial trouble, drug abuse, Zumwalt media use, 277–80
and Rickover, 118, 270, 315, 317, 327, 340–41, 409n20
and Schlesinger, 322, 324, 326, 329, 338, 341, 354–55, 372
and Shear, 327, 436n29, 447n8, 452n108
Soviet Navy, 260, 308, 339
successes and failures as CNO, 358–60
VCNO, Kissinger, naval aviation, Hayward, Rickover, 315–17
and Warner, 255, 326, 328–29, 372
warship construction, fleet obsolescence, Soviet Navy, Battle Force Fleet, NWP-1, Rickover, SALT II, 337–44, 450n68, 450n83
Z-Grams, racism, opposition, Zumwalt service on JCS, 279, 285–86, 291, 306, 440n66, 442n99
Zumwalt as CNO, 255, 315, 327, 330–31, 437n55, 441n79
Holloway, James L., IV, 118
Holloway, Jane, 118
Holloway, Jean Hagood, 113
Holloway, Lucy, 118
Holloway Plan, 114
Holloway Report, 375
Hollyfield, Ernest E., 58
Hon Gai, North Vietnam, 56, 246, 251–52
Hon Mat Islet, North Vietnam, 50
Hon Me Island, North Vietnam, 49–50, 53, 56
Hon Nieu Island, North Vietnam, 49
Hong Kong, 7
Honolulu, Hawaii, 90–91, 120
Hopwood, Herbert G., 9
Horner, Charles A., 113
hospitals, 116, 147, 163–64, 297, 301, 336
hot pursuit, 52–54
House, W. H., 162
housing, 141, 146, 173, 182, 186, 278
Hue, South Vietnam, 65, 106, 112, 124, 226–28
Hughes, Thomas L., 91, 386n96
Hughes, Wayne P., Jr., 433n104
Human Goals Program, 287, 303, 327, 335
human resources, 254, 266, 301
human rights, 330
humanities, 425n25
Humphrey, Hubert, 171, 416n74
Hung, Dinh Manh, 188
Hussein, Saddam, 377

Hutchinson, Homer G., Jr., 112
hydroelectric plants, 105
hydrofoils, 263, 273
Hyland, John, 142, 176, 385n80, 402n40
   operational control, 109, 112, 399n42
   and Sharp, 45, 64, 100
   and Zumwalt, 177, 265, 418n105, 418n106

I Corps, South Vietnam, 109–12
Ignatius, Paul, xiv, 133–35, 139–40, 150, 156–59, 178, 408n14
Iklé, Fred, 344
Illegal or Improper Use of Drugs, 142
Imperial Japanese Navy, 153
imports, 104, 235, 243, 251
In Retrospect (McNamara), 120
Inchon (LPH-12), 296
Incidents at Sea Treaty, 235, 256
Independence (CV-62), 349
India, 218, 312–14, 325
Indian Ocean, 3, 312–14, 445n39
India-Pakistan War, 325
indigenous peoples, 9, 11
Indochina, xix, 13, 40, 42, 67, 71, 80, 84, 162, 348, 364–66, 397n20
   air operations, 74, 76, 79, 116, 240, 362
   conflict in, 16, 23, 36, 212, 221, 363, 386n93
   French involvement, 7, 61, 111, 231
   Mao's considerations, 62, 65
   US withdrawal from, 222, 318, 349
Indonesia, 58, 95, 108, 158, 389n129
Industrial College of the Armed Forces, 194
industry, 63, 92, 274, 330, 341
infantry, 147, 357
   Army, 89, 106, 175, 181, 217, 279, 419n118, 422n164
   enemy, 61, 175, 229
   Marine, 85, 107, 112
   South Vietnamese, 181, 210–11, 228
infiltration, 67, 80, 348–49, 396n88
   by sea, xxi, 21–22, 25–26, 82, 88, 191, 385n80, 418n97
   from Cambodia, 32, 34, 162–64, 178
   Ho Chi Minh Trail, 105, 124, 161
   Operation Market Time, 108, 156, 161
inflation, 231
inland waterways of South Vietnam, 21, 106, 167, 235
inspections, 279, 281
Inspector General of the Navy, 290, 440n71

institutions of higher learning, 303
insurgencies, 17, 69
intelligence, 13, 66, 93, 96, 132, 160, 178, 202, 210, 291, 321, 419n114, 425n16
   China, 36, 74
   infiltration, 65, 85, 162, 191, 205
   operations re: North Vietnam, 15, 28, 30, 46–47, 50, 54, 56, 58, 213, 241, 243, 248, 391n11, 427n65
   ships and aircraft, 138, 198, 356
intercontinental ballistic missiles, 265, 308, 343
intercultural relations programs, 266, 267
interdepartmental task force, 21
interdiction, 77, 82, 92, 105, 124, 152, 156, 165, 199, 206, 364, 382n41
international crises, 8, 204, 325, 372
international relations, 271
interservice relations, 111, 356
intervention, 23, 26, 95
   Laos, 10, 16, 381n28
   Sino-Soviet, 36–37, 56, 59, 61, 65, 69–70, 74, 95, 102, 230, 233, 363, 396n82, 402n47, 431n44
   US, 64, 66, 68
intimidation, 17, 19, 91
Intrepid (CVS-11), 296, 442n101
investigation, 218, 267
Iowa-class battleships, 374, 450n83
Iran and Iraq, 375–77
Israel, 96, 132, 318–19, 325, 446n53
Israeli-Egyptian rapprochement, 319
Iwo Jima battle, 86

J-3 Operations, Joint Staff, JCS, 402n37
Jackson, Henry, 137, 319, 322, 372, 446n61
Jacksonville, Florida, 238
jamming, 215, 242
Japan, 3, 5, 9, 45, 49, 59, 132, 198, 231, 266, 273, 346, 357, 409n26
Japanese Maritime Self-Defense Force, 409n26
Jason Summer Study Group, 104, 124
JCS Concept Plan, 199
JCS target list, 80
Jesse Brown (DE-1089), 287
Jews, 164
Jinmen (Quemoy) Island, Republic of China, 7
John F. Kennedy (CVA-67), 296
John R. Craig (DD-885), 47
Johnson City, Texas, 145
Johnson, Harold K., 37, 86

Johnson, Lyndon B., xv, xxi, 12–13, *121*, 132, 145, 148, 159, 162, 199, 216, 239, 250, 256–57, 361–66, 376, 407n136
   air operations in Laos, North Vietnam, 72–82
   comparison with Nixon, 233, 236, 237, 412n68
   fear of Sino-Soviet intervention, 61–71, 396n82, 402n47
   Gulf of Tonkin crises, 42–60, 392n24
   height of bombing campaign, 120–30
   in-country war, 106–11
   mining Haiphong, 230–31
   pressuring North Vietnam, 29–37
   Rolling Thunder, 90–105
   US intervention in South Vietnam, 85–89
Johnson, Roy L., 50, 52, 54–55
Joint Chiefs of Staff, xix, xx, xxiii, 8, 11, 32, 99, 132, 178, 207–8, *208*, 305–6, 317, 324, 360–61, 383n43
Joint General Staff, South Vietnamese armed forces, 34, 423n185
Joint Planning Group, Department of State, 69
Joint Security Area, South Korea, 358
Joint Staff, Joint Chiefs of Staff, 55, 69, 97, 232, 322, 341, 355, 447n71, 452n108
   Rolling Thunder, 77, 99–100, 402n37
Joint Task Force 116, 10
Jones, David C., 354–55, 372, 452n108
Jones, John Paul, 14, 165
Jordanian crisis, 1970, 238
Jouett (DLG-29), 277
journalists, 12, 31, 42, 247, 352
junior officers, 147, 167, 278, 282, 295, 303, 330, 368
Junk Force. *See* Coastal Force, Vietnam Navy

kamikaze, 5
kangaroos, 419n115
Kansas, 4
Kansas City, Missouri, 453n118
Karch, Frederick J., 86
Kauffman, Draper L., 146, 285, 287
Kelley, Roger, 295, 442n96
Kelley, Thomas G., 164, 414n48, 422n172
Kennedy, John F., xiii, 20, 40, 42, 47, 60, 104, 361, 387n108, 421n144
   counterinsurgency, 18–19, 362
   Laos, 11, 15, 381n28
   limited partnership, 23, 41
   special forces, 26, 29, 32

INDEX   485

Taylor and McNamara, 12–13, 380n12
Kennedy, Robert, 125
Kep airfield, North Vietnam, 104
Kerr, Alex A., 155, 397n3
Kerr, Howard, 162, 171, 265, 270, 284–85, 322–24, 416n74, 416n76, 439n22
Kerry, John, 167, 179, 192, 323, 415n55
Kerwin, Walter T., 176
Key Biscayne, Florida, 151
Khe Sanh, South Vietnam, 106, 111
Khmer Rouge, xxii, 201, 351, 355
Khomeini, Ayatollah, 375
Khrushchev, Nikita S., 19, 62, 66
Kidd, Isaac, 329, 448n11
Kiem, Do, 181, 188
Kien River, North Vietnam, 30
Kim Il-sung, 132–33, 356, 358
King, Ernest J., xx
King, Jerome H., Jr., 134, 187, 232, 255
Kirkpatrick, Jeane, 444n15
Kiska, Aleutian Islands, 153
Kissinger, Henry, xxi, 123, 149, 366–70, 372, 414n33, 425n16, 429n14, 441n77, 444n31, 445n38
  axe murders, 354–59, 453n118
  Cambodia, Laos, 197–213
  differences with Zumwalt, 307–25, 445n32, 449n64
  Easter Offensive, 221–30
  Haiphong mining, 231–37
  and Holloway, 341–44
  Linebacker, 238–46
  post–Paris Agreement, 348–49
  White House troubles, 218–20
kitchen cabinets, 180, 292, 303
Kitty Hawk (CVA-63), 38, 210, 288, 290, 292–95, 440n66
Klusmann, Charles F., 38–39, 389n131
Koh Tang Island, Cambodia, 355–56
Komar-class missile boat, 246
Kompong Som, Cambodia. *See* Sihanoukville
Kontum, South Vietnam, 229
Korean peninsula, 65, 371
Korean War, 6, 59, 80, 84, 102, 134, 204, 259
  bombing, 105, 111, 113, 123, 389n124
  intervention, 60–62, 64–65, 402n47
  leaders in, xv, xx, 45, 63, 77, 112, 153
Korth, Fred, 270
Krulak, Victor H., 30, 36, 93, 108, 110–12
Kuwait, 376–77
Kwangsi Province, China, 63

La Jolla Country Club, California, 434n4
La Maddalena, Italy, 266
LA-7 fighters, Chinese, 7
Lach Troung/Hon Me area, North Vietnam, 56
Laird, Melvin, 142, *183*, 229, 309–12, 320, 385n93, 393n46, 425n16, 427n65
  Cambodia, 196–97, 201–2
  Lam Son 719, 209–12
  Linebacker, 236–37, 245
  mining of Haiphong, 230, 233, 235, 431n43
  and Moorer, 221, 223–24, 227–28, 250
  Nixon's animus toward, 198–99
  protective reaction, 213–16
  Radford affair, 218–19
  social issues, 285, 300
  Vietnamization, xxii, 151, 170–71, 193, 203, 349, 423n192
  Zumwalt connection, 159, 184, 207, 253–55, 264, 272, 278–79, 281, 291, 308, 325, 365, 367, 434n4, 434n5
Lam, Hoang Xuan, 210, 213
landing craft air cushion vehicles, 374
"Land of a Million Elephants," 9
Langley (CV-1), 48
Lao Cham Island, South Vietnam, 30
Lao Kay–Hanoi railroad, North Vietnam, 28
laser-guided bombs, 237, 240
Last of the Titans (Hébert), 293
Lavell, Kit, 163
Lavelle, John D., 216, 427n63, 428n71
law of war, 433n96
Lawrence, William P., 244
Le Duan, 33, 67, 71, 222, 230, 348, 391n19, 424n6
Leading Chief Petty Officer of the Navy, 140. *See also* Master Chief Petty Officer of the Navy
leaks of information, 197, 219
Lebanon crises, 375
LeBourgeois, Julien J., 272
Lee, Kent L., 139, 145, 409n18, 409n20, 448n11
Lee, Robert E., 178
legal services, 15, 57, 141, 155, 301, 397n3
Legion of Merit, 5, 118
Lehman, John, 155, 203, 341, 430n23
  and Holloway, 345–47, 367, 450n68, 450n83
  Linebacker, 342–43
  and Rickover, 270, 409n21
  600-ship navy, 371, 374
  social issues, 288, 290, 331
  strategic arms limitation, 309, 344
  and Zumwalt, 263, 367

LeMay, Curtis, 12, 37, 68, 129, 204–5, 411n64
Lenihan, Rita, 297
Lexington (CV-2), 5
liberalism, 159, 255
Liberty (AGTR-5), 132
liberty and leave, 279, 289, 292
light at the end of the tunnel, 24
limited partnership, 23, 25
limited war, xx, 9, 19, 61, 129, 362
Linebacker campaign, xxii, 123, 237–49, 252, 288, 315, 366, 431n60, 431n61, 433n96, 452n109
Little Americas, 267
Loc Ninh, South Vietnam, 228
locks, 105
Lodge, Henry Cabot, 30, 33
logistics, 13, 103, 152, 167–68, 189, 193, 203, 365
Lon Nol, 175, 200–201, 351
London, UK, 98
Long Beach (CGN-9), 216
Long Binh Jail, Long Binh, South Vietnam, 143
Long Tau River, South Vietnam, 169, 353
Long, Robert L. J., 380n8, 448n15
Long-Range Objectives Group, Navy staff, 49
Los Angeles County, California, 249
Los Angeles-class submarines, 269
Louisiana, 293
low-altitude delivery tactics, 79
low-level reconnaissance, 38
low-risk policy, 58
Lucky Bag, Naval Academy yearbook, 146
lunches, 6, 54, 95–96, 100, 124, 184, 297, 333
Lynn, Doyle, 39

M-72 antitank rockets, 229
MacArthur, Douglas, 8, 178, 402n47
Macbeth, 72
Mach Nuoc, North Vietnam, 59
Mack, William P., *324*, 401n35
Macmillan, Harold, 15
Maddox (DD-731), xxi, 50–57, 70, 393n42
Maginot Line thinking, 105
Mahan, Alfred Thayer, 153
Malaya, 17
Malaysia, 158
Manila, Philippines, 120
manpower, 175, 295, 327
"Manual on Equal Opportunity and Treatment of Military Personnel," 145
Mao Zedong, 7, 9, 36, 60–67, 104, 231, 235, 351, 393n54, 395n65
Mariana Islands, 45, 153
marijuana, 141–42
Marine Air Station, Kaneohe,

Hawaii, 143
Marine All-Weather Attack Squadron 224, 234
Marine Corps, US, 12, 26, 87, 107, 160, 296, 342, 352
  amphibious doctrine, 109–10, 130
  on JCS, 201, 208
  Sharp, 363, 404n78
  social issues, 142–43
Marine expeditionary brigades, 86
Marine security detachments, 352
maritime operations and forces, 34, 42, 68, 234, 250, 259, 264
  coastal patrol, 83–84
  Operation 34A, 30, 49
  seaborne infiltration, 26, 82
  SEALs, 26–28
  US advantage, 19, 311, 339, 346
maritime strategy, 258, 347, 360, 371, 373–74
Mark 50 sea mines, 54
Marrow Foundation, 354
Marshall, George C., 97
Martin, Graham, 353
Marxist-Leninist ideology, 62, 363
Massachusetts Avenue, Washington, DC, 254
massive retaliation, 9, 40, 224
Master Chief Petty Officer of the Navy, 140–41, 150, 331, 334, 359
material condition of the fleet, xx, xxii, 17, 139, 258, 446n49
Mauz, Henry H., Jr., 377
Mayaguez crisis, xxii, 354–56, 360, 362, 371, 452n108
McCain, John S., Jr., xiv, 113, 192, 201, 233, 241, 243
  and Abrams, 227, 231
  Laos, 206, 213–14
  and Moorer, 149, 224
  selection as CINCPAC, 147–48
McCain, John, III, 138, 149
McCann, Richard, 162
McCarthy, Eugene, 125
McCauley, Brian, 249
McConnell, John P., 79, 92, 122–23
McCrory, Mary, 247
McDonald, David L., xiv, 34–38, 59, 74, 83, 121, 140, 144, 317, 329, 372, 389n133, 411n64
  Mobile Riverine Force, 106, 403n60
  self-evaluation as CNO, 98–99
  Tonkin Gulf incident, 47, 58
McGovern, George, 244
McKee, Fran, 301
McKee, Kinnaird, 224
McMaster, H. R., xix
McNamara, Robert S., xiii, xxi, 27, 36, 60, 76, 81, 105, 107, 146, 156, 161, 165, 230, 362n64, 398n40, 408n7, 411n64
  antipathy toward military, 14, 42
  civil-military friction, 77–78, 95–99, 129, 134–35, 147, 150, 250, 291, 361, 382n34, 401n35, 401n36, 405n94
  counterinsurgency, 20–22
  Diem era, 23–25, 32–33
  end of Rolling Thunder, 120–27
  Laos, 15, 35, 38–40
  nuclear-powered carriers, 137–39
  Operation 34A, 29, 49, 386n96
  qualifications, 11–13
  Rolling Thunder, 90–94, 100–104, 400n3
  Sino-Soviet intervention, 69–71
  social issues, 143–45
  Tonkin Gulf incident, 53–59
  US intervention in South Vietnam, 88–89
McNaughton, John T., 72–73, 77, 81, 90, 99, 102, 396n2, 397n3
Medal of Honor, 6, 51, 164, 415n48, 422n172
medals, 45, 49, 113, 162, 277
media, 33, 211, 279, 348
  Constellation protest, 289, 291
  and Felt, 31, 386n100
  and Holloway, 118–19, 139, 372
  and Moorer, 202, 217, 247
  and Zumwalt, 235, 272, 277–78, 280, 283, 298, 302, 307, 325
medical care, 27, 31, 66, 141, 167, 353
Mediterranean, xiv, 238, 267, 273, 294, 311, 338, 442n96
Meet the Press, 323
meetings, 86, 176, 200, 285, 300, 313, 382n41, 411n64, 452n108
  Joint Chiefs of Staff, 306–7, 309
  Nixon White House, 208, 237
  Texas ranch, 96
  Tuesday lunch at Johnson White House, 95–96, 100
Mekong Delta, xiv, 27, *160*, 163, 195, 203, 315, 353–54, 375, 377, 415n46
  Abrams, 158, 160
  allied successes, 174–75, 418n67
  ARVN operations, 31, 188
  infiltration, 25, 33–34, 161, 201
  Mobile Riverine Force, 106, 140
  Vietnamization, 254, 365
  Zumwalt, xxii, 158, 160
menu operations, 197
Merchant Marine, 420n131, 445n44
merchant ships, 161, 169, 351, 377
mess hall, 279
messages, back-channel, 319
Metropolitan Club, 350
Mexican American community, 60
Meyer, John C., 246
Miami, Florida, 145
Mickey Mouse regulations, 281, 292
micromanagement of military operations, 14, 39, 187, 363, 400n57
Middendorf, J. William, II, 340, 347, 372, 447n76
Middle East, xxiii, 5, 238, 259, 311, 318–19, 373, 376, 445n44, 446n51, 446n53
Middle East Force, 5
midshipmen summer cruises, 152
MiG bases, xiii
MiG fighters, 60, 66, 82, 119, 122, 214–16, 234, 394n58, 408n2
military advisor at the White House, 12
Military Advisory Group, Chinese, 61
Military Assistance Advisory Group, Vietnam, 17
military assistance, 173, 194, 215, 245, 256, 349
Military Assistance Command, Vietnam, xix, 25, 42, 47, 84, 106, 149, 206, 283
  Abrams, xxii, 158, 211
  Felt, 27, 40
  operational control of forces, 77, 109–12, 149
  Sharp, 77, 110–12, 130
  Westmoreland, 84, 94, 106, 109, 211
  Zumwalt, 159, 176–77
military construction, 173
military honor, 92
military mind, 73, 156
Military Operations to Terminate Aggression in Southeast Asia, 35
Military Region I, South Vietnam, 226
military retaliation, 35, 198
Military Sealift Command, US Navy, 351
Miller, Gerald, 121, 264, 284, 296, 305–6, 327, 401n36, 408n9, 417n95, 418n106
Miller, Henry L., 20
Mine Countermeasures Force (Task Force 78), 251
mine warfare, 49, 169, 231–32, 266, 424n9
mines, 54, 102, 105, 161, 206, 233–35, 251, 375–76

INDEX 487

minesweeping, 64, 83, 160, 251
Minh, Hoang Co, 185–89, 192
minimum risk approach, 29
mining, xv, xxi, 198–99, 237–38, 245, 431n43, 433n102
  early considerations, 28, 35–36, 54, 92, 230, 400n10, 402n47, 424n1, 424n9
  Moorer, 49, 68, 83, 231–35, 249–50, 366
    Sharp, 69, 102, 121–22, 230
    Zumwalt, 156, 230, 232, 235
mini-staff, Zumwalt's, 292, 454n3
Ministry of Defense, Hanoi, 199
minorities, 145, 285, 335–36, 367
minority affairs, 276, 284–87
Mirage F-1 fighter aircraft, 376
missile research center, 49
missile sites, 100, 215
"Missions of the U.S. Navy" (Turner), 264
Mississippi, 16
Missouri (BB-63), 376
Mitchell, John, 218–19
Mobile Riverine Force, 106, 140, 162, 174, 177, 186, 403n60. *See also* Riverine Assault Force; Task Force 117
Mod Squad, 265, 273, 368, 436n39
Momyer, William W., 91, 110, 112, 206, 406n124
Mondale, Walter, 137
monitors, 160
monsoons, 39, 116, 205, 226
Montagnards, 27
Montgomery, Alabama, 48
Moore, Joseph H., Jr., 77
Moorer, Carrie Ellen Foy, 48, 254, 453n1
Moorer, Ellen Butcher, 453n1
Moorer, Hulda Hinson, 48
Moorer, Richard F., 453n1
Moorer, Richard R., 48
Moorer, Robert H., 453n1
Moorer, Thomas H., xiv, xv, xx, xxi, xxiii, 16, 33, 36, 45, *46*, 81, 97–98, *118*, 125–26, *133*, *148*, 155, 162, 171, *200*, *255*, *324*, 361–69, 372–75, 383n43, 401n22, 402n37, 405n94, 408n5, 408n7, 408n14, 408n17, 411n64, 411n66, 412n68, 416n68, 421n158, 422n173, 425n14, 427n51, 431n44, 453n1, 454n8
  air operations in Laos, Lam Son 719, 205–13
  air operations short of war in Laos and North Vietnam, 73–74, 76
  approval of ACTOV, 420n129
  approval of Holloway, 329, 445n44
  bombing, invasion of Cambodia, military advice to Nixon, 196–205
  civil-military discord, 14–15, 72, 77, 134, 150
  early life and career, 48–49
  Easter Offensive, 222–30
  establishment of MCPON and Navy personnel issues, 139–46
  Gulf of Tonkin incident, 51–52, 55, 391n11, 392n22
  international crises, White House, 311–15, 318–20, 444n31, 445n38, 446n53
  JCS service in support of wartime strategy, 146–50, 354
  leadership and resource management of Navy, 134–39
  Liberty, *Pueblo*, and CNO's global responsibilities, 132–34
  maritime interdiction and troop deployment to South Vietnam, 82–89
  mining of Haiphong, Linebacker, 230–38, 400n10, 429n14, 244–49
  Operation 34A and Desoto Patrol, 46, 49
  operational control of air, naval gunfire, and amphibious forces, 112
  opposition to micromanagement, 38, 79
  POWs, 214, 217, 244, 318, 349, 427n65, 432n80
  proposals to deter Hanoi and support Saigon, 68, 70–71
  protective reaction, air operations in Laos, North Vietnam, 213–16, 428n71
  Soviet Navy threat, 259, 306, 444n15
  strategic arms control, 308–10, 322
  successes and failures, 249–50
  support of NAVFORV and Zumwalt, 152, 157, 159, 176–77, 184, 187
  US, DRV response to Gulf of Tonkin incident, 57–58
  White House liaison office and Radford affair, 217–21, 426n38
  and Zumwalt, 306–8, 316, 324, 414n33, 443n6
  Zumwalt communication to fleet, personnel policies, 281–83
  Zumwalt lack of fleet command, liberalism, 254, 264–65, 414n32, 435n11
  Zumwalt opposition to Rickover, 270, 274, 314–15, 317, 409n22, 425n25
Moorer, Thomas R., 453n1
morale, 192, 212–13, 240, 266, 278, 300, 333, 372, 396n2, 442n92, 442n96
morality, 217
mortars, 49
Morton (DD-948), 58
Moscow, Soviet Union, 36, 65–66, 120, 225, 228, 231–35, 256, 309, 312, 322, 362
motor gunboats, 25
motor torpedo boats, 29, 386n95
motorcycles, 281
Mount Willing, Alabama, 48
Mountbatten, Lord Louis, 8
moustaches, 139, 281
movies, 297
Mu Gia Pass, Laos, 73, 214
Mullen, Michael, 453–54n3
munitions, 22, 25, 36, 42, 63, 82, 161, 191, 203, 236–37, 249, 377
Murphy, Terrence, 64
Murray, Albert K., 439n34
Mustin, Henry, 120, 260, 262, 333
Mustin, Lloyd, 60, 69, 102–3, 105, 120, 396n88, 402n37
mutiny, 294
My Chanh River, South Vietnam, 226, 229
My Father, My Son (Zumwalt), 157
My Lai, South Vietnam, 217, 293, 428n74
My Tho, South Vietnam, 186
mythical Chinese hordes, 69

Nakhon Phanom, Thailand, 205
Nam Tha, Laos, 15
napalm, 217
Nape Pass, Laos, 73
Naples, Italy, 266
Nasser, Gamal Abdel, 63
Nasty-class fast patrol boats, 29, 386n95
National Command Authority, 425n16
National Guard, US, 143
National League of Families of American Prisoners and Missing in SEA, 314
National Liberation Front, 62
National Security Action Memorandum 288, 37
National Security Action Memorandum 328, 68, 88
National Security Advisor, xix, 103, 197, 219
  Kissinger, 203–4, 207–8, 254, 310–14, 317, 319, 325, 369
  McGeorge Bundy, 77, 95
  Moorer, 203–4, 208, 319
  Scowcroft, 354, 357
  Zumwalt, 207, 254, 310–14, 317, 319, 325, 369
National Security Agency, 50, 55, 425n16
National Security Council, 59, 88, 154, 200, 372, 382n4, 396n88
  Mayaguez, 343, 354, 356
  Zumwalt, 312–13

National Security Council
  Memorandum 68 (NSC-68),
  154
national security establishment,
  13, 42, 74, 86–87, 127, 135,
  264, 312, 321, 361–62, 366
national security policy, 6, 12,
  343
National Society of Former
  Special Agents of the Federal
  Bureau of Investigation,
  426n25, 446n49
National United Front for the
  Liberation of Vietnam, 185
National War College, 5, 154,
  301, 315
Naval Academy Academic
  Advisory Board, 445n44
Naval Academy Foundation,
  445n44
naval advisors, 25, 171, 301, 307,
  311, 321. See also advisors
naval advisory group, 84, 171,
  173
naval aide, 154–55, 157, 264,
  413n18
Naval Air Station, Miramar,
  California, 242
naval air stations, 5, 242
naval aviation, 5, 204, 265
  Holloway, 137–38, 315–16,
    340, 359, 364, 445n44
  Moorer, 48, 137, 157, 204
  women in, 336, 371
  Zumwalt, 262, 315–16, 340,
    359, 364
naval bombardment, gunfire
  support, 49, 52, 83, 93, 112,
  223, 226, 262, 432n72
naval construction units. See
  Seabees
naval districts, 140, 146
naval facilities, 25, 54, 68, 267
Naval Historical Center,
  421n141, 443n6
Naval Historical Foundation,
  445n44
naval intelligence, 36, 54, 232
naval intelligence liaison officers,
  419n114
Naval Investigative Service, 287
Naval Observatory, 254, 335
naval operations, xv, 34, 84,
  152, 166, 170, 176, 183, 342,
  418n98, 433n104
Naval Ordnance Test Station,
  China Lake, California, 49
naval personnel, 160, 171, 176,
  182, 243, 277, 287, 336
naval policy, xiii, 139
naval power, Soviet, xx, 306,
  308, 368
naval power, US, 84, 240, 250,
  313, 341, 449n64
  re: China, 35–36, 59, 62, 65,
    70, 152, 228
  re: North Vietnam, 36, 38,
    70, 152, 228
  projection ashore, 262–63,
    274, 346, 371

naval quarantine of Cuba, 13, 45
Naval Reserve, 60, 114, 144, 278,
  299, 342
Naval Reserve Officers Training
  Corps (NROTC), 114, 144,
  301, 303
Naval Security Group, 50
naval special forces, 19, 26. See
  also SEALs
naval support activities, 160
Naval War College, 5, 16, 49, 75,
  154, 264, 268, 270–71, 335,
  420n131
*Naval Warfare Publication No.
  1: Strategic Concepts of the U.S.
  Navy*, 339, 371
Navy Affirmative Action Plan,
  336–37, 359, 371
Navy Carrier Program, 136
Navy Cross medals, 5, 452n109
Navy Drug Exemption and
  Rehabilitation Program, 276
Navy exchanges, 286
Navy Lodge, Norfolk Naval
  Base, Virginia, 141
Navy Nurse Corps, 299
Navy staff, 11, 19–20, 45, 136,
  139, 238, 409n26
Navy Unit Commendation
  medal, 5
Navy women, 296–300, 336
NBC *Today* show, 235
Neak Luong, Cambodia, 170
negotiations, 7, 105, 231, 235,
  318–19
  in Paris, 123, 207, 214–15
  Paris Agreement, 230, 248,
    250
  Rolling Thunder, 92, 101,
    103, 124, 129, 152, 364
  strategic arms limitation,
    228, 309–10, 325, 343, 369,
    372, 444n20, 446n51
neutralists in Laos, 9
Never Again Club, 84
New Guinea, 60
New Hampshire, 125
New Mexico (BB-40), 45
New Orleans (CA-32), 48
New Orleans, Louisiana, 293
New York, 294
New York Times, The, 242, 279,
  370
New Zealand, 3
Newport News (CA-148),
  241–42, 432n72
Newport, Rhode Island, 5, 49,
  452n108
newspapers, 118–19
Ngo Quang Truong, 228
Nguyen Hue Offensive. *See*
  Easter Offensive
Nha Trang, South Vietnam,
  172, 351
Nichols, John B., 240
Nicholson, Richard, 265
Nimitz (CVN-68), 137, 316
Nimitz, Chester W., xx, 27, 283
Nimitz-class nuclear-powered

  carriers, 138, 374
Nitze, Paul, xiv, 26, 36, 112,
  158, 207, 291, 305, 364, 369,
  398n40, 406n110, 406n122,
  413n16, 435n24, 444n15,
  446n61, 454n3
  and Clifford, 125, 408n5
  and McNamara, 13–14, 96,
    99, 156, 383n43
  and Moorer, 135, 150, 157,
    159
  Navy social issues, 140, 145
  and Rickover, 269–70
  strategic arms limitation,
    308–10, 322, 368
  US commitment to South
    Vietnam, 258, 388n119
  and Zumwalt, 154–56, 254,
    367, 413n18
Nixon Doctrine, 256, 263, 273
Nixon, Richard M., xxi, xxii, 65,
  142, 162, 178, *200*, 254, 258,
  288, 298, *328*, 342, 348–49,
  357, 361, 365, 368, 412n68,
  414n33, 421n144, 424n1,
  424n6, 425n13, 425n164,
  429n85, 447n76
  air operations in Laos and
    Lam Son 719, 205–13
  bombing and invasion of
    Cambodia, 196–203
  Constellation protest, 291,
    303
  Easter Offensive, 222–30
  Holloway's service, 328,
    372–73
  Linebacker, 236–49
  mining of Haiphong,
    230–35, 424n9, 433n102
  Moorer connection, 204–5,
    220–21, 425n14
  Nixon Doctrine, 256, 263,
    273
  Paris Agreement, POWs,
    Operation End Sweep,
    249–52
  POWs, 432n80, 433n102
  protective reaction, 213–16
  Radford affair, 217–20
  Vietnamization, 170–71,
    173–74, 416n68, 416n74
  withdrawal from Vietnam,
    151–52, 159, 364, 366
  Zumwalt's opposition,
    307–26, 369
Nolan, Robert, 140
Nolting, Frederick, 22, *24*
non-communist governments, 7,
  9–10, 57, 185
non-judicial punishment, 280,
  295
Norfolk, Virginia, 26, 141,
  333, 338
Norman, William S., 276,
  284–87, 454n3
North Atlantic Ocean, xiv, 138
North Atlantic Treaty
  Organization (NATO), 238,
  346, 373

INDEX

North Korea, 46, 102, 130–34, 198, 356–58, 384n63, 389n124, 407n1
North Vietnam. *See* Democratic Republic of Vietnam
North Vietnamese 325th Infantry Division, 67
northeast monsoon, 199
Norway, 29
nuclear weapons, 154, 321, 341, 344, 369
　alternative to, 7, 9
　Chinese and Soviet, 41, 63
　use of, 11, 35, 80, 111, 198, 388n117
nurses, 296, 299
Nyce, Barbara, 301

Oahu, Hawaii, 130
O'Connor, George C., 106
O'Connor, Patricia, 45
offensive operations, 35, 124, 273, 347
office of legislative affairs, 138
office of the secretary of defense, 97, 121, 219, 303, 307, 316
officer candidate school, 299
officer clubs, 333
offshore islands, North Vietnam, 54, 58
Ohio-class attack submarines, 265
oil platforms, Persian Gulf, 376
Okean 70 Soviet Navy exercise, 259
Okean 75 Soviet Navy exercise, 339
Okinawa Island, Japan, 5, 59, 135, 143
Oklahoma City (CLG-5), 241, 352
Old Nam Can, South Vietnam, 168
old Vietnam hands, 232, 267, 368, 373
Oliver Hazard Perry-class guided missile frigates, 263, 375
Olympia, 16
On Watch (Zumwalt), 157, 259, 261, 269, 285, 300, 365, 370, 301
one-Navy concept, 301
Ong Doc River, South Vietnam, 168
Operation Plans: 32-59, 16; 32(L)-59, 9; 34, 29; 34A, 29, 30, 37, 46; 36-84, 35; 37-64, 37; 37-65, 67; 38-64, 35; 39-65, 59; 111-69, 162
operational accidents, 122, 136
Operational Archives, Naval Historical Center, 421n144, 443n6
operational arts, 13, 129, 271
operational control, 107, 109, 111, 112, 399n42
operational efficiency, 405n94
operations: 34A, 29–30, 37, 41, 46–49, 58–59, 67, 70–71,
84, 386n96, 386n97, 393n48; Badger Tooth, 111; Barrel Roll, 72–74, 88; Commando Hunt, 152, 205–6; Dagger Thrust, 108–9; Desert Storm, 377; Dessert, 197; Dinner, 197; Duck Hook, 198, 220; Eagle Pull, 351; Earnest Will, 376; End Sweep, 251–52, 266, 452n109; Flaming Dart, 74–79, 88; Freedom Bait, 214; Freedom Train, 227; Frequent Wind, 352; Giant Slingshot, 164–65; Igloo White, 205; Jackstay, 109; Lam Son 719, xxi, 206–12, 220–22, 249, 325; Lion's Den, 241; Lunch, 197; Market Time, xxi, 83, 88, 108, 156, 161, 191, 398n40, 422n176; Pierce Arrow, 55–57, 60, 71, 81, 103, 393n45; Pocket Money, 234–35; Praying Mantis, 376; Proud Deep Alpha, 215; Pruning Knife, 199; Rolling Thunder, xxi, 75–82, 88–104, 113, 116, 119–20, 123–26, 130, 156, 213, 236–43, 246, 362–63, 373, 390n139, 396n2, 431n60; Rolling Thunder Alpha, 236; Sea Dragon, 93; Sea Float, 163, 167–68, 179–81; Snack, 197; Solid Anchor, 168, 181; Starlite, 107; Strangle, 80; Supper, 197; Yankee Team, 38–39
oral history, 37, 106, 114, 144, 147, 176, 191, 232, 249, 350, 382n41, 452n108
Orange County, California, 249
Oriskany (CVA-34), 136
outboard motors, 167
OV-10 Bronco attack aircraft, 163, 165, 415n46
Oval Office, 197, 310
overseas deployments, 288
overseas homeporting, 260, 266
over-the-beach logistic support, 83
Oxford University, 271

P-3 Orion patrol aircraft, 83, 191
P-4 torpedo boats, 50, 54, 56
P-5B Marlin seaplanes, 83
P-6 fast patrol boats, 242
Pacific Air Forces, 77, 100
Pacific Command, US, xix, 9, 41, 50, 53, 147, 250, 313, 363, 384n63, 452n109
　Felt in charge, 3–4, 40
　operational authority, 27, 42, 87, 224, 314
Pacific Fleet, US, 3, 26, 77, 83, 294, 346
Pacific theater, 27, 40, 127, 346, 361
Pacific war, 152
pacification, 174, 178
Packard, David, 307–8, 444n15
Pakistan, 9, 312–13, 325
palace guard, 293, 441n82
Palmer, Bruce, 209, 306
Panama, 218
Panama Canal Treaty, 218, 453
Panmunjom, North Korea, 102, 105
paper tigers, 357
Paracel Islands, South China Sea, 25
parallels, 17th, 18th, 19th, 20th, 17, 25, 82, 90, 93, 120, 214, 243, 248, 406n124
paramilitary, 16–17, 19, 21, 31, 41, 169
Paris Agreement, xxi, 191, 250–51, 318, 343, 347–49, 351, 366, 373, 434n106
Paris, France, 123, 152, 166, 213, 215, 230, 243–44, 248, 250, 258
Parker, Jackson K., 436n39
Parrot's Beak, South Vietnam, 164, 202
Passover Seder dinner, 164
Pathet Lao, 11, 15, 28, 70, 389n131
patrol frigates, 263
patrol gunboats, 83
Patrol Squadron 22, 48
Patton, George S., 166, 212
Paul Doumer/Long Bien Bridge, North Vietnam, 237
pay, 13, 140–41, 173, 331–32
PBY 5 flying boat, 48
peaceful coexistence, 62
Pearl Harbor attack, 48
Pearl Harbor, Hawaii, 3, 42, 130, 366
Peet, Raymond, 135, 434n4
Peiping, China. *See* Peking, China
Peking, China, 56, 73
Pensacola, Florida, 5, 48
Pentagon. *See* Department of Defense
People's Liberation Army, 61, 64, 84, 205
People's Liberation Army Navy, 63
People's Republic of China, 7, 61, 231, 313, 388n119
Perle, Richard, 444n15
permissiveness, 283, 292, 441n76
Persian Gulf, 376–78
Persian Gulf War, 45, 276
Personal Response Program, 182, 189, 267, 437n41
　chief of, 114, 145
　Holloway policies and programs, 327–59
　naval personnel, 29, 140, 146, 154, 159, 167, 173, 243, 265, 268, 410n34
　problems, xx, xxii, 22, 139, 253
　in South Vietnam, 160, 176
　training, 28, 171, 182
　Zumwalt policies and programs, 277–304, 367–68,

372, 434n2
petroleum, oil, and lubricants, 56, 92, 236, 318, 376, 398n32
Petropavlovsk, Soviet Union, 235
petty officers, 277, 281–82, 296, 303, 332, 336, 442n96
Phalanx close-in weapon system, 265, 375
Phelps (DD-360), 153
Philadelphia, Pennsylvania, 309
Philippines, 3, 17, 59, 83, 158, 164, 190, 218, 288, 353, 424n9
Philippine Sea (CV-47), 7
Philippine Sea, 45
Phnom Penh, Cambodia, 170, 175, 203, 351, 354
photo reconnaissance, 38
Phoumi Nosavan, 10
Phu Qui, North Vietnam, 81
Phu Quoc Island, South Vietnam, 172
Phuc Yen airfield, North Vietnam, 104
Pickavance, William W., 242
Pickerel (SS-177), 45
pigs-and-chickens program, 173, 182, 185–86
pilots, xiii, 34, 54, 60, 63–64, 81, 116–17, 147, 206, 389n133, 431n44
pipelines, 11, 212, 214, 349
Piper Cub aircraft, 249
Pipes, Richard, 444n15
Pirnie, Alexander, 294
Plain of Jars, Laos, 10, 38–39
Plato, 157
Pleiku, South Vietnam, 74, 88
Podhoretz, Norman, 444n15
police, 17, 33
Politburo of North Vietnam, 33, 67
political-military affairs, 5, 40, 128, 154, 244, 362
political turmoil, 80, 103, 267
political warfare, 164, 185
pontoons, 167
pope, 101
Popeye the Sailor Man, 149
popular uprisings, 19
population centers, 41, 106, 175, 177, 206, 222, 237
Port Tobacco, Maryland, 157
postwar navy, 275
Potomac River, 157
poverty, 152
Powell, Colin, 262, 376
power projection, 337, 450n86
Prairie View Agricultural and Mechanical College, 144
Pravda, 63
precision-guided munitions, 236
prejudice, 145, 334–35, 409n25
presidential assistants, 220
presidential elections, 59, 68, 223, 290, 344
Presidential Palace, Saigon, 353
Presidential Program, 21
President's Blue Ribbon Commission on Defense Management, 445n44
President's Task Force on Combating Terrorism, 445n44
press-gangs, 332
pressure campaign, xxi, 46, 57, 72, 76
Price, Arthur, 106, 169
prime ministers, 10, 15, 38, 266
principles of war, 204
prisoners of war/missing in action (POW/MIA), xiii, 138, 211, 244, 318, 389n131
   Holloway, 366, 373
   Moorer, xxi, 217, 244, 349, 427n65, 432n80
   repatriation, xxi, 243–44, 250–51, 349, 366, 373, 432n81, 433n102, 452n109
   Son Tay prison, 214, 244, 427n65
   wives, 244, 314, 432n80
prisons, 57, 119, 214, 217, 244, 389n131, 427n65
professionalism, 94, 117, 192, 246, 294, 360, 447n4
Project 100,000, 143, 145
Project Sixty, 260–65, 271, 273, 333, 339
projection of naval power, 240, 262, 274, 371
promotions, 6, 26, 187, 285, 297, 307, 312, 333, 409n25
   Holloway, 333, 359
   Zumwalt, 154, 184, 207, 307, 367–68
propaganda, 30, 175, 207, 241, 419n120
prostheses, 354
protective reaction, 213–16, 220–21, 427n63
protocol, 208, 299
Providence (CLG-6), 241
Providence, Rhode Island, 173
Prussia, 13
psychological actions, 11, 16, 21, 30, 37, 72, 111, 122, 204, 246, 419n115
public affairs, 155, 277–78
public enemy number one, 142
Public Law 90-130, 298
public speaking, 152
publicity, 119, 139, 247
Pueblo (AGER-2), 96, 110, 132, 134, 198, 356, 407n2, 407n4
Puerto Ricans, 285
Purple Heart medals, 49
Pursley, Robert, 184
Pyongyang, North Korea, 105, 133, 357, 407n2
pyrotechnics, 51

quality of life and service, 278–79, 282, 289, 302, 334
Quang Khe, North Vietnam, 56, 81
Quang Ngai City, South Vietnam, 85
Quang Tri City, South Vietnam, 226–27
Quang Tri Province, South Vietnam, 229
quarterdeck, 284
Quarterdeck Society, 152
Quemoy-Matsu crisis, 1958, 113
Qui Nhon, South Vietnam, 75, 88, 351
Quigley, Robin, 297–301

RA-5C Vigilante reconnaissance aircraft, 240
race relations, 144, 146, 150, 267, 285, 287, 295, 329, 331, 334–35
racial turmoil, xx, xxii, 143–46, 303, 369
Racial Harmony Councils, 279, 287
racism, 143, 292, 294–95, 327
radar, 47, 50, 54–55, 58–59, 64, 66, 119, 213–15, 240–42, 347, 375
radar intercept officers, 64, 214
Radford, Charles E., 218–20, 224, 428n81, 429n88
radio, 51, 56
Raiders of the Lost Ark, 421n144
raids, xxi, 28, 35, 80, 83, 104, 109, 208, 419n120
railroad station, Hanoi, 199
railroads, 28, 68, 235
Ramage, James D., 209, 283, 293, 403n66, 418n105, 447n4
Ramage, Lawson, 6, 402n40
Ranger (CVA-61), 74, 76, 103, 210
Rangers, US Army, 85
rap sessions, 277, 287
Rauch, Charles F., 168, 171–72, 267, 301, 416n76, 420n133, 454n3
Raborn, William, 103
Reader's Digest, 124, 149, 398n32, 407n136
readiness, military, 8, 9, 16, 63, 173, 221, 239, 242, 257, 266, 341, 375
recoilless rifle, 49
reconnaissance, 38–39, 72, 81–83, 114, 116, 213, 240
recruitment, 287, 327, 335
Rectanus, Earl F., 178, 180, 232, 430n35
Red Army, 153
Red River Delta, North Vietnam, 104, 123
reeducation camps, 354, 421n137
reenlistment, 279, 333
reforms, 193, 265, 271, 281–83, 293, 303, 327–31, 337, 359, 367
refugees, 351, 353
rehabilitation, 142, 276, 438n5
reinforcements, 205, 210, 346
relieved of command, 180, 192
religious turmoil, 32
repair and maintenance, 171, 192, 257, 332, 338, 370
Report on the War in Vietnam, 106

INDEX 491

reporters, 118, 202, 247, 278
Republic of Vietnam (South Vietnam), *18*, 18–19, 157, 182, 187, 348, 352, 411n47
 armed forces, 17, 27, 173
 Easter Offensive, 222, 245
 territory, 166, 168
 US support for, 33, 176, 194, 249–50, 349, 366, 454n8
Republican National Convention, 357
Republicans, 294
resistance movements, 185
rest areas on Ho Chi Minh Trail, 11
retaliatory air strikes, xxi, 37, 39, 58, 67, 79, 81, 103, 213–14, 238
retention of personnel, 140, 150, 278–80, 283–85, 293, 298–303, 327, 331
retirement, 368, 418n105
 Chafee, 232, 434n2
 Felt, xxiii, 9, 37, 363, 373
 Holloway, 260, 373
 Moorer, 159, 244, 282, 297, 373, 443n6, 453n1
 Sharp, xxiii, 70, 95, 100, 128, 230, 373, 398n32
 Zumwalt, 155, 159, 259, 261, 270, 299, 312, 324, 348, 369–70, 373, 418n105, 434n2, 437n51, 443n6
Revolutionary War, 370
RF-8A Crusader photo-reconnaissance aircraft, 38
Rhodes Scholarship, 271
Richard S. Edwards (DD-950), 58
Richardson, David C., 104, 116, 146, 255–56, 379n5, 435n11
Ricketts, Claude V., 35–36
Rickover, Hyman G., xiv, *118*, *269*, 271, 409n21, 425n25, 437n44, 437n48, 437n51, 446n49
 aircraft carriers, 136–39, 150
 Enterprise, 117–18, 405n96, 409n20
 fleet composition, 338–41, 345
 and Holloway, 117–18, 136–39, 315, 317, 327, 329–30, 359, 372, 409n25
 and Moorer, 136–39, 150, 315, 409n22
 Project Sixty, 262–63
 and Zumwalt, xxii, 268–70, 274, 314–15, 328, 369, 414n33
rifles, 49, 62, 65, 82, 161, 226, 395n72
Rights and Opportunities for Women, 298
riots, 141
River Division 574, 165
River Force, Vietnam Navy, 27, 34, 174, 191–92
river patrol, 21, 165, 169, 176
River Patrol Force, US, 106, 160, 162
River Warfare Force, 26
Riverine Assault Force, US, 160. *See also* Task Force 117; Mobile Riverine Force
Rivero, Horacio, 34, 83, 137, 403n60
Rivers, Mendel, 140
roads, 27, 65, 72–73, 174, 205–6, 237, 349, 417n88
Robinson (DD-562), 153
Robinson, Rembrandt C., 122, 198
Robison (DDG-12), 241
Rock Creek Park, Washington, DC, 4
Rockefeller, Nelson, 201, 354
rockets, 49, 73, 76, 229
Rockeye cluster bombs, 242
Rocky Mountains, 260
Rodman, Peter, 203
Rogers, Bernard, 278–79, 287
Rogers, William, 197, 236, 310
Rolling Blunder, 117
Rome, Italy, 101
Rome Plows, 169
Rommel, Erwin, 178
Rose Garden, 197
Rostow, Eugene, 444n15
Rostow, Walt, 95, 103
Rota, Spain, 266
Route 1, South Vietnam, 226
Route 9, South Vietnam/Laos, 210–11
route packages, 77–78, *78*, 88, 130
Rowan (DD-78), 241
Rowney, Edward L., 32
Royal Navy, 8, 49, 231
rules of engagement, xiii, 81, 115–16, 119, 213–16, 236, 363, 409n18
Rumsfeld, Donald, 335, 343
Rung Sat Special Zone, 109, 169, 416n66
rural population, 17, 22, 31
Rusk, Dean, 23, 95, 102, 125, 444n15
Russians, 5, 153, 216, 235–36, 245, 262, 322, 339, 350
Ryan, John D., 205, 208, 216, 305
Ryujo (Japanese aircraft carrier), 5

S-3 Viking attack aircraft, 375
SA-2 Guideline surface-to-air missiles, 66, 80, 248, 396n2
SA-7 Strela surface-to-air missiles, 223
sabotage, 27, 30, 35, 52, 297
Saigon Naval Shipyard, 173
Saigon River, South Vietnam, 165
Saint James School, Hagerstown, Maryland, 113, 445n44
Saipan, Mariana Islands, 153
Salt Lake City (CA-25), 48
Salzer, Robert S., 162, 176, *190*, 292, 334–35, 419n118, 422n158
 combat record, 174, 190
 evaluation of the Vietnam Navy, 187, 191, 193–94, 422n164, 422n185
 Navy social issues, 276–77
 Vietnamization, 192–94, 256
 Z-Grams, 280, 284, 286
 Zumwalt, 276–77, 280, 284, 286
Samuel B. Roberts (FFG-58), 376
samurai sword, 51
San Clemente, California, 201
San Diego, California, 155, 289, 301
San Francisco Bay, California, 118
San Francisco, California, 3, 117–18, 144, 152, 421n137
sanctuaries, 16, 59, 196, 201
Sanctuary (AH-17), 301
Saratoga (CV-3), 5, 45
Saratoga (CVA-60), *200*, 237, 288
Sardinia, Italy, 266
Sasebo, Japan, 266, 409n26
Sather, Richard C., 56
Schade, Arnold F., 23
Schaub, John, 294
schizophrenia, 224
Schlesinger, James R., 127, 312, 319–26, *324*, 329, 338, 341, 354–55, 372
schools, 22, 66, 168, 301
Schreadley, Richard, 127, 420n123, 421n144
Schwarzkopf, Norman H., 45, 376
Scowcroft, Brent, 354, 356–57
Sculpin (SSN-590), 191
sea control, 257, 259, 262, 337, 346, 436, 451n86
Sea Control Ships, 263–65, 273, 436n36
Sea Force, Vietnam Navy, 25, 193
sea lanes, 273
sea lines of communication, 339, 373
Sea of Japan, 132, 198, 357
sea patrol, 22
Sea Plan 2000, 347, 359
sea/shore rotation, 279
Seabee technical assistance teams, 21–22, 27, 41
Seabees, 20–21, 27, 168, 173, 186
seaborne evacuations, xxii
seaborne infiltration, 21–22, 25–26, 82, 191, 418n97
SEAL Teams 1 and 2, 26
SEALORDS (Southeast Asia Lake, Ocean, River, Delta Strategy), 162, 164–68, 174, 177–78, 191–92, 365, 415n55, 419n114
SEALs, xxi, 27–28, 41, 167, 169
seapower, xiv, 134
search and rescue, 39, 84
seasickness, 153

SECNAV Notice 5420, 140
secrecy, xxi, 197, 207, 221, 318, 369
secretary of defense, 13–14, 39, 49, 78, 87, 125, 132, 137, 142, 213, 255, 312, 314, 344, 354, 361, 376, 393n46
    Cambodia, 196, 202
    Gulf of Tonkin incident, 53–55
    Johnson, 52, 60
    Kennedy, xiii, 11–12
    Laird and military women, 298, 303
    Laird, Zumwalt, 183, 253, 272, 324, 365, 367
    McNamara, xiii, 382n41
    Nixon, Laird, 198, 221
    relationship to JCS, 97, 99
    Rolling Thunder, xxi, 90, 101–2, 107, 112, 116
    Rumsfeld, 335, 343
    Schlesinger, 319–20
    Schlesinger, Holloway, 326, 341
    Schlesinger, Zumwalt, 322–23, 329
    Sharp, 121, 363, 407n136
    Vietnamization, xxii, 151, 175, 245
    withdrawal from Vietnam, 171, 223
secretary of state, 23, 95, 167, 319, 444n15
    air operations, 123, 125, 197, 236
    bypassed, 207, 310
    Kissinger, Holloway, 341, 344
    Kissinger, Zumwalt, 321, 370
    post-Vietnam crises in Asia, 354, 356–57
Secretary of the Navy, 26, 29, 36, 135, 155, 232, 263, 268, 270, 289, 298, 347, 398n40, 435n24, 447n76
    Chafee, Moorer, 255
    Chafee, Zumwalt, 73, 273, 365, 367
    Middendorf, Holloway, 271–72, 340–41
    Navy social issues, 139–40, 145
    Warner, Holloway, 326, 328
    Warner, Zumwalt, 281, 329, 454n7
Section 3, North Vietnamese PT Squadron 135, 50
selection boards, 154, 279
self-immolation, 33
self-promotion, 139, 365
Senior Enlisted Advisor of the Navy, 140
senior enlisted personnel, 140, 281–82, 295–96, 368, 372
senior petty officers, 277, 286, 296, 303
sensitivity training, 182, 334–35
sensors, 105, 165, 205, 262

Seventh Air Force, US, 76, 91, 110, 206, 212, 216
Seventh Fleet, US, xxii, 7, 46, 54, 63, 102, 115, 130, 215, 226, 239, 240, 254, 273, 288, 329, 433n92, 445n39
    coastal patrol, 22, 25, 83, 161
    end of war evacuations, 351–53
    Laos crises, 10, 15, 38
    Linebacker, xxii, 241–42, 246, 250, 315, 365, 372
    mining of enemy ports, 233, 235
    Operation End Sweep, 251–52
    Operation Sea Dragon, 93–94
SH-60B Seahawk light airborne multipurpose system helicopters, 265
Shakespeare, 204
Shanghai, China, 153
Sharp, Grant, 45
Sharp, Patricia Ann, 45
Sharp, Patricia O'Connor, 45
Sharp, Thomas F., 45
Sharp, Ulysses S. G., xiv, xv, xx, xxi, xxiii, 11, 14, 20, 30, 43, *46*, *53*, 64, *75*, *94*, *107*, *108*, 114, *121*, 147, 149, 199, 216, 230, 294, 361–64, 373, 389n133, 396n88, 396n89, 399n46
    air operations short of war in Laos and North Vietnam, 73–76
    civil-military discord and the air war, 95–102
    control of air power in Southeast Asia, 76–80
    early life and career, 44–45
    end of Rolling Thunder, 120–23, 407n136
    Gulf of Tonkin incident, 50–54
    MACV, riverine and amphibious operations, 106–10, 403n66, 404n78
    maritime interdiction, deployment of US troops to Vietnam, 82–89
    Operation 34A and Desoto Patrol, 46–47
    operational control of US air power, 110–13
    Pierce Arrow retaliatory air strike, 54–57
    POL campaign, 102–6
    proposals to deter Hanoi and support Saigon, 67–71
    Rolling Thunder, naval bombardment, troops to South Vietnam, 90–95
    successes and failures as CINCPAC, 123–31
    Washington, Hanoi response to Gulf of Tonkin incident, 57–59
Shear, Howard E., 268, 327,

436n29, 447n8, 452n108
Sheets, Roger, 234
shipbuilding, 263–64, 269, 274, 308, 330, 340, 344
shipping, 35, 234
shore batteries, 93
Shoup, David, 121
showing the flag, 391n11
Shultz, George, 369, 444n15
sideburns, 139, 281
signal flags, 51
signals intelligence, 50
Sihanouk, Prince Norodom, 161–62, 197, 200
Sihanoukville, Cambodia, 156, 161–62, 175, 201, 351
Silver Star medals, 45, 49, 60, 164, 167
Sims, William S., 272
Singapore, 58
Singing Sam (Hanging Sam), 17
Singlaub, John, 357
single management of air power, 112
Sino-American relationship, 235
Sino-Soviet alliance, 60
Sino-Soviet bloc, 70, 92, 94, 100
sit-downs, 289
Six-Day War, 1967, 96, 132
slavery, 9, 146
small arms, 26, 82, 193, 394
Small Craft Assets, Training, and Turnover of Resources (SCATTOR), 171
smart weapons, 240
Smedberg, William R., III, 145
Smith, Gerard, 322
Smith, Margaret Chase, 223
smoking gun, 55
social changes, 283, 315
social programs, 277, 371–72
Socialist Republic of Vietnam, 185
Socrates, 157
Son, Nguyen Xuan, 186
Son Tay prison, North Vietnam, 214, 244, 427n65
Sorley, Lewis, 206, 431n45
sorties, aircraft, 100, 104, 120, 197, 377, 409n18
    Easter Offensive, 224, 228–29
    Laos, North Vietnam, 212–15
    Linebacker, 234, 237, 289
South China Sea, 10, 15, 105, 169, 235, 315
South Korea, 3, 218, 356–58
South Pacific, 48
South Vietnam. *See* Republic of Vietnam
South Vietnamese armed forces. *See* armed forces of South Vietnam
Southeast Asia, 11, 23, 38, 61, 66, 105, 130, 141, 154, 202, 220, 234, 246, 257, 314, 350, 353–56, 366, 396n91, 412n68, 454n8

INDEX 493

command in, 76, 100
communist aggression, 8, 9, 35, 59, 68, 389n129
conflict in, xxi, 13, 19, 59, 63, 68, 151, 197, 230, 240, 244, 368
defense of, 16, 57, 83, 85, 111
deployments to, 224, 227, 236, 349
failure of US policy, strategy, 127–28, 363
withdrawal from, 203, 347
Southeast Asia Treaty Organization (SEATO), 3, 24, 313
Souvanna Phouma, 10, 15
Soviet ambassador to the United States, 101, 231, 310
Soviet global interests, 19, 66
Soviet Navy, 22, 132, 259–60, 275, 306–7, 310, 314, 339, 358, 369, 371, 435n22
Soviet Pacific Fleet, 313
Soviet Union, 19, 80, 125, 135, 153–54, 233, 256, 266, 270, 312, 351, 359–60, 374
  assistance to allies, xv, 11, 63, 65–66, 223
  Cold War conflict with, 96, 258, 273, 369
  ideological conflict with China, 62, 65, 231
  Nixon policy toward, 159, 196, 220, 309, 350, 373
  nuclear capability, 41, 154, 259, 344
  risk of war with, 92, 258, 260, 319, 346–47
SP-2H Neptune patrol aircraft, 83
spare parts, 189, 193, 345
Special Assistant for Counterinsurgency and Special Activities (SACSA), 30
special assistant for minority affairs, Office of the CNO, 286
Special Assistant for National Security Council Affairs, 59
special forces, 17, 19, 26–27, 85, 202
Special Landing Force, Seventh Fleet, 85, 107
Special Operations Group. *See* Studies and Observation Group, 30
Special Warfare Center, US Army, 22
Spence, John C., 166
spheres of influence, 315
Spivak, Lawrence E., 447n76
Spruance, Raymond A., xx
Spruance-class destroyers, 262
SPY-1A phased array radars, 375
spying, 218, 219
Stalin, Joseph, 5, 64
standard of living, 173
standing authority, 215
Stark (FFG-31), 376
State of the Union, 124

States Rights Party, 293
Steele, George P., 351–52, 453n113
Stennis, John C., 122–23, 137, 308
Steward Branch, US Navy, 144
Stilwell, Richard, 357–58
Stockdale, James B., 51
Stockdale, Sybil, 244, 314
Stoner, Robert H., 166, 179
Strait of Hormuz, 376
Strait of Malacca, 312
Strait of Taiwan, 62, 130
Strategic Air Command, 229, 246
strategic arms, 228, 231, 306, 308–11, 369
Strategic Arms Limitation Talks (SALT), 308–9, 310, 413n18
strategic bombing, 49, 92, 231
Strategic Plans Branch, Navy staff, 306
Strategic Plans Division, Navy staff, 45
Strategic Plans Section, Navy staff, 6
strategy, xv, 13, 56, 120, 129, 146, 154, 203, 350, 364
  bombing, 91, 121
  Carter administration, 264, 346–47, 359
  counterinsurgency, xxi, 41
  failure of, 86, 88
  global, 45, 350
  Maritime Strategy, 258, 359–60, 371, 373–74
  McNamara, 96, 129
  Naval War College, 271–73
  SEALORDS, 162, 174
  US, xix, xx, xxi, xxii, 70, 76, 86, 90, 305–6, 350, 368, 380n12, 411n64
Strategy for Defeat (Sharp), 70, 106, 127–28, *128*
"Street Without Joy," 226
Strike Warfare Division, Navy staff, 136
Studies and Observation Group (Special Operations Group), 30
study groups, 34, 104, 298, 300
Stump, Felix B., 45
Styx surface-to-surface missiles, 247
Subic Bay Naval Base, Philippines, 288–89
submachine guns, 82
submarine chasers, 191
submariners, 136, 292, 359
submarines, 22, 83, 63, 238, 274, 313, 340, 343–44, 368, 377, 416n76, 445n38
  attack, 262–63, 269, 334, 371, 374
  ballistic missile, 253, 262–63, 265, 269–70, 308, 371
  nuclear-powered, 117, 191, 273, 315, 317, 329, 339, 341, 371
  Soviet, 138, 235, 259, 375,

382n41
World War II, 6, 45
substance abuse, 141, 277
Sullivan, William H., 73–74
summits, 225, 231, 233
Superintendent, US Naval Academy, 113, 324
supplies, 169, 193, 229, 238, 240, 257, 346, 350, 377
  Cambodia, 156, 161–62
  infiltration of, 25, 34, 62, 82, 101, 177, 230
  interdiction, 92–93, 102, 105, 206, 214, 236, 239
  Soviet provision of, 10, 66, 235
support vessels, 3, 353
Supreme Allied Commander, Europe, 333
surface action group, 374
surface ships, 5, 22, 117, 215, 237, 257, 259, 343, 374, 377
surface warfare officers, 113, 134, 136, 187, 231, 262, 292, 315, 359
surgeon general, US Army, Vietnam, 142
swamps, 109, 165, 169
Swartz, Peter M., 167, 181, 188, 267, 417n85, 436n25
  animal husbandry, 173, 178
  Project Sixty, 263, 339
  Zumwalt and counterinsurgency, 258, 262
  Zumwalt's character, 164, 178, 419n121
Swift boats, 29, 83, 161, 163, 167, 170, 179, 192. *See also* fast patrol craft
Swing Strategy, 346
sycophants, 420n123
Symington, Stuart, 122, 137–38
Syria, 259
systems analysis, 135, 155–56, 260, 269–71, 306, 408n14
Systems Analysis Office (Division), Navy staff, 134, 271

T-333, T-336, T-339, 50
tactics, 7, 45, 79, 95, 181, 236, 239, 327, 400n3, 405n96, 433n104, 453n113
Taiwan, 7, 130
Taiwan Strait Crisis, 1954–1955, 7, 16, 42, 62
Taiwan Strait Crisis, 1958, 9, 10, 16, 35, 42, 62
Talos surface-to-air missiles, 215–16, 237
Tan Son Nhut, South Vietnam, 76, 84
Tanaka, Kakuei, 266
Tank, the (JCS conference room), 305, 310
tank landing ships (LST), 25, 83
tankers, 114, 238, 284, 338, 376
tanks, 65, 85, 191, 193, 210, 212, 226, 229, 353, 377, 395n72
Task Force 74, 313

Task Force 115, 84, 161, 167, 179. *See also* Coastal Surveillance Force
Task Force 116, 10, 160. *See also* River Patrol Force
Task Force 117, 160. *See also* Riverine Assault Force
Task Force 194, 162, 164. *See also* SEALORDS
task forces, groups, units, 55, 241–42, 266, 313–14, 340
tax collectors, 167
Tay Ninh, South Vietnam, 165
Taylor, Maxwell D., 23, 32, 35, 69, 78, 97, 389n124, 399n48, 404n78, 411n64
  actions re: North Vietnam, 36, 90
  counterinsurgency, 20, 68, flexible response strategy, 8, 37
    Kennedy favorite, 12–13, 380n12
    Sharp, 86–87
Taylor, Rufus L., 36
Tchepone, Laos, 15, 211
technical skills, xv, 143, 332
technology, 91, 136, 287, 317, 333, 425n25
Tehran, Iran, 376
telephone and telegraph office, Hanoi, 199
telephones, 279
television, 232, 235
Terrier surface-to-air missiles, 215
testimony, 97, 122–23, 135–38, 216, 294–95, 345, 369, 428n71, 442n96
Tet Offensive, 1968, 110, 125, 131–32, 152, 161, 206, 221–22, 364
  Mekong Delta, xxii, 166, 175, 203, 365, 423n185
  Mobile Riverine Force, 106, 177, 403n63
  Sharp, 126, 149
Texaco Company, 453n1
Texas, 60, 96, 98, 144–45, 354
Thanh Hoa Bridge, North Vietnam, 240
Thanh Hoa, North Vietnam, 214
That Man, 120–21
Peloponnesian War, The (Thucydides), 272
Theodore Roosevelt (CVN-71), 345
Thieu, Nguyen van, 152, 209–12, 222, 230, *239*, 243, 245, 318, 348–49, 352
III Corps, South Vietnam, 417n88
Third Fleet, US, 335, 440n53
Third Front, 63, 395n65
III Marine Amphibious Force, 107–8, 110
Third World, 156
Tho, Le Duc, 243, 245

Thoai, Ho Van Ky, 186, 194
Thompson, William, 155, 277–78, 283, 326, 408n14, 448n14
Thompson, William (Senator), 4
Thong, Nguyen, 181
Thucydides, 272
Thurmond, Strom, 137, 293
Ticonderoga (CVA-14), 50–51, 54, 56–57, 296
Tidd, Emmett, 262, 436n25, 454n3
Time magazine, 49, 283
tit-for-tat air strikes, 37, 41, 69, 79, 250
toilets, 186
Tomahawk land attack cruise missiles, 308, 343, 374, 377
Tonkin Gulf incident, xxi, 56, 64, 66, 72
Top Gun school, 242
Topeka, Kansas, 4
torpedo attack, 50, 55, 153
torpedo boats, 29, 50, 241, 386n95, 391n19
torture, 133
Tory, 370
Train, Harry, 398n40, 439n33
  and Holloway, 341, 347, 354, 452n108
  and Moorer, 141, 148, 219, 354, 409n22, 411n66, 414n32, 425n14, 427n65, 434n8, 436n29
  and Zumwalt, 293, 320, 354, 420n123, 434n8, 441n82
training, 5, 19, 47–48, 66, 145–46, 182, 257, 283, 288, 409n19, 419n115
  Holloway, 334–36, 345
  South Vietnamese military, 25–27, 171–72, 186
  Zumwalt, 287, 300, 334–35
Tran Hung Dao, 182
Tran Khanh Do (HQ-4), 191
transportation, 73, 90, 161, 177, 230, 398n32, 417n88
Travis Air Force Base, California, 144
trawlers, North Vietnamese, 26, 161, 191
treaty of peace and friendship (Soviet-Indian), 312
Trenton (LPD-14), 296
Trident II (D-5) ICBM, 265
trolling, 213
troop transports, 317
truck parks, xiii, 11, 246
trucks, 66, 161, 205–6, 230, 297, 349
Truman, Harry S., 144
Trump, Donald, xix
Truong, Ngo Quang. *See* Ngo Quang Truong
Tuesday lunch meetings, 95–96, 100, 124
Tulare, California, 152
Turkish Navy, 264
Turner Joy (DD-951), 51–57, 70,

393n42
Turner, Stansfield, 260–62, 264, 271–72
turnover to Vietnam of ships, craft, bases, 88, 171–72, 181–82, 189
two-ocean navy, 345, 359

U-boats, 45
U Minh Forest, South Vietnam, 165, 168, 181
UN forces, Korean War, 61
UN resolutions, 312
Uncertain Trumpet, The (Taylor), 8, 380n12
Unconventional Activities Working Group, 19
unconventional warfare, 7, 16, 22
Under Secretary of the Navy, 347
underwater demolition teams, 20, 146
uniforms, 281–82
Union of Soviet Socialist Republics. *See* Soviet Union
unions, 262
United Daughters of the Confederacy, 146
United Nations, 357, 377
University of North Carolina, xix
unless otherwise directed (UNODIR), 105
US ambassador to Cambodia, 351
US ambassador to Laos, 73–74
US ambassador to Portugal, 284
US ambassador to South Vietnam
  Bunker, 148, 224
  Lodge, 30, 33
  Martin, 353
  Nolting, 22, 24
  Taylor, 68, 86–87, 404n78
US ambassador to Thailand, 73
US defense policy, 8, 96
US Embassy, Phnom Penh, 351
US Embassy, Saigon, 352
US global interests, 223, 249, 346
US ground forces, xxi, 20, 59, 82, 85–86, 92, 202
US House of Representatives, 57
US maritime dominance, 259, 311
US Military Academy, xix
US military establishment, xxi, 224, 254, 366, 375
US military forces, xx, 3, 16, 28, 131, 168, 338, 351
US military mission to Russia, 5
US Naval Academy, xxi, 114, 144, 182, 425n25
  Felt, 6, 16
  Holloway, 113–14, 315, 324, 330–31, 344, 359, 372, 409n20, 445n44
  Moorer, 48, 146, 204, 324
  Sharp, 44–45
  women at, 300, 336, 359
  Zumwalt, 114, 152–54, 315,

INDEX

321, 324, 330, 370, 372, 434n4
US Naval Forces, Vietnam, 152, 157–58, 162, 170, 187, 190, 364, 365
US Naval Institute, 114
US non-nuclear forces, 9, 40, 338
US Senate, 57, 59, 97, 155, 203, 261, 427n51
US Strategic Bombing Survey, 49, 231
US West Coast, 3, 45
US withdrawal from South Vietnam, 79, 125–26, 192, 237, 249, 348, 360
US-Japan alliance, 266, 273
US-Japan Security Treaty, 346
US-PRC rapprochement, 65, 313, 325

VAL-4 Light Attack Squadron Black Ponies, 163
valedictorian, 48, 152
Valley of Death, 116
Vann, John Paul, 229
vehicles, military, 66, 97, 165, 175, 193, 205–6, 211, 349, 383n44
vertical/short-takeoff-and-landing aircraft, 263–64, 273
veterans, xiii, 267, 272, 275, 295, 354, 370, 374, 376, 417n85
Veth, Kenneth L., 152, 176–77, 418n97
Vice Chief of Naval Operations, 6, 35, 159, 271, 276, 327, 347, 435n11, 452n108
　Holloway, 252, 266, 277, 279, 306, 316–17, 326, 329, 332, 333
　Rivero, 34, 137
Vice Chief of Staff, US Army, 306, 322
Vice Commander, Pacific Air Forces, 77
Vice President of the United States, 322–24, 354
victories-to-losses ratios, 31, 167, 242
Victory (*Chien Thang*) Plan, 34
Vienna, Austria, 310, 343
Vientiane, Laos, 10
Viet Cong, xxi, 28, 43, 62, 67, 69, 70–71, 80, 87, 89, 92, 106, 114, 166, 222, 229, 418n97, 419n120
　attacks, 31, 41, 68, 74, 84–85
　insurgency in South Vietnam, 17, 21–27
　Marine operations, 107–8
　seaborne infiltration, 62, 82, 161, 191, 201
　SEALORDS, 165–69, 174–80, 188, 420n126
Viet Minh, 61, 111
Vietnam at War (Davidson), 127
Vietnam Delta Infiltration Study Group. *See* Bucklew Report
Vietnam Navy, xxii, 25, 34, 83,
148, 168–93, 353, 365, 417n85, 422n176
Vietnam unification, 41, 62
Vietnamese Communist Party, 33
Vietnamese culture, 13, 187
Vietnamese Worker's Party, 16
Vietnamization, xxii, 151, 230, 349, 423n192, 430n23
　Cambodia, 196, 202–3, 221
　Easter Offensive, 222–23, 229, 245
　Lam Son 719, 206–7, 210–12, 221
　Moorer, 249, 254, 366
　SEALORDS, 165, 168, 365
　Vietnam Navy, 170–71, 180–81, 184–85, 189, 192–94, 365
　Zumwalt, 176–77, 256, 258, 318, 418n105, 423n189
Vincennes (CG-49), 376
Vinh Long, South Vietnam, 423n185
Vinh, North Vietnam, 54, 56
Vinson, Carl, 270, 293
visits, 24, 118, 164, 182, 278, 293, 334, 338
Vladivostok, Soviet Union, 235, 314
Vo Nguyen Giap. *See* Giap, Vo Nguyen
volunteers, 28, 80, 258, 287, 298
Voting Rights Act, 1965, 60
Vulcan Phalanx close-in weapon system, 265
Vung Ro Bay, South Vietnam, 82
Vung Tau, South Vietnam, 352, 417n88, 420n131

Wages, Clarence J., 169, 454n3
Walker, John A., Jr., 267, 419n115
Walker, Robert J., 331, 334, 359
Wall Street Journal, 103
Walleye TV-guided bombs, 237
Walt, Lewis, 107–8
war effort, 31, 65, 111
　allied, 84, 160, 178, 365
　enemy, 67, 74, 102, 104, 200, 222
　South Vietnam's, 185, 396n88
　US, 99, 129, 223, 230, 323, 342, 363–64
Ward, Alfred G., 35
Ward, J. D., 294
Ward, Norvell G., 84, 418n97
wardrooms, 286
Warner, John, xiv, 147, 282, 289, *328*, 435n22
　and Clarey, 255, 442n92
　and Holloway, 326, 328–29, 372
　and Navy women, 298–99
　and Zumwalt, 255, 281, 289, 329, 439n27, 454n7
Warsaw, Poland, 105
warships, 238, 265–67, 301, 346,
353, 376–77
　bombardment, 93, 227, 237, 240–41, 246
　construction, 253, 263, 338
　Gulf of Tonkin incident, xxi, 54, 58, 393n48
　nuclear-powered, 315, 369
　in Pacific Command, 3, 53, 59, 130, 236
　Soviet, 259, 312, 435n22
Washington, George, 10
Washington Navy Yard, 232
Washington Post, 31, 218, 247, 370
Washington Special Action Group, 313, 357
Washington Star, 247
Washington state, 293
Wasp (LHD-1), 374
water wells, 22
waterborne guard post tactic, 165, 191
waterborne supply, xv
Watergate crisis, 256, 291, 318, 321, 323, 349
Watkins, James D., 332
weather, 13, 81, 93, 210
　bombing in North Vietnam, 74, 76, 79, 103, 116–19, 214–15, 227, 246
　Gulf of Tonkin incident, 53, 59
Weinberger, Caspar, 376
Weinberger Doctrine, 376
Welander, Robert O., 218–19
Weschler, Thomas, 439n22
West Point. *See* US Military Academy
West, Francis, 347
Western Atlantic, 45
Western Pacific, 49, 59, 63, 84, 107–8, 231, 239, 288
Western White House, 201
Westmoreland, William C., xix, 32, 37, 47, 58, 68, 73, 93, *94*, 106, 121, 109, 110, 114, 120, 127, 147, 176, 306, 404n78, 411n64, 418n98
　chain of command, 94–95, 125, 363
　coastal patrol, 82–84, 161
　JCS, 220, 305, 427n54
　Lam Son 719, 208–11
　operational control, 76–77, 87, 108, 111–13, 130, 399n42
　re: micromanagement, 39, 400n57
　Rolling Thunder, 90, 101, 105, 124
　troops to South Vietnam, 84–88
wheelchairs, 354
Whidbey Island (LSD-41), 374
white colonialism, 23
White House, xxi, 74, 80, 126, 130, 201, 323, 329, 345, 368, 425n16, 447n76
　Foreign Intelligence Advisory

Board, 291, 321
Kissinger, 155, 254, 310, 312, 314, 368
Laird, 171, 250
liaison office, 198, 218–19, 224, 312, 426n38
military representative, 12, 97
mining of Haiphong, 232, 234
Moorer, 77, 148, 217–18, 221, 224, 250, 310, 368, 426n38
Radford affair, 218, 224
Sharp, 77, 121
Tuesday lunches, 54, 95, 100, 124
Zumwalt, 178, 235, 254, 310, 312, 314, 322–23, 429n85
White House tapes, 200
White House Years (Kissinger), 319
White Russians, 153
Whitmire, Donald, 352
Whiz Kids, 38, 99, 150, 155–56, 401n35, 413n15
"Why We Lost in Vietnam" (Record), xix
Williams, Samuel T., 17
Winder, Georgia, 145
Wisconsin, 151, 223
Wisconsin (BB-64), 153
wise men, 125
wives of POWs, 244, 314, 432n80
Women Accepted for Volunteer Emergency Service (WAVES), 299–300
woodcutters, 167
Woolsey, R. James, 347
world opinion, 358
World War I, 146, 248
World War II, xv, xx, 6, 8, 12, 27, 30–31, 45, 60, 77, 92, 97, 114, 123, 129, 135, 146–47, 151, 204, 212, 240, 257, 291, 297, 346, 366, 446n49, 452n109
Felt service in, 5, 16, 40
Holloway service in, 113, 241–42
Moorer service in, 51, 231
operational control, 111, 130
Sharp service in, 45
Zumwalt service in, 152–53
World War III, 358
WPB US Coast Guard cutter, 161
Wulzen, Donald W., 86
Wylie, Elizabeth G., 297

Xom Bang, North Vietnam, 81

Yalta Conference, 5
Yalu River, 61
Yankee Station, 51, 114, 116, 119–20, 136, 146, 255, 288, 290, 364
Years of Upheaval (Kissinger), 319
Yokosuka, Japan, 266
Yom Kippur War, 318–19, 325, 341
Yost, Paul A., 166, 179–80, 419n118
Yugoslavia, 259
Yunnan Province, China, 63

Zakheim, Dov, 454n8
Zeilin (APA-3), 153
Z-Grams, 277, 278–84, 289, 302, 316, 440n71, 443n111
Zhou Enlai, 62–64, 389n129
Zumwalt, Elmo R., Jr., xiv, xv, xvi, xx, xxii, xxiii, 14, 73, 96–98, 114, 125, 134–35, 138–39, *158*, *163*, *183*, *190*, 209, 230, *255*, *286*, *316*, *324*, 326, 345–50, 355, 361, 364–65, 372–73, 407n2, 407n4, 408n7, 408n14, 454n3, 454n8
assignment to Vietnam, 157–62
and Chafee, 135, 415n46
changes for Navy women, 296–302
early life and career, 152–56, 412n4, 413n11
early successes and failures as CNO, 273–74, 436n39
Easter Offensive, 227–28
Holloway adaptation of Zumwalt reforms, 331–36
Holloway and Linebacker, 238, 242, 252, 433n92
Holloway re: High-Low Mix, Soviet Navy, emphasis on experience, 336–40
interaction with Nixon, Kissinger, Schlesinger, 317–25, 342, 362, 449n64
JCS service, Moorer, White House, strategic arms, 305–11, 414n33, 443n6, 444n15, 444n20, 445n32, 447n76
Jordan crisis, India-Pakistan War, POW wives, new VCNO, 311–17, 446n51
mining of Haiphong, 232, 235, 250
Nitze connection, 96, 125, 154–59, 388n119, 413n16, 413n18
overseas homeporting, Japan, Greece, 265–67, 437n41
personnel reform programs, 284–88, 440n53
post-retirement for refugees, Vietnam veterans, 353–54, 420n137
Project Sixty, 260–65, 436n27, 437n55
promotion to CNO, Navy problems, Soviet Navy, 253–60, 434n4, 435n11
retention, drug abuse, racial tension, media, 144–45, 275–78, 327
Rickover, changes in OPNAV, Naval War College, 267–72, 437n48, 437n51
SEALORDS, leadership traits, innovative thinking, 162–69, 365, 398n40, 418n97, 419n114, 419n121, 420n123
service on the JCS, bypassing of Laird, 207–8, 219–20, 224, 227–28
social revolution successes and failures, 302–4, 327, 367–70, 439n27, 441n79, 441n82, 448n15
successes and failures in Vietnam, 174–87, 421n144
support for Bagley, Holloway as CNO, 328–30, 447n8, 448n11
Vietnamization, naval campaign after Zumwalt, 187–95, 422n173, 423n189
Vietnamization/ACTOV, Abrams, US withdrawal from Vietnam, 170–73, 216n74, 417n95, 418n105, 418n106, 422n164
warship disturbances, Hicks hearings, 288–96, 441n76, 442n99
Z-Grams, opposition to changes, 278–84, 439n34, 439n39, 441n74
Zumwalt, Elmo R., III, 179, 413n8
Zumwalt, James G., 407n2, 413n8
Zumwalt, Mouzetta, 413n8
"Zumwalt's Big Mistake" (Fussell), 334
Zumwalt's Wild Ideas, 178, 368

www.ingramcontent.com/pod-product-compliance
Lightning Source LLC
Chambersburg PA
CBHW021847230426
43671CB00006B/290